THE LIVING PAST

IVAR LISSNER

THE LIVING PAST

*The great civilizations
of mankind*

TRANSLATED FROM THE GERMAN BY

J. MAXWELL BROWNJOHN

M.A. (Oxon.)

THE REPRINT SOCIETY LONDON

FIRST PUBLISHED IN GREAT BRITAIN 1957
REPRINTED 1961
THIS EDITION PUBLISHED BY THE REPRINT SOCIETY LTD
BY ARRANGEMENT WITH JONATHAN CAPE LTD. 1960

Originally published in Germany
under the title *So Habt Ihr Gelebt*

PRINTED IN GREAT BRITAIN IN THE CITY OF OXFORD
AT THE ALDEN PRESS

CONTENTS

List of Authorities   15

Introduction   17

MESOPOTAMIA

7000 years and 4000 gods   27
Babylon was well lit at night   40

EGYPT

First-rate sewing-needles — 4600 years old   47
Where does Pharaoh Sekhem-khet lie buried?   52
Eternal Sun — origin of life   57
Do not be sad in life   71

ANATOLIA

The Hittites   81

PHOENICIA

They never had time . . .   93

PERSIA

When Ahasuerus could not sleep   99
The kings died — the bureaucracy seemed everlasting   109

PALESTINE

O Absalom, my son!   121
They fought against polytheism: sixteen prophets   128
Man is of few days and full of trouble — the Book of Job   133
Christ lived   137

INDIA

The greatest enigma in human history: Mohenjo-Daro and Harappa   141
An atom can never understand the Universe   148
Who created the image of Buddha?   154
Rebirth   159

CAMBODIA

Angkor lies abandoned in the jungle   165

CONTENTS

CHINA

China's ancestor lived 500,000 years ago 169
Confucius and Lao-tse 174
The eighth wonder of the world 180
Li T'ai-po is only immortal when he is drunk 188
Peking, the most beautiful city in the world 193

CENTRAL ASIA

Jenghiz Khan and Tamerlane — hated, cursed, loved and admired 199

JAPAN

Some day the bear will return: the Ainu 207
A people in love with art 213
Nature is not an alien force 220
The green houses of Yoshiwara — Utamaro 224
Starve if need be . . . but paint! Hokusai 229
They painted 'the moving world': Harunobu — Sharaku — Hiroshige 233

AUSTRALIA

Where the dead live on 241

POLYNESIA

Experts in the art of doing nothing 247
The unsolved mystery of Easter Island script 253

MELANESIA

Coconut and shellfish civilization 259

NORTH AMERICA

The arrival of the Indians 265

SOUTH AMERICA

We shall never know — Tiahuanacu 269
In rarefied air 12,000 feet up. The Incas 277
At midnight . . . I shall come 283
Atahualpa tumbled into the dust 288
Pizarro's death 295

CENTRAL AMERICA

Their gods were always hungry: the Maya 305
They built pyramids: the Teotihuacáns and Toltecs 312
I overthrew large and powerful nations — Hernando Cortez 318

CONTENTS

CRETE

A labyrinth 5000 years old   327
The mysterious downfall   335

GREECE

The city of Priam: Troy   345
Graves tell secrets: prehistory   354
The world's first democracy   361
That is what earthly immortality means   368
Alcibiades, Athens' most dangerous friend   378
Socrates, the saintly teacher   385
But I will obey God   390
Little horses of Venus   394
Cursing their master behind his back   400

ITALY

The mysterious Etruscans   405
The Land of Calves   412

CARTHAGE

Elephants and galleys   417
The tragedy of Hannibal   424

Index   431

ILLUSTRATIONS

MESOPOTAMIA   *following page*   64
THE SUMERIANS
EGYPT
PHOENICIA

PERSIA   112
PALESTINE
INDIA

CAMBODIA   176
CHINA
CENTRAL ASIA
JAPAN

JAPAN *continued*   240
AUSTRALIA
POLYNESIA
MELANESIA

MELANESIA *continued*   288
CENTRAL AND SOUTH AMERICA

CENTRAL AND SOUTH AMERICA *continued*   336
CRETE

TROY   368
GREECE

GREECE *continued*   400
ITALY
CARTHAGE
   A*

MAPS AND DRAWINGS

MESOPOTAMIA   31

EGYPT   49

PERSIA   111

SINAI PENINSULA, EGYPT AND THE HOLY LAND   123

EXCAVATED SITES OF INDUS CIVILIZATION   143

POLYNESIA   249

OBVERSE OF WRITING TABLET PECULIAR TO EASTER ISLAND   255

SOUTH AMERICA   271

CENTRAL AMERICA   307

CRETE   329

OLDEST SYLLABIC CHARACTERS OF EUROPE   334

CRETAN NUMERALS   334

REPRODUCTION OF CHARACTERS ON A TABLET INSCRIBED IN 'LINEAR B'   343

TROY AND ITS ENVIRONS   347

THE LARGE FORTIFIED TOWNS OF THE MYCENAEAN PERIOD   356

ANCIENT GREECE   377

THE EXTENSION OF ETRURIA   407

CARTHAGE   422

ACKNOWLEDGMENT

I should like to express my warmest gratitude to these eminent authorities who have aided me in my work by offering advice and many valuable suggestions, and also by checking the sections dealing with individual civilizations:

Professor Dr Hanns Stock, Professor of Egyptology at Munich University, Director of the Egyptian State Collection, Munich, for checking and amplifying the sections on Mesopotamia, Egypt, Phoenicia and Persia;

Professor Dr Ludwig Alsdorf, of Hamburg, for looking over the chapters on the Indian and Persian civilizations and offering valuable suggestions on the section about Mohenjo-Daro and Harappa;

Dr Richard Schröter, Departmental Director at the Museum of Ethnology, Hamburg, for his hints on planning the chapter dealing with the Khmer civilizations of Cambodia;

Dr Peter Wilhelm Meister, Museum of Arts and Crafts, Hamburg, for supplementing the chapters on China and Japan;

Professor Dr Annemarie von Gabain, Lecturer in Turkish at Hamburg University, for looking over the chapter on Mongolia;

Dr Herbert Tischner, Curator and Director of the Indo-Oceanic Department at the Museum of Ethnology and Prehistory, Hamburg, for looking over the sections on Australia, Polynesia and Melanesia;

Dr Hans Dietrich Disselhoff, Director of the Museum of Ethnology, Berlin, for his interesting hints on the treatment of early American civilizations;

Professor Dr Ernst Sittig, for manifold suggestions on dealing with the language and script of ancient Crete;

Professor Dr Phil. W. Brandenstein, Professor in Ordinary of Comparative Philology at Graz University, for his perusal of the chapter on Troy and important expositions of the stratification of the Homeric city;

Dr Reinhard Lullies, Chief Curator, Munich, for valuable interpretations of certain examples of the Greek plastic arts;

Professor Dr Siegfried Lauffer, for checking the chapters on classical Greece;

Professor of Sociology Dr Hans L. Stoltenberg, authority on German

ACKNOWLEDGMENT

etymology and elucidator of the Lycian language, for his help in composing the chapters on the Etruscans, Hannibal and Carthage.

All these scholars have contributed to the success of my work. If there are instances in the text where my wording does not correspond with their interpretations, they have done their best to ensure that my picture of the great civilizations of mankind is not at variance with scientific thought.

AUTHORITIES

ANDREWS, ROY CHAPMAN, American expert on Asia, 199

BANERJI, R. D., Indian archaeologist, 141
BATCHELOR, JOHN, student of the Ainu, 209
BELL, H. I., British papyrologist, 140
BLEGEN, CARL W., American archaeologist, 340, 341-2, 343, 345
BONI, GIACOMO, Italian archaeologist, 413
BRANDENSTEIN, W., Austrian Indo-European philologist, 23, 345
BRUNTON, GUY, British archaeologist, 50

CARTER, HOWARD, British Egyptologist, 67
CATON-THOMPSON, GERTRUDE, British archaeologist, 50
CHADWICK, J., British philologist, 341
COOMARASWAMY, ANANDA, Indian archaeologist, 162, 166
CUMONT, FRANZ, authority on Mithraism, 114

DELATTRE, R. P., French archaeologist, 418
DIBELIUS, MARTIN, German evangelical theologian, 139
DISSELHOFF, HANS DIETRICH, German Americanist, 23, 315
DODGE, THEODORE AYRAULT, American army officer and historian, 426, 427
DÖRPFELD, WILHELM, German archaeologist, 345, 346, 352-3
DUBOIS, EUGÈNE, Dutch doctor and anthropologist, 241

ERMAN, ADOLF, German Egyptologist, 74
EVANS, SIR ARTHUR, British archaeologist, 327, 328-30, 332, 335-6, 338 ff.

GAETANO DE SANCTIS, Italian historian, 426
GARDNER, E. W., British archaeologist, 50
GARSTANG, JOHN, British archaeologist, 122-3
GHONEIM, ZAKARIA, Egyptian archaeologist, 53-4
GROTEFEND, GEORG FRIEDRICH, German historian, 27

HABERLANDT, MICHAEL, Austrian ethnographer, 254-5
HALL, British ancient historian, 47
HELMOLT, HANS F., German historian, 27
HERZFELD, E., archaeologist, 101, 105-7
HEYERDAHL, THOR, Norwegian zoologist, student of Polynesia, 258, 267
HUMBOLDT, ALEXANDER VON, German scientist, 278, 305

JUNKER, HERMANN, Austrian Egyptologist, 50

KÄMPFER, ENGELBERT, Assyriologist, 28
KERAMOPOULLOS, A. D., Greek archaeologist, 358
KINGSBOROUGH, VISCOUNT, Irish archaeologist, 315
KOBER, A. E., American philologist, 341
KRAMER, SAMUEL NOAH, American Assyriologist, 38
KRAUS, F. R., Dutch Assyriologist, 38
KOUROUNIOTIS, K., Greek archaeologist, 340, 343

LAYARD, SIR AUSTEN HENRY, British archaeologist, 28
LIBBY, W. F., PROFESSOR, American archaeologist, 354
LOFTUS, W. K., British archaeologist, 28

MALLOWAN, M. E. C., British archaeologist, 33
MARSHALL, SIR JOHN, British Indologist, 141, 145, 146
MENGHIN, OSWALD, Austrian ethnologist, 50
MÉTRAUX, ALFRED, French student of Polynesia, 258
MEYER, EDUARD, German ancient historian, 47, 89, 340, 373
MOMMSEN, THEODOR, German historian, 420, 427
MONTET, PIERRE, French archaeologist, 96
MOUHOT, HENRI, French Sinologist, 166
MYRES, JOHN, British ancient historian, 341

15

AUTHORITIES

O'NEALE, LILA MORRIS, American archaeologist, 272
OPPERT, JULES, French Assyriologist, 28
OSBORNE, HENRY FAIRFIELD, American authority on Asia, 199

PENDLEBURY, J. D. S., British archaeologist, 336, 337
POSNANSKY, ARTHUR, German Americanist, 269, 273-6
PRESCOTT, WILLIAM HICKLING, American authority on Peru, 305-6

RANKE, LEOPOLD VON, German historian, 368, 369, 376, 390
RAWLINSON, SIR HENRY, British Assyriologist, 28
RÉMUSAT, ABEL, French Sinologist, 166
ROBERTS, C. H., British papyrologist, 139-40
RODENWALDT, G., German archaeologist, 358
ROUTLEDGE, KATHERINE, ethnologist, 256

SCHACHERMEYER, FRITZ, German authority on the Etruscans, 406
SCHARFF, ALEX, German ancient historian, 47, 89
SCHLIEMANN, HEINRICH, German archaeologist, 273, 327, 345, 350-3, 358
SCHMIDT, ERICH F., German archaeologist, 101, 105
SCHULTZE-JENA, LEONHARD, German geographer, 312
SITTIG, ERNST, German philologist, 23, 334, 341
SKEAT, T. C., British papyrologist, 140
SMITH, EDWIN, Egyptologist, 78
SPEISER, E. A., American archaeologist, 29-30
STAMATAKES, Greek archaeologist, 358

TAYLOR, British archaeologist, 28
THOMSON, American authority on Polynesia, 254-5
TSOUNTAS, C., Greek archaeologist, 358

VENTRIS, MICHAEL, British philologist, 340-1, 343

WACE, ALAN J. B., British archaeologist, 340, 341-2, 357, 358
WHEELER, SIR MORTIMER, British archaeologist, 144
WILAMOWITZ-MÖLLENDORFF, ULRICH VON, German ancient historian, 367
WOOLLEY, SIR LEONARD, British archaeologist, 28-9, 33-6

YEIVIN, Egyptologist, 71

INTRODUCTION

Now the first men, since none of the things useful for life had yet been discovered, led a wretched existence, having no clothing to cover them, not knowing the use of dwelling and fire, and being totally ignorant of cultivated food. And though the sounds which they made were at first unintelligible and indistinct, yet gradually they came to lend articulation to their speech.

Diodorus Siculus (circa 25 B.C.), Universal History.

'THERE's a whole city down there,' the fisherman said. He was right: you would only have had to step out of the boat into the water to find yourself standing on broad slabs of marble, balconies, walls and ruined houses. The old man told me that on clear nights he had often seen the dim outlines of the submerged city below the surface.

We were off Comacchio, where the calm waters of the Valle del Mezzano lagoon cover the ruins of the ancient metropolis of Spina. Legends thousands of years old tell us about this important Etruscan city, which reached its prime five hundred years before the birth of Christ and once dominated the Adriatic. The low-lying area at the mouth of the Po, a land of endless marshes and lagoons, has already yielded up vast quantities of Etruscan-made articles: vases, mirrors, candlesticks, clay figurines, bronze vessels, jewellery, examples of goldsmith's work and a Graeco-Etruscan cemetery of some thousand graves. All these things can be seen in the *Museo di Spina* at Ferrara, yet the city of Spina itself still lies buried, its site guessed at but hitherto unexcavated.

I had a queer feeling, standing there above the ruins of a once refined and pampered civilization. How many of the Etruscans' cities still lay hidden and undiscovered? Where exactly in Asia Minor was Tursa, their city of origin? Where had they come from, these men who called themselves Tyrsanians or Tyrrhenians, after the name of their city? A whole sea, the Tyrrhenian, bears their name; yet Tursa is still unlocated. The Etruscans or Tyrrhenians who emigrated from Lydia in Asia Minor and settled in Italy have provided us with a clear indication, in their burial-places, of the magnificent achievements which can spring from a meeting between East and West. There has rarely been an art which made a more human and vital impression or begged eternity for continued existence more fervently than the Etruscan.

By far the greater part of mankind's thoughts, dreams, deeds and material achievements, lies beneath the ground: under marshes, like the vanished city of Tartessus in the estuary of the Guadalquivir; or under the seas, like Gondwana, the former bridge of land between south Asia and Australia.

INTRODUCTION

When will we discover Wasukanni, capital of the Mitanni Empire, which must have stood somewhere on the southern slopes of the Armenian mountains? When will Kussara be unearthed, the erstwhile seat of Anitta, first king of the Hittites? Who is going to discover Nesa, entombed in the soil of eastern Anatolia, or identify the site of Arzawa, the kingdom which flourished in western Asia Minor about 1400 B.C.? And when will they excavate Sodom and Gomorrah or the other cities in the Vale of Shittim at the southern end of the Dead Sea?

In the year 400 B.C. a man arrived in Athens who had already, even in those days, won a great reputation. Hard working and hungry for information, he was steadfastly resolved to acquire a wide knowledge of the workings of Nature. He was so indifferent to fame and so anxious to avoid being recognized in Athens that he frequently withdrew into solitude, one of his favourite haunts being a graveyard. He discoursed with Socrates, the greatest Greek philosopher, yet not even Socrates recognized him. The world, he taught, consisted of innumerable, infinitesimal atoms. These atoms were only quantitatively definable, but the shapes which they could assume were infinitely variable, and they whirled about unceasingly in boundless space. They could either unite or disperse: they could even become so dense that they formed whole stars. The man who had evolved this theory was Democritus, who was born at Abdera in Thrace and lived from 460 to 370 B.C., dying at the age of ninety. His many attainments included a knowledge of perspective and the technique of arch-construction, and he was a brilliant mechanic and inventor. He raised the status of natural science to hitherto undreamed of heights, a task in which he was greatly aided by his wide knowledge of mathematics and astronomy. What won him most fame, however, was his atomic theory. He actually used the term 'atom' or *atomos*, the Greek for indivisible, and held that atoms moved about in the Universe whirlwind fashion, agglomerating and forming composite substances like fire, water, air and earth.

Democritus had taken over the rudiments of his atomic theory from Leucippus of Miletus, but he had a more restless mind and was a greater scientist than his former teacher. Eager to know the world, he collected information from all quarters, spending the bulk of his private means on travelling expenses. He saw Babylon, visited Egypt, and roamed across large tracts of Asia, probably reaching Persia, the Red Sea, and even India. In fact, most of Democritus' scientific knowledge was acquired from Chaldean theologians in the temples of Mesopotamia, and from the astronomers of Babylon and Egypt.

Another man who travelled widely in the East was Thales of Miletus, who lived about 600 B.C. He adopted the Egyptian division of the solar year into

365 days and learned how to foretell eclipses from the Babylonians. It was he who accurately forecast an eclipse of the sun for May 28th, 585 B.C. Anaximander imported the idea of the sun-dial from Babylon in 560 B.C., and was the first man to attempt to draw a map of the known world. Pythagoras armed himself with a letter of recommendation to Pharaoh Amasis and travelled to Egypt, where he learned the Egyptian language. He also spent some time with the Chaldeans and the Magi in Babylon and Persia. Hipparchus, who was probably the most important of all the Greek astronomers, identified more than 850 stars. He was born in Bithynia, in modern Turkey, and the East had a decisive influence upon his scientific researches. Ptolemy, who lived between A.D. 100 and A.D. 178, was born in Egypt, and was the last great natural scientist in antiquity.

The number of notable Greek scholars who acquired the fundamentals of their knowledge from the East is extraordinarily large, and it was this knowledge which, developed and amplified, Greece and Rome handed on to the Western world. The Greeks and Romans were our masters, yet it was they who in a sense paid for our schooling, for they exhausted and weakened themselves so much in the process of exchanging and giving away ideas that they ultimately brought about their own downfall. Christ spoke Aramaic, a Semitic language, and his teachings conquered the world on the wings of Hellenism. In literature, we are still using the same themes which men evolved, expounded and performed long ago in ancient Greece, and Euripides is a mute and constant collaborator in all our modern playwrights' most 'original' ideas. Plato and Aristotle were the founders of our philosophy and ethics, and Athens and Olympia the home of our ideals of sport.

We have all been linked together for many, many thousands of years now, and the ties which bind us are not only ancient but remarkably far-reaching: they stretched nearly all the way round the world, long before the great age of discovery arrived. The gulf between Mesopotamia and China, for instance, was bridged by the Asiatic steppe-civilization of the Scythians, who made use of Mesopotamian and Chinese examples in evolving an art of their own. Not only was it very long-lived, but it travelled over enormous distances, borne along in the Scythians' waggons and on the backs of their pack-animals. Between the 8th and 3rd centuries B.C. the Scythians dominated the greater part of what is now Russia. It is an astonishing thought that the golden fish, sixteen inches long, which was found in Germany in 1882 at Vettersfelde, Brandenburg, was a Scythian work of art dating from about 500 B.C., and that these same Scythians were in cultural communication with countries as far away as Turkestan and China.

In China, the history of copper and its alloy, bronze, goes back to 1400 B.C. What is interesting, however, is that the idea of casting bronze was actually imported into China from the 'Far West'. East and West were, in fact, interchanging cultural ideas 3500 years ago. But there are still greater surprises in store. During the Shang Dynasty, an era of great culture, lasting roughly from 1500 to 1050 B.C., whose bronze-craftsmanship was of a remarkably high order, we repeatedly come across the image of Tao-tie on sacrificial bowls. This theme was also adopted by the magnificent bronze-smiths of the Chou emperors, whose line survived for almost a thousand years until 249 B.C., when the last of the dynasty abdicated. Tao-tie is the head of an unidentified beast whose origins lie far in the prehistoric past and may perhaps have stemmed from a vague memory of some ogre or long extinct man-eating monster. Astonishingly enough, the likeness of this monster travelled as far as America, where Tao-tie reappears as Quetzalcoatl, the plumed serpent. More than that, the mysterious animal is to be found not only in the Olmec civilization on the coast of the Mexican Gulf, but also in the Chavin civilization of ancient Peru, where it recurs unmistakably as a gold mask in the shape of a beast of prey.

Five hundred years before the birth of Christ, the Pythagoreans taught that the earth neither occupied a central position in the cosmic system nor enjoyed any special privileges over other heavenly bodies: it was a mere speck of dust in the Universe, like millions upon millions of others. The middle of the Universe was occupied by a 'central fire', from which the inhabited parts of the earth were averted, and towards which the sun and moon were turned. Aristarchus of Samos announced in 260 B.C. that the sun remains motionless, while the earth gyrates about it on its axis. This startling piece of information lapsed into obscurity for two thousand years, until the 16th century, when Copernicus, closely following out the ancient Pythagorean line of thought, defied the whole of contemporary ecclesiastical opinion by expounding his heliocentric system.

This was how ideas, discoveries and inventions travelled back and forth across the world. Our whole Western way of life is descended from civilizations which once flourished in Mesopotamia, Egypt, Central Asia and the islands of the Aegean. Yet the span of time embraced by the advanced civilizations known to us is incredibly brief. Ten thousand years are like a day in the lifetime of human evolution. We are in possession of sewing-needles, pipes, flutes, harpoons and magicians' wands, for instance, which date back twenty thousand years to the Magdalenian period, so called after Abri la Madeleine near Tursac in Dordogne, France. Man has been roaming the earth as a two-legged creature endowed with intellect since the first Ice Age, or about 600,000 years ago. We of today are not only burdened with the countless afflictions and everlasting mistakes of past millennia, but are also heirs to the discernment and knowledge which they have brought in their train. We owe the brief happiness of what we call our existence to countless millions of men who returned to dust long ago.

Every age mistakenly considers itself to be the most important in world history: hence those irritating and well-worn phrases which are always occurring in public speeches: 'We stand at a turning point in history', or 'We are living in a new age'. When was there ever *not* a 'turning point' or a 'new age'? The golden ages of the great civilizations are merely peaks protruding from a boundless ocean of barbarity. Yet not even the loftiest peaks of creative achievement ever guess how close they are to Heaven, or recognize themselves for what they are. That is why sublime art and utter primitivity are so often found living cheek by jowl. An interval of hundreds or thousands of years must elapse before men can recognize exactly where and when *homo sapiens* scaled the steepest heights of human endeavour and achievement. I refer, of course, to artistic and not scientific achievement, for a work of art is unique and never recurs, while scientific advances can take their time. What one generation leaves undone another century will see accomplished, and, were there no such thing as danger or man as the enemy of his own kind, technological discoveries would always occur exactly when they were needed.

There is nothing new about our way of life or the age in which we live, nothing very new about our ideas or scientific methods. We have taken over much more from the East, from Greece and Italy, than we realize. All our modern sciences move along the same lines, concerning themselves almost exclusively with the nature of material things and living creatures. We imagine that our wide knowledge in these spheres represents progress, and care far too little about man's inner self, his mind and soul. Yet I submit that the nations and eras which did not merely strive for material comfort, but kept eternity before their eyes in all they did, were probably more 'progressive' and certainly wiser than ourselves.

The Greeks were fond of telling lies, a trait which explains their natural gift for poetic composition. They learned the fundamental secret of how to blend imagination and reality in order to produce a work of art. More important to them than anything else was the investigation and study of the human being and his potentialities in the mental and spiritual realm; and in this respect they were always truthful and sincere. Whether we of today, with our 'exact sciences', are pursuing more perilous chimeras than the ancient world ever did, is not yet clear. The only certainty is that if the intellectual development of the West goes on lagging, as it has been doing, behind our indisputably great advances in the field of natural science, we shall one day be like small children playing with large and dangerous toys which they do not understand, or like specialist technicians pressing buttons and unleashing forces whose moral effects they are no longer capable of assessing.

What would happen if we could look back and see with our own eyes all the sufferings and struggles which man has experienced during his hundreds of thousands of years as a human being? Would we turn to salt, like Lot's wife?

I do not think so. For it was not Sodom and Gomorrah that brought us through the aeons to our present state, but nations and individuals, endowed with an endless store of patience, who always built afresh upon the ruins of death and devastation, accumulating a vast treasury of ideas which their more recent descendants one day committed to stone, clay and parchment.

I did not write this book today or yesterday, nor did I write it with the hasty intention of cashing in on the well-known hunger of our own day for information about the past. When I was assembling material for this book, people's attentions were quite otherwise engaged. I have worked on it for many years, always trying to reduce the vast amount of available material to smaller and more concise proportions, and always keeping an eye on the latest scientific discoveries. I owe a great debt of gratitude to the numerous specialists who have gone over each of my chapters and offered so many suggestions. There is not an idea or a figure which I have included in these pages without careful reflection, and I have learnt in the course of my work that the foremost authorities frequently hold the most divergent opinions about the statistics of many an ancient city's population or the date of a ruler's birth or death.

Various sections of this book have been published separately in European periodicals since 1949, which has given me a chance to examine criticisms and make certain amendments. It has taken me many years to form a living picture of this world with its diverse inhabitants, their activities and their past history.

In my view, the known span of human history is so brief that we may for once be pardoned if we try to isolate and define the essential features of the past, its nations, countries and civilizations. We only learned how to write four or five thousand years ago, but the salient events in our history occurred at widely separated points in that tiny portion of earth-time. Every civilization, every race, has furthered at least one side of human development in its own inimitable fashion; and in the prime of every civilization lie the seeds of its death.

This is not a history book, nor is it exclusively concerned with ancient civilizations. All past history once lay in the present, and all present history is rooted in the past. If I were asked which I considered the most important landmarks in the history of mankind, I should probably reply: the invention of writing by the Sumerians; the Book of Job and the Prophets' wealth of ideas; democracy in Athens during the Periclean Age; the life and death of Socrates; the art of Japanese wood-engraving; and the poems of Li T'ai-po. These items all seem to lack cohesion and to vary a great deal in comparative worth, I admit, but when you have wandered around the world a few times as I have, things take on a different perspective.

We must always be on our guard against the temptation to apply the restless, progressive standards of the West to civilizations which should be assessed by quite different criteria. Our Western standards are not by any means applicable to every race on earth. Neither dynamism nor progress, in the Western sense, necessarily make for human happiness. The slumbering, dreaming existence of the Pacific races, for instance, with its careless tranquillity and unconsciousness of sin, its elemental rhythms of joy and sorrow, is probably much closer to the secret of living. Arrested civilizations appear to have a much longer expectation of life than dynamic civilizations, which is why the Polynesians have survived for so long. The whole of humanity has made much greater and faster advances in the past seven thousand years than ever before; yet *homo sapiens* managed to survive 600,000 years of slow and undisturbed existence without writing, chemistry, or machines. Progress, in our sense of the word, is probably a poor guarantee of mankind's longevity: hence the greater wisdom of men like Li T'ai-po and the Japanese masters of wood-engraving who 'painted the moving world'.

I am not saying that the West is likely to meet its downfall any sooner than the East. That would be a contradiction in terms, for the East is appropriating all the most dubious achievements of the West and furiously copying them. China, Japan, India and Asiatic Russia are much more obsessed with progress today than the West. There seems to be little to choose between any of the sections of modern humanity: they have all lost the art of living.

It was in 1932 that I first set out to visit all the places whose past history has most contributed to our own way of life: Athens, Carthage, Rome and Constantinople. I travelled along the Nile, the Euphrates and Tigris, the Indus, the Yangtze and the Hoang-ho. All the world's greatest civilizations were born in these river-valleys. They are still inhabited by farmers and merchants with the experience of thousands of years behind them, enlightened men who are wise in the ways of the world and sometimes even of eternity, thrifty and not over-hospitable men who know that a tide of invading humanity will one day make them poor.

And I got to know other races, too: warm-hearted, generous people like the wandering Polynesians of the Pacific and the nomadic inhabitants of the endless steppes, grasslands and deserts of the world; people who never cling to their possessions because their herds keep them constantly on the

move, people who often look up at the starry skies and are better equipped
to realize the futility of material things. I talked to nomads in Arabia, drank
many bowls of tea in the tents of Mongolia, and lived among the wandering
Tunguses in the forests of the north Manchurian *taiga*.

We are a tenacious and inventive species. Perhaps our modern technology
will enable us to survive the next Ice Age in 50,000 or 100,000 years' time.
Who knows? There have been four Ice Ages and three temperate periods
during the past 600,000 years, so men have already managed to survive spells
of cold lasting up to 100,000 years on four separate occasions, each time without the help of modern science.

Yet, in another respect, our ideas are imperfect and limited. We forget
that we are only an insignificant link in the endless chain of people who have
made us what we are and brought us as far as we have come, men who
survived not because they strove for success, but because of their immense
reserves of fortitude and endurance. Our horizons are alarmingly restricted
because we always greatly over-estimate the significance of the convulsions,
upheavals and so-called 'New' Orders of our own small age.

We should always remember that man is far from being a necessity.
The earth would still go on rotating about the sun even if he ceased to exist.

THE LIVING PAST

MESOPOTAMIA

7000 YEARS AND 4000 GODS

Without the ancient Orient we should not be what we are; without an understanding of it we shall never know ourselves. Countless fruits of civilization have been passed on to us by the Sumerians via the Assyrians, Babylonians, Egyptians, Greeks and Romans. The excavations in the Land of the Two Rivers have acquainted us with the origins of our own intellectual development. Our alphabet, our religion, our legal system and our arts all presuppose an interminably long chain of evolution. From Mesopotamia and the Sumerians came what is perhaps the most decisive starting-point of all civilization: the art of writing.

'OF the history of the Sumerians we know nothing.' This sentence occurs in Helmolt's *History of the World*, a work comprising nine volumes which appeared at Leipzig in 1913.

Yet in the space of less than forty years we have succeeded in unearthing human epochs which have trebled the temporal extent of our historical knowledge. It is in the valleys of the Tigris and the Euphrates, or what is now Iraq, that the most ancient of all the advanced civilizations of mankind has been wrested from the depths of the desert sand — an enthralling, almost fabulous world which had long lain buried and forgotten.

The Greek historian Herodotus had never heard of the Sumerians. Berossus, a Babylonian scholar who lived about 250 B.C., had only heard tell of them in dim legends. He wrote of a race of monsters who were supposed to have emerged from the direction of the Persian Gulf under the leadership of a certain Oannes. It was not until two thousand years after the time of Berossus that the Sumerians were rediscovered.

Only a hundred years ago, scholars were still gazing uncomprehendingly at the mysterious characters, chiselled in stone, which the Sumerians had left behind them. It was the German scholar Georg Friedrich Grotefend who first discovered a method of deciphering this picture-writing. The 'cuneiform script' of the Sumerians is in fact the earliest known system of writing in the world. The word 'cuneiform' comes from the Latin *cuneus*, meaning wedge. It was a method of writing practised by many of the Mesopotamian peoples: in other words, those living between the Tigris and the Euphrates, and also by the Elamites, or Old Persians, and others.

The ancient Sumerians lived from 3500 B.C. onwards in the region between modern Baghdad and the Persian Gulf, and between the Tigris and the Euphrates. Their own records, which reach back into times far beyond our ken, never mention any other land of origin. It was here that they

27

invented the picture-writing which developed, in the course of time and through the adoption of clay tablets as a writing surface and hollow stems as graving-instruments, into cuneiform characters. It was here – and only here – that the earliest evolution of cuneiform writing came about, for we find no suggestion by the Sumerians that they borrowed the idea from elsewhere. The beginnings of this writing date from about 3000 B.C. The characters were inscribed with specially fashioned hollow reed-stems upon tablets of clay, which were subsequently hardened. Oppert, the French scholar, christened the people who first discovered this system of writing 'Sumerians', and Engelbert Kämpfer called the cuneiform method *Keilschrift*, or wedge-script.

In Sir Henry Rawlinson the English possessed a man, like Lawrence of Arabia, of wide interests, rich imagination and great gifts. He was working as political agent in Afghanistan and Arabia, and was an indefatigable traveller and researcher. During a stay in Persia, he studied the 'cuneiform inscription' of Behistun and, while Consul at Baghdad in 1844, managed to decipher this ancient tablet, upon which was also engraved a translation in Babylonian.

In 1854 the Englishmen Taylor and Loftus started digging in the ancient cities of Ur, Eridu and Erech (Uruk). Erech had apparently been a king's capital before the Great Flood, and Gilgamesh had once ruled there. At the end of the nineteenth century, French archaeologists digging at Telloh brought to light the remains of the city of Lagash. Here they discovered stones bearing the first clues to the history of the Sumerian kings. Sir Austen Henry Layard uncovered ancient Nineveh under the hill of Kouyunjik on the right bank of the Tigris, opposite the present-day city of Mosul. There, amid the ruins of the palace of the Assyrian king Assurbanipal (668–626 B.C.), he unearthed a large library of clay tablets, among them whole 'dictionaries' in clay which listed Sumerian words together with their Semitic-Assyrian equivalents. King Assurbanipal's library was exceedingly old, and the clay tablets contained transcripts and collections of texts dating from about 2000 B.C.

Among the tablets was a very precious find, the Gilgamesh Epic, or history of the Flood, which proved to be an astonishingly accurate confirmation of what the Book of Genesis tells us about Noah. The Gilgamesh Epic was inscribed upon twelve tablets, each of which contained a more exciting revelation than the last. The whole work consisted of 3000 lines. Fragments of all twelve tablets were found under the ruins of the King's palace at Nineveh, and of the full text about 1500 wholly or partially complete lines are known to us. Tablets VI and XII are better preserved than the rest.

Shortly after the First World War, Professor (later Sir Leonard) Woolley directed an Anglo-American team of archaeologists working jointly for the University of Pennsylvania and the British Museum in excavating the small site at Al Ubaid (Tell el 'Obed), north-west of Ur. They unearthed temples, residential districts, pottery and sculptures. It was realized by this time that the Sumerians had already attained a high level of civilization 5000 years ago. The effect of these researches was to lift the veil from an ancient race whose existence covered a span of time perhaps twice as long as the history of the West from the birth of Christ until the present day.

Christ's contemporaries never ventured to think back so far into the past. In his day Sumer had long ago been forgotten. It lay in the twilight of past millennia, and mountains of desert sand covered what remained of the bright mosaics, fine sculptures, mighty temples, vases, pots, ornaments and cosmetic implements which had once belonged to human beings very like ourselves. But more than that: this flourishing life reached back into an age which already seemed immeasurably old to the Sumerian scholars and priests of 2300 B.C. Priests, who were the historians of their day, compiled lists of their kings which went back for 432,000 years!

Now the Sumerian priests were certainly guilty of an exaggeration when they wrote in terms of 432,000 years, for the Sumerians did not arrive in Mesopotamia, the Land of the Two Rivers, until 3500 B.C. But, of course, it is quite possible that these early settlers had previously lived for thousands upon thousands of years in other cradles of civilization. After all, Western civilization travelled from the Land of the Two Rivers and the Nile Valley into Palestine and Greece, from Greece to Rome, from Rome to Spain, France, Germany and England, and from England to North America. So perhaps the Sumerians had left a similar westerly trail behind them before they finally arrived at the place which is probably the Paradise of the Bible. Perhaps they were the 'Americans' of the years around 3000 B.C.

To reach the bottom of the ruins at Nippur entails no less than 70 feet of downward digging — an excavation deeper, in fact, than the height of most houses in a modern metropolis. At Nippur, this seventy-foot depth betokens an age of about 5000 years.

In very recent times, archaeologists have discovered something more: no matter how far they delve into this early cradle of mankind, the beginnings of life always lie buried a little deeper in the past. In 1927, Speiser, of the University of Pennsylvania, discovered a hill in the region to the north of Mosul which rises some sixty-five feet above the plain of the Tigris. The townsfolk of the neighbourhood call this hill Tepe Gawra. Upon excavating it, Speiser laid bare no less than twenty-six strata, each belonging to a different period; only the topmost six fall within historical times. The latest excavations which have been carried out in the Land of the Two

Rivers are leading us ever backward in time, into the 4th, 5th and 6th millennia B.C., and the excavations near Hassuna, to the south of Mosul, have once again pushed what we once regarded as prehistoric back into the dimness of the past by a not inconsiderable period. Iraqi archaeologists found clay vessels there, as well as representations of a Mother-goddess, little amulets, the remains of rush mats and sickles of flint and bitumen. The first half of the 4th millennium B.C. has been named the Halaf, Samarra and Eridu period, after the most important archaeological sites in northern, central and southern Iraq. One particular curiosity belonging to the period was discovered for the Museum of Baghdad: the neck of a large earthenware vessel decorated with a painting of a woman's head. On each cheek she bears three blue lines, just like the ones which are still a familiar sight on the faces of tattooed Bedouin women of today. It was at Eridu that the earliest known houses in the world were unearthed, as well as the oldest temple-precincts as yet discovered. Above this temple lay no fewer than thirteen other temples, one layer upon another, each of which was carefully laid open.

When Jarmo, in northern Iraq, was excavated by Chicago University, the oldest town-settlement known to us was discovered, dating back 6000 years before Christ. A few little clay figurines found there must be the earliest examples of sculpture in existence, being, as they are, almost 8000 years old.

Probably the most interesting ruined site of all is the one which was excavated not long ago in the central region of the Euphrates Valley, on Syrian soil, not far from the Iraq border. People had been passing by the ruins on the hill of Tell Hariri for two thousand years without ever giving them a second thought; and yet beneath, entombed in sand, there lay the once mighty city of Mari. It was only after some Bedouins had accidentally come upon the fragments of a small statue that archaeologists began to be interested in the hill of Tell Hariri.

In January 1933 the French set their shovels to work on a large excavation project. In twenty years they have uncovered the city of Mari and its history, a history which stretches from the beginning of our chronology to a point 2000 years earlier. Even now there is no end in sight. The layers of Mari's ruins dating from 4000 B.C. lie at a depth which has never been reached before.

The exhibits unearthed here, articles of stone, clay and shell, paint a world so vivid that the time which has elapsed between today and the year 3000 B.C. seems to shrink into nothing. The civil servants of the day stare at us with wide eyes; the tiny faces of the 'caricature sculptures' of those times grin at us; rulers pray with folded hands; a pious man leads a small goat to the sacrifice; court stewards peer with cunning and inquisitive expressions out

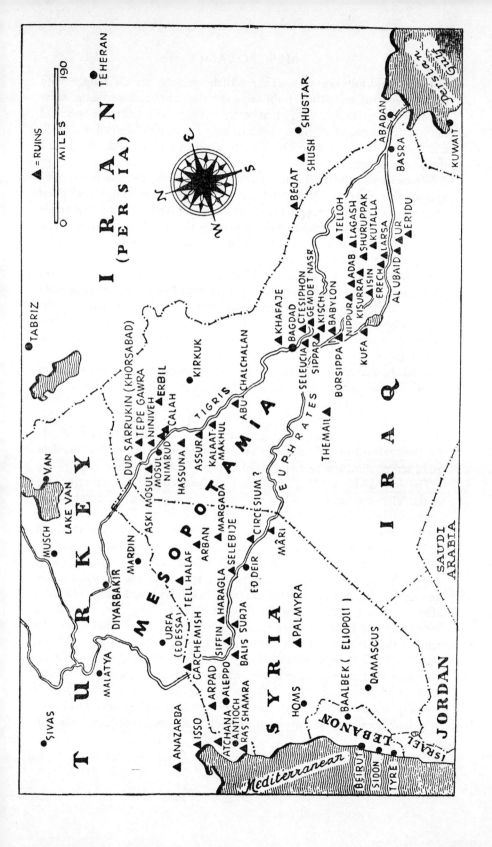

of their world into our own. There sits the great singer Ur Nanshe with perfect deportment, as though she were just about to break into song; there a bronze lion gazes at us with a hint of disillusion in his inlaid stone eyes; and the headless statue of a prince shows us how beautifully adorned with frills and tassels were the court robes of Mari, almost two thousand years before the birth of Christ.

We know that the inhabitants of Mari were Semites, and thus not racially akin to the Sumerians. However, Mari's civilization is certain, like all great civilizations, to have sprung from many different sources. So it is that beside the grave and hardy qualities of the Sumerians we find the humorous, subtle cynicism and the rather more 'Parisian' interpretation of life which prevailed among the inhabitants of Mari.

All the thoughts, activities and endeavours of the Sumerians were focused upon the future. Could we be happy if we always knew what lay in store for us? Well, the prophet-priests of the Sumerians, the *baru*, knew everything. They controlled the doings of their people for 3000 years. For generations and centuries they went on comparing the turn of events with the condition and appearance of sheep's livers, and in this way they finally claimed the ability to expound the future accurately from an inspection of them. This meant that the whole life of Sumer was ruled by a knowledge of the inevitability of fate.

And Fate was their god. The city belonged to him, as did all the cultivable land. He could dispense either happiness and plenty, or want and death. The Sumerians believed implicitly in the god of their city and his attendant gods, served him, and were prepared to sacrifice everything to him.

The god had his city, but he also had his *State*, and the political prototype of the 'city-state' is, next to the art of writing, the most important single contribution made by the Sumerians to the civilization of Mesopotamia and the ancient world in general. These city-states were strongholds of advanced civilization, and first place among them was held by Uruk, the Erech of the Bible. German scholars have been digging here, in what is now Warkah, and publishing their scientific findings since 1929. No one can stand today among the lofty ruins of the Zikkurat of Warkah without feeling even now, after 4000 years, something of this thought: that here, long ago, the god and his children and his city once formed a true unity. Only thus could the temple, the Zikkurat, have become such a mighty 'mountain', and only on that account did the people of Uruk pile the fruits of their faith and fanaticism into the heavens, nearer to him, their god Anu. Anu was the father and king of all other gods. At Uruk his cult was closely associated with the worship of Inanna (or Innin), the Mother-goddess and Mistress of Heaven who later became more important to Uruk than Anu himself, and who was called Ishtar by the Semites. Female deities were possessed of great significance for the Sumerians.

In the temples of Nippur they worshipped Enlil, the God of the Air, together with his consort Ninlil. The Sumerians had an especial relationship with the moon, for their seers foretold the future by observing the characteristics of its phases. The city of Ur once belonged to the important Moongod, Sin, whose sacred number was 30. Sippar and Larsa were cities of the Sun-god Shamash. Eridu worshipped Ea the Water-god, whose son Marduk later became the national god of the Babylonians. There was even a city, Borsippa, whose god was Nebo the Scribe. Nebo's function was to list the decisions of the other gods. In addition, he was the patron of the Sumerian scribes, mankind's earliest pen-pushers and stenographers.

It is possible that the Sumerians were the first men ever to conceive the idea of building their god a house, or at least a terrace where they could be near him and where he could reside. Every city possessed one or more such terraces. They dominated the scene, being in course of time built higher and higher, one level upon another, until they finally became man-made mountains or towers, the 'high places' of our Bible. Man felt it a duty to build his god a sacred place. Only the power of faith, *true* faith, only a strong inner feeling of yearning for god could have accomplished those miracles in brick, those links between heaven and earth, those artificial mountains reaching into the sky, those temple towers we call *zikkurats*. The word means simply height or point, and was the Mesopotamian expression for temple or terraced tower. The Sumerians and later the Babylonians left us magnificent examples of these zikkurats: at Uruk, Eridu, Al'Uqair, Khafaje, Ur, Assur and at Babylon. And since the great city-gods of the Sumerians originated in the distant darkness of prehistoric times, many a zikkurat has crumbled away into wind and dust and earth.

The Sumerians were acquainted with astrology and had, moreover, an amazingly good knowledge of astronomy. They undoubtedly believed in resurrection after death, and so it cannot have been too terrible for the attendants of the Sumerian kings to allow themselves to be buried alive in the company of their dead masters.

Two hundred and twenty miles to the south of Baghdad lie the ruins of the city of Ur. There, in the autumn of 1922, Professor Leonard Woolley excavated a royal cemetery. During the ten years between 1922 and 1932 he and his assistant Mallowan, who has subsequently become well known in his own right, methodically dug up this burial-ground, and thereby shed the light of day richly and conclusively upon the true spirit of Sumerian civilization for the first time. Woolley found 1850 graves. From accompanying discoveries, scholars were able to place most of them in their chronological order. Only 751 out of the 1850 contained no objects of a datable nature.

Sixteen graves were distinguished from the rest by their especial opulence, construction and mode of burial. In these 'royal' graves were found human sacrifices whose number varied between six and eighty. Woolley distinctly perceived that in every case only one of the bodies had been buried, and that the rest had been sacrificed. As we shall see later, this sacrifice did not take place under duress.

The presence of human sacrifices could only be ascertained in graves which contained vaults constructed of stone. They were not found exclusively in graves provided with rich appurtenances. For instance, Prince Mes-Kalam-Dug's grave was much more splendid than the king's grave to which Woolley gave the designation PG/1054. But whereas no skeletons belonging to human sacrifices were found in the Prince's grave, PG/1054 contained eight. Woolley also unearthed a queen's burial-chamber. This grave too has been catalogued, and goes in archaeological records by the name of PG/800. The queen's name was Shub-ad.

How do we know that? Woolley found a cylinder seal on the queen's right shoulder which bore her name. And we know more still: she was 4 feet 11½ inches tall, and of a delicate bone-structure. She had small feet, small hands and a large, narrow head. Woolley also thinks that he can establish that she spent most of her time in a kneeling position, like Japanese women. Prince Mes-Kalam-Dug was about 5 feet 5 inches tall. Woolley has deduced from the build of his skull that he was left-handed. Both the queen and prince belong, according to Woolley, to the 'proto-Arabian' race. The graves are about 4500 years old, and date from the 1st Dynasty of Ur. A hundred years either way in this estimate of the date do not make much difference. The queen and the prince may have been laid in their graves in about 2600 B.C. Woolley puts the time at between 3400 and 3100 B.C.

What was the method of burial in those days?

Queen Shub-ad was found lying stretched out on her back. Her corpse had simply been laid on a wooden bier. At her head crouched a female attendant, while the remains of a second were found at her feet. These attendants died a sacrificial death, for the burial-chamber had been ceremonially sealed.

Down the ramp leading to the chamber came a procession of courtiers, soldiers and other men and women attendants. These latter had donned brightly coloured robes, and wore golden hair ornaments and golden ear-rings, chaplets of lapis lazuli, cornelian and gold-leaf, silver hair-pins and ornamental combs, necklaces and large robe-pins. They all took up their position in the pit, far below ground-level, and following them down the ramp came carts drawn by oxen and donkeys, complete with drivers and grooms. Each man and each woman held a small receptacle of stone, earthenware or metal in their hand. In the middle of the pit stood a large copper vessel. Apparently, they had all filled their cups from this and taken poison. Even the animals must have been killed in some manner. The whole grave was then filled in with earth. This is the only way in which Professor Woolley can account for his having found the victims tidily ranged in their rows and giving such an impression of utter calm, and why he was unable to detect any signs of violence whatsoever. Not even the girls' coiffures had been disarranged. Probably all of them died in a prone or seated position, as though they had quite quietly and suddenly decided to die. Indeed, Woolley could see that the musicians among them had been playing until very near their end.

Every member of the retinue in every king's grave was always found holding a cup in his hand, and the copper vessel was always to be found down there, too. Woolley is convinced that the courtiers not only died quite peacefully, but also of their own free will. He thinks that the animals appear in every case to have died after their grooms, but they, too, died in their allotted places.

It is certain that these live burials were not bride-sacrifices to the gods, as many scholars have supposed. Actually, there were more men than women found among the principal people interred. A bride who had been selected for a god would have had to be young and beautiful, yet Woolley ascertained that Queen Shub-ad was about forty years old. Even so, it must be remembered that this opinion is based on the examination of a woman who had been dead for almost 5000 years.

As for the rest of the things which Woolley brought out of the royal burial-ground and into the light of day, they surpass one's wildest imaginings. Queen Shub-ad's shell powder-box, her little reticule of blue malachite, golden pins, rings, bracelets, necklaces, the wonderful amulets with their enchanting colours, the queen's diadem, the many varieties of head ornament covered with finest gold-leaf, all these things are so wonderful, even by modern standards, that no goldsmith of our own day could even begin to conceive them. Woolley found massive golden bowls of beautiful design among the objects in the queen's and the prince's graves, and so many bright and lovely things were unearthed as to be almost uncountable: harps and lyres, gaming-boards, figurines of wood, metal, stone, shell and lapis lazuli, little boats, a royal standard inlaid with frieze-work in mosaic of white marble, drinking-vessels of lapis lazuli, bowls and basins—all of extraordinarily simple shape and design which give them a look of costliness and modernity. There were golden daggers as well, together with axes, lance-heads, carriage-shafts and bridle-rings; and, finally, that most famous object of them all, the 'Ram in the Blossoming Tree', a magnificent composition in precious metals and coloured stones.

Imagine how it must feel to discover graves like these! They lie quite undisturbed, with body-servants still inside the tomb, soldiers on guard at the entrance, grooms holding their beasts' bridles, musicians at their instruments, and the ladies of the court stationed respectfully near the king's chamber — the mass burial of a whole retinue, loyal to their sovereign lord even in death. These people entered the death-pit firmly believing in a life after death, and must have felt completely secured by the close proximity of their god-prince against any dread of the eternal night to come.

Among the other city-states which flourished in the central region of Sumer early in the 3rd millennium B.C. was Lagash, city of the god Ningirsu, and the place which is now Telloh. Lagash was only a provincial city of Sumer, but clay tablets were discovered there, and that is why we know something about this particular place. The citizens spoke Sumerian, and were cattle-dealers, fishermen, merchants or craftsmen. Like every other city in Mesopotamia, Lagash was built around its temple. The citizens of Lagash loved their freedom, enjoyed ownership of property and were only obliged to obey the decrees of the city-god and his temple in so far as they had to maintain the public water-supply, the drainage-system, and other necessities.

In about 2500 B.C. disaster overtook Lagash: foreign rulers conquered the city and all Sumer with it. It is interesting to read how clay tablets written by an 'historian' of those days describe the conditions then prevailing. Boat-officials took over the boats, cattle-officials took over the cattle, large and small, and fishery-officials appropriated the fisheries. Any citizen who sheared a white sheep in front of the palace was obliged to pay a tax of five shekels. Each divorce that took place brought in five shekels for the ruler and one shekel for his minister. The best agricultural land belonging to the city-god was earmarked for the foreign ruler's onions and cucumbers. Death itself was taxable, and innumerable priest-officials robbed bereaved relatives. The whole countryside swarmed with tax-collectors. The palace became rich, its harem grew fat.

Then, when things were at their worst, a new ruler came to power in Lagash. He was the famous king Urukagina. He did away with the authorities and priest-officials who were battening upon the citizenry like a swarm of drones. The priests had once more to become servants of God, and the city's governor, the *Ensi*, the first servant of his city. This great social reformer looked after the property and well-being of all, and must have been able to boast in his old age that he had really given his people their freedom. Unfortunately, his reign lasted less than ten years.

Later, out of the neighbouring country of Umma, came the Sumerian ruler Lugalzaggisi, who overthrew Urukagina, destroyed the right of property, slaughtered many inhabitants, pillaged the temples and founded a new empire in Uruk. There was no weeping, no complaining. Everyone accepted it as fate. The gods had their reasons.

When was the Sumerians' dying hour? Well, they never died at all. They were merely assimilated, like the Tunguses by the Chinese, or the Etruscans by the Romans, or the Wends by the Germans. For at the zenith of their civilization, in about 2350 B.C., the Sumerians were succeeded by the Semites who had settled in the district of Akkad after their immigration from the Arabian Peninsula.

Sargon I is an historical figure who has become legendary. He was the founder of the Akkadian Empire and also of an era — we call it the Akkadian period — which lasted from 2350 until 2150 B.C. The king now became a god, and the Akkadian Empire a god's kingdom. This Semitic dynasty was made up of a succession of extremely able men. Sargon, his sons Rimus and Manistusu, and his grandson Naramsin, were all undoubtedly rulers of great competence.

Sargon himself was the son of La'ipu the Semite. His mother is said to have been a priestess, and Sumerian legend relates a story about her which is reminiscent of Moses. The priestess laid her new-born child in a little basket of osiers bound with clay, set it afloat on the Euphrates, and then went quietly back to her duties in the temple. A gardener called Akki found the little basket, and the boy later became cup-bearer to King Ur-Zababa of Kish. He dethroned his master and made himself ruler of Kish in his stead. He defeated Lugalzaggisi and exhibited him alive in a cage in front of the temple of Enlil at Nippur. Then he subjugated the whole of Sumer, finally washing his weapons in the waters of the Persian Gulf. He eventually reached Anatolia and founded the first large empire in world history.

The Semitic kingdom of Akkad was once again destroyed by a foreign people, the Guti, and in the end we find ourselves back in a world of city-states, and in Lagash, where a late-Sumerian dynasty held sway. Frigid diorite statues of Gudea, the king who ruled there, survive in the Louvre and many other museums in the world. Sometimes the prince is portrayed in a sitting posture and sometimes standing, but always extraordinarily composed and tranquil, with folded hands and feet pressed firmly together. Gudea was a large-scale owner of real estate, as many foundation-stones attest, and the crowning glory of his life was the new temple he caused to be built for Ningirsu, the city-god of Lagash.

At the beginning of the 3rd millennium B.C., the Sumerians began to write on clay tablets. By the latter half of the 3rd millennium the Sumerian art of writing was fairly far advanced. About fifty years ago, several thousand clay tablets of this period were dug up in a town near Nippur, some hundred miles from Baghdad. They are now in the University Museum of Philadelphia, and in the Museum of Oriental Antiquities at Istanbul, while several hundreds more, which were mainly bought up by dealers in antiquities in the East, repose in the British Museum, in the Louvre and at Berlin. They are an amazingly rich store, ranging from quite short textual fragments to innumerable hymns, myths, prose narratives, proverbs and fables. Sumerologists have naturally only been able to decipher a few of the tablets during the past fifty years. Many of them are smashed, but many others fortunately exist duplicated several times over, so that, by dint of much piecing-together and restoration, experts have finally been able to read them. The work will last for years and decades to come, but several good translations of Sumerian literature are already in existence today.

King Ur-nammu was probably the first man to convert one of the terraced temples into a stepped tower, or so-called zikkurat. It is very likely that a zikkurat of this type was the parent of the Tower of Babel. Ur-nammu was the founder of the 3rd Dynasty of Ur, and reigned about 2050 B.C.

Professor Samuel Noah Kramer of the University of Pennsylvania tells us how he came upon an extremely interesting law deriving from this king. In 1951-52, when staying in Istanbul, F. R. Kraus, Professor of Cuneiform Studies at the University of Leyden, recommended him to make another attempt to 'read' clay tablet No. 3191 from the Nippur collection at Istanbul Museum. Kraus had earlier reconstituted this tablet out of two broken pieces. Kramer put No. 3191 on his desk in Istanbul and sat himself down in front of the small, sun-baked, pale brown clay tablet, which measured a mere eight inches by four. After days of arduous work, he realized that before him lay one of the earliest laws which had ever been found. We read that the king dismissed corrupt officials, that he introduced honest weights and measures, and that he looked after orphans, widows and the needy, for 'He who has a shekel shall not fall prey to him who has a mina' (sixty shekels). Anyone who cuts off another man's foot has to pay him ten shekels. Anyone who breaks another man's bones, a silver mina. But anyone who cuts off another man's nose only has to pay two-thirds of a silver mina. Professor Kramer rightly commented that in his opinion this law must have been preceded by even more ancient codices.

The celebrated legislator King Hammurabi, of the Amoritic or West Semitic dynasty of Babylonia, lived three hundred years later. He reigned for forty-two years, and under him the Sumerians and the Semites became a single nation: the Babylonian nation. The supremacy of the Semites was thus finally assured, and they held sway over the ancient 'land between the rivers'. At the same time, however, the history of the Sumerians began to fade farther and farther into the past, only to be dug up once more in our own century. And even as you read these lines, printed in characters which ultimately owe their existence to a Sumerian invention, digging is still going on.

BABYLON WAS WELL LIT AT NIGHT

'I came to Babylon and saw you not. Ah, I am so sad.'

THE region in which Babylonia and Assyria once lay is today known as Iraq. This name means 'land of the river-banks'. It is an appropriate name, for the country has literally been manufactured by the rivers Euphrates and Tigris out of the alluvial silt deposits which have made possible sowing and harvesting, flourishing civilizations, thousands of ancient cities and, in fact, the beginning of our Western history altogether.

Once upon a time the two rivers flowed down to the sea and into the Persian Gulf independently of each other. But in the course of some thousands of years they deposited such huge masses of mud, and pushed out so much new land into the sea, that today the estuary of the Euphrates and the Tigris lies about ninety-five miles farther to the south-east than it did in the golden age of Babylon and Assur. And so anyone who wants to unearth ancient cities should not dig for them in this new ground. However, the soil 'between the rivers' is so rich in buried cities, towns, temples and artistic treasures, that people will be making valuable finds for many years to come.

We have already formed a good idea of what life was like among the Babylonians and the Assyrians, that is to say, in an era which lies between 2500 and 4000 years in the past. Even now, only about one per cent of all the submerged cities has been dug up. The other ninety-nine per cent are still lying there waiting for the field archaeologist and his picks and shovels. Magnificent royal graves still slumber beneath the ground with their contents of gold, jewels and precious stones. Between thirty and sixty feet below ground-level there still sleep hundreds of fortresses, towns and temples. Whole libraries await the attentions of scholars who in these days could easily read them, once they were unearthed. It is fortunate that the Babylonians and Assyrians wrote in cuneiform characters upon clay tablets, for of our own literature, printed as it is upon paper, not the slightest trace would have remained after 4000 years. Anyone who travels through the arid desert country near the Euphrates and the Tigris finds it hard to conceive that cities once flourished here, or that mighty kings reigned and gods were worshipped in their temples by hundreds of thousands of men. It is a region of limitless solitude, ruled only by death. Not a pillar, not a single archway remains standing. Everything has crumbled away to dust. Only the fox peeps from his earth, and a deathly hush reigns, occasionally broken by the plaintive howl of a jackal. It would never occur to anyone not well acquainted with archaeological excavation that thousands of human habitations lie buried with their secrets beneath this desert land, or that graves have lain here undisturbed for thousands of years. The plain is dotted with small hills. There are hills wherever one looks, and under each hill reposes a town. Why especially under hills?

Towns grow upwards. All the wood, stone and other materials which people amass in one particular place, all the refuse, sweepings and rubble, go to form a large mound when their town is destroyed or falls into decay; But on top of every town that perishes a new one is erected, and the hill therefore grows in size. That is why excavations have to be conducted with the utmost care, because the historical periods lie right on top of each other in layers, the oldest at the bottom, and on the surface, perhaps, a modern village.

Thriving civilizations are repeatedly razed to the ground when they reach their zenith and have on that account become weak and apathetic.

What is civilization, in fact? It is the breathing-space between the two dominions of jungle and steppe.

When urban civilization has reached a peak, and people no longer care for anything save beautiful clothes, perfumes and baths; when they have become peaceable and law-abiding and are no longer interested in playing the soldier; that is always the signal for a steppe-race to fall upon them — usually from the east — and destroy all their pomp and splendour. It has been like that for thousands of years now.

The man who visited Babylon about 3000 years ago would have seen from far off a mighty edifice rising two hundred feet into the air, its seven lofty storeys towering above the spires of the city. It was rather like a tower of steps. The glazing on the bricks in its walls sparkled in the Mesopotamian sun. High up, forming the top storey, was a temple. Inside the temple, so Herodotus informs us (I, 181), were a golden table and an ornate bed, carefully prepared. At night a girl lay on it, ready to welcome the god of the Babylonians. This building was the Tower of Babel. Biblical tradition has it that the Babylonians originally intended to build it as high as the sky (Genesis ii, 4). However, God in his wisdom would not sanction building so high in those days. There is fundamental truth in the thought that splitting the atom and reaching for the skies are the first steps towards the destruction of mankind. Even the gods of the Babylonians had eventually to surrender to the god Yahweh.

To the south of the tower of steps stood the gigantic temple of the god Marduk, and below this temple Babylon lay spread out, a city of broad thoroughfares and narrow lanes, of rubbish-strewn streets, of foetid smells mingled with the scent of myrrh, of noise and bustle, a city boasting bazaars and a sacred avenue flanked by one hundred and twenty brazen lions. One end of this avenue led through the famous Gate of Ishtar, which German scholars transported back to the Pergamon Museum in Berlin.

The golden age of Babylon lasted, with certain interruptions, from 1750 until 562 B.C. Two particularly outstanding kings marked the beginning and the end of this epoch: Hammurabi and Nebuchadnezzar. The succession of the Babylonian kings was broken early on by the sovereignty of the Kassites. They were a savage race from the mountains and steppes, a non-Semitic people from the mountains of eastern Iran. The Kassites overran Babylon about 1675 B.C. Thirty-six of their kings reigned for a total of 577 years over the world empire on the Euphrates. During that period Babylon lost its early predominance over western Asia. Syria and Palestine remained independent, and the high priests of Assur made themselves kings of Assyria.

It was Hammurabi who left behind him a code of laws which, although it no longer rates as the oldest, is certainly one of the most famous in existence. He tells us that, like the Moses of our Bible, he received his laws direct from God himself. Hammurabi is depicted on the famous diorite stele or stone pillar which bears his code of laws as a man with a long beard wearing a toga-like robe and a turban, like King Gudea. Opposite him sits the Sun-god Shamash, giving him divine inspiration. Hammurabi erected the massive diorite block bearing his laws in the temple of Marduk at Babylon. The stele was later — during the 12th century B.C. — carried off by the Elamites to Susa, where it was dug up by French archaeologists between 1897 and 1899. Today the stone is probably the most valuable piece in the Louvre museum at Paris.

Hammurabi was not only a legislator but also a fine stylist and letter-writer, a great builder of cities and a victorious general. He destroyed cities as well as built them, for it was he who laid Mari in ruins.

This most remarkable figure of his age ruled over the whole of Sumer, Akkad and Assyria and reigned for forty-two years, from 1728 to 1686 B.C. Apart from the diorite stele, there is another fine sculpture of the king's head in existence, executed in black granite. The bearded countenance, the strong markings round eye and forehead, the intelligent mouth, all contribute to give us an impression of a great ruler and a man whose abundant experience had made him wise and enlightened. The artists of those days did not attempt to reproduce every feature exactly according to nature, yet even to-day the king's spirit speaks to us with extraordinary vivacity and directness out of the black marble which, like the stele, can be admired in the Louvre. His laws were really 'legal judgments' or court decisions, no longer couched in the old Sumerian tongue but in Akkadian — 'Law and justice in the language of the country'. His penal code was still a *lex talionis* governed by a harsh retaliatory principle. Penalties were literally based on the principle of 'an eye for an eye'. For instance, the putting out of an eye was punishable by blinding, and the causing of grievous bodily harm by physical punishment of like severity. A man who struck his father lost his hand. A man who boxed the ears of a 'superior' received sixty lashes with a bull's pizzle. If a doctor performed an operation successfully he got his fee; if the patient died, the physician had one of his hands chopped off. Slaves were branded, and any surgeon who removed a branding-mark without instructions from the slave's owner also lost a hand. Furthermore, doctors were obliged to perform operations for officials of high rank at a cheaper rate than for ordinary citizens. Should a house collapse and its proprietor thereby lose his life, the architect was put to death. If the son of the proprietor died, the architect's son likewise forfeited his life. Anyone who killed a strange girl incurred the death of his own daughter, and anyone who bore false witness or made unfounded accusations was called severely to account. Unfortunately we also read that it was possible to be indicted for witchcraft. The accused person was forced to undergo 'trial by water' — in other words, to submit himself to divine judgment. Hammurabi tried to protect the poor, the widows and orphans; but, generally speaking, his 'cuneiform judgments' are quite as unyielding as the stone upon which they are inscribed.

When we come to Nebuchadnezzar, at the end of Babylonian history, we can already recognize the signs of decadence. He ruled over the whole of the known world as far as Egypt, and made Babylon one of the wonders of the ancient world. He built a number of palaces and fifty-four temples. He drove canals from the Euphrates and the Tigris far out into the country, to make the land fertile. Even today one can follow from an aeroplane the tracks of the Babylonian canal system which dried up so long ago.

However, towards the end of his reign, in 562 B.C., Nebuchadnezzar became intoxicated with his own power. Tormented by delusions and insomnia, he imagined himself a beast of the field, crawled bellowing through his palace on all fours, and ate grass.

In his successor Nabonidus, Babylon no longer possessed a warrior-king but a scholar. He spent his time in archaeological pursuits, and carried out research into a Sumer which was already old in his day.

The Book of Daniel in the Old Testament tells us about Belshazzar. It demonstrates only too clearly the weaknesses and fears of a dying dynasty. Belshazzar read the end, and death, in the fiery letters which appeared on the wall. In the same night he was murdered.

The Assyrians waged a struggle lasting hundreds of years with the Babylonians for the hegemony of western Asia. They were a tough, hardy race who lived in the valley of the upper Tigris and its mountainous borders.

The pillagings, burnings and massacres of the Assyrians belong among the bloodiest chapters in all the history of mankind. Assurbanipal, Tiglath-Pilezer and Sennacherib are the most important Assyrian kings — not least 'important' in their role of ferocious conquerors. Sennacherib, for example, razed 89 towns and 820 villages to the ground, and carried 208,000 prisoners off into exile. He fought a fierce battle for Babylon, captured the city, and burned it down to its foundations. Men and women, young and old, he slaughtered them all. The corpses lay piled so high in the streets that any would-be fugitives found themselves trapped before the city began to burn.

History is usually passed on to us at second hand, which is why it so often seems dry and boring. In the case of Babylonia, however, we have an eye-witness's description by Herodotus the Greek, who lived about 450 B.C. and saw the city of Babylon only 150 years after the death of Nebuchadnezzar. We know that Herodotus is often given to romanticizing, but his descriptions do have the value of direct, if at times rather exaggerated, experience. According to Herodotus, the city wall was fifty-three miles long, and broad enough to allow a team of four horses to be driven along its top in comfort. Through the centre of the city, bordered by palm trees, flowed the Euphrates. Bridges spanned the river, and there was even a tunnel leading beneath its bed from one bank to the other. Large numbers of bricks were found in the ruins of Babylon. In ancient times, bricks were stamped with the name of their royal owner, and many of Babylon's bricks bear the inscription 'Nebuchadnezzar, King of Babylon'. It was under him that the city blossomed for the last time before the coming of the Persians.

Herodotus also tells us about Queen Semiramis of Babylon. So many fables and legends were spun about the person of this Chaldean princess, even in the age of antiquity, that it is nowadays very difficult to distinguish between historical truth and poetic fiction. On the other hand, how could the Greeks have accounted this princess's famous hanging gardens as one of the seven wonders of the world, if Semiramis herself had never existed?

Semiramis is the Greek version of the Babylonian name Shammuramat. A pillar which was discovered in 1909 describes Shammuramat as 'a woman of the palace of Shamsi-Adad, King of the World, King of Assyria . . .' The inscription establishes the fact that Shammuramat enjoyed a unique position and that she survived a change of government. She lived about 800 B.C., and it seems likely that she conducted a military campaign against the Indo-European Medes, as well as against the Chaldeans.

That much at least is fact. Legend knows, as always, much more. The princess, it is said, was a Mede. She was never able to acclimatize herself to the hot sun of Babylon and yearned for the mountains of her northern home. She therefore had many feet of earth piled on top of the upper terrace of her palace. Many kinds of plants and flowers were planted there, and even the tallest varieties of tree were allowed to take root. The airy botanical gardens were irrigated by water pumped from the Euphrates by machines concealed in the supporting pillars and kept working day and night by relays of slaves. It was there, high above the city in the shade of her trees, that the princess sat, an imperious lady attended by the women of the harem.

Babylon was well lit at night, for the Babylonians had already discovered how to extract petroleum from the Mesopotamian soil. Alexander the Great (356-323 B.C.) took this information for an old wives' tale. He dipped a boy's head in the liquid and set fire to him with a flaming torch, feeling certain that the lad would not catch fire. Unfortunately he was wrong.

Babylon undoubtedly had its 'garden suburbs'. To quote from a letter sent from one of these suburbs to King Cyrus of Persia in 539 B.C.: 'Our property seems to me to be the most beautiful in the world. It lies so near Babylon that we enjoy all the advantages of the big city, and yet, when we come home, we are out of all the noise and dust.'

In spite of all this, or because of it, slavery existed there as it did everywhere else. The purchase price of slaves was fixed according to their age and capabilities. Female slaves were cheaper than male slaves. Their masters often handed them over to other people for a certain period in payment of debts, at the end of which time they were returned. On the other hand, debtors could also 'hire out' their wives or sons until their indebtedness had been worked off. One could be a slave for any of several reasons: by being born of parents who were slaves; by being taken a prisoner of war; as a form of punishment; or by voluntarily selling oneself. Slaves were completely in their master's power. He had the entire disposal of their man-power, their property and their children. He could sell them and punish them, although he was not allowed to kill them. Most slave-owners had children from their female slaves. These children remained slaves until their father's death, when they became free. However, they could not inherit from their father unless he had publicly adopted them as legitimate children during his lifetime. It was considered good form for a slave-owner to look after the feeding and housing of his slaves, as well as to pay their doctor's bills and provide for them in times of unemployment and old age. It sometimes happened that slaves whose services had won them particular favour with their master were released. Only very few achieved this doubtful good fortune, however, fraught as it was with the dangers of economic insecurity. Most of them were fully reconciled to their lack of freedom, bore their lot like people who had never known any other, and never regretted that their children were slaves by birth. In course of time this apathetic and under-privileged class grew larger and larger and at the same time gradually more refractory and menacing, particularly in times of external danger.

MESOPOTAMIA

The Babylonians solved the problem of arranging marriages in such an ingenious way, according to Herodotus' account, as almost to invite our copying it today. On a given day, all the marriageable girls were collected together in the market-place. A crier bade them stand up one by one and auctioned them in turn. The most beautiful of them was the first to be sold, and naturally brought in the most money. Then came the second most beautiful, and so on, one after the other, down to the ugliest. The proceeds of the auction were then placed in a chest and, from the 'half-way mark' on, each man who declared his readiness to marry an ugly girl got some money with her. The uglier the girl, the more money her future bridegroom received. To quote Herodotus: 'In that way the beautiful girls brought the ugly and deformed ones to husband.' He closes this interesting chapter (I, 195) with the words: 'This, then, was their wisest custom.'

But now comes, as Herodotus puts it, 'the Babylonians' most loathsome practice'. Every girl in the land of Babylonia was obliged on at least one occasion to go and sit in the temple of Mylitta and 'entertain' a stranger. The daughters of the well-to-do drove to the sacred grove in closed carriages, taking their serving-women with them. The girls seated themselves in neat rows, with straight paths running between them in every direction. 'Then the strangers strolled along and picked out the one they wanted.' The first stranger to toss a coin into any girl's lap could take her with him. Afterwards the girl was consecrated to the goddess, went home, and never, as Herodotus expresses it, did it again, unless she got married. 'Girls who were pretty and shapely soon came home again. The ugly ones, on the other hand, had to wait a long time before they satisfied the requirements of the law. Many of them sat there in the sacred grove for as long as three or four years.'

Clay tablets have been dug up with little love-poems, songs and letters engraved on them in cuneiform script. One of these letters has an amazingly up-to-date ring about it. It exemplifies the yearning and loneliness of a young heart in love. A young man has arrived in the huge, cruelly impersonal city, only to find that she, Bibiya, is not there.

To Bibiya. May the god Shamash and the god Marduk for ever endow you with good health. I sent a messenger to inquire your whereabouts. Please tell me how you are. I came to Babylon — and saw you not. Ah, I am so sad.

And again, what a tender ring there is about the words of this love-song, the beginning of which appears in a catalogue found at Assur: 'I brought a girl hither. Her heart was like a stringed instrument. I thought of you to-night.' And what did the lovely child look like who was in the mind of the poet when he wrote these lines: 'You came to the gate, light of mine eye. Until this evening! Until tonight!'

EGYPT

FIRST-RATE SEWING-NEEDLES —
4600 YEARS OLD

In those prehistoric times Egypt looked considerably different from the way it does nowadays, when it is one of the most arid and treeless regions in the world. In those days there was still an appreciable amount of wooded country, and large tracts of territory, especially in Lower Egypt, would have presented a jungle-like appearance.

Alexander Scharff

THIRTY dynasties reigned in Egypt between about 2850 and 332 B.C., the date when Alexander the Great took possession of the country. The famous German historian Eduard Meyer put the 1st Dynasty even as early as 3200 B.C. The German scholar Scharff, the Englishman Hall and other historical researchers place the start of Egypt's history in 3000 B.C. In recent times the supposition has been favoured that Menes, the first king of the 1st Dynasty, ruled no later than 2850 B.C., and that that is the date which marks the beginning of Egypt's amazing three thousand years of history. Of course, 'historical time' is really only an artificial classification. We possess clear evidence of the Egyptians' cultural achievements dating from 2000 years earlier.

Long before the 'beginning of Egyptian history', 15,000, 20,000, or even 30,000 years earlier, man already existed on the high ground near the Nile, which at that time flowed through a marshy valley. What this man looked like we do not know; we only know his tools. The tools of the Old Stone age (also called the Palaeolithic age), the oldest stone implements of mankind known to us, are, whether they come from the Nile Valley or its neighbouring desert, similar in type to all those of the same period which have been found in the whole of North Africa and western Europe. *Homo sapiens* of 30,000, 50,000, or even 80,000 years ago seems to have owned a common civilization, whether he lived in Europe or Africa, a state of affairs which mankind has never again achieved.

During the middle of the Palaeolithic age — we are still speaking of a period which lies about 15,000 years in the past — man developed a flint-knapping technique, that is to say, a method of chipping hand-tools out of flint, which is characteristic of the whole large region of North Africa and Egypt.

During the late Palaeolithic age, between 12,000 and 5000 B.C., this puzzling and still unclarified period of cultural unity prevailing in the Mediterranean area disintegrated.

Fireplaces of burned earth and kitchen refuse of this period have been found along the former banks of the Nile and by the side of prehistoric lakes. Fish-bones were unearthed, together with animal-bones, shells, ivory and burnt ash. Stones which had been hollowed out for use as corn grinders betray the fact that 10,000 years ago in Egypt man was already making flour. What is more, he engaged in agriculture and harvested cereals. He knew how to use the bow and arrow, too, as many arrow-heads of stone, ivory and bone bear witness. It appears, though, that the early inhabitants of Egypt did not as yet manufacture earthenware vessels.

In the Neolithic age, roughly between 5000 and 3000 B.C., man turned more and more to agriculture, and began to breed cattle, build houses, make pottery and weave cloth.

From about 5000 B.C. onwards, an extraordinary natural phenomenon took place. The land bordering the Nile began to dry out. Man was accordingly forced either to succumb to the will of Nature or to become inventive, and build himself a civilization. Thus, in Egypt, Nature made great demands upon the ingenuity of *homo sapiens* from the very start. For, the moment man withdrew from the drying banks of the Nile and took up a settled abode, he was forced to provide for the irrigation of his arable land. He had to fight against flooding, build dykes and lay out canals. And so it was that the mighty, capricious Nile compelled puny man to develop his natural gift for organization. It introduced him to ideas of civilization earlier here than in many other regions of the world. It is generally true to say that large rivers and their valleys always seem to have been the best teachers and educators of humanity.

Neolithic graves in the vicinity of Tása in Middle Egypt demonstrate to us that even the Egyptians of this prehistoric period already believed in a life after death, an existence which would be similar to their daily life on earth. A dead man was laid on his left side in an oval pit with his knees drawn up in a foetal position, as if he were sleeping in his mother's womb. His head pointed south and his face was turned towards the west. The body was wrapped in hide, mats or cloth, and the head was often supported by a leather cushion. Into the grave with him went brown and grey-black bowls filled with food and drink, little palettes of alabaster or slate containing eye- or face-cosmetics, ivory bracelets, necklaces, little cosmetic spoons, mortars for grinding grain, polished stone axes, stone knives, stone saws and so on.

It is true that the broad skulls and jaw-bones of the inhabitants of Tása differentiate them anthropologically from the later historical peoples of Egypt. But, even so, it seems that the ideas about death, and a life after

death, which were later accepted without question in Egypt's early historical times and which influenced the Pharaohs to become pyramid builders, were directly passed on from this dark period of prehistory.

The unwearying efforts of Gertrude Caton-Thompson and G. Brunton in their excavations at Badari, from 1925 onwards, brought to light a civilization which was already baking its clay pots in ovens, and could carve combs and spoons out of hippopotamus tusk. They even unearthed statuettes of women which were designed to accompany the dead. But the civilization of Badari found its highest fulfilment in the making of jewellery. It is here that we first meet the technique of quartz-cutting which was later to play such an important role in the Egyptian glass and faience industries. However, the Badari civilization teaches us even more. It shows us that the people of Middle Egypt were already in contact with central Africa. Ivory was introduced from the south and from Nubia, shells were brought from the coasts of the Red Sea, turquoises from the Sinai Peninsula.

Further excavations carried out in the north, in Lower Egypt, by E. W. Gardner and Gertrude Caton-Thompson since 1925 at Fayum, and by Junker and Menghin at Merimde-beni-Salaam from 1928 onwards, have brought to light bone needles and fishing-hooks, ladles, spoons and articles of jewellery. Dwelling-places were at this time constructed of wicker-work, wood and reed mats, and were frequently built in a circular shape. The people of the period buried their dead in 'grave-dwellings' above the ground, and 'shared' their daily meals with them.

Between 3500 and 3000 B.C. there flourished the 'first Negade civilization', christened after the site of its discovery at Negade in Upper Egypt. Here were found articles of copper, something which was probably a fishing-hook, a harpoon and polished red ceramic ware with white ornamentation on it depicting people, animals, birds, ships and trees.

Even finer are the ceramics of the second Negade period which is also known as the Gerzeh period, after another archaeological site, and which existed between 3000 and 2600 B.C. Here we can already find representations of groups of people, beasts fighting, birds on trees, crocodiles, gazelles and giraffes. Flat-headed copper axes were discovered, together with copper basins and needles, not to mention some first-rate sewing-needles, quite like those which we use today. There were also a number of remarkably exciting finds made, such as bowls with spouts very like the cans of the same period which have been found in Mesopotamia, and cylinder seals with friezes of animals on them, vessels with corrugated handles moulded on to each curved side, and vessels in the shape of animals. All of this makes it certain that relations already existed between Egypt and the Jemdet-Nasr period of Mesopotamia, in the early part of the 3rd millennium B.C.

At Hieraconpolis a chamber was found which measured 8 feet by 6 feet 6 inches and was divided into two parts. One of them had probably contained the dead man, while the other contained articles for his use. The walls of the tomb were decorated with river scenes, ships and scenes of hunting, battle and dancing, just like those found on pre-dynastic vases.

Many ancient royal graves have been found dating from the close of the Negade period onwards. They are large, flat, four-cornered constructions with oblique outer walls built of mud brick. A burial-shaft leads downwards from the surface through the rock floor into subterranean chambers. It is certain that graves like these were developments of those of the Neolithic age. Native workmen of today call these bench-like grave-mounds *mastaba*, an expression which comes from the Arabic word for bench. It is in graves of this kind, located north of Sakkara, at the edge of the Nile Valley, that kings of the 1st Dynasty were buried: Horus Ahai, Horus Zer, Zer's wife Merjet-Neith, Horus Wadjet, Horus Kaa — in fact, most of the early Pharaohs known to us.

What does the word 'Horus' before a king's name signify? In prehistoric times, Horus was the chief god of Upper Egypt, and the Nile Delta had already been conquered by the rulers of Upper Egypt before history began. Ever since that time, the kings were themselves called Horus, as being visible and earthly embodiments of the god of their realm. Thus god and king were identified in one person. The symbol of Horus was a falcon.

The earliest historical figure in the Egyptian realm and the founder of the 1st Dynasty, was King Menes. This king is not a mythical figure, although his name was not originally Menes but an honorific epithet meaning 'The Eternal One'. He lived about 2850 B.C., and was responsible for the unification of Upper and Lower Egypt. It is thought probable that he was the founder of Memphis, and we also know that he conquered Lower Egypt from the south, that is to say, from the direction of Upper Egypt. A grave found near Negade in Upper Egypt has been attributed to him. The first prominent personalities in Egyptian history were King Zoser and a scholar named Imhotep. The latter was an architect, a doctor, priest, magician, author, a composer of epigrams and, above all, personal adviser to King Zoser. He lived about 4600 years ago, and probably designed the plans for Egypt's oldest large monument, Zoser's 'step-pyramid' at Sakkara.

What is this step-pyramid, and how did Imhotep the master-builder or Pharaoh Zoser arrive at the idea of erecting a pyramid out of blocks of stone piled on top of one another in tiers?

WHERE DOES PHARAOH SEKHEM-KHET
LIE BURIED?

On his empty sarcophagus lay a branch of giant fennel.

THE propellers have been droning their way across the Mediterranean the whole night long. The sun has not yet risen, but it is already light. The sky is a mixture of rose-red and yellow. The Nile Delta lies shrouded in its eternal mist. And then, suddenly, there is the desert and Heliopolis.

Cairo's suburbs extend for ten miles outside the main city. Heliopolis stands in a higher, drier, more healthy position than Cairo. It is a huge artificial creation, and every drop of water has to be piped to it. The distance between Cairo and the village of Abusir is nineteen miles. Abusir, like Sakkara, stands beneath the escarpment of the western desert. Both of these large villages are inhabited by the descendants of the people of Memphis, Egypt's earliest capital.

The pyramid is always in sight, standing high up on the plateau like a queen, near her much smaller sisters out of later times. Like all the pyramids, that of Sakkara looks yellow-brown, but it differs from them in one important respect: it displays its steps. Before the time of Zoser, a king's grave was never more than a single, large, four-cornered massif of bricks — the pile, in fact, which the Arabs call a mastaba. Zoser's towering construction of six such 'benches' is therefore not really a pyramid so much as a stepped-mastaba.

King Zoser erected this huge monument, or rather, had it built for him by Imhotep, during the nineteen years of his reign. Zoser and his four successors comprise the Pharaohs of the 3rd Dynasty. He reigned about 2600 B.C., and was responsible for constructing the first monumental building in the world to be made of natural stone. Until his day, mud bricks had been the only building-materials.

What exactly is a pyramid? It is a colossal burial-mound built of stone. Yet the pyramids and the whole grave-precincts are even more than that: they are a reflection of the city in which the Pharaohs lived. Thus Zoser's tomb is a sort of reproduction of Memphis, his royal seat which lay in the valley below. What was there built in mud, wood and reed mats, arose here in the desert built in stone.

This, then, is what distinguishes King Zoser from all the other Pharaohs: he was from every point of view the first great Pharaoh, and the first Pharaoh who ventured to build a pyramid. And the pyramid was only a part of the grave, for it was encircled by a mighty wall enclosing government buildings, courtyards for the celebration of festivals, huge store-chambers, a second grave, and a sacrificial temple – all of which belonged to the dead king's residence.

The step-mastaba of Pharaoh Zoser now lies in the midst of thousands of graves; so he rules, even now, over a host of dead subjects. It is a land of the dead pervaded by the silence of death. An aerial photograph revealed that near Zoser's step-mastaba another burial-precinct lay mapped out in the desert sand.

Aerial photographs are the archaeologist's X-ray pictures. They have an uncanny way of revealing the outlines of cities, walls and graves which have long ago disappeared, especially when taken after rain.

So it seemed that for thousands of years two vast and mysterious rectangular outlines had been lying there in the sand. It was not until 1951 that Dr Zakaria Ghoneim, Chief Inspector of the Antiquities Service at Sakkara, started excavating this site.

Zoser's immediate successors only reigned for six years each. The Pharaoh who built the grave-precinct which was discovered in 1954 undertook a most peculiar course of action. To begin with he did as Zoser had done, and erected a step-pyramid. When he had reached the third tier, however, he changed his mind and stopped short. He obviously had no wish to lie beneath a 'grave-mound' as the shepherds and nomads of Upper Egypt had once done, but preferred to be buried in a 'house', like the peasant-kings of the Lower Egyptian Delta. So he filled in the whole area bounded by the perimeter wall up to the height of the three tiers already built. In the process, he covered over a portion of the perimeter wall, namely the long side to the north, and extended his grave over it. In this way a huge mastaba was formed, its dimensions being roughly 760 by 215 yards. It is worth reflecting that this area is much larger than that of the Pyramid of Cheops, which is only about 260 yards square.

The first surprise which attended Zakaria Ghoneim's excavations was the discovery of the covered portion of the wall. This had been preserved unaltered and undamaged in the same condition as it was when first built, 4550 years before.

At about the same time, Ghoneim uncovered three of the slanting outer walls which had belonged to the original step-mastaba. It now lay below the level of the desert, of course, for 4000 years of wind and weather had completely covered it with drift-sand. The great problem now was where to find the entrance to the subterranean chamber beneath the mastaba massif. The actual burial-chamber must lie somewhere down in the depths below the immense earth-work. But where was its access?

It was during the winter of 1953-54 that Ghoneim finally discovered it, north of the mastaba massif, a passage-way which led obliquely downwards through the rock. That was in itself an immense achievement, for the ground area is prodigious, and the passage or tunnel is only a tiny slanting 'crack' in the monumental construction. However, it must be remembered that only just over 500 yards away lies Pharaoh Zoser's burial-ground, the step-mastaba whose already familiar ground-plan could serve as a guide to the investigation of the new grave. And so, just as Zoser's step-mastaba had provided his successor with a model, so it now provided a plan for our present-day archaeologists to follow.

Ghoneim began by clearing out the passage-way into the burial-chamber which he had discovered. In the course of this work, some shoring-material fell in and crushed one of his workmen to death. Deeper and deeper into the rock-face burrowed the archaeologist, until he had reached a depth of over 120 feet, where, at last, he came to the burial-chamber. An uncomfortable, clammy, musty heat reigned there. In the middle of the vault stood a massive sarcophagus of solid alabaster.

Two circumstances were remarkable: in the first place, the sarcophagus was not in the exact centre of the vault, and, secondly, it was standing a little obliquely. Was it an indication that the sarcophagus might be empty? We are in ancient Egypt, and the ancient Egyptians were never careless about the installation of such an important article of religious worship as this.

The fact that the sarcophagus was still closed came as a great surprise. Nearly all the royal vaults hitherto discovered in Egypt contained sarcophagi which had been forced open and rifled. Out of hundreds, only a very few had been found intact, as for example those of Tut-ankh-amun, Osorkon, Psusennes and Queen Hetepheres.

So here, once again, was the extremely rare phenomenon of an undisturbed grave. The Pharaoh must surely be lying inside. And if a Pharaoh did repose there, then vast treasures of intrinsic and artistic value dating from earliest times were also to be anticipated — the oldest art-treasures in human history.

On Saturday, June 26th, 1954, the massive lid of the 15-ton alabaster sarcophagus was lifted in preparation for the ceremonial opening. They peered through the first crack into the interior. They shone torches inside. The sarcophagus was empty. It was not only empty, but immaculately clean. There was not the slightest trace of any object inside.

How was this to be explained? Was the Pharaoh buried elsewhere? Was he lying in a second burial-ground? Was there yet another royal vault in the same burial-ground? Was this merely a sham grave? This was a possibility, for the Pharaohs of that epoch used to construct one grave each for Upper and Lower Egypt, just as Zoser, this Pharaoh's predecessor, had done shortly before, inside his perimeter wall.

Here we come to something which brings the time of this Pharaoh strangely close to us. We do not know what took place in this burial-vault, but the people who lingered down here 5000 years ago left us a curious memento: on the sarcophagus were found the remains of a large branch. In the passage of 5000 years it had decayed so badly that it went to powder when touched. Botanists have established beyond question, however, that it was *ferula*, or giant fennel, a thorny plant yielding a kind of resin which can be used for medicinal purposes, and which may have been used in the embalming process. Why should they have put the branch on the empty sarcophagus? Perhaps it was a form of symbolic burial. Perhaps the Pharaoh reigned on, and was buried, when he eventually died, in another vault.

There is an unfinished look about the interior of the whole building, a hint of improvisation and inexplicable haste. One is involuntarily reminded of the briefness of the Pharaoh's reign. Of the Pharaoh . . . but which Pharaoh?

We know the most important title of the Pharaoh who built this burial-ground. That was soon discovered. Certain clay jug-stoppers which were found in the new vault all bore the same title. It was Sekhem-khet.

And here we come to yet another remarkable fact about this 5000-year-old greeting from the other world. The title Sekhem-khet was altogether new to us. It was a quite unfamiliar title, although its form and composition placed it unequivocally in the 3rd Dynasty. For instance, Zoser's title was Netjer-khet, and the word *khet* means 'body' in each case.

It may be assumed that Sekhem-khet was Zoser's successor, which would mean that he died in 2575 B.C., and would explain why his tomb is both near to, and shares certain common features with, that of King Zoser. If all this is correct, the king whose title is Sekhem-khet would have borne the name Zoser-Atoti, for that is the name which follows Zoser's in the tables of Egyptian kings.

As is the case with all pyramids, the sliding-way or ramp down which the sarcophagus was originally dragged into the vault was sealed in two places by blocks of stone. In front of one of these obstructions, in the passage deep in the rock, were found the remains of a little jewel-casket. The casket had crumbled into dust, but the jewellery remained intact. It consisted of twenty-one golden arm-bands, a golden necklace, a pair of golden tweezers, and a golden sea-shell. The two halves of this shell, beaten out of pure gold, fit perfectly together and are joined by a hinge.

What did the discovery of this shell mean to us? We had found the loveliest and earliest example of the Egyptian goldsmith's art; more — we had found the most enchanting and at the same time the very earliest product of the goldsmith's art in the world. Its incredibly delicate filigree-work must, in its minuteness, make it the finest exhibit which Cairo Museum possesses. The shell has a diameter of just over 4½ inches.

What queen, what delicate princess, once carried this trinket? What graceful woman may once have used the shell as a little casket for jewels, perfumes or cosmetics?

And how mysterious that the find should have been made precisely at this spot, in a passage leading to a sarcophagus where no dead king lay. The shell, like the branch of *ferula*, would seem to indicate that a king *must* lie buried somewhere here — or perhaps a queen.

Exploration and research will continue for years to come, but we shall probably never fathom all the mysteries of this tomb.

ETERNAL SUN—ORIGIN OF LIFE

WITHIN an incredibly short space of time the Egyptians learned how to shift the most gigantic blocks of stone ever known in the history of architecture, and how to erect their amazing pyramidal buildings. A span of only fifty years separates Pharaoh Zoser, who built the huge step-mastaba which represents the earliest monumental stone construction in history, from the Pharaohs who reared the great pyramids at Gizeh. In this brief period the Egyptians had abandoned brick and converted themselves into master-builders in natural stone such as the world has never seen before or, it can safely be said, since. In less than a hundred years the Egyptians' God-and-Pharaoh worship had soared from the level of the desert, from slab graves and unpretentious mastabas, to Zoser's miracle-building and to the 480-foot-high summit of the Pyramid of Cheops. From then on, pyramids began to get smaller.

Facing Old Cairo across the Nile stands the village of Gizeh. Nearly five miles to the west, on the edge of the desert, three pyramids rear their lonely and gigantic forms into the deep blue sky.

These world-renowned tombs were erected by three kings; Khufu, Khafre and Menkaure. Khufu means *khnum*, or 'protect me'. Khafre means 'The Sun-god (Ra) rises shining'. Menkaure means 'Eternal are the realities of Ra'.

During a visit to Egypt, the Greek historian Herodotus made inquiries about the Pharaoh Khufu, who had been dead for 2000 years even in those days. By that time, the Pharaoh's name had come to be pronounced 'Cheops', which is why Herodotus calls him by that name. Khufu sited his pyramid near the precipitous north-east edge of a rocky plateau. Khafre's stands farther to the south-west, on higher ground. The third pyramid, that of Menkaure, is the smallest.

'All the world fears time, but time fears only the pyramids,' so runs one Arabic proverb.

Those who visit these pyramids would do well to reflect that Herodotus, the 'father of history', once stood here in 450 B.C., gazing in wonder at these titanic monuments; that Antony strolled here with Cleopatra; and that Julius Caesar, Caesar Septimus Severus, and Napoleon once stood here, too. 2000 years are as nothing, and 4500 years like a mere second in the lifetime of mankind. It is as though the Pharaohs and Caesars of that minute portion of earth-time which we call history were stretching out their hands to us in welcome. The mighty Pharaoh Cheops, Herodotus the Greek, a man with an imagination and a gift for observation which embraced every realm of humanity, unbending Caesar Severus and the small ambitious Corsican — are they not all of one family with you and me, when we consider the 30,000, 50,000 or 80,000 years of prehistorical past enjoyed by the people who live on the banks of the Nile? For the pyramids were only built 4500 years ago, when the *homo sapiens* who first shaped a chisel out of flint was already 'old'.

Half lion, half king, the Sphinx crouches motionless on its limestone base to the right of the road leading up from the valley to the funerary temple of Khafre's pyramid. It was this protruding outcrop of rock which probably induced the Pharaoh to choose it as the spot in which to realize his huge example of the plastic art. The dual-being gazes far out over the moribund landscape. It seems to smile, still jealously guarding its eternal secret. The Sphinx has been painted, measured and photographed. Its total length is 230 feet, and it is more than 65 feet high. Its ear measures 4 feet 6 inches, and its mouth is about 7 feet 6 inches wide. This much we know. What was for a long time not known, however, was the identity of the creator of this largest sculpture in the world. The Sphinx stands near the valley temple of Pharaoh Khafre, below and to the east of his pyramid. It has lately been assumed with confidence that Khafre himself was the author of the building. What led people to that conclusion? The pyramid of Pharaoh Sahure, a king who reigned during the 5th Dynasty about 2430 B.C., provided the clue. A relief found in the temple of worship belonging to it portrayed the king as a Sphinx slaughtering his enemies. If Pharaoh Sahure was depicted as a Sphinx in the vicinity of his pyramid, it is therefore reasonable to suppose that the Sphinx near the valley temple of Khafre depicts none other than Pharaoh Khafre himself, and that it was he who had it built. The Great Sphinx is not a personification of the Sun-god Ra, as many have supposed. It represents King Khafre, whose pyramid still dominates it.

King Cheops, Khafre's father, wanted to snap his fingers at time and build for eternity, so he erected Egypt's largest pyramid: 100,000 of his subjects — it could have been fewer — had to labour continuously for twenty-three long years to assure their king of eternal life. They had to man-handle no less than 2,500,000 huge blocks of dressed stone, some of them weighing 150 tons. (The largest modern lorries can only manage 40 to 50 tons at the most.) These immense loads of stone had to be transported to the site over large distances. In fact, some of them were floated down-river for hundreds of miles before they were finally hauled into position up a series of ramps. The granite freestone quarry at Assuan lies 500 miles away.

The main bulk of the pyramid was built of stone taken from the surrounding country. What is impossible to visualize today, and what must once have endowed the pyramid with an almost unimaginable beauty, was its white facing. Imagine what a gleaming picture it must have made beneath the sunny skies of Egypt, for the facing was composed of snow-white limestone. This limestone was brought across the Nile from the eastern side during the flood season.

Khufu's gigantic edifice, the Pyramid of Cheops, reaches a height of about 480 feet and contains just under 3,300,000 cubic yards of masonry.

Anyone who reads about the pyramids can hear in imagination the cracking of whips, the harsh commands of the overseers, and the sound of curses and groans, but it was not like that. In that golden age of the 'Old Kingdom' an individual's whole life was focused upon the God Pharaoh. Through the Pharaoh he had a purpose in life, and through the continued existence of the Pharaoh after death, something to hope for. And so the 100,000 laboured not only under the compulsion of the whip, but out of religious devotion; for no beating or physical coercion could forcibly have engendered the fanaticism which freely and willingly translated the God-Pharaoh concept into stone. In those days there was no other end, no other task, nothing at all which so completely claimed the energies of the Egyptian people as the building of the pyramids. Of course, a certain degree of coercion was used. Priests and officials saw to that, for the eternal city of their dead God-King was worth any, absolutely any, sacrifice. After all, if anyone did succumb under the rigours of the work, the eternal life of the Pharaoh was assured, and the life of the individual in him. Each man represented a puny little component in a neat, firmly knit conception of the world where there was a good reason for everything, where nothing ever happened without due cause, and where death had lost its terrors. Naturally, this happy notion of things did not last long, for periods of irresolution, doubt and impotence in the history of mankind have always held the field longer than the creative periods during which man knows where he stands.

It was never the Egyptian Pharaohs' ambition to win fame by their pyramids. The thought would never have occurred to them. They had no desire to become renowned and admired by posterity for their monumental buildings. They had no idea of building 'eternal architecture' as such. They wanted to live, to live on after their death, not just modestly or anyhow, but in greatness and security, undisturbed and imperishable. The Pharaohs believed, just as in later times every Egyptian came to believe, that the body was inhabited by a second being, the *ka*. The body might die, but the *ka* never perished. The *ka* lived on whatever happened. If the *ka* had no body, however, it merely slept and was incapable of action, so it was worth any effort to preserve the lifeless body and secure it against desecration and decay. This, then, was the purpose which the pyramids and their inner burial-chambers served. It was intended that the embalmed body should rest there, eternal and unchanging, and that the pyramids should endure throughout successive ages. How successful was the Pharaohs' fantastic plan?

In the passage of 4500 years, the Pyramid of Cheops has lost about twenty-two feet in height. The wind takes its time, but it works away conscientiously, and the original surface of the huge structure has already disappeared. Part of it simply slid off. It was and is still being overheated by the sun, which has burned its limestone away to chalk. This process is still going on today. The fellaheen are forbidden to remove any limestone from the funerary temples or the cemeteries. Stones bearing inscriptions of any kind are also protected, although limestone fragments without writing on them may be taken away.

Anyone who walks today down the long flights of steps leading to the burial-chambers in the heart of the pyramids (in Cheops' case the steps lead upwards) will recognize the futility of man's struggle against the ravages of time and Nature. There he stands with a pounding heart in the dead, musty stillness of the vault, a place where the silence of the grave literally reigns. Once upon a time Cheops reposed there in the impenetrable darkness, shut off from the outer world by walls which even modern aerial bombs could not have shattered. The Pharaoh's granite sarcophagus is still there, but it is open. The vault was plundered and the body of the king stolen, never to be found. Other Pharaohs who wished, like Cheops, to escape the eyes of man for all time to come have likewise been torn from their graves, robbed, even in death, and left to turn to dust somewhere in the desert, where the winds carried them up to heaven after all. Still others lie in the poor glass cases of some museum, for timid and wondering eyes to gloat upon.

Egypt's three thousand years of history may seem an amazing achievement in the art of living, self-preservation and culture, but there are other races which exhibit the same peculiar 3000-year 'rhythm'. A people starts its history with the art of writing. It experiences cultural zeniths and periods of foreign domination. It is defeated, its blood is adulterated with that of other races, and, somewhere about the middle of its lifetime – after 1500 years or so – it enters upon its age of dictators and generals. It plunges into the depths again, revives to enjoy new days of greatness, and ends its history after about 3000 years. We find this span of existence in the case of the Greeks, too, if we let their history begin about 1400 B.C. and end in A.D. 1453 with the conquest of Byzantium by Mohammed II. We can gauge the life-span of Europe and America in the same way, if we assume central European or Western history to have started in A.D. 451 with the Battle of the Catalaunian Fields. If we adopt the principle of a 3000-year historical 'rhythm', then we are now situated exactly on the half-way mark of our life-span. We are in the age of generals and dictators. We are at the stage which Egypt had reached after the Middle Kingdom. We can expect wars and annihilation followed by a golden age. According to this theory, Europe is still far removed from her last plunge, her final decadence and her hour of death. We still have 1500 years before us.

Ancient Egypt produced great figures in her time, some terrible and some good, some cruel and some gentle, Pharaohs who made territorial conquests, robust Pharaohs and Pharaohs of extreme sensitivity like Nebkaure, Sesostris I and Amenophis IV, who had a high regard for literature and art. The statue of Khafre shows us a proud, fearless man with penetrating eyes. Sculptured in stone, he now reposes in Cairo Museum. His pyramid is a memorial to an inflexible will. Then there is Amenemhet I. He ushered in an age of artistic greatness, and lived about 2000 years before Christ. In the twentieth year of his reign, that is to say in 1971 B.C., this wise Pharaoh made his son Sesostris I co-regent, and father and son reigned together for ten years. Amenemhet I adopted the name Amenemhet in honour of Amun, the god of Thebes. Later, after the Pharaoh had been murdered, his son Sesostris declared in a collection of precepts: 'Be harsh with your subjects. The people only obeys those who use force. Draw close to no one unattended, and make no one your brother. Do not believe in friends. When you go to bed, have yourself well guarded, for a man does not have a single friend in times of danger.'

These sentiments have been communicated to us via the famous Millingen Papyrus. Pharaoh Sesostris was their author, and he attributes them to his father Amenemhet.

Sesostris erected his pyramid thirty miles south of Memphis and a little to the west of the town of Lisht. It was a brick construction whose interior was built of blocks taken from the funerary temple of Cheops. Sesostris' mummy was never found. His grave had been ransacked.

At about this time a canal was built from the Nile to the Red Sea. It was in fact the 'Suez Canal' of pre-Christian history.

It is interesting to note, incidentally, that huge quantities of foodstuffs, stores and flowers were found in Sesostris' funerary temple. Stores like these were always provided for departed Pharaohs, of course, but in this particular case they had all remained preserved until our own day. There were fowl, both plucked and unplucked, sides of beef, garden lettuces, cucumbers, numerous loaves of bread and white and blue lotus lilies. In addition, there were representations of the royal butchers at work slaughtering and preparing oxen. An ambulant wooden statue of Sesostris was also found. It was only about two feet in height and depicted the king wearing a red crown and carrying a sceptre. He was dressed in a short apron, with the upper part of his body and his legs bare. The statue has such a life-like, natural, and one might almost say 'modern' appearance, that one can only marvel at the sureness of touch, the delicacy, the success in catching the essentials of their subject, and in general, the advanced technique which the artists of this epoch display.

Every advanced human civilization is like an island in a sea of barbarity. Whether we like it or not, we live in the present, and scholars, artists, poets and all freedom-loving people should live in daily awareness of the happy condition which is known as peace. For there came a day, about 1675 B.C., when nomadic tribes came storming out of Asia and laid Egypt low. They overran the Nile Valley just as the Kassites had overrun Babylonia a short while before, just as the Romans were to conquer Greece, as the Huns were to invade Italy, and the Mongols to sack Peking. Who were these conquerors? The Egyptian priest and historian Manetho, who lived about 280 B.C., devoted some space in his histories to a description of this foreign invasion and the setting up of the empire of the 'peasant-kings'. His description has best been preserved for us in Josephus' account of it, although the latter unfortunately remodelled it a good deal to the advantage of Israel. More reliable accounts of the 'Amu', the nomads who occupied the city of Auaris and from there proceeded to plunder northern Egypt, come from the Egyptian kings Kamosi and Ahmosi, and from Queen Hatshepsut. If the peasant-kings really were Amu, or Syrian Semitic kings, then they were probably either Canaanites or the very same Churri who invaded Mesopotamia in 1680 B.C. and subsequently founded a great empire on the Euphrates and the Tigris, the empire of the Mitanni.

The fact that the peasant-kings were able to conquer Egypt at all was attributable to the decades of anarchy which had been prevailing in the country prior to their arrival. Fifty years before, everything had gone to pieces. After the close of the 12th Dynasty the country lacked any form of central authority, and various generals had attempted to seize power. Such were the circumstances which delivered an impotent Egypt into the hands of her nomadic enemies.

It is a rule of history, however, that once a race of conquerors has settled down in a fertile river-valley they become fat, lazy and weak. Under the rulers of the 17th Dynasty at Thebes, the Egyptians' struggle for liberation began, and at the beginning of the 18th Dynasty the Pharaohs finally chased the Hyksos peasant-kings out of the country and founded a large and powerful kingdom.

One of the personalities prominent in this portion of Egyptian history was a woman, the Queen Hatshepsut mentioned above. She reigned from 1501 to 1479 B.C. Since the rulers of Egypt always had to be 'sons' of Amun, their god, the idea of a woman as Pharaoh was inconceivable. Queen Hatshepsut solved this difficulty by simply constituting herself a man and, like all the Pharaohs, declaring herself to be the son of the god. She had herself portrayed in masculine attire, wearing a beard. She enhanced and enlarged the temple at Karnak, and erected two large obelisks there. She also built herself a magnificent funerary temple at Der el Bahari, and eventually did what both her father and grandfather before her had considered necessary: she had yet another secret burial-place hewn out for herself in the rock of the sand-swept mountain massif on the western side of the Nile which later became known as 'the Valley of Kings'. Sixty royal graves are carved into the rock there, and in time there arose on both sides of the Nile at Thebes an enormous city, the quarter of the living on the east bank, and that of the dead on the west.

The brother of the celebrated Queen Hatshepsut, Tuthmosis III, became the founder of an empire which extended from the Sudan to the Euphrates. He was the most powerful Pharaoh of his epoch. While he was still very young he was married to Hatshepsut, who was his half-sister. She was so greedy for power that she seized the government for herself. When her brother grew up, however, he had her murdered, together with her lover Senmut, and thereupon had every reminder of his 'beloved sister' erased. It really seems as though, from then onwards, Tuthmosis III gave free rein to the tide of energy which had for so long lain suppressed and pent up in him. He conquered the whole of Palestine, the whole of Syria, and all the countries between Egypt and the Euphrates. Records of his sixteen years of military campaigning are inscribed in stone on the walls of the temple at Karnak.

Amenhotep II was a great archer and huntsman. He personally put down a revolt in Syria, and provides us with noteworthy example of the severity which the Pharaohs exercised towards their enemies. It is reported that he brought seven Asiatic kings to Thebes in chains. Six of them he hanged from the city walls without delay, and the seventh he later hanged at Napata in the Sudan. Many daring exploits are related of this Pharaoh, and he seems to have been able to boast of more than a few during the course of his twenty-six years on the throne. A stele which stands between the paws of the Great Sphinx depicts Amenhotep II as a bowman.

Amenhotep III reigned from 1400 B.C. onwards, and during his reign the empire abounded in prosperity, wealth, luxury and elegance. In his time, Thebes was a magnificent city on the scale of, say, modern Paris. Goods from all over the world were sold in the markets of the metropolis, and its temple-precincts do not suffer by comparison with the buildings of even a large modern city.

Dozens of subject States made tributary payments to the Pharaoh. The rulers of the great Asiatic kingdoms of Mitanni, Assyria, Babylonia and the Hittites sent their daughters to Amenhotep's harem, and considered themselves fortunate to have secured his friendship. The temples of Thebes were heaped with gold, and the city's magnificent villas, vast palaces and artificial lakes outshone anything the world had known hitherto. Amenhotep III was the originator of the temple at Luxor and the Colossi of Memnon, which stood on guard in front of his huge funerary temple (now completely disappeared), looking out over the plain to the west of Thebes.

The most singular character in the great procession of Pharaohs was the son of Amenhotep III and his wife Taia, who was not of noble birth. Amenhotep IV came to the throne in 1330 B.C. This youthful Pharaoh was just fourteen years old at the time, and his efficient mother Taia continued to handle affairs of state for the time being.

Amenhotep IV was from his earliest youth onwards an ardent worshipper of the Sun-god of Heliopolis. It is possible that the priesthood of the Sun-god Ra had already existed at Heliopolis for a long time, in opposition to the priesthood of Amun at Thebes. The Sun-god Ra was older than the god Amun, whose importance only dated from the 12th Dynasty.

It had not yet come to an overt struggle between the two gods. Both of them had a place in the Egyptian pantheon. Amun grew in importance because he was held to be an outward form of the god Ra. He had now become Amun-Ra.

The young Pharaoh venerated the Sun-god particularly in his visible manifestation as the sun's disk, or Aten. This is the only correct reading of the name, incidentally. Aton is wrong.

Aten was the visible source of all life, all creation, growth and action. The king had temples erected everywhere for his Sun-god, and in honour of the new national god he adopted the name Akhen-Aten. After years of tension and continual quarrelling and friction with the priesthood of Amun, the Pharaoh finally abandoned Thebes as his capital. Akhenaten established his new residence in the region of El Amarna, calling it Akhet-Aten, 'City of the Horizon of Aten'.

Akhenaten composed what is perhaps the most beautiful poem known to us in the whole of Egyptian literature: 'Lordly thou climbest the heavenly mountain of light, eternal sun, origin of life . . . Thou hast created the world after thy liking. Thou gavest sustenance to all living creatures for ever. Thou apportionest to each his span of life. Thou art the pounding of my heart. All that we perceive in thy light shall perish, but thou shalt live and

Iraqi archaeologists laid bare the foundations of this house at Eridu, originally occupied in about 4000 B.C. A raised fireplace is visible in the foreground (centre), and to the right of it is a large clay oven roughly six feet in diameter. The foundations of the house consisted of mud bricks and the walls of reeds coated on both sides with clay

Babylon shortly after its excavation at the turn of the century. In the left foreground can be seen the Gate of Ishtar, which was later re-erected by German scholars in the Pergamon Museum at Berlin. The ruins of Babylon yielded thousands of clay tablets whose cuneiform inscriptions throw light on contemporary history

A Basalt statue, about 4,500 years old, found in Northern Iraq. A cuneiform inscription on the back of the figure indicates that it portrays Dudu, the court scribe. It is among the finest sculptures of the Early Sumerian artistic period

Statue of a priest found in a grave at Sakkara, and about 5,000 years old

top right:
Nefertiti, wife of Pharaoh Amenhotep IV (Akhenaten). [Berlin, Staatl. Museum, Bildarchiv Foto Marburg

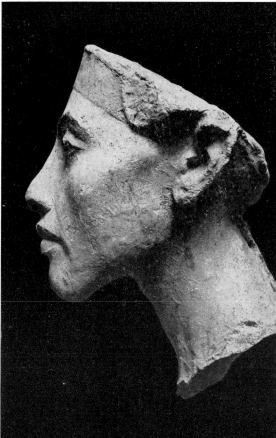

Pharaoh Amenhotep IV. [Bildarchiv Foto Marburg

130 feet below the level of the desert lies the burial-chamber of *Pharaoh Sekhem-khet*. His sarcophagus, hewn out of solid alabaster and weighing nearly fifteen tons, was empty. On it lay a branch of giant fennel which had almost crumbled away to dust. The stone slab (facing) could be let down

Amenhotep IV (Akhenaten) was only t̃ years old when he married ten-yeã Nefertiti. He is here shown kissing c his small daughters, while Nefertiti the other two in her arms. Pharaoh

A reconstruction, following specifications given by Professor Hanns Stock, of the as yet unexcavated mastaba of Pharaoh Sekhem-khet. Dr Zakaria Ghoneim started work on the tomb in 1951. On June 26th 1954 the sealed sarcophagus was opened. It was empty

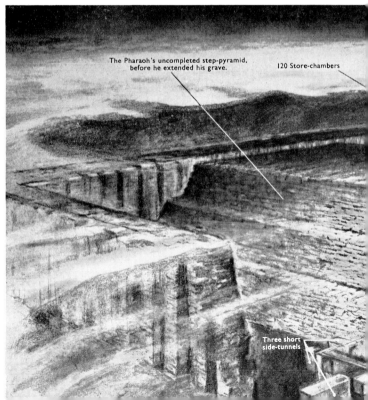

The Pharaoh's uncompleted step-pyramid, before he extended his grave.

120 Store-chambers

Three short side-tunnels

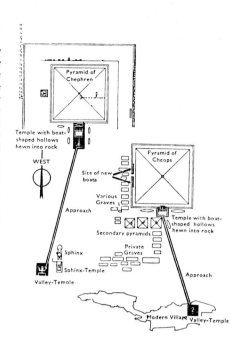

Ground plan of the pyramids of Khafre (Chefren) and Khufu (Cheops), showing the position of their 'boats'. For a long time the only boats to be found were merely boat-shaped hollows carved out of the rock. It was only in 1954 that a really large wooden boat was discovered, the first in the history of Egyptian archaeology

Pyramid of Chephren

Temple with boat-shaped hollows hewn into rock

WEST

Site of new boats

Various Graves

Approach

Pyramid of Cheops

Temple with boat-shaped hollows hewn into rock

Secondary pyramids

Private Graves

Sphinx

Sphinx-Temple

Valley-Temple

Approach

Modern Village Valley-Temple

o been unapproachable in their sanc-
d it was quite a new departure for
o be portrayed with their families.
humanization' of Egyptian art is
as the 'Amarna Period'

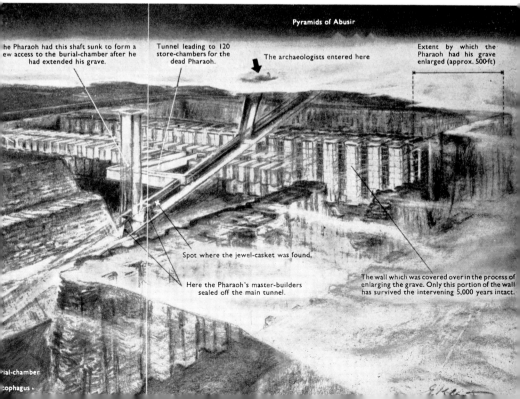

Pyramids of Abusir

he Pharaoh had this shaft sunk to form a
ew access to the burial-chamber after he
had extended his grave.

Tunnel leading to 120
store-chambers for the
dead Pharaoh.

The archaeologists entered here

Extent by which the
Pharaoh had his grave
enlarged (approx. 500-ft)

Spot where the jewel-casket was found.

Here the Pharaoh's master-builders
sealed off the main tunnel.

The wall which was covered over in the process of
enlarging the grave. Only this portion of the wall
has survived the intervening 5,000 years intact.

ial-chamber

:ophagus

The Sphinx, a personification o
Pharaoh Khafre (4th Dynasty) prob
ably erected by himself. In the back
ground is the Pyramid of Khuf
(Cheops) near the village of Gize

Brewing beer almost 5,000 years ago. Beer used
to be made out of water and fermented
bread. Small models like these accompanied
the dead into their graves. Height: $15\frac{3}{4}$ inches

The Temple of Luxor of Thebes, bu
by Amenhotep III between 1413 at
1377 B.C.

The magnificent funerary temple built at Der el Bahari (Thebes) by Queen Hatshepsut (1501–1479 B.C.),
the wife and half-sister of Tuthmosis III

Two male masks, caricatures in clay typical Phoenician faces, which we discovered in Carthaginian graves

Phoenician deity in bronze. This statuette probably belongs to the period 1200 B.C.

A unique civilization which flourished in the 7th and 8th centuries B.C. has been identified on the island of Sardinia, where archaeologists are digging up tower-like fortifications – so-called 'nuraghs'. The builders of these erstwhile fortresses and places of refuge left us no form of written memorial, but Christian Nervos and Gennaro Pesce have unearthed some very lifelike little figures in bronze near the Nuraghic ruins. These small figurines are now on view in the National Museums at Cagliari and Sassari. They betray Phoenician and early Etruscan influence

prosper for evermore.' We are always coming across the Hymn to Aten in Egypt, on the walls of graves and temples, and indeed, wherever Akhenaten built.

We should try to imagine what it must have meant to the inhabitants of the ancient royal capital of Thebes when the Pharaoh moved out, taking his huge household with him. We should try to visualize how fearful and angry the priests of Amun were at the prospect of losing the aura of regal splendour which they had always enjoyed until then. And as if that were not enough, Akhenaten ordered that the god's name should be erased from all the holy places. Everything which belonged to the god Amun, and which for that reason did not serve Aten, had to be destroyed. Amun's name was everywhere obliterated. The State archives were carefully combed through, and the Masters of the Rolls were obliged to make sure that the proscribed god's name did not appear anywhere in the papyrus documents. The priests of Amun lost their official positions and emoluments. Only the visible Sun-god might now be worshipped. It was a spate of iconoclasm such as Egypt had never witnessed before.

How did the young Pharaoh come to carry out such a fundamental reformation? Was he a religious fanatic? Was the priesthood of Ra at the back of it all? Or his mother Taia? Was he activated by oblique political motives of some kind?

None of these suppositions does justice to Akhenaten's personality. He was, in fact, the harbinger of a new era, and of an idea which had grown in, and out of, a mind of unshakeable convictions. He was an idealist. Somewhere within him there existed a mysterious spark of genius. It was the driving force of his times which worked in him. It was the manifestation of an historical period which, on the brink of a gradual decline, can yet give vent to one last burst of creative energy. For there now came into being an utterly new era of artistic achievement. The products of the ateliers at Akhet-Aten in this period are among the finest known examples of Egyptian sculpture. We are now confronted by the 'Amarna period'.

The Amarna period saw a rediscovery of Nature, an enhancing and re-vivifying of all the media of expression, a humanizing of Egyptian art which was very strongly influenced by Crete and represented a break with many strict and hitherto inviolable laws. It also implied an artistic decline – not from the point of style as divorced from other considerations – but a decline when compared with the zeniths of artistic achievement in Egypt. The king, who had until now been unapproachable in his sacrosanctity, suddenly became a human being, a person whose everyday habits could now become common knowledge, and who could even be portrayed performing routine functions. The veil of utter secrecy which had until now screened the State apartments of the king's wife was at last lifted, and the celebrated Nefertiti emerged. Many portrayals of her exist, all wonderfully true to life. We are suddenly allowed to see the little princesses being embraced by their royal parents. The artists were permitted to make of Nature exactly what they wished. They had only to paint and sculpt things as they really saw them. That is why we possess such magnificent sculptures of Nefertiti, the Pharaoh's wife, sculptures which could never have achieved such beauty otherwise, sculptures painted in glorious colours showing us a woman of ineffable perfection and delicacy of feature.

Who was Nefertiti?

As we have already heard, Akhenaten's father, Amenhotep III, had among other Asiatic princesses in his harem two princesses of Mitanni. The city of Mitanni stood between the Euphrates and the Tigris, at the spot where the two rivers lay farthest separated from one another. King Tushratta ruled over Mitanni at this period, and the Indo-Aryan princesses whom he sent to the Pharaoh's court were called Taduchepa and Giluhepa. On the death of Amenhotep III, both princesses were taken over into his son's harem. It is not beyond the bounds of possibility that it was the daughter of one of these princesses who later became the wife of the important Pharaonic reformer — in fact, that we rediscover this daughter in the world-renowned figure of Nefertiti. If this were so, Nefertiti would have had Indo-Iranian blood in her veins.

Amenhotep IV was a mere twelve years old when he married Nefertiti, then a little girl of ten. Throughout his reign she was always there at his side, sharing the conduct of affairs. She thus bore no resemblance to the usual picture of an Asiatic queen, whose principal duty was to remain out of sight in the harem.

The happiness of the young king and his beautiful queen was not destined to last for long. Amarna, the new royal seat, was from the very start a city of parvenus. Nobility and tradition, property and rank all remained vested in Thebes. The king was too sensitive and weak for his immense task. The opposition of the priesthood of Amun did not subside, but fed and grew in secret. What was more, the Pharaoh took absolutely no interest in external policy, and as soon as the dependent, tributary countries noticed that the throne of Egypt was no longer occupied by a ruthless tyrant but rather by a sensitive reformer, they suspended their payments. Egypt's position of power in the Near East began slowly but surely to crumble. Akhenaten became lonely. Many of his friends deserted him. When he was scarcely thirty years old, in 1358 B.C., he died. A bust of the Pharaoh found at Tell el Amarna displays a remarkably fine profile and a gentle, almost effeminate face of exceeding sensitivity and intelligence, large, dreaming eyes and a degenerate body.

When Akhenaten died, Nefertiti believed that her only means of preserving the throne for her children, and perhaps for herself, lay in turning to the distant King of the Hittites for aid. She appealed to him to send her a Hittite prince, intending to marry him and use Hittite power to bolster up her own throne. Her project failed, however, for the prince was murdered while on the way to her. We do not know how Nefertiti died. Her overtures to the Hittite king were very likely regarded as high treason, and she was probably assassinated.

The fact that Nefertiti turned to the Hittite king at all (being, as he was, an Indo-European) is extremely interesting. It may well be an additional indication that she was of related stock and that she really was the daughter of one of the princesses of Mitanni. Neither Akhenaten's nor Nefertiti's mummy has ever been found.

The reign of the great reformer was followed by a period of great confusion. First came Semenkhare, Akhenaten's son-in-law. Nobody lived very long in those days, and Semenkhare soon died what was undoubtedly not a natural death. His successor Tutankhamun was likewise a son-in-law of Akhenaten. He was the Pharaoh who became well known through Howard Carter's excavations. His original name was Tutankh-Aten, but pressure exerted on him by the priesthood of Amun at Thebes forced him to change it. Furthermore, he was obliged to transfer the royal seat from Amarna to Thebes once more, and to renounce the cult of Aten. He also died early in life.

For decades, Egyptologists racked their brains for some indication of how old Tutankhamun was when he died. When his grave was discovered in 1922, the young Pharaoh's name swept the world. On opening his sarcophagus, Howard Carter found a second one inside. He unsealed it carefully. It held yet a third, this time made of pure gold. It was a coffin in the shape of a man, and in it lay the young Pharaoh's mummy. At last they knew . . . he was a youth of only eighteen when he died.

The biggest traitor and intriguer of this period was Ay, an official and priest of the Theban cult of Amun, who had been forging his dark plans even during Akhenaten's lifetime. He eventually managed to become king, but he was not allowed to enjoy the fruits of his intrigues for long. He too had a stubborn opponent in Horemheb, the commander-in-chief of the army of Lower Egypt. After four short years, General Horemheb succeeded in assassinating Ay, and mounted the throne in his turn. The history of Egypt is like a vast and trackless ocean, ever ready to drown the would-be traveller in its unfathomable depths.

Anyone who travels along the Nile these days will often hear the cry: 'What! Rameses again?' For Rameses II was, so to speak, a 'mass-producer'.

He is responsible for a lot of ruins because he erected statues of himself everywhere. He was an egoist and a monomaniac. As king, he was so fond of building that almost half of all the ruins in Egypt which survive today originated in his reign. He completed a gigantic hall at Karnak and extended the temple at Luxor. He built himself a huge funerary temple, known as the Ramaseum, and erected colossal statues of himself all over the country. He renovated the canal from the Nile to the Red Sea. He had about a hundred wives, a circumstance less remarkable in ancient Egypt than it would seem to us, since most of the Pharaohs married a large number of women. Rameses II is reputed to have had a hundred sons and fifty daughters; many of the latter he married himself—once again, not an unusual practice in ancient Egypt.

Within a hundred years of his death his name was an object of universal hatred, and his dynasty died out on the demise of his successor. However, his mummy has survived with a fineness of feature which neither 67 years on the throne, 90 years of living, nor over 3000 of death have materially affected.

Under Rameses III the wealth and power of the God Amun reached amazing proportions. The priests of Amun now lived in veritable opulence. Their store-chambers were filled to bursting-point, and they commanded the services of 107,000 slaves. Like many ancient statistics, the latter figure may be an exaggeration, but it does serve as some indication of their number. If we put the contemporary population of Egypt at five to six million, it means that one out of every fifty or sixty persons must have been temple property. The British Museum contains the longest ancient Egyptian manuscript in existence, the famous 'Harris Papyrus'. It is over 130 feet long. The text, which is extremely well preserved, contains detailed lists of all the gifts and bequests which Rameses III made to the temples of Egypt during the course of his reign. If we accept the accuracy of these detailed estimates, we must conclude that the god Amun and his priests owned one-seventh of all cultivable land, 169 cities in Egypt, Syria and Kush, a fleet of 88 ships, 53 dockyards large and small, and a herd of 500,000 head of cattle.

In those days there were as many feast-days as working days, an arrangement which swelled the coffers of the priests of Amun to a boundless extent. The king became no more than a servant of the men of God. In order that the gods could continue to exist, the power and position of the king had to suffer more and more. The Pharaoh's circumstances grew increasingly precarious. He was now compelled to rely on an army largely composed of mercenaries. The plot to assassinate Rameses III, whose threads, like so many others in the history of the East, were spun in the harem, is very characteristic of this period. Wishing to secure the throne for her son, one of the queens of the harem managed to enlist the aid of the wives of six officers in the harem guard in her plan to remove the Pharaoh. The support of other influential persons was also secured. When the conspiracy was betrayed and Rameses summoned a high court to mete out due punishment to the guilty parties, the accused ladies of the harem actually managed to visit two of the judges in their homes and win them over. It was then the turn of the judges to be tried. Their ears and noses were cut off, and one of the men so punished committed suicide. Thirty-two officials of high and low rank received a very lenient sentence: they were permitted to take their own lives. However, the old Pharaoh did not survive all these excitements by very long and died in 1167 B.C. These, then, were the signs of the times: domination by the priesthood, harem intrigues, treachery and resorts to foreign aid. In this way, Egypt gradually approached its end. The country was invaded first by the Libyans, then by the Ethiopians, and then by the Assyrians. Egypt was conquered by the Persians under Cambyses. Alexander made the country a province of Macedonia. In 48 B.C. Julius Caesar took the Egyptian capital, Alexandria, and gave Cleopatra the son who could never sit upon the Egyptian throne. In the end, Egypt became a mere province of the metropolis on the Tiber and the granary of the Roman Empire. A vast kingdom and three thousand years of history had been extinguished.

What still remain are pyramids, temples, rock-graves, kings' statues in limestone, alabaster and diorite, pictures, inscriptions and rolls of papyrus. What still remain are the rainless, burning sky and the annual flooding of the Nile, the date of whose commencement, July 19th, the ancient Egyptians adopted as their New Year's Day. What still remains is the fertile black mud of the Nile, after which the Egyptians of antiquity named their land *keme*, or 'the black one', the word from which the 'black art' of the Middle Ages and our expression 'chemistry' have evolved. The Egyptians, too, remain much as they always were, in spite of racial intermingling and foreign invasion. What these people, once so abundantly endowed with artistic and creative energy, have lost, however, is the titanic courage, the imagination, the will for eternal life and the urge towards elemental art which marked their great religious epochs. They lost their god, and with him, all sense of endeavour. They lost their faith, and with it, their creative strength. Once upon a time the Nile was their greatest teacher. It was the Nile which compelled them to build dykes and canals. It was the overflowing waters of the Nile which led them out of poverty into abundance, which inspired them to form a society, to undertake public works, and so to create a State. That was how Egyptian civilization came into being, but the river-water and the floods which once provided such an impulse and blessed natural spur to activity have long since lost their effect with the advent of huge dams and their attendant machinery.

EGYPT

What still remains is the hot south-easterly wind which blows between March and May, bringing the all-pervading sand with it. What still remains is the sweet breath of the north-easterly wind which prevails for the remainder of the year. The sand, the wind and time itself — all conspire to nibble away, corrode and consume the great civilization of Egypt, although the extreme aridity of the country remains as always a great conserver of its cultural relics, at least in the places where the Nile's grasping fingers cannot reach. And even the Nile can only destroy the tangible portion of what survives. It can destroy the works, but not the spirit which conceived them.

The value of what Egypt bequeathed to humanity and passed on to Western civilization is well-nigh inestimable. She gave us the trade of the smith, architecture, the pillar, the art of stonemasonry, monkhood, large portions of the religious conceptions of the West, monasticism, the principles of governmental organization — some of which were assimilated by the Roman Empire — the civil service, the invention of glass, the discovery of the calendar, chronology and geometry, fine clothing and jewellery, furniture and houses, a postal service, astronomy and medicine. All these things were passed on to us by Egypt when she was in her golden age and we were still dwellers in forest and steppe. Sculpture and painting attained heights among the Egyptians which scarcely any subsequent age has managed to scale again. Passed on to us via the Phoenicians, Syrians and Jews, via the Cretans, Greeks and Romans, Egyptian culture plays an important part in our life today. The astounding duration of Egyptian life once it had taken shape, the example and at the same time the inimitability of Egyptian art, the fanaticism and energy of the Egyptian Pharaohs, craftsmen and artists, the constant search for a firm idea of the 'whence' and 'whither' of life, the unbelievable value to mankind of what was, after all, merely a small people dwelling by a huge, sluggish river — none of these things will ever occur or ever again be achieved in the cultural history of mankind. Egypt provided a stage for the dramatic spectacle of a civilization which soared almost to the heavens and has not, even now, returned to earth — the greatest civilization which has ever flourished on our planet.

And this civilization was once life sustained by beating hearts and rooted in the human soul, springing from true faith, and for that reason so strong and sublime. For where there is no seed, nothing can grow.

DO NOT BE SAD IN LIFE

'I lay in bed — and I was awake.' Jottings like this have been found on rolls of papyrus thousands of years old.

I T is strangely enthralling to look at the face of a mummy, still as alive and expressive in death as if its owner had only yesterday closed his eyes for the first time. Many mummies have waited 5000 years for their resurrection, yet research has established that the soles of mummified feet 2000 or 3000 years old are still soft and pliable.

In death, the soul leaves the body. But the ancient Egyptians believed that upon the burial of a dead body, the soul was recalled by the officiating priest and reunited with it. It was because the body had to be intact for this critical moment that the Egyptians embalmed thousands, hundreds of thousands, even millions of their dead — and not only kings, it may be added, but everyone who could afford it.

Even in A.D. 700, when the Egyptians had virtually abandoned the practice of preparing their dead for eternity, some 100,000 persons were embalmed. Thousands of well-preserved mummies are still lying in the graves of Egypt, never having been dug up. The mummies of many Pharaohs repose in museums, but others remain undisturbed. (Alexander the Great, who was embalmed in wax and honey, has never been found, either.)

There are three methods of preserving a dead body: by cold-storage; by the modern method of injecting bacteria-killing agents into the blood-vessels; and, finally, by desiccating the body and maintaining it in a dry condition. It was the latter method which was favoured in ancient Egypt. Since 75 per cent of the human body consists of water, it is not easy to dry it out completely. The Egyptians probably used fire for this purpose, or, in less frequent cases, the heat of the sun. In the City of the Dead at Thebes, a chamber was discovered inside the grave of a certain Hatiay containing a large number of mummies piled almost to the ceiling. In the opinion of Yeivin, the Egyptologist, these mummies had been dried over a slow fire, an assumption which traces of soot found on the walls of the vaults would appear to substantiate. A second theory, however, is that the soot-stains may have been due to fires kindled with brushwood at the entrance to the burial-chamber by people who had surprised some tomb-robbers at work. The desecrators had simply been 'smoked out'.

There are other methods of achieving desiccation besides heat, of course, such as the use of dehydrating or moisture-removing agents like chalk, salt, or natron. Chemical analysis has established the presence of all three

71

substances in Egyptian mummies and, in some graves, researchers have actually found vases and pots which had once contained natron.

According to Herodotus' description, which tallies in the main with the results of modern research, the dead were embalmed in the following way: first, the brains, intestines and stomach-contents were removed, the heart and kidneys, however, being retained. The interior of the body was cleansed with wine and herbs, and then packed with myrrhs, cassia and aromatic essences, together with linen cloths, sawdust, sand, natron and even — occasionally — an onion or two. Chemical substances were injected into the arteries and blood-vessels, and the exterior of the body was anointed with oil of cedar and rubbed over with myrrhs and other fragrant essences. (It is amazing how even after several thousand years, many mummies still exhale the scent of these essences.) The corpse was then swaddled in linen cloths soaked in tar and other medicaments. The face was often covered by a mask of linen and plaster or gold, carved stone and precious metals. The mummy was laid on its left side in a sleeping posture with its head resting on a support, and the coffin was then closed. Specially designed embalming-tables which have been unearthed bear witness to the care lavished on the embalming process, and still exhibited traces of natron and salt. According to one inscription, the process sometimes took as long as ten months to complete. In earlier times, a dead man was accompanied into the grave by all his household effects, the grave itself taking on the shape of his house or palace, as the case might be. Later on, however, the only things which went into the tomb with him were meat and drink and perhaps an earthenware model of a house with miniature granaries attached to it, and the figures of labourers emptying sacks of grain into them. He was also accompanied by statues of varying sizes representing serving-women who were supposed to spin and weave and wait on their master just as they had done during his lifetime. Again, we find the figurines of richly adorned girls bringing their lord his looking-glass or his meals, or of a woman grinding grain. Small figurines of naked girls with the lower portion of their legs missing were also placed in the grave. The reason for this mutilation was as follows: in earliest times the court retinue of a king were buried alive with their master; later on, these unfortunate victims were replaced by dolls, but so that the dolls should not 'escape', they were simply fashioned with the lower part of their legs missing. The Egyptians took a vast quantity of things into the grave with them, such immense treasures, in fact, that we can only be amazed at how many centuries it took for their race, like its dead, to sink into the dust.

But the Egyptians were not only skilled in the art of surviving death. They knew how to live, too. In spite of all their superstitions and worship of the dead, they were a truly practical race. They combined a rich sense of humour — as their brilliant caricatures demonstrate — with remarkably few scruples about taking life.

They whiled away the time with games played on boards of twenty and thirty squares, like the ones found in some graves. They had an original version of snakes and ladders which they played on a circular board with pieces representing lions and dogs. They played dice and made fine toys for their children; they were fond of wrestling and sport. Serving-men and slaves were obliged to fight wrestling-matches for the enjoyment of their noble masters and mistresses, and prosperous households maintained their own champions trained in the art of fighting with quarterstaffs. Opponents in such matches were not allowed to spare each other, one of the pair often having to be carried out of the ring. Girls trained in ball-play and gymnastics were also kept, and artistes, female dancers and musicians beguiled the time of the wealthy. They played the harp, the flute, the lute, and what was not actually a native Egyptian instrument, the oriental lyre. Male singers always clapped out the rhythm of their songs, while female singers merely beat time with their hands. It was the servants' business to provide their masters with every kind of entertainment. Young girls fanned away the flies, and dwarfs looked after the household jewellery and clothing. They also exercised their master's or mistress's pet dogs and monkeys. Humpbacked jesters were very popular, too, and many a Pharaoh had his 'household dwarf'.

On feast-days the Egyptians had themselves anointed and garlanded with flowers by their servants. They drank wine and beer; they 'got into the mood'; they became, to quote a contemporary description, 'like a broken ship's rudder, which no longer answers either to port or starboard'. Indeed, one picture from the New Kingdom period portrays an unfortunate society lady in the act of vomiting. A serving-woman is hurrying up holding an outstretched bowl, somewhat dismayed and altogether too late!

The Egyptians were a handsome race, and their aristocrats bore themselves like kings. The men were robust and muscular. They had narrow hips and broad shoulders, full lips and serious, forceful expressions. Wealthy Egyptians set much store by being slim. We find many beautiful oval faces among the Egyptians, with long straight noses and wide, expressive eyes. Their skin was white at birth, but was soon burned brown by the hot Egyptian sun. Artists always depicted men with reddish and women with yellowish skins. The latter, after all, exposed themselves less often to the light of day.

Fashions continued to change throughout the whole course of Egyptian history, very gradually, it is true, but nevertheless so markedly that one can usually employ fashion as a clue to period. In the time of the Old Kingdom, or from about 3000 to 2270 B.C., men only wore an apron, and for a period of at least 700 years — it had probably been so since time immemorial — the upper part of the body remained bare. At times the apron was worn short and narrow, while at others, as in the reign of Cheops, it became longer and wider. The apron was also worn draped in many different styles, according to the prevailing fashion. During the Middle Kingdom, or somewhere between 2100 and 1700 B.C., men wore a double apron — a narrow short one of stiff linen as an under-garment, and a longer one, also of linen but transparent, over it. A short, loose tunic made its appearance at the same time as the 'revolutionary' double apron, and we also come across a close-fitting striped robe which reached from throat to ankle, a garment principally worn by the aristocracy. In later times only the humblest servants and peasants still wore the short apron, and during the New Kingdom, 1550 to 700 B.C., men kept the upper part of their bodies covered.

Naturally enough, differences in dress existed between the various social strata, and peasants, herdsmen, labourers and slaves usually wore nothing but a short loin-cloth or girdle. Men in strenuous occupations often went naked, for the feeling of physical modesty was scarcely known. As Adolf Erman the celebrated Egyptologist says: 'After all, some of the commonest hieroglyphic characters represent things which we ourselves are not exactly in the habit of depicting.'

By comparison with the diversity of masculine attire, women's clothing was very monotonous. From the earliest beginnings of Egypt's history, or at least of her pictorial art, all women dressed alike in a long straight chemise which clung quite closely to the body and clearly revealed the lines of their figures. This chemise began beneath the breasts and reached to the ankles. The breasts were only covered by the shoulder-straps which held the garment up. These shoulder-straps were the sole article of dress which was subject to changes in fashion. Sometimes they were worn straight on the shoulders, sometimes obliquely or crossed, sometimes they covered the breasts entirely, sometimes less so, sometimes not at all, and sometimes again, they were adorned with rosettes which fitted over the breasts. The chemises were usually white, less commonly red, yellow or green, and were practically always plain and unadorned. The most surprising thing about feminine fashions in Egypt, however, is still the fact that from the queen down to the poorest girl in the land no difference in dress existed. It was only later, at the beginning of the 18th Dynasty, that it became 'the done thing' to wear two articles of clothing, and a roomy outer garment was added to the tight-fitting chemise. Both articles of clothing were made from such fine linen that the outlines of the body were clearly visible through them.

Serving-women dressed almost exactly like their mistresses. If they ever had heavy work to do, however, they naturally found it impossible to move freely in their narrow chemises, and in such cases wore nothing but a short apron like the men. Female dancers, too, kept the upper part of their body and their legs bared, and young serving-girls of the New Kingdom offered round the dishes at banquets completely naked except for an embroidered girdle worn about their hips.

The Egyptians kept their fine white linen scrupulously clean, and the washing, wringing and beating of clothes went on unceasingly under the eye of the laundry superintendent. Clothes which had been stained by ointments and oils were cleaned by a special process, probably involving the use of soda. All Egyptians went barefoot except in cases of extreme necessity, when they wore sandals.

The Egyptian aristocrat kept his hair clipped and wore either a close-fitting cap or a wig over it. Wig-making was a great art in Egypt, and the most wonderful confections of plaits and ringlets were produced. In many pictures one can distinguish places where natural hair peeps out from under a wig. Every woman in the Old Kingdom wore her hair long and smooth, but fashionable women kept their hair slightly shorter and occasionally wound it into plaits. We can see from the Egyptian wigs in our museums that they were not manufactured out of human hair, but sheep's wool.

The women of ancient Egypt painted their lips, lacquered their nails and oiled their skin and hair. A variety of creams and rouges was a necessity to any young Egyptian woman interested in her appearance, both during her lifetime and in her grave. The lower eyelid was tinted with a green cosmetic made from malachite, while the upper lids and eyebrows were painted with a black preparation of lead sulphide. The effect of this was to make the eyes appear larger and more lustrous. Samples of cosmetics such as these have been found in graves. They were applied with so-called cosmetic pencils, little sticks fashioned out of wood or ivory. Cosmetics were kept in small oblong boxes of ivory, stone, faience, or wood. Whole mountains of toilet articles have been unearthed, including metal mirrors with handles of wood, ivory and faience, mirrors fashioned like slim, naked girls, mirrors of gold and silver with magnificent containers to match, ointment-boxes of alabaster, combs, hair-curlers and hair-pins, powder-boxes, razors and little ointment-spoons made of wood, ivory, alabaster and bronze. And, of course, in a pampered civilization like this, perfume was also used.

Both men and women wore rich jewellery, such as necklaces of pearls, cornelian, malachite, lapis lazuli, amethyst and faience, arm-bangles of ivory, bone, horn, copper or flint, anklets, collars of strung pearls, earrings and large ear-pendants, which the men abandoned from the 19th Dynasty onwards and left for the women to wear. From the very earliest times, Egyptians also wore rings of gold, silver and blue and green faience. The king wore a crown, and the noblemen of every Egyptian dynasty carried rods and sceptres. Where cosmetics and jewellery were concerned, there is nothing we could have taught the Egyptians. On the contrary, it is we who might adopt a great deal from their wealth of achievement in this field.

The Egyptian aristocrats were very keen sportsmen. They went hunting water-fowl in boats, bringing them down with the throwing-stick, a peculiar form of boomerang shaped like an elongated S, with which they must have been extremely dexterous. Fowl for the kitchen were caught in outspread nets. Even geese were caught in this manner, to be kept for fattening in large hedged enclosures on country estates. Pictures on the walls of graves show us the unfortunate birds being stuffed with paste-balls. Curiously enough, the Egyptians also used to fatten cranes. Ducks and pigeons were captured in small clap-nets which functioned automatically. The nobility were very fond of the sport of fish-spearing, but fish were also caught with hand-nets, baskets and drag-nets. Fish were usually dried in the sun, and formed the staple diet of the poorer classes, being cheaper to buy than corn. Shooting-drives were often organized for the king, the quarry including gazelle, ibex, sabre-antelope, maned sheep, deer, wild ox and hippopotamus. Wild animals were often captured by lassoing, and hyenas caught in this way were also fattened. It is reported that Tuthmosis III killed 120 elephants in the course of a single hunting expedition. Rameses II owned a tame lion, and an Egyptian nobleman of King Khafre's court made much of his pair of pet baboons. Small long-tailed monkeys were also kept as pets, and little apes on leads were a common sight. Girls kept cats as playthings, and dogs were an integral part of every well-to-do household. Some murals even show us Egyptians leading tame hyenas. Greyhounds were very highly prized, and the dachshund was also known. Savage and homeless dogs roamed the streets of Egyptian towns, even in those days.

We still possess Egyptian school 'exercise-books'. Of course, they are really exercise-rolls, for all writing was done on papyrus, which was kept rolled up. School discipline was very strict, and obedience was enforced with the aid of a stick. One pupil writes to his teacher: 'You beat me. That is why your teachings have entered my ear.' We read again: 'A boy has a bottom. He listens when he is beaten,' and: 'Never be idle, or you will be thrashed.'

'Paper' was manufactured by cutting papyrus plants into strips, laying them side by side, and then placing other strips crosswise on top. The whole was then pressed, and produced a durable material which has in certain cases remained well-preserved and legible even after 5000 years.

The Egyptians became acquainted with the script of the Sumerians at the beginning of their commercial relations with them, and it was this which inspired them to evolve one of their own. Their script depended upon the use of pictures which were 'read' in each word in turn. Some words consisted only of one consonant and an accompanying vowel, and others of two or three consonants. Since it is an invariable practice in the East to write consonants only, and merely to add vowels when speaking, it was quite possible to express a word of two or three consonants in terms of pictures. Thus the picture for 'the sacred dung-beetle' displays the beetle itself once (*chpr*), and then the word 'become' (*chpr*), written with the aid of the beetle-symbol but differentiated from it by the addition of a supplementary mark. The existence of words of one consonant only has enabled us to identify all the letters in the alphabet, although the Egyptians themselves never got as far as doing this. It was the Phoenicians who first collated an alphabet of the Egyptian script. It contained no less than 600 different symbols, each corresponding to an object.

Numerous writings have survived from the period between 2000 and 1000 B.C. Rolls of papyrus have been found stored in jugs, labelled and systematically arranged. Papyri such as these often contain the most remarkable adventure stories, diaries of travel, fables and poems. In one papyrus dating from about 1220 B.C., the so-called 'Orbiney Papyrus' in the British Museum, we can read the story of an adulteress who turned two good brothers into enemies. It might stand for all time as a locus classicus of jealousy and fraternal love and hatred. In another roll, the 'Petersburg Papyrus', we can read the fascinating experiences of a shipwrecked sailor who is cast up by the stormy waves on a lonely island, where he has the strangest encounter with a golden snake. Again, the life and adventures of Sinuhe among the Syrian Bedouin read like an immensely exciting travel-story of our own day, even though the action takes place in the time of Sesostris I, somewhere between 1980 and 1935 B.C. The complete text is preserved on a papyrus in Berlin Museum.

Egyptian numerical notation and calculation were rather inconvenient, clumsy and slow. The Egyptians were familiar with the decimal system, however. One stroke signified '1', two strokes '2', nine strokes '9'; '10' was represented by a fresh symbol, derived from a sort of curved contrivance for tethering grazing cattle. Two such symbols denoted '20', and so on up to 100, which was represented by yet another symbol. There was a new symbol for 1000 in the shape of a lotus-leaf, another for 10,000 — the picture of a finger, and another for 100,000 — a tadpole. The symbol for 1,000,000 was a man holding his hands above his head, almost as though he were amazed that such a figure could exist at all. It can be seen that in order to write down a three-figure number, one frequently had to employ more than twenty individual symbols. Multiplication was rather complicated, as it was done in the head by 'doubling', so that the sum '4 × 4' was reached by the stages 4, 8, and finally, 16. Division was even more laborious, and fractions as we know them were unknown. The idea of 'one-fifth + one-fifth + one-fifth' existed, for example, but not that of 'three-fifths'. For all that, the science of mathematics was highly developed in Egypt — otherwise her architectural achievements would never have been possible. The Egyptians observed the movement of the stars over a period of thousands of years. Even in those days, they drew an accurate distinction between planets and fixed stars, and catalogued stars of the fifth magnitude which are invisible to the naked eye.

Medical treatises of extreme interest have been preserved for us, among which are two important rolls of the 'Great Medical Papyrus' in Berlin Museum and the 'Ebers Papyrus', formerly in Leipzig Library. The Egyptians made a study of anatomy, the circulation of the blood, and the functions of heart, stomach and spleen. It was recognized that the heart 'speaks in the vessels of every limb'. One of the most interesting of the medical papyri, named after its discoverer Edwin Smith, is a roll about 16 feet in length and 3600 years old, containing descriptions of 48 surgical operations. It seems that the medical science of the day clearly understood that the movement of limbs is controlled by the brain. Egyptians were not exempt, it may be noted, from the majority of our present-day ailments, although we come across no mention of syphilis or cancer, and dental decay seems only to have appeared during the last few centuries of Egyptian history, as a consequence of civilization. Astonishingly enough, we read accounts of the atrophy of the little toe quite far back in Egyptian times, from which it can be deduced that it is not the result of wearing shoes, since the Egyptians almost always went barefoot. Many hundreds of medicaments are listed in the 'Ebers Papyrus'. One-tenth of all these were remedies for eye-diseases, which were probably very widespread. Certain of the prescriptions, such as human and animal dung, fly-dirt and urine, rather tend to make us shudder, but there were other less repulsive remedies like those for drawing blood out of a wound, for example, which included wax, fat, date-wine, honey and boiled corn. Whole medicine-chests were found in some graves. Baldness was combated by rubbing the scalp with fats. But apart from curing their ailments, the Egyptians also tried to preserve their health. Listen to what they say: 'Most of what we eat is superfluous. Thus we only live off a quarter of all we swallow: doctors live off the other three-quarters.' Herodotus the Greek wrote: 'Next to the Libyans, the Egyptians are the healthiest race in the world.'

The Egyptians conveyed food to their mouths with their fingers — just as we still did at the time of Shakespeare, it may be remembered.

In order to preserve the purity of the blood royal, the Pharaohs often married their own sisters. Whether this custom had any injurious effects in the long run, we cannot tell. At all events, the Egyptians did not think so, even though they had several thousand years' experience of the practice. Marriage between brothers and sisters prevailed among three-quarters of the population of Arsinoë until the 2nd century A.D. Incidentally, the Egyptian mode of address between lovers was 'brother' and 'sister'. The Pharaoh owned a large harem which included not only the daughters of the aristocracy, but also women captured on military campaigns.

The great majority of the Egyptians, however, practised monogamy, and the stability of their family life is only matched by that of Christian countries. Divorce was generally rare, and the status of women was about the same as in our own day. There was perhaps no other people of antiquity which so honoured and deferred to its womenfolk as that which lived by the Nile. Greek travellers, accustomed in their native land to keep their women on a very short leash, were amazed by their 'progressive' Egyptian counterparts. Diodorus Siculus, a Greek who lived in the latter half of the 1st century A.D., relates, somewhat indignantly, that on the Nile it was the man who was bound under the terms of a marriage contract to be obedient to the wife. Diodorus gained the impression that it was the woman who courted the man and did the proposing. She was not always so diffident about it, either. 'Oh, my handsome friend,' runs one letter, 'it is my desire to become your wife and the mistress of all your possessions.'

They were a hot-blooded folk on the Nile. Girls were ready for marriage by the age of ten, and pre-marital promiscuity was rife. One courtesan is supposed to have built a whole pyramid out of the proceeds of her amatory escapades.

The largest collection of love-poems still surviving is to be found on the obverse of the so-called 'Harris Papyrus 500' in the British Museum. 'The loveliest thing is to go out into the field to meet the man one loves', we read in one of them. Among the proverbs of Ptah-hotep, who was Chamberlain to King Asosi and lived about 2600 B.C., we find many a valuable precept reminiscent of the Proverbs of Solomon. This collection of proverbs is preserved for us on the 'Prisse Papyrus' in the Bibliothèque Nationale in Paris. 'If a son accepts what his father says, none of his plans will go awry,' we read. 'When you speak, take care what you say.' 'If you wish to forge an enduring friendship with the household in which you are master, brother, or friend, take care to shun the women: the place where they abide is not good.' 'The truth endures for evermore. It goes down to the City of the Dead with him who practises it.' That lovely passage comes from the 'story of the eloquent peasant', and dates from the period between 2000 and 1800 B.C.

The following few sentences from deciphered rolls of papyrus may serve to bring everyday life in ancient Egypt quite close for a moment. They are taken from letters, little notes, jottings and the like.

Lovers longed to be always together, just as they do nowadays. And so 'he' writes: 'I go for a walk, and you are with me in every beautiful place, and my hand is in your hand.'

One cannot help wondering what the man was thinking of, who wrote, a few thousand years ago: 'I lay in bed — and I was awake.' Or what had annoyed the girl who scribbled the following: 'Another time you need not come.'

A man called Anna addresses visitors to his tomb with the following words: 'Hear ye! May ye do the good that I have done, that ye be likewise done by.' And an unknown girl cries to her lover across thousands of years: 'I am hateful to your heart — but why?'

A meditative poem — it is 4000 years old — reminds us of the impermanence of human life: 'Nobody comes from the other world to tell us how he fared . . . Make joyful holiday. Do not be sad in life. For see, nobody takes with him what he owns, and nobody returns who has once departed.'

And here is a really timeless little love-poem: 'It disturbs me to hear your voice. My whole life hangs on your lips. To see you is better than all food and all drink.'

ANATOLIA

𐤎

THE HITTITES

Therefore the queen of Egypt . . . sent a messenger to my father and wrote to him thus: 'My husband has died. A son I have not. But to thee, they say, the sons are many. If thou wouldst give me one son of thine, he would become my husband. Never shall I pick out a servant of mine and make him my husband! I am afraid!' When my father heard this, he called forth the Great Ones for council, saying: 'Such a thing has never happened to me in my whole life!'
The Deeds of Suppiluliuma as told by his son Mursili II. (Translated by Hans Gustav Güterbock, Oriental Institute, University of Chicago.)

THERE are many vanished races in the world whose names we know, but whose history and culture are still a mystery to us. Four thousand years ago, on the Anatolian Plateau in the heart of modern Turkey, there lived a race which was only rediscovered at the turn of the century. Hattusa, their national capital, lay some hundred miles to the east of Ankara, near the modern village of Boghazkeui. The Hittites' role in world history was brief but of the utmost importance, for it was they who left behind the oldest written examples of an Indo-European language. They ruled over the bend of the Red River, 3000 feet above sea-level in Anatolia, for about six hundred years (roughly between 1800 and 1200 B.C.) and their influence extended far to the east and south. Yet they too, like so many others before them, eventually went down into the great grave of nations which we know as the history of mankind.

The 'Red River', or in Turkish, Kizil-Irmak, flows into the Black Sea. In antiquity, the river was called 'Halys' and the Black Sea 'Pontus Euxinus'. It was the highland plateau enclosed by the Halys, one of the least known areas in Asia Minor, which became the heart of the Hittites' dominions.

In 1902, the Norwegian Orientalist J. A. Knudtzon examined two tablets from the royal archives at El Amarna, Egypt. Both of the tablets were written in a completely unknown tongue, but Knudtzon ventured to suggest that he recognized in them traces of an Indo-European idiom. This was a bold enough theory in those days, and, needless to say, it was repudiated by all the Indo-European experts of the time. However, the lonely inscriptions on the walls, ruined buildings and rockfaces at Boghazkeui, east of Ankara in Anatolia, had long been an object of interest to scholars, and it was also known, thanks to the work of E. Chantre, that some of the fragmentary inscriptions there were written in the same language as the two remarkable tablets at El Amarna.

Between 1906 and 1912, the German Oriental Institute began excavating the ancient city of Hattusa at Boghazkeui under the direction of Dr Hugo Winckler. No less than ten thousand cuneiform tablets came to light, and it was at last recognized that Knudtzon had been on the right track: the two Amarna tablets were inscribed in Hittite characters. The difficult task of deciphering them was undertaken by a very brilliant Czech scholar, Bedrich Hrozny, who finally proved beyond any reasonable doubt that the people who had left these written records were Indo-Europeans. This discovery was of the utmost importance, for it provided the earliest historical evidence of the penetration of the Near East by Indo-European settlers.

In 1931, long after the First World War, the excavation of Hattusa was resumed under the leadership of Professor Kurt Bittel. Nine years later, the ancient city's principal features had been unearthed.

The name Boghazkeui is a very apt description of the region in which the village stands, its literal translation being 'gorge-ravine village'. Ever since the near-by ruins became so famous, incidentally, the place has borne the name *Boghazkale*, or 'ravine-fortress'. The highest point in the ancient city, the southern gate of Yer-kapu, stands at about 4075 feet above sea-level. Why did the Hittites select this desolate highland region as a site for the capital of their empire? In the first place, the firm and rocky ground made it less liable to the effects of the earthquakes which are so common in Anatolia; secondly, fast-flowing waters and constant winds kept the district free from malaria; and, finally, the uneven terrain with its deep gorges and rugged peaks made the place an ideal site for a fortified town. Kurt Bittel and Rudolf Naumann carefully excavated and examined the ground-plan of the Hittites' massive city, and the exciting results of their research were published in 1952.

The city is probably the Indo-European prototype of all European fortified towns. Hattusa contained a citadel, Büjükkale, in which the rulers of the Hittite Empire used to live, and whose walls were so closely adapted to the natural structure of its rocky site that it must have been virtually impregnable. There was a massive temple, too, the Hittites' largest religious building, complete with warehouses and store-chambers which housed the national treasury. The city's mighty walls enclosed a further four temples, residential quarters whose flat-roofed houses rose in terraces up the steep hillsides, massive towers, impressive gateways, a secret tunnel through the rock designed for sorties against the enemy in time of war, steep flights of steps, posterns and paved streets. The skill with which the citadel was dove-tailed into the landscape justifies one in regarding it as an example of advanced building technique. In Bittel's opinion, the massive, elemental nature of this architecture and the impression it gives of organic unity with the craggy countryside around make it something quite unique. Its originators brought their own individual conception of the world with them into the Orient. Excavations clearly show that Hattusa was the centre of a large empire. Thousands of hands helped to build the city, thousands of stone-masons, labourers and artisans. There are 200,000 bricks alone in the section of the city walls running from the King's Gate, via the lofty gate of Yer-kapu, to the Lion Gate: and that does not take into account the bricks in the projecting battlements or the outlying walls. For all that, Bittel puts the total population of Hattusa during the Hittites' prime at no more than fifteen or twenty thousand.

Walls, battlements and turrets all conform to the landscape. Whole crags and sections of mountainside were removed, holes were drilled into the rock, blocks of stone pinned together with metal plugs, and deep embrasures carefully filled in. Whatever happened, the wall (which was $17\frac{1}{2}$ feet thick round the citadel) was to constitute an impregnable fortification.

Inside the citadel archaeologists discovered the buildings where the Hittites had stored their archives. In this ruin, known to science as 'Archive A', were found 3294 clay tablets and fragments of which 1922 were lying in one room alone. These tablets may once have been stored in wooden chests, like those at El Amarna. All the Boghazkeui specimens were flat on one side and curved on the other, which must have made them easy to lay out on wooden shelves. They were labelled and even catalogued, likewise on clay.

Only a few graves dating from Hittite times were found. In the corner of one house excavators dug up the bones of a very young girl, wearing a thin, flat, gold ring in her right ear and a fine bronze bracelet on each forearm. Near a fireplace was found the skeleton of a fully grown man, lying on his left side with his legs drawn up. His skull was smashed, unfortunately, and very few traces of his bones had survived. Another grave, also containing only poorly preserved bones, had belonged to a child. The German anthropologist Sophie Ehrhardt devoted a great deal of study to the lower jaw-bone of this child, who was between thirteen and fourteen years old, but the poor condition of nearly all the Hittite skeletons made them almost worthless for purposes of anthropological research. The Hittites sometimes buried their dead inside their houses, but they also practised cremation.

Boghazkeui revealed other secrets, too. Discoveries of bones enabled scholars to reconstruct the animal world of those days. Portions of seven canine skeletons indicated that the inhabitants of Hattusa kept medium-sized dogs, probably rather like the Australian dingo in build. Horses were used here as draught-animals and beasts of burden, and the remains of six were discovered. Evidence of slaughtering and butchery proved that oxen must have been the city's principal source of meat, but other animals identified included goats, sheep, pigs and, among wild game, lion, aurochs, bison, elk, red deer, onager, fox, beaver and hare.

There is an indefinable atmosphere of tragedy about the ruins at Boghaz-keui. Hattusa was the capital of a large empire, yet archaeologists have always felt that the mountain city was never more than an artificial creation which could not have survived indefinitely, and that it was not really suitable as a road junction or as a link between the available oases in the Anatolian steppe.

This gigantic monument to human endeavour met a violent end. Where-ever Bittel and his colleagues dug, whether in the living-quarters of Temple 5 or in the walls of Yazilikaya, they found traces of a devastating conflagra-tion. Every inflammable object had been destroyed, brickwork had become fused by intense heat into a red, hard, slaggy mass, and limestone had burst or splintered. Bittel occasionally got the impression that the buildings would not normally have contained enough combustible material to account for such a degree of heat. In his opinion, some human agency had intentionally fed the flames, some unidentified enemy who had stormed the place during the Aegean Migration, bringing inflammable materials with him. Not a house, not a temple or hut had escaped the all-consuming flames, and nowhere did the excavators find evidence of even the most modest attempt to rebuild the city during Hittite times. Some of the inhabitants must have been massacred, others were probably carried off and sold into slavery, and the remainder fled to northern Syria. From 1200 B.C. onwards the city lay abandoned to the silence of death.

Where did the Hittites come from? What route did they follow? What did they bring with them? Where did they get their name? What was their script like? How far back into the past can we trace their history?

The Hittites did not always live in the bend of the Halys. They were not, to put it scientifically, autochthonous. Three clay tablets bring us some extremely interesting information on the matter. One of them was found in 1937, in the south-eastern store-chambers of the Great Temple, while the other two date from excavations before 1914. The text in question owes its authorship to a certain King Anitta, and Heinrich Otten, the authority on the Hittite language, regards the events described in it as historically accurate. Anitta lived about 1800 B.C., long before the earliest Hittite kings previously known to us, and is separated from Labarna, the first of them, by a gap of 100-150 years. The tablets have been translated as far as the ravages of time will allow, and the text, which is in an early Hittite idiom, reads like good, fluently composed history.

King Anitta lived in a place called Kussara, and he tells us that his father Pithana conquered the city of Nesa. (Kussara and Nesa may have stood in eastern Anatolia, perhaps in the interior of the Halys bend, but they have not yet been located.) King Anitta further informs us that after his father's death, he followed in his footsteps by going to war, defeating all the lands which opposed him. He was twice attacked by Pijusti, king of Hatti, but took Hattusa by storm in the course of a single night. 'In its place I sowed weeds. He who becomes king after me and peoples Hattusa again, him may the Storm-god of Heaven strike down.'

Did King Anitta originally write in Hittite (the tablets found were actually transcripts of a somewhat later date), and can his narrative stand as proof that even as early as this, in the 19th and 18th centuries B.C., Anatolia was inhabited by an Indo-European population?

Heinrich Otten brings forward ingenious arguments to prove that Anitta's text was, in fact, originally written in Hittite, and that the Indo-Germanic Hittites were already resident in Anatolia in the 19th century B.C. Bittel, too, assumes that the king employed the Hittite language in recording his war- and hunting-experiences for posterity, and, consequently, that the Indo-European Hittite tongue was already known in central Asia Minor in the 19th and 18th centuries. And that is the present extent of our knowledge of the Hittites. We cannot trace their history beyond this point.

As we have seen, King Anitta laid a curse on anyone who attempted to repopulate the city which he had conquered. Yet later Hittite rulers who, like Anitta, hailed from Kussara, selected Hattusa as their capital. What can we deduce from this? Hattusa and King Pijusti had been there long before the advent of the first Hittites. Hattusa bore a non-Indo-European name, and was a non-Indo-European (if also a non-Semitic) city whose inhabitants spoke 'Hattili'. The Indo-Europeans who conquered the city and settled there changed its name to Hattusa and called themselves 'men and women of Hatti' or 'sons of Hatti'. That was how the Hittites came to bear a Near Eastern name, although they themselves came from quite another part of the world.

It was for a long time assumed — and many scholars still adhere to this view — that the Hittites immigrated from the west. This is a convenient theory, since many authorities believe that the Indo-Europeans' original home was in central Europe, and the easiest route out of that area leads eastwards. Professor Ferdinand Sommer, on the other hand, the eighty-two-year-old scholar who is still lecturing at Munich University, has advanced very plausible arguments to prove that the Hittites probably arrived in Anatolia from the north-east, surging into Asia Minor across the neck of land between the Black Sea and the Caspian. Like most other racial migrations, it was not a concerted invasion, but a gradual process which lasted for many years. The Indo-Europeans first arrived in the Anatolian highlands at about the turn of the 2nd millennium B.C. Using Kussara and Nesa as a bridge-head they conquered the cities of the interior, eventually gaining control of the whole area and its ancient highland civilization. The celebrated Hittitologist Anton Moortgat considers that the term for the Hittite language was really 'Nesian', from the city of Nesa.

When the Hittites migrated into Asia Minor from the east, they brought with them an archaic type of cuneiform writing which they had acquired in the course of their wanderings. The trading-settlements of the East used an old Syrian cuneiform script considerably different from the Hittites', whose own script had an affinity with that of the 3rd Dynasty of Ur. All the records and correspondence in the archives at Boghazkeui were written in the Hittite mode.

The language of this cuneiform script was Indo-European, and there is no further doubt today about the Indo-European structure of the Hittite language. One can see at a glance how the Hittite word *uatar* became *water* in English, *Wasser* in German, and *woda* in Russian; or how *genu* became our own *knee*; or how *kardi* became *cor* (genitive: *cordis*) in Latin, *heart* in English, and *Herz* in German; or *pahhur* the English *fire*, the German *Feuer*, and so on. Admittedly, all the research carried out so far has shown that only a minority of Hittite words were actually Indo-European. But words are not the only decisive guides to the classification of a language. Inflexion, modes of declension and conjugation, etc., are much more important, permanent and invariable factors, and the inflexions in Hittite mark it unequivocally as an Indo-European language. It is quite certain, too, that it was a spoken tongue, not merely one that was employed for literary or official purposes.

There are two more languages which are closely related to Hittite: Luvian and Palaic. Luvian was spoken in the territories of the Taurus mountains. Of Palaic, only about four hundred words have survived. All three languages, Hittite, Luvian and Palaic, were about as closely related as English, Swedish and German are today.

In addition to their cuneiform script the Hittites used a hieroglyphic or picture-writing, remnants of which, dating from between the 15th and 8th centuries B.C., survive today. The bulk of all the important specimens of this script were found at Carchemish, near the modern village of Jerablus, and, during the 2nd and certainly the 1st millennium B.C., Carchemish must have been the principal home of Hittite hieroglyphics.

Why did the Hittites retain this second method of writing? It was only used for seals, monuments and inscriptions in stone generally, and was thus of much less importance than the universally popular cuneiform script. Although our only examples of Hittite hieroglyphics date from between the 15th and 8th centuries, they must certainly have been preceded by a long period of development, for they already exhibit a certain tendency towards the cursive and their pictorial symbols are simplified and stylized. Bittel believes that the script was already in use during the latter half of the 3rd millennium B.C. The simplest way to account for the script's invention is to assume that it was designed for a language related to Hittite. This is the theory held by Güterbock, and it seems a plausible one. Hieroglyphic-Hittite is very probably a dialect related to Luvian. At all events, it is certainly a member of the Hittite-Luvian linguistic family.

The story of the hieroglyphic script's discovery and elucidation is an enthralling one. It has only recently been published, and even now not in its entirety. In the autumn of 1947, H. T. Bossert and his Turkish collaborators made a sensational discovery. On the mound of Karatepe, which stands in the foothills of the Taurus range in eastern Cilicia near the river Jejhan, Bossert unearthed some inscriptions in Phoenician and hieroglyphic-Hittite. Although the texts were not identical, they were similar enough to provide a means of deciphering the fundamentals of the Hittites' hieroglyphic script. Ambiguities still exist, of course, and much of the information had already been known, but Bossert's find, coming as it did after years of painstaking research by numerous students of the Hittite hieroglyphics, remains the most important landmark so far reached in this field. Very recently, in 1956, another discovery was made. During the excavation of the royal palace at Ugarit-Ras-Shamra a number of seals were unearthed. The scientific importance of this find lay in the fact that round the Hittite hieroglyphics on the seals ran a legend in Akkadian script, a circumstance which enabled E. Laroche to amend and identify a large number of additional symbols.

Cuneiform and pictographic texts alike point to Hittite as an Indo-European language, and the Hittites can, in fact, be classified as members of the Indo-European linguistic group. Their physical characteristics, on the other hand, were constantly subject to adulteration and alien admixtures, sometimes strong and sometimes less so. It would be interesting to know who were culturally more advanced, the invading Indo-Europeans or the indigenous population of Hattusa (known to science as 'proto-Hattians'). We gather that newcomers and original inhabitants got on quite well and learned a lot from each other, but it is not certain which group made the more valuable contribution to their joint way of life. Moortgat and Sommer both think that the original, subjugated inhabitants were in many respects the cultural superiors of their new masters; and Bittel, who has spent years of research on the actual site of the ancient city, also surmises that although they speedily assimilated the old Anatolian civilization, the immigrant Hittites were at first culturally inferior.

The Hittites were foreigners from far away, yet, once they had established themselves in eastern Anatolia, they took the indigenous civilization of the region and raised it to heights which received universal recognition, even in the world of that time. But despite all the fruits of the ancient Anatolian civilization which they adopted, the Hittites remained totally distinct from the Babylonians in their beliefs, ideas and customs. They had their own individual style in everything: in dress, ornamentation, monumental sculpture and town-planning.

Hattusa was a fortified metropolis, and its crowning glory was Büjükkale, the citadel. The principal feature of the famous cities in Mesopotamia, by contrast, was always the temple of their city-god. The king of the Hittites could not exercise his authority as arbitrarily as other eastern potentates. He was supreme lord of his people both in war and peace, but his powers were circumscribed by the nobility. We find no indication that the Hittites persecuted and tortured defeated peoples, as was the habit of the Assyrians and Medes. Punishments were less severe, too. The practice of mutilation was unknown, and sentence of death was only rarely passed on non-slaves.

If the male Hittite wished to get married, he purchased a wife, and even slaves were allowed to acquire free women in marriage. The Hittites did not, however, follow the Egyptian custom of marriage between brother and sister. We have precise information on this subject, in the shape of a clay tablet written by King Suppiluliuma to a certain Hukkanas from the land of Hajasa: 'A brother may not take his own sister or cousin, for it is not right. Whosoever does such a thing in Hattusa does not remain alive, but dies.' Suppiluliuma remarked that while it might be quite customary in Hajasa to marry one's own brother, sister, or cousin, such a thing was prohibited at Hattusa. The king was justified in writing to Hukkanas in this fashion because he had ennobled the simple but able man and given him one of his sisters as a wife. He was therefore at pains to establish proper relations between his family, his court and his new brother-in-law. The king strikes a very human note as he continues: 'If, then, one of your wife's sisters or a half-sister or cousin comes to you, give her to eat and drink; eat and drink together and make merry. But do not lust for her. That is not allowed, and merits the death penalty: so do not try it. Even if someone should tempt you, pay him no heed and do not do it.' There is something reminiscent of Solomon's shrewd proverbs in this advice.

Suppiluliuma reigned from 1380 to 1340 B.C., and was probably the most powerful ruler in the world at that time. He skilfully exploited Egypt's political weakness under Akhenaten the reformer, incorporated the whole of northern Syria down to the Lebanon border into the Hittite Empire, conquered the countries of Asia Minor, and destroyed the Mitanni nation.

A man of his calibre naturally expected orderly behaviour within his own household. Hence this additional warning on the clay tablet addressed to Hukkanas: that his new brother-in-law should not go too near any woman of the court, whether a freeborn lady or a slave-girl in the service of the temple. 'Go not too near her, nor speak a word to her. Nor let your serving-man or maid approach her. Be very wary of her. As soon as a lady of the palace approaches, leap out of the way and let her pass.' In the course of his covenant with Hukkanas, the able king told him a small story designed as an object-lesson. It seems that, one day, a certain Marjas let his glance rest on a hierodule, or female temple-slave, who was passing by. He, Suppiluliuma, the Father of the Sun, happened to be looking out of a window at the time, and saw the mild preliminary flirtation going on. Ordering the unfortunate Marjas to be arrested, he demanded: 'Why did you look at the slave-girl?' If the Father of the Sun asked such a question, it was tantamount to a sentence of death — and Marjas was, in fact, executed 'on this account'. But the king went a step further: he was determined that his new brother-in-law should not slip back into the old immoral ways even in Hajasa, his own country. There, too, he was in future to abstain from touching his brother's wives and his own sisters. On the other hand, he would be permitted to retain the women he already owned as concubines.

We have heard in a previous chapter how the widow of Pharaoh Akhenaten wrote to a Hittite king and asked him to send her one of his sons as a prospective husband. The Hittite, who incidentally must have been quite flattered by this suggestion, was none other than King Suppiluliuma, and the Egyptian queen was probably Nefertiti. We are not entirely sure if this unusual request, coming as it did from a queen of Egypt, was really made by Nefertiti or by the widow of Tutankhamun, Akhenaten's successor. Eduard Meyer and Alexander Scharff both assume that it was actually Nefertiti who entertained these startling matrimonial plans. Güterbock, however, believes that the author of the sensational proposal was Tutankhamun's widow, and the Egyptologist E. Edel shares this view.

The story of this dynastic scandal, which took place about 3300 years ago and was certainly not made public at the time, is told in *The Deeds of Suppiluliuma*, written by his son Mursili II. The fragmentary clay tablets bearing this extremely interesting text were carefully assembled by Güterbock between 1954 and 1956 at Frankfurt and Ankara, and were then translated by him into English. The Egyptian queen's letter is the most reliable portion of Mursili's account to have been preserved for us.

Let us go back three hundred years to the time when the Hittite throne was occupied by Labarnas II, also known as Hattusilis I. This king left us a bilingual text in Hittite and Akkadian. It was his last will and testament

written as he lay dying. His queen consort and the heir apparent seem to
have been in league against him. His son shed no tears and showed his dying
father no sympathy: 'Cold he is, and heartless! I, the king, summoned him
to my bedside, but he is my son no longer. Then his mother bellowed like
an ox.' But the king remained unmoved. 'His mother is a serpent', he went
on. 'Time and again my disloyal son will heed the words of his mother, his
brothers and his sisters, and then he will wreak revenge. There will be a
blood-bath.' The king warned against revolution and civil war. Instead of
leaving his throne to the crown prince, he designated the latter's son, Mursili,
as his successor. Mursili was still young, he said, 'so bring him up to be a
hero king'. Hattusilis must have been an excellent psychologist, for he
commanded that his young grandson have his grandfather's decree read to
him once each month.

It is easy to deduce from the clay tablets of the Hittite kings that they were
men who had accumulated the experience of many generations and applied
it to their own circumstances. Where treaties were concerned, they were
never satisfied with mere pacts of mutual assistance. They were able psycho-
logists who were well aware of all the weaknesses and temptations to which
even friends and relations are prone. That was why they went much further
in their security measures than our modern statesmen. They emphasized
that their treaty partner must never waver in his loyalty, carefully laying it
down in writing that he was not to let himself be influenced by any outside
party. Anyone who was an enemy of the Sun (and the Hittite king was
always referred to as 'the Sun') must also be an enemy of his ally, and anything the ally heard which was to the king's disadvantage must always be
reported to him. It is rather touching to hear how Mursili II, who reigned
from 1339 to 1306, addresses his ally Kupanta-Kal, enjoining him not to put
any faith in false rumours. Here are his actual words: 'Humanity is corrupt.
If rumours fly, and someone comes to you and whispers that the Sun is
doing you wrong, that he is going to take away your house or lands and do
you a mischief, you must inform the Sun without delay.'

In concluding pacts like these, the contracting parties always swore by
the thousand gods of the Hittites. 'We have called the thousand gods to
the tribunal', ran the formula. The Sun-god of the sky, the Sun-goddess of
Arinna, the Storm-god of many places, Ishtar the Queen of the Firmament,
and countless other gods and goddesses were called to witness, all of whom
were to destroy anyone who disregarded the king's decree.

There came a time, however, when the gods of the Hittites failed. Hattusa
went up in flames. Citadel, temples, store-chambers and houses crashed to
the ground, and the sky glowed red as the Hittites met their downfall in
the place which had once been the seat of their power. From 1200 B.C.

onwards, all reference to the Hittites ceases abruptly. Their life in eastern Anatolia was at an end.

The death of a nation is like the death of an individual: it is always hard to comprehend. Anyone who sees the truly remarkable fortifications of Büjükkale and allows his imagination free rein will recognize the elemental will-power which must have belonged to the builders of Boghazkeui. And he will recognize something else: that these men built for eternity, never questioning the permanence of their handiwork. They sank wells, worked at their vineyards, tended their apple trees, tilled their fields, grazed their sheep, and, if the king so ordered, built chariots and went to war. They bought and sold slaves. Paragraph 14 of their legal code lays it down that anyone who punched a slave-woman on the nose was fined three silver shekels, while the same assault upon a full citizen cost a whole *mina*, or sixty shekels. If a slave escaped and was recaptured for the owner by someone else, the finder received a reward.

If, after a man had paid the price of a bride, her parents subsequently decided not to part with the girl after all, they were obliged to repay the sum twice over. On the other hand, it also happened that a girl who had been promised to one man was suddenly married off to another. In that case, the successful bridegroom was only bound to repay his rival the equivalent of his expenditure to date. Perfumiers and herdsmen were held in low esteem, apparently, for any girl who married one automatically became a slave for three years.

The Hittites' laws vividly illuminate their colourful way of life. A man who sneaked off after a woman into the lonely mountains and raped her was sentenced to death. When another man assaulted a woman in her own home, her complicity was taken for granted, and she too had to die. (A slave-woman's honour was not legally protected.) Somebody killed a snake, uttering the name of his enemy while doing so. Dangerous magic of that kind incurred a fine of one silver mina, and a slave who did the same thing forfeited his head. There must also have been at least one Hittite who was so enraged that he lifted a door off its hinges and carried it away, for a law was invented to cover such a contingency. The eccentric miscreant had to replace all the livestock which the owner of the house lost as a result of his act (possibly because of the severe cold), and pay a silver mina in addition.

The Hittites were a vigorous, hot-blooded race, and life seems to have been more eventful in the east Anatolian highlands in those days than it is now. We can visualize how the Hittite bridegrooms used to wade through the waist-high snow, lashed by the bitter north or north-east wind, to collect their brides; how the people used to rejoice when the steppe put on its bright mantle of green; how they celebrated the short-lived, tumultuous feast of colour which only lasts until July and then yields once more to the greyish-brown monotony of the arid landscape; how they endured the scorching summers and the bitter winters with their heavy falls of snow; how they triumphed over the infinite loneliness of their mountain home, filling the melancholy Anatolian highlands with life and laughter. Yet there came a day when they succumbed to the most dangerous thing on earth, something far more implacable than Nature at its most destructive: the enemy in human form.

PHOENICIA

X

THEY NEVER HAD TIME...

'Rogues, bringing countless trinkets with them in their dark ship.' *Homer*, circa 800 B.C.

WE know exactly what race they belonged to, but we do not know very much about their history. They have left us few written records and scarcely any literature. They simply never had time to write. However, we know where they came from, we know their cities, and we know where they went on their voyages. . . .

The most astonishing thing about the Phoenicians is that although they were probably the greatest seafaring people in the ancient world and built cities on every coast, scarcely any other race is so puzzling and difficult to investigate, for they left no large or enduring kingdom behind them in their native land.

The Phoenicians' ancestors were Semites, and belonged to the Canaanites of whom we read in the Bible. The name used at that time to be pronounced 'Kinahni', and we come across it in the 'Amarna Tablets', which were letters inscribed in clay addressed to the Egyptian court about 1400 B.C., and which were discovered at El Amarna in Egypt.

If the Phoenicians were really Semites — and their language also points to that conclusion — it is remarkable that they ever developed such an un-Semitic love of the sea. Fearless and endowed with infinite powers of endurance, they sailed away across the seas to places where no one before them had ever dared venture. Ancient Phoenicia comprised the coastal areas of modern Syria, the Lebanon and Israel, and it was along these coasts that the Phoenicians built their sea-ports: Byblos, Tyre, Sidon, Marathus, Ugarit, Beirut and many others. The name 'Phoenician' is probably derived either from the Greek word for a date-palm, which was *phoinix*, or from the adjective *phoinos*, meaning red. It may be that the Greeks called them by the latter name because the Phoenicians possessed a reddish, or rather, brownish-red skin. Or again, perhaps it was on account of the purple-dyed cloth for whose manufacture the Phoenicians became famous.

When Herodotus the Greek visited Phoenicia, he was told that Tyre had been founded '2300 years ago'. If the date of his visit was about 450 B.C., it would mean that Tyre was founded in 2750 B.C.

When once these remarkable seafarers had freed themselves from Egyptian domination, they became the undisputed masters of the eastern

Mediterranean. They manufactured articles of glass and metal, precious vases, weapons and jewellery. They traded in grain, wine and cloth, bartering these goods along every coast in the Mediterranean and transporting them to the most distant shores. Lead, gold and iron they obtained from the southern shores of the Black Sea; they loaded their ships with copper, cypress and other woods and grain from Cyprus, ivory and gold from Africa, wine from southern France, tin from the Atlantic; and everywhere they went they shanghaied foreigners for the slave-trade. They supplied the harems of the contemporary world with the girls they seized. They maintained trade with Tarshish, probably the place in south-western Spain which we know as Tartessus. They imported so much silver from there that it is even said they made their ships' anchors out of that metal. From Gadeira, or modern Cadiz, they sailed out into the Atlantic Ocean to the 'Tin Isles', which were probably the Cornish coasts of England.

The Phoenicians are reputed to have circumnavigated Africa 700 years before the birth of Christ, which would mean that they discovered the Cape of Good Hope 2000 years before Vasco da Gama! Their low, narrow galleys, often 100 feet long, raced along in all weathers, the galley-slaves who toiled at their oars being assisted by a large square sail. Soldiers were stationed on deck, and the Phoenician watchword was: 'Trade or fight!' However, the Phoenicians had a high regard for trade, and only used their weapons when people showed no signs of succumbing to verbal persuasion. Ships like theirs, with a draught of only five feet and no compass on board, naturally had to hug the coasts whenever possible. Nevertheless, Phoenician helmsmen eventually learned how to steer by the stars, and the Pole Star later became known among the Greeks as the 'Phoenician Star'.

The Phoenicians installed trading-stations and garrisons at every strategic point in the Mediterranean: at Cadiz, Carthage, Marseilles, on Malta, Sicily and Corsica, and probably even on the distant shores of England and other islands in the Atlantic which were only later rediscovered by our forefathers. The Phoenicians controlled Cyprus, Melos and Rhodes. They put slaves to work in their mines, and were never averse to combining business with a bit of robbery when it seemed worth while. They robbed the weak and swindled the gullible, and were only honest when they were dealing with the ablest merchants. Furthermore, they practised piracy, inviting foreigners on board their ships to look round, and then simply sailing off with them. The Greeks, who were not above a little piracy themselves, used 'Phoenician' as a general term for any pirate-chieftain, and the poet Homer, who lived about 800 B.C., remarks pertinently in his *Odyssey*: 'Then came the Phoenicians, renowned mariners, rogues bringing countless trinkets with them in their dark ship.' (*Odyssey* XV, 415.)

But the Phoenicians were not only merchants and pirates. They were also bearers of civilization in the truest sense of the word. They imported scientific knowledge and the art of writing from Egypt, Crete and the Near East into Greece, Africa, Italy and Spain. They linked East and West commercially, and acted as 'middle-men' between Babylon and Egypt. Civilization travelled to Europe in their holds full of barrels and bales, and liberated the new continent from cave-life.

The commercial aristocracy of Phoenicia were fonder of good business than of war, which was why their cities became so immensely wealthy. Byblos was probably the oldest of their metropolitan cities, and papyrus, or paper, one of their most important trade-goods. That was how the Greeks came to call any book *biblos*, and how we got our 'Bible', via the Greek *ta biblia*.

Some fifty miles south of Byblos and also situated on the coast, stood Sidon. This city provided King Xerxes with practically the whole of his fleet, and the sea-battles fought by the Persians against the Greeks were principally conducted with Phoenician ships, which really made them Graeco-Phoenician wars. When the Persians eventually besieged and took Sidon, the proud Phoenician big business men set fire to their own city, the Hamburg of antiquity, and 40,000 people died in the conflagration.

The most important Phoenician city, however, was Tyre. Built on an island some miles off-shore, it possessed a magnificent harbour. Slaves drawn from every country in the Mediterranean man-handled bales, chests and barrels to and fro between warehouses and ships. King Hiram I of Tyre (969-936 B.C.) was a friend of both David and Solomon, and supplied them with cedar-wood, carpenters and stone-masons. In 520 B.C., Tyre was so rich that it owned silver 'as the dust' and gold 'as the mire of the streets' (Zechariah ix, 3).

The city only had a circumference of just over 2½ miles, but its buildings were tall enough to allow 25,000 people to live in it. The total population of the city was larger still, however, for there was a mainland city on the shore opposite the island, known as 'Old Tyre'. We read that Nebuchadnezzar besieged this city for thirteen years, but there is no mention of his ever having captured it.

Alexander the Great only succeeded in gaining access to the island-citadel by first destroying the mainland city of Tyre and then building a causeway out of its ruins. During the course of centuries, alluvial deposits have built up a neck of land there which is today 650 yards across at its narrowest point.

Carthage was yet another Phoenician foundation (878 B.C.), and the Carthaginians were a Phoenician people. Hannibal was a son of this unique race of merchants and seafarers. It was Phoenician inspiration which created the citadel of Carthage, with its tall blocks of flats and narrow streets running like ravines between them. Carthage held out against Rome for a long time before her merchant inhabitants succumbed to the superiority of the Roman soldiery. The latest excavations have shown that her streets ran at right angles like those of New York; 700,000 people lived there in the year 149 B.C.

The Phoenician Carthaginians had a very simple method of ensuring that the whole trade of north-west Africa flowed through their own sea-port. They always permitted foreign merchants to come to Carthage — indeed, they made them very welcome. But if they ever found foreign merchants in any of their African colonies, they tied stones to their legs and threw them into the sea.

Many gods were worshipped by the Phoenicians, and each of their cities had its own 'Baal'. The Baal of Tyre was called Melqarth. He was as strong as the Greeks' Hercules, and performed feats which even Baron Munchausen would have envied. The Phoenicians took over Ishtar, the goddess of fertility, from the Babylonians, and the handmaidens of Astarte at Byblos also had to sacrifice their long tresses to the goddess and 'entertain' any strange passer by in the forecourt of her temple, just as the virgins of Ishtar Mylitta did at Babylon. Finally, there was Moloch, the frightful god to whom the Phoenicians used to offer living children as a burnt sacrifice. When Carthage was besieged in 204 B.C., her inhabitants immolated one hundred boys of noble birth on Moloch's altar to propitiate the god and raise the siege.

Like the Egyptians, the Phoenicians placed great importance upon the enduring burial of their dead. In 1921-23, French archaeologists under the direction of Montet dug up Ahiram's beautiful sarcophagus in the neighbourhood of Byblos, or what is now Jebeil. On it is one of the oldest Phoenician inscriptions known to us.

The Phoenician merchants were practical men. They were neither visionaries nor poets. Like the inhabitants of all large cities, they just 'never had time' for such things. That is why so little belonging to their race has survived. The majority of their monuments were destroyed or have crumbled away over the years, and while rolls of papyrus have remained legible and in good condition for thousands of years in the dry climate of Egypt, everything rots away quickly on the humid coasts of Syria. Scarcely more than a dozen inscriptions in stone have been unearthed in Phoenicia itself. Of the mighty sanctuary of Melqarth at Tyre, not one stone remains upon another. The cities are destroyed, and such few works of art as have been found almost always display a similarity to those of Egypt and Babylon.

Since the Phoenicians were responsible for introducing so many countries to the modern technical and artistic achievements of their day, it was for a long time assumed that they were themselves the inventors of glass, coinage, faience ware and even of the alphabet. However, the latest scientific research indicates that while they may have been great imitators and transmitters of culture, they were not great inventors. They brought all these fine things on to the market, it is true, but the original ideas sprang from elsewhere. Arithmetic, weights and measures and coinage came from the Babylonians. The making of moulded glass and faience was known to the Egyptians much earlier than to the Phoenicians. It was only later on that the glass industry of Sidon became world-famous. The alphabet, too, had a long series of 'elaborators' before it reached the Phoenicians.

It is even uncertain whether the Phoenicians were the original manufacturers of purple dye, although their mastery of this art made them worldrenowned in antiquity. They extracted the much sought-after dye from a gland in the murex, or purple sea-snail. Tyrian purple was not, as is frequently imagined, a scarlet colour, but a dark violet approaching black, comparable with the colour of congealed blood, although looked at obliquely or from below, or in harsh lighting, it took on a paler tone. Egyptian society women, and indeed, smart society throughout the Mediterranean, had a high regard for materials which had been dyed at Tyre.

On the southern side of what used to be the island of Tyre, thick layers have been discovered which are in fact composed of stone-hard conglomerations of waste matter from former purple factories. The Greeks used to wrinkle up their noses at the very mention of Tyre, for the numerous dyeworks there produced a repulsive stench, rather reminiscent of garlic. However, cloth dyed in purple was very costly, and the wearing of purple robes became a mark of royalty.

The Phoenicians used to catch the molluscs alive in racks rather like oysterbaskets set in the sea. The shells were opened up and the glands extracted. The juice of these was then simmered in cauldrons over a gentle fire for ten days, and clarified by constant skimming. When the liquid had become adequately condensed, the fabrics which were to be dyed were dipped in it and left to dry in the sun. Only then did the colours display themselves in their true splendour and, since it was only through exposure to light that they appeared, they did not subsequently fade.

When Alexander the Great overthrew the city of Tyre in July 332 B.C., the far-flung empire of the Phoenicians came to an end. 8000 Tyrians were massacred and another 30,000 sold into slavery. The cities of Aradus, Sidon, Tyre and Tripolis had one more lease of life in the time of Pompey (64 B.C.), but they adopted Roman customs, started to speak Latin and Greek, and married foreign wives. Eventually, this mysterious race of courageous seafarers stepped from the arena of world history.

PERSIA

✗

WHEN AHASUERUS COULD NOT SLEEP

When King Xerxes was reviewing his land and sea forces [in 480 B.C., before the sea-battle of Salamis] he wept, and said: 'Truly, it grieves me when I reflect how short the whole life of man is. For out of all these men, not one will still be alive a hundred years from now.'
Herodotus

THE known span of human history is so short that it is always the most interesting problems which are lost in the twilight of the past. It is very probable that some 100,000 years ago our earth was inhabited by a universal kind of man, and that all 'races' are subsequent variations of this same two-legged creature, mere nuances of the *homo sapiens* who adapted himself in the course of his earthly life to varying climates and kinds of food, varying types of terrain and hunting facility. If a complete history of the world comprised a thousand volumes, we should only be able to read the last chapter of the last volume. What this last section deals with is the eclipse and domination of the oriental peoples of the Near East by Indo-Iranian or 'Aryan' races. The ancestral domain of these conquerors may have been the great steppes of the Asian interior, the plains of southern Russia, or the shores of the Baltic Sea. Old legends tell of a long-lost land called 'Airyanem Vaejo' and of migrations by nomadic peoples into Persia and India via Bokhara and Samarkand.

The Old Persian Empire, that greatest empire in the ancient world only flourished for some three hundred years, from 600 to about 300 B.C. During the course of these three hundred years, however, there unfolded on the Iranian plateau and in the whole of the Near East a drama so fascinating, a spectacle so fabulous and incredible, that we cannot fail to be dazzled by the insane genius, the atrocious deeds, the extravagance, and also by the greatness of some of the Median and Persian kings who were making history there more than 2000 years ago.

The Persian Empire was built upon the ruins of the former supremacy of the people we know as the Medes. Where did these Medes come from?

Their point of immediate departure was evidently in south Russia. They reached Persia by traversing the mountains between the Black Sea and the Caspian. Some of them (Indians) trekked on farther to India, while others settled in Iran. They were a tall, white-skinned race of nomads and herdsmen, and the most important cultural innovation which they brought with them was the horse. It was not long before they and their descendants were holding sway over the kingdom of Babylonia, Assyria and Syria.

The first king of the Medes of whom we know was Deioces. He established Ecbatana, his capital city, on a hill, and crowned it with a temple which glittered in the sun. The city is said to have been enclosed by seven walls, the innermost of pure gold, the second of silver, the third of gleaming orange-coloured bricks, and the others of blue, scarlet, black and white. Nothing is left of this fairy-tale city, although one wonders whether the solid gold walls will ever be dug up. Ecbatana probably flourished where Hamadan stands today. Herodotus tells us that none of its inhabitants was ever allowed into their king's presence, and it was commonly believed that he was of a different shape from other mortals.

The most important Median king was Cyaxares, who sacked Nineveh and eventually besieged Sardis. It is said that an eclipse of the sun put such dread into the hearts of besieged and besiegers alike that they forthwith concluded a peace. They exchanged two bowls of human blood and ceremonially poured them out on the ground to symbolize the ending of the umpteenth 'World War'. (The world was not yet round in those days!)

Not a single stone, not a line of writing, no correspondence and scarcely any works of art belonging to the Medes still survive.

In 585 B.C., Astyages assumed the government from his father Cyaxares. He took his place on the Median throne at Ecbatana, modern Hamadan, fully determined to preserve and enjoy his sovereignty for a long time to come. He introduced gorgeous fashions and every conceivable kind of extravagance. Gentlemen of his day wore embroidered trousers, a garment which was a complete innovation and owes its invention to the Medes. Ladies used to take good care of their fine skin, and were much interested in cosmetics and jewellery. In a country which was constantly exposed to cavalry invasions from the steppe lands of the north and east, horse and rider were united in a life and death association, and the animals were arrayed in quilts embellished with gold. The glittering capital city, Ecbatana, was the scene of one festivity after another.

Reckless splendour such as this always carries with it a suggestion of the eleventh hour, and doubt, and imminent downfall, and the terror which accompanies ugly dreams of the future. Man usually behaves in an unseemly way when he is at the peak of his power. King Astyages had learnt from interpreters of dreams that his daughter's son would one day rule all Media. He accordingly married his daughter Mandane not to a Mede, but to Cambyses, the Persian prince of a vassal State. Any child of such a marriage could be done away with later, Astyages thought, for the Medes, so far from regarding the Persians with any great respect, were rather inclined to despise them. No sooner had Mandane, the Median king's daughter, presented Cambyses the Persian with a son, Cyrus, than Astyages ordered his chief minister Harpagus to kill the child. Harpagus did not obey these instructions, however, and gave little Cyrus into the keeping of a cowherd. It was there, among the blustering winds of the highlands to the north of Ecbatana, that the boy who was later to become the greatest statesman of his age grew up.

Herodotus tells us a horrible story about the outcome of this act of mercy. One day, Astyages found out that Harpagus had spared young Cyrus's life. As a punishment, he served him up a joint of roast meat. It was Harpagus's own son, with the head, feet and hands lopped off. While they were still at table, Astyages had the Chancellor shown the head of his dead son. Harpagus preserved a strict outward calm. 'All that the King does is good,' he said. From then on he played a clever waiting game until Cyrus grew up, when he allied himself to him, admitted him into the land of the Medes, and abetted his victory. It is interesting to note that, on the very threshold of his immortal career, Cyrus permitted Astyages to live out his life in honourable freedom after his defeat and subsequent capture.

So the land of the Medes fell into the hands of their Persian cousins, who were likewise of Indo-European stock. The Persians had settled in Anzan in southern Elam. Their capital city was Susa, and their royal house that of the Achaemenides, named after their first king, Achaemenes, who reigned somewhere between 700 and 675 B.C. He was followed by Teispes, Cyrus I, Cambyses I and Cyrus II. Some 320 miles south of Susa, the Achaemenides owned a second very ancient stronghold called Parsagarda or 'Camp of the Persians', a fortress which the Greeks named Pasargadae. The actual history of the Persians begins with Cyrus II, the heart of whose possessions was the land of Parsa, or Persis. E. Herzfeld, digging at Madar-i-Sulaiman in 1928, not far from the River Pulvar and about 25 miles from the modern town of Shushtar, unearthed the ruins of the royal residence at Pasargadae. While flying over the area in 1935, Erich F. Schmidt discerned the outlines of an ancient fortress. There in its lonely simplicity Cyrus's tomb still stood, having defied the blazing heat of the sun and the winds of the plain until the present day. At one time it had been surrounded by a park, with walls and colonnades. On a pillar were found the words, inscribed in cuneiform lettering: 'I am King Cyrus, the Achaemenid.' But the grave was empty, and the golden sarcophagus in which Cyrus the Great once lay had been stolen long before.

With the conquest of Ecbatana, Cyrus became master of all Media at a single blow, and thereby the founder of the Persian Empire. To the Persians, he represented their perfect ideal of masculine beauty. However, it was probably not so much that they loved him because he was handsome as that they found him handsome because they loved him. Plutarch tells us that the Persians considered a hooked nose a mark of beauty. Why? Because Cyrus had one! We do not know very much about this particular Cyrus, for what Xenophon tells us of him in his *Cyropaedia* or 'Boyhood of Cyrus' is less of an historical work than a hymn in praise of monarchy and an educational treatise of a purely Greek character. It was written for a later Persian prince, Cyrus the Younger, and is strongly coloured by the philosophy of Socrates, who was a friend of Xenophon. Cyrus's first step was to raise a powerful army, with which he proceeded to conquer Lydia and the famous city of Sardis.

Seen from our own day, King Cyrus's triumphal progress truly seems one of mankind's brightest morning hours, conducted as it was with the mysterious magic of a statesmanship worthy of Caesar, led by a spirit of emancipation, and guided by magnanimity and true human greatness.

Caria, Lycia and Ionia surrendered to the Persian king's generals.

In the east, Cyrus protected his empire against the audacious raids of the Saka tribes of the Turenian steppes. He laid his mighty hand on Bactria, Margiana and Sogdiana, and far away on the Jaxartes, to the north of modern Samarkand, he founded the powerful frontier fortress of Cyreshata. He also subjugated Babylon, at that time discontented with its ruler Nabonidus. On October 29th in 539 B.C. he entered the ancient city amid scenes of public rejoicing, liberated the Jews who were imprisoned there, made sacrifice to the Babylonian god Marduk, and put an end to the Semitic domination of western Asia which had lasted a thousand years. In this way, the Persian world empire became the greatest administrative organization in the pre-Roman world.

Cyrus seems to have been sympathetically inclined towards the religions of other races. He respected their gods, made obeisance in their holy places, and apparently considered it advisable to put himself under the protection of their gods and idols, for he maintained their temples and looked devoutly on while the incense rose before each sacred image. He never indulged in extermination, but always tried to win people over. He was the new spirit of western Asia, and its most gifted and important figure until Alexander the Great appeared on the scene.

It was no wonder that people hailed him with such joy, no wonder that he occupied Babylon with the support of most of the citizens of that ancient city and that Belshazzar's army melted away, no wonder that generals and princes and the people of Sumer and Akkad fell at his feet and kissed them. He was a truly broadminded man, and he may have guessed that, outside his own religion and apart from Ahura Mazda, a God ruled the world whom he did not yet know. It is certainly no mere fable that it was this particular Cyrus who rebuilt the ruined temple of Yahweh in Jerusalem for the Jews.

Cyrus did not die in bed, at home in his own city of Ecbatana. He threw himself into the fray against an invasion by Asiatic bowmen, the Massagetic horsemen of the north who had stormed out of the steppes of Turkestan, incited by the Scythians. In the course of his heroic struggle against this menace to Persia, the great Achaemenid died in the summer of the year 530 B.C., presumably a victim of the wily tactics of his steppe-riding adversaries and their dangerous bowmanship.

The statesmen of our own day could learn a great deal from Cyrus. He may have lived 2500 years ago, but it seems fairly apparent that the intelligence of politicians has not increased one jot since that day. Here is an example: the King of Lydia was that renowned and envied man, Croesus. His fabulous wealth depended on the output of numerous gold and other mines. Croesus' capital, Sardis, was a glittering stronghold of the arts and sciences. When Croesus asked the philosopher Solon what he thought of so much happiness and wealth, Solon quietly answered that no one should ever call himself happy until he has lived out his life to its end. Shortly afterwards, Cyrus conquered the city of Sardis, and the Persians prepared to burn Croesus at the stake. Sitting there on his pyre, very near to death, Croesus suddenly remembered Solon's prophetic words and murmured the philosopher's name. Overhearing him, Cyrus asked for an explanation. When Croesus had told the whole story, Cyrus in his wisdom freed the defeated king who had been Persia's arch-enemy, gave him large tracts of land, a high position at court, and appointed him his personal adviser. Croesus served the shrewd king for thirty years, and his successor Cambyses after him.

Cambyses, the son of Cyrus, corresponds more closely to our picture of a modern dictator. He was in every respect his father's opposite. He murdered his brother Smerdis. He extended his empire to the Egyptian Nile, slaughtering any prisoners he took on the way. He is reported to have thrown the Egyptians' gods into the dust. He opened up their royal graves and took out the mummies — which in those days was still considered a crime — his avowed intention being to cure the Egyptians of their 'superstitions'. However, since he eventually became a megalomaniac or epileptic, the Egyptians had the last laugh, for they were convinced that their gods had punished him for his war-crimes. Towards the end of his life Cambyses must have become something of a Nero. He killed his sister by hitting her in the stomach with his fist, and murdered his wife Roxane. He mortally wounded his son Prexaspes with an arrow. For a little variety, he had twelve of the Persian aristocracy buried alive. He sentenced Croesus, of whom we have already heard, to death. He had scarcely pronounced the sentence when he regretted it and began to weep. However, discovering that the execution had not been carried out, he flew into another rage and punished the officers who had not obeyed his orders. These insane goings-on resulted in a revolution. A religious fanatic arrived on the scene alleging that he was Smerdis, the brother whom Cambyses had in reality murdered long before. Later, a second revolution overthrew this Smerdis and set Darius upon the throne.

Darius I is familiar to us from the pages of Greek history, and was the king who was defeated at Marathon in 490 B.C. Herodotus attributes the failure of Darius's Greek campaign to his having followed a woman's advice. The king, he relates, put his foot out of joint while leaping from his horse during a hunting trip, and sent for an Egyptian doctor to put it to rights. (In those days, Egyptian doctors were still regarded as the best, although this was no longer a fact. At the date of this story, 492 B.C., Greek doctors were patently superior to their Egyptian colleagues.) At all events, the Egyptian doctor tried to wrench the King's foot back into joint by force, causing him so much pain that he could not sleep for seven nights. Now the King had heard of the Greek doctor Democedes of Croton, and he gave orders for him to be speedily summoned. He was brought to Darius chained and dressed in rags. Much knowledge is sometimes dangerous, and Democedes was about as much in demand then as atomic physicists are today. And so, fearing that if Darius realized how competent he was, he would never let him go home again, he denied all knowledge of medicine. Darius had goads and scourges brought, and threatened the dissembling doctor with them. This did the trick. Democedes cured the King's foot, and Darius presented him with two golden chains as a fee. Democedes was something of a Sauerbruch in his day, and Crotonic medicine owed its fame to him. The doctor now remained in attendance on the Persian king, but he yearned for his native land. If Greece had been united with Persia at that time, he could have travelled home but, as things were, there was an 'Iron Curtain' which prevented his return. Now Darius's wife, Atossa, was suffering from a cancer of the breast. At first she concealed the malady, but when it continued to grow she sent for Democedes. He promised to cure her on one condition: that she persuade the King to conquer Greece. Atossa was cured, and so one night in the royal bed-chamber she began to wheedle her lord and master as follows: 'March against Hellas,' she said, 'for I wish to have serving-women from Sparta, Argos, Athens and Corinth. After all, you have a good adviser who knows conditions in Greece — our doctor Democedes.' The King let himself be persuaded, and that was how the campaign against Greece, which ended with the battle of Marathon, came about — or so the Greeks explained the event, anyway!

However, the Darius who was defeated was only the 'European side' of

Darius, so to speak. In western Asia he reconstructed the huge Persian Empire once more.

He put down dangerous rebellions which smouldered and flared up in many of his provinces. He controlled the Persian Empire and the kingdom itself by the rigid bureaucracy of his government departments and officials, and welded the huge administrative apparatus together by the introduction of a diplomatic lingua franca: Aramaic.

In 520 B.C., near Behistun (now pronounced 'Bisitun'), Darius had a whole cliff above the royal highway leading from Babylon to Ecbatana through the Zagros range covered with reliefs and inscriptions. This catalogue of the King's achievements is set so high up that it could never have been legible from the road. But Darius was not thinking of his own time so much as of times to come. What he in fact did was to create a huge memorial which has defied the ravages of time and weather until our own day. Water has been trickling over the edge of the cliff for 2500 years, but its continuous passage has not done much to affect the inscription on the rock-face. It has been called, with justification, the queen of all the inscriptions in the world. Executed in three languages, Persian, Elamitic and Babylonian, it is still quite legible today.

Darius was one of the greatest rulers in world history, an organizer of the first order, and a better practical economist than any king before him. His occasional over-insistence on the collection of tributary payments won him a name for miserliness, but he was not a bad strategist and, where the dangerous wastes of Russia were concerned, a wiser general than Napoleon. He led his armies across the Bosphorus, northwards through Thrace, and as far as the Danube. He crossed the river with a force of between 70,000 and 80,000 men and marched off into the uncharted wilderness, under constant attack by Scythian horsemen. It is uncertain how far north he pushed, but we know that lack of water forced him to retreat without having reached the Dniester. Leaving his sick and stragglers behind, he and his exhausted army re-crossed the Danube. He was never able to inflict a decisive defeat on the Scythians. On the other hand, he marched through Afghanistan to the valley of the Indus, gaining gold for his coffers and many millions of foreign subjects for his empire.

In his native land of Persis he founded a new capital, Persepolis. The ruins of this erstwhile seat, twenty-five miles south-west of Pasargadae as the crow flies and the same distance from the modern town of Shiraz, were excavated between 1931 and 1934 by Ernst Herzfeld, working under the auspices of the Oriental Institute of Chicago University. From 1935 to 1937 Erich F. Schmidt took over the direction of these diggings. Between them, these two distinguished archaeologists uncovered the huge artificial platform or terrace upon which Darius began to build in 518 B.C., and where building continued for over fifty years, until 460 B.C., under Kings Xerxes and Arta-xerxes. In his own foundation inscription, King Darius calls this terrace 'citadel' and 'fortress', but it can also be described as a royal seat, with huge palaces, a 'hall for a hundred thousand', houses for the harem of Darius and later that of Xerxes, accommodation for the harem guard, quarters for officials and for thousands of serving-men and women, buildings for the financial administration and government, cisterns, fortifications and graves. The large network of subterranean tunnels installed there was probably part of a fresh-water system. Herzfeld found 30,000 clay tablets inscribed in Elamitic at the north-east corner of the terrace, which are now being examined and worked on in the Oriental Institute of Chicago University. The tablets contain detailed accounts relating to the immense buildings, wages lists, registers of expenditure on materials and so on.

Soon after his defeat by the Greeks, Darius started preparations for a new campaign against them. As ruler of the largest empire in history and undisputed master of millions upon millions of people of all races, he saw Marathon merely as an accidental mischance. In the autumn of 486 B.C., however, when he was in the midst of preparations for what was to be a decisive campaign against Greece, the mighty conqueror died.

Darius had built himself an eternal resting-place during his lifetime. The burial-chambers of Darius the Great and his successors are situated in the steep rock-face at Naksh-i-Rustam, not far from Persepolis. Each grave consists of three apertures carved into the living rock, the centre aperture which forms the entrance being larger than the other two, so that the tombs look like crosses cut into the side of the cliff. The tri-lingual inscription which King Darius installed in his grave is one of the most interesting ancient texts we possess. Ernst Herzfeld has managed to render it legible. It runs: 'A great god is Ahura-Mazda, who . . . has done this work which . . . is manifest. By the will of Ahura-Mazda I am of this kind: that which is just, I love; injustice I hate. It is not my pleasure that the lowly should suffer injustice at the hands of his superior. . . .'

The king who succeeded Darius is known to us from the Bible. He was Ahasuerus, who reigned at Susa and made Esther his queen. The Ahasuerus of the Old Testament is called Xerxes by Herodotus. Like Cyrus, he was a very handsome man, tall and powerfully built. Handsome men are usually vain and in constant danger of being twisted round some woman's little finger. Xerxes owned a whole harem of ambitious women, and to the end of his days he never knew which he loved or which loved him. Scandalous stories about his excesses were whispered in the streets of Susa, and it is not surprising that the finest building he ever erected in Persepolis was his harem.

Amazing as it may seem, any modern visitor to Persepolis can still see the harem which once belonged to this royal individualist. Using plans drawn up by Ernst Herzfeld, the architect Friedrich Krefter has reconstructed the huge building exactly as it must have been about 2500 years ago. It gives a remarkably modern and functional impression, and its simple, clean lines make it a thing of great beauty. Herzfeld first recognized that he was actually dealing with the ruins of the King's harem when he came across numerous small rooms of similar design, sometimes connected by one long or two smaller chambers. Attached to these were long corridors and rooms designed for the attendants and servants of the ladies of the harem.

King Xerxes was an ostentatious gentleman. He immersed himself in wine-drinking, banqueting and vast building projects. It was his fleet which was vanquished by the Greeks at Salamis. This defeat at sea, coupled with the debacle at Plataea and, above all, the annihilation of a second large Persian army on the Mycale Peninsula — the 'victory of the spear over the bow' — had the effect of forcing the Persians to remain in Asia from then on, and prevented their ever becoming a European power. After twenty years of court intrigues and maladministration, Xerxes was — appropriately enough — murdered in his bed. He was buried with great pomp, mainly because everyone was so glad to be rid of him.

Cyrus and Darius built the Persian Empire. Xerxes inherited it and allowed it to decay in a welter of excess and extravagance. Under his successors we can trace its downfall, for it was with them that the fatal series of murders and assassinations began.

Xerxes' murderers were executed by King Artaxerxes, whose successor, Xerxes II, was murdered by a half-brother. He in turn was murdered by Darius II. Blood flowed in torrents. Darius II put down a rebellion with the maximum ferocity. He had his wife hacked to pieces and his mother, brothers and sisters buried alive. Artaxerxes II killed his son and then died of a broken heart on learning that another son, Ochus, was in turn planning to murder him. Ochus succeeded him and reigned for twenty years, after which time he was poisoned by one of his generals. The vast Persian Empire drowned in a sea of assassinations, murders, cruelty, tears and blood.

Alexander had only to cut down something which was already rotten and internally sick. Nevertheless, it was an immensely exciting moment in human history when, in November of the year 333 B.C., Darius III, the last of the Achaemenides and surnamed Codomannus, opposed Alexander at Issus with an army of perhaps 30,000 to 40,000 men. Alexander only had 20,000 foot-soldiers and 5000 cavalry under his command, but what principally contributed to his victory was his oblique order of battle and the fact that, when he charged, Darius fled from the Persian centre in his battle-chariot, leaving his army leaderless. By the time the battle was over, Alexander had only lost 450 men, while the Persians had lost perhaps ten times that number — certainly not more, for the figures given by the Greeks (a Persian army of 600,000 and losses of 110,000) are grossly exaggerated. The exaggeration is understandable, of course, for it made Alexander's victory seem even more impressive. In his flight, Darius abandoned his royal pavilion, leaving his mother, his wife, two daughters, his imperial carriage and all the golden jewellery, precious stones and riches which went with them.

If we can believe the accounts of Greek historians, the victorious Alexander behaved with all the chivalry of a Prince Charming. He treated Darius's relations with great courtesy, and married his daughter Roxane. Darius's mother grew so attached to her Macedonian grandson-in-law, in fact, that she voluntarily starved to death when he died.

Old Persia had fallen. Her fascinating history lies in ruins before our eyes. Patiently, stone by stone, scholars are digging up the relics of this once glorious world empire. It always means the death-warrant of a people and its kings when the man who conquers them is much greater and more magnanimous than those he conquers. Darius was murdered by his own officers, but Alexander condemned the murderers to death and gave Darius a State funeral at Persepolis. It was such a grand and splendid occasion that the people of western Asia were still talking about it centuries later. The Persians flocked to Alexander in their thousands, dazzled by his manliness, his youth and his magnanimity. His name outshines even those of the most outstanding kings of Persia — Cyrus and Darius.

THE KINGS DIED—THE BUREAUCRACY
SEEMED EVERLASTING

*'What is the fifth most sorrowful thing in the world? Thereupon Ahura-Mazda answered:
It is, O Zarathustra, if the wife or son of an innocent man be borne off as booty along dry
and dusty roads, and the prisoners weep.' Avesta, Chapter 3 of the 'Vendidad'.*

UNDER King Darius I (Darius the Great, 521-485 B.C.), the Persian
Empire comprised twenty 'satrapies' each administered by a *Ksha-trapavan*, or satrap. The world empire had reached the limits of its
expansion. It stretched from Egypt, via Palestine, Phoenicia, Phrygia,
Ionia, Cappadocia, Cilicia and Armenia, as far as Assyria. It extended over
the Caucasus, Babylonia, Media, modern Persia and Afghanistan, Baluchistan, India west of the Indus, Soctria and Bactria. It went as far as the
steppes of central Asia. No one king had ever wielded his sceptre over such
a large area before. People of many races, probably numbering 50 millions
in all, lived within the boundaries of the Achaemenides' world empire, while
the inhabitants of the nucleus of the empire, Persis, numbered no more than
about 500,000. For two hundred years, this handful of Persians were masters
of the world.

The racial group of hardy mountain peoples whom we call Indo-Germans
should really be termed Indo-Europeans. They had long white European
faces and were the forefathers not only of the Germans but of the majority
of European peoples. They came from south Russia across the Caucasus,
having earlier traversed Afghanistan. In 1500 B.C. they roamed into the
valley of the Indus.

Many tongues were spoken in the Persian Empire, but the language spoken
at court in the time of Darius I was Old Persian. This language is related to
Indian Sanskrit, and it was long ago established as a remarkable fact that
many words both in Europe and in the valley of the Indus share a common
derivation.

Who would think that, far away in an ancient river valley bordered by
steaming jungle, the Old Indian equivalent of our word 'brother', for
instance, was *bhratar*? In the Old Persian of the *Zend-Avesta* it becomes *bratar*,
in Greek *phrater*, in Latin *frater*, in Old Irish *brathir*, in Old Slavonic *bratru*,
in Old High German *bruoder*, and in German *Bruder*. The Sanskrit and Old
Persian word *pitar* becomes *pater* in Greek and Latin, *Vater* in German, and
'father' in English. 'Mother' becomes *mater* in Sanskrit and Old Persian, *meter*
in Greek, *mater* in Latin, *match* in Russian, *Mutter* in German. Again, the
word 'stand' is found in Sanskrit as *stah*, *cta* in Old Persian, *istemi* in Greek,
sto in Latin, *stajatch* in Russian, and *stehe* in German.

For purposes of cuneiform writing, the Persians adopted 36 letters out of some 300 Babylonian syllabic symbols. They regarded writing as an unmanly skill, however, hunting and the harem being a good deal more important to them. To 'degrade' themselves so far as to produce literature struck them as disreputable, which was why they did not leave any written records of much importance. All we have inherited from them is the story of their great prophet, which was handed down by word of mouth and in a few written accounts. Long before the birth of Christ there appeared in their ancestral home-land, Airyanem Vaejo, a certain Zarathustra, whom the Greeks called Zoroaster. His disciples took down his prayers and precepts in writing, and this Zoroastrian 'Bible' later became known as the 'Zend-Avesta', which can be roughly translated as 'Interpretation and Text'.

The Roman historian Pliny informs us that the work originally comprised two million verses, and the Persians report that the original text was kept in the great library at Persepolis, written in golden letters on 12,000 cow-hides. When Alexander the Great burned down the palace at Persepolis, this original text is said to have gone up in flames. One book and a few fragments are all that survive.

When did Zarathustra live? Modern research places him about 700 B.C., although the Greeks believed him to have lived 5500 years before their own time.

We do not know much about Zarathustra. His real home may have been in eastern Iran or Bactria. Like Christ, the prophet is supposed to have withdrawn into the wilderness and spent a period of isolation from human society. The Devil tempted him, but without success. He was subjected to ridicule and persecution, prevailed against it, lived to a ripe old age, and finally ascended into heaven in a shaft of light.

Many words and phrases in the Avesta resemble those of the Indian Vedas, while others are reminiscent of ancient Babylonian traditions. Thus we are told that the earth was created in six stages, that everyone is descended from a first man and a first woman, and that there was an earthly paradise. Zarathustra believed, like the prophets of our own Bible, in one supreme god. As a religious founder, he entered a world which was dominated by the ancient folk-gods of the Indo-Europeans. Admittedly, these gods were invisible like his; admittedly, they were probably never represented by the Aryans of Old Iran in human or animal shape; but the idea of a *single*, all-embracing and invisible god had never hitherto been conceived.

Before the coming of Zarathustra, worship of the gods had been controlled by the Magi. Very little information has reached us about these people. They were an extremely imaginative and highly religious Median

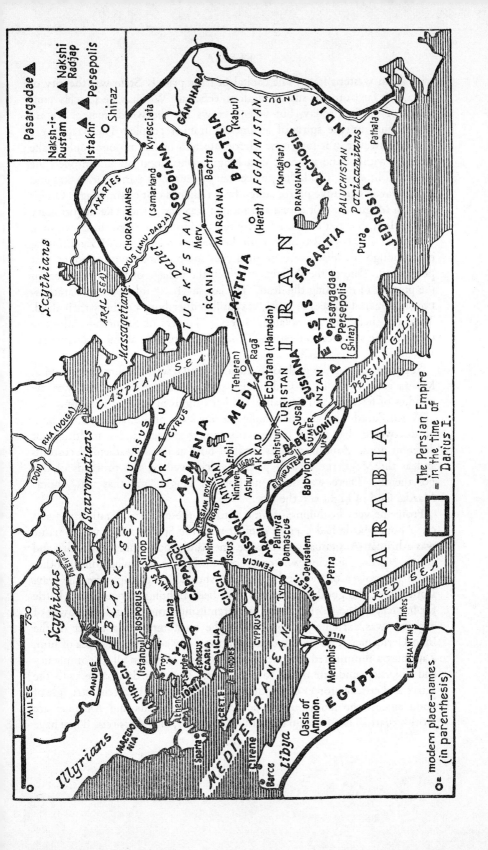

MILES
0   750

Scythians

Illyrians

MACEDONIA

THRACIA

DANUBE

DNIEPER

(VOLGA) RHA

DON

Scythians

Sauromatians

CAUCASUS

BLACK SEA

Sinop

BOSPORUS (Istanbul)

Ankara

CAPPADOCIA

Troy

LYDIA

Sardes

Ephesus

IONIA

CARIA

RHODES

CRETE

Athens

Sparta

Barce

Cyrene

Libya

MEDITERRANEAN SEA

Oasis of Ammon

EGYPT

Memphis

NILE

Thebes

ELEPHANTINE

RED SEA

CYPRUS

Tyre

PALEST.

Jerusalem

Petra

FENICIA

Damascus

Palmyra

ARABIA

CILICIA

Issus

Melitene

PERSIAN ROYAL ROAD

ARMENIA

ASSYRIA (ATHURA)

Niniveh

Erbil

TIGRIS

Ashur

AKKAD

EUPHRATES

Babylon

SUMER

BABYLONIA

URARTU

CYRUS

ARAXES

CASPIAN SEA

MEDIA

Ecbatana (Hamadan)

Behistun

LURISTAN

SUSIANA

Susa

ANZAN

PERSIS

Pasargadae

Persepolis

(Shiraz)

The Persian Empire
= in the time of
Darius I.

Ragā

(Teheran)

PARTHIA

Merv

MARGIANA

IRCANIA

TURKESTAN

Dahet

Massagetians

ARAL SEA

OXUS (AMU-DARJA)

CHORASMIANS

JAXARTES

SOGDIANA

(Samarkand)

Kyresciata

GANDHARA

Bactra

BACTRIA

(Kabul)

AFGHANISTAN

(Herat)

DRANGIANA

(Kandahar)

PARICANIANS

ARACHOSIA

SAGARTIA

I R A N

BALUCHISTAN

Pura

JEDROSIA

INDUS

INDIA

Pathala

PERSIAN GULF

ARABIA

○ = modern place-names
(in parenthesis)

Pasargadae ▲

Naksh-i-Rustam ▲   Nakshi Radjap ▲

Istakhr ▲   Persepolis ▲

○ Shiraz

tribe from western Iran. The capital of their priestly State was the city of Raga, not far from the site of modern Teheran. We may be scarcely conscious of the fact today, but whenever we use the word 'magic' we are summoning up the spirit of an ancient Iranian people. The Magi were priests, however, not sorcerers. Herodotus tells us that no one could make sacrifice without the presence of a Magus, who stood by and intoned the sacrificial liturgy. The killing of certain creatures, in particular snakes and birds, was an exclusive prerogative of the religious cult of the Magi. On his death, a Magus was not encased in molten wax and buried like the ordinary folk of Iran, but put out to be devoured by birds and dogs. In later times, Zarathustra has been associated with the Magi or the Magi with Zarathustra, even though his ideas were originally in sharp conflict with those of that priesthood. One of the differences which the passage of time has effaced is the practice of exposing the dead. The last surviving followers of Zarathustra, 90 thousand Parsees in India, may still neither burn nor bury their dead. They lay them out on isolated towers — 'Towers of Silence' — and leave them for the vultures to devour. Today there are only about 10,000 Zoroastrians left in Persia itself.

Supreme among the gods of Iranian antiquity were Mithra and Anahita. Mithra was originally an Old Iranian god of war, while Anahita was the goddess of fertility, and probably had her origins in Semitic Babylon.

When Zarathustra arrived among the ancestors of the Medes in 700 B.C., he discovered that people were worshipping animals and a multitude of different gods. Zarathustra was enraged both at these 'heathenish' customs and at the Magi, the race of priests which lived off the proceeds of this polytheism. There was only one god, he taught, and that was Ahura-Mazda, God of Light and the Sky.

From the very beginning of time until the present day, Zarathustra went on, Ahura-Mazda had been in conflict with the Spirit of Evil whose name was Ahriman-Angramanyu. On the one hand stood truth, light, fire and Ahura-Mazda, the being who embraced all those things, while on the other stood the power of evil and darkness, Ahriman, ever eager for the fray. Both forces, the good and the evil, had been fighting an everlasting battle for mastery of the world. It was an unremitting struggle, and the power of darkness was extremely resourceful. The most interesting aspect of the Indo-Germanic Devil was his creative power. By adopting this idea of him, Zarathustra illuminated the quest for the origin of evil in all its complexity and diversity, and attempted to explain it. Thus Mazda's battle with the active and creative forces of darkness actually becomes the eternal struggle of good against the unimaginable power of evil. Mazda and Ahriman are worlds apart. They have no ties with one another, only divisions. They have

This man lived at Susa in about 600 B.C. He may have been either a Persian proper, or a member of the race which inhabited Susa before the Persians' arrival. In 400 B.C. the Persians were considered the handsomest people in the known world, and were objects of universal renown and envy

This bull adorned the capital of a pillar in the great hall of Darius' palace. Dating from the 4th century B.C., it is made of grey marble, and was found at Susa. The beast's back supported massive wooden ceiling beams

The tomb of King Darius II in the cliff face at Naksh-i-Rustam, near Persepolis. The 'façade' or portico with its four supporting pillars was a replica of the King's palace. Further along the same cliff to the left are the tombs of Artaxerxes I and Darius I

The 'Egerton Papyrus', written only 70 to 120 years after the Crucifixion. It is based on and is an early confirmation of the four Gospels

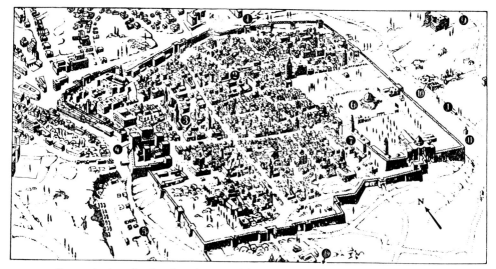

Panoramic view of modern Jerusalem. 1. Jericho Street, 2. Via Dolorosa – Christ's route to the Cross, 3. Church of the Holy Sepulchre, 4. Tower of David, 5. The road to Bethlehem, 6. Dome of the Rock, 7. Wailing Wall, 8. Tomb of David, 9. Mount of Olives, 10. Garden of Gethsemane, where Jesus prayed, 11. Absalom's Tomb. (Jerusalem – Urusalimmu in Assyrian)

The upper window (now walled up) in Damascus, through which St. Paul escaped

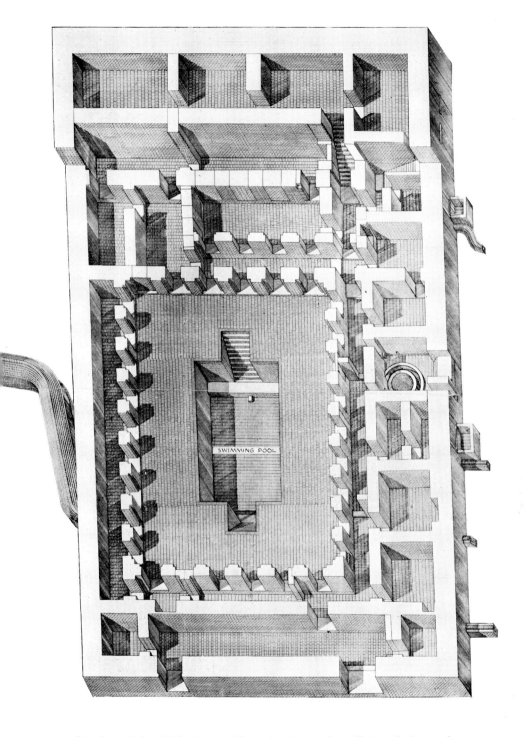

SWIMMING POOL

Reconstruction of the Great Bath at Mohenjo-Daro. The swimming-pool is still virtually intact after 5,000 years. The water was changed by means of an outlet drain (left) and a subterranean conduit

Statue of Buddha from the Gupta period, the golden age of Indian art which began A.D. 320, with the accession of King Chandragupta. The writing on the pedestal belongs to the 5th century. The statue clearly exhibits the influence of Greek art which allied itself to the indigenous art of north-west India

Bronze statuette of a dancing-girl from Mohenjo-Daro

One of the towers of the Bayon, or 'Central Mountain' of Angkor Thom, with quadruple faces of Brahma

The temple of Bayon at Angkor Thom comprises fifty towers like these, each ornamented with four faces of Brahma. [*Photograph:* Meissner

nothing in common 'neither thought nor teaching, aims nor beliefs, word nor deed, our self nor our soul'.

But what did Zarathustra do with the old nature-gods? In his teachings they became the demons or 'daevas' to whose number Mithra and Anahita also probably belonged, the deities which rallied to the cause of the Evil Spirit and, like all false gods, corrupted the minds of men.

Man was a spectator of this spiritual battle between Ahura-Mazda and Ahriman. He was free to choose between the two, but choose he must, and go on choosing, until the time, three days after his death, when he stood before the tribunal of the living and the dead. There the godless, the evil and the liar could anticipate the eternal pangs of hell, and the righteous man, clemency, and the immortality of his soul.

Besides this court of judgment over the individual there were also an end of the world, a resurrection of the dead, and a last judgment. It was at this world court that the battle between light and darkness would ultimately be decided. The good spirit would prevail, mankind would be redeemed, and evil would cease for all time. All good men would enter Paradise with Ahura-Mazda, while the evil would fall into an abyss of eternal darkness. The duty of each, as the Avesta describes it, is threefold: to make his enemy his friend, to convert the evil man to goodness, and to bring the ignorant to knowledge.

This victory of Ahura-Mazda in the teachings of Zarathustra is of paramount importance. For despite its 'dualism', its twin powers of 'good and evil', Zarathustra's religion is really monotheistic, and teaches the existence of a single god. He saw this god as the preserver of the firmament and the earth, lord of all the winds, clouds and water, ruler of the suns and the stars, maker of plants and animals, and creator of the soul. Prayers could be addressed to him anywhere one chose, and the religion had no room either for pictures or houses of the god. Nobody ever built a temple to Ahura-Mazda, and no religious buildings have ever been found in the citadels of Pasargadae or Persepolis, although fire-altars on the surrounding hills may once have saluted the god of Zarathustra with the smoke of their burnt-offerings. We learn from the Greeks how greatly the Persians of Darius's time looked down upon races who represented their gods in human or animal form and confined them in a cramped little abode, quite unbefitting the god of all creation.

The Kings of Persia, the Achaemenides, did not stick to the letter of Zarathustra's teachings and the commandments contained in the *Gathas* — the verses of the Avesta. They recognized and worshipped the gods of subject nations. While this may have been a matter of policy on their part, it is more probable that it was because Zarathustra's religion took 200 years to become firmly established. Darius I was the first king to accept Zarathustra's doctrines and do away with the ancient gods and the priesthood of the Magi — that is to say, more or less so. People certainly went on clinging to their nature-religions and the Magi never died out, even though Darius officially proclaimed the Zoroastrian faith as his State religion. How far the Persian kings before Darius believed in Zarathustra is not certain, for apart from the five words on Cyrus's tomb no inscriptions from their day survive. Darius was the only one to speak of 'the greatest of all gods', and Ahura-Mazda occupies a predominant position in his inscriptions. Darius held Mazda to be the author of the earth, the sky, the Universe, of mankind, and, in particular, of his own personal welfare.

Darius's successors would seem to have drawn away from Zarathustra once more. Artaxerxes addressed his prayers not only to Ahura-Mazda but also to Mithra and Anahita. Berossus, the Babylonian priest of Bel, reports in 250 B.C. that Artaxerxes was the first king to have taught the Persians to worship gods in human form. In his reign the cult of Mithras and of the goddess Anahita received State recognition and, once it had drunk its fill of the Mystery-cults which thrived in Asia Minor, the Mithraic faith eventually conquered the whole world. During Roman times it became the soldiers' religion, and it turned out to be early Christianity's greatest adversary.

And Zarathustra? Where did the doctrines of that valiant old man, so amazingly creative in the religious sphere, find their eventual home?

Zarathustra had not evolved a national religion. His teachings were directed at the world in general, and everyone could receive the same god. Old Persia's political history ended with Alexander's destruction of Persepolis, but her formative spirit, and that of Media, lived on in the religious history of the East and, later, of the West. There is in fact present in the history of religion, as the great Mithraic scholar Franz Cumont has emphasized, not only a 'Hellenism' but also an 'Iranism', a mysterious and scarcely discernible creative force of great antiquity. Ahura-Mazda is perhaps the earliest synthesis of all the forces in the religious history of mankind which regard morality and rectitude as the supreme law. The light of Zarathustra's teaching shines deep into the history of European beliefs. The Jewish conception of Yahweh owed its development to him, as did that of a universal god of heaven, of a dualism between God and Devil, and of redemption and a last judgment. Good and evil wrestle everlastingly for mastery of the world.

Where among the steppes and mountains of eastern Iran did Zarathustra's birthplace lie? Where exactly did he live? Such questions are less important than the fact that, somewhere, sometime, his God appeared to him, and that he saw with uncanny clarity that thousands of years hence humanity would still be carrying the torch of goodness forward into the darkness ahead.

Zarathustra lived and taught about 700 years before the beginning of our chronology, and Mohammed about 700 years after it. Between the two stands the Christ of our own religion.

The apex of governmental organization in the largest pre-Christian empire was the king, and all other rulers were his vassals. That is why he called himself: 'King of Kings, King of the lands of many different peoples, King of this great wide world.'

The king owned many wives. In addition, he had a very large harem of concubines, 'as many as there are days in the year', the Greeks inform us. None of them ever visited the king's bed twice 'except the King delighted in her', as we are told in the second chapter of the Book of Esther (v. 12 *et seq.*). 'In the evening she went, and on the morrow she returned into the second house of the women, to the custody of Shaashgaz, the King's chamberlain, which kept the concubines.' Each woman had first to undergo a twelve-month course of purification with oil of myrrh, balsams and other beauty preparations.

Herodotus reports that every Persian aristocrat had numerous regular wives, 'but he took many mistresses into his harem in addition'. There were a large number of foreign women among the King's wives, and Cyrus and Cambyses both had Median and Egyptian princesses. Darius I took over Cyrus's harem and married two of his daughters, Atossa and Artystone. Atossa, who had previously been married to her brother Cambyses, was the mother of Darius's successor, Xerxes. Artaxerxes II even took two of his own daughters into his harem.

The harem was guarded by eunuchs. As part of her annual tribute, Babylonia castrated five hundred boys each year and sent them to the Persian king's court as pages, for instruction in this profession. By reason of their influence on women who were close to the king, the eunuchs became the biggest intriguers and gossip-mongers in every Persian court. Their influence grew so great that they overthrew kings, plotted palace revolutions, organized assassinations, and generally used the petty jealousies of the womenfolk to their own advantage. In the latter years of the Persian Empire, succession to the throne was principally determined by murder and revolution. The Persian kings based their power on huge armies in which a babel of different tongues prevailed. They put their faith solely in numerical strength, and it is not surprising that they were often defeated. According to Herodotus, Xerxes' expeditionary force against Greece numbered 170,000 men. Even if this figure is a gross exaggeration (a tenth of it, or 17,000 men, would have been a mighty army in those days), we can still visualize what a spectacle this wild, desperate horde, with its motley assortment of races, must have made after its defeat, as its endless columns wound their way back into

Asia Minor. In view of the mixed composition of the army, the retreat itself was a great achievement in the Persian art of war.

The king was supreme judge, and his word was law. His monarchy was absolute. Justice was administered by royal judges holding commissions from the king and appointed for life. They could only be dismissed for crime or corruption, and frequently bequeathed their office to their sons. The courts of Persia not only meted out penalties, but also distributed rewards. King Cambyses stamped out corruption among his judges by having one of them beaten to death, upholstering the judgment seat with the dead man's skin, and setting his son upon it as judge in his father's place. Small misdemeanours were punished by from 5 to 200 strokes of the horse-whip. Serious crimes were expiated by crippling, blinding, imprisonment or death. It was no laughing matter if anyone went too near one of the ladies in the king's harem, and a man who fancied the idea of sitting on the king's throne gambled his life away. Crucifixions, hangings, stonings, live burials, hot ashes and even worse cruelties were the punishments which held the Persian Empire together.

Nevertheless, the empire was not merely a political organization devoted to injustice and cruelty. Herodotus asserts that no one, whether free or slave, was ever sentenced to death except on adequate grounds. A good king like Darius I never allowed himself to be swayed by caprice. He respected Ahura-Mazda's commandments and endeavoured not to infringe the rights of his subjects.

The twenty satraps who governed the various provinces were members either of the nobility or of the royal family. A satrap administered the provincial government, represented the interests of king and State, and looked after public order and safety. He was also the supreme judge of his province.

Power is like a salt which creates the thirst for absolute authority, and every viceroy of a distant province became by sheer virtue of his geographical location a latent or potential rebel. Accordingly, safety-measures were devised. Each satrap was allotted a royal secretary whose permanent responsibility was to ensure that liaison with the royal residence was maintained intact. He controlled the receipt and dispatch of royal correspondence. Dispatch-riders galloped along the royal post-roads from one end of the empire to the other, from Ephesus and Sardis to the capital, Susa, more than 1250 miles away, from Babylon through the Zagros range and past the cliffs at Behistun to Ecbatana and the Bactrian and Indian frontiers, a total distance of over 1800 miles. The roads were measured in *parasangs*, and royal post-horse stations and hostels were erected at regular intervals along them. Royal commands and government dispatches carried by relays of riders raced along night and day towards their destinations 'swifter than the cranes', as the Greeks described it. It is even said that there was a system of telegraphy by fire-signals.

Each satrapy possessed a garrison and a fortress commander. This general kept an eye on the satrap, and the satrap in turn kept an eye on the general. Finally, there was the 'King's Eye', a very high official — usually a brother or son of the king — whose job it was to travel from one satrapy to another with an armed body of men, turning up unannounced to inspect the administration. 'His Majesty's Eye and Ear' always appeared suddenly and unexpectedly. He checked governmental expenditure and other transactions. Thus satraps, garrison commanders and royal secretaries alike constantly had to be careful and circumspect. Cleverly designed controls like these were remarkably successful in securing the king's god-given sovereignty over his vast empire. However, they only functioned as long as the supreme ruler was a statesman, and not the mere puppet of his harem.

In spite of enormous taxes, in spite of the sovereign's extravagances, and in spite of revolts and wars, the Babylonians, Phoenicians, Palestinians and other subject peoples lived quite contentedly under Persian domination. They always felt that their own generals and tax-officials would rob them even more effectively than the Persians. Under Darius I, the Persian Empire became a brilliantly efficient political organization such as the world was not to see again until the times of the great Roman Emperors Trajan, Hadrian and Antoninus.

There was also bureaucracy among the satraps, however. The kings died, but the bureaucracy seemed everlasting. The satraps built themselves extravagant palaces, maintained large harems, and ran magnificent hunting-preserves — parks which the Persians used to call 'paradises'. The cost of maintaining the satrap's court and the administration in general was borne by the subject population, which also had to render taxes to the king. Each satrapy sent him its tribute in the form of gold or silver talents. A Persian-Euboean gold talent contained about 55½ lb. of pure gold, and a Babylonian silver talent 74 lb. of silver. The combined satrapy of Babylonia and Assyria paid the largest tribute. It poured no less than 1000 silver talents every year into the treasure-chests of the Persian king. Then followed Egypt with 700 talents, the coastal satrapies of Asia Minor, Lydia and Mysia, with 500 talents, and Caria with 400. The Cilicians, who paid 500 talents, also had to set aside 140 talents a year for the cavalry garrison which was stationed in their province, and supplied the court with 360 snow-white horses of the finest breed. Since Persis, the heart of the empire, paid no tribute but probably only sent the king presents, the total number of satrapies which poured their tributes into the royal exchequer was nineteen. Between them, these nineteen satrapies paid a grand total of 7600 Babylonian silver talents, or, reckoning £255 to the talent, £1,938,000 – not such a very large sum, as one can see. However, even after deducting the 8000 talents which Darius III took with him in his flight after being defeated by Alexander the Great, the latter still obtained no less than 180,000 talents in minted and unminted gold and silver from the coffers of Susa, Persepolis and Pasargadae – a sum roughly corresponding to £97,000,000 in modern money.

Apart from these monetary tributes, each province paid the king taxes in kind. Cappadocia supplied a yearly total of 1500 horses, 2000 cattle and 50,000 sheep, and Media paid nearly twice that. The Arabs were not obliged to pay any tribute. Instead, they sent 'the King of the World' 1000 talents' worth of incense. Interminable caravans of camels burdened with the Gerrhaeans' and Minaeans' precious commodity – they were the merchant-folk of Arabia – swayed over the famous incense-roads towards the Persian metropolis. 'But the land of Arabia also smells heavenly', says Herodotus. Purchased slaves straggled back over the same endless route, too. We have a Minaean inventory listing slave-girls who were obliged to dedicate their lives to the gods. We read in it that one each came from Ammon and Moab, 3 from Qedar, 6 from Dedan, 7 from Egypt and 24 from Gaza. Ethiopia sent the Persian king 200 trunks of ebony, 20 large elephant-teeth and five negro boys.

Set in this extravagant, sanguinary, often cruel, but in the main tolerable political framework, people of many different races lived more or less happily, more or less free, just as we do. They were good-natured and extremely hospitable folk, as the Persians of today still are. They loved, they hated, they laughed and they wept.

Persons of equal rank exchanged greetings by kissing each other on the lips. Inferiors kissed their superiors on the cheek, and citizenry bowed low before officialdom – a failing of which man has never been able to cure himself since the days when Persia ruled the world. Spitting, blowing one's nose and eating in the street were forbidden. The pollution of rivers was also strictly prohibited – a very hygienic rule which seems to be unknown today – and infectious diseases were subject to quarantine. Until the zenith of Persian world sovereignty, that is to say until the time of Darius I, the Persian lived a healthy life, partook of only one meal a day, and adhered strictly to his nature-religion or to Zarathustra's commandments, which designated lying as the most disgraceful sin of all. Horsemanship, archery and telling the truth were the usages which the young males of Persia were brought up in, from their fifth to their twentieth year. Gradually, however, the Persian Empire fell a prey to the heterogeneity of its own racial composition. The Persians culled every kind of luxury from their empire, being much given — as Herodotus tells us — to the adoption of foreign customs in general. As time went on, the aristocracy began to ply themselves with ever increasing quantities of food. They drank liberally and with gusto, and frequently transacted important affairs in a state of intoxication. Sober once more, they reviewed the decisions they had made. Then, if they could not agree on them, they discussed the whole matter again — under the reconciliatory influence of wine.

Herodotus reports that the Persians regarded the abduction of a woman as an evil action, but that they considered any man who tried to avenge it a fool. It was obvious, they thought, that no woman could be abducted against her will. In view of the king's need for soldiers, polygamy was allowed. Children were married off by their parents, and marriages between brother and sister, father and daughter, and mother and son were possible. Women could walk about unveiled and without hindrance. They administered household affairs, and could conduct business transactions in their husband's name. Only the wives of the nobility were not permitted to be seen in public with men, or even to set eyes on their closest male relatives.

Sons were more in demand than daughters. A man who had a goodly number of sons was rewarded by the king. Nobody prays for a daughter, the Persians used to say, and daughters are not numbered by the angels among the blessings of mankind. Medicine was a combination of magic and medical skill. In cases where a surgeon, a herbalist and a priest were all available, it was considered best to fetch the latter — the doctor 'who heals with the sacred word'. Psychiatry was regarded as preferable to a surgical operation, for while there was no danger involved in healing the soul, the scalpel could prove fatal!

The Persians had beautiful houses and fine gardens, costly furniture, magnificent bed-chambers, vessels of gold. They bought most of their beautiful things from foreign craftsmen, since they themselves had enough to do with the administration of government, wars and their agricultural estates. Only in the field of architecture did the Persians achieve anything of their own. The palace of Xerxes I at Susa must really have been a building of amazing grandeur, as we can conclude from excavations and Old Testament descriptions in the Book of Esther. Diggings at Persepolis continue to reveal the grand scale on which the Persians' royal palaces were built. The size of the pontoon bridges which the Persian kings threw across rivers and straits during their military campaigns still have the power to amaze us today. Wind and wave soon destroyed them, of course, but Herodotus' description of the feats of engineering accomplished by slaves and soldiers about 2500 years ago still borders on the fabulous.

Greek travellers returned from their visits to the Persian Empire filled with admiration and told stories of halls, palaces, and the wonders of contemporary Persian luxury. But while the Persians' extravagance and the splendour of their clothes and jewellery all increased from decade to decade, and while their civilization grew brighter, richer and more magnificent, their kings became more and more feeble and crazed. This remarkable and glorious empire finally choked in its own luxury and the good things of life — an empire which had already come to believe in *one* god, but did not survive long enough to witness the coming of Christ.

PALESTINE

✗

O ABSALOM, MY SON!

'And the king . . . went up to the chamber over the gate, and wept: and as he went, thus
he said, . . . would God I had died for thee. . . .' 2 Samuel xviii, 33.

LITTLE Palestine has had a greater influence on the life of humanity, on
its thought, its morality and its beliefs than Babylonia, Assyria, Persia,
Egypt, India or China. The cultural heritage which Palestine left
behind her has accomplished more in its effects than the whole culture of
Greece. This smallest of countries has bequeathed to the world a religion
pervaded by an unprecedented dynamism: Christianity. The Bible, that
'Book of Books', has outlived the Egyptians' Book of the Dead, the Indians'
Mahabharata, the teachings of Confucius and of the Chinese, and the gods of
the Aztecs. Irresistible and uninterrupted, the history of Yahweh and his
chosen people lives on from generation to generation.

No other work has so often been burnt as the Bible, no other work so
much translated, none so often impugned, none so revered. It is the most-
printed book in the world, and the literature which has grown up around it
is like a vast ocean of whose waters a man can only drink a mere thimbleful
in his lifetime.

The Jews are a Semitic race — like the Babylonians, Phoenicians and
Arabs — which was already resident in Palestine in very early times. During
their nomadic period they were called *Khabiri*.

The name 'Jew' is derived from 'Judah', and the Jews were originally
descendants of Judah, the fourth son of Jacob and Leah. Although the designation 'Jew' only appears from 516 B.C. onwards, the history of the Jews is
several thousand years older than that.

Abraham, the tribal founder of the Jews, is described in the Bible as 'the
Hebrew' (Genesis xiv, 13). He lived about 1700 B.C., and came from Ur in
Mesopotamia. He built altars to the living god, altars whose novelty lay in
the fact that they incorporated no statues. Abraham had recognized the
spirituality of God. He was undoubtedly an historical figure, and indeed
modern archaeology is constantly bringing to light new proofs of the authenticity of the Old Testament in general. It seems that Abraham's name in the
Chaldean tongue of his native country was 'Orham', and that he was a
prince of Ur. He is credited with having replaced human sacrifice with the
sacrifice of rams.

It was almost 4000 years ago when Abraham arrived in Canaan. After long years of spiritual development beset by every kind of misconception, he had come to believe in holding fast to God's promises, nor did he abandon this faith when he was put to the test. The story of Isaac appears to have been a protest against the Canaanite custom of human sacrifice. God tested Abraham, saying: 'Take now thy son, thine only son Isaac, whom thou lovest, and . . . offer him . . . for a burnt offering.' Abraham bound his son, laid him on the altar, and was just taking up his knife to kill him, when an angel appeared and absolved him from the sacrifice.

Later, Abraham made his 'eldest servant' swear that he would not choose his son a Canaanite wife. The servant took ten camels and set off for Abraham's country of birth, Mesopotamia, where he travelled from place to place until he found the girl Rebecca, a daughter of the city of Hatran. Isaac married Rebecca and, when his father died, he and his brother Ishmael buried him in fraternal concord. He reaped a hundredfold, for the Lord blessed him, and his love of peace overcame his enemies. He dug two springs, handed them over to quarrelling herdsmen, and then dug a third for himself. Isaac's successor was Jacob, whose surname was Israel. He had twelve sons, each of whom became a founder of one of the twelve tribes of Israel.

From 1500 B.C. onwards, Palestine came under Egyptian domination. The Amarna tablets throw some light on the conditions prevailing in Palestine somewhere between 1400 and 1350 B.C. They are 350 letters from Near Eastern princes to the Egyptian kings Amenophis III and IV, and were found at El Amarna, Egypt, in 1887. After their period of slavery under the Egyptian yoke, the children of Israel were welded into a nation by Moses, who led them on a long and arduous march through the desert to Canaan. This migration did not all take place at once, but lasted for forty years. The Israelites made numerous halts on the way and led a nomadic existence. Their train on this divinely inspired march included women and children, great herds of cattle and donkeys burdened with goods and chattels. They married, begot children, and discovered their God, only to fall from grace on certain occasions by dancing round their 'golden calf'. In the course of these forty years, Israel accepted the Twelve Commandments of Sinai and became 'a kingdom of priests and an holy nation', and Moses received the tables of the Covenant. Moses, who saw Yahweh as a god of the thunderstorm and the burning bush, was one of the greatest geniuses of all time. General and preacher, organizer and historian, he often seems gloomy and inclined to irascibility. In common with Tolstoy, he saw all civilization as disloyalty to Yahweh.

Moses is not a Jewish but an Egyptian name. Professor Garstang of Liverpool University believed that he had discovered evidence in the royal graves at Jericho which indicated that Moses was rescued as a small child in 1487 B.C. by the Egyptian princess who later became Queen Hatshepsut, and that he was brought up by her at court, later to escape from Egypt.

Until Christ's coming, the religious literature of the Jews had been assembled in thirty-nine books written in the Hebrew and Aramaic languages. This literature — the Old Testament — is divided into three large sections: the Torah (the Law), the Nebiim (the Prophets) and the Ketubim (the Holy Writings). The Torah consists of five books. Moses is credited with the authorship of these 'five rolls', which were later called by the Greek name 'Pentateuch'. All five books enjoyed the status of law among the Jews.

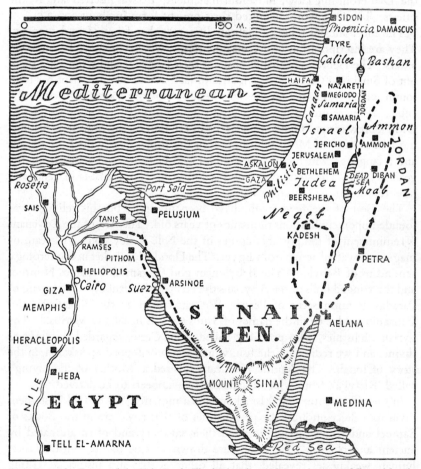

Sinai Peninsula, Egypt and the Holy Land. The broken line indicates the route followed by the Israelites in their migration under Moses from Egypt to the Dead Sea, where Moses died

When, where and by whom were they written down? Actually, these are pretty intimidating questions, for a literature of about 50,000 volumes has been written in an attempt to answer them. To reduce these 50,000 volumes to a common denominator: science classifies the oldest elements in the Bible, that is to say, the various versions of the story of the Creation which bear a resemblance to one another, under the initials 'J' and 'E', one part calling the Creator Jehovah (Jahve), and the other calling him Elohim. The 'Jehovistic' accounts are supposed to have been written in Judah, and the 'Elohistic' in Ephraim. In 719 B.C., after the fall of Samaria, the two collections were amalgamated. A third group, known to science as 'D', contained the 'Deuteronomic Law', and a fourth element, 'P', was inserted later by the priests. The four works acquired their present form in about 300 B.C.

The most ancient relics of Hebrew literature date from around 1200 B.C. They are inscriptions in Old Canaanite script, which contained twenty-two letters. The Hebrews probably brought their language and script with them out of Sinai into Canaan. As a matter of fact, an old Semitic script has been found which was in use on the Sinai Peninsula before 1600 B.C. Besides the Bible, there are only a few inscriptions which provide us with examples of Old Hebrew script. One of these is the inscription on the Mesa stele belonging to the King of Moab who figures in the Bible. It is written in a script and a language which closely resembles Old Hebrew, and dates from the year 855 B.C. The stone was found at Diban in Transjordania in 1868, and now reposes in the Louvre at Paris.

The God of the Jews might have been invisible, but his religion was founded upon civilizations thousands of years old. The Ark of the Covenant is reminiscent of the portable houses of the Nile Valley gods. A breath of magic was wafted across from Egypt. The Flood and a belief in numerology remind us of Babylon. The Babylonian god Gilgamesh becomes Nimrod, and the winged bulls of the Assyrians the Hebrews' cherubim. The legend of Paradise is reminiscent of Persia. We can recognize the Phoenician and Canaanite god Baal in the names of Saul's sons, Eshbaal and Meribaal. The Syrian Philistines, who probably hailed from Crete, regarded the dove as divine, and we rediscover the fish, which was worshipped at Askalon, in the story of Jonah. The Semitic Arameans revered a 'Mother of the Living', called 'Khavva', from which the name 'Eve' appears to be derived.

In the tenth century B.C., Israel became a monarchy. The Old Testament gives us a description of the personalities of that royal era in the Books of Samuel and Kings. Magnificent in their savagery and often animated by ancient and childish beliefs, they are drawn so true to life, with all their human weaknesses revealed, that all other poetry and historical writing pales beside these descriptions of them. And the authenticity of the Old

Testament cannot be doubted, for history has hardly ever been painted with such vividness as in these 'Sacred Books'.

Saul was a handsome and chivalrous man. In 1025 B.C. he was called by Samuel to become king of Israel. He was calm and magnanimous, of a religious disposition, and at once valiant and victorious in battle. He was always obedient to his God, but the older he grew the more impatient, irresolute, restless and quick-tempered he seems to have become, until at the end of his life he was as spiteful as a raging demon. When he found that God was not answering him any more, he started going to soothsayers and eventually died by his own hand.

Saul was succeeded not by his son Jonathan, but by David, who was the greatest king of Israel. David's achievements included the unification of his people, victory over neighbouring countries, the founding of Jerusalem, and the linking of throne and altar. He appears as a titanic character, possessed of many good sides and yet a prey to all the usual human weaknesses. He defeated Goliath. He loved his son Absalom tenderly, but he also loved numerous women. He used to dance wild dances in the nude, play the harp, and sing magnificent songs. He ruled with great competence for forty years, yet it was he who abducted Bathsheba into his large harem and then sent her husband Uriah into battle to get rid of him; who had the beautiful woman brought to him after seeing her at her bath one hot summer evening from the terrace of his palace; who forgave his ungrateful son Absalom for having plotted a conspiracy against him, and later wept when he heard that he had been killed, crying: 'O, my son Absalom, my son, my son!' In old age his bones grew chilly, so they brought Abishag the Shunammite girl and laid her beside him to warm him. When David felt that he was near death, he called his son Solomon to him and said: 'I go the way of all the earth: be thou strong therefore, and show thyself a man.' He further recommended him to take vengeance on some of his old enemies, and to spare certain others. David reigned from 1012 to 972 B.C. He was an historical figure, and one who, while still a barbarian at heart, already exemplified the typical Eastern autocrat. In addition, he was one of the greatest poets and singers the world has ever known. Contemporary study has confirmed the age-old supposition that this royal singer was the author of most of the Psalms.

Solomon, who succeeded him, must really have been one of the wisest kings in the history of mankind. Who but a wise man could have combined a life of such fantastic opulence and exquisite luxury with such a punctilious fulfilment of all the duties of a king? The name Solomon comes from *shalom*, meaning peace, and King Solomon lived up to it not only by accustoming his people to law and order, but also by assuring them of peace. Under his shrewd administration, Jerusalem became one of the wealthiest cities in the

Near East. Phoenician merchants brought their caravans through Palestine to Jerusalem, and Israel's produce was exported to Tyre and Sidon in exchange. King Solomon's fleet sailed the Red Sea, and he maintained trade with Africa and Arabia, where he established gold-mines. The powerful Queen of Sheba courted his friendship. He recruited armies of forced labourers, brought the Ark of the Covenant into the Temple, spoke the prayer of consecration and blessed the congregation. For all that, he loved life as scarcely any other man before him. He collected wives, and his passion for this hobby seems but little diminished by the results of exact research into the subject, which bid us reduce the traditional estimates crediting him with 700 wives and 300 concubines, to 60 and 8 respectively.

From 1925 onwards the Oriental Institute of Chicago University carried out extensive excavations at Megiddo. The first layer disclosed ruins of Babylonian and Persian times, and the second contained ruins of Assyrian palaces. Layers 3 and 4 were Israelite, and the latter stratum revealed traces of building by Solomon, who had constituted this city the capital of the fifth administrative region of Israel. Royal stables came to light, as well as the palace built for Baana, who was once governor of Megiddo, as we learn in the Bible (1 Kings iv, 7 and 12). The diggings were further extended between 1935 and 1938, and it was confirmed that Megiddo had originally been founded in about 3500 B.C. Three temples and an altar for burnt sacrifices were discovered, all dating from about 1700 B.C. — the time of the Patriarchs, Abraham and his successors. The altar was the first to be found in Palestine in a fairly intact condition.

After Solomon's death in 932 B.C., a revolution broke out. Ten of the twelve tribes of Israel severed themselves from Solomon's son Rehoboam and established the Kingdom of Israel. Rehoboam stayed behind in Judaea with the remaining two tribes, while Jeroboam became King of Israel and ruled over the renegade ten.

From this time onwards there was a Kingdom of Judaea and a Kingdom of Israel. However, the larger of the two, Israel, only survived for two hundred years and came to an end in 721 B.C. with the conquest of Samaria by the Assyrian king Sargon II; 27,000 members of the Ten Tribes were deported to Inner Asia, and have since then vanished from the historical scene. We have never heard what became of them, and their fate remains one of history's unsolved riddles. Indeed, it has become a favourite pastime of historians to 'rediscover' the Ten Tribes. The finding of stones bearing Jewish hieroglyphics in China has led some scientists to believe that that is where they finally settled, while others suppose the Anglo-Saxons to be the latter-day descendants of these 'deportees', and the 'Anglo-Israelite' theory possesses its own extensive literature.

Men have thought that they have discovered the final destination of the ten lost tribes almost everywhere in the world: in Mexico where Cortez was awaited as the 'White Saviour'; in Africa; and even in North America among the 'white Indians'. The 'Book of Mormon' is an outcome of the latter theory.

The modern Jews are the descendants of the smaller kingdom of Judaea. They were borne off to Babylon by King Nebuchadnezzar in 586 B.C., for the duration of what is known as the 'Babylonian Captivity'. In 538 B.C. Cyrus of Persia allowed them to return to Palestine and rebuild the Temple, a task which they finally completed in 516 B.C. Jews from all over Judaea poured into Jerusalem to pray to Yahweh and see the building which they regarded as one of the wonders of the world.

The central theme of Judaistic theology was that of sin. The flesh was weak, and the laws all-embracing: therefore, sin was unavoidable. Whenever there was a prolonged drought, or plagues raged, or cities were destroyed, the Jews always saw sin as the cause. They did not believe in Hell, but in a subterranean kingdom of darkness, Sheol, which good and bad alike had to enter. Only the elect, like Moses, Enoch and Elijah, were exceptions to this rule.

The Jews did not at first believe in the immortality of the soul, or that punishments and rewards existed elsewhere than on earth. It was only after they had lost all faith in the ultimate triumph of their history — forced to that conclusion by their external contact with Persia and possibly with Egypt — that there awoke in them a belief in the resurrection. Devastation and hopelessness, endless suffering and the fate of millions of people who sought consolation — these were the factors which paved the way for Christianity.

And there is fundamental truth in the theory that nothing great, enduring or eternal, has ever sprung from prosperity and happiness. Heaven reveals itself only to the seeker, to the man who calls on it out of the depths of suffering.

THEY FOUGHT AGAINST POLYTHEISM
Sixteen Prophets

I F someone of our own day were asked what a prophet is, he would probably reply: 'That's easy. A prophet is a man who foretells the future.'

However, the prophets of the Old Testament were not solely concerned with the future. It was not merely that they claimed to be enabled by divine enlightenment to know the future, or that they predicted the coming of the Messiah. Their character and significance was quite different.

Prophetes is a Greek word. The concept of prophecy could not be expressed in the Hebrew tongue by one simple word. *Nabi* is the Hebrew term for a prophet, and *Nebiim* was what the Hebrews called the prophetic books of the Bible. But the word *nabi* was not indigenous to Israel, and it will be worth while to pursue its origins farther, since they may throw light on its fundamental meaning. We find the word *nabaa* both in the Assyrian-Babylonian languages and in Arabic. In Assyrian it means 'talk', 'speak', 'proclaim' or 'designate'. There was a Babylonian god called 'Nabu', and we find the word again in the names of kings such as 'Nabo-polassar' and 'Nebuchadnezzar'.

Arabic is perhaps the most rewarding source to draw upon in any scientific investigation of the Semitic languages, since it is even closer to Old Semitic than Sanskrit is to Old Indo-Germanic. In Arabic, *naba'a* means 'announce', and it is here that we arrive at the idea that the speaker is not saying something of his own but, rather, passing on someone else's instructions. The *nabi* is therefore a spokesman, a man who has a message to deliver or a certain communication to make. With that, we have reached the heart of the matter. The prophets were not conscious of speaking on their own authority, but rather as the instruments of a superior. They felt that they were 'the mouth of God'.

It may be added that even the Greek word *prophetes* is not to be identified with prediction: the force of *pro* is not so much 'fore' as 'forth'.

The prophets' basic conviction and their one certainty were that their thoughts issued from Yahweh. 'Thus saith the Lord' is a frequent preface to their discourses.

If their name comes from Arabia, then perhaps Arabia was also the original home of these early seers, with their powers of 'ecstatic divination'. There is undoubtedly a hint of the desert in their character. Elijah, the first prophet of whom the Old Testament tells us, came from east Jordan, a region where

Jews and Arabs were racially quite intermingled, and Samuel still went under the name of 'seer'. Like everything else in the evolution of mankind, prophecy also has its history. At first the prophets were 'seers'; then they became the verbal transmitters of religious thought and mood; and finally, they started to put down their prophetic utterances in writing.

When we speak of the prophets of the Old Testament today, we are thinking principally of the 'literary prophets', the first of whom was Amos. They number sixteen in all — men whose names we learnt at school and have since forgotten. The body of written prophecy extends from Amos, who lived about 750 B.C., to the unknown author who wrote Zechariah, Chapters ix-xiv in 275 B.C. In the course of time, the prophets' characteristic quality of wildness waned and vanished.

We can best recognize the difference between the prophets' realm of ideas and the other Oriental conceptions of divinity by reading the Koran. Mohammed (A.D. 569-632) was at such pains to emphasize the omnipotence of God that he often paints him as a self-willed despot. In fact, if God were really as incalculable and capricious as Mohammed suggests, it is difficult to know how the Universe could go on fulfilling its functions of time and motion. To the prophets, God's omnipotence never conflicts with Nature. His authority may be absolute, but one can build and rely on it as surely as one can rely on the stars above. The outcome of this conception of Yahweh was that the prophets could often proclaim in advance what sort of destiny He was going to mete out. Science can never have power to refute such a god.

The prophets saw God as Lord of Nature. They had an unconscious realization of this in the 8th century B.C., and perhaps even earlier. This feeling found expression in the story of the Creation, for Yahweh was also the lord of world history. Anyone who tries to search for first causes and to identify the unfathomable forces which activate humanity will come very close to the laws of Nature and the Universe, and ultimately to the creator of them.

Nevertheless, there were certain things which did not lie within the scope of Yahweh's design. If any individual or nation acted at variance with Nature and so against the Law of God, he brought something evil into the world, something reproductive and deadly. Somewhere, sometime, it would and must have a sequel, and this sequel was retribution.

And that is where the prophets' true greatness lies: they were not mere dreamers or clairvoyants, they did not foretell the future as such, and above all, they laid no claim to magical powers — yet at a time when the world was still governed by sorcery, black magic and evil spirits, they found a new heaven and a new earth, unshakeable ideals for mankind, and the way to a

new god. Taking a lone stand against the convictions of the whole contemporary world, they evolved ideals for countless future generations, ideals
which still govern our whole life today. Jonah and the whale and Daniel
and the lion's den are ancient fables, underlaid by a deeper meaning, it is
true, but which have nothing whatsoever to do with prophecy. Israel's
prophets despised charlatans and magicians. Spiritually, they stood head and
shoulders above their country's numerous neighbours. Spiritually, they
remained unshaken either by natural catastrophes or foreign subjection.
Spiritually, they enjoyed a superiority over the rest of the world which has
lasted for thousands of years beyond their time. The rest of their contemporaries were terrorized by ghosts, golden bulls, cannibalistic Molochs,
Baals hungry for sacrifices, and magicians.

The great religious teachers whom we call the prophets never asserted that
they could perform miracles. Elijah and Elisha led lives full of miracles, of
course, but they departed without leaving posterity a single written word,
even though Elijah lived only fifty years before Amos. With the coming of
Amos, the first literary prophet, all these miracles ceased.

The prophets were the storm-birds of world history. They saw God's
hand in the destiny of mankind. They were the embodiment of the nation's
conscience, saw ephemeral things through the eyes of eternity, and perceived
the universal direction of God. If we wanted to put it 'scientifically', we
might say that they led mankind for the first time to the frontiers of that vast
realm which is not susceptible of measurement by any criterion, whether
physical or chemical, nor visible even with the finest telescopes which modern
astronomy has at its disposal. This immeasurable and eternal realm is not
witchcraft nor idols of stone and gold, but God himself.

This, then, was what they recognized. And if it seems self-evident to us
now, we should reflect that in those days human knowledge was not bounded
by the concepts of infinite time and space. It was an age when sorcery reigned
supreme, making life a hell and infinity the playground of demons.

The prophets were a remarkable band of men. Ezekiel suffered from
periodic spells of dumbness. It was as though his tongue cleaved to his palate
until his mouth suddenly chose to open again. For a while he was also lame.
Isaiah went around naked for three years. It can well be imagined why
children followed him about and people wagged their heads at him.
Jeremiah used periodically to go around with a yoke on his neck, like an ox.
Hosea named his daughter 'Unpitied', and took back his wife, who was
notorious for her unchastity.

It was a characteristic of the prophets that they did peculiar things like
these. Was it that they wished to attract attention? Were they prompted by
'ecstacy'? Who will venture to judge the actions of a genius or sit in judg-

ment on men like these, who described the thoughts of God and overflowed with passion and burning exaltation, men whose spirit transported them to spheres beyond the range of thought?

All sixteen of the prophets are historical personalities. Factual detail like that which is given in the Books of the Prophets could never be mere invention, and the comparative study of texts is bringing to light more and more evidence of the authenticity of these men.

Amos was a shepherd and grower of mulberry-trees from Tekoa. He kept a sharp eye on the ungodly luxury of the mighty and the oppression of the poor. It was probably some violent thunderstorm or earthquake which first induced him to put his discourses into written form, and his verses are constantly tinged by recollection of the occurrence (Amos iii, 8). His style is extremely artistic and utterly original, and he was a past master in the art of graphic description.

Hosea had a tragic life. He loved his wife as dearly as any man could, but she left him for a series of lovers and was finally sold into slavery. He took her back again, and by so doing demonstrated the meaning of really great and divine love, clothing it in the written word for the first time in human history.

Isaiah lived in Jerusalem, was married and had two sons. Teaching between 740 and 700 B.C., he stands like a giant among the historical prophets, and is the classical genius of Judaism. In him, speech and thought alike found their highest consummation. He was a great statesman, mingled freely with kings and politicians, and was perhaps the most brilliant theological teacher in Israel before Christ. Of all the prophets, it was probably he who wielded the greatest influence.

Micah (750-685 B.C.) lived on the great international highway between Egypt and Assyria. He was conversant with all the racial and political trends in western Asia, and he well knew what sort of historical future his own race might expect. At times, the violence of his language reaches great heights of dramatic expression. It does not matter whether verses 1-3 of chapter v of the Book of Micah were written by him or by someone anonymous: generation upon generation of Christians will kneel down in wonder and devotion before their prophetic significance. 'But thou, Bethlehem Ephratah, though thou be little among the thousands of Judah, yet out of thee shall come forth unto me that is to be ruler in Israel; whose goings forth have been from of old, from everlasting.'

Jeremiah was only a young man when he received the call to become a prophet. He came from a family of priests. For forty-one years he prophesied and admonished, and he was himself responsible for the compilation of his utterances. His public career lasted from 626 to 584 B.C., and no other prophet ever made such a deep impression on his contemporaries or on posterity as he did by the sheer force of his personality. He laid bare his own inward struggles with unique candour, never able to remain silent for the inner voice which left him no peace. He only had to open his mouth to make everyone his enemy. He suffered immensely under the burden of his vocation, and was nearer to Christ than any other prophet. No one before Christ was so vehement in demanding absolute religious sincerity, and no one before Christ ever waged a battle against the laws and dogmas of the external world with such singleness of purpose. Unmarried and solitary, he suffered, endured and prayed – like the Sufferer of Gethsemane.

Ezekiel was borne off into Babylonian captivity in 598 B.C., together with many other Jews. His utterances combine a passionate vehemence with shrewdness and circumspection. He was an erudite and cultured man, who looked back to the beginnings of humanity and traced them forward to the moment when the peoples launched their final self-destructive assault upon the House of God.

King Darius of Persia was in the second year of his reign when Zechariah appeared on the scene, but very little is known about this prophet's life.

Haggai was born in Babylon. He called upon the great men of his country to recommence and complete the building of the Temple. All the cathedrals in the world are summoned up by Haggai's words: 'The glory of this latter house shall be greater than that of the former.'

In the year 275 B.C., prophet-hood ceased. The prophets were secretive about their personal experiences, but they all revealed their thoughts – a characteristic which both Homer and Shakespeare share with them. The sixteen present an almost unbroken succession of great minds. They all fought against polytheism and foreign religious cults. Always before their eyes was a comprehensive picture of the future, Yahweh's 'grand design', what, perhaps, Western civilization in the truest sense of the term might have become – and should have become. Some day, they declared, the greatest of all the prophets would come, a man who would meekly submit to death, and about whom his disciples would say: 'He is risen again.' In the end, there would be a new Creation and a new golden age.

The prophets recognized something deep and fundamental: they knew what lies hidden in man, and they deduced from it that there is One who exists beyond human ken, and who orders the Universe. They lived, they suffered and they died for the sake of a better world.

In reality, none of us has any other end in life.

There is no finer one.

MAN IS OF FEW DAYS AND FULL OF TROUBLE

The Book of Job

'All the world agrees that the Bible deserves to be entitled the greatest book of mankind. It is the book in which our whole civilization has learnt to read, from which we have conceived all our moral, artistic and literary ideas, and out of which there has come, like a stream of fructifying water, an inexhaustible store of sanctity and spirituality.'

Paul Claudel, December 1940

ALMOST all the great civilized races possess their own store of legends, but the development of Jewish legendary poetry seems to have been arrested. Such heroic sagas as do exist were mostly taken over from very ancient foreign sources and elaborated by prophets and priests for instructional purposes. Israel had no theatre, either. Dramatic composition was impossible because a live performance on the stage would have transgressed the law against human representation.

It was only in the field of lyric poetry that the Hebrews reached a magnificent stage of development. 'Lyric' comes from the Greek word *lyra*, meaning lyre, and lyric poetry was once upon a time sung to that instrument. Lyric poetry is largely differentiated from legendary (epic) poetry and from dramatic poetry by its closer association with music. Thirty of the one hundred and fifty psalms in the Old Testament carried musical directions at their head, for psalms were poems designed to be sung. At the same time we find a parallel development in epigrammatic poetry in the Proverbs of Solomon and in Ecclesiastes, while the Book of Job combines both song and proverb in a very beautiful manner.

The 'poetic' or didactic books of the Old Testament consist of Job, Psalms, Proverbs, Ecclesiastes, and the Song of Songs — five in all. The Bible of the Roman Catholic Church, known in its Latin translation by St Jerome as the Vulgate, contains in addition the 'Book of Wisdom' and the 'Book of Jesus Sirach', making a total of seven. In the Hebrew Bible, these books belong to the Ketubim or 'Writings'.

We do not know who the author of the Book of Job was. We can only gather from the didactic poem that he was an Israelite. However, even that is open to question. He may have been an Arab who was ignorant of the Hebrew law. It has even been suggested that the story of Job may have come from Babylon. Fragments of a 'song of the righteous man in affliction' have been found both in King Assurbanipal's library at Nineveh and also at Sippar. This tells the story of a pious king who becomes crippled by disease and is on that account adjudged a great sinner. He has to put up with every kind of abuse before, in the midst of his sufferings, he suddenly discovers his

133

sin. It is that he has compared himself with his God. In the end we see him restored to health and happiness once more, and the god Marduk appears to him in a dream. Nevertheless, there is a considerable difference between the Babylonian and the Biblical stories: Job was innocent, while the Babylonian king had actually sinned.

It is possible that Job lived about 1700 B.C. at the time of the Patriarchs — Abraham, Isaac and Jacob — near the Arabian Desert on the eastern border of Palestine. In fact, the name Job is already to be found in Egyptian documents of about 2000 B.C., as well as in the Amarna Letters of about 1400 B.C. However, by the time the Book of Job was written, its subject had already become a sort of legendary figure. When was the book actually written?

Many erudite works have been written on this subject and, as so often happens, scholars cannot agree about it. The book must have appeared somewhere between 600 and 200 B.C. The only point of universal agreement is that this sacred work is the finest masterpiece in the whole of Hebrew literature. Goethe, Victor Hugo and Tolstoy are all unanimous in calling the Book of Job the most considerable poetic work which mankind has ever produced. It is an all-embracing epic of spiritual life.

Taking what was obviously an old folk-story as his theme, the poet wove into the framework of Job's story a spiritual drama translated into words. Towards the end of the book, a certain Elihu makes his appearance. His discourses appear to be interpolations, since they are couched in a language which exhibits a stronger Aramaic flavour than the rest, and they were probably added later.

'There was a man in the land of Uz, whose name was Job; and that man was perfect and upright, and one that feared God, and eschewed evil. And there were born unto him seven sons and three daughters. His substance also was seven thousand sheep, and three thousand camels, and five hundred yoke of oxen, and five hundred she asses, and a very great household; so that this man was the greatest of all the men of the east. . . .

'Now there was a day when the sons of God came to present themselves before the Lord, and Satan came also among them. And the Lord said unto Satan, "Whence comest thou?" Then Satan answered the Lord and said, "From going to and fro in the earth, and from walking up and down in it." And the Lord said unto Satan, "Hast thou considered my servant Job, that there is none like him in the earth, a perfect and an upright man, one that feareth God, and escheweth evil?" Then Satan answered the Lord and said, "Doth Job fear God for naught? Hast thou not made an hedge about him, and about his house, and about all that he hath on every side? Thou hast blessed the work of his hands, and his substance is increased in the land. But put forth thine hand now, and touch all that he hath, and he will curse thee to thy face." And the Lord said unto Satan, "Behold, all that he hath is in thy power; only upon himself put not forth thine hand. So Satan went forth from the presence of the Lord".'

That is the story within a story — God's wager with the Devil, the object of the wager being Job's faith.

From then on there is a procession of messengers, each bearing 'Job's tidings': an armed raid has taken place, Job's herds have been driven off and his servants massacred; lightning has struck from the sky and burned up his sheep and his servants; the Chaldeans have fallen upon his camels; a great wind has killed his sons and daughters. 'Then Job arose, and rent his mantle and shaved his head, and fell down upon the ground, and worshipped, and said, "Naked I came out of my mother's womb, and naked shall I return thither: the Lord gave, and the Lord hath taken away; blessed be the name of the Lord." '

Having made no impression on Job, Satan goes to the Lord once more, and says: 'Skin for skin, yea, all that a man hath will a man give for his life. But put forth thy hand now, and touch his bone and his flesh, and he will curse thee to thy face.' God puts Job entirely into Satan's hands, with the sole proviso that he must spare his life. Satan afflicts Job with virulent boils from the soles of his feet to the crown of his head, and Job sits among the ashes and scrapes himself with a potsherd. 'Dost thou still retain thy integrity?' asks his wife, but Job is unshaken, and answers: 'Thou speakest as one of the foolish women speaketh. What? Shall we receive good at the hand of God, and shall we not receive evil?' Job's friends Eliphaz, Bildad and Zophar visit him to express their sympathy and to offer him comfort. Not recognizing him at first, they weep and tear their garments. In the end Job breaks his silence, and curses the day he was born.

There follows an exposition of the insoluble problem of retribution. In three sets of discourses — Job counters each of his friends' arguments in turn — they search for the cause of Job's afflictions. Is it the unwarranted wrath of God? Is it an act of kindness on God's part, intended to convert Job from his errors? In general: how do justice, wisdom and power operate in this world? Conscious of his innocence and from the depths of his misery, Job launches a vehement attack on God. Even so, he remains true to Him in his innermost heart, hoping against hope that he will one day be vindicated and reinstated. Eventually, with a plea that God should send him a judge, he reduces his friends to silence. An arbitrator does arrive upon the scene, in the shape of Elihu. 'Why dost thou strive against Him?' he asks, 'For God speaketh once, yea twice, yet man perceiveth it not. In a dream, in a vision of the night, when deep sleep falleth upon men, in slumberings upon the bed . . . He is chastened also with pain upon his bed.' Elihu reproves Job for his presumptuous attitude. Affliction is not only a form of punishment, but also a means of improving and purifying the innocent and devout.

Finally Yahweh himself speaks. He opens Job's eyes to something very great. He shows him the nature, the omnipotence, the wisdom and the love of the Creator inherent in the whole infinity of Creation and the structure of the Universe. All the apparent enigmas, secrets and anomalies in Nature are only part of a well-considered if incalculable plan. Job is reduced to silence. Eventually he speaks: 'I know that thou canst do everything, and that no thought can be withholden from thee . . . I uttered that which I understood not; things too wonderful for me which I knew not.'

The Lord thereupon restores Job's good fortune; indeed, he increases his possessions so that they number double what he had before. Job lives on for another hundred and forty years, finally to die old and full of days. Satan has lost his wager.

This book owes its novel, unique and revolutionary character to the fact that it casts the age-old theory of retribution to the winds. Happiness and misery are not dispensed according to merit or demerit. God's plan embraces the whole world and the whole Universe, and all divine action is ultimately directed not at the individual man or nation, but at totality and the world in its entirety. The innocent man who suffers can thus retain his good conscience. On the other hand, he should not believe in God merely because he looks for recompense in the world to come, for that would be just another selfish motive. The idea of the next world only rears its head once in the Book of Job, when Job cries: 'O that thou wouldest hide me in the grave . . . If a man die, shall he live again? All the days of my appointed time will I wait, till my change come.' But the hope which only Christ could have supplied fails him once more, and he goes on: 'Thou prevailest for ever against him [man], and he passeth: thou changest his countenance, and sendest him away.' The Book of Job is the most moving testimony to man's violent and eternal struggle with his God.

To implement the ultimate truth which this book contains would be a task beyond man's ability. It would entail his mentally tearing himself free from the limitations of a human comprehension of God and conception of devotion, and from an earthly assessment of life's values.

That is where the spiritual drama in Job lies: in the eternal flounderings and strugglings of humanity faced with the huge mystery of Creation; in a realization of the essential futility of all scientific research and knowledge; in a hint of the other, vaster and more far-reaching thing which we cannot know. Our only surviving conviction is that nothing and none of us within the Universe ever goes astray, and that a pure heart is the only key to this infinite problem.

CHRIST LIVED

The Books of the New Testament and their contents are probably better authenticated than any other human traditions. 'It is precisely the fury with which so many people attack Christ which proclaims that he is not yet dead.' Giovanni Papini in his *Storia di Cristo*.

I N the fourth year before the beginning of our chronology, in the reign of King Herod, there was born at Bethlehem the Christian Saviour, Jesus, the son of Mary. 'Christ' comes from the Greek word *christos*, meaning 'the anointed'. Jesus was crucified in the twenty-ninth or thirtieth year of our era. He really did live, and he really was nailed to the Cross.

For about 1900 years, people have been seeking to murder him a second time. They have tried to prove that Jesus was a fictional character, asserting that he never existed at all. Writers of fiction and visionaries have between them attempted to reduce the Gospel Story to the status of a myth.

Giovanni Papini, the Florentine author who wrote a life of Christ asks this question of all such sceptics: 'What would take the place of the great man you reject? His grave was dug ever deeper, yet no one ever managed conclusively to bury him.' No amount of refutation, falsification, criticism, erasure, destruction or prohibition has yet succeeded in driving Christ from the world. We are still living in the 'Christian era'. It has still not come to an end. Had any genius invented the life of Christ, he would have been even greater than Christ himself.

Where does our knowledge of Jesus and his life and works come from, and what 'historical sources' do we possess? Our sources are the writings of the New Testament, which is not a single book, but a small library of books written by different people at different times which the Church assembled during the course of the first few centuries. These are the Christian sources of information about the life of Jesus.

The earliest testimony about Jesus to be given by a Christian is contained in Paul's Epistles — in particular those to the Romans and Galatians and the two Epistles to the Corinthians. Paul, or Saul, as he was originally called, was born at Tarsus, the capital of Cilicia. His parents were Jews, but of Roman citizenship. While he was still a young boy they sent him to Jerusalem, where he sat at the feet of Gamaliel and diligently learned 'the Law' and — as a side-line — the tent- and carpet-maker's trade. Saul strove with uncompromising fervour after perfect righteousness and the observance of the Jewish law. He put men and women who had become Christians in chains and sent them to gaol, persecuting them because they worshipped their crucified Christ as the Messiah, and because Jesus' doctrine of the love of God destroyed the force of the ancient law. He had the High Priest empower him to continue his work in Damascus, where he intended to arrest other heretics and bring them back to Jerusalem for punishment. On his way to Damascus, however, a great light suddenly shone down on him out of the sky, and he heard a voice saying: 'Saul, Saul, why persecutest thou me?' As soon as he reached Damascus he had himself baptized. This probably happened in the year A.D. 35. Paul was the first man to carry the news of the Redeemer out into the world. His life was one of the most heroic that has ever been lived, and his watch-word was always: 'Not I, but HE in me!' Ancient tradition has it that Paul suffered death at the hand of the executioner in Rome on July 29th, A.D. 67.

The New Testament contains thirteen of Paul's Epistles – or fourteen, if we include the Epistle to the Hebrews, which differs from the rest in form, style and mode of thought. They are the earliest evidence of the life of Christ to come from a Christian source. All the rest of the Epistles in the New Testament are of post-Pauline origin.

Paul and the twelve Apostles of Jesus were the chief missionaries of Christianity – the 'ones sent forth', as the Greek derivation of the word 'apostle' implies. When these men began to die off one after the other from the year A.D. 60 onwards, an urgent need arose to commit the Gospel of Jesus to writing. The word Gospel, derived from Old English, and its less common equivalent the Evangel, derived from Greek, are both compounds meaning 'good tidings'. We possess four different accounts of the Gospel of Christ: Matthew, Mark, Luke and John. The first three constitute a group distinct from the fourth. They present a similarity of construction, choice of material and verbal detail, when 'looked at together', which has gained them the name of the 'synoptic' Gospels – a term, once again of Greek derivation, which has now been in use for about one hundred years.

There once lived in Jerusalem a much respected Christian woman who was a friend of Peter, and at whose house the Apostles often used to meet. Her name was Mary, and she had a son, Mark, whom Peter converted and baptized. Mark became acquainted with the words and deeds of Christ through Peter's accounts of them, and between A.D. 65 and 67 he wrote them down, accurately, though not in order of their occurrence. Justin the Martyr, an historical figure who was born in A.D. 100 and put to death at Rome in A.D. 165, called Mark's book the 'Gospel of Peter'. Papyas, who lived about A.D. 100, held that Mark had never personally heard or followed Christ. On the other hand, it is possible that Mark really was the 'young man' who was present when Christ was arrested and who fled naked, leaving his garment behind in the hands of those who tried to seize him. If that were so, the passage in St Mark xiv, 51, 52 would be autobiographical.

Matthew was one of the twelve Disciples, and earned his living as a

Customs official at the Roman Custom-house on the Lake of Tiberias. Writing between A.D. 70 and 80, he tells the story of Jesus with a magnificent sense of history.

Luke came from Antioch in Syria. That we know upon the evidence of an historical figure, Eusebius. Luke was a doctor by profession, and wrote his Gospel in the year A.D. 70.

John was a fisherman's son from Lake Galilee. His mother Salome was the sister of Jesus' mother, and followed the Saviour to the Cross. It was John to whom Jesus entrusted his mother Mary before he died. John himself died at a ripe old age in A.D. 79. He wrote his Gospel at the request of friends, probably in Ephesus.

The New Gospel was written entirely in Greek. The accounts of Matthew, Mark and Luke were passed on by word of mouth in Aramaic before they were committed to paper, and so, in the case of the three synoptic Gospels, Aramaic verbal tradition preceded their actually being written down. Christ's own mother-tongue was almost certainly Aramaic too. In the first century of the Christian era, however, the language of literature was Greek and, since the Gospel was intended to be carried out into the world at large, it had to be in a language which the world could understand.

Jesus' native land was Galilee, the frontier between the Jewish and the Hellenic worlds, and it is quite possible — as Martin Dibelius believes — that Jesus and his Disciples understood and perhaps even spoke Greek. Undoubtedly, the Evangelists could speak and write the language in addition to their own.

What we know about Jesus is therefore neither mythical, legendary, nor visionary, but based on what was written down in black and white only thirty to seventy years after his crucifixion. Even if we have not — hitherto, anyway — found the Evangelists' original manuscripts, we do possess fragments of very, very old copies of them. The most ancient of these are papyrus manuscripts. In the time of the Roman Emperors, the period when the writings of the New Testament appeared, there existed large factories and export houses devoted to the manufacture of 'paper' from papyrus reeds. Great quantities of such papyri have been discovered and are housed in the vaults of all the large museums in the world. Many of them are as yet undeciphered or unread, and it is anyone's guess what discoveries may still remain to be made.

However, what we already possess today is amazing enough: 1931 saw the publication of 126 sheets of papyrus from the Chester-Beatty collection which duplicated certain portions of New Testament books and were written between A.D. 200 and 300. In 1935, C. H. Roberts published papyrus fragments of St John's Gospel dating from the time of Hadrian, who died in

A.D. 135. These pieces of documentary evidence relating to Christ must therefore have been written only about a hundred years after the Crucifixion. In the same year, H. I. Bell and T. C. Skeat published a largish piece of papyrus from the British Museum containing a fragmentary account of the life of Christ. This text is based on all four Gospels, and is on that account known by the name 'Harmony'. Research has established that this fragment dates from between A.D. 100 and 150. The Egerton Papyrus can hardly fail to inspire us with a certain degree of awe, when we reflect how directly it attests to the life of Christ.

Almost all the papyrus fragments of New Testament books in our possession have been discovered within the past forty years, and nearly all of them were found at Oxyrhynchus in Upper Egypt. The ground there is so dry that it preserves perishable materials remarkably well, which is why this ruined town just under a hundred miles from Cairo has become a sort of happy hunting-ground for New Testament research.

The other great medium of literary tradition in antiquity was parchment, a younger material than papyrus. Parchment is the carefully prepared hide of goats, donkeys, sheep, calves, or antelope. The process was perfected during the 2nd century B.C. at Pergamum, from which city parchment gets its name.

The four most famous New Testament manuscripts are known to science under the designations B, א, A and C. 'B' is the 'Codex Vaticanus' of the fourth century, the oldest of all the parchment manuscripts which have survived from antiquity. 'א' is the 'Sinaiticus', which was discovered by Tischendorf on his visit to Sinai in 1854, and also dates from the fourth century. 'A' is the 'Alexandrinus' from the fifth century, and 'C' is the so-called 'Codex rescriptus', also from the fifth century. Those are the four earliest and best-known complete manuscripts of the New Testament.

The Books of the New Testament are probably better authenticated than any other documents in the literary heritage of mankind. The year 1874 saw science already in possession of 120,000 only slightly divergent New Testament manuscripts of an early or very early date. In 1892 there were 150,000. Today there are more versions of the New Testament than there are words in it, but even though these manuscripts all vary to a greater or lesser extent, the substance of their contents remains unaffected.

Out of a veritable flood of early Christian literature, the Church has extracted the oldest texts and those which were already accounted the most reliable only a short time after Christ's crucifixion. However much mankind destroys and however many churches it bombs or burns down — if people uproot every cross in the world, smash one altar after another, vandalize sacred pictures and desecrate images of the Virgin Mary — the life of Jesus will still pervade this world for all time to come.

INDIA

THE GREATEST ENIGMA IN HUMAN HISTORY
Mohenjo-Daro and Harappa

This Indus civilization takes us back 3600 years to a prehistoric era which can only be described as 'ultra-modern'.

IN the year 1856, during the reign of Queen Victoria, the British were engaged in building the East India Railway between Karachi and Lahore. The operation was under the direction of two brothers called John and William Brunton. John was laying the southern section of the track, and William the northern section up to the Punjab.

The construction of a solid railway embankment calls for firm ground and ample supplies of stone, and John Brunton was perpetually racking his brains for a suitable source of stone. Not far from his route stood the ruined medieval town of Braminbad. Veritable mountains of bricks were readily available there, and the resourceful engineer accordingly satisfied his needs from them. He informed his brother William of how he had mastered the problem of stone supply, and William began to reconnoitre the country on either side of his own stretch of track between Multan and Lahore. Very soon he too discovered an old ruined city, on whose rubble the small modern township of Harappa had been built. 'Some good solid bricks at last!' he said to himself. They were exactly what he needed for his embankment, and so the ruins of the city at Harappa were cleared away with all dispatch. Trains travelling between Lahore and Karachi today thunder along over nearly a hundred miles of track laid on bricks made 3600 years ago. The product of one of the earliest highly developed civilizations in the world, they are still so solid and indestructible that even modern locomotives have failed to reduce them to dust. Yet Harappa's stone-masons had been dead for over 1500 years by the time Christ was born. . . .

In 1922, when the Indian archaeologist R. D. Banerji was engaged in excavating an old Buddhist monastery dating from about A.D. 300 and situated on the lower Indus at Mohenjo-Daro, the 'Hill of the Dead', he established that the bricks which the early Buddhists had used dated from very much earlier times, and that beneath the monastery and the 'Hill of the Dead' a very ancient city lay buried. At about the same time, the Director of the Indian Archaeological Service, Sir John Marshall, began to carry out extensive excavations at Harappa. It was soon further established that the sites of this prehistoric Indus civilization stretched as far as Baluchistan, and it was concluded that long before the so-called Aryans migrated to India from the Caspian Sea about 1500 B.C., a much more ancient civilization must have existed in north-west India. This advanced prehistoric civilization flourished between 1700 and 1500 B.C. What confirmation is there for this estimate of when the builders of Harappa and Mohenjo-Daro lived?

Scarcely any documentary evidence has been found in the Indus valley – only seals bearing unidentified and hitherto undeciphered characters. So no answer to the mystery lies along that line of investigation. However, the archaeologists who dug up Sumerian towns in the area of the Euphrates and the Tigris found quite similar seals and a few pieces of broken pottery which unmistakably originated in the ancient cities on the Indus. Since Sumerian cuneiform inscriptions had been deciphered and precise dates could be established for them, the date of Harappa and Mohenjo-Daro was deducible from the layers of earth which the Indus seals shared with datable Sumerian objects. On that basis of reckoning, the inhabitants of Mohenjo-Daro and Harappa were contemporaneous with a Sumerian period fixed at between 1700 and 1500 B.C.

Where did these ancient city-builders come from? Very little is known. All that is certain is that their cities were flourishing long before the 'Aryan'-speaking immigrants arrived in northern India. It may be that the inhabitants of Harappa were themselves intruders who had set out on a large-scale migratory trek from somewhere beyond the north-west frontier of India. They were certainly in an advanced state of civilization when they began to build their cities. The fact that their writing has only been found on seals (they are probably amulets) and on a few pottery fragments and tools, and that the lettering found at different levels of the excavations at Harappa and Mohenjo-Daro (i.e. belonging to different periods) exhibits scarcely any sign of modification, indicates that these people only underwent a slight measure of intellectual development after their arrival in India – perhaps as a consequence of the enervating climate. On the other hand, the reason why no extensive documentary evidence has ever been found there could also be that larger written documents were executed on bark, cotton, leather, palm-leaves, or wood, all of which materials would obviously have decayed away to nothing long ago, buried in the damp and saline earth of India.

Several groups of skeletons were found during the excavations at Mohenjo-Daro. One group, fifteen strong, was lying in a large room, while another, consisting of six skeletons, lay in a street. The contorted attitudes of the dead indicated that they died a violent death. Archaeologists have thought that Mohenjo-Daro and Harappa were abandoned by their inhabitants simultaneously, though the reason for this naturally remains a mystery.

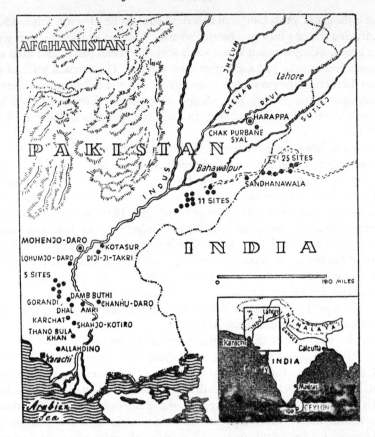

Excavated sites of Indus civilization

Both cities appear to have been built to a careful plan. The streets of Harappa run almost parallel to each other, and are traversed at right angles by other parallel streets. These ancient cities on the Indus had no winding lanes such as were common in the cities of medieval Europe, and town-planning seems to have rested in competent hands. In fact, Mohenjo-Daro and Harappa between them represent the oldest examples of town-planning in the world.

It is also interesting to note that hardly any of the houses ventured to encroach upon the street, their frontages forming fairly straight lines. The main streets ran through the city from east to west and north to south. They were probably built in this fashion so that the prevailing northerly winds kept them well ventilated. 'Street No. 1', as it has been designated, which is about a thousand yards long, ran in a dead straight line from north to south and divided the city into two parts. Several of Mohenjo-Daro's streets were quite broad, being as much as ten yards wide in certain places, and carts and carriages could easily pass each other two abreast. The external walls of the houses bordering the excavated main streets, not yet fully cleared of earth, already go down twenty feet. Some house-fronts have even been laid bare to a depth of twenty-six feet, and still the foundations have not been reached.

Houses at street intersections were rounded off so that beasts of burden and pedestrians could not 'catch' themselves on the corners. Almost every building in Harappa and Mohenjo-Daro is constructed of baked bricks which more or less resemble our own in shape. The remarkable feature of Mohenjo-Daro is the simplicity of its buildings. There is scarcely any kind of ornamentation, no pillars, balconies, sculpturing or windows – only narrow doorways and flat roofs. Windows were unpractical in the hot valley of the Indus, and many of the houses are veritable labyrinths. Perhaps their owners liked to feel quite secure in their depths. Nevertheless, it is possible that ornamentation did exist on the houses, but carved out of wood, as is still the general practice in India today. In that case, of course, none of it would have survived after 3500 years.

Anyone who strolls through the ruins of Mohenjo-Daro and Harappa can see that the houses which once stood there were provided with 'all mod. cons.', so to speak. No amenity was lacking. There were baths, lavatories, drainage and fresh-water tanks, handsome interior courtyards – like the ones which are still to be seen throughout the East – comfortable bedrooms, guest-rooms, dining-rooms and porters' lodges. And all of it is 'prehistoric'. It all existed at a period when central Europe's only form of housing accommodation was the cave.

The most important construction which has so far been excavated at Mohenjo-Daro is the great bath-house. This included among its amenities hot air, steam and water, a fine swimming-pool, changing-rooms, small bathrooms, running water, cold showers and the like. No one who examines the layout of these premises can fail to be astounded by the ultra-modern building technique which these people possessed over 3000 years ago.

To the west of the great bath-house lay a huge granary, which was excavated in 1950. The individual grain-bins were so constructed that constant air-circulation prevented stocks of cereals from becoming damp. The building must originally have measured 164 by 82 feet, but it had at some period been enlarged on the south side. Sir Mortimer Wheeler invites us to visualize how the commodity which was the most important factor in civic prosperity used at one time to be administered and distributed by officials, and how government tithes must have filled and re-filled the grain-bins. He points out that, in a moneyless period of history, this granary must really have represented the public treasury.

However, the mightiest building of all has not yet been dug up, for a Buddhist shrine, or stupa, stands above it, and would have to be demolished before we could explore the secrets it hides. Unfortunately, the Indians do not want their stupa to be damaged, and so there is no possibility of getting at this subterranean miracle, which may be a 4000-year-old temple.

Many female statuettes have been found at Mohenjo-Daro and Harappa. They probably depict a goddess, but her name is not known. The greatest and most knowledgeable of all the authorities on the Indus civilization, Sir John Marshall, believes her to be the Mother-goddess who is still worshipped by some Indians today, and who obviously dates from prehistoric times. She is portrayed on some of the amulet-seals as a seated figure surrounded by animals, and has rightly been regarded as a forerunner of Siva, one of the two major divinities in present-day Hinduism. In addition, there were animal-gods, sacred fig-trees and a whole menagerie of idols of various kinds. If the Mother-goddess's clothing is any guide, the women of Mohenjo-Daro wore nothing but a sort of skirt which barely reached their knees and was held up by a girdle. There may also have been a cloak which covered the arms but left the breasts bare. We possess a nude statuette of a dancing-girl in bronze. The men probably wore a kind of loin-cloth, and over it a robe which went across the left shoulder and tied beneath the right arm.

Many jewels have been found cached in silver, copper and bronze vessels, as well as necklaces and jewellery in gold, electrum (an alloy of silver and gold), silver, copper and bronze. Great quantities of other objects were unearthed, including rings, bracelets, nose-ornaments, examples of almost every precious and semi-precious stone known to us, bronze mirrors with wooden handles, cosmetics, razors and even a saw with serrated teeth, the very first of its kind. Large numbers of hooks betray a knowledge of fishing, and some of them even had cotton lines still attached.

There are small inscriptions on many of the tools and weapons. They may be names, or perhaps numbers. Also discovered were a large number of weights made of alabaster, quartz, jasper and limestone. They were found to have a unit weight of 0·0302 oz., and rise in the following series of multiples: 1, 2, 4, 8, 16, 32, 64, 160, 200, 320, 640, 1600, 3200, 6400, 8000 and 12,800. The inhabitants of Mohenjo-Daro were apparently an honest bunch of people, for hardly any 'crooked' weights were found — that is to say, weights which did not adhere to the scale given above. The scales consisted of a bronze bar with copper pans attached. A linear measure was found, too. It was a strip of shell divided into units of 2·1999 feet. The error, or departure from the norm, on this measuring instrument amounts to only 0·00299 inch.

These people could spin and weave cotton, as many spindles bear witness. Their pots and vessels are far from primitive, and display not only an extremely advanced technique but also a considerable variety of design. They are the products of a people which already enjoyed a tradition of craftsmanship hundreds if not thousands of years old. For all that, they cannot be compared with the utensils found in Sumer or Egypt. Designs were probably evolved on the Indus at a much earlier date, and were adhered to without modification.

The children of Harappa and Mohenjo-Daro could amuse themselves quite as well as the children of modern cities. They possessed all kinds of toys, from miniature oxen pulling carts and brightly decorated rattles with small stones inside, to model animals and birds. One of these little birds, complete with its tiny toy cage, has its beak open in a silent song which has lasted 3500 years. Pipes were also found, and a small animal – which zoologists have hitherto been unable to classify – climbing up a stick. While no dolls were discovered, there were pieces of doll's crockery with the finger-marks of their childish makers still imprinted in the clay. One particular model of an ox must have delighted the children of Mohenjo-Daro and Harappa greatly: it could nod its head.

The people of these cities loved, drank and played games. Their dice were beautifully fashioned. Each side bore a number (we have even been able to identify them) running from 1 to 6; 2 is on the other side of 1, 4 of 3, and 6 of 5. The numbers are not arranged as on our dice, where the sum of two opposite sides always equals 7.

It is certain that meat was eaten here. That assumption is confirmed by remains of deer, buffalo, pig, tortoise, goat and ox. The people of the Indus valley took their meals sitting on mats, but they probably used tables and chairs as well, as certain pictographic symbols seem to indicate. The large quantity of horn which was dug up at Mohenjo-Daro has inclined researchers to think that it may have been used in its powdered form for medicinal purposes, a practice which is still favoured in India and China today.

The general significance of the excavations at Mohenjo-Daro and Harappa has been to show us that we will for ever be re-writing our account of history. Before these discoveries were made, India's prehistoric age was assumed to be a dark and uncivilized era of barbarity. It is now recognized that long before the 'beginning of all civilization' a much more ancient and yet exceedingly advanced stage in human development already existed. It borders on the fabulous to hear an extremely knowledgeable scholar like Sir John Marshall declare it his considered opinion that the jewellery of these

Indus people is so perfectly and brilliantly cut that it could more easily have originated in London's present-day Bond Street than in a prehistoric house over 3000 years ago!

At the period when Queen Nefertiti and her much beloved husband Pharaoh Akhenaten were living in Egypt, a high degree of civilization had also been reached here on the Indus, a modern urban life whose foundations are hidden deep in the mists of prehistoric times. And the most amazing thing is that it is always the oldest pieces from the Indus civilization which display the greatest perfection and convey the strongest cultural impression.

What was dug up here was therefore only the product of an already waning evolution. Its splendid origins remain to this hour the greatest enigma in human history.

AN ATOM CAN NEVER UNDERSTAND THE UNIVERSE

Shapeless as yet, the spirit of India was groping its way out of the darkness of primeval times. And then came Buddha.

O UT of the darkness of an age long past, 3000 years ago or perhaps much longer, India sends us these words: 'Study and learning bring joy, self-possession and freedom. We benefit from them day by day, sleep peacefully, and become our soul's best doctor. Mastery of the senses, joy in being alone, growth of knowledge, authority and maturity will be the result.'

Whose was the mind which shaped these words?

Where did those who thought thus, live?

Where can we read more of the same?

The origins of India's history lie hidden in impenetrable obscurity. We do not know what people first inhabited the continent of India. We do not know what happened to them. . . .

The earliest advanced civilization to be unearthed from the soil of India is that of Mohenjo-Daro and Harappa. This civilization lies 3500 to 4000 years in the past, and as such, is prehistoric.

Later on, perhaps 1500 years before the birth of Christ, the Aryans invaded northern India. They left no mementoes of their immigration in stone or earth, no writings, no tangible evidence of their existence. In their stead, we possess an almost uncanny heritage which can be traced back to these people, a heritage of thought which has been handed down by word of mouth from century to century. These thoughts were never written down, nor inscribed anywhere, nor translated into terms of the written word. The oldest poems of mankind, the *Iliad*, the *Odyssey* and the Germanic sagas, were likewise never written down, but passed on verbally from one generation to another.

So it is with the Indian Vedas. It was only in the 7th or 8th century B.C. that Hindu merchants brought back a Semitic script with them from western Asia. All subsequent Indian alphabets are derived from this so-called 'Brahmi script'. During the course of the succeeding centuries the Vedas were recorded in writing. Sacred hymns, sacrificial rituals, magical invocations, ceremonial instructions, theological-cum-philosophical discourses — all these things are contained in the Vedas, an amazing spiritual monument which was built for all time by these Aryan — we also call them Indo-European — immigrants, and which developed more and more as centuries went by. The oldest collection in this great Vedic literature is the

Rig-Veda, containing about a thousand hymns made up of some ten thousand verses. The other components of the Vedic literature are the Sama-Veda, the Yajur-Veda, the Atharva-Veda, the Brahmanas, the Aranyakas, the Upanishads and the Sutras.

The most important works of later periods are the Mahabharata and the Ramayana. The Mahabharata consists of 100,000 double verses, and is thus about eight times as long as the *Iliad* and the *Odyssey* put together. Besides being a great heroic epic, it is also a huge pool of sagas, legends, myths and didactic treatises of every kind.

The Ramayana, consisting of 24,000 double verses, is a poem describing the extraordinary adventures and heroic deeds of King Rama. We know that the man who composed this epic was called Valmiki.

It is easy to see that the only people likely to learn such immense works by heart and hand them on through the centuries were those to whom 'study and learning brought joy'. (This particular sentence comes from the Brahmanas.)

The 3500- to 4500-year-old thoughts in the Vedas embrace all that one could ever dream of, think of, or imagine. There is Indra, for example, the god who embodied Siegfried, Adam and Noah in his one person. 'He slew the serpent, made an outlet for the waters, and clave the groins of the mountains. He slew the dragon which stretched itself out on the mountain . . . Just as a tree-trunk is felled by the axe, so the dragon lay felled flat upon the earth.' There is a Pilate, too, washing his hands in innocence: 'Take away all that is sinful in me, ye waters; if I was faithless or have cursed, and every lie.' And here is a noble passage about night: 'O Night, you have filled the earthly space according to the commandments of the Father of All. You spread in the height to the heavenly abodes. Star-sparkling darkness draws nigh.'

It is obvious how clearly the author of the following good advice perceived the impermanence of all material prosperity: 'The prosperous man should give to him who has fallen upon evil days and consider the long road ahead; for riches turn like waggon-wheels, for ever coming to a different man in turn.'

Here are some instructions about the choice of a wife: 'A man should marry a girl who is intelligent, beautiful, virtuous, lucky — and healthy. Of course, the signs of luck are hard to recognize. . . .'

A word about the virtues of getting up early: 'Like Indrani, an early riser, you should wakefully await the dawn which precedes the glow of the fire.' Some observations on sleep and dreams: 'In that you are neither alive or dead, O Sleep, you are the heavenly child of the gods. You set an end to things, you are death; thus we know you for what you are, O Sleep. Keep us, O Sleep, from evil dreams.'

And here we are confronted with an example of a woman's jealous love for a man, dating from a time when people could sing but had not yet learned to write: 'I am the spokesman, not you. You can be spokesman in the assembly, for aught I care. You shall belong to me alone. You shall never once speak of other women.' But what woman could have resisted the man who made such demands as these? 'As the liana holds the tree entwined, so cling to me because you are in love with me and will never be untrue to me.' And he not only wanted her body, but her soul as well: 'As the griffin flying upward with both wings holds fast to the ground, so do I hold fast to your soul.'

A word about insanity: 'May Agni calm your spirit if it be unhinged. I am skilfully preparing a remedy, that you may be freed from madness.'

A story of Creation: 'In the beginning was darkness veiled in darkness. This whole world was a chaos past recognition. The seed of life which was surrounded by the void, the One, was born by virtue of its urgent heat. To it was added, from the beginning, the craving for love.'

'In the beginning this world was neither being nor yet non-being. It was, and it was not. It was but thought.'

'This world and everything in it is rooted only in thought, when all is said and done. This thought is Brahman, which here means "tomorrow-better".'

Some words on the effects of time: 'Through time the purifying wind blows, through time the earth is great. The great heavens repose in time.'

A lonely man's fear: 'He was afraid, as a man is afraid who is all alone. But he reflected: If there is nothing here except myself, of whom should I be afraid? Then his fear abated.'

It is hard to grasp how, here in the obscurity of India's early history, man in his insignificance struggled to gain knowledge of great things; hard to grasp how touchingly human his efforts so often seem, and yet how daringly his intellect probed the unfathomable depths of space and time, providing him with gods and practical rules for existence. Nothing was as yet hard and fast, nor moulded into formulas. Man was still waging a free and unprejudiced battle with all his problems.

Schopenhauer says of one portion of the Vedas, the 'Upanishad': 'It makes the most rewarding and uplifting reading in the world: it has been the solace of my life and will be that of my death.'

What began by pulsing with blood and life, however, gradually degenerated into a hotch-potch of false doctrines, witchcraft, magical beliefs and superstitious notions. Many people became 'nihilists', despising the priesthood and disbelieving in all gods. One teacher, Sanjaya by name, discarded all knowledge and demanded that the sole objective of philosophy should be the attainment of peace. Purana Kashyapa taught that the soul was merely an ungovernable slave of chance. Maskarin Gosala believed that fate decided everything, regardless of human merit. Ajita Kesakambalin declared that, when once their bodies have perished, wise men and fools alike are destroyed and that after death they become nothing.

Into the midst of all this came Buddha, the founder of what was later to become the greatest Asiatic religion. As he grew up, he heard philosophers, merchants and peasants in the houses, streets and forests of northern India conducting interminable arguments without any firm basis for their thoughts whatsoever. It was a period when quibblers and orators as slippery as eels were preaching the absurdity of all virtue.

In about 560 B.C., a son was born to the rich prince Shuddhodana and his wife Maya. They lived near Kapilavastu in what is now Nepal. Close by, the Himalayas soar into the sky from the plain of the Ganges, and about 250 miles from Buddha's place of birth stands Mount Everest, majestic in its solitude.

The name Buddha is a theological title meaning 'the Enlightened'. The subsequent bearer of this title was known among his contemporaries by his family name, which was Gautama. Gautama spent his early years in luxury and self-indulgence, but when, at the age of twenty-nine, he realized that the end of man is old age, sickness and death, that existence entails suffering, and that everything is transitory, he left his wife and child and became a wandering ascetic. He subjected himself to such rigorous forms of physical privation that he became thin and weak to a degree where death itself loomed before his eyes. Then, abandoning self-torture, he persevered in the profoundest meditation on life and its meaning. Enlightenment finally came to him after a night spent awake beneath a pipal tree at Uruvela, or what is now Buddh Gaya in Bengal.

Gautama had become Buddha, the Enlightened, and he resolved to proclaim his findings to the world at large. He started by converting five ascetics who were his companions and lived near Benares. Before long, sixty more disciples rallied to his cause, and he sent them forth as missionaries. He personally converted a thousand people in Uruvela and won a supporter in King Bimbisara, who presented him with a park where he and his followers could live.

We hear little of Buddha's preaching and teaching in the forty-five years which followed these events. He probably roamed the eastern regions of the Ganges Valley, only spending the rainy season in permanent lodgings or caves.

Neither Socrates nor Christ nor Buddha ever thought of writing their teachings down. What they taught was passed on by their disciples.

Buddha was a man of iron will-power and great powers of persuasion. Proud, yet most amiable in speech and manner, he never asserted himself to be the agent of a god. He meditated day and night on ways to prevent the destruction of life, tried to reconcile enemies, and brought peace wherever he went. Like Christ, he strove to requite evil with good, and listened quietly to anyone who attacked him. In contrast to the heroes of this world, Buddha had a sense of humour. He realized that metaphysical knowledge and an inability to smile make an arrogant combination.

He roamed tirelessly from town to town and from village to village, accompanied by 1200 devotees. He cared little for his physical well-being and never worried about the morrow. He shocked his disciples on one occasion by taking a meal in the house of a prostitute. Buddha was convinced that suffering and misfortune overshadow the better aspects of life to so great an extent that it would be better if one were never born at all. 'More tears have flowed upon this earth than there is water in the four oceans.' He saw all pleasures in a dubious light because they were so fleeting. He laid down five moral precepts: 'No one should kill a living creature. No one should take what is not given him. No one should lie. No one should get drunk. No one should be unchaste.'

Buddha was not at home in the company of women. 'What should we do when women speak to us?' asked one disciple. 'Be very cautious,' replied Buddha.

'Never in the world did hate put an end to hate. Hate can be displaced only by love.' Buddha's one and only interest was in human conduct. He never demanded worship or theology. The most interesting trait in this holy man of Asia remains the fact that while he was the founder of a world-wide religion, he steadfastly declined to enter upon any discussion of eternity, immortality, or God.

'An atom can never understand the Universe.' Buddha was averse to guessing at enigmas — like the beginning and end of the world, for instance, or whether the soul is of the same substance as the body, or whether even a holy man ever goes to some kind of heaven. He dismissed all such questions as 'webs, thickets and deserts'. The only people with whom Buddha dealt at all sharply or angrily were the priests of his day. He denied that the Vedic literature was divinely inspired, and he attacked the caste system. 'Rich and poor, young and old, we are all one,' he said. Buddha established a religion without a god. On the other hand, he regarded reincarnation as a fact. This idea was probably the only one which he accepted without reservation. All his thoughts and energies were directed towards the attainment of nirvana. What nirvana is, however, we shall not attempt to explain here, for whole libraries of books have been written on the subject.

By the end of his life, the old man's followers had begun to worship him. He was by now 80 years old and very weak and thin, yet he roamed on and on, for ever teaching and preaching. While travelling to the ancient town of Kusinara, he was taken ill after eating some bad pork. His last admonition to his disciples was that they should henceforward make his precepts their supreme master, and strive in all earnestness to fulfil them. He died in 483 B.C.

'Now then, O monks, I speak to you. All material things are destined to perish. Strive ye in earnest.' Those were his last words.

As the centuries passed, however, Buddha's doctrines started to die out in India, overwhelmed by the sheer weight of the country's age-old religions. They foundered on Hinduism, their much more ancient rival, and on the Indians' traditional predilection for polytheism, miracles, mythology and witchcraft. Buddhism adopted numerous legends from the Hindu religion and took over its rituals and gods, until scarcely anything of the original Buddhist doctrines remained. In about A.D. 750, after a life-span of roughly 1000 years, Indian Buddhism died out. Outside India, however, Buddhism lived on. It took root in every country in the Far East, conquering almost the whole continent of Asia from the Siberian borders to the hot islands of Indonesia, from the lamaseries of Tibet to the tinkling gongs and incense-candles of the Zen priests in Japan.

WHO CREATED THE IMAGE OF BUDDHA?

The more I ponder on Buddha's philosophy, the more convinced I become that death is the true mother of all religions.

IF Buddha really existed, he was undoubtedly the greatest, wisest and most brilliant man India has ever produced.

The Buddhism which has become a world-wide religion is something quite foreign to its founder's original conception. Only two hundred years after the death of this genius from Nepal, eighteen variations of the Buddhist doctrine were already in existence, and the main forms of Buddhism, 'Mahayana' and 'Hinayana', have divided the Buddhist world into two halves. China and Japan (with the exceptions of Tibet, Bhután, Sikkim, Nepal and Mongolia, who adhere to it in the form of Lamaism) follow Mahayana, the 'Great Vehicle'. Ceylon and Indo-China follow Hinayana, the 'Little Vehicle'. Mahayana is the endeavour, born of compassion for the world, to be reincarnated as a future Buddha (Bodhisattva), to the welfare and happiness of all. The adherents of Hinayana seek only their personal salvation.

Did Siddhartha, the man whom half of all humanity follow today, if more often with lip-service than sincerity, really exist?

Again, statues of Buddha are to be found all over Asia. Do these effigies bear any real relation to the features of the man who once taught people by the Ganges to 'overcome rage with kindness'?

The authenticity of Gautama Buddha's life is attested by many detailed accounts which have been handed down from the past. We know his place of birth, we know his parentage, we know his name and we know what towns he visited. Buddha is said to have been cremated after his death, his remains being distributed among numerous princes and aristocratic families as sacred relics. His own family, the Sakya, also received a share, which they interred in a stupa at Kapilavastu. (A stupa is a conical, doorless structure, a sealed, bubble-shaped tumulus with a sort of protrusion at its summit.)

In the year 1898 this stupa was discovered in the neighbourhood of Piprava in Tarai. An inscription in Brahmi script recorded that the urn containing Buddha's relics was 'dedicated by the brothers, sisters, children and women-folk of the Exalted One'. It seems certain that the stupa was not opened between the time of its erection and the year 1898, which is yet another proof of Siddhartha Buddha's authenticity.

Everything has an origin of some kind. Buddha's philosophy, or at least the germs of it, must have been evolved by *someone*. Concrete accounts, stories and legends only grow up around figures who have really existed.

As we shall see later, modern research and archaeological excavation have transformed numerous Greek legendary figures into historical personalities.

However, if there is a lack of precise information about the man who became Buddha, and if no one knows exactly what he looked like, how can we explain the fact that the statues of Buddha which are to be found throughout India, China, Japan and eastern Asia are all somehow related? How is it that the more effigies of Buddha we study, the more convinced we become that the same flesh and blood personality lies behind all of them?

Buddha came from Nepal. The earliest images of Buddha, however, came from what is now Afghanistan, from the district which was once known as Gandhara. Stone statues of Buddha were made there as early as 200 B.C. When speaking of Gandhara as the birthplace of Buddhist sculpture, we are now thinking less in terms of a geographical unit than of a cultural area whose frontiers extend far beyond the ancient region of Gandhara itself. It was within this indefinable area that the portrayal came into being which was to underlie all subsequent representations of Buddha. It seems astonishing, doesn't it? Why should the spirit and countenance of Buddha have been translated into stone just there, some way outside India in what is now Afghanistan? The riddle is soon solved when we reflect that a combination of two factors was necessary: the idea of Buddha, and the existence of people who could lend that idea artistic shape. The idea came from India, but the only artists capable of putting it into a concrete form in those days lived in Gandhara, and they were not Indians.

The man who was responsible for the propagation of Buddhism outside the frontiers of India was the Indian king Asoka, who reigned roughly between 260 and 232 B.C. It was during his time that Buddhist missionaries reached Gandhara, and we know for a fact that the Buddhist apostle Madhyantika visited Kashmir and Gandhara in 242 B.C. What sort of civilization did these missionaries find in Gandhara?

When Alexander the Great died in 323 B.C., his dominions were divided among his generals. That was how the kingdoms of the Diadochi or Successors came into being. Alexander's Indian possessions went to Seleucus Nicator, the ruler of Syria. In 256 B.C., during the reign of his grandson Antiochus II (261-246 B.C.), the governor of Bactria, a Greek named Diodotus, rebelled and constituted himself king in his own right. That was how the Graeco-Bactrian kingdom originated.

Before long, it split up into numerous small states ruled by Greek kings. Even then, however, the process was not complete. Into this racial melting-pot, in the year 140 B.C., came the Yue-Chi, a Scythian tribe which had been chased out of eastern China by the Huns; 190 years later, in A.D. 50, they founded an Indo-Scythian kingdom under the Kushan dynasty. This dynasty produced a ruler who is quite unknown to us in Europe, yet became one of the greatest figures in world history. His name was Kanishka. This king came to the throne in A.D. 144, adopted the Buddhist faith, and expanded his domain from the Aral Sea in the north to Chotan in the east and from the plain of the Ganges to Benares in the south. His influence on Gandhara art must have been of the utmost importance, for as king and Buddhist convert he concentrated the whole of State-sponsored artistic activity on the great Exalted One from Nepal. It was during Kanishka's reign, in fact, that Gandhara art reached its prime.

So we see that, in Gandhara, Buddhism encountered a Hellenistic civilization, a civilization compounded of Greek and oriental elements. The orientals in Gandhara (there must certainly have been some pure-blooded Greeks and Romans there as well) began to make statues of Buddha. In making these statues they followed out their idea of Buddha, as he appeared to them from his career and his doctrines. From the very first, therefore, the Buddha image has been no more than an idealized conception which bears no relation to the prince's son called Siddhartha.

Since the artists of Gandhara were either of Greek descent or products of the racial melange which existed there within the framework of a Hellenistic civilization, they thought in Greek forms. That was why, when they decided to create an idealized picture of the man whose doctrines they had adopted, they dressed him in Greek clothing. And at every period since that time, no matter where Buddhism has gained a hold, Buddha has always been portrayed in Greek attire. Of course, styles have varied to a greater or lesser degree, but the heavy folds which lend dignity to the human figure have always been in evidence.

The seated Buddha is purely Indian in conception. This posture is typical of that which Indian ascetics of every period have been accustomed to adopt. The standing Buddha, on the other hand, belongs to the classical Greek realm of ideas. Thus the artists of Gandhara expressed an Indian ideal using techniques which originated in ancient Greece.

Buddha is supposed to have possessed physical attributes which distinguished him from other mortals. They are the thirty-two and the eighty minor 'bodily signs of the great man'. The Indians thought that Buddha must have been differentiated from other men not only spiritually but physically. What is interesting, incidentally, is that several of these 'signs' betray a tendency towards effeminacy or hermaphroditism. It is as though Nature had blurred the sexes in Buddha, giving expression to something supra-sexual and divine.

People are only too eager to designate the art of Gandhara as 'Graeco-Buddhistic'. This is not quite accurate, however, for the Greek elements in

it bear less relation to classical Greece than to Hellenism, which is by defini-
tion a blend of Greek and alien idioms. Gandhara even reveals echoes of
Roman and early Christian art. Hence the similarity between many representations of Buddha and early Christian sculptures of Jesus. In general,
modern research is inclining towards the theory that Gandhara art was the
eastern outpost of Roman civilization, with the oasis of Palmyra as a possible
intermediate link.

Gandhara's conception of Buddha's personal appearance became the
pattern upon which all later portrayals of him were modelled, whether in
Java, Siam, China or Japan. In the same way, Gandhara's representation of
the *mudras* became standard throughout eastern Asia. *Mudras* are the symbolic positions of the fingers adopted during religious meditation. There
are various constantly recurring gestures, each of which has a different
significance. One posture symbolizes 'turning the wheel of the Law'. Another, in which the hands lie in the lap, is a posture of meditation. Yet
another signifies 'calling the earth to witness', and consists in touching the
ground.

No paintings have been found in Gandhara itself, but it is fairly certain that
paintings and probably a school of painting did exist there. The glorious
frescoes in the cave-temple at Ajanta, dating from the second century A.D.,
show us likenesses of Buddha which were quite patently influenced by far
earlier paintings in Gandhara.

The Buddha sculptures of India could never have existed without Gandhara originals. The Indians did not merely copy Gandhara prototypes,
however, but adopted the various styles and added their own artistic ideas
to them.

There were Buddhist monasteries in China by the first century A.D., but
the earliest Chinese stone sculptures of Buddha date from the period A.D. 400.
Buddhism was introduced into Korea in A.D. 372. In A.D. 552 it reached
Japan, and in A.D. 632, Tibet.

Curiously enough, if you want to see the most beautiful statues of Buddha,
you must go to Japan. The Japanese have always made a point of collecting
fine Chinese originals, and they have evolved their own magnificent school
of Buddhist art. Gandhara style has survived in many of their sculptures
with an astonishing degree of purity.

The Chinese, on the other hand, portrayed the figure of the religious
founder in a far stronger native idiom. Their Buddhas often exhibit a
marked Chinese flavour. The celebrated Daibutsu statue at Kamakura in
Japan displays a Japanese cast of feature, it is true, but the rich folds of its
heavily draped robe bring it much closer to the Gandhara figures than many
Indian or Chinese sculptures of Buddha.

No one who stands before the Daibutsu Buddha and surrenders to the huge figure's sublime tranquillity, no one who absorbs the ultimate quality of its absolute composure will fail to recognize something of the spirit of this Nepalese genius: the removal of all pain, the quenching of all desire, the cessation of self-concern, and the extinction of personal identity like a candle-flame, which is nirvana, the condition of non-suffering.

REBIRTH

There is something above and beyond mankind's eternal round of petty cares, something higher than a preoccupation with worldly activities.

IF you are interested in religions, your first port of call should be India. Hinduism, Buddhism, Jainism, Mohammedanism and countless fragmentary sects all combine to make this land a theologian's happy hunting ground.

The Hindu religion is based on age-old Indo-Aryan traditions. The Indians embody all the sacred traditions relating to their early history in the word *Veda*, meaning 'knowledge'. A Veda is thus a book of knowledge, and this 'book' is in effect a whole literature.

Upa means 'near' in the Sanskrit language, and *sat* means 'sit'. It was the 'sitting near' or proximity of a religious instructor which gave birth to the word *Upanishad*, carrying with it a hint of the secret doctrines which a teacher imparts to his most promising pupils. The Upanishads are the thoughts and teachings of numerous wise men who regarded religion and philosophy as one and the same thing. Evolved between 700 and 500 B.C., these works strive to embrace all the secrets of life and the world hereafter, and mark the first important milestone in the history of philosophical thought. In them we find a belief in transmigration, in an eternal cycle of existence (*samsara*), and in reincarnation in human or animal form as a consequence of good or evil conduct. The Sanskrit term for this important process is *karma*. Yajñavalkya, one of the greatest Upanishad philosophers, expresses it in the following way (Brhadaranyaka, Upanishad 4, 4, 5): 'Just as a man acts, just as he changes, so will he be born; he who does good will be born good; he who does evil will be born evil; he will become holy through holy works and evil through evil. Wherefore is it truly said: man is entirely composed of desire; just as his desires are, so is his intelligence; just as his intelligence is, so are his actions; just as his actions are, so it fares with him.'

No matter how aspiring and sublime a religion may be, it is always in danger of becoming corrupted by petty human inadequacies. We shall never know how many anonymous religious founders sacrificed their lives in prehistoric times for pure and noble ideals which were later distorted by luxury-glutted priests. By 600 or 500 B.C., Brahmanism had already degenerated into a vast and petrified system of intricate rituals, whose punctilious performance by the priests or Brahmans was a person's only method of gaining salvation. Superstition, a continual emphasis on the efficacy of magic, the misappropriation of sacrificial offerings, self-torture as a means to supernatural powers, and lifeless religious formalism combined to inspire a revolt against the Brahmans and their religion. They had strayed far indeed from the erstwhile ideals of Indo-Aryan priesthood. Claiming that they alone were entitled to expound the sacred Vedas, they abused their religious monopoly in the most tyrannical manner and assuaged people's spiritual needs according to their own self-willed and often unjust standards. A crop of sceptics, fatalists, materialists and new religious founders grew up, took their stand against the Brahmans' lack of spirituality, and showed men fresh ways to salvation of their own devising. And, since secular power is always jealous of spiritual power, the Brahmans' opponents found an effective source of support in the warrior-caste, or *Kshatriya*.

It was during this period of 'great spiritual upheaval', as the Indologist Waldschmidt puts it, that the incalculable heavens bestowed on India two of the greatest religious founders that ever lived. One of them was Buddha, of whom we have already spoken. The name of the other is relatively unfamiliar to us in the West.

Mahavira Vardhamana was born in 540 B.C., at about the same time as Buddha. Like him, Mahavira was the son of a rich nobleman. His place of birth was on the outskirts of Vaishali, in modern Bihar. His parents belonged to a sect which, in common with all Indian religions, wrestled with the problem of reincarnation and its attendant suffering. They were worshippers of an itinerant ascetic called Parsva, who 250 years earlier laid the foundations of what were subsequently to become their son's religious ideas. They believed that suicide as a means of accelerating the cycle of reincarnation was a sacred right and, when Mahavira was thirty-one years old, they voluntarily starved themselves to death. It may have been this experience which impelled the gifted young man to become a naked ascetic and roam from place to place through what is now the province of Bihar. After thirteen years of purification, the light of infinite knowledge dawned in Mahavira. His disciples proclaimed their master as a *Jina* or conqueror, invested him with the title 'Great Hero', and called themselves Jains.

Mahavira's doctrine, or in other words, the Jain faith, is one of the most remarkable and interesting religions in the spiritual history of mankind. All earthly truth is limited. Each man sees only his immediate environment and judges things from his own standpoint: hence the distortion of all his perceptions. The truth is only revealed to *Jinas*, redeemers who appear on earth at rare intervals. The Jain religion is fundamentally atheistic. That is to say, it does not assume the existence of a creator or a first cause. A cause must itself have a cause, say the Jains: thus there cannot have been an original creator. The world has existed from all eternity, without a beginning or a god. In place of a god the Jains worship their twenty-four *Jinas* or *Tirthan-karas*, men who in earlier times attained 'absolute perfection'.

How is this absolute perfection to be attained? Well, an ordinary man can never hope to attain it. A monk may possibly do so, but even that is doubtful. The path to redemption is only open to the man who by continual ascetic penance and abstention from any resort to violence reaches complete *ahimsa*, an expression which is familiar to us in the English equivalent always used by Gandhi: 'no violence'. No one should injure another, and above all, no one should rob another living creature of its life. No one should kill, lie, or take what has not been given to him. Each should preserve his chastity, renounce all worldly desires, and become completely independent of external things.

Of course, all this is easier said than done. It is scarcely practicable to observe even the first of these prohibitions, that against taking life. No peasant can be a Jain in the strictest sense, for by tilling the soil he destroys insects and worms. The orthodox Jain monk wears a veil over his mouth in case he breathes in a fly and kills it. He must cover his lamps because their light may attract moths, and he is not allowed to use artificial lighting. He also sweeps the ground before him while walking in case his naked foot crushes the life out of some small creature.

Like all Indian religions, Jainism has disintegrated into numerous sects. There are the Swetambaras, who dress in white robes, and those who go around naked, the Digambaras. In actual fact, even the Digambaras usually wear clothes nowadays, although by rights they should not, for clothing is comfort, and comfort is the indulging of bodily desires. Only a very few holy men still wander around unclothed. There are 1,168,000 Jains among India's 340 million inhabitants, of which 80,000 live in Greater Bombay. Their influence is greater than their numbers would imply, however, for Jainism includes India's richest merchants among its adherents. Country-folk can never make good Jains, anyway, for they have to kill worms and even — if they are cattle-breeders — animals as well. Hence the Jain peasants are, or should be, constantly worried about their spiritual welfare.

There are many similarities between Buddha and Mahavira. Both men rebelled against the rigidity of Hinduism, both came from aristocratic families in eastern India, and both abhorred a life of self-indulgence and luxury. Like all the other religious founders in history, they both went into retreat, Mahavira when he was twenty-eight and Buddha at the age of thirty. Both of them reached the state of enlightenment beneath a tree, both believed in the blessings of a true and sincere morality and in a high standard of ethical behaviour as the minimum prerequisite and first step on the long, steep and arduous road to salvation. Both men founded monastic and lay orders.

Neither had any god, neither believed that the world had a beginning, and neither preached in Sanskrit, the ancient, classical tongue of the Vedas and Upanishads, but in the language of their native regions.

There were differences between them, too, however. For Buddha, re-birth had nothing whatever to do with the transmigration of souls. The Jains, on the other hand, place great emphasis on the soul. All things have souls. Left to itself, Nature would produce some very pure and serene souls, but the material world intrudes into everything. Only by strict asceticism can a man prevent this intrusion and evade all craving, desire and activity. Buddha set no great store by mortification of the flesh. He taught a 'middle path'. But the Jains see a decisive significance in the complete renunciation of all physical and material claims, in the true 'abandonment' of the body, and thus in self-mortification.

In common with almost all religious founders, neither Buddha nor Maha-vira left any written works behind. The teachings of both these great geniuses were only committed to writing long after their death.

The loveliest Jain shrines in India are to be found on Mount Abu in Raj-putana. They are the five celebrated Dilwara temples, two of which should really be reckoned among the wonders of the world. One of them was built by a minister and general called Vimala in A.D. 1032, and the other by two brothers, Vastupala and Tejpala, orthodox Jain merchants who decided to serve their religion by making vast financial sacrifices. Each of these temples is dedicated to one of the twenty-four Jinas, the earlier adherents of Jainism who attained true perfection. They are constructed entirely of white marble, which is really what makes them such miracles of architecture, since their wealth of stone carvings is scarcely rivalled anywhere else in the world. The well-known Indologist Ananda Coomaraswamy describes this as one of the rare instances where 'superabundance becomes beauty'.

The temples are not dead and deserted. Day by day the faithful come to pray before the twenty-four statues, bringing sacrifices (not bloody ones, naturally) such as flowers and sandalwood. The chief figure in the cult, the Jina to whom each temple is dedicated, has his sanctuary in the holy of holies, which is in semi-darkness. Apart from this the temples are completely open, like forests of pillars surmounted by a roof. Neither in Hindu nor Jain architecture is there such a thing as a real arch. Indian architecture is thus in complete contrast to our own, the whole weight of its roof-structures press-ing vertically downwards towards the ground.

If you stand among these pillars and ceilings with their boundless wealth of ornamentation, you get the impression that all the traditional rules of architectonics have been abolished. It is as though you are in some fabulous submarine world, surrounded by pearls and columns of coral and dazzled by a superabundance of beauty which has attained the same perfection as that bestowed by Heaven upon the Jinas themselves.

It is here at the pulsing heart of this almost extinct religion that one can still detect a measure of the nobility which once pervaded the conception of Jainism in ancient India.

Why do the good suffer? Why must a man who commits no sin, a man who lives righteously and never transgresses the commandments, have to undergo sickness, misfortune, death and decay? Like Job, the Christian religion wrestles everlastingly with this vast and unanswered problem. The ancient religions of India, Hinduism, Buddhism and Jainism all solved it long ago. They believe in cyclical rebirth either as a human being or as an animal. The problem of suffering thus holds no more mysteries for them. Anyone who seems to suffer without due cause must have incurred his unhappy lot in a previous life. In the same way, everyone readily accepts the fact of his having been born into a particular caste as just another facet in the destiny of his birth, for that, too, is something which was determined in a previous life. Since suffering predominates in all reincarnations, however, the Indian has only one desire: to extricate himself from the eternal cycle of rebirth. And the only way to do this is to attain perfection.

It is this 'growing out of and above oneself', this self-restraint, this escape from the eternal cycle, this cessation of rebirth, in fact, which constitutes the sole aim of Jainism. And to the Jains the only men to have travelled the road to perfection and shown others the way to the goal of ultimate peace are the twenty-four true Jinas who are worshipped in their temples. Symbols of harmony, calm, victory and gentleness, they alone stand or sit there in timeless tranquillity, their faces far withdrawn from the world, proving to the faithful that there is something above and beyond mankind's eternal round of petty cares, something higher than a preoccupation with worldly activities.

CAMBODIA

✠

ANGKOR LIES ABANDONED IN THE JUNGLE

Only a hundred years ago, the most remarkable temple and city ruins in Asia were wrested from the jungle. The man who roams through these gigantic ruins will suddenly find himself among the gods of India in an epoch long submerged.

THE year 1524 saw the birth at Lisbon of a very remarkable man. His father, the captain of a large sailing-ship, was drowned off the coast of Goa. The boy was a good-for-nothing, a rebel and a dreamer, yet he later became the greatest poet his native land ever produced. Luíz de Vaz de Camões was intoxicated with the greatness of his country's seafaring past. He was a Christian and a child of the Renaissance who revered the beauty of classical antiquity. Spiritually, he was the brother of Dante, Petrarch, Ariosto and Tasso.

Great talent is often allied with a passionate temperament. Camões fell in love with a lady of the court. He would draw his sword on the slightest provocation, especially where affairs of the heart were concerned. He was banished and, in desperation, became a soldier. He fought against Morocco with the Portuguese fleet, writing his poetry in the thick of naval battles. His right eye was put out by an arrow off Ceuta. One-eyed like Nelson, he sailed off to India in 1553. He wrote poems celebrating the prowess of contemporary Portuguese sailors. He also wrote satires, however, and was rewarded for this talent by the punishment which is every poet's passport to world-renown: exile and imprisonment. Free once more, he sailed off across the seas to write what is, after Homer's *Odyssey*, the greatest sea-epic of all time.

His caravel was dashed to pieces in the estuary of the Mekong in Cochin-China, and we can picture him swimming ashore through the warm sea, holding his most treasured possession above the waves. It was the manuscript of his great epic poem, *The Lusiads*.

King Sebastian was still a child, but he was master of a world empire, master of Portugal. It was a great moment both for the young king and for Camões when the poet presented his sovereign with *The Lusiads*. But Sebastian soon fell at the battle of Alcazar, a royal line died out, and Portugal left the stage of world history.

At night, in the pale moonlight which faintly illuminated the darkened streets of Lisbon, a slave used to go out and beg. His master, the king of all the poets in the world, was starving, and he himself, a dark-skinned descendant of the Kings of the Mekong who had been abducted from the primeval forests of Cambodia, was begging so that Camões could go on writing.

What was a fabulous feat of daring in Camões's time, the sea-voyage to Cambodia, can now be done in a mere twenty-five days, on board ships that glide along almost noiselessly over sunlit seas, past bright horizons fringed with the green of distant coconut palms.

'Five pineapples on a hill' — that was how the celebrated French novelist Paul Claudel described the most magnificent temple ruins in Asia. He was referring to the towers of the temple-city of Angkor Vat. They glow red in the setting sun and shimmer grey-green in the pale light of dawn. At night, when moonlight bathes the virgin forest, they look an unearthly shade of blue. Pierre Loti, the author of *Pêcheur d'Islande*, gazed in wonder at these ruins, and they have been visited by the kings, statesmen, poets and philosophers of every nation.

Temples, cities and shrines all reposed here for centuries, camouflaged by the luxuriant jungle and forgotten: forgotten, that is to say, until the arrival of some Jesuit Fathers in 1815; until Abel Rémusat translated old Chinese accounts of cities which had been thought extinct; until 1858, when a French explorer on his arduous trek along the valley of the upper Mekong looked through the undergrowth and saw the huge temple overgrown with lianas, miraculously slumbering like some Sleeping Beauty of the jungle, massive blocks of its stonework burst asunder by jungle trees in the eternal triumph of Nature over man's handiwork; until Henri Mouhot published the story of his voyage round the world in 1863; in fact, until it was finally realized that the ruins of Angkor had been rediscovered. Scientific explorers accoutred in frock-coats and wing-collars toiled their way slowly through the jungle. Then de la Porte brought the first sculptures back to Paris, and the Guimet Museum was thronged by top-hatted gentlemen and be-bustled ladies toying with their lorgnons. On December 15th, 1898, Paul Doumer, who was at that time Governor-General of Indo-China, founded the Far East School at Hanoi. Its aims were the study of Indo-China's history and architecture, as well as those of India, Indonesia, China and Japan.

Even in our own day, more and more temples and cities are being wrested from the jungle and their old splendour reconstructed, and the work of measurement, deciphering, translation and research is still going on. Today, Angkor is one of the wonders of the world.

'All roads in Asia lead from India,' says Ananda Coomaraswamy, the famous Indian archaeologist. India's art accompanied her religion to Ceylon, Java, Cambodia, Siam, Burma, Tibet, Turkestan, China, Korea and Japan, just as the Buddhism of China, Japan, Tibet and south-east Asia also originated in India. The ruins of Angkor Vat likewise betray Indian inspiration (although it is admittedly much older than Buddha), in the same way as the temple ruins at Borobudur in Java also portray India's vision of the world in stone.

The main tower of Angkor Vat soars 230 feet above the level of the jungle. With its three terraces and nine towers, the temple covers an area of about 48,000 square yards. The outer moat surrounding the precincts is nearly 360 feet wide, and forms a watery defence 12½ miles in circumference. Angkor Vat is a gigantic rectangular construction, a hymn in stone to gods who failed and were not strong enough to preserve their temple. A four-cornered plane surface surrounded by water, it was intended as a replica of the world and its oceans. Divinity was embodied in the king, and the mountains of the world were represented by the highest tower, which radiated the power of God to every quarter of the heavens.

But who were the builders of these prayers in stone? At the time of the Saviour's birth in Bethlehem, Cambodia was inhabited by a race called the *Khmer*. Their racial and linguistic characteristics seem to have sprung from two different worlds. The Khmer are taller, darker and slimmer than their neighbours, and their eyes are like those of the Indo-European races. By contrast, they are linguistically related not only to the peoples of Indonesia and the South Seas, but also to the Melanesians and Polynesians. But while Polynesians, Mongols, Chinese and Japanese all have smooth black hair, the Khmer's hair has a tendency to curl. They are probably a product of continuous interbreeding with the many races with whom they have come into contact. It must also be remembered that China's human avalanches have been rolling to the north and south for countless centuries, and that it was the consequent overpopulation of Indo-China which led to the daring sea-voyages of the Polynesians, who eventually reached Easter Island at the eastern end of the Pacific. Indeed, it is even possible that north-east Asia dispatched related races to the highlands of South America, to become the people whom, using Columbus's description, we still call 'Indians' today.

When, in 1296, Kublai Khan's ambassadorial secretary Khuta-Kuan paid a visit to the Khmer's capital city, Angkor Thom, he found them a remarkable people who toiled ceaselessly to lay out rice fields and build temples for their gods. The king of the Khmer had five wives, a principal wife and four others — one for each of the cardinal points of the compass. Apart from them, he had 4000 concubines at his disposal. He was virtually wading in gold and jewels. Pleasure-boats idled upon his lakes, and royal elephants swayed ponderously through his streets. Over a million people lived in Angkor Thom alone. Attached to the temples were hospitals complete with nurses and doctors.

Angkor Vat was built for King Suryavarman II between the years 1113 and 1150 by slaves and prisoners of war. As an example of architectural construction it is as impressive as the great buildings of Egypt and Greece, and as massive as the cathedrals of Europe. Thousands of slaves cut away the jungle trees and hauled the great blocks of stone into position, while artists sculpted and priests kept the evil spirits away. To get enough slaves for his purposes, the king conducted a number of wars. But wars are chancy affairs, and the temples and cities were eventually overrun by the Siamese, until all that remained of them was ruins.

The Khmer are reputed to have owned large libraries, but nothing has survived of them, and their 'immortals' are as dead as their mortals. Angkor Vat contains about 7875 feet of stone reliefs. They show us that men and women used to wear mosquito-nets (and anyone who walks round the ruins today will quickly realize how necessary this precaution was).

Between 2000 and 500 B.C. the sacred Vedic literature came into being in India.

The god Vishnu is the central figure in the Sanskrit texts of the Mahabharata and Ramayana. Siva and Brahma are two other gods who also originate in ancient Indian literature. It was here on the Mekong that the gods of these sacred Indian texts found their shrines and cities. The spirit of Buddha, who lived from 560 to 480 B.C., is associated with them, too, and we also meet the fan-shaped head of Naga, the sacred snake, everywhere in Khmer art. Eventually, all the gods found a common home in Cambodia.

It is always the same story: people like to skim the cream off every religion. Just as the Romans, whenever they had conquered a new race, put its gods into their own temples, just as Mohammed took over into Islam all the prophets from Abraham and Moses down to Christ himself, and just as the Christians adopted the pagan festival of Christmas, so the Khmer appropriated every god in the Indian pantheon.

The native inhabitants of modern Cambodia are descendants of the Khmer, but the mighty have fallen with a vengeance! Whereas their ancestors used to build for eternity on a scale which is still an object of admiration among modern archaeologists, the latter-day Khmer live in stilted huts with ladders leading to them. At night they pull these ladders up, always leaving the topmost rung hanging down in deference to the spirit which perches on it and guards the sleeping house from demons.

CHINA

CHINA'S ANCESTOR LIVED 500,000 YEARS AGO

'All the people about whom we know anything at all possess at least the germs of a civilization. Even the Peking Man (*Sinanthropus pekinensis*) manufactured implements and knew
the use of fire.'   *Kaj Birket-Smith*

IT all began with some chicken-bones. Not so very long ago, the bones
and skeletons of a large number of birds were dug up on a hill some
thirty miles south-west of Peking. The local Chinese took them for
chicken-bones, christened the small mound 'Chicken-bone Hill', and thought
no more about it. Archaeologists, examining the bones under a microscope,
established that what confronted them were in fact the fossilized bones of
birds, rodents and even of beasts of prey. Chicken-bone Hill took on a
fresh interest, and the whole surrounding district, which is known as Chou
K'ou Tien, became a favourite haunt of European archaeologists.

It is a significant fact that the European races are far more interested in
archaeology than the Oriental. Europeans want to know; Orientals want to
live. It must have been a European who took the first bite out of the apple in
Paradise, certainly not an Oriental. The European investigates things,
destroys and creates them. The Oriental simply lets them decay.

Among other things discovered beneath Chicken-bone Hill was the molar
of a man-like creature. More and more were found, and over a thousand
cases of fossilized bones were brought back to Peking, where they were
examined and sorted. Human jaw-bones and fragments of skull were identified and, when the whole splendid discovery was reviewed, it was confirmed
that the bones belonged to no less than twenty-five different individuals.

Then came the year 1929, and with it a real sensation. A complete skull
was unearthed – the skull of the so-called *Sinanthropus pekinensis*. This
gentleman is not the Adam of mankind, having an even earlier forerunner
in the two-legged ape-man of Java. Nevertheless, the Peking Man had been
lying in his hole under Chicken-bone Hill for a considerable length of time –
about 500,000 years, in fact. If he had been able to write, he would have told
us what our world looked like half a million years ago in the earliest period
of the Stone Age, what his worries were, and what he thought about. We
know for certain that he could think. The capacity of his skull was 58·8
cubic inches, slightly less than modern man's 61 cubic inches. His centre of
speech was studied, too, and it was confirmed that he could speak. What

was more, his teeth and jaws indicated that he was related to the Mongols, Eskimos, Chinese and Japanese. If that is anything to go by, then the Chinese, whom we regard as part of the Mongolian race, have been resident in northern China for aeons without number.

But amazing as these discoveries were, they were not enough to satisfy the archaeologists. They determined from traces of yellow ash that the Peking Man was already familiar with fire; 3000 bones which had been fashioned into a uniform shape by human agency proved that a small 'industrial centre' had once existed there. Thousands of quartz stones had been knapped with powerful blows of a hammer, and the remains of buffalo, deer and other forest animals indicated that the area had contained marshes, lakes and forests and been subject to a warm, damp climate. Today, the region round Peking is treeless, dry and extremely cold in winter.

Near Chicken-bone Hill and still in the same Chou K'ou Tien district, a second site of discovery was unearthed – the so-called 'Upper Cave'. The early inhabitant of this region was already an artist; 3000, 4000 or 5000 years ago, pretty girls were already wearing necklaces, as twenty-eight animal teeth found there show, and bone utensils were painted red.

There is yet another important site of discovery which sheds light on this early Stone Age civilization. This is at the Ordos Bend. The people here were even more 'up-to-date'. Traces of charcoal mark the former site of their camp-fires, and fragments of rhinoceros, hyena, antelope, cow and buffalo bones, together with egg-shells belonging to an extinct species of giant ostrich, give us an indication of what their bill of fare was like. Are we only dealing with a highly developed ape? By no means. *Homo sapiens*, man himself, left his own memorial here. It is only a single tooth, yet it is enough to illuminate the monstrous obscurity of the past.

From the early Stone Age – also called the Palaeolithic Age – onwards, i.e. between 500,000 and 2500 B.C., there lies an immeasurable span of time which we know nothing about.

What had happened? Had mankind died out? Had the Noah of a Chinese Flood taken refuge on some mountain-top?

We do not know. The next message from man comes from Yang-shao. This time – it was in the year 1921 – a whole village was discovered. We are here confronted by an advanced civilization 4000 or 5000 years old whose history of evolution remains shrouded in mystery. It is just like Mohenjo-Daro in India: not a sign of anything before it, and then all at once a completely civilized, fairly sizable population. Clay disks attest to the existence of some kind of spinning-wheel and the cultivation of fibrous plants, and earthenware vessels bear the imprint of woven cloth. There are tools made of bone and horn, sewing-needles with very fine eyes cut in them, pots with necks and handles, elegant, fragile vases with slender necks, and large urns, some depicting people, dogs and horses, and some with abstract ornamentation. The figure of a cat, only just over a tenth of an inch high, suggests that this animal was probably a household feature even in those days. It is even possible that this period, which is called the Stone-Bronze Age, possessed its own form of writing, for the earliest indications of a hieroglyphic script have been found in graves in the province of Kansu. The skeletal remains of some 120 men and women found at Kansu prove that they were members of the Mongolian race. However, we do not know whether these 4000- to 5000-year-old 'Chinese' of the Stone-Bronze age were descended from the 500,000-year-old Peking Man.

By the time the earth had revolved round the sun another thousand times or so, man was already burying his dead in graves. We have evidence of this in the graves of the Shang, also known as 'the graves of the Yin', which were only opened in very recent times. They lie in what is now Anyang in Honan Province, some 75 miles north of the Yellow River. The Shang Dynasty is the first Chinese dynasty about whose existence we have really reliable information. This imperial line was founded in 1450 B.C. and lasted until 1050 B.C. The heavens themselves were responsible for shedding the first light on this dynasty, for in the year A.D. 1079 a mighty storm ripped up the ground and disclosed the grave of a Shang emperor.

The Chinese of this region found a number of bronze vessels, and — practical as they always are — speedily sold them at the nearest market. Later, a village was built on the site, and feet trampled gaily around on the relics of past millennia. For centuries, peasants at their ploughing went on turning up animal bones and tortoise-shells covered with inscriptions.

It is an inveterate Chinese habit to regard anything which is mysterious and only semi-edible as medicine. The 4000-year-old bones and tortoise-shells were accordingly ground into powder and sold to apothecaries' shops, where they were bought by the local population and eagerly swallowed as an elixir for the prolongation of life. The human stomach can stand more than is commonly supposed, but archaeology suffers a great deal by such practices! The new medicines stayed on the market until the arrival of inquisitive white men, who quickly bought up the bones and tortoise-shells in question and dispatched them to museums all over the world. Still more 'white barbarians' arrived, and the Chinese peasantry looked on in astonishment as they bought up the boring old bones by tens of thousands.

These finds bore examples of China's oldest written characters. Such messages from 4000 years ago constitute a treasure-trove of inestimable value to the study of human history. The tortoise-shells and bones from the graves of the Shang emperors not only give clear examples of the questions which people used to put to their local 'oracle', but also provide the answers to them. There are questions asked of gods and ancestors, questions about journeys, fishing and hunting, questions about harvests, illnesses and the interpretation of dreams. And the long-preserved bone and tortoise-shell 'documents' give answers to all of them. As we read them, a picture of Chinese civilization is conjured up from the mists of the past.

Here is an example: 'Tonight it will rain; an elephant must be caught.' So there were elephants in central China in those days.

Again: 'A prayer to grandmother Yi for rain.' Evidence of ancestor-worship almost 4000 years ago.

The pictographic symbols for 'fishing' show us that the Shang people used lines, rods, nets and bait. The symbols for 'hunting' prove that they were familiar with arrow and spear. Also to be deduced from their writing symbols is the fact that horses were used to pull carts. The word 'man' was expressed by a combination of the symbols for 'strength' and 'field.' The symbols for grain show us corn, millet and rice. Mulberries were cultivated, too, and silk was manufactured here at a time when the majority of mankind was going around naked or clothed in skins, and only the civilizations of the Mediterranean and Central America were familiar with woven fabrics.

The graves of the Shang yielded articles of bronze, but the Shang people also knew how to smelt copper, tin, iron, silver and lead. Astonished scholars marvelled at the sacrificial vessels, wonderful bronze vases with animal designs, bronze mirrors and incense-burners which this extremely mature civilization produced.

But it was not only scholars who marvelled. Any common or garden visitor to northern China could go into a curio-shop and buy genuine bronze bowls of the Shang period. Nobody who lived in Peking during the last war will ever forget Mr Chuan. His splendid shop stood in a dusty side-street, where, for the sum of 50, 100, or 500 American dollars, the astonished visitor could acquire a genuine Shang bowl – a fabulously beautiful piece which had been made 1450 years before Christ proclaimed his Gospel to the world. It must be added that this era of advanced bronze-craftsmanship was also a very gory period. Thousands of people were sacrificed to the Earth-god, and their blood poured into sacrificial vases. The imperial house of Shang grew degenerate on an unvarying diet of debauchery and high living. Just as Rome had her Nero and her Heliogabalus, so the close of this great epoch saw the advent of the last of the Shang, the monstrous Chou Hsin. He was as strong as Samson and could slay wild beasts with a single blow of his fist. 'He used his oratory to refute all good counsel, and his wit to conceal his mistakes.'

The day of reckoning came. Abandoned by his warriors, Emperor Chou

Hsin could see no way out of his predicament. Putting on his most gorgeous robes and bedecking himself with jewels, he set fire to his palace and perished in a sea of flames. As for the concubines who had been his companions in debauchery, they were taken over by the victorious invaders.

They smiled.

For they were weaker and yet wiser than their late master the Emperor.

CONFUCIUS AND LAO-TSE

'If you do not know life, how shall you know death?' Confucius
'Never be the first in the world.' Lao-tse

EVERY age believes that it has reached the acme of all wisdom. Men have always referred to 'our progressive age', always despised the past, never been envious of the future. But if anyone wished, after reviewing all the hundreds and thousands of years of past history, to award one particular epoch a prize for the greatest intellectual achievement, he would, in my opinion, have to select the sixth and fifth centuries B.C. For the period between 600 and 400 years before the birth of Christ saw a dazzling outburst of religious, philosophical and literary activity in almost every quarter of the world.

Humanity therefore won its 'Oscar' for moral teaching roughly 2500 years ago. At about this time, Buddha was teaching in India and Zarathustra in Persia. In Palestine, Jeremiah, Ezekiel and Isaiah were preaching the coming of the Messiah, and the Old Testament was taking shape. In Greece, democracy was lifted from its cradle by Solon and Cleisthenes, and between 480 and 430 B.C. Athens enjoyed her golden age of power and culture. These centuries also witnessed the birth of China's two most important philosophers: Lao-tse and Confucius.

Greece, Judaea, Persia, India and China still had very few mutual connections at this time, and it must almost be regarded as an astrological miracle that mankind's greatest thoughts should have been evolved with such simultaneity among such different races and in such different corners of the world.

China's greatest philosopher, Confucius — in Chinese, K'ung-tszu — was born in 551 B.C. in what is today Shantung Province. We know very little about his childhood, except that he was a serious, thoughtful boy and that when his father died he had to work after school hours in order to support his mother. Confucius having become the important moral teacher he is, we can easily understand why the Chinese are in doubt as to whether he ever had an earthly father! As a young boy he quickly mastered the arts of bowmanship and music. He married when he was nineteen and got divorced at the age of twenty-three, for a moral philosopher should remain celibate, as Socrates' marriage to Xanthippe bears testimony. Confucius soon gained fame as a moral teacher, mainly because he did not launch attacks on other philosophers or waste any time in refuting their arguments. He was strict with his disciples, yet he loved them dearly. When one of them, Yen Hwui, died, he wept, and said: 'He loved to learn. I never yet had a pupil who learned as willingly as he. His time was short, and there is not another like him.' Evidently Yen Hwui must have been a sort of St John to his master.

Confucius lived in what we call the 'feudal period' of China. It was a time when feudal lords ruled in walled towns surrounded by arable land and hunting-reserves. These feudal towns were to be found in modern Honan and in parts of Shansi, Shensi and Shantung. Ch'i and Ch'in eventually became the most important of these city-States, and Ch'in finally gained mastery over all its neighbours, to found the united empire from which China probably derives its name. It may be noted that the Chinese are the only people in the world who do not know 'the Kingdom of the Centre' as 'China'.

In Confucius' day, however, the feudal States had not yet been united, and the master spent his time roaming from one to another of them. He recognized the universally low standard of governmental administration which prevailed, became incensed by it, and suggested methods of improving it. One or two princes gave him an opportunity of holding actual office in their administrations, but it was probably never long before Confucius grew tired of losing his temper with officials and princes. Perhaps, too, he was ill at ease in an environment which continually offended against his standards of wisdom and integrity.

'When I was fifteen,' he said, 'my mind was occupied with learning. When I was thirty I held firm views. At forty I was free from doubts. At fifty I knew the laws of heaven. At sixty my ear was an obedient recipient of truths. At seventy I could apprehend whatsoever my heart desired without abandoning the path of righteousness.' Confucius died at the age of seventy-two. There came a morning when one of his disciples heard him crooning sadly: 'The great mountain must crumble, the strong beam must break, the wise man must wither away like a flower.' Then another disciple hurried up, and Confucius called out: 'No intelligent ruler arises. No one in the whole land will make me his counsellor. It is time for me to die.' So saying, he lay down, and after seven days gave up the ghost. But Tze Kung, the disciple who had loved his master best, sat by the great teacher's grave for another three years, mourning for him in solitude.

What exactly did this titan of practical morality teach? He left behind five volumes, known in China as the five classics. It is probable that Confucius was not himself the author of these writings, but merely passed on the traditional wisdom of the past. He dedicated himself to the publication of the ancient classical texts which went on influencing the thought and culture of China until the twentieth century. While he undoubtedly left the imprint of his own mind upon the age-old doctrines which he edited and passed on, it was solely in an effort to gain acceptance not for his own ideas but for the knowledge and morality of the ancients.

Mesopotamia, Judaea, Arabia and India are the regions which gave birth to the great religions of mankind. China has always been the land of the great philosophers, the land of the practical moral teachers. The Chinese have never worried about God, or a world to come, or theology, but they love life, and life as it really is. They recognized what was and what had to be: rich and poor, good and evil, generals and kings, the bright rainbow and the pale moon. They love arched bridges and their reflection in pools, lotus-blossoms and tea, silk and incense, dainty women and good food, grasshoppers in cages and sails in the evening breeze. China's novelists write about the little things of everyday life: good fellowship, holiday feasts, the tittering of young girls, dark clouds over the moon, wild duck making for the water, family festivals, marriage, childbed, dutiful sons and obedient daughters-in-law — the whole enthralling beauty of life in its hours of joy and tragedy. But for immortality, for a life after death, for thoughts that do not spring from the good earth, for what goes on in heaven or what lies beneath the ground, the Chinese simply have neither time nor inclination. That was why Confucius never constructed a philosophical system, but founded a school of clear thinking. That was why he never conducted theological discourses, but concentrated his thoughts upon the creation of rules for individual and governmental conduct. That was why he never tried to establish a theocracy, but did his best to strengthen and improve the strict and aristocratic government of his day. When someone questioned him about the admittedly important problem of death, he answered: 'If you do not know life, how shall you know death?'

The whole of Confucius' teachings may perhaps best be summed up in the following sentences: 'The ancients, wishing to set an example of supreme virtue in the land, first put their country in order. In putting their country in order, they worked on themselves. In working on themselves, they purified their hearts. In purifying their hearts, they endeavoured to be sincere in their thoughts. In being sincere in their thoughts, they extended their knowledge. In extending their knowledge, they explored matters. When these matters had been explored, their knowledge became comprehensive. When their knowledge was comprehensive, their thoughts became sincere. When their thoughts were sincere, they themselves became decorous. When they themselves were decorous, their families became orderly. When their families were orderly, their country became well governed. And when their country was well governed, the whole world lived in peace and contentment.'

Wisdom, therefore, like charity, should begin at home. Confucius is at

Girls of the Khmer race, whose ancestors built the cities and temples of Angkor

Neck of a burial-urn with human features, from the Stone-Bronze age civilization of Yang Shao. It is 4,000 to 5,000 years old. The eyes betray a distinct Mongoloid slant

China's earliest written characters. Read from left to right, they signify: son, grandson, cockerel, cart, elephant; and, on the extreme right, the modern equivalent of the same thing

Buddhist saint in glazed clay from the T'ang Dynasty (A.D. 618–906)

The Great Wall of China

K'ung Fu-Tze (551–479 B.C.), teacher, philosopher, statesman, sociologist and upholder of ancient morality

Clay statuette of the T'ang period (*c.* A.D. 600–900). This Taoist goddess was found in a grave

The Summer Palace of the Chinese Emperors outside the walled city of Peking

Kublai Khan (A.D. 1216–1294), a grandson of Jenghiz Khan

Jenghiz Khan (A.D. 1162–1227), whose dominions stretched from Korea to Hungary

ane provided himself with this durable
eum (known as Gur-i-Mur) during his
. It is in Samarcand, which is now in
he Soviet Republic of Uzbekhistan

Tamerlane (A.D. 1336—1405)

The weeping rakan. This remarkably lifelike sculpture is preserved in the Horyuji, the celebrated monastery which is reputed to be Japan's oldest wooden building. It stands in the sacred temple grove at Nara

one with all the geniuses of this world in holding that a man should first set his own soul in order before he begins to organize the outside world. Confucius was really a very shrewd man, for it was his implicit belief that decent behaviour on the part of the individual was the key to an orderly world and a peaceful life. But he went far beyond this demand on the individual He was possibly the greatest teacher of sociology the world has ever known. He strove to regulate the relationship of men to each other, just as he did that of citizens to their government. When he was asked: 'Is there any one word which can serve as a practical rule throughout life?' he answered: 'Reciprocity', meaning by that the interdependence of all things, the interdependence of all actions, and the interdependence of all doctrines and people. He meant forgiveness. He meant an amicable relationship between all men on earth. As Dostoievski put it: 'Each is responsible for the other.'

Above all else, Confucius loathed obscure allusion and muddled thinking. He regarded indecision as the mother of national catastrophe. 'Act before you speak, and then speak as you have acted.' It was a safe policy, at all events. 'The "superior" man so acts that his actions blaze a common trail for all generations. He so conducts himself that his conduct becomes a law for all generations. He so speaks that his words are a valid precept for all generations.' Confucius was probably the most persuasive advocate of the golden rule: 'Do unto others as you would be done by.' But he went even farther, for when someone asked him: 'What do you say to the theory that evil should be repaid with good?' he replied: 'In that case, with what could one repay good? Repay evil with justice, and good with good.'

Confucius' teachings constitute a vast kaleidoscope of extremely practical instructions. If we were to follow them, we might not have a god or a religion, it is true, but we should at least have a tolerable life here on earth. Confucius has never been regarded by the Chinese either as a god or as a religious founder. All that is to be found in his temples is the tablet bearing his name and the smaller tablets bearing his teachings. It was only several centuries after his death that his rules of conduct became the universal moral code of aristocratic Chinese society. 'Only two sorts of people can never change,' he asserted, 'the very wise and the very foolish.' Confucius was one of the very wise, and he did not suffer fools gladly.

His contemporary Lao-tse was also a very wise man, but he loved simple folk. Even less is known about Lao-tse than about Confucius. He was probably a real person, although even that is open to question. However, it is hard to imagine how his name and his teachings could have sprung from nothing. There is a story that Confucius once met Lao-tse and spoke with him. Whether it is apocryphal or not, one thing is certain: two such dissimilar natures would never have found each other congenial company. Confucius belongs to the city, Lao-tse to the country.

Lao-tse merely means 'old master' in Chinese, but the philosopher's actual family name is said to have been Li, or 'Plum'. His claim to literary fame rests in a collection of disjointed pieces of information called *Tao-te-king* or (roughly) 'Book of the Way and of Virtue'. Confucius attempted to organize the mutual relationships of humanity. Lao-tse's teaching was one of the most important and certainly the most impudent ever to be devised. He did not make things as easy for himself as Confucius, for it was precisely towards the less well intellectually endowed that his teachings were directed; and very comforting and effective they are, too. 'The way' means in essence 'the way to think', or rather, 'the way not to think'. Thinking, we are told, is only good for quarrels, while poverty of thought secures peace. We should therefore live modestly, always efface ourselves, love the land, be content with the tranquil contemplation of Nature, and do what Voltaire says is the wisest thing left for man to do: till our fields. Knowledge has nothing to do with wisdom, and the 'intellectual' is as far removed from happiness and wisdom as the moon is from the earth. To have a philosopher in charge of the State would be a horror to end all horrors. Lao-tse's ideal ruler is a kindly, straightforward man. The more people think, build, discover and achieve, the nearer catastrophe looms. (Lao-tse may indeed have a point there. Look at the latest product of human knowledge and ingenuity: the planned exploitation of the atom.) Like Rousseau, Lao-tse called for a return to Nature. He is much nearer the true spirit of the Chinese people than Confucius, and his doctrines were probably very, very ancient. They sprang from China's earliest conviction, which was that a man is only free for as long as he is absolutely uncomplicated, and that a good government is one which does nothing. 'Never be the first in the world,' taught Lao-tse, and 'the wisest thing in life is never to get oneself involved in anything'. Chwang-tsze, his greatest adherent and a brilliant and vivid stylist, had assessed Lao-tse's teachings quite correctly when he summed them up: 'To follow the stream as a drop of water does, and not conduct oneself arbitrarily therein.'

It is this sort of attitude to life, with its patience, long-suffering, resignation and self-subordination, its laissez-faire and negative strength, which has determined the rhythm of life throughout the civilizations of the Far East. Lao-tse's genius lies in his having devised the most successful of all the philosophies of self-preservation. It is the philosophy of hiding oneself, of avoiding violence and creeping beneath the covers, of shunning argument and therefore never coming to harm. It is the theory of strength through ignorance and of stupidity as the surest form of defence against the tyrants of this world. Like Solomon, Lao-tse recognized the futility of all aspiration, the advantages of the simple, the strength of the weak, and the genius of the man who makes his life a game of blind-man's-buff. Anyone in China's history who became a great statesman — and perhaps even a good and just one — was almost certainly a follower of Confucius. But the ruler who fled the world, plucked apples from the trees as if he were in the Garden of Eden, and stayed alive, belonged to the school of Lao-tse.

'Only because everyone beneath the heavens recognizes beauty as beauty is there such a thing as ugliness.' 'He rules wisely who makes hearts light, fills bellies, destroys intelligence, braces himself and endeavours to protect his people from knowledge and keep them free from desire.' 'The force of words is soon expended. It is far better to keep what is in one's heart to oneself.' 'In ancient times,' Lao-tse tells us, 'Nature made men straight-forward and peaceable, and the whole world was happy. But then man acquired knowledge, and life became complicated. Mankind made dis-coveries and lost its innocence. Mankind moved from the fields into the towns and began to write books. Then misery was born, and tears welled in the eyes of philosophers. The wise man will avoid towns and the corrupt-ing and enervating toils of laws and civilization. He will hide himself in the lap of Nature, far from towns and from books, from spiteful officials and unsuccessful social reformers. The secret of enduring happiness lies in obey-ing Nature and wandering simply along the quiet ways of the earth.'

And is there any better dictum than this? 'All things in Nature do their work quietly; they become nothing and they possess nothing. They fulfil their purpose and crave nothing. All things accomplish their ends; then we see them recede again. When they have reached their prime, they return to their source. This withdrawal is peace and the fulfilment of destiny. This ebb and flow is an eternal law. To know that law is wisdom.'

THE EIGHTH WONDER OF THE WORLD

'If a son be born to you, beware and do not take him up; if a daughter be born to you, feed her and rear her; she need not mark how corpses and bones lie heaped together at the foot of the Wall.'   *Shui-chiang-ch'u*, Chapter 3

I T is the largest thing man has ever built, and a gigantic monument to human will-power. Over 2000 years old, its lonely grandeur makes mock of the whole of modern building technique. The Chinese call it Wan Li Ch'ang Ch'eng, or 'wall of the ten thousand li', a li being about 550 yards. Does this mean that the Great Wall of China is over 3000 miles long?

We do not know, just as we do not really know very much about China in general. It takes longer than the 50, 60, or 70 years of a human lifetime to understand this country with its 600 million inhabitants and 5000 years of history. We can only say that the largest nation in the world built the largest wall in the world, for the dimensions of this stone serpent are so staggeringly vast that no explorer, cartographer, traveller, or human criterion of measurement has yet proved equal to the task of assessing them.

The Wall itself is perhaps 'only' about 1500 miles long, but the Chinese built branch-walls off it on a scale which could enclose countries the size of Belgium — double and triple bands of masonry which would, if laid end to end, reach all the way across the Atlantic from England to America. The Wall runs along the whole of China's northern frontier, separating agricultural land from steppe, China from Mongolia, the Chinese from the Mongols, peasants from nomads.

Projecting from the Wall are 40,000 towers. These towers were there in the first place, and were only later linked by the Wall, which was originally an earthwork of immense length. Today it is built of brick.

I have wandered along the Wall myself. One can walk westwards along it for days, weeks and months, yet the farther one goes the more incomprehensible the whole edifice seems to become. When it meets mountains it traverses them at their highest point, invariably winding its way along the loftiest ridges. It towers steeply into the sky and then falls precipitously from the dizzy heights into the depths beneath. The scenery is one of unending loneliness, with barren brown mountains and deserted steppes for ever lashed and stung by the wind.

The Wall was a huge defensive work so vast that whole regiments could be marched along it and carts could pass one another in comfort — wherever it was not too steep, of course. It was furnished with accommodation for military units, forts, signal stations, granaries for the commissariat, loopholes, shelters and dungeons.

We were recently informed in a press announcement that the Chinese government was permitting its citizens to dismantle the Wall and use its bricks to build houses. This cultural loss is to be regretted, of course, but the Wall merely laughs at such stupidity. People have been 'dismantling' it for 2000 years. For 2000 years they have been purloining its stones and masonry, with about as little effect as a bird might have on the Himalayas by sharpening its beak on them.

The Wall is a genuinely Chinese construction. No other race could have summoned up the unimaginable diligence and energy which the assembling of such an avalanche of stone must have required. The Chinese loves to shut himself up. Walls surround his house, and walls surround his towns. If the Great Wall and all the town-walls in north China were laid end to end, they would encircle the Equator.

In 214 B.C., when the building of the Wall began, the peoples of the distant Mediterranean recognized seven wonders of the world. These were:

(1) The 'Hanging Gardens of Babylon', which towered 430 feet into the air in distant welcome of the approaching traveller. Bold arches supported terraces on which flowers grew, pools gleamed in the sun, and trees thrust upward into the blue of the sky, while climbing plants clothed the whole structure in their tendrils. Pumps worked day and night to water this garden in the sky, which was built by the King of Assyria as a love-nest for Shammuramat, the queen whom the Greeks called Semiramis.

(2) King Khufu's pyramid at Gizeh, the only one of the seven wonders of the ancient world still standing today.

(3) The Temple of Diana at Ephesus, which was started in 772 B.C. and took thousands of people 200 years to erect. On the night Alexander the Great was born, a man called Herostratus set fire to it. His motive: a desire for everlasting fame.

(4) The Jupiter Olympus by Pheidias, a statue in gold and ivory which he completed at Elis in 435 B.C. It was a work of such perfection and beauty that it was thought that nothing would ever surpass it. Chiselled on its plinth were the words: 'Pheidias the Athenian made me.'

(5) The tomb of King Mausolus (from which the word 'mausoleum' was coined), built by his wife at Halicarnassus in Caria in 354 B.C. Thirty-six Ionic pillars enclosed this fabulous construction. Mausolus was never actually laid in his tomb, however. His loving widow shook her husband's ashes into a draught of rare wine and drained the appalling concoction to the dregs. It was her way of ensuring that he was 'buried' in her!

(6) The lighthouse at Pharos, whose beam was visible nearly a hundred

miles out to sea. The tower was completed in 283 B.C., and a beacon burned continuously on its topmost platform for no less than 1500 years.

(7) The Colossus of Rhodes, a gigantic ancestor of New York's Statue of Liberty, and big enough for a large sailing-ship to pass between its legs. It was completed in 280 B.C., after twelve long years of work. The huge metal casting was so large that the statue's thumb was too big for a man's arms to encircle. Glass lenses suspended from the giant's neck formed an early kind of telescope which enabled the viewer to look twenty-five miles out to sea.

These, then, were the seven wonders of the ancient world. The Great Wall of China, the largest wonder of the world, was not reckoned among them. China was not only too far away, but it was also — something which we find difficult to grasp nowadays — regarded at that time simply as a traveller's tale (if and when any information about China ever reached the Mediterranean at all).

In 218 B.C., one-eyed Hannibal's elephants lumbered their laborious way across the Alps. The North African Carthaginians were marching on Rome during the second Punic campaign against Italy. It was at that time, when the ancient world was approaching the close of its greatest age of building, that there arose in the mind of a half-crazy genius the idea of building the Great Wall. The man who conceived this vast project was Ch'in Shih-huang-ti, the first emperor of the Ch'in Dynasty. He intended that his dynasty should last for ever, that all emperors after him should be entitled 'the second', 'the third' and so on, that his empire should endure for all time, and that work on the Wall should never cease. He was a man with a very hooked nose, small eyes set close together, a body like that of a bird of prey, and a voice like a jackal's. He decided that the whole of Chinese history prior to him and the memory of all the Chinese States which had fought him for supremacy should be erased.

Bamboo archives and scientific records crackled and blazed. Confucius' Book of Songs went up in smoke. The words of intellectuals and the logical arguments of disputing States burned merrily. The spirit of tradition was to be done away with once and for all.

When scholars protested to Emperor Shih-huang-ti about this wholesale destruction of the past, he had them 'thrown into the pit' and shut them up by stoning them. Other carping critics and malcontents followed them, and a crop of plump melons grew over their place of summary burial.

Ch'in Shih-huang-ti was no believer in half measures. He had the great earthwork which later became the Great Wall thrown up as a defence against the Mongols or nomadic Huns (in those days they were popularly called 'the demons') who represented a continual threat to China's northern frontier. Hundreds of thousands of people were sent off to work in the barren mountains. They included soldiers, prisoners of war, criminals, dignitaries convicted of bribery, scholars who had not surrendered 'black-listed' books for burning and members of the unhappy intelligentsia and the only too happy bureaucracy. Fortresses and watch-towers sprang up like mushrooms on the craggy heights and garrisons were established in the valleys. In winter, winds from Siberia stung the swarming army of labourers without respite, while in summer a scorchingly hot breeze filled the luckless men's eyes and ears with fine dust. The Wall was the birth-place of many yearning poems, homesick letters and melancholy songs. The sad and heavy-hearted chant of men plodding along on horseback in the puddles beneath the Great Wall rang plaintively out over the desolate countryside.

No words can convey how much blood, tears and suffering was walled up in this Calvary in stone. Yet even this was not enough for the first ruler of the world. To reinforce his sovereignty, he concentrated all the rich and powerful men in the country at his capital Hsien Yang, not far from modern Hsianfu, where he could keep a sharp eye on them and at the same time use their presence to lend his capital city a certain glamour. He divided his empire into forty-one provinces, established a new system of weights and measures, standardized the method of writing, and installed canals and a vast network of roads. His armies overran all the countries as far as Canton, and his influence extended into what is now Tonking in French Indo-China. He was perhaps the most powerful emperor in world history.

The Emperor had several palaces built in the vicinity of his capital Hsien Yang, and even today there is a spot, just over three miles north-west of the city, where an earth wall with embrasures for gates is still discernible. His summer residence stood in an imperial park known as 'His Majesty's Forest'; 700,000 prisoners helped to construct the 'Ah Fang Palace', as it is called, and the Emperor had no less than 170 other palaces built within a radius of 60 miles. To furnish them he appropriated works of art, precious stones and rare woods from all the countries he had conquered — not to mention the loveliest women in the contemporary Chinese world.

The Emperor's main palace is said to have contained so many rooms that it would have taken him 36 years to go round them all, living in a different one each day. This brings us to the heart of the tyrant's secret: like every other Asian dictator, he suffered from persecution mania. People got to know his weakness and exploited it by warning him never to sleep in the same room for two nights in succession. So he changed his bedroom each and every night, and a mute procession of eunuchs and ladies of the harem bearing cushions and silken sheets wound like a nightmarish frieze along the inter-minable corridors of his palace.

Ch'in Shih-huang-ti was obsessed by an indomitable will to work. He travelled backwards and forwards across his dominions, supervising building projects and governmental administration. Whenever anyone made a joke about him, the Emperor was sure to appear at his elbow like an evil Jack-in-the-box — which was the signal for a pit to be dug where the mockery could be appropriately buried. Anyone who disobeyed him was instantly put to death.

The Emperor himself, on the other hand, intended to live for ever, and the magicians who were the chemists of those days worked night and day to manufacture 'elixirs of life'. When the Emperor heard that there were geni on the islands of P'eng Lai (probably Japan) who tended the 'Herb of Life', he sent 3000 youths and women across the sea to gather some of it. It was said that all the animals there were snow-white, and that the palaces and gates were of gold and silver. The inhabitants were a fortunate race, it seemed. However, contrary winds prevented this 'Children's Crusade of the 3rd century B.C.' from landing, and the Emperor had to die after all, which he did in the year 210 B.C.

'But he *can't* be dead!' whispered the palace eunuchs and ministers. Accordingly, they installed the lifeless Emperor in his sedan-chair and bore him through the countryside, to give wordless audiences from behind a curtain and live on after his death. His corpse eventually began to give off an unpleasant smell, and huge barrels of salt fish were placed near the Emperor's sedan-chair so that the smell of fish would cancel out 'the imperial odour'. Chinese history owes its splendour to a close blend of wit, poetry and grandeur. Finally — after nine months — even the fish admitted defeat, and the Emperor had to be buried.

He was interred beneath the hill called Li, 'mountain of the black horses'. His last resting-place, on which he had been working since the beginning of his reign, was quite as splendid as his palaces, so he could not have been quite as confident as all that of the efficacy of his magicians' elixir of life. Hundreds of thousands of labourers worked on this tomb. The Emperor had its interior flooring encased in bronze and furnished it with splendid works of art, models of his palaces and administrative buildings, gold, silver, jewels, and, finally, his sarcophagus. Rivers and seas of quicksilver poured noiselessly into the depths of the tomb, driven by machines, while automatic cross-bows were installed to ensure that anyone who desecrated the place met with certain death. The vaults were lit by artificial torches which were intended to keep the darkness away for a long time to come. All the women of the Emperor's palace who were unlucky enough never to have borne any sons were buried alive with their dead lord. As for the artisans who knew all the tomb's secrets, their fate was quickly sealed. Just as they were making their way up into the light of day, their tasks completed, a trap-door cut them off from the land of the living for all eternity. Finally, the whole magnificent edifice was planted with trees and flowers. The Emperor slept ... but the Wall lived on. Like every fortification, it was only a bastion against attack when it was manned by troops of high morale. As soon as the spirit of resistance grew feeble, the Wall lost its point. And indeed, during most periods in the past 2000 years, it proved the most useless piece of building in human history.

To wander along the Wall, with Mongolia on your right and China on your left, is to tempt yourself to dream long dreams about China's vast sea of history. Soon after the first emperor's death, all his palaces vanished from the face of the earth in the smoke and flames of revolution.

Then came the flourishing age of the Han emperors, who reigned from 206 B.C. until A.D. 220 and founded their new metropolis Ch'ang An, 'the city of the long peace', near the ruins of Hsien Yang. This dynasty produced some really great rulers, like Emperor Wen, 'the Cultured', and his son Ching, 'the Radiant'. 'The Cultured' was a very thrifty man who wore nothing but simple black silk robes. He was ashamed of the great fortune which he had inherited from his father.

Emperor Wen did not build any palaces or summer residences. The people of the time were so rich and contented that the Chinese still regard 'sons of Han' as an expression for men blessed with good fortune. Another of these Han emperors was Wu Ti, or 'the warlike'. Between the years 141 and 86 B.C., he transformed China into a great power in the Far East. He was also a brilliant diplomat, and tried to form an East–West alliance against the Huns, or Hsiung Nu. To this end, he dispatched a certain Chang Ch'ien on a journey across half the world to Bactria and Sogdiana. The news of this journey reached Rome, where it aroused much amazement and discussion about 'Serica', or the 'Land of Silk', as China was called. Silk used to travel along the interminable caravan routes to Rome and Greece, and we find Ptolemy referring to the silk-capital, or 'metropolis of Sera'. Peaches and apricots, then known as 'Chinese fruits', also reached Europe in those days.

The Wall creeps endlessly over mountain ranges and through deserts, much as China's history went on creeping through the succeeding centuries. We can still hear the wild battle-cries of the Tartars as they scrambled over the Wall between the years A.D. 200 and 400, and see how the weak dynasties of the time had to give ground before them. Again, between 618 and 906, we can see the T'ang emperors on the Chinese throne in an era of the greatest culture — if also of luxury, frivolity and dalliance. This was the great age of Chinese poetry.

China had reached her cultural zenith. It was the most dazzling period the world had ever known. Any review of the literary achievements of this age must include a large annotated edition of Confucius' works, 12,300 major poets, 48,900 poems, and an imperial library of 54,000 volumes. Buddhist monks arrived from India, missionaries from Persia, Nestorian Christians from central Asia. The Emperor — T'ai Tsung — attracted all the religions and sciences of the world to his court, while personally remaining a straightforward Confucian. This was the time of China's most brilliant poet, Li T'ai-po. It was the time of the ferocious Empress Wu Hu, who chopped off the arms and legs of one of her rivals and turned her into 'human pork'. It was the time of Yang Kuei-fei, the emperor's mistress who eventually had herself strangled of her own free will by a eunuch, and even today plays her doomed role in the great Chinese dramas. It was a time when the dead were buried in beds full of pearls, when statuettes were carved out of rubies and bowls out of jade, when the elaborate masterpieces of a refined culinary art were served upon tables inlaid with green precious stones. It was a time when thousands of workers sat before humming bobbins in silk factories. It was the zenith of China's sculpture and one of her golden ages of painting.

Then came further centuries of chaos, poverty and disunion, followed by the important three hundred years of Sung rule, which saw a renascence of literature, art and Confucianism, and produced wonderful paintings and porcelain.

New conquerors arrived, ushering in the age of the Mongols. Jenghiz Khan raced westwards and Kublai Khan east. The Great Wall once again proved no obstacle, and Kublai sat proudly on the Dragon Throne at Peking. Marco Polo set out from Venice, roamed through the whole of Asia, and paid homage to the Mongol emperor.

Fresh armies of labourers were sent to the Great Wall, hundreds upon hundreds of thousands of them. The Ming emperors (1368-1644) were now on the throne. They built themselves magnificent tombs ornamented with massive stone animals at Nanking, not far from Peking — a wise precaution, for they too were destined to go the way of all flesh.

Out of the northern forests, or what is now Manchuria, came other ambitious princes, who fought their way slowly down to Peking. They were Tunguses, a race of foreign overlords who abandoned their native forests for the silken cushions of the south, where they ultimately became quite at home.

But the element which survived all these changes was the grace and charm of the dainty women of China. Each dynasty succumbed to them in turn, and the rugged princes from the Manchurian north were no exception. They grew more and more Chinese in their Chinese sweethearts' embraces. The people of China amiably adopted the Tunguses' pigtail, and the Tunguses looked on in wonder. Under the Manchus, who reigned from 1644 to 1912, Peking became what is probably the most beautiful city in the world. And at this very moment, while the north wind still gnaws at the stones of the eternal Wall, the last descendant of the Manchus, Emperor Pu Yi, is sitting in a gaol at Vladivostock, unable to comprehend how this fabulous tradition could ever have perished.

And it really does seem incomprehensible.

LI T'AI-PO IS ONLY IMMORTAL WHEN HE IS DRUNK

'Your Majesty, this genius unfortunately has one failing: he drinks.' Ho Chih-chang

THE darkness of the early Middle Ages still hung over Europe. In Arabia, the prophet Mohammed was beginning to propagate his doctrines.

Meanwhile, China stood on the threshold of her most flourishing period, the T'ang Dynasty. Emperor T'ai Tsung (627-650), Empress Wu Hu (684-704) and Emperor Hsüan Tsung (713-755) — these are the great and resounding names which dominate the three golden centuries of the T'ang period. The fertile valleys of the Yellow River and the Yangtze glowed under the pale green mantle of their rice-fields. Peasants ploughed their way contentedly between the waters of sparkling canals and gleaming lakes. Ch'ang An, the capital, which is now the city of Hsianfu in Shensi Province, was the wonder of its day. Apart from the main palace with its nine gates, a further thirty-six palaces towered above the city, pillared with gold, and the villas of the various princes surpassed one another in splendour. The streets swarmed with people, with prosperous men on horseback and mandarins in coaches drawn by black oxen. Lovely girls, their faces pale as the moon, danced in the many places of entertainment. The life of China was permeated by the spirit of Buddha, Confucius and Lao-tse. Ch'ang An was a cosmopolitan city which attracted within its walls Syrians, Arabs, Persians, Tartars, Tibetans, Koreans, Japanese and Tonkinese. Calligraphy, mathematics and music were taught there. The shelves of the imperial library held over 200,000 volumes, and the city could boast drama schools, sculptors, painters and musicians. Of the 3000 palace maidens, Yang Kuei-fei outshone all the rest in beauty.

Poetry held first place among the arts during the T'ang period. Everyone who was 'anyone' in those days was a poet. This is no exaggeration, either, for the 'Anthology of the T'ang Dynasty' comprises 900 books and contains more than 48,900 poems by over 2300 poets. Furthermore, the fact that the collection was not assembled until the 18th century makes it certain that it only contained such works as had not been devoured by the ravages of time. It is almost impossible to grasp what a prolific and enchanted forest of poetry sprang up in the fertile soil of the T'ang period.

In view of the foregoing, we can imagine what it meant when the Chinese unanimously declared that of all this vast host of immortals Li T'ai-po was the greatest and most important. To them, he was not only the greatest poet of the T'ang period, but the greatest poet of all time. One Chinese wrote of him: 'Li Po is T'ai, the titanic peak which soars above ten thousand mountains and hills. He is the sun in whose light millions of stars lose their flickering brightness.'

Perhaps Li T'ai-po happened to live just when things were ideal for a poet. He witnessed an age of peace and general prosperity, a great period of cultural isolationism. He encountered hospitality and an understanding for literature. He heard tales of distant wars, saw the court intrigues of his day, and finally experienced national catastrophe, revolution, Tartar invasion and the fall of Emperor Hsüan Tsung — a drama of unimaginable grandeur.

On the night of Li T'ai-po's birth (the year is traditionally 701), his mother saw the planet Venus in a dream. Since the Chinese call Venus 'the great white star', or in their own tongue, 'T'ai Po Hsing', and Li was the poet's family name, he was called Li 'great white', Li T'ai-po.

Li T'ai-po could read by the time he was six. At the age of ten he had studied the books of Confucius and knew all the classical texts by heart. It was at this early age that he started to write poetry. Before long he withdrew into solitude. It should never be forgotten that all the greatest geniuses in history have at one time or another spent a period of seclusion in the wilderness, the mountains, or prison. Li T'ai-po chose as his retreat the mountains of northern Szechwan, where he dwelt with a hermit who collected rare birds and animals about him, much as St Jerome did. When the local magistrate invited the two unusual companions to visit him, they calmly declined. Li T'ai-po had learned at an early age how to say 'no' and despise the great of this world.

At the age of twenty he wandered down the Yangtze. He married the daughter of a retired government official, and then went on to Shantung. 'I am thirty years old', he wrote to a friend, 'and am tirelessly writing poetry, while carriages and horses pass my hut.' His first wife took their children and left him — not an uncommon experience for a poet! Far from dismayed, Li T'ai-po found a way of life much more to his taste: he settled down in a bamboo grove with five other kindred spirits who were also poets. 'The Six Idlers of the Bamboo Grove' drank liberally and scribbled verses to their heart's content.

China's greatest poet was also her greatest exponent of the art of living. He drank without cease, travelled and roamed about a great deal, and loved beautiful women. One of his aristocratic patrons built him a wine-tasting room. Li T'ai-po used to make pleasure-trips with this gentleman, whose name was Tung Tsa-chiu, and never forgot to take a few attractive singing-girls along.

The poet's thirty-seventh year saw him back in Shantung once more. It was there that he encountered his greatest rival and China's second immortal poet, Tu Fu. Like two comets which roam the Universe and only come into contact every few million years, the two men were irresistibly drawn to each other. They became great friends and went on exchanging poems until the end of their lives. They lived in the same house, slept beneath the same coverlet, and went about hand in hand like brothers.

Li T'ai-po used to stand in drunken reverie on old arched bridges. He wandered dreaming among the ruins of ancient palaces and steeped his eyes in the things of long ago. He sat by lakes and admired the lotus-blossoms. Filled with a yearning to embrace the whole world, he strode along up hill and down dale, spurred on by wine. At last, in the year 742, he stood before the gates of Ch'ang An, the capital. Ho Chih-chang, a guest of the Emperor, was enchanted by Li T'ai-po and, quickly grasping the poet's need for wine, traded a piece of golden jewellery for a barrel of wine for him. He commended the poet to the Emperor with the words: 'I have in my house the greatest poet who ever lived. Your Majesty, this genius unfortunately has one failing which can scarcely be overlooked. He drinks, and sometimes he drinks too much. But his verses are magnificent. Sire, judge for yourself!'

'Bring him here,' said the Emperor, after quickly scanning a few of his poems. So Li T'ai-po declaimed his verses before the Son of Heaven in the Hall of the Golden Bells. The Emperor was an unemotional character, but even he was intoxicated by what he heard. A banquet was spread in Li T'ai-po's honour on the Table of the Seven Jewels. The poet was granted a chair at the Han Lin Academy, where he had nothing to do save write poetry — when he had a mind to. He dined with princes and ladies of the court. He made solitary excursions to the taverns of the city, got drunk to his heart's content, and immortalized his boon companions in verse.

Life is so short that we should make the most of every second. That was what the Emperor used to think when beautiful Yang Kuei-fei was lying in his arms. One day there was an imperial feast in the Pavilion of the Aloe. Peonies imported from India bloomed in all their splendour. Musicians from the 'Garden of Pears' were in attendance, and the wine came from the exquisite grapes of Hsi Liang. The question was, how could the moment be preserved? How could these glorious hours which drifted by like smoke be held in thrall?

'Call Li T'ai-po,' ordered the Emperor. Li T'ai-po swayed in. He was drunk. Courtiers poured cold water over his head and handed him his writing-brush. Impelled by genius, Li T'ai-po dashed off some strophes with fluent strokes of his brush. He sang the praises of the divine Yang Kuei-fei, accompanied by the Emperor on a flute of jade. Kao Li-shih, the influential palace eunuch, surveyed the scene in secret envy. The power which the poet and his verses wielded over the Emperor and his mistress knew no bounds. There came a day when Li T'ai-po was lying in the palace, dead drunk yet again, and the Emperor bade the eunuch take off the 'immortal's' shoes. This humiliation stung the scheming eunuch like a slap in the face. Eunuch by the grace of the Son of Heaven, he alone had the right to visit the moon-pale Yang Kuei-fei in her private chamber, he alone save the Emperor. 'Hearken, Kuei-fei,' he told her, 'the poet has written a satire about you. He compares you with the "Flying Swallow", the courtesan of the Han Dynasty who was unfaithful to the Emperor and never became Empress.'

Yang Kuei-fei was not only beautiful; she was also ambitious, and the eunuch had sowed the poisonous seeds of hatred in her heart. Li T'ai-po was forced to set off on his travels once more. Yet he was quite happy as he roamed through China's glorious countryside, halting wherever and for as long as he chose. He made the most of his short lifetime, transforming it into something which all future generations could envy. Ten years went by like a single day.

It was a moonlit night, and Li T'ai-po was travelling down the Yangtze towards Nanking. He donned royal court-dress. He sat up in the boat and laughed. He laughed until the distant banks rang with the sound. He laughed at the stupidity of a little world which would never understand his great soul. He knew by now that his world-renown was assured. But what was the world, after all? A speck of dust in the Universe, a mere nothing. And what was he himself? Li T'ai-po could only laugh, and the river-banks sent back their uncanny response.

Then came A.D. 755, the unhappy year in which Emperor Hsüan Tsung died of a broken heart. In the confusion of war, Li T'ai-po escaped from Lo Yang. The rebel leader An Lu-shan occupied the city, and the waters of the river Lo ran red with blood. Li Po took refuge in the mountains near Kiu Kiang in the province of Kiangsi. He was summoned to join the staff of Prince Li Ling. Later, he was sentenced to death, but he was by now a grey-haired old man, and his death-sentence was commuted to one of banishment. Li T'ai-po was forced to leave his country, but as long as he could see mountains, valleys, blossoming peach-trees and tranquil fish-ponds, he forgot all his cares. And so, taking his time, he wandered happily westward. For some months he stayed with the governor of Wu Chang. On many a night brilliantly lit by the harvest moon he would lie cradled in a boat, gently rocked by the waters of Lake Tung Ting. He crossed the boiling gorges of the Yangtze and reached the town of Wu Shan. He was granted an amnesty, and visited Nanking once more. He had friends everywhere now, and everywhere he went he was greeted by the sound of his own poems.

He died in the town which is now called T'ai P'ing, in the province of Anhwei. How did he meet his death? He calmly let it approach. Indeed, he even went a little way to meet it. It was a beautiful night, and the moon-beams were dancing on the water. Draining his last pitcher of wine, Li T'ai-po decided to do what only China's greatest poet could have done: he leant over the gunwale of his boat, put his arms about the moon's reflection, and sank from sight. So even his death became a poem.

It was Li T'ai-po's wish to be buried in the green hills near T'ai P'ing. He had spent the better part of his life in the open air, walking the roads beneath blossoming trees and the stars. Nature herself guided the brush which penned his eternal poems. He well knew that he would live on in another world. 'Why am I now beneath the green hills?' he wrote. 'I laugh, yet I cannot answer. My soul is now quite pure. It tarries in another heaven. And the earth belongs to no one. The peach-trees blossom, the waters flow and flow.'

He wanted his poems never, never to fade. That is why he still speaks to us today, after 1200 years:

> I paint letters, attended by solitude
> The bamboo surges like a sea. From bushes
> the dew falls like strings of pearls.
> I cast verses on to the gleaming paper
> as peach-blossoms are scattered in the snow.
> How long does the scent of the mandarin-fruit endure
> if a woman carries it in her arm-pit?
> How long does snow thrive in the sunshine?
> But may this poem which I write down now
> last for ever, and for ever, and for ever!

PEKING, THE MOST BEAUTIFUL CITY IN THE WORLD

'On coming to the Gate of the Eternal Order, one can see in the distance the five pavilions on Coal Hill, towering high into the air, and the maze of galleries in the palace buildings, shrouded by mist and rain.' From *The Palaces of Peking* by Hsieh Chu, 1938.

A MAN who has seen all the great cities in the world and wants to award one of them first prize for beauty will probably choose Peking. Rio de Janeiro lies in the loveliest bay in the world, Venice stands dreaming amid her labyrinth of canals, New York is breathtaking, and Tokyo goes on waiting for the next earthquake, with snow-capped Fuji-yama visible on clear days from the terraced roofs of her modern skyscrapers.

But Peking has everything: beauty and tranquillity, fairy-tale palaces like Sleeping Beauties and streets teeming with exuberant life, the greatest past history and the most modern street-system in the world, secluded ponds and incomparable gardens, fabulous temples and shops and stores which overwhelm the eye with their profusion of wares. Men who have travelled the whole world over, Englishmen, Frenchmen, Germans, merchants, scholars and collectors, have chosen to spend the rest of their days in Peking. Tourists have visited Peking to see the sights, wandered through one palace after another, gazed at the temples, statues of Buddha and countless works of art, immersed themselves ever more deeply in the beauties of fine porcelain, embroidered silks, lacquer-work, ivory and jade. And then, awaking from their reveries, they have found that twenty years have gone by without their having assimilated more than a tiny part of this inexhaustible city.

I knew a German army captain who had once — during the First World War — helped to defend German Tsingtao against the Japanese. He lived in Peking without doing much work, but comfortably, like all foreign residents. Perhaps he collected old bronzes and sold a piece or two occasionally — or again, perhaps he did nothing at all. Foreign residents in Peking were always so generous to their fellow-Europeans that none of them could ever come to grief. The captain told me all about Tsingtao.

'And then?' I asked.

Well, then came a spell in a Japanese prisoner-of-war camp.

'And then?'

Then? Well, he came to Peking.

'And what did you do here?' I asked.

'I don't know,' he said quietly. 'It seems as though I only came here yesterday, and yet twenty-five years have gone by since then. You're just here, that's all. Time slips by, and each day is lovelier than the last.'

Peking has seen everything in its time. In 1121 B.C. a village stood on its site; 2000 years later, in A.D. 936, the Tartars attacked and took the city. In 1151 the Chinese reoccupied it. Another hundred years, and the Mongols lay encamped beneath the city's mighty walls under the leadership of Jenghiz Khan, the most feared man of his day. When all the metal inside the city had been used up for cannon-balls, the defenders started melting down silver and eventually gold, and their ancient muzzle-loaders poured golden shot into the Mongols' camp! In the end the city was taken and destroyed, later to be rebuilt by Kublai Khan. Each new conqueror to arrive undertook fresh building: the Ming emperors, the Manchu emperors, and finally even the Europeans, who established the small garden-city known as the legation quarter. Between 1421 and 1928, Peking was the capital of China. Today new masters are lodged within the walls of the ancient fortress, and Peking is once more the capital of a people of 600 millions who calmly accept their new regime just as they did all the others which preceded it.

Just under forty miles from Peking the Great Wall winds westwards over endless stretches of mountain and steppe. Nearly twenty miles of masonry surround the two large quadrilateral sections of Peking. The northern part is the Tartar city, and the southern part the Chinese. Six gates lead into the former and nine into the latter. Inside the Tartar city stands the rectangular walled enclosure which contains the forbidden quarter of the imperial palaces.

It was the third ruler of the Ming Dynasty, Emperor Yung Lo, who made Peking his capital in 1421. The palaces he erected there surpassed in magnificence all the buildings of his age. Even today, Versailles itself must pale beside the bold and splendid design of these palace precincts. Yung Lo built temples and altars and laid out many gardens, bridges and ornamental ponds. Apart from the imperial buildings, a further fifteen palaces for the various princely families sprang up. The walls of Yung Lo's city are sixty-five feet thick at their foundations.

Two hundred and twenty-five years later, in 1643, the last Ming emperor was standing on his belvedere with a telescope, watching his enemies marching to the attack. In despair, he stabbed his daughter and then hanged himself from a tree, which incidentally can still be seen to this day, enclosed by an iron chain.

It is well nigh impossible to put into words what really constitutes the enchantment of this most beautiful city in the world. Perhaps it is the symmetry of the sloping roofs, stone replicas of the tents of ancient nomadic tribes, their four corners supported upon posts. Perhaps it is the red and yellow tones in the glazed brickwork, which shines afar in the sunlight. Perhaps it is the splendid vistas which stretch from gate to gate and palace to palace. Perhaps it is the broad, straight streets. Perhaps it is the artificial lakes, or the arched marble bridges, or the venerable old trees. Perhaps it is simply the courage which caused these bold visions in stone and wood to materialize.

It is almost eerie to stand in the exact centre of the open-air Altar of Heaven and find that every call or sound you make produces a fifteenfold echo from the palace buildings and distant hills around. Yet it only works if you stand in exactly that spot. If you step a mere yard away from the centre of the altar, the echo is silent.

There is something fantastic in the thought that it was here in Peking, as long ago as 1279, that Old China established the earliest modern astronomical observatory in the world, where the movements of the sun, moon and stars were studied. Not far from the observatory stand the examination halls where civil servants were obliged to undergo their written tests. The final examinations were so stiff that they drove many candidates literally out of their minds. The halls contain 10,000 cells, each measuring about 10 feet by 5 feet. A small aperture in the wall was the examinee's sole source of light and food, the whole system being designed to ensure that he did not 'crib'. Each individual was submitted to a thorough physical check-up before the examination and then locked in for its duration, which could be up to a week or more. Nobody could hope to pass this examination without having studied for many years. The huge columns inside the palaces, the filigree-work of their ceilings, the massive beams towering above the wondering and insignificant visitor, the dark green walls hung with silk, the works of art, bronzes, porcelains and idols — all are so overwhelming that the study of this civilization makes a human lifetime seem like the second-hand on some eternal clock. Green jade is a very valuable semi-precious stone, especially if almost transparent. Even a piece of opaque green jade as big as a man's fist is worth a considerable sum of money, but in the forbidden city there is a sacrificial basin too heavy for three strong men to carry, and it is carved out of a single block of green jade. The Ming period, and in particular the fifteenth century, produced the very finest porcelain the world can boast. Of the Manchus, it was Emperor K'ang-hsi and his successor Yung-cheng who had the finest and best porcelain manufactured in the ancient imperial factory at Ching-te-Chen. The Chinese porcelain factories always tried to produce 'pairs' of everything, which is to say, two specimens of each vase or basin or large bowl they made. These 'pairs' of the Ch'ien Lung period (1736-96) are only rarely to be found in the great metropolitan museums of the world, and their value runs into thousands of dollars, especially when they belong to the black, green or rose-coloured 'families' — i.e. when these colours predominate in them. Yet there are thousands upon thousands of such pairs in the palaces of Peking, ranging from tiny, almost transparent bowls to vases taller than a man.

Even during the Second World War, there was no conceivable whim which this city could not fulfil. You could purchase gold ingots, silver plate, glorious dark-red amber necklaces, pieces of jade, diamonds, pearls, emeralds, every semi-precious stone imaginable, coral from Turkestan, hand-carved ebony furniture, silks and brocades adorned with marvellous embroidery, Persian, Indian, Chinese and Mongolian carpets, Mongolian silver jewellery with its invariable garnishing of coral, trained falcons and cormorants taught to catch fish. Each Peking street had its own speciality. There was a Jade Street, a Flower Street, a Book Street, a Silver Street and even a Gold Street. There was a street whose dozens of shops displayed nothing but the most fascinating selections of bows and arrows. There were streets of choice restaurants specializing in duck dishes, whose pervasive aroma tempted the visitor as he rolled along on the noiseless wheels of his rickshaw. You could drug yourself on heroin and opium; you could pay girls to sing and boys to dance, or vice versa; you could buy things in the antique shops which any museum in the world would have accepted from you with gratitude — and all this for a comparatively small outlay.

Some interesting people used to live in Peking, too. There were stranded millionaires, art-collectors of world-renown, experts on Mongolia, White Russian generals, Swedish missionaries' sons who could conduct you into the depths of Mongolia and introduce you to its princes, dealers in camel-hair and pale Sinologists. One elderly American woman used to make a practice of riding through the city in her rickshaw for hours each day. She was slightly crazy, and maintained a handsome, sturdy rickshaw coolie who used to trot through the streets with her at a diabolical pace, the Stars and Stripes streaming out behind over the back of her seat. You could also meet a Frenchman who had married a Russian taxi-dancer from Harbin and only let her wear Chinese clothes, or a Portuguese gentleman who was legally married to five Chinese women. At the large Rockefeller Hospital, which was staffed by excellent doctors of all nationalities, there was a Hungarian who made a living by rearing lice on his own body and selling them for purposes of medical research.

Although they were still extremely attached to their lands of origin, all these people had grown new roots in Peking. Their hearts beat with a double rhythm, as it were, leaving them no peace. Each year that passed saw foreigners, Americans, Englishmen, Frenchmen, Swedes and Japanese alike sending one treasure after the other back home to their own countries. Yet Peking remained inexhaustible, and even her poorest Chinese inhabitants seemed contented.

PEKING, THE MOST BEAUTIFUL CITY

Peking is a clear confirmation of the truth of Gautama Buddha's dictum: 'He who sits still, wins.' China's revolution was not initiated by Mao Tse-tung, nor even by Sun Yat-sen. It is fifty centuries old, and a miraculous example of the survival of one race in one place. Babylonian and Egyptian supremacy and the golden ages of Greece and Rome flared up and died on the funeral pyre of history. China survived them all intact. She never brooded on the past or doted on the future. Like no other country in the world, she lived for the present with a shrewdness which overcame all her difficulties and an immense store of patience which preserved her from rash action. Her only weapon was time. She never tried to conquer or die in the attempt. She lost thousands of battles without ever having fought 'to the bitter end', knowing that a decisive war spells danger and that it is better to withdraw than reach a decision, for withdrawal means life. Lao-tse, the wise old man of China, said: 'Who can clear muddy water? If it keeps still, it clears of its own accord.'

At a time when the whole world was on the move and hungry for progress, the 'Kingdom of the Centre' slumbered on, lost in the depths of its own unreality. Every foreign visitor to the country was gripped by an almost debilitating sense of the greatness, timelessness and earth-bound quality of Chinese life. China's immense vitality, her great powers of endurance, her instinct for compromise, her scepticism and her adaptability were all tried and sterling qualities. Her whole civilization was based on the tenet that it is better to fight one's way through than fight to the death. The Chinese sometimes died for an unattainable ideal under compulsion, but never just for the sake of being heroes.

That is how it was . . . How will it be in the future?

The Chinese lost their ancient religions long ago, and the only things that survived were their ancestor-worship and their consciousness of family obligations. Now even the family is to give way before a new ideal. China is to become revivified and the tempo of her life heightened by the introduction of machines and marching, State police and a police-State.

Should these new Chinese be led back and forth a few times across the whole of northern Asia to the Urals and to Europe at this restless new pace, what sort of blood will then flow in the veins of the people who live between Shanghai and Danzig?

CENTRAL ASIA

X

JENGHIZ KHAN AND TAMERLANE—
HATED, CURSED, LOVED AND ADMIRED

Jenghiz Khan united the peoples of the steppe, and Tamerlane used them to rule cities.

FROM the Hungarian Puszta across the Ukraine, the Caspian lowland and western Turkestan to Iran, and from the steppes of the Kirghiz across Dzungaria and Mongolia to Manchuria, there extends a huge ribbon of steppe-land stretching from eastern Europe almost to the Pacific. From time immemorial these regions have been inhabited by nomadic races.

Roy Chapman Andrews, who has undertaken numerous expeditions on behalf of the American Museum of National Sciences, and Henry Fairfield Osborne, have between them established that central Asia represents a vast sea of human history. In fact, they regard the Gobi Desert as the original birth-place of mankind. Two or three million years ago there were men living in a great forest paradise where Mongolia now keeps her lonely vigil, awaiting the crucial hour when she must choose between East and West. Andrews found forests of petrified trees which had died millions of years ago in the days when their foliage was still fodder for dinosaurs. The bed of an erstwhile river disclosed the remains of early mammals and fresh-water shell-fish. Furthermore, the skeleton of a pre-Mongolian man was unearthed, a human being over 6 feet 6 inches in height who must have hunted in these parts long before King Tutankhamun did in Egypt.

Attila, Jenghiz Khan and Tamerlane — those are the three great names which ring in our ears whenever we think of the Huns' and Mongols' immense marches of conquest. Attila was killed on the Marne in 451. Jenghiz Khan and Tamerlane were never defeated. Quite how far these people with their high cheek-bones and narrow eyes actually penetrated into Europe from the eastern end of Asia across the Urals — in other words, how far Tartars (more correctly 'Tatars'), Turkestanis, Mongols, Kalmucks and Buriats are ethnologically related — is a scientific jungle which it would be pointless to try to explore. It must not be forgotten, however, that Finnish, Estonian and Hungarian are closer to Mongolian than they are to any other language of western Europe.

Only 700 years ago, a single man managed to conquer almost the whole of

Eurasia. During their campaigns, Jenghiz Khan and his horsemen covered nearly a hundred degrees of latitude. Such cities as did not submit voluntarily were trampled into the dust. Jenghiz altered the course of rivers and peopled deserts with hosts of refugees and dying men, leaving their burial problems to be solved by the attentions of wolves and vultures. He was only a nomadic hunter and a herdsman king, yet he managed to outwit three world empires in the game of strategy. He had never seen a city nor learned how to write, yet he laid down a code of laws which served a large number of nations. He ruled the world from Korea to Hungary and from China to Iran. Moscow, before whose gates both Napoleon and Hitler came to grief, was captured ten years after Jenghiz Khan's death.

The area between the sources of the Kerulen, the Onon and the Tula is an uncharted region of green grassland and high, wind-swept plateaux, lit during the icy winter nights by the mysterious glow of the aurora borealis, and covered with huge flocks of birds in summer — a countryside which only knows the language of freedom and the open air. Here lay the home of the Huns, the Turks and the Mongols, and here Jenghiz Khan was born. The children in this corner of the northern Gobi never had to be toughened to withstand hardship. They were born tough! Their baby-foods were mother's and mare's milk. Babyhood once past, they were obliged to take the places farthest from the tent fire, there to reflect on the hardships of life when young and the hopelessness of cold and hunger. Even in springtime, when the mares and cows produced most milk, their training continued; then they went hunting wolf and antelope. In winter the strongest men always ate first, while the women, old people and children laid about each other unmercifully for the sake of the bones and scraps. And the children not only had each other to contend with, but the dogs, too. Towards the end of winter, when the community's stock of cattle had dwindled away and no more animals could be slaughtered, they simply learned to put up with hunger. As long as the world went on being conquered by virtue not of superior machines but of greater human endurance, it was easy to account for the victorious campaigns of Islam, the Arabs and the Mongols.

Jenghiz Khan was born in a tent of felt, known as a *yurt*. These yurts were mobile dwellings transported on carts drawn by dozens of oxen. Temuchin, as young Jenghiz Khan was called, had a very beautiful mother, Yulun Eke. She had been abducted by Jenghiz Khan's father while actually on her bridal journey, but she had resigned herself to her fate.

One day while Temuchin was still a youth, he and his father were entertained by a strange warrior in his tent. Temuchin caught sight of a little girl sitting in one corner. She was very pretty, and he asked his father whether he might marry her. The girl's father said that although his daughter was still rather young, being only nine years old, Temuchin was welcome to look her over. Next day the transaction was completed and she was betrothed to Temuchin. A few days later, however, Temuchin's father was poisoned, and from then on the lad was always on the run, constantly pursued by enemies who feared that the young prince might try to assume his father's leadership. He was captured and put into a wooden yoke, escaped with his hands and arms still lashed to it, was freed, and fought for his life. It was all good schooling for the generalship which was to follow.

After interminable battles against numerous Tartar tribes, Jenghiz Khan was finally proclaimed Khan of the united Mongol and Tartar peoples.

At this juncture, the Khan declared that he had been called by Heaven to conquer the world. This implicit belief in his divine vocation communicated itself to his troops, and he led them on from one victory to another. The land of the Uigurs in the middle of central Asia submitted to him voluntarily, and Jenghiz Khan became overlord of all the Tartars. In the year 1211, when he was probably fifty-six years old, Jenghiz Khan led hundreds of thousands of Mongols against the Great Wall. He stormed the gate-forts with relative ease, but the conquest of China took him five long years. It was not until 1215 that the capital, Yen-King, or modern Peking, was taken by storm and pillaged. Jenghiz Khan sent ambassadors to Turkestan, only to have them murdered by the commander of a frontier-fortress who mistrusted him. An army 700,000 strong followed them. Bokhara and Samarkand were stormed, plundered and burned. Samarkand was a royal capital, and one of the greatest commercial centres in the world. It was enclosed by walls and fortifications two and a half miles in circumference, and garrisoned by a force of 110,000 men equipped with more than twenty war-elephants. Whenever the insatiable Khan had taken such a city he used to single out the artisans and present them as slaves to his sons and generals. Samarkand supplied no less than 30,000 such prisoners and, in addition, Jenghiz Khan earmarked a similar number of able-bodied men for military purposes, transport and so forth. All the prettiest girls were taken into the Khan's 'inner chambers', of course, and the rest of the inhabitants were beheaded. Any of the enemy who managed to escape, like the Kankalis, for instance, were defeated by cunning. Jenghiz Khan generously granted the Kankalis permission to don Mongolian uniform. They did so, marched happily into his camp, and were 'collectively liquidated'.

The conquest of Merv al-Shahidshan, one of the oldest cities in the world, brought Jenghiz Khan's reputed score of massacred victims to 1,300,000. The city was so thoroughly razed to the ground that practically nothing was left of it. Jenghiz Khan dispatched his victorious armies as far as the banks of the Dnieper, and in 1226, when he was probably seventy-one years old, he marched once again at the head of his warriors against north-west China. After several successful battles, he handed over the task of annihilating the enemy army to his sons.

Jenghiz Khan's invariable maxim was: 'The conquered never become their conquerors' friends. The destruction of the conquered is the conquerors' best guarantee of safety.'

In the summer of the year 1227, Jenghiz Khan retired to the mountains of Liu-pang, west of Peking. Uneasy of mind and perhaps guessing that he was soon to die, he went to Shan-si, where he was struck down by a severe fever. As he was dying, he turned to his friend Kiluken Bahadur and said: 'Be a true friend to my wife Bortai,' (she was the nine-year-old girl he had taken as his first wife) 'and be a friend to my sons Ogotai and Tule. A man's body is not imperishable; without a house or a resting-place it decays. What you have to do, do with all your might. Do not be influenced by the wishes of others, and you will win the support of many. I must take my leave of you and depart. The boy Kublai will some day sit upon my throne, and he will guard your welfare as I have done.'

Having been throughout his life not only a ruthless conqueror but also a brilliant statesman, organizer and planner, Jenghiz Khan still continued to administer the most important affairs of state from his death-bed. He commanded his youngest son Ottshigin to undertake a further campaign against China, employing a plan which he expounded in great detail. As for his empire, he divided it between his five sons.

The dead Khan's body was secretly conveyed to Mongolia. So that no one could break the unbelievable news of the great ruler's death prematurely, the escort of his funeral train slaughtered any travellers or tribes who were unlucky enough to meet it on the way. It was only when the procession had reached the great *ordu*, or tented city, which stood at the source of the Kerulen that the Khan's death was made public. The coffin was carried into each of his many wives' yurts in turn, so that they might all have an opportunity of joining in the lamentations. Thousands of his wives, children and grandchildren were summoned together, and forty beautiful daughters of the nobility were burned on his pyre.

Jenghiz Khan owned about 500 wives and concubines, among whom were beautiful captives from every race in Asia and Europe. He had a much more efficient method of choosing 'beauty queens' than the judges of our modern contests. Every captain in his army turned the most beautiful girls taken from a defeated city over to the colonel; the colonel, after an intermediate weeding-out process, turned them over to the general, who, after further careful selection, passed them on to the army commander. The army commander then sent this 'cream of the nations' to Jenghiz Khan. In that way, every land was carefully combed for the benefit of the Khan's 'inner chambers'. Besides his first and dearest wife Bortai, he owned another four principal wives. They wept loudly over his grave, but Bortai grieved in silence for the conqueror of the world whom she had once enchanted when he was still Temuchin. She was nine years old when he bought her, but he did not make her his wife until she was seventeen.

In the history of Asia, 110 years are like a single day. A.D. 1336 saw the birth of Timur, the fabulous Tamerlane, at Kesh in western Turkestan. Jenghiz Khan was a Mongol. Timur was of Mongolian extraction, but his language was Turkish. While not a direct descendant of Jenghiz Khan, he was a true son of the steppes. He became chieftain of his tribe at the age of thirty-four, after a spell as joint regent with his brother-in-law Hussein. One day he became tired of sharing authority, so he murdered his rival, put his small kingdom in order, and set out to conquer the world. During one battle he received a wound in the foot which made him limp for the rest of his life. That is how the Persians came to call him *Timur i leng*, or 'Timur the Lame'.

The 'Lame One' subjugated Persia and then central Asia, from the Great Wall to Moscow. In 1398 he pushed on towards India. Where cruelty was concerned, this gentleman put Jenghiz Khan well in the shade. He purloined Syria from the Mamelukes, overran the Turkish Sultan's empire with his immense army, and in 1402 defeated Bayezid the Ottoman on the plain of Angora. In 1450 he prepared an expedition against China. Then death overtook him.

Like Jenghiz Khan, this dictator and conqueror was also a brilliant statesman. He required his political officials to combine justice with strictness, to look after the peasantry, and to protect trade. He insisted that his officers keep their troops well equipped. Each horseman had to have two mounts, a bow and a well-filled quiver, a sword, a battle-axe, a saw, some twine and ten sewing-needles. Moreover, one tent had to be provided for every eighteen men in camp.

Timur was a patron of the arts and sciences, and even developed a personal talent for writing. He was a Napoleon with the disposition of a Himmler. Serious, gloomy and an enemy of gaiety, he blended cold calculation with incredible toughness and generosity. He knew how to defer to others and withdraw into the background when prudence demanded it. In his youth he spent a month roaming in the wilderness, and underwent a period of temporary captivity. During this term of imprisonment his beloved young wife was kept locked up in a cow-shed swarming with fleas and vermin. But like her husband, she could 'take it'.

In later years it was Timur's habit to recuperate from the great hardships of his military campaigns at his city of summer residence, Samarkand, where he assembled huge quantities of booty, including the finest works of art from every country in the Asiatic world and numerous princesses complete with dowries, slaves, servants, artists, musicians and scholars. It was at Samarkand that he held the drunken orgies at which thousands of guests ate food from golden dishes and drank wine from golden beakers; at which whole roast horses were sampled, and ladies of the court paraded in gowns of silk, velvet and satin, or in red silken robes adorned with gold lace and furnished with trains so long that it frequently took fifteen maidservants to carry them. Here could be seen helmet-like hats set with pearls, rubies, emeralds and long white feathers which hung down over a woman's eyes and endowed her face with an especial charm when she moved.

Timur possessed great personal courage. After his fourth campaign against Khwarizm, one of his adversaries hit upon the bizarre idea of replacing the wholesale slaughter of pitched battle by hand-to-hand combat between himself and Timur. He made his dangerous opponent a proposition which might well interest us all today. 'How much longer must the world suffer pain and misery for the sake of two men? The welfare of mankind and the nations demands that they should enter the lists alone and try their fortune.'

Timur was delighted with the challenge, and was the first to arrive at the place of battle. But when he called for his opponent in a loud voice, he was nowhere to be found.

Human life, whether his own or other men's, was as little sacred to Timur as that of an insect. Yet he was capable of mourning deeply for relations or friends when they died. If need arose he could also play the Islamic fanatic, and he was as adept at selecting the appropriate role from his large repertoire as any versatile character actor.

Jenghiz Khan's aim had been to unite all the nomadic peoples of the world in overthrowing the settled civilizations. Timur had no fixed aims. Although still a nomad himself, he was hopelessly in love with the culture of the settled races, and luxuriated at Samarkand while his armies fought in tents.

'Pray for my soul,' he told his assembled wives as he lay on his death-bed in Otrar at the age of seventy-one. 'Do not wail or grieve,' he bade them feebly, 'for lamentation is pointless. No one has ever yet driven death away by weeping. Instead of tearing your clothes and running madly about, beseech God to be merciful to my soul.'

It was a stormy night in January. The wind howled without respite, and the weaker the dying man became the louder the thunder rolled, while priests intoned incessant prayers from the Koran.

Hated and cursed, loved and admired, Timur breathed his last. No other figure in history is so rich in contradictions. No other tyrant or ruler has been responsible for so much destruction and devastation, no autocrat was ever such a brilliant administrator, none at once so dreaded and so admired. Far from abating, this admiration of him grew with the passage of time, and kings of Europe and tsars of Russia alike marvelled at his deeds for many centuries after his death. The people of Asia still sing his praises today, and the peasants of modern Pamir point proudly to the miles of drainage installations which he built into the rock. Directing the foreign visitor's attention to roads, canals, diverted rivers, wells and dams, they say: 'Timur did all that.' And even today, when Mongol mothers suckle their children at halts on their endless wanderings, they still sing them songs of Timur i leng and great Jenghiz Khan.

JAPAN

⚔

SOME DAY THE BEAR WILL RETURN

The Ainu

A small and nearly extinct Indo-European race of Siberian origin still surviving on Hokkaido and Sakhalin.

IT seems fantastic that in the midst of all the Mongoloid peoples of eastern Asia there should still survive an isolated racial group of Caucasian stock, a little band of 'Old Siberians' who are related to west Europeans in physique, skull formation and colour of skin. The last descendants of a dying race, some 15,000 of these Ainu are still living on the large island of Sakhalin at the northern extremity of Japan. The Ainu have presented ethnologists with a number of problems of which the greatest, namely the question of their place of origin, remains virtually unanswered to this day. The problem becomes even more obscure when it is related to the fact that this very ancient Caucasian (Indo-European) race at one time occupied all the Japanese islands, long before Polynesian and Mongoloid peoples ever set foot on them. The Ainu had already been established there for a long time when Japan's first emperor, Jimmu Tenno, came across from the southern island of Kyushu to the main island of Yamato in 660 B.C.

There are, in fact, mountains and places throughout the whole of Japan whose names are derived from the Ainu language. Hokkaido's capital, Sapporo, Mauka on Sakhalin and Tarato in Siberia are all Ainu names. Yes, even the extinct volcano Fuji, the most beautiful mountain in the world, owes its name to the Ainu. The Ainu's ancient household god and father of their race is called Skisei koro Ekashi, and his wife, the divine grandmother of fire whose throne floats invisibly in the heart of the flames on the hearth, is called Fuji. It may be that once upon a time, long before history began, the Ainu actually witnessed the birth of Fuji-no-yama the fire-mountain as it sprang from the ground, spewing masses of lava and basalt into the sky, eventually to reign in stately supremacy over all other mountains. Fuji must have been a sacred mountain long before there was such a place as 'Japan', and before the men who were to make Nippon a world-power ever arrived at her shores.

The cultural period which followed the Ice Age was a time when the earth already enjoyed a warm, dry climate, and is known to science as the

Neolithic Age, that is, the later Stone Age, from the Greek *neos* (= recent) and *lithos* (= stone). During this period, somewhere about 3000-1800 B.C., man was already carving and drilling stone to make implements and weapons. He had a permanent abode and was cultivating wheat, barley, millet and leguminous plants, storing his supplies in barns, taming and training domestic animals, among them dogs, and using wood for building houses. But before man thought of building houses he lived in caves, and the Japanese originally called the Ainu *Tsuchi-gumo*, which means 'earth-spiders'. Translated into the Ainu language that would have signified 'cave-dwellers', and in fact the Ainu did at one time live in caves.

So this puzzling creature the Caucasian or Indo-European Ainu was already resident in Japan during the Neolithic period. There are two different kinds of earthenware to be found in the graves dating from Neolithic times. They belong either to the 'Jomon' or the 'Yayoi' type. The Jomon type are more commonly found in the north and east and are considered to be earlier in date. While technically inferior to the Yayoi, they are artistically much more beautiful. A thorough examination of the bones or fossils taken from Neolithic graves has led scholars to the conclusion that the Jomon people corresponded in physique to the Ainu who still survive today, and that the Ainoids had spread their Jomon culture over the whole of Japan before some other race or races started to catch them up with the Yayoi style.

We can well imagine what terrible wars these different races must have waged against each other; how the new arrivals must have driven a wedge into the Ainu, forcing them to withdraw farther and farther to the north and south; and how the last Ainu in the south must ultimately have been killed off, leaving a remnant of these 'Indo-Europeans or 'Old Siberians' to subsist on Hokkaido and Sakhalin in the far north. Even in A.D. 720 they were still putting up such a desperate resistance that the Japanese were obliged to muster soldiers from nine different provinces before they managed to defeat them. However, as time went by the Ainu expended so much of their strength in internecine struggles that they eventually became exhausted and were left to await their final extinction on Hokkaido and Sakhalin.

In about 1600 there were still 50,000 Ainu on Hokkaido as compared with 12,000 Japanese; in 1700, 30,000 Ainu and 20,000 Japanese. By 1800 the scales had tipped in favour of the Japanese, with 20,000 Ainu and 30,000 Japanese, and today a mere 15,000 Ainu are eking out a poor existence there while the 3,000,000 Japanese inhabitants turn them to good use in the tourist trade as an 'ethnological miracle'. The inexorable mathematics of the Ainu's steady decrease in population make it possible to forecast the actual date when the last of the Ainu will return to dust, and when the sentence of extinction will finally be carried out.

It seems as though history gives every race on earth its one big chance, its golden age, its span of life, its 'season'. Humanity's stop-watch ticks on unnoticed, until suddenly the dying hour is at hand. One is tempted to wonder what difference it would have made to the course of history had the Ainu, the Old Siberians, maintained their hold on the islands of Japan.

The question is a hard one to answer, for races not only constitute distinct entities but also intermingle to the best of their ability and taste. The Ainu and the Japanese mingled in this way from the dawn of history onwards, and Ainu blood flows in the veins of the Japanese just as surely as that of the Mongols and the people of the South Seas does in the veins of the Ainu.

In the year 1877 a young and energetic theologian went out to visit the Ainu. His name was John Batchelor, and he was a scientist and missionary. He got to know the Ainu really well, made a study of their language and customs, won their affection, and remained their staunch friend until the end of his days. He affected a very long beard, incidentally, just like the Ainu men. As a very old man he wrote from Hokkaido: 'I have more than reached the age of retirement. Yet I am still here on the spot, where I can go on helping the Ainu.' The Japanese made Dr Batchelor an honorary member of the Hokkaido government, and in the twilight of his fantastic life he was awarded a pension in recognition of his services to the Ainu race.

It is Batchelor whom we have to thank for our deepest insight into the speech, grammar and way of life of this dying race. Almost every piece of information we possess about the Ainu is the result of Dr Batchelor's painstaking research. No one who wanders through the squat grey Ainu villages on Hokkaido today can fail to notice the feeble reflection of an ancient life which was close to Nature and on intimate terms with spirits and departed ancestors.

The spirits are still there today, perching everywhere, lurking, hovering on the breezes. Even now the old Ainu men hear their voices, struggle with them, feel themselves persecuted by them and reminded of the inevitable annihilation of their race. The clothes-chests of the Ainu still contain ancient and beautifully ornamented robes of elm bark. The call of the mountains still echoes alluringly from the primeval time when the mountains of northern Asia were sacred. You will often find an Ainu wandering on the slopes of a volcano, yet if you ask him why, he will not be able to tell you. The Ainu still wear fine furs and skins — bear, seal, dog, fox and reindeer — for Hokkaido has always been cold in winter, and an icy wind blows across from the Okhotsk Sea. They still have their totems, too, those animistic clan symbols which link all the civilizations of the Pacific so mysteriously.

The Ainu seem to have been inspired from earliest times by the belief illustrated in the Old Testament story of Samson: that physical strength reposes in a man's hair. They always believed, and still do, that strength and hair go together, and take great care to lose none. The men wear long beards and regard the adornment as sacred. The Ainu have been nicknamed 'the Tolstoys of Hokkaido'. Only a woman who has lost her husband may tear out her hair — and then she probably has good reason, for all authorities unanimously agree that Ainu men treat their womenfolk well. Indeed, women were so highly esteemed in the old days that the Ainu practised poly- andry, or a plurality of husbands to one wife. Later, however, polygamy became customary, and one man could marry several women.

In early times Ainu women used to have their hands, arms and forehead ornamentally tattooed, and their mouths enlarged by a ring of blue-black tattooing. This was carried out when the subject was still in early childhood and was effected by a series of knife incisions which could never be erased. The cuts were then anointed with juices extracted from tree-bark, which made the process an extremely painful one. The origin of the custom is unknown, but it may possibly have been a primitive method of branding women who had been captured in battle from defeated tribes to make escape impossible for them.

One is so easily tempted to dismiss any dying race as 'primitive'. On the verge of extinction at the end of a cultural evolution lasting thousands of years, very little survives of the Ainu's world, yet it was once a very thriving place. Their gods were as numerous as the multiplicity of the natural pheno- mena which they represented, for the Ainu religion has always been a form of nature-worship. Amorphous and invisible beings dwelt in every place where one could walk or look. Rocks, fish, trees, the sun, and, in particular, fire, were all worshipped as sacred things. Witchcraft and magic dominated the Ainu's existence, and the invisible link between man and superhuman forces was maintained by their witch-doctor, or *shaman*.

There is something of the Tunguses in the Ainu, something of the Siberian forest-peoples' civilization in their unshakeable belief in the animation of inanimate objects, or 'animism', something of the demonic spirits which infest the forests, mountains and marshes of the Taiga of north-east Asia.

All the various Tungus tribes believed that the bear, being the most man- like creature in their natural environment, constituted a mediator between this world and the next. North-east Asia is full of bear stories based on this belief. The bear speaks, acts and intervenes in the destiny of man. He both sympathizes with and suffers like man himself. He is the 'exalted being who lives among the mountains'. That is exactly what the Ainu call him: *kim- un-kamui*. The word *kamui* is probably the original form of the Japanese word *kami*, meaning deity.

Every race on earth has concerned itself with the problem of man's relationship with the dead. We are born, we live, we toil, we laugh a little, we cry, we die. While each generation of men contributes something new to the store of experience, they would be so much wiser if only the spirits of all those who have gone before could assist them in their task. A man's lifetime is so short that he cannot achieve or learn very much. If there were no means of communicating with one's forefathers and the spiritual world of departed souls, life would be unbearable. But how is this liaison with the spiritual realm of earthly and bodily dissolution to be effected?

That is exactly what the bear is there for, the Ainu tell us. When a bear is stripped of its skin, it looks alarmingly like a man. So that is what it is — a human being in furry clothes. The Ainu see the bear as a mediator between their own harsh world and the world of disembodied souls. Exactly when they came to this conclusion, no amount of research will ever disclose, but the Ainu just *know*, and that is that. That is why their most important festival is the *iyomande*, or sending home of souls. In it, a bear is killed and his soul sent forth alive out of his body to visit his bear ancestors. Some day the bear will return, only to be dispatched once more. His flesh is eaten, his blood is drunk, and his soul performs its mission. To the Ainu, that is the divine order of things, the eternal cycle, the be-all and end-all of things, and thousands of years have done nothing to shake their belief.

A bear-cub is carefully reared, fed and nursed. He is even assigned an Ainu wet-nurse who suckles him at her breast — until the young bear's claws become too sharp, when he is shut up in a cage.

The villagers regularly come to visit the bear in his abode, greeting him in the most friendly fashion. Master Bruin goes on living like this for two years, and then comes the big festival with its preparations and invitations. 'I, so-and-so, living at such-and-such a place, am going to send my dear little bear-cub back to his home in the mountains. Come, masters and friends, to the feast. We wish to celebrate the joyful departure of the exalted one, come!'

The guests arrive, a few of the women coming early to help the lady of the house with her preparations. The bear is led round the huts for the last time to receive the friendly salutations of all the villagers (a proceeding which naturally irritates him). Then he is taken to the place of 'transformation', where he is addressed as follows: 'We greet you. We have nourished you with great care because we love you so much. Now that you are fully grown, we are sending you off to your father and mother. When you arrive, speak well of us, and tell them how good we have been to you. Come back to us again, and we will hold a new festival and send you off once more.'

After that the bear is tied up, tormented by all the guests, shot full of arrows and, while still not dead, thrashed. The more frenzied the animal becomes, the more overjoyed the guests are. As soon as he begins to grow weak he is 'dispatched on his homeward way' by strangulation, or, less commonly, by being tied to two stakes and killed by an arrow in the heart. After part of the meat has been eaten raw and the blood drunk, the remainder of the animal is boiled. The meal is improved by the invisible co-operation of Fuji, the goddess of fire, and her daughter, 'the maiden of the cooking-pot'. The men anoint themselves with the bear's blood, which is considered a sovereign means of ensuring success in hunting, and the bear's skull is exhibited outside the house facing east, for purposes of worship. When the unfortunate beast's soul is assumed to have left its body and to be rising heavenwards, the men loose off a few more arrows in a north-easterly direction.

We come now to the most mysterious thing about the bear-cult. After its death, the bear is known as *chinukara-guru*, which signifies 'prophet' or 'guardian'. The Ainu use the same word to describe the Pole Star in the constellation of the Lesser Bear. So it seems that the distant civilizations of the Mediterranean and the Ainu have both associated this constellation with the bear from very ancient times. It is there that the soul of the creature which the Ainu believe to be their redeemer and mediator finds its final destination.

On the way from Mororan to Sapporo I passed through the village of Chitose. I went through a large number of little Ainu villages on Hokkaido and visited Yurappu, Oshamamu and Shiraoi. The Ainu told me: 'They've forbidden the bear-festival. They think it's cruel.'

'Do you still believe in the home-coming of the bear's soul?' I asked. 'Do you really believe that it can return?'

They laughed. 'Of course we don't,' they said. 'What do you take us for!'

It was cold and dark. The first stars were beginning to twinkle above the volcanoes of the Shishima range. I had just left the low-built Ainu hut when the little girl who had been plying us with saké (Japanese rice-wine) ran out after me.

'Do you know what we do now?' she whispered. 'We kill foxes and crows and sparrows and send *their* souls off — *instead*, you understand!'

A PEOPLE IN LOVE WITH ART

Hanawa Hokiichi, the celebrated blind scholar, was reading the *Genji Monogatari* with his pupils. Suddenly the wind blew their lamp out. Hanawa quietly went on 'reading'. His pupils started to fidget. 'The light has gone out,' they said. 'That only shows you,' answered Hanawa, 'what a nuisance it is to have to rely on your eyes.'

FOUR large islands, 600 smaller ones, and 8000 minute islets which are often little more than mountain peaks sticking out of the sea: that is Japan.

Eleven ranges comprising 192 volcanoes extend over the whole length of the islands from Kyushu in the south to Hokkaido in the north; 58 of these volcanoes are still active. Fuji-no-yama is Japan's highest and at the same time her most beautiful mountain. This 12,395-foot king among mountains is in fact a volcano which has been extinct since 1707.

However, if you want to see the biggest crater in the world you must climb Aso-také, the lip of whose crater measures nearly a hundred miles in circumference. But take care — it makes a dangerous walk. For Aso is still sending the smoke from its subterranean furnaces into the skies, and large fragments of magma come hurtling down out of the clouds into its depths.

There are hot springs, wonderful natural parks and rugged mountains to be found everywhere in Japan. Only a fifth of her surface is suitable for agriculture.

The Japanese experience a perceptible earth-tremor at least once every three days. On September 1st, 1923, an earthquake killed 120,000 people, and since that day there have been no less than 12,000 earth-tremors in the 'very noticeable' category.

Fuji-no-yama is said to have sprung blazing out of the ground one dreadful, haunted night in the year 286 B.C. It has created the most beautiful landscape in the world, and no one who stands on the summit of the mountain to watch the red disc of the sun come leaping up over the Pacific horizon can fail to understand why Japan is called 'the land of the rising sun'.

On clear days the snow-capped peak of Fuji-no-yama is visible from Tokyo, and during the war American pilots found their way to the city with deadly accuracy merely by pointing the noses of their roaring aircraft at the dream-like beauty of its summit. It was not the first time that Fuji-no-yama had brought death.

To say that these islands are close to the gods is not just to quote legends or myths fostered by ancient visionaries. Every morning and evening the mountain peaks soar into the clouds above their swathing mists just as they

213

did when Ninigi, the forefather of Jimmu, Japan's first emperor, climbed down them out of heaven.

The official history of Japan begins in 660 B.C. Japanese historians expressly state that this year marks only the *earthly* inauguration of the oldest imperial dynasty in the world. The Emperor's ancestors existed in heaven a long time before that, and history and legend alike link their origins directly with the story of Creation. The first god Izanagi and his consort Izanami created an original island where they settled down and produced more islands and gods. Izanami died in giving birth to her son the Fire-god, and, like Eurydice, went down to the underworld. Orpheus-fashion, Izanagi followed her with the intention of bringing her back, but as he was leading her out of the underworld he turned to look at her, a thing he had been expressly forbidden to do. Izanami immediately vanished, and Izanagi was left to escape from the realm of the dead on his own.

The Greek story of Orpheus and the Izanagi myth of Japan display a perfect similarity. Separated by a hemisphere, these two ancient themes nevertheless agree in almost every detail. What is the reason? We just do not know, and we shall never find out. After all, in the beginning was the word, and in the beginning its validity seems to have extended all the way round the globe.

But why did Japan's first emperor climb down out of the *sky*?

The Japanese can give us the precise reason. Izanagi granted the sovereignty of the sky to the Sun-goddess Amaterasu-Omikami. Her brother, the Storm-god Susa-no-o, was an uncouth character who spent his time devastating rice-fields and ditches and wreaking all kinds of mischief. The Sun-goddess Amaterasu took refuge from her brother in a cave, and the world became darkened. Eight myriad gods (the Milky Way, perhaps) took up their station outside her cave and debated how best to persuade the touchy lady to come out. Meanwhile, Amano-Uzume, the ballet-dancer of heaven, performed a somewhat indecent dance which brought roars of laughter from her divine audience. (The Japanese gods were no prudes!) Becoming curious to know what was going on outside her cave, the Sun-goddess pushed the stone which blocked its mouth a little to one side, just to have a peep. The earth was bathed in sunlight once more.

Shortly afterwards, the Sun-goddess sent her grandson Ninigi-no-Mikoto down to earth. He landed on the island of Kyushu equipped with a jewel with a flaw, a sword and a mirror. One of Ninigi-no-Mikoto's great-grandchildren was Jimmu Tenno, the first Emperor of Japan.

If there is a race of artists in the world, a race which really unites art with life, a race whose houses look as though they were mere continuations of Nature, and whose painting, lacquer-work and wood-cuts have scaled the heights of human achievement, if there is a race which has made a ceremony out of tea-making, given flowers a 'language' and forced the trees themselves to grow to a man-made pattern, it is the Japanese. They are so in love with art that it would never occur to them to question whether the story of Tenno's heavenly origins is really true or only a myth. The legend of the Sun-goddess was so beautiful that in this scattered chain of islands lying half in the ocean and half in the sky it became transformed into both history and religion. And after all, Ninigi-no-Mikoto did bring with him circumstantial evidence of his heavenly origins in the shape of the jewel, the sword and the mirror.

So how can the Japanese doubt the truth of this story or question the divine origins of their Emperor, when the insignia of State are still preserved today: the jewel in the imperial palace at Tokyo, the sword at Atsuta Jingu, and the mirror at the great shrine of Ise? This 'Shinto' shrine, the most sacred in all Japan, stands by the banks of the Isuzu near the town of Uji-Yamada in the district of Mie, served by a chief priest with seventy-four priests under him. The three insignia of royalty have been passed on from emperor to emperor in unbroken succession until the present day. Every Japanese has to pray before the Ise shrine at least once in his life and, until the year 1945, every Japanese Prime Minister used to visit it on taking up office. The shrine itself is the abode of the Sun-goddess.

It is this belief in an imperial dynasty which has survived uninterrupted from the time of Creation until the present day, this belief in 'Tenno', who, as we have seen, is in all reality a son of heaven, this belief in Japanese history, in fact, which constitutes the Shinto religion. Until the end of the war, Japan boasted no less than 306 national shrines, 49,579 shrines in the various prefectures and villages, more than 60,000 private shrines and 129 soldiers' shrines. The most important shrine in the last category is the Yasukuni-jinja at Tokyo, where the ashes of every Japanese soldier who has ever died for his country are kept in small white chests. Hence the Japanese soldier's farewell greeting: 'See you in Yasukuni.'

To ensure the continuance of the imperial line, the Emperor was permitted to take as many wives and concubines as he pleased. The right of succession did not always fall upon the eldest son, but rather on the most 'suitable'. Sometimes the most suitable son happened to be the strongest and shrewdest, but sometimes the string-pullers at court managed to see that he was the weakest. Japan has had one hundred and twenty-four emperors. Many of them were good and upright men, some were great and influential, some eccentric, and some downright wicked. One of them became a monk and entered a Buddhist monastery, while another forbade the starving inhabitants of his island realm to eat fish. Emperor Yozei, who died in 949, was cruel even as a child. When he came to the throne he developed a taste for ordering his subjects to climb trees and then shooting them down like so many sparrows. Such members of his audience as did not laugh at this unpleasant sport he punished severely. He used to seize young girls in the street, tie them up with lute-strings, and throw them into ponds. Emperor Yozei was mad about riding. When he was feeling in particularly high spirits he would gallop through the streets of his capital lashing the subservient population with his horse-whip. This by no means exhausts His Imperial Majesty's list of spare-time recreations. Japan's Nero had a large number of other hobbies which we shall not dwell on here. In the end, a true miracle occurred: he was deposed.

In 794 the seat of Japanese government was transferred from Nara with its rustling tree-tops to Kyoto, where a golden age prevailed for 400 years. In 1190 no fewer than 500,000 people lived in Kyoto, more than in any European city of the same period with the possible exceptions of Constantinople and Cordoba. Influential aristocratic families like the Fujiwara, the Taira and the Minamoto installed and deposed one emperor after another at will. During the time of Daigo (898-930), Japan's culture and way of life leaned towards that of China, which was at that time experiencing its early classical period under the T'ang Dynasty.

From its very beginning until the present day, Japanese history has been filled with dramatic tension, sanguinary greatness and incalculable impulses. It has been a great Shakespearian theatre peopled with kings, executioners, generals and slaves, and pervaded by love, hatred, suicide and murder. It did not become this reluctantly, but was created so by a people who retained their individuality and transformed everything they adopted into their own idiom. They turned the Buddhism which they took over from China into something essentially Japanese, just as they did with Chinese writing, poetry, administration, music, art and architecture. The Japanese assimilated Chinese culture over a thousand years ago, just as they are assimilating the culture of Europe and America today. They have always been inquisitive and predisposed to snap up everything foreign, yet they have also been eternally mistrustful of it, and have always adapted foreign importations to their own mould.

There is one particular figure in Japanese history who has always fascinated me. This is Yorimoto, who lived from 1147 to 1199. He was a very handsome man and a great favourite with the ladies. He often fell in love, and he was faithful, too. But he had one failing: he could never bring himself to remain faithful if he ever caught sight of someone more beautiful than his current amour. On one occasion, when a certain Hojo Tokimasa's daughter was due to wed a powerful governor, the bridegroom turned up at the appointed hour to find himself alone. Like Ibsen's Peer Gynt, Yorimoto had borne the bride off into the mountains — an escapade in which the young lady joined only too wholeheartedly!

Yorimoto was constantly on the run, constantly harried by pursuers, but in the end he settled at Kamakura in beautiful Sagami Bay, and turned it into the most powerful city in Japan. He became Japan's first *Shogun*.

Kamakura remained the heart of the empire for one hundred and fifty years. In those days the metropolis had a population of some 800,000: today it is a fishing-village once more. However, Yorimoto's tomb is still there. It is a small stone pagoda situated on the slopes of a hill behind the local grammar-school on the way to the shrine of Kamakura. I have been there. It is a lonely spot. Moss is creeping over the pagoda standing behind its stone fence, and Yorimoto's tomb lies there forgotten, an ideal place in which to meditate on the fleeting glories of this world.

From now on, there were virtually two emperors, one in the north and another in the south, for behind the Emperor loomed the authority of the Shogun. Splendid buildings sprang up in the imperial capital of Kyoto. Kamakura was twice burned to the ground. It was an age of warring princes, warring knights, highwaymen and lawlessness. The Portuguese introduced a new factor into the Japanese scene by importing fire-arms. Gradually a state of chaos arose. Three great personalities dominated Japan in succession: a Japanese Wallenstein, a Japanese Napoleon, and a strict paternal autocrat rather similar in character to the father of Frederick the Great.

'The first made the cake, the second baked it, and the third ate it,' the Japanese say, referring to Nobunaga (the Wallenstein), Hideyoshi (the Napoleon) and Tokugawa-Iyeyasu, the warrior-king.

English scholars have always fiercely debated the underlying motives for Hideyoshi's attempted conquest of China in 1592. Almost as an afterthought, they mention that he wanted a Chinese princess as his wife. Perhaps he dreamed of strolling through the gardens with a beautiful Chinese girl on his arm, picking his way over the stepping-stones in the ponds of his palace grounds towards Nagoya or Fushimi. Perhaps he dreamed that he asked her the question which Japanese have always asked: 'Isn't it beautiful here in Japan?' and perhaps his high-born Chinese girl looked at him a little disdainfully and answered as the Chinese have always answered: 'Oh yes, it's beautiful here, but nothing compared with China.' Perhaps Hideyoshi stared at her and thought to himself: 'You must become Emperor of China and Korea as well as Japan, you son of a peasant.' Be that as it may, he certainly wrote a letter to the King of Korea asking him to march with him against China. But the King of Korea, Lien Koku O, only replied: 'So you want to conquer China? Then you are like the shell-fish that wants to drain the sea dry, or the tiny bee which exhausts itself in trying to sting the tortoise through his armour.' Hideyoshi was furious, possibly taunted by the mocking laughter of his Chinese dream-girl, so he invaded Korea with an army equipped with foreign cannons. His campaign was a failure, however, and his life's work crumbled just as Napoleon's was to do.

When Tokugawa Iyeyasu came to power, he abandoned the Korean adventure. He made Edo, or modern Tokyo, his capital city. He and the great Hideyoshi are in fact the fathers of Tokyo. The Tokugawa 'Shogun Dynasty' lasted for 265 years, until 1868, during which time the emperors played second fiddle to the Shoguns. For two and a half centuries Japan remained divorced from the rest of world history. The system brought the country 250 years of peace, but it could only be maintained for as long as no foreign interference or immigration was tolerated.

Since the islands of Japan were no larger in those days than they are now, this isolationist policy had murderous results, and within her overpopulated confines mass-slaughter became the normal method of birth-control. The more the Japanese population increased, the smaller the fields and the *samurai's* rice crops became. There came a day when the *daimyo*, the feudal lords who had once employed the samurai to fight for them, could pay them no longer. A leaderless band of men, the samurai roamed through Japan. They were now called *ronin*. They were warriors no more — just so many bellies to fill. They had no internal or external policy, no outlet for their abilities. They could not hold any civil office because officials sat entrenched behind the barriers of a caste-system on the Chinese model, under which rewards were allotted on a basis of nepotism rather than efficiency. The officials controlled the administration, the priests beat their gongs, and the mercenaries stood boredly at their posts. The brush-strokes in the officials' ledgers dried and grew dusty, the dull booming of the gongs rang out emptily over the weary paradise, the sentries fell asleep. And the Shogun was in duty bound to finance the idling machinery of government, for that was why Heaven had created him.

Outside Japan, however, the world advanced — and at what a pace! The Americans raced from their eastern seaboard to California in the west; India and Canada were occupied; Captain Cook sailed round the southern tip of the world to distant Australia. Whole continents were seized, distributed or partitioned at the whim of the empire-building nations. Merchant-ships ploughed through the seas of the world. It was a time of awakening, a time when any nation which loitered at home would rue it for centuries to come. At last the gates of Japan were thrown open, but not from within — from without, and by foreign hands.

Iron has never grown out of wood, let alone bamboo, and wooden gates are no defence against cannon-balls.

It was in 1853 that Commodore Matthew C. Perry of the U.S. Navy broke open the gates of Japan's fairy-tale castle. It must have been a most remarkable encounter when Perry, commanding the frigate *Mississippi*, and the Governor of Uraga met in Edo Bay like two creatures from different planets. And even more fabulous must have been the time, five years later, when the American Consul-General expounded the basic principles of international law to the astonished Daimyo of Bichu and his officials, men of ancient ceremonial who had hitherto governed according to their own ideas and the even more ancient ideas of China.

History repeats itself, as one can see.

NATURE IS NOT AN ALIEN FORCE

'My dream roves through parched fields.' *Basho*

M EN really are remarkably strange. It is quite amazing how they leave the best things alone and take something mediocre instead.' This sentence occurs in *Sketch-book under the Pillow* by the Japanese lady-in-waiting Sei Shonagon. Living about 1000 years ago, she was a keen and accurate observer of people and things, with slightly blasé tastes, an acute mind and a sarcastic tongue. It is extremely entertaining to dip into her diary.

She describes her 'greatest enjoyment' as 'fording a river on a bright moon-lit night, with the water splashing up at every step the ox takes, as though crystal were being shattered to pieces.' She tells us what looks ugly: 'White silken robes worn by someone with scanty hair'; 'a toothless old woman eating plums'; 'mallow blossoms in curly hair'. She is revolted by: 'The inside of cats' ears'; 'the reverse of a piece of embroidery'; or 'hairless young rats falling out of their nest'. She is charmed by: 'The face of a child biting into a melon'; 'a little girl in convent uniform, throwing back her head to shake the hair out of her eyes when she wants to look at something'. Among the things which she regards as rare are: 'Subordinates who never revile their superiors, and daughters-in-law who are well-disposed towards their mothers-in-law'; while 'people who can live in close proximity, yet keep their distance and never become in the slightest degree lax' are something she never meets.

There is no other race on earth which can fashion the little things of this world so perfectly as the Japanese: small bowls, for instance, or little curved coloured platters for serving fish, lacquer boxes, small caskets for writing-materials, the elegant art of floral arrangement, the controlled growth of dwarf trees, little ponds, miniature grottoes, mountains with peaks only waist-high, miniature gardens, miniature bridges and miniature pavilions. The Japanese are masters of the world of small and dainty things. No other nation ever produced poets who could so vividly capture the fleeting thought like the famous Basho, for instance, when he wrote: 'Ancient fish-pond. A frog leaps. A sound in the water.' The Japanese call miniature poems of this type *haikai*, and the last haikai which this laconic giant among poets ever wrote, ran: 'Weary of wandering, my dream roves through parched fields.'

In fact, these island people of the north-east Pacific have always been strangers to massive, spacious themes on the grand scale. Yet they have a bold, gifted and inventive eye for painting, the arrangement of colours and the choice of silk patterns, and a talent for dancing, acting and, above all, for portraying the small things of life on their cramped, scattered chain of islands with a pleasant and affectionate touch. The Japanese have often fallen prey to the very characteristics which have made them such great artists: their naive and childlike qualities. Yet they have always realized how small man is in comparison with the vastness of Nature. Hiroshige's picture 'The Grotto of Enoshima' is a haunting example of this discernment. Spruce-trees bend before the storm, the sea is still menacingly calm, but in the background a single foaming white wave plucks with giant fingers at the tiny figures of three men.

The Japanese have always been, for better or worse, at the mercy of their cramped island home with its perilous earthquakes and its smoking volcanoes. Always close to the sea, they have for ever been prisoners of their natural environment. And because they know so much about Nature they have never bothered to tame it, never framed their pictures nor barricaded their houses against the elements, never tried to counteract the winter's cold with stoves nor wept when an earthquake engulfed their mothers, wives and children. To this day, I have never fathomed how the Japanese manage to bury the victims of natural catastrophes with such an apparent absence of grief. It is due partly, I think, to their view that Nature is not an alien force, and partly to a courteous desire not to extort sympathy from anyone with their tears.

Eternally submissive towards Nature, the Japanese have always bowed down to the sun and revered the chief product of their fields, the precious rice which feeds them and also supplies straw for the mats upon which they sleep at night. They have always been obedient and self-controlled, and have known how to die without sorrow.

It is not easy to practise humility and, if the men of Japan were resolved never to master this art completely themselves, they at least compelled their womenfolk to become perfect exponents of it.

Humility is a charming quality. Charm is not susceptible of organization, but it makes life more beautiful. That is why small Japanese girls are taught to move gracefully from a very early age. It is an aesthetic delight to see a Japanese woman dressed in kimono and obi and walking on her getas, to watch her as she kneels down and squats on her heels, or offers a bowl of tea, or withdraws backwards from the room, opening the sliding-door and closing it softly behind her.

There is charm in the very language of the Japanese, in their mode of greeting — even in their simple 'yes', which is expressed by the word *haai*. No one who has a feeling for such things and, above all, can keep his patience, will fail to be delighted by even such a small thing as the Japanese telephone operators' soft and friendly voices which greet him as he lifts the receiver. The same girlish Japanese voices are to be heard over the loud-speakers on every main railway station in Tokyo, thanking travellers on their arrival and departure. So the innate amiability of Japanese womanhood has not quite been overcome even by the incredible bustle which prevails in this huge metropolis. One is still met in the foyer of every good Tokyo restaurant by a row of such women, bowing low and chorusing their welcome. Cinema usherettes, sales-girls in the big stores, waitresses and bath-attendants are all eager to greet you with the friendly sing-song of their voices, whose charm is greatly enhanced by the fact that no two consonants ever directly follow one another in the Japanese language, vowels and consonants always occurring alternately.

It is all very lovely, and neither war nor American influence nor democracy will ever transform the Japanese from rice-eaters into bread-consumers, or convert them from kimonos to lounge-suits and from straw mats to floorboards. For the Japanese have a deep conviction that beauty can only repose in Nature, or what is a development of Nature. Perhaps the loveliest thing about Japan is the cherry blossom which flutters down in the spring breezes when it has reached the acme of its rose-pink beauty. 'They died like the cherry blossom' was the Japanese epitaph on three young soldiers who sacrificed their lives as human bombs in the battle for Shanghai.

Death itself is part of Nature. Shinto temples are dovetailed into their natural surroundings with complete sureness of touch, and the sacred groves are part of Nature. The whole of Japanese history springs from Nature, and the Emperor himself is a descendant of the sun. Japanese houses are just a continuation of their gardens, house and garden seeming to melt into one another. As soon as they pull off their shoes, get out of their Western clothes, and remove the dust from their pores with a hot damp face-cloth, the Japanese leave behind them all the miseries and burdens of Western civilization. Their homes display no harsh colours, no carpets, no knick-knacks, no furniture, even — only polished natural wood of fine workmanship, mats of resilient straw, windows of the wooden trellis-work covered with paper which is such a work of art in Japan, subdued lighting, the customary alcove (*tokonoma*) perhaps containing a single scroll-picture (*kakemono*), and a vase holding a single branch or some artistically arranged flowers. Japanese straw mats are always the same size, 3 feet by 6 feet, and the floor-area of a Japanese room is calculated according to the number of straw mats (*tatami*) it takes to cover it. The sliding doors (*karakami*) which divide up the Japanese house can be removed to transform it into a single large room.

There are wonderful little hotels nearly all the way round Japan's coasts.

NATURE IS NOT AN ALIEN FORCE

You can have your pillows laid out on the mats at night and lie on your back, the whole wall of your room facing the sea removed, watching the sun come up or listening to the roar of the surf and dreaming that you are racing along, high above the waves, on board some huge ship. It is the same inland, too. Your first impression on waking is that you are lying in the garden. You will always find this so, because a Japanese housewife considers it her duty to let the morning air and the sun into her rooms punctually at six o'clock in the morning. And, obedient as Japanese women are, that is one thing you can never stop them doing.

Trees possess souls. An old tree is almost as greatly revered as an old grandmother.

The Japanese think it a sin or a crime to cut down an old tree. Poor though their cramped islands are in fuel resources, they own vast tracts of wooded country and huge parks, and no one who has heard the wind rustling among the conifers of Nikko, Hakone, Beppu and Lake Biwa will ever be able to forget them.

The Japanese undertook a remarkably bold task when, with Polynesia on the wane, they constituted themselves the sole race to preserve the culture of Oceania and the Pacific. They are the only nation to have taken over all that was valuable from the continent of Asia and at the same time to have adopted the civilization of Europe and America eagerly and inquisitively, while still remaining true to their own character, the character of their island home. Even today the Japanese weep with emotion when they see their Emperor. Even today they sing: 'May the imperial house flourish until a little stone grows into a moss-covered rock.'

THE GREEN HOUSES OF YOSHIWARA

Utamaro

'The soul of man, it comes and goes, fluttering away like sunflowers.' Hokusai

WORLD-FAMOUS Yoshiwara stands where it has stood since 1657, about a mile north of Asakusa Park in Tokyo. It used to be a little town in its own right, with hundreds of houses, broad streets and narrow alleys – a sleepless town which knew no night, unrivalled for its bright lights and for ever pervaded by a mysterious hum, a restless quality of trembling anticipation.

Thousands of girls used to squat there in long rows behind iron grilles. They came from every province in the country, sold into Yoshiwara by their needy families. Daughters were usually so fond of their parents that they not only acquiesced in this sacrifice but sometimes even volunteered for it of their own free will. On their arrival from the country they exchanged their simple clothes for gorgeous dresses, and underwent a period of careful training. They learned how to speak a special, deep-voiced form of classical Japanese, and were instructed in the arts of music, singing and poetry.

The highest class of this kind of courtesan, the *oiran*, had two little girls to wait on her, called *kamuro*. These children were bought by the proprietors of Yoshiwara establishments between the ages of five and eight, and could entertain the hope of one day becoming oiran themselves. When an oiran reached the age of twenty-seven she was usually discharged, and the Japanese of the 17th and 18th centuries looked upon her, amazingly enough, as an entirely respectable and marriageable person. Amazingly enough, it must be added, because there is no country in the world today where the girl who caters for unchastity is more despised than Japan.

Yoshiwara never had more than one entrance and one exit, both of which gates were constantly guarded by police to ensure that none of the girls escaped. Every visitor was given a white kimono upon admittance, on the principle that equality should reign supreme in a place where all were united by the bonds of delight.

The grilles crumbled with the passage of time. The white kimonos were no longer distributed, and the age of courtly etiquette and the samurai knighthood faded away.

But Yoshiwara survived. It kept its two gates and its watchful police, its establishments and bright lights, its sleepless atmosphere and hum of activity. Now, however, the houses stood open to the street, and at the back of their lobbies — an innovation of our own 'progressive' age — photographs of girls with white, powder-frosted faces and lofty coiffures were displayed in the harsh glare of neon lighting. Hundreds, even thousands, of such faces stared out from photographs, peeped from behind bamboo curtains, called softly, or beckoned.

Even so, a sense of calm and orderliness still pervaded the place, to remind the visitor that, after all, he was in Japan. This strange and wonderful world with its nightly activity survived until the day when the great bomb fell in 1945. Yoshiwara burned. The town of bamboo and gold lacquer went up in flames and many of its girl inmates with it, just as it had done in 1923 during the great earthquake.

Absolutely nothing of the old splendour remains. I have strolled through the grey streets of Yoshiwara. The only reminder of its romantic past is the little cemetery whose headstones bear mute testimony to so many dramas of love and death. Modern blocks of flats are growing up on the ground which once knew so much glamour, so much luxury and poverty, joy and grief, intrigue and romance.

Yoshiwara witnessed moments of great drama and deeds of desperation, lovers faithful to death, abductions, acts of jealousy and despair, poisonings and suicide-pacts.

About three hundred years ago there lived a young Japanese called Shirai Gompachi. He was a brave young man, but he was unlucky enough to kill one of his liege lord's retainers in a quarrel over a dog, and was forced to leave home. On the way to Yedo (modern Tokyo), he spent a night at an inn. He was suddenly awakened by the voice of a very beautiful girl, who told him that her name was Komurasaki, and that she had been carried off by a band of robbers who were now planning to kill him and steal his samurai sword. Gompachi lay in wait for the robbers, killed them, and brought Komurasaki home to her parents' house. Then he continued on his way to Yedo, leaving the lovely girl to sit and pine for her young deliverer. Gompachi found the gay night-life of the city much to his taste and, hearing talk of a very charming girl who sat behind the grilles in Yoshiwara, he went to pay her a visit. He could scarcely believe his eyes when she turned out to be Komurasaki. Her parents had fallen upon evil days, and she had sold herself into Yoshiwara to ease their burdens.

Gompachi visited her every day, and every day a little more of his money passed into the hands of the business-like proprietor of the establishment. He became poorer and poorer, until one day the gates of Yoshiwara were closed to him. Desperate to see his beloved, he murdered a man, robbed his body, and went to Yoshiwara on the proceeds. The unhappy man repeated this expedient until he was finally arrested, sentenced to death and beheaded.

When the unfortunate Komurasaki learned that her lover was buried in the Meguro quarter of Tokyo, she stole out secretly into the forbidden city, threw herself weeping upon his freshly turned grave, and stabbed herself with a dagger. It is appropriate that Japan's own true version of the story of Romeo and Juliet was set in Yoshiwara.

For Yoshiwara was not just a den of vice. It was a rendezvous for artists and poets, a place where they could enjoy a fleeting taste of the romance and fantasy which the everyday world could not offer them, and which shone forth each night in the reflected splendour of their obedient Muses' submissive, white-powdered faces.

And that is why so many of Japan's great painters, who may well be the greatest in the whole cultural history of mankind, drew their inspiration from Yoshiwara, reviled and glorified, celebrated in song and as often condemned.

Toyoaki Utamaro, whose real name was Kitagave Yusuki, was born at Kawagoye in the province of Musashi in the year 1754. When he was still a child, his mother sent him to study painting under the celebrated master Sekiyen. Utamaro began to observe, study and draw every living creature he saw in the most minute detail. He was only a young boy, yet he could paint little miracles of Nature, like the flies or grasshoppers he caught, with such amazing attention to detail and so mature an eye for composition that master Sekiyen declared that his pupil's brush was guided by his heart. The great work in colour which made Utamaro famous in his own right was his book of shell-fish. In this he illustrated thirty-six groups of shell-fish in the mysterious blue depths of the sea with an overwhelming richness of colour and the most exquisite technique. He employed glitter-dust, powdered mother-of-pearl, gold-dust and gold-leaf in addition to a large range of more conventional colours. However, this absorption with the glittering, staggering, thrilling quality of the great out-of-doors was only the start of Utamaro's unique skill. He became Japan's greatest painter of women, and found his immense store of models in Yoshiwara. He painted characteristic, dreamy beauties with extraordinarily slim figures. He worked incessantly day and night, dividing his time between the labyrinths of Yoshiwara and his studio. He painted for as long as he could stand on his legs, only granting himself a modicum of rest when they threatened to give way under him. He became at once the most brilliant, self-willed and lyrical painter of women which his age produced.

Through Utamaro, the all too perishable beauties of Yoshiwara gained immortality. Utamaro studied them as they danced and painted. He watched them when they were sad, probably brooding on their captivity. He listened to their classical music and took part in their tea-ceremonies. He drugged himself with the harmony of colours, the lights gleaming upon silk, the secret whisperings, the soft notes of the samisen, the movement of heads under the coal-black glory of their elaborate hair-style with its bouquet of pins, and the scent of perfumes. His pure and splendid imagination transformed all these things into pictures richer in colour and movement than any the world had ever seen before. He saw the eternal essence of femininity in everything, and in so doing he at last discovered the great secret which lay hidden in the faces of the poor peasant girls whom Yoshiwara's delusive glamour had turned into princesses of love: with their infinite patience and their instinctive ability to console, they were all mothers at heart. Fundamentally, they were all images of Nature, the bountiful force which squanders itself in the perpetual furtherance of human life. Utamaro painted them and, carried away by a talent which ennobled everything it touched, invented the children to go with them.

Taking as his models the unhappiest girls in the world, the captive flowers who languished in the cells of Yoshiwara in their gorgeous kimonos and enamel make-up, Utamaro bludgeoned his amazing talent into producing faces of the sublimest beauty, and thereby idealized the Japanese woman in a fashion which no nation or age can ever hope to rival. His impulsive genius and daring intellect sought to express not only the essence of all mortal beauty, but also its yearning to endure, to conquer time and finality. Therein lies the hint of melancholy discernible in the faces of all Utamaro's Yoshiwara beauties. It comes from a realization that some things are unattainable, and that consolation is never quite complete.

In the course of time, Utamaro's girls became slimmer and slimmer, their faces longer and longer. Their necks became flower-stems supporting heads which swayed above shoulders too narrow to be true. The bold, sickle-shaped arch of their coiffures towered ever higher, and their gorgeous dresses swathed figures so fragile as to be unearthly. By the year 1800, Utamaro had reached the stage where his beauties had heads three times as long as they were broad.

Utamaro was determined to get nearer and nearer his conception of perfect beauty. Although he was by this time acknowledged to be one of the really great artists of the world, he was no businessman. A certain art dealer and publisher called Jusaburo had very early on secured the rights of the shell-fish book, thereby gaining a great reputation in artistic circles. It was Jusaburo, keen connoisseur that he was, who used this initial success to establish his own atelier, where he installed the indefatigable Utamaro and allowed him to work. This publisher, whose first name was Tsutaya, should not be thought of only in connection with Utamaro. He was a very influential man in every respect, and brilliant at co-ordinating the joint efforts of the numerous craftsmen whose co-operation was necessary to the production of a single woodcut, a man with a true spirit of enterprise who attracted and secured the services of the greatest contemporary masters in the art of wood-engraving. Utamaro lived in his publisher's house and ate at his table, while Jusaburo turned all his protégé's work into gold.

Utamaro grew taciturn, often standing before his sketches wrapt in thought. He was overwhelmed by a sudden realization that all the girls in Yoshiwara were in a sense his sisters. For was he not, like them, confined in a golden cage? He loved glamour, he revelled in playing the grand seigneur, and he wanted to remain a welcome visitor to the 'Green Houses' which through the medium of his prints had become a subject so highly prized by the art dealers of the world at large. Utamaro was the highest paid artist of his day. Yet living as he did at Jusaburo's house near the gates of Yoshiwara, he was for ever dependent upon his employer and source of income. During the day he worked in his astute patron's atelier, as if in a delirium. But as soon as night came down over Tokyo and the evening mists rose to meet it, as soon as the lights of Yoshiwara shone out into the darkness, Utamaro plunged like a man possessed into the night-life of the enchanted world. With eyes red-rimmed for want of sleep or rest, he worked as he lived, on a prodigious scale, spurred on by his employer to the limits of his endurance, and gaining an unrivalled reputation.

Always experimenting, always enhancing and improving his technique, always painting women and studying their faces, hands and figures, he finally, at the age of forty-three, discovered his ideal model. She was very young and extremely talented, with eyes like cherries and pitch-black hair so long that it could be dressed magnificently high. Utamaro married her, and until his death the beautiful girl washed the master's brushes, mixed his paints and knelt and bowed before the amazing man who was her husband.

Utamaro was also a poet, which was why Fate laid its ponderous hand upon his ardent, passionate life. The military junta of the day took exception to one of his small satires, and Utamaro was thrown into gaol. It was there amid the grindstones of the prison administration's mill that his constitution, which had never been strong, finally gave way. One moment Utamaro was enjoying freedom, light and colour, and the next he had simply crumpled up and died. The great man's young wife knelt beside his body and wept.

STARVE IF NEED BE...BUT PAINT!

Hokusai

'It is good that life seems unending....' Hokusai

UTAMARO may have been a giant, yet by comparison with Hokusai, he seems like a dwarf. Next to Leonardo da Vinci, Shakespeare and Lope de Vega, he was one of the most prolific geniuses in the whole cultural history of mankind.

Incredible as it may seem, Hokusai passed on to posterity not only an impressive array of novels and hundreds of glorious poems, but more than five hundred illustrated books and over 35,000 pictures. He was a fanatical worker, and the scope and grandeur of his life's output has seldom if ever been exceeded. It simply surpassed any normal human criterion. Hokusai used countless pseudonyms, among others the significant one 'The Painting-maniac'. So rich and inexhaustible were his talents that he generously donated his pseudonyms to pupils, who used them to gain a brilliant start in their careers.

Hokusai's father was a mirror-cutter by trade, and when Hokusai was a little boy he used to gaze into his father's stock of mirrors and see enchanted worlds which seemed to lie beyond the frontiers of reality. Wishing to become a craftsman like his father he decided to learn the art of wood-engraving.

An apprentice had to follow his master's instructions to the letter. The Japanese have always set great store by obedience, and they held that before a boy could 'develop freely', he must first acquire ability. Every day saw new drawings and pictures in colour arrive in the workshop. The apprentice was given delicate cutting-knives, and had to adapt himself to the varying styles of many different artists. He had to cut his blocks of wood so that their impression gave an exact reproduction of the original brush drawing. It was a risky operation, too, for one false cut entailed the making of an entirely new original. This was because the original drawing was gummed down on top of the wood and destroyed in the process of engraving. The artist merely supplied a drawing done on transparent paper, which the apprentice first had to copy several times over. A five-colour picture required five wooden blocks for its reproduction, and a ten-colour picture, ten. It was also the apprentice's job to mix the paints, which had to correspond to the artist's specifications with extreme accuracy.

Hokusai was fifteen years old when he prepared his first drawing for subsequent printing. He was fifteen, too, when he wrote his first poem, and by sixteen he had written his first novel. At the age of eighteen he entered the atelier of Shunsho, who was at that time the most famous painter of actors. Shunsho's studio was a hive of feverish activity, for the master had to keep pace with the latest productions at the Kabuki Theatre. The public wanted to see their favourite stage personalities. And the actors? Well, they were just as fond of publicity then as they are now, and so Shunsho's establishment was much frequented by mimic actors of considerable repute. It was an atmosphere in which singing and poetry flourished, and Hokusai himself later wrote some very successful short poems. He worked day and night at his poetry and painting. Again and again he succeeded in making two of his pseudonyms so famous simultaneously that the inhabitants of Yedo, as Tokyo was called at that time, could not grasp the fact that they both belonged to one and the same painter, novelist, or poet.

Hokusai was an inveterate wanderer, changing his studio and his lodgings more than a hundred times in the course of his lifetime. He was always poor and often hungry. He roamed drunkenly through the countryside in the autumn winds like a tramp. At one time he turned street-trader and peddled his own drawings, while on another occasion he sold red pepper in a market. The motive power within him grew with each year that passed, spurring him on to ever greater achievements. On the one hand he attained great successes, and on the other, he lived in poverty. In fact, poverty dogged him throughout his life, for he had such a fundamental disdain both for money and fame that he only tried to throw them away.

Hundreds, thousands of pictures took shape under Hokusai's brush. For a time he joined forces with Utamaro. He painted Fuji thirty-six times — then a hundred times, depicting the sacred volcano in an amazing diversity of moods. Hokusai's views are so grandiose that he might almost have seen the mountain from an aeroplane flying many miles up. Nothing seemed beyond the reach of his brilliant observation of Nature.

Hokusai strove to evolve entirely novel techniques. He painted with his fingers, with his left hand, now working from the bottom upwards, now from left to right, now the other way round, sometimes using a bottle, and sometimes an egg. He drew and dissected plants and painted enthralling sea-scapes full of cliffs and pounding breakers. Looking at prints of his wood-cuts, one often forgets all about the engraving technique which produced them, so bold are they in colour and design.

Hokusai mingled with the people. No Japanese painter has ever portrayed the faces of common folk with such sincerity and obvious delight. Here Hokusai was in his element. He ridiculed people, he caricatured them, he showed up their grotesque little idiosyncrasies, as in his 'Ghost-dance of the Capital' (at that time Yedo). He rarely painted beautiful women, because the subject did not interest him.

The public marvelled. The public laughed, as they always do when they cannot understand genius. 'So you laugh, do you?' cried Hokusai. 'Am I too small for you then?' And he began to paint a gigantic picture of such dimensions as the world had never seen before. He ordered a sheet of paper no less than 635 feet square. To keep it taut, he had a thick layer of rice-straw and wooden blocks spread over it as ballast. It was feared that otherwise the wind would tear the paper and blow it away. A vast framework of scaffolding was erected on the wall of a temple to support rollers on which the picture could be raised by means of long ropes. Dozens of casks stood ready, and paints were transported to the site in huge pails. The miraculous scene was thronged by a vast crowd of interested spectators.

At midday Hokusai appeared, dressed in an entirely new style of garment of his own design, which left his arms and legs bare. A procession of pupils carrying bronze pails followed the master as he painted. Hokusai's brush was an immense besom. Dipping it into one of the pails of paint he drew an enormous nose, then an eye, then a second eye. Gradually a *daruma*, or wizard, took shape under his strokes. Working at top speed, Hokusai drew in mouth, ear, neck, hair and beard in turn. His pupils came panting up dragging a huge bronze basin. This time Hokusai's brush was a bundle of rice-sacks tied together. Dragging it after him by means of a cord tied round his neck, and taking small steps backwards, he painted in the daruma's clothes, quickly colouring in the traditional red spots on the wizard's costume by scooping the paint out of a bucket with a ladle.

Night had come down over Tokyo unnoticed. Everything was quite still. The crowd held its breath. The daruma's picture was finished. It was dragged up into the sky on its rollers. As it hung there for a moment above the crowd, it must almost have looked like a piece of cake in the midst of an ant-hill.

People were entranced, terrified, dumbfounded. A few women cried. Hokusai's huge painting was a *succès fou*. The painter's name was on everyone's lips, and he was obliged to endure public acclamation. To demonstrate his skill once more, he painted a giant horse.

The Emperor of Japan summoned the new darling of the people into his presence. He wanted to see his skill for himself. Hokusai bowed low. He lifted one of the great temple doors off its hinges — it was faced with paper, in the Japanese fashion. Plunging his hand into a paint-pot, he threw some indigo on to the paper and smeared it over its surface. Then he opened a basket which he had brought with him and took out a live cockerel. Dipping the bird's feet in red ink, he let it walk around on the paper. Finally, he bowed to the Emperor once more. The whole of the court entourage knew immediately what Hokusai had painted: it was Tasuta, the River of the Poets, with red maple-leaves floating upon its surface.

Hokusai was enthusiastically acclaimed. He was the only commoner ever to be received by a Japanese emperor of the Tokugawa period. For weeks and months his house was besieged by mobs of people, each wanting a personal drawing bearing the celebrated signature. Hokusai soon withdrew from the public gaze, however, and went to live under assumed names. He worked like a man possessed. It was during this period that he painted his terrible Ghost Pictures. In a symphony of colours he painted the most imposing waterfall which ever held an artist under its spell — the cataract of Yoshino, its huge spidery fingers groping their way into the depths below. Another of his pictures shows a horse shying, with two little mannikins holding anxiously on to the reins. He painted some glorious azaleas with a cuckoo swooping out of the blue sky above them, a dragon-fly hovering over kikyo flowers, and — these last over and over again — Fuji, clouds and the sea. No other painter ever attempted such bold and at the same time splendid pictures.

Hokusai wrote an educational manual and compiled a fifteen volume pictorial encyclopaedia, in which he touched on every aspect of the life of the common people. No matter where he sought refuge from publicity, no matter what pseudonym he used, people always recognized him. Yet he was a poor man, and had his worries.

Hokusai married twice, but his only son turned out to be a ne'er-do-well, as the sons of genius so often do. Ragged, verminous and destitute, Hokusai lodged for five long years in an unheated garret. He went begging, but only to raise enough money for brushes and paints. He might starve, but he would go on painting. It was good that life seemed unending. Hokusai was seventy-three years old before he thought he understood Nature. At eighty he pronounced himself ready to start making progress. At ninety he proposed to begin exploring the mysteries of the material world. And when he was a hundred and ten, or so he prophesied, he would have reached the stage where his strokes and dots had a life of their own.

This giant among men was a world in himself. He had an inexhaustible power of observation, and his genius allowed him to capture the intrinsic nature of a subject without ever sacrificing his eye for detail. His application and energy bordered on the miraculous, and all his works reveal that, in spite of his dire poverty, this genius never lost his sense of humour.

Hokusai was not always popular with the Japanese, for he was an intellectual giant who did not take his little compatriots too seriously. The Western world regards him as one of the greatest artists of all time. He died on May 10th, 1849, in his ninetieth year, and his last words were: 'Had Heaven granted me another five years, I might have become a painter.'

THEY PAINTED 'THE MOVING WORLD'

Harunobu — Sharaku — Hiroshige

To rob the moment of its impermanence, that is art.

JAPANESE coloured woodcuts are a fairy-land of their own, an art which inspires anyone who steeps himself in it with admiration, love and amazement in turn. For the degree of artistic ability and craftsmanship which contributed towards the production of a Japanese coloured woodcut is almost unbelievable.

The Japanese woodcut was probably the finest, the most mature and the last artistic product of eastern Asia. Its masters did not strive to achieve mere replicas of Nature. They had an understanding of the atmosphere, the soul, the true ring and the whole tumultuous rhythm of life. The artist did not paint a picture 'just like that'. He first had to have a painting clear in his mind's eye down to its very last detail. Then he broke his mental picture down into its component colours. And finally, he painted several pictures, one for each colour which occurred in the complete version. Sticking them down on a piece of wood, he cut away the unpainted areas until only the painted portions remained, and sent the individual pictures off one by one to the wood-engraver's workshop. The reproduction of a picture containing fifteen colours thus entailed the making of fifteen individual one-colour pictures. As soon as the printer had the fifteen blocks in his workshop, he was ready to begin. He moistened each of the blocks with the requisite paint and impressed them on paper, one after the other. It was only then that the artist saw his work for the first time. Making a coloured woodcut was therefore rather like composing a symphony.

The individual colour-prints had to correspond to one another with great precision. An infinitesimal discrepancy between one block and another could mean an altered facial expression. Every line had to 'register', not only once, but as many times as there were colours being employed. Only when one learns that the Japanese never used any tracings, but cut each separate block accurately to a fraction of an inch relying solely on memory, does the full wonder of this art become apparent. Only men whose memories had mastered each subject in its entirety could have done such a thing freehand. Three years after delivering the blocks for one of his pictures, the celebrated Hokusai suddenly decided that some additional colours might improve it. Without a guide of any kind, he made paintings for the additional colours: they fitted down to the last detail. In an art such as this, any slipshod work, indistinct outlines or blurred colours were unthinkable. There was no way of correcting a cut once it had been made, and the advance selection of colours was a mental feat of the first order. The masters of the Japanese polychrome woodcut who gained world-wide reputations possessed real genius. They had to have an amazing feeling for composition, they had to be brilliant calculators, and they had to have a sense of perspective and an ability to visualize the interplay of colours without actually seeing them. On top of that, they had to be brilliant craftsmen. But above all, when they were doing a portrait of a girl, for instance, they did not just paint a graceful girl and leave it at that. They had to portray 'the essence of grace'. Their form of art was called 'The moving world', or in Japanese, *Ukiyo*. And the man who gave the Japanese coloured woodcut its name called himself Ukiyo Matabei. It was he who founded the Ukiyo-e school of painting. The masters of the woodcut who followed his lead in painting 'the moving world' never concerned themselves with pure fantasy, but painted the contemporary world. The ageless quality of their work is part of the fundamental secret of all great art, which is to rob the moment of its impermanence.

Anyone who knows Japan will also know what a great role is played there by a small article which we Europeans rather disdain: the toothpick.

About two hundred years ago there stood near the Kwannon temple in the Asakusa quarter of Tokyo the shop of a worthy toothbrush and tooth-pick merchant called Niheiji-Yanagi-ya. His small establishment went by the name of The House of Willows. Tokyo may have been called Yedo in those days, but her cherry-trees blossomed just as gloriously, her gold-fish ponds sparkled as brightly, and her gingko-trees flaunted their foliage as bravely, silver-green and as glossy as patent leather. And then, just as now, there were some very pretty girls in Japan.

There was also, just as there is now, a great demand for toothpicks. There was something about Niheiji's shop, however, which particularly attracted the masculine members of his clientele. It was his beautiful daughter Ofuji. Since she sold not only toothpicks, but also perfumes, flowers in rice-wine, scent-shells and other toilet requisites, she knew how to use them — just as the sales-girls in modern Tokyo establishments do today. Ofuji was just sixteen years old, and so beautiful that dramatists were already — in 1769 — naming their heroines after her, and children singing little songs about her in the streets. One day, a gentleman in a dark robe walked into the shop. Ofuji inclined her head. After the gentleman had paid several visits to the shop, she put a few cherry-blossoms into the bowl of saké which it was usual to offer every good customer. The stranger was Harunobu the painter, and he had fallen in love with the girl. She began to figure in many of his pictures. In one of them she is seen kneeling in her shop smoking 'tobacco', with Harunobu himself sitting beside her. The House of Willows stood in the shade of a gingko-tree and, although it is not visible in Harunobu's dainty picture, its fallen leaves can be seen on the ground. The look passing between the two sensitive faces is not easy to define, but it has a tenderness and delicacy, a yearning and timeless quality which scarcely any other artist has ever achieved.

Harunobu could never paint unless he was in love, and he only fell in love with very young girls who still had the charm of naivety. He painted sweet, flower-like creatures with tiny faces and hands and arms of incredible delicacy and childish grace. For all that, his style is never mawkish. It remains a mystery how Harunobu managed to imbue his young creatures with so much life, quite apart from their tranquil grace. In his eternal craving for beauty, the artist had discovered another sixteen-year-old girl even before he found Ofuji. Her name was Osen, and she was employed by the Kagiya tea-house at Kasamori. Kasamori was the site of the Inari shrine, and contemporary Japanese records inform us that pilgrims visited the shrine less from a desire to pray than to be served by charming Osen in the Kagiya tea-house. Her hair was black as night, her face was shaped like a melon-seed, and her lips were vermilion-red. Osen was really a peasant-girl, and wore a long comb in her hair and humble clogs on her feet. No rouge or powder adorned her fresh face, yet if ten men passed her by, ten men turned to stare.

Osen had the humility proper to all well brought up Japanese girls, and loved her parents. She was conscious of her beauty and made a patient artist's model. She is perhaps the only girl in history who sang the praises of her own beauty in classical verse and not only failed to irritate anyone by doing so, but gave all who heard her song a brief moment in heaven.

> 'Out of violet-coloured clouds of steam
> she steps, as if
> lacquered all over in gold and silver . . .
> She sits by the tea-filled kettle
> musing, musing all alone,
> thinking, ever thinking of this and that
> and stroking her little head with a silver pin.
> — He who would rest his legs a while
> should do so at Kasamori
> in the shade of a tree.'

Young Osen composed that herself, in 1769. The poem goes on: 'In the morning I make Japanese tea, in the evening I roll dumplings . . . Even if my name never figures in the history of the goddesses, at least my likeness is to be found in the brocade pictures of the east country, Harunobu's own brush has painted me, and they spread my fame abroad in folk-songs. My name is being repeated in all four corners of the heaven, and everyone who has eyes and a mouth is saying: Osen, Osen. . . .'

Harunobu idealized his enchanting models after his own fashion. He wanted to stir the beholder's tenderest emotions, and was less concerned for effect than to express the absolutely timeless concepts of love and grace in an absolutely timeless way. In one of his pictures a frail and lovely girl is seen crossing a bridge in a snow-storm. Another delightful child is blowing soap-bubbles for her brother in the garden. Another is listening to a cuckoo, and another to the evening bell tolling from a temple near by. Another is seen buying a fan, another taking leave of her lover, and yet another entrusting a love-letter to a little girl.

Two of Harunobu's models were so beautiful that they were engaged to dance at a ceremonial consecration of the effigy of the god Shoshi at the Yushima temple in Yedo. Their names were Onani and Omitsu. We also hear of another girl who came from the Tsuta-ya tea-house in the Asakusa quarter. Her name was Oyoshi, and she too was a famous beauty.

Harunobu had the profoundest contempt for everything coarse and vulgar. He was an aristocrat, both by brush and by birth. The theatre was a particular *bête noire* of his, because actors had such unsavoury reputations. Harunobu wanted to raise the level of Ukiyo-e art. Even when he painted Hinatsuru, the famous courtesan from the House of Cloves in Yoshiwara, he made her so innocent and fine, so lily-like and unselfconscious that any hint of the ephemeral nature of his model's real everyday life was quite absent, and all that remained was the artist's own conception delicately expressed in line and colour. Harunobu painted Hinatsuru many times, but if he had only painted the courtesan once, as he did in 'Pictures with contourless white robes', it would have been enough to set her on the throne of immortality.

Hinatsuru, incidentally, was 'bought out' of Yoshiwara by a rich admirer of hers. When the beautiful bird had left her cage, one of her former companions in misfortune wrote her the following letter. It gives us a good example of feminine Japanese style:

It is with a feeling of extraordinary relief and joy that I hear that you will today leave the 'fiery house' of Yoshiwara, that you are departing, and that you will henceforth live in more temperate and seemly surroundings. I can find no words to express my envy of the future which awaits you. Your own nature corresponds to wood, and your husband's to earth, just as Fate has ordained. It is a magnificent meeting of the active and passive elements in Nature. For the earth feeds and protects the tree as long as it lives. It is truly a good omen, and augurs well for your future happiness and well-being. So I send my greetings to you on the day of the happy union into which you are entering.

Your Usugumo — Soft Clouds

As we have seen, the masters of Japanese wood-engraving did not copy Nature. They went on mentally collecting pictures until they had a clear perception and exact idea of them and could finally paint the essence of their subject. If they were familiar with oil-paints, they were wise enough never to use them.

The Japanese had been painting in water-colours on silk and paper long before the invention of woodcuts, and the *makemono* or *kakemono* could be rolled up. Ukiyo-e is above all a style of painting. The long list of brilliant Ukiyo-e exponents testifies to the fact that no really great artist has ever suffered by starting out as a faithful imitator of his master, that this does not necessarily lead to a life-long career as a copyist, and that an individual style and great personal ability can develop from an initial talent for imitative craftsmanship.

Four people had to co-operate in the making of a coloured print: the publisher, the artist, the wood-engraver and the printer. Perhaps this list should also include the paper-manufacturer, the man who supplied the wonderful hand-made mulberry-bark paper which enabled the colours to blossom forth in the true splendour of their gentle radiance. Until the 19th century, the Japanese extracted their paints from plants.

The Japanese were always aware that art should be more than a slavish imitation of Nature. As draftsmen, the Ukiyo-e artists have never been rivalled by any others in the world. The masters of Japanese wood-engraving concentrated above all upon bringing out the essentials of their subject in line and colour. Nothing ever intimidated them, and it can be said that Hokusai, for instance, turned the disorder in Nature into order, though it may be added that his kind of order was an uncommonly dramatic one.

It is far too often forgotten that the exponents of Japanese wood-engraving exerted a very considerable influence upon modern European painting. It was Japanese works which helped the French impressionists to recognize the essence of a subject — its 'impression', in fact; which helped them to see atmospheric effects, the play of light, and colour tones, not as they appear under close scrutiny, but rather as they are affected by light and natural reflexes. The Paris exhibition of prints by Hokusai, Utamaro and Hiroshige in 1867 made a great sensation. The most celebrated French impressionist, Manet, saw in their works quite novel methods of achieving realism, and his contemporary Monet realized that colour was not inherent in an object, but depended on its lighting.

Europeans began to buy and collect Japanese woodcuts, and museums all over the world followed their example. America is today spending hundreds and thousands of dollars on Japanese prints.

Of all the Japanese masters, however, it is now Sharaku whose works command the highest prices. He is really a European discovery, for the Japanese themselves did not begin to be interested in him until European and American art-dealers had turned his prints into 'best sellers'. All too belatedly, the Japanese began to investigate his life, but the only thing they found out was how very little they knew about him. His real name has been forgotten, and the date of his death is unknown. He was a gentleman and the vassal of a princely house, received a regular income from his prince, knew neither poverty nor hunger, and never worked for money.

Japan has always been a land of the theatre. The Kabuki Theatre owed its origins to the Nō dramas of the aristocracy, Japanese dancing and the puppet theatre. Even princes took part in stage productions, and Sharaku was also a performer.

Actors need publicity. This is not just a Hollywood discovery, for Yedo was well aware of the fact, and her theatres used portraits of actors as advertising posters. It was in the spring of 1793, during Yedo's theatrical 'silly season', that Sharaku suddenly appeared on the scene. Under the magic of his dancing brush there appeared a whole series of heads and full-length portraits of the mimic actors of the day, with their large pale faces. Sharaku painted in a most arresting way. He produced such bizarre, terrifying and repulsive compositions that the viewer's attention could not fail to be caught and held. The Japanese hated Sharaku, and it was probably the public's hatred which drove him back into obscurity.

Glaring pupils, grimaces, very slanting, piercing eyes, dark mica backgrounds, all these things were symptoms of his diabolical struggle with the invisible souls which remained, for all his audacity, beyond his powers of expression. Sharaku wrestled eternally with Fate and with the limitations which the material world imposed upon him. He was like some giant fighting with an invisible force stronger than himself. It seems almost uncanny that everything we have by Sharaku was painted within the space of a single year — between 1793 and 1794. None of the Nō dancers or actors had ever painted before.

Sharaku vanished as suddenly as he had appeared. It was probably his prince who forbade him to give 'the despised race of actors' a chance of immortality. So much mystery surrounds this great master of the woodcut that today he might almost be a ghost, despite his neglected grave at Tokushima. Yet the man about whose life we know so little presented the humble actors of his day to an audience larger than they ever dreamed of — the whole world.

Utamaro was Japan's most brilliant painter of women. Hokusai was her prodigy, her Leonardo da Vinci. Harunobu was her amorous painter of naive feminine grace. Sharaku was the comet which illuminated the Japanese theatre in its darkness. Finally there was Hiroshige, Japan's most truly national painter in that he painted the Japanese landscape, showing helpless little mortals caught in the toils of their menacing natural surroundings.

All the wonder of the Japanese islands is portrayed in Hiroshige's coloured woodcuts: the thirty-six views of sacred Fuji-no-yama, the eight different views of Lake Biwa, the countryside round Yedo, snowy mountain landscapes peopled with stooping, hurrying figures, so lifelike that one only has to look at them to shiver with cold, the racing rapids at Naruto, snowflakes, a slanting downpour of torrential rain, tardy raftsmen punting upstream against the current, lonely moonlit landscapes, hungry seas.

Before Hiroshige, artists looked on the human being as their most important subject, and landscapes were merely a background. Hiroshige ventured to lay a bold hand upon Nature itself, upon the moon, the ocean, the wintry skies, the incomparable symmetry of Fuji-no-yama — on 'the great out-of-doors', on something which was not to be taken in at a glance, but felt.

Hiroshige's father was an officer in the fire-service, a profession which conferred official positions, honours and privileges upon its members. Hiroshige's life was closely linked with the fire-service, and he travelled about the country a great deal on its affairs, for a time acting as superintendent of the nine miles of road separating Yedo from the imperial city of Kyoto. It was tours like these which inspired the fifty-three pictures in the 'Tokaido'. Hiroshige painted thousands of pictures, yet in his own day he was far better known as a poet than as a painter. He also kept a very conscientious diary in which he recorded the weather, the inns where he stopped the night, the many people he met, and all the little experiences he had on his travels. His pictures are boldly conceived, and always express a mood of some sort. If they often seem unrealistic to our eyes, it is only because we do not know Japan. Japan really looks the way Hiroshige painted it. Mountains soar into the air out of their banks of mist, and Nature is always lurking there ready to spring, while man, her puny slave, scurries quickly through life. Hiroshige came uncannily close to the day-fly called 'man', to timelessness, and to the omnipotence of Nature.

2

1. *A young girl from Yoshiwara, painted by Utamaro* (1753–1806). She wears the sign of her establishment on her purple dress

2. *Portrait by Sharaku of the actor Ichikawa Ibitso IV*, playing at the Kajiri Theatre in Yedo (now Tokyo) in January 1794. All Sharaku's brilliant paintings were produced within the space of a single year

Two lovers under an umbrella, by
Utamaro

Torii Kiyonaga's favourite subject was the unsophisticated charm of beautiful women of the people. He lived in Yedo (now Tokyo) from 1752 to 1804

A young girl at her morning toilet, by Toyokuni (1768–1825)

Ainu mother and child on the island of Hokkaido. 15,000 Ainu still survive on Sakhalin and Hokkaido, but the race is dying out. [*Photograph:* Hecht

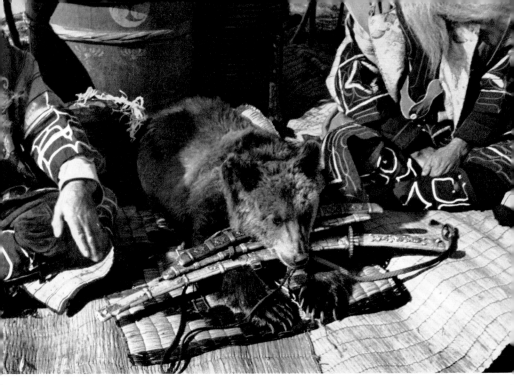

The Ainu bear-festival, which ends with a feast over the slaughtered animal's body. The dead creature's soul floats up to the constellation of the Lesser Bear. [*Photograph:* Hecht

Early Australian aborigines' cave-drawings found on cave walls near the Humbert River, Northern Territory

The ancestors of the Worora tribe are buried in a cave near Port George IV. From time immemorial, each descendant to visit the sinister place has left his hand-print on the rock wall. Hence the ghost-picture

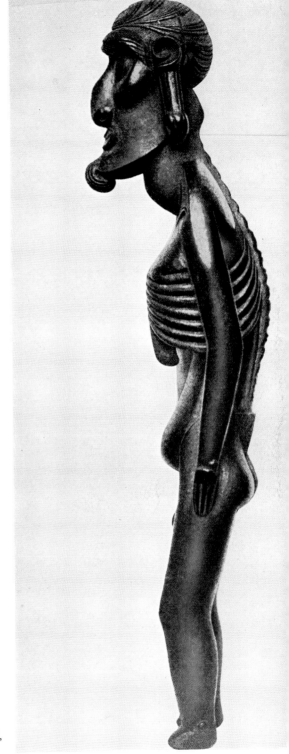

...den figure from Nukuhiva, in the *...uesas* group, carved with primitive implements. [Völkerkunde-Mu-..., Munich. *Photograph:* Herbert List

Wooden statue from Easter Island, carved from driftwood

Wooden shield surmounted by the head of an ancestor, from New Guinea, which served as a reliable magic protection and an effective deterrent. [Völkerkunde-Museum, Munich. *Photograph:* Herbert List

AUSTRALIA

X

WHERE THE DEAD LIVE ON

The continent of Gondwana was engulfed. Men were already living in Australia a million years ago.

A GREAT Dutchman died in 1941, in the middle of the Second World War. Although he left behind a large number of erudite works, he took a great proportion of his knowledge to the grave. Eugène Dubois was a doctor, and it was he who dug up the oldest human skull which the earth had ever surrendered.

Dubois, a professor of anatomy, did not discover this skull (it was really only the roof of a skull) purely by chance. Before leaving Holland for Java, he announced that he would very probably find the remains there of a primitive creature which was related to man. And Java was, in fact, the site of the great discovery. Digging in the neighbourhood of Trinil, Dubois unearthed the remains of *pithecanthropus erectus*, the 'Adam' of anthropology. The age of this member of a society which was even in those days, fairly human in character, is estimated at 500,000 years. His brain capacity was 54·9 cubic inches, as compared with a gorilla's (33·55 cubic inches), and a modern man's (73-91 cubic inches). Most authorities assign *pithecanthropus* to an extinct branch of the *hominoides* (cf. Boule-Vallois, *Les Hommes Fossiles*, Paris 1952, p. 127). The nature of his bone-structure places him in a category half way between modern man and his earliest *human* ancestor, and so the designation *pithecanthropus*, from the Greek *pithekos* (ape) and *anthropos* (man), is not well chosen.

Because *pithecanthropus erectus* resembled man, even he, early ancestor of man that he was, must have been preceded by hundreds of thousands of years of human evolution. It is certain that neither he nor his forefathers would have recognized the earth in its present guise. Since his time the continents, mountains, islands, oceans and even the positions of the poles have altered, and they have altered more markedly than the appearance of man himself. Some portions of the earth's crust were swallowed up by the oceans, while others reared themselves out of the water.

Australia, the most distant continent, the most recently discovered, and the area of the world with the most unusual anthropological past, was not always an island continent. It was at one time connected with south-east Asia by a bridge of dry land. It is even possible that South Africa, India and

Australia were all linked together by the now submerged portion of the earth which zoologists call 'Lemuria', and geologists 'Gondwana'. However, since man existed long before the continents were severed, Australia today represents mankind's own 'anthropological museum'. It cannot be mere coincidence that 'Man No. 1' was dug up on the neighbouring island of Java.

The most important discovery relating to Australia's earliest inhabitants was made at Talgai in south-east Queensland in the year 1884, when a fairly well preserved skull was exposed to the pitiless light of day. Although no other human bones were found in the vicinity of the skull, remains of extinct animals were unearthed, including bones belonging to the *diprotodon* (an early kangaroo), the *nototherium* and certain horned reptiles. After a recent study of the 'proto-Australian's' skull, Dr S. A. Smith has come to the conclusion that it bears a resemblance to that of the modern Australian aboriginal. In view of the fact that the aborigines have so far exhibited no signs of developing a 'national consciousness', we may add that Dr Smith recognized characteristics in the proto-Australian which bear a greater resemblance to the ape than to any other race of man, living or extinct. Further finds of human bones were made in the Wellington Caves, and the fossilized foot-prints of an early Australian aboriginal were found in Tertiary rock at Warrnambool, 125 miles south-west of Melbourne. All this points to the fact that men were living in Australia during the Tertiary period, which is to say at least a million years ago, and probably much earlier.

Then came the catastrophe. We do not know precisely when the waters rolled between Australia and Asia. We only know that Gondwanaland was engulfed, and that the event is much less of a myth than the story of 'Atlantis'. We know that a vast continent was submerged, and that Australia survived.

And her human inhabitants survived, too. They let time pass them by, no longer menaced by the overpopulation of southern Asia or the incursions of seafaring races thirsty for conquest. Australia had very few dangerous animals, there was good hunting, and it was many thousands of years before the sun's heat dried up the endless tracts of fertile land. Completely cut off, and thus insulated against all human inroads, the early aborigines sat there on their lonely and isolated continent, confronted on three sides by a watery void. There, over 9000 miles from the shores of South America and 5000 miles from Africa, men and animals developed independently of the rest of the world.

Australia remained quite undisturbed until 1605, when the Dutch navigator, W. Janszoon landed at the Gulf of Carpentaria, followed by Dirck Hartog who reached Western Australia in 1616; and finally Captain James Cook, who discovered 'Terra Australia' in 1770. The continent's existence

had, incidentally, been presupposed, since it was held to be indispensable to
'terrestrial equilibrium'. Cook landed at Botany Bay, near Sydney, and
presented King George III with a continent!

In discovering Australia, mankind had laid its hands not only upon a
whole new continent but also upon a 'living museum', where it was possible
to study an early species of man which had scarcely developed at all for
thousands and probably hundreds of thousands of years, and where plants
grew which were to be found nowhere else in the world. (Nine-tenths of all
Australian plants flourish only on that island continent, a fact which is in
itself enough to establish the long duration of Australia's independent existence.) The 'land of the living fossils' had at last been discovered. Animals
still survived there in a form only to be found in early periods of the earth's
history. There were more than a hundred and fifty kinds of marsupial in
Australia, from the opossum to the giant kangaroo, mammals which laid
eggs covered with skin-like shells, like the duck-billed platypus, and birds,
like the cassowary and the emu, which had lost the art of flying because they
no longer had any hereditary enemies. And the vast eucalyptus forests were
populated by Nature's own toys, the koalas, clambering around like animated
little teddy-bears.

It was in this lost and isolated world that the tribes of mankind's oldest
racial group used to hunt and roam. They still had living connections with
original human stock. Captives of the age-old cults which had been handed
down from generation to generation, rigid upholders of their ancient customs and rites, dismembered into 500 different tribes and alienated from one
another by as many different languages and dialects, living ever more frug-
ally on their continent as it grew drier and drier with the passage of centuries,
and always in quest of water, these Robinson Crusoes of mankind had reduced their whole material existence to its simplest fundamentals in a struggle
for mere survival. Their demands upon life became ever more negligible
and their skulls ever thicker in their effort to withstand the scorching heat
of the sun.

As late as 1914, there were still some aborigines in Australia who had
never yet encountered a white man. It is estimated that at the time of the
white man's first appearance in Australia — putting the date at 1788 — there
were approximately 300,000 aborigines living on the continent.

Slowly, like some malignant disease, the Europeans pushed forward into
the Australian interior. The life of the blacks degenerated under the impact
of this white invasion. They became weak and sickly in their sudden greed
for the thousand new things which affected their traditionally tough and
rigorous way of life so injuriously. No sooner had the white tide rolled over
their young men, bringing them into contact with that most destructive and

unsettling of all influences which we call Western civilization, than they lost all inclination to obey the ancients who had defended their tribal customs and their totems — the symbols of ancestor-worship — for so many thousands of years. The black men began to die out. They became indifferent huntsmen. They grew degenerate. They started to unlearn the thousands of little skills which were essential to the preservation of life on their continent. For the first time they had water and to spare, yet they withered away in their new clothes and corrugated iron huts like so many flowers in a dank cellar. The 300,000 dwindled to 60,000 and then to 50,000, of which only 25,000 still led the nomadic life of their forefathers.

Australians like these, who had really become a match for their continent, were eventually only to be found in the hot central regions of Australia, an arid wilderness of sinister desert where they still hunted kangaroo and emu and their women caught edible snakes, rats, frogs, lizards and grubs; where they still gathered lily-bulbs and acacia- and grass-seeds for food; where they still conquered thirst, in a desert where in years of extreme drought literally not one drop of rain fell, by extracting water from roots — an art which even the ablest white explorers never mastered. The aborigines never used vessels of any kind for boiling water or food, but cooked their meat simply by leaving it in hot ash, earth, clay or mud.

All the tribes had their own residential and hunting areas, and very seldom infringed each other's boundaries. It is generally true to say that nomads are far better at keeping within their frontiers than settled races, because the nomad is far better acquainted with the farthest limits of his country than the 'river-valley dweller'.

The Australian aborigines hardly ever waged war on neighbouring tribes. On the tribal level they were invariably peaceable, and the fact that some explorers claim to have heard the distant sound of wooden clubs thudding dully on heads at night does not invalidate this generalization. Thwacking your wife on the head a few times with a piece of wood has from time immemorial been regarded by the aborigines as a useful little educational measure, and, as we know, the sun has made their skulls extremely tough! Duels in which male or female opponents beat each other on the head with wooden clubs were always conducted in a very fair and sportsmanlike manner. If the contestants were women, the men normally sat quietly by and watched, only interrupting the proceedings occasionally if they became too rough. If men were fighting, their womenfolk would participate by interposing their own heads as a form of shield.

No 'civilization' can be judged by comparison with another which is quite alien to it, and no civilization can be assessed by another's criteria. I have seen Australian aboriginal dances, and I have to admit that there is no other communal dance in the world quite so enthralling and impressive as the corroboree, performed under the stars with much stamping and rhythmical leaping around hissing red fires, and an accompaniment of guttural, primeval voices. These dances tell whole animal stories in mime. They portray birds catching fish, for instance, or relate the history of the totem or tribal ancestor. Primitive though the designs on the aborigines' shields, bodies and cave walls may be, it was still a splendid imagination which gave birth to them. Astounding drawings, whose immense age does not rob them of an almost eerie animation, have been discovered in the caves along the Humber, Glenelg and Forrest rivers, as well as in the Musgrave range. Among them is the sketch of a *diprotodon's* paw, which permits us to conclude that the artist was a contemporary of that now extinct species of early kangaroo. The hand-prints of the Worora tribe in the cave at Port George are reminiscent of a nocturnal conspiracy of ghosts. The aborigines' pictures of animals are at once naive and compelling, and fish swim along the rocky walls as if in a petrified aquarium.

Civilization has no beginning or end. Just as the discovery of the wheel was an epoch-making cultural achievement, so the invention of the Australian spear likewise marked a step on the road to civilization. And as for the *woomera*, or boomerang, the 'long arm' of the aboriginal which enables any expert to out-distance the world javelin record with consummate ease, it constitutes a masterpiece of human ingenuity.

It was a rich and splendid life that perished here. It ranged from one horizon to another with its countless acquired skills in the mastery of Nature at her harshest and most inimical, and its intimate relationship with heaven and earth and with the foaming, roaring breakers which have pounded away at the shores of the world's fifth continent for so many thousands of years.

For ever on guard before the northern coast of Queensland stands the Great Barrier Reef. It is a gigantic rampart of coral — the largest coral formation in the world, in fact — and forms an infertile and uninhabitable natural breakwater 1250 miles long, shaken by the everlasting thunder of the surf.

Between the Barrier Reef and the mainland, just under fifty miles north of Townsville, lie the Palm Islands. It was there that I saw Australia's last terrible awakening from the dream which has lasted for so many thousands of years. For these islands are a reservation where aborigines who have come into contact with white civilization are concentrated. This is where the great hunters of old now live, in clothes which do not become them, in huts which they managed to do without for 100,000 years, and under modern hygienic conditions which are sapping their resistance to disease. They live on, yet they died long ago. They go on dancing, and the ocean sings their requiem.

POLYNESIA

ℵ

EXPERTS IN THE ART OF DOING NOTHING

'Without doubt the Pacific Ocean is aeons older than the Atlantic or the Indian Ocean. When we say older, we mean it has not come to any modern consciousness. Strange convulsions have convulsed the Atlantic and Mediterranean peoples into phase after phase of consciousness, while the Pacific and the Pacific peoples have slept. To sleep is to dream: you can't stay unconscious. And, oh heaven, for how many thousands of years has the true Pacific been dreaming, turning over in its sleep and dreaming again: idylls: nightmares.'

D. H. Lawrence

'BEFORE us lies the horizon. It is the horizon which is for ever vanishing, the horizon which always seems close at hand, which arouses dread doubt and oppresses us with fear — the horizon, with its unsuspected and primeval power, which no ship's bow has ever yet cut asunder. The intangible skies hang above us, the wild seas roar beneath. The untrodden path lies before us — our ship must away!'

That is a Polynesian song, a song of the great seafarers who, centuries before the Vikings or Columbus, conquered a maritime region three times the size of North America.

The Polynesians discovered thousands of islands, 'Gardens of Eden' large and small, volcanoes towering above the sea, coral reefs, inhospitable cliffs and islands luxuriant with virgin forest. They became masters of an ocean as studded with islands as the sky is with stars, rulers over the triangle bounded by Hawaii, New Zealand and Easter Island. It is quite certain that they reached the shores of South America long before Cabral, Amerigo Vespucci, da Gama or Magellan, and modern research is continually finding fresh parallels between the Polynesian and American-Indian civilizations. The Polynesians were always a race of seamen, and needed no Pacific version of Atlantis to help them reach the west coast of America dry-shod. Thus the 25,000 books which geologists, biologists and archaeologists have written about the 'Pacific Atlantis', or 'Mu', still rest on rather shaky foundations.

No other race upon earth has ever inhabited so large a geographical area as the Polynesians. The Polynesian world extended over 69 degrees of latitude and 70 of longitude, covering the 4700 miles between Hawaii and New Zealand and the 3700 between Tonga and Easter Island. It was a world of outriggers and huge war-canoes manned by crews of up to 300 men, of voyages lasting months or years, of interminable wars and migrations. These seafarers had no compasses or iron. They left us no written history. The Easter

247

Island inscriptions have never been deciphered, and as for the waves – who knows how much evidence they have swallowed up?

But the Polynesians have always been a people of song. They passed on their legends and sagas from one generation to the next, storing up the origins of their race in their unencumbered minds and repeating them to their children. They firmly believed that anyone who recited an important tradition incorrectly would be killed by the wrath of the gods. In modern terminology, they were word-perfect in something which had never been written down. That is why we owe so much to the Polynesians' good memories. The Maoris of New Zealand relate, for instance, that it was a chieftain from Tahiti called Kupe who discovered New Zealand, forty generations before the arrival of the Europeans.

Another Maori legend tells of a land called *Uru*, which had at one time been their forefathers' native land. People have tried to identify Uru with Ur of the Chaldees in Mesopotamia, although in the Maori dialect of the Polynesian language Uru simply means 'west'. The Polynesians are also familiar with a land called *Irihia*, and some enterprising scholars decided to regard Irihia as a corruption of *Vrihia*, an old Sanskrit name for India. Again, the Polynesian word 'sun' is *ra*, and it was not very long before certain 'authorities' were claiming that the Polynesians must at one time have lived in Egypt, since 'Ammon Ra' was the ancient Egyptians' name for their Sun-god.

Another mythological link between Polynesia and its original Asian home-land is represented by the widespread *Hawaiki* saga. The Hawaiki version of the story of Creation is to be heard everywhere in Polynesia (except in Samoa and Tonga), always with many small variations, it is true, but always with the same basic theme. 'We come from great Hawaiki, from far Hawaiki, from distant Hawaiki', the Maoris sing. Hawaiki was the Polynesians' erstwhile Paradise, the place they left behind them when they set off over the seas, sailing on and on into the rising sun, to discover and colonize their island world. It is only the souls of their dead which wander westwards into the land of the setting sun, back to Hawaiki. But where was Hawaiki?

In general, science has come to the conclusion that the ancient Polynesians came from Indo-China via Indonesia, though the question has not altogether been resolved. There are also many numerous cultural similarities between the Polynesian and Indonesian races. Like the Indonesians, the Polynesians kept dogs, pigs and chickens, and in both Indonesia and Polynesia fire was produced by rotating a vertical stick in a hollowed piece of wood placed on the ground. Thousands of Polynesian words are related to Indonesian words both in sound and meaning. The Indonesians are Malays, and the Polynesian and Indonesian languages have so much in common that, together with the

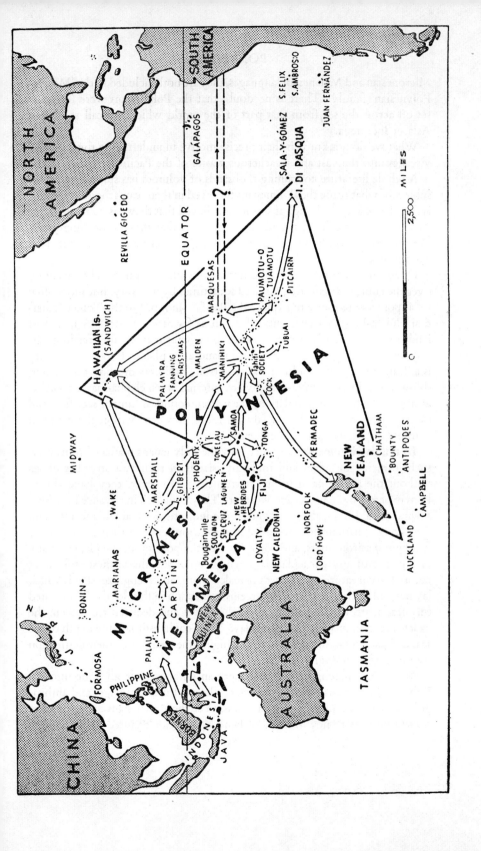

Micronesian and Melanesian languages, they are both included in the 'Malayo-Polynesian' family. There is no doubt that the Polynesians were forced to set off across the sea from that part of the world which we call south-east Asia or Indonesia.

What we do not know is their precise motive in undertaking these suicidal voyages into the vast and treacherous wastes of the Pacific.

A whole literature containing thousands of volumes has sprung up on the subject of what route the Polynesians followed in their leap-frogging journey across the ocean. Although it was long believed that they passed through the Melanesian archipelago, the modern theory is that they chose Micronesia, the group of islands which used to belong to Germany before the First World War.

Of course, these migrations did not all take place at once. They went on over the course of centuries, inspired sometimes by necessity, but more often by a spontaneous desire to explore the Pacific. In A.D. 650 the Tongan chieftain Hui-te-Rangiora even pushed down as far as Antarctica. A nation of land-hungry master-mariners obsessed by a wild craving for freedom, the Polynesians discovered and colonized island after island. Polynesian history is a dramatic tale of expulsion, exile, pursuit, explorers meeting tragic ends, shipwrecks, sinkings, inter-island wars, internal wars, elephantiasis, abortion as a remedy for overpopulation, starvation, countless human sacrifices and even of cannibalism, which is always more prevalent within the cramped confines of islands than on continents.

To this day it remains a mystery how the Polynesians managed to traverse such immense distances and find tiny islands in such vast stretches of sea without the aid of navigational instruments. However, they have always been experts on the winds and weather. They could tell in advance how long a wind would hold, they recognized the indications of storm and tide, and they knew what currents prevailed in the various parts of their ocean. They were good astronomers, and could forecast the position of the planets at any given hour of any particular day. They could 'see' the farthest atolls long before the curvature of the earth revealed them, and recognize islands which lay beyond the horizon by their greenish reflection in the clouds. They noted tiny fragments of plants floating on the waves and deduced from them the exact direction in which an island lay. They could estimate the depth of the sea, and had an infallible instinct for gauging the nearness of their destination by observing the flight of birds.

American, French, English and German scholars have all gone into the Polynesians' past history, their voyages, their culture, languages and anthropology, with the utmost thoroughness. Yet the Polynesians are constantly presenting us with new riddles. When Captain Cook visited Tahiti and the

250

Sandwich Islands (Hawaii), he estimated their populations at 300,000 and 400,000 respectively. Today there are only 30,000 natives in Tahiti, 21,000 in the Sandwich Islands, and about 300,000 in Polynesia as a whole. Here in the middle of the ocean as elsewhere, white man's civilization seems to be having a fatal effect on the indigenous populations. Missionaries and colonial officials tried to wean the Polynesians from everything which belonged to their ancient 'coconut civilization', with its atmosphere of sun and salt breezes. They tried to accustom the Polynesians to clothes, soap, church-going and schools, and, wherever their attempts to 'civilize' succeeded, the true Polynesia ended for good and all. It still lives on in modern guise in Hawaii, it is true, but the influence of modern singing and dancing rhythms and the admixture of Japanese, Chinese, Portuguese and American elements has made it a place quite alien to the ancient ocean world of which it was once a part.

Polynesia's ancient civilization used to be something altogether different. It embraced free love between boys and girls until marriage, the adoption of children on a liberal scale, the prohibition of any kind of communication between brother and sister (in western Polynesia), a disdain for maidenly modesty and an equally deep disdain for excessive sexuality, marital fidelity coupled with unconditional divorce if so desired, and strict segregation of the sexes during the eating, and even during the preparation, of meals. As soon as King Kamehameha did away with these customs in Hawaii, the old civilization was finished. The Polynesians possessed one virtue above all others, however, and they have not yet lost it: they are the world's greatest experts in the art of doing nothing. From the cultural standpoint, their way of life is surely the best that any man could wish for. Its naive joy in living for the moment, its complete indifference to material possessions, its shrewd insistence on the one indispensable thing in life — a serene freedom from care — all make it something which can be summed up in a single word: paradise. Polynesia's leisurely character and her propensity for artless existence without ambitions or pretensions are survivals from Stone Age times.

European planters, colonial administrators, missionaries and scholars — the people whom we call 'bearers of civilization' — have all foundered on the Polynesians' splendid indifference to work, industry, ambition, wages, the 8-hour day and the 5- or 6-day week. People are very far from the mark when they call the Polynesians lazy. Any work that must be done, they co-operate in eagerly, but only until the 'must' has been accomplished. After that, they go back to their timelessness, their delight in games, their hospitality and their fine sense of humour where 'yours and mine' and debit and credit are concerned. It was this latter Polynesian characteristic which formed the strongest impression I gained from my visits to the islands between

Honolulu and Auckland. An extraordinarily endearing trait, it is often discon-
certing and always unforgettable. I have seen foreigners who found the price
of coconuts, copra or bananas too high reduced to crimson-faced embarrassment when Polynesians greeted their attempts to haggle by smilingly handing
over all their wares and walking quietly away. The fact is that the Polynesian
is firmly convinced that the acquisition of money which he does not immediately need, and the earning of which interrupts his permanent state of
holiday, really signifies a lowering of his standard of living. He works in
order to live. It never occurs to him to live in order to work.

A hundred and thirty long years of painstaking 'cultural education' have
not availed the West in its attempt to alter the Polynesians' way of life, except
perhaps in a few seaport towns. Far from getting down to the work which
we consider essential, the Polynesians devote their time to aesthetic pleasures,
inter-village festivals, music, dancing, wood-carving (for the benefit of their
gods rather than the furniture industry), the painting of tapa cloth and
free love untrammelled by any moral scruples.

In spite of all the catastrophes of the past, the Polynesian islands remain the
last surviving paradise on earth. They are a world of carefree tranquillity
and joy, a world which lives for today and is as indifferent to tomorrow as it
was to yesterday, a fairy-tale world which we forfeited long ago.

THE UNSOLVED MYSTERY OF
EASTER ISLAND SCRIPT

2500 miles west of Valparaiso a small and lonely basalt island protrudes from the waves. It is the easternmost island in the Polynesian world. Massive stone statues, some of them colossuses up to 46 feet in height, stand or lie tumbled on the island's beaches, hillsides and volcanic slopes. The Polynesians called their small rocky domain *Te pito te henua*, and the Tahitian name for Easter Island was *Rapanui*. It represents the greatest prehistoric enigma in the South Seas. The Easter Islanders' script has never yet been deciphered.

EASTER Island was discovered by the Dutch admiral Jakob Roggeveen on Easter Sunday in the year 1722. The island lapsed into oblivion once more, however, until Captain Felipe Gonzáles y Haedo rediscovered it in 1770. Captain Cook paid it a visit in 1774, La Pérouse in 1786, and Otto von Kotzebue in 1816. Then, in 1862, some Peruvian pirates appeared on the scene. Finding the place occupied by between 3000 and 4000 native inhabitants, they summarily carried off 900 of them to the Guano group of islands. A year later the survivors of these 900 — a mere 15 — were brought back to Easter Island suffering from smallpox. The disease quickly spread, and before long the indigenous population of Easter Island had dwindled to 650.

So much for the promising start of 'Western colonization' among the members of the only little Polynesian race which still commanded the ability to read and write a script of their own. Today the art is dead.

Eugène Eyraud was a pious lay brother. He lived all alone on his small triangular island in the middle of the ocean and did his best to acquaint its brown-skinned inhabitants with the blessings of Christianity. One and a half centuries after the original discovery of Easter Island, this first missionary made a discovery of his own. It consisted of some long wooden tablets — the largest were over six feet long — bearing neat lines of some form of hieroglyphic script incorporating the outlines of human beings, animals, plants, stars, harpoons, paddles and other objects not identifiable. The tablets were of *toromiro* or drift-wood, and the inscriptions had been scratched on them with pointed stones (obsidian knives) or sharks' teeth, often on both sides.

It was Eugène Eyraud who discovered Polynesian writing, but the pious brother was not an erudite man, and he had no inkling of the immense significance of his pieces of wood. Such of the natives as adopted the Christian faith used the tablets as firewood. No sooner had they been baptized than they set about burning their 'books', though they did so with mixed emotions. On the one hand, they were not completely convinced that the old gods would tolerate the destruction of their sacred tablets, while, on the other, the treeless nature of their island home meant that they were always short of fuel.

A colleague of Brother Eyraud, Father Zumbohm, brought back a fragment of one of the tablets to show Tepano Jaussen, the Bishop of Tahiti, and a certain Father Roussel brought back a further five, better preserved than the first. We are also told that the natives sent the Bishop a long cord, spun out of human hair, as a gift, and that this cord was wound round a piece of wood — one of the writing tablets, in fact. At all events, it is Bishop Jaussen whom science has to thank for the discovery of Easter Island writing, and for the preservation of the last surviving tablets. The most important collection of these is to be found in the Congrégation des Sacrés-Cœurs de Picpus, the pious religious order of which Bishop Jaussen was a member, and which is still doing so much widespread and valuable work today.

Troubled by a bad conscience as regards both the old god and the new, one of the islanders had made himself a new fishing-boat out of the 'speaking timber'. When the boat fell apart, he carefully saved the pieces and later built himself a new canoe out of them. It was this traitor to both faiths, the island's first 'nihilist', so to speak, whom Thomson, the American expert on Polynesia, had to thank for one of the last surviving tablets. When Thomson visited the island in 1886 he found an old man called Ure-vaeiko who could read the tablets to a limited degree and was familiar with some of their contents. Unfortunately, Ure-vaeiko had by that time become a good Christian and, citing the missionaries' prohibition of 'sacred tablets' as an excuse, he refused to read them. Trembling with fear, he hid himself in the interior of the island, where he sat in his house and quaked under the twin threats of purgatory and 'pumping' by inquisitive scientists. It was only on the evening before Thomson was due to leave that he managed to surprise the unwitting islander in his hut. Adopting the course usually taken by a man who wants to stop someone reading something, the shrewd investigator plied his brown-skinned friend with alcohol until at last, late that night, he consented to take a look at photographs of some of the tablets and read them. Thomson soon found out, however, that Ure-vaeiko was not reading the individual symbols so much as reciting something from memory. When taxed with this, the man excused himself by saying that, although it was true that the meaning of individual symbols was lost, he could recognize the purport of the tablets by certain unmistakable details, and that the gist of his account was correct. The man who acted as interpreter during these proceedings was a French-Tahitian half-caste called Paea Salmon, and it was his translation of the ostensible texts of the five tablets in question which Thomson later published. The Austrian ethnologist Michael Haberlandt

Not yet deciphered. Obverse of one of the writing-tablets peculiar to Easter Island. This tablet was inscribed to mark the occasion of a festival which lasted for weeks. Even after 1914 there were still natives on the island who could recite parts of this text from memory, but today its real significance is unknown. Many such tablets have been found and certain of the symbols can be identified, since a proportion of them clearly refer to the objects they represent: the moon, a star, a fish, a crab, a fishing-hook. An examination of the swarm of characters reveals that some of them recur frequently.

Looked at from the bottom, only the characters in the 1st, 3rd, 5th and 7th rows are in an upright position, while those in the 2nd, 4th, 6th and 8th are upside-down. Reader and writer alike began at the right of the bottom line and on reaching the extreme left, turned the tablet round and retraced his steps along the line immediately above, rather like an ox ploughing a field. Hence 'boustrophedon', the term applied to this method of writing, from the Greek *bous*, meaning ox, and *strophe*, turn.

gives it as his opinion that these texts are – to put it mildly – incomplete, since the number of words they contain is far exceeded by the number of symbols on the tablets. But what casts the gravest aspersions on worthy old Ure-vaeiko's accuracy is the fact that when Thomson secretly swapped some of the photographs in mid-translation, the good fellow gaily went on reciting the text he had already started.

The two tablets which Thomson himself managed to obtain on the island are now housed in the United States National Museum at Washington.

Between March 1914 and August 1915, Easter Island had a woman visitor in the shape of Mrs Routledge, a competent ethnologist who devoted her time to finding out all that there was left to know about the script. She showed the natives photographs of various tablets, which the good-natured islanders were only too happy to read for her. Usually they all read out the same text, quite regardless of which particular tablet Mrs Routledge pointed to. Eventually, Mrs Routledge found an old man who knew how to write a second form of script which had formerly been used for keeping historical records. She tried to question this man, whose name was Tomenika, on the meaning of individual symbols. It may be added that her investigations were attended by a considerable degree of risk, since he was a leper. The old man had forgotten a good deal, and what little his decaying mind still vaguely remembered he could not express in words. His brain grew more and more fogged, and his replies more and more muddled and hesitant. In the end he died under the very eyes of his courageous interrogator while he was actually engaged in spelling. The dying man's last words were: 'The words are new. The letters are old.' Through him, Mrs Routledge has left us a vivid picture of the old priest-king who was still in office at the time of the Peruvian raid. His name was Ariki Ngaara, and he ruled over the Miru tribe which had its settlement on the island's northern coast. He could trace his ancestry all the way back to Hotu Matua, the first immigrant ruler of Polynesia. Ngaara was a short, fat man, so thickly ornamented with tattooing that his skin looked nearly black. Wooden figurines suspended from the front and rear of his body clattered together as he walked. No one was permitted to watch the fat man eating, and only a few special servants were allowed to enter his quarters. Alas for poor Ariki Ngaara! Magical considerations forbade him to partake of Easter Island's most prized delicacy – roast rat. Ngaara's chief responsibility was to induce the islanders' chickens to persevere in their egg-laying, and because rats are not naturally well-disposed towards chickens or their eggs and the chieftain might, if he partook of the joys of rats' meat, absorb a measure of their 'hen-hostile' nature, it was considered that his own 'hen-friendly' qualities might thereby be impaired. An elderly native called Haha had in his youth served Ngaara as a messenger. It seems that when

Ngaara caught his servant gnawing a rat's bone one day, the old priest flew into a towering rage.

It is interesting to reconstruct a picture of Easter Island as it once was. Chief Ngaara used to sit enthroned on the head of one of the celebrated stone colossuses whose method of construction and transportation are still puzzling the scholars of today. Newly tattooed natives were then paraded before him, and he used to sort out those who had been well tattooed from those who displayed slipshod workmanship. It was always the signal for a great yell of derision to go up from the assembled tribe when the fat priest abandoned the latter to their ridicule.

Apart from fulfilling the functions already mentioned, Ariki Ngaara was also, in a manner of speaking, president of the island's literary society. It was he who supervised the great art of reading the tablets. The study of these hieroglyphics was the prerogative of a small and select circle called the *rongo-rongo*. These learned men lived in special huts away from their wives. They had pupils and gave lessons. Beginners used to write on banana-leaves, while advanced students used sharks' teeth and *toromiro* tablets. Like Charlemagne, Ngaara was himself an assiduous calligrapher and school-inspector. Regular *rongo-rongo* conventions were held, at which hundreds of the erudite men would forgather while the general public sat round to watch. Then there were tribal feasts and important examinations, which were presided over by Ngaara (and his son Kaimokoi after him), ensconced on piles of writing-tablets. If one of the young men bungled his reading he was merely reproved. But if an old man showed that he was not word-perfect, one of the young men took him by the ear and led him out of the assembly and down to the beach. The conference and its accompanying celebrations were rounded off by the presentation of something which every worthy citizen should have in his pot on Sunday: a chicken. Each member of the *rongo-rongo* received one of these clucking awards.

During the latter years of his life poor Ngaara had much to contend with. Small as the island was, it was afflicted by intertribal feuds. The Ngaure tribe defeated the Miru and enslaved them. Together with his son and grandson, Ngaara spent five long years in captivity, at the end of which time the Miru managed to ally themselves with a third tribe, the Tupahotu, and liberated the old man shortly before his death.

Some of the numerous tablets which Ngaara left behind are still supposed to be lying hidden in one of Easter Island's many caves. The quest for these tablets would make a commendable project for some of the news photographers, reporters from illustrated magazines and young hopefuls who seem nowadays to be setting out on voyages of exploration every other week.

I

257

According to Easter Island tradition, Chief Hotu Matua, the first arrival, brought sixty-seven tablets with him from his original home. It is possible, therefore, that in the inscriptions on the tablets which survive we may have the remains of an age-old and in earlier times much more extensive script. There are many indications that the hieroglyphs are extremely ancient, and that the *rongo-rongo* of latter days only employed a poor form of shorthand based on them. Certainly, when the Spaniards officially took control of the island in 1770, its chiefs and dignitaries signed the treaty in hieroglyphic characters which resemble the script on the tablets.

Easter Island writing consists of ideograms, which is to say pictographic symbols expressing particular ideas. Each character was designed to portray the intended object as faithfully as possible, but, although we can interpret a symbol here and there, the full significance of the script remains an enigma.

What is also an enigma is the question whether Easter Island is a relic of some now submerged archipelago, or whether it has survived in its present shape for thousands of years.

The archipelago theory is combated by the *ahu*, or stone images, which still stand stiffly round the island's shores. Neither the beginning nor the end of Easter Island's civilization can be explained by geological modifications. Easter Island is not the relic either of a submerged continent or a submerged archipelago, nor was the downfall of its civilization attributable to volcanic eruptions. Some scientists think that Easter Island's culture is so individual that it should not be lumped together with the rest of Polynesia, even though the natives were Polynesians at the time of its discovery.

Alfred Métraux of the Bernice P. Bishop Museum at Honolulu in Hawaii, puts forward a number of arguments designed to draw Easter Island into the Polynesian cultural orbit. It is to be feared that the parallels between Easter Island and South American Indian civilization so dear to the heart of Thor Heyerdahl, the author of *Kon-Tiki*, are only wishful thinking, although the discovery of two Easter Island spear-heads in a grave in Chile is scientifically indisputable.

It is probable that the Easter Islanders left the central Polynesian orbit before the individual Polynesian civilizations had fully developed, and that their seafaring skill deteriorated because of their island's lack of boat-building materials. Wood was as rare on Easter Island as jade in New Zealand, which was why the Easter Islanders always made their 'jewellery' out of it.

The Easter Islanders' only native invention seems to have been their wooden tablets. But the 'speaking timber' has lost its voice. It beckons the researcher but will not answer him. The tablets lie there in museums and the years roll by. The ocean waves which break upon the shores of the lonely island remember nothing, or, if they do, guard their secret well.

MELANESIA

※

COCONUT AND SHELLFISH CIVILIZATION

Scarcely any other race in the world has set scholars as many problems as the Melanesians. The origins of the native inhabitants of this island world have never been definitely ascertained. In ancient times the Melanesians may have lived under a system of group-marriage. It may be that they hold the key to the mystery of the totem. This much is certain: Melanesia is one of the last living museums for dying races, and a veritable anthropologist's El Dorado.

THE Pacific is not the limitless, empty expanse of water it often seems in our school atlases. It is an ocean containing over 10,000 islands – it could be 30,000, for they are virtually uncountable. The Tuamotu group is called in the language of its inhabitants 'Cloud of Islands'. It is made up of 80 major islands and innumerable 'fragments'. There are very many such clusters of islands in the Pacific, the Philippine group alone comprising 7000 islets. A single atoll, or ring of coral surrounding a central lagoon, may really be composed of a multitude of small islands protruding from the sea.

The Pacific is larger than any continent in the world. Its island archipelagos are like constellations, and its peoples, Indonesians, Melanesians, Micronesians and Polynesians, are as unfathomable in their culture and ancestry as the ocean which surrounds their island homes.

A million years ago, the west coast of the Pacific basin may have stretched from Japan to New Zealand via the Carolines and the Fiji Islands. Epoch after historical epoch has been submerged by the waters of the Pacific, and the true history of Oceania goes back many, many thousands of years into the past.

Oceania's first inhabitants were the Pygmoids, a short and dark-skinned race with crinkly hair who were driven out of Asia during the latter portion of the Ice Age. At that time the waterways separating the world's land-masses were much narrower than today, for vast layers of polar ice kept the oceans small and the land-masses dry. When the Ice Age came to an end about 14,000 years ago, it inundated vast tracts of dry land and turned mountain-tops into islands, 'Ararats' on which human beings probably took refuge. We know little or nothing of what actually happened. It is possible that the Pygmoid migrations into what is now Oceania did not last only a hundred thousand years, but several hundred thousands.

Emerging from the area of Malaya, a second tide of humanity swept down to New Guinea and Australia. These Oceanic forefathers were quite unlike the little Pygmoids. Their skin was lighter, their hair straight instead of crinkly, and their bodies hirsute. They belonged to a very ancient white racial stock, the 'Ainoids', similar to the racial type which is still to be found on Hokkaido, Japan's most northerly island. These white people spread over western Oceania and intermingled with the Pygmoids, but the latter must have been a much more vigorous, prolific and hardy race than the Ainoids, for the light-skinned race 'drowned' in the blood of the blacks.

The Ainoids were followed by other peoples, hunters and food-gatherers of the pre-agricultural period known as 'Veddids', who bore a physical resemblance to the Veddas, or early inhabitants of southern India. It is possible that Mongoloid peoples also accompanied them.

In the island world which we call Melanesia the negroid element is far more pronounced than the other three, which is how Melanesia got its name, from the Greek compound meaning 'Black Islands'.

Three, and probably very many more races, three or more civilizations, and at least three or more languages interlocked and intermingled here, only to split up once more into a variety of different dialects, different customs and different social orders. While the huge maritime area of Polynesia exhibits a considerable degree of cultural and racial uniformity — its natives looking almost like brown-skinned Europeans — the far more ancient Melanesian region is a mosaic of hundreds of different civilizations. There is nothing really typical about the world bounded by New Caledonia, New Guinea and the Fiji Islands. There is no other ancient cultural region so heterogeneous as Melanesia, whose dark-skinned, woolly-headed, mysterious inhabitants make mock of scholars and all their attempts to classify them.

Even today the islands of Melanesia give clear evidence of migratory trends. In the course of centuries, later arrivals settled around their coasts and chased the older inhabitants, the primitive negroid peoples, into the forests, mountains and marshes of the interior. Water is often a better link than land and, while the coastal peoples of the various islands developed close cultural ties, the communities in the interior became more and more isolated. The result is that one can clearly distinguish between the 'coast native' and the 'bush native'. The Papuan languages are spoken almost exclusively in the interior of certain large islands, notably New Guinea and New Britain. There are countless Papuan tongues, all so different that the inhabitants of one village can scarcely make themselves understood by those of the village next door. Meanwhile, the coastal inhabitants speak Melanesian. Take Bougainville in the Solomons, for instance. It has about 35,000 native inhabitants. Eight different Papuan linguistic groups live in the interior and in the south, while Melanesian-speaking peoples — belonging to seven linguistic groups — occupy the coastal and northern regions. The island exemplifies just what makes it so hard for anyone to classify the various races in the area: linguistic and cultural assimilation. Not long ago, some Melanesian-speaking natives from the Shortland Islands landed on the east coast of Bougainville. They are now 'Melanesianizing' the Papuan communities of the interior. By contrast, the coastal Melanesians of the southwest are gradually abandoning their unhealthy seaside villages and migrating inland, where they are becoming thoroughly 'Papuanized', not only linguistically but culturally. Just to complicate Bougainville's picture still further, the inhabitants of the southern part of the island are tall in stature, while those of the mountainous interior are almost pygmy-like. And yet all the indigenous inhabitants of Bougainville, whether Melanesian- or Papuan-speaking, coastal or inland residents, tall or short, are black as soot — blacker even than the Papuan-speaking people in the most inaccessible nooks and crannies of New Guinea. As for New Guinea, part of its native population is predominantly Melanesian, and the rest belongs to the negroid Papuan race.

There are really only five island areas which are indisputably Melanesian: (i) parts of the Solomons; (ii) the Santa Cruz group; (iii) the New Hebrides and the Banks Islands; (iv) New Caledonia and the Loyalty Islands; and (v) the Fiji Islands.

Melanesia may be the ethnologist's nightmare, but it is a living museum devoted to primitive forms of civilization. No other region in the world contains so large a number of diverse civilizations within so small a compass. Among the very few factors common to them all are: chipped stone tools, the bow and arrow, spears, pig-rearing, domestic dogs, chickens, fishing, agriculture and the gathering of wild plants, animism or the belief that inanimate objects have souls, secret male societies and initiation ceremonies, ritual masks and finally, 'exogamy'.

Here we come to the most interesting aspect of Melanesian civilization. Exogamy means marriage with someone from outside one's own strictly defined community. There is no more important tenet in the Melanesians' realm of ideas than this division of everyone into two or more groups. No marriage may ever take place inside one and the same group. A person who belongs to group A, for instance, must marry someone from group B or group C. It is not clear how or when these groups came into being, but they exist, and they are rigidly maintained. Membership of a particular group is passed on to children by their mother, the mother's group membership always being the deciding factor. Sons and daughters thus belong to the same group. Neither geographical location nor clan nor tribe have any bearing upon the limits within which a marriage may be made — only the mother's membership of this or that group. The groups have no other significance, whether of a political or tribal nature. An exactly similar system prevails in Australia. To a Melanesian, all the women of his generation are either prohibited 'sisters' or potential brides, while to a Melanesian woman, all men are prohibited 'brothers' or potential suitors.

In Melanesia, as in Australia, this method of marrying individual persons probably originated in some age-old system of 'group-marriage', under which all the women in one group were the communal wives of all the men in another. Scholars have tried to base this supposition on the fact that in certain Melanesian languages the expressions for 'mother', 'spouse', 'wife' and 'child' only exist in the plural. They have deduced from this that there was once a time when the whole of life was dominated by group relationships, and individual relationships were unknown. With the single exception of New Caledonia, marriage within one's own group has always been unthinkable in Melanesia, whose natives classed it as a capital offence. This penalty applied equally to a man who seduced a girl in his own group.

Another thing common to all Melanesians is 'totemism'. This extremely complex phenomenon is also to be found in the civilizations of Australia and America. The word 'totem' is derived from *ototeman*, which occurs in the closely related Ojibwe and Algonquin languages of the American Indians, and means literally 'one's-brother's-sister-relative'. Totemism is a belief in one's descent from, and identity with, an animal, a plant, a star, or a flash of lightning, and forms a link between a related group of people. This lively belief in totemism has given birth to artistic creations of haunting grandeur, to taboos or sacred prohibitions, and to important festivals at which the totemistic union is renewed. Whole families and clans are named after certain animals and plants. Some family groups in New Caledonia, for instance, regard the large gecko as sacrosanct and inviolable, while other clans hold the sparrow-hawk, lizard, or shark in like esteem.

In complete contrast to the brighter and more light-hearted atmosphere of Polynesia, Melanesia's world was always a gloomy place governed by witchcraft and magic. Head-hunting and cannibalism existed on certain Melanesian islands, and it used to be a common practice to kill off the aged and infirm. It has equally been established that the natives of many Melanesian islands used to do away with the seriously ill. When questioned about their reasons, the natives invariably replied that they did it out of fellow-feeling.

Linguistic relationships existed between the various Melanesian islands, of course, but on the whole an utter babel of tongues prevailed. There are about twenty different languages and dialects in New Caledonia alone. There were no grammars of native authorship for any of these languages, yet the Melanesians hardly ever make any grammatical errors in speech. Their meticulous care in speaking is founded upon a profound realization of the power of words. Every Melanesian knows that the spoken word is inhabited by a dangerous magic, a magic which must not be annoyed, a force which grows angry when it is disregarded.

It is a remarkable world. The long Pacific swell rolls up its beaches in an everlasting succession of breakers, and coral seas gleam where race after race dreamed away thousands of years. Volcanoes erupt from its tiny islets, myriads of minute sea-creatures labour to build its coral reefs and atolls, tidal waves rear up and engulf whole islands, moonbeams glitter nightly upon the water, and the Milky Way, seven hundred thousand light-years distant, looks down at its reflection in the island world below. Frenchmen, Englishmen and Americans have between them wrested the South Sea islands from their slumbers.

Western scholars are laboriously investigating these coconut and shellfish civilizations and their ancient taboos, trying to get to the bottom of the Oceanians who found so much happiness in a life of unchanging tranquillity.

But there is no going back. The ancient and enchanted worlds are tumbling before the onset of science and progress, and the largest of all the oceans is being forced into unconditional surrender for the first time, its ancient peoples wrenched from the quiet changelessness of their natural existence.

NORTH AMERICA

THE ARRIVAL OF THE INDIANS

They left Asia and wandered across the Bering Straits, reaching North America between ten and twenty thousand years ago.

About four million years have gone by since the day when a most remarkable ape-like being stood up and walked on only two of its four legs. By doing so, the amazing creature gradually became able to develop the two limbs which it no longer needed for purposes of locomotion into aids in the struggle for existence and the search for food. Later — we do not know when — something altogether new declared itself in the creature's head, something which the earth had never known before, the gift of intellect and volition, and the idea of work. The two disengaged limbs could accomplish so much more if they gripped a stone — a tool. Two-legs discovered the use of fire and learned how to articulate. What was more, he learned how to use his eyes in a manner quite unlike any other living creature in the world.

There can scarcely be a more interesting science than one which is devoted to investigating the traces of the first people on our earth, the traces of that mysterious creature called 'man'. A fragment of chipped stone, the remains of a slaughtered animal, huge bones from some fish long extinct, or just the ashes of a fire — those are the sort of clues which endow the science of anthropology with such endless fascination.

The oldest human remains so far brought to light, 'fossils' which had lain under their protective covering of stone and earth awaiting discovery for quite half a million years, were found in Europe, Asia, Africa and Java. 'I was here. I lived here.' It is almost eerie, the way man greets us over a span of hundreds of thousands of years from his abode in Java (*pithecanthropus*), near Peking (*Sinanthropus*), in Rhodesia and in the Neanderthal. Yet in America we have never found any human bones, human skulls, tools, or, indeed, any traces of human habitation which are more than 20,000 years old.

The advanced nature of the Mayan and Aztec civilizations in Central America and of the Peruvian Incas tempts one to suppose that such peaks of human culture and achievement could only have been the culmination of a very long period, and that men must have lived in the same spot for 30,000 or 50,000 years before they could have attained such heights. But this is a fallacy, for, as we have seen, the advanced civilizations of Mesopotamia and the Nile and Indus valleys took only a few thousand years to reach their greatest heights, and then relapsed into nothingness. The earliest known civilization in South America, the Chavin civilization, which flourished on the highland plateau and in the coastal regions of northern Peru, lasted from 100 B.C. to A.D. 500. The oldest Mayan city, Uaxactún in Guatemala, was founded in A.D. 328. There is absolutely no indication in North, Central or South America of any product of an advanced civilization dating from earlier than 200 B.C. We are left with the question of when the people whom ever since Columbus's day we have called 'Indians' — the people whom we now regard as the original inhabitants of both the Americas — actually arrived there.

North America has yielded many finds of arrow-heads and spear-points revealing obvious signs of human manufacture which were discovered close to the fossilized bones of animals now extinct in America, such as camels, early species of bison, giant sloths and prototypal American horses. The dates of these finds were deduced from the age of the rock in which the fossils and objects were embedded. The oldest finds belong to the so-called 'Folsom', 'Sandia' and 'Cochise' civilizations, although none of the three groups of implements should really be classed as civilizations, but rather as industries or types of craftsmanship. The Folsom 'industry' derives its name from the site of its initial discovery in the north-east corner of New Mexico in 1926. Folsom articles were also found on the eastern side of the Rocky Mountains at Alberta, Canada, and scattered over almost the whole of North America east of the Rockies. The Sandia articles were discovered in a cave in the Sandia Mountains of New Mexico; and the Cochise articles in South Arizona, in company with fossils belonging to bisons, mammoths, camels and horses. These 'industries' are 10,000, 15,000, or at most, 20,000 years old. Indigenous to the whole of North America, they were carried on by people who were familiar with fire — as traces of charcoal prove — and lived a nomadic, hunter's life. If there is anything older than Folsom and Sandia in America, it has never yet been discovered.

So we know that human beings have been living in North America for approximately 20,000 years, and that it was not until about the time of Christ's birth that advanced civilizations began to develop in Central America, and later in Peru. We do not know what these people did between the time of their arrival in North America and about 200 B.C., although excavated layers in the Ventana Cave in southern Arizona throw a certain amount of light on the matter. The lowest layer contained tools of the Folsom type, the next, articles of the Cochise type, and the top layer, vessels of almost modern Indian manufacture. Can it be that the Ventana Cave was continuously occupied for 12,000 years?

There are whole libraries of books devoted to the origins of the American Indians. There is Atlantis, for instance, and the legend of Mu, the submerged Pacific continent. There are the similarities between the Indians and the Egyptians, and there are the theories which credit them with Phoenician ancestry. There are people who place them in Polynesia and people who place them in Melanesia, there are Heyerdahl and his *Kon-Tiki*, and a thousand other hopeful theorists. Whenever a Polynesian boat is dug up on the South American coast, or an Inca god seems to resemble one of the stone colossuses on Easter Island, or a certain implement is found to exist in both the Polynesian and American Indian worlds, all it means is that once upon a time a man or a group of men were cast up out of the ocean wastes on the shores of America. But anthropology cannot go far on such pieces of evidence, for only a comprehensive picture complete with a large number of cultural and anthropological similarities could decide the issue.

The question remains: where did the Indians, the first inhabitants of North and South America, come from?

All groups of North and South American Indians have certain physical characteristics in common: blue-black hair, skin ranging from yellow-brown to red-brown, dark eyes, prominent cheek-bones, large faces. In other respects, characteristics tend to vary enormously between one tribe and another. Thus we meet straight hair and crinkly, flat noses and aquiline, thick lips and thin, small stature and large.

Where colour of skin, eyes and hair is concerned, the Indians resemble the Mongolian race. Their cheek-bones likewise testify to an Asiatic origin, and so all their most marked physical traits point in the direction of Asia. We can at least say that the American Indians are more closely related to the Mongolian race than to the white or negroid races. They are not Chinese, therefore, but are possibly descended from a pre-Mongolian type of which both they and the people of east Asia are off-shoots.

Nobody who has seen Indians in both North and South America can fail to recognize that the skull formation and build of the various Indian tribes of North, Central and South America are in many cases so diverse as to render it almost impossible to talk in terms of a single Indian race. America has probably experienced many human influxes from the Bering Straits in her time, influxes separated by intervals of thousands of years. Thus the various Indian races are probably the product of migrations by various Asiatic races into North America. All the tools and hunting-weapons which have been found indicate that the colonization of North America preceded that of South America, for North America is where the earliest articles — those of the Folsom, Sandia and Cochise types — were discovered.

Since the continents of America and Asia almost meet at the Bering Straits in the far north, it must be assumed that it was there in the far north that the first crossing from Asia into America was made. We know, in fact, that a neck of dry land did exist between the Tchuktchen Peninsula and Alaska for thousands of years, enabling mammals to wander freely back and forth between northern Asia and North America.

Proof that subsequent migrations from Asia to America took place is offered by the various products of Asian culture which America adopted: ceramic ware with bands of ornamentation, for example, the composite hunting-bow, moccasins, tailored clothing, the art of ivory-carving and countless sagas and legends. Everything else, like agriculture and architecture, pottery, the art of writing, the calendar and, above all, an arithmetical system, the Indians invented for themselves. The Mayan arithmetical system of Central America was a piece of native ingenuity which central Europe never matched. We inherited a clumsy system from the Romans which was only superseded in comparatively recent times by our present Arabic numerals.

Europe's gifts to the American Indians have included the Christian religion, alcohol, negroes, skyscrapers and dollars, Rockefeller and Pizarro, Eisenhower, democracy and the atom. In return, the Indians have given us chocolate, rubber, tobacco, ground-nuts, the garden strawberry, pineapples, tomatoes, maize, manioc, quinine and cocaine.

In discovering America, Columbus lifted the door of our world off its ancient Mediterranean hinges.

SOUTH AMERICA

WE SHALL NEVER KNOW

Tiahuanacu

Professor Posnansky's theories about Tiahuanacu seem fanciful. He regarded these ruins as 'the cradle of American man'.

FOR nearly 3600 miles along the South American coast run the Andes, a continental system of mountain ranges 100 to 400 miles in width and containing 57 peaks of over 17,350 feet in height.

It was in these highlands that the greatest South American Indian civilizations once flourished, and it is here that the largest surviving Indian populations are to be found. It is here — especially in the mountainous highlands of Bolivia and Peru and in the deserts on the west coast of Peru — that the civilizations of the American Indian races lie buried, cities and abodes of the dead which not even the next thousand years will see fully unearthed.

While man left traces of his existence in North America 20,000 years old, very little evidence of prehistoric man has been discovered in South America which dates from earlier than 5000 years ago. A type of nomadic huntsman was roaming in southern Patagonia before that time, it is true, but all we know about him is that he was a landsman who was unfamiliar with the canoe. In 1921 a human skull was discovered at Punin, Ecuador, which undoubtedly appeared to be much more than 5000 years old, and the Peruvian coast has yielded up large mounds of shells, the relics of some unidentified race of fisherfolk who lived at a time when agriculture was as yet unknown in the region.

Our knowledge of human history in South America only goes back to about the time of Christ's birth. Everything earlier than that still reposes in stubborn obscurity. It may be that archaeologists have not dug deep enough or that they have been so impressed by all their finds dating from historical and early historical times that their investigation of prehistory has suffered by it; or again, it may be that men did not arrive here in any great numbers until a late date.

Peru and Bolivia constitute a single archaeological field made up of civilizations lying superimposed upon each other a hundred times over. Many races have lived, built and become crystallized there, only to vanish once more. Nevertheless, some characteristics are common to all of them. In their archaeological past, the people of Peru and Bolivia lacked all knowledge of the wheel or bow. They were equally ignorant of writing as we know it. They had no burial urns. They were agriculturalists. They planted maize, beans, potatoes, cassava, quinoa and oca. They used to chew a mixture of coca-leaves and lime — but not tobacco, curiously enough. They bred llamas and alpacas. They wove cloth out of wool and cotton, they carved wood and made baskets. In all their centuries of development, these Peruvian and Bolivian civilizations remained almost wholly independent of the other regions in both the Americas. Peru and Bolivia were highly enough developed and well enough organized to counter any external invasion, until the Spaniards arrived. All that the first Spanish conquistadors elicited from the surviving Incas was a rather deficient history of the thirteen generations of their royal dynasty. The Inca Empire's period of greatest expansion began only 123 years before the Spanish conquest.

It was not until 1936 that we started to form an idea of the most important pre-Inca civilizations, or rather art-forms, which flourished somewhere between Christ's birth and A.D. 500. Notable among these is the Chavin style, named after a site called Chavin de Huantár in Peru. Products of the Chavin civilization have been found in many places in the northern highlands and coastal regions of Peru.

In fact, of course, we are not so much talking of a civilization as of a realm of ideas. Darkness still reigns over the people who lived in the centuries when this realm of ideas prevailed. One thing which does assert itself in the products of the Chavin style of art is fanatical religious belief. The men who wielded the wooden moulds and chisels which gave birth to them were permeated by a fervent strength and fanaticism which testify to an almost frightening greatness and determination. Although it occurred at the beginning of all the advanced American civilizations known to us, and lay in the earliest period within reach of archaeological research, this style attained amazing heights at its very inception, heights which were never subsequently surpassed and could only lead to inevitable decline. One of the ruins at Chavin de Huantár — the so-called *castillo* or fortress — not only contained halls, galleries, ramps, steps and corridors, but was also provided with a system of ventilation which still supplies its deepest chambers with fresh air today. The castillo was probably the seat of a religious cult.

Between two and three hundred years after the Chavin art-form came the Nasca style, which flourished in the Ica and Nasca valleys on the south Peruvian coast. Burial-places found in the sides of these valleys contained grave-shafts varying in depth from twenty inches to fourteen and a half feet. Some of the skulls discovered there displayed artificial deformities. An elongated head was apparently considered 'the latest thing' during the Nasca

period. Pots decorated with paintings of birds, mice, llamas, bats, fishes, human heads, fruits and unidentified monsters exhibit a range of up to eleven colours. Cloth was already being woven from wool and cotton during Nasca times, and it was often dyed a variety of colours. In fact, L. M. O'Neale announced in 1939 that she had managed to distinguish no less than one hundred and ninety different shades. The only metal known in the Nasca period seems to have been gold.

For the past fourteen years, scholars have been industriously probing the obscurity which veils the earliest civilizations of Peru and Bolivia, and they believe that the many discoveries they have made are enabling them to distinguish ever more accurately between individual styles and civilizations, such as the 'Paracas', 'Mochica', 'Recuay' and others.

One of the least explored civilizations is that of Tiahuanacu, whose ruins still stand for all to see. During the course of centuries the Tiahuanacu people expanded their sphere of influence northwards over the whole of Peru, dominating the coast as far as Trujillo and perhaps even reaching Ecuador.

The ruins of Tiahuanacu stand in the Bolivian highlands, some thirteen miles south of Lake Titicaca. They cover an area measuring about 1100 yards by 500 yards, and the sandstone and basalt of which they are built must have been brought to the site from at least three miles away. The transportation of quarried blocks of stone weighing up to a hundred tons implies careful organization and supervision, and the dressing and positioning of the massive blocks must have called for great technical ability and armies of labourers.

According to the findings of archaeologists, the Tiahuanacu civilization falls into four periods: an early period, a second period, a classical period and finally, a period of decline. Its largest building, the Acapana, now resembles a natural hill, but it must at one time have looked like a step-pyramid. A water reservoir and several buildings probably stood on its summit, and the whole edifice may have been a kind of fortress or place of refuge. Northwest of the Acapana stand the ruins of another massive construction, known as the Calasasaya. Exactly what this building was remains a mystery, but it includes the famous Gate of the Sun and a large number of stone statues. West of the Calasasaya stand the ruins of the 'Palacio', which was at one time enclosed by a double ring of earthworks, while to the east lies a semi-subterranean building. In addition to the main group of ruins there is also Puma Puncu, a platform constructed out of a large number of sandstone and lava blocks, all of which are smashed and have been shifted from their original positions.

Wendel C. Bennett, Professor of Anthropology at Yale University, has warned us against reading a symbolic astronomical significance into every building, stone and relief at Tiahuanacu, as some have tried to do. The harsh climate of the highlands, the Altiplano, encourages him to suppose that life once went on here much as it does today. Llamas and alpacas were bred here 1400 years ago just as they are now, as finds of bones would indicate. Nor was the extent of agricultural land any greater or less poor in quality then than in our own day. Tiahuanacu may, during its classical period, have been a sort of Mecca, visited by pilgrims, but Professor Bennett does not think that any very large race of people could ever have subsisted up there. Nature simply would not have permitted it.

Bennett's view is important, for just as Troy found its Schliemann, so another man, Arthur Posnansky, devoted his whole life to the ruins of Tiahuanacu. This fanatical student of early Andes civilization completed his monumental work *Tiahuanacu, the Cradle of American Man* in the year 1914. Professor Posnansky was an engineer, an anthropologist, and the holder of many scientific qualifications and awards, and his work is so many-sided and romantic, so full of imagination, so breathtaking even, in its theories and conclusions, that Bennett's more recent and cautiously conservative verdict is really rather saddening, in spite of its greater likelihood.

Posnansky, a 'Professor of Royal Bavaria', made Tiahuanacu his own personal site of exploration about fifty years ago. In his ardent zeal for his subject he enlisted the services of astronomy, geology, meteorology, archaeology — in short, every conceivable science, to prove the correctness of his theory that Tiahuanacu was the cradle of American man. If you dig in the highland plateaux of Tibet, the Andes and Mexico, you will be able to trace the story of man's evolution from its earliest beginnings to the splendour of its advanced civilizations in an almost uninterrupted chain of development. It was an evolutionary ladder of this type, ranging from primitive cave-dwellers to advanced astronomers, which Posnansky believed he had discovered here in Tiahuanacu. Indeed, he even disputes the Eurasian double-continent's claim to have been the site of the Garden of Eden and the scene of man's first appearance. He believed that American man existed earlier — a theory which is demonstrably false.

The cultural development of a large race would never have been possible in the High Andes under the climatic conditions which prevail there today. After an extensive study of geomorphology, or the science of geological evolution, Posnansky reached the conclusion that the highland plateaux of the Andes were at one time neither as high nor possessed of as cold a climate as they are now. He pointed to the fact that even during Pliocene times (ten million years before the beginning of our chronology), and frequently since then, our earth has undergone structural alterations. Even today the west coast of Greenland is subsiding, while the east coast of Labrador is rising ever higher above sea-level. The eastern shores of the United States between the 30th and 40th parallels are sinking, and the west coast of the Gulf of Mexico is rising. Again, portions of the South American continent near Bahia in the Amazon Bay, Brazil and on the eastern sea-board of Patagonia are imperceptibly yet continuously emerging farther and farther from the sea. Posnansky cited many further instances of such changes in altitude before finally coming to Tiahuanacu and Titicaca, the lake which deserted its oceanic mother, the Pacific, and made for the clouds. That Lake Titicaca really is just an elevated ocean trough is demonstrated by the similarity between its fauna and that of the Pacific. We come across the hippocampus or little sea-horse, for instance, as well as various species of ocean shell-fish in the waters of Lake Titicaca, although many of the ocean creatures must have died off after their transference from the warmer environment of their original home to the much lower temperatures which prevail at 12,000 feet.

According to Posnansky, Tiahuanacu was once a vast political and religious metropolis whose influence extended over the whole of the South American continent, a place of death-cults and great burial-grounds, a South American Athens, a Rome, a Byzantium. Then a terrible catastrophe occurred, a huge earthquake which caused the waters of Lake Titicaca to overflow and volcanoes to erupt. Thirty miles from the Calasasaya there is a volcano called the Cayappia, and Posnansky established that the ruined site was covered with layers of lava. He attributes the downfall of this cradle of American civilization to a combination of natural catastrophe and civil war. The early Tiahuanacu people suffered their first great disaster in about A.D. 500. In A.D. 900 Tiahuanacu went under for the second time, but civilization had by then become disseminated over the whole of Peru and, after an epoch marked by the existence of many small and flourishing principalities, the age of the Incas arrived. The Incas called the ruins of Tiahuanacu 'The City of the Dead', and Tiahuanacu had in fact been lying lifeless and ruined for hundreds of years when they came to power.

Cieza de León, who visited the ruins of Tiahuanacu in the year 1540, was able to see large portions of its magnificent buildings still standing in their original state. Since then the unique Sun-temple has been gradually demolished over the centuries and its stones have been carried off to help build houses and bridges in La Paz and other places. Whole waggon-loads of such stones went to La Paz, and until only a few years ago architects were helping Nature and her catastrophes to eradicate the ancient glories of the Tiahuanacu era. An exceedingly incompetent archaeologist called Georges Courty was responsible in 1904 for introducing yet another element of confusion into the ruins by senselessly removing stones and demolishing walls for the sole purpose of finding buried gold.

Many theories have been advanced as to the identity of the people who built Tiahuanacu. The place now belongs to the Bolivian district inhabited by the Aymará or Colla Indians. The Colla race is undoubtedly descended from the people who lived up in the Andes 1500 or 2000 years ago. They were there when the Incas arrived, and archaeological research discloses the fact that Tiahuanacu civilization flourished until almost that time. The Colla priests and rulers must certainly have belonged to a special caste, for they were excellent astronomers who had preserved the experience and traditions of many foregoing centuries. The Sun-temple in the Calasasaya proves that they must have enjoyed a wide knowledge of astronomy, for it demonstrates that they knew how to determine the seasons, dates and equinoxes, and that they were familiar with the sun's rotation round the earth. They evidently believed that the world was the centre of the Universe and Tiahuanacu the centre of the world.

When they had reached the summit of their erudition, they set about building the Sun-temple. Completely ignorant of theodolites, sextants or astronomical calendars, and employing only the most primitive methods, they achieved remarkably dependable results. They devised a stone calendar which divided the year accurately into twelve months, and the months into thirty days. September was not only the beginning of spring (we are in the southern hemisphere, of course), but also marked the beginning of the year.

Posnansky even went so far as to undertake the classification of the various ornamental marks which decorated the sculptures and ceramics found at the ruined site, and also the frieze on the Gate of the Sun. The Tiahuanacu people had no form of writing, but they had obviously evolved certain religious and astronomical ideograms. There was a stairway symbol signifying earth or sky, and there were ideograms representing fish, snakes, winged eyes, mouths, ears, quarters of the moon, arms, legs, tails, wings, crowns, sceptres, human faces and many other things. The men of the Tiahuanacu civilization are even supposed to have compiled a whole almanac.

In Posnansky's opinion, the Gate of the Sun was only the centre-piece in a massive wall bearing records relating to the calendar. This gate is the most remarkable of all the buildings of the splendid third Tiahuanacu period. It remains an unsolved mystery why virtually none of the buildings round Lake Titicaca was ever completed by its architect. Even today, archaeologists are able to confirm that every one of them was abandoned at one stage or another. Classical Tiahuanacu resembles some megalomaniac's project, rather like the Tower of Babel; had it ever been completed it would

— at least in Posnansky's view — have surpassed every other man-made construction in the world.

At 12,000 feet the thin air renders fast walking, mountain-climbing and, indeed, any form of physical exertion difficult. One wonders how the Colla or their slaves ever managed to transport the massive blocks of stone which constituted their building-materials. If Posnansky's theory about Tiahuanacu's erstwhile lower altitude is correct, then everything is easily explained. But it is such a fantastic theory that we can scarcely entertain it today. Yet, if we discard it, the problem posed by the Gate of the Sun becomes even more fantastic. How could this gate, a monolith carved out of a single block of stone, ever have been transported to its site? It is composed of rock which is quite unobtainable anywhere within a wide radius of Tiahuanacu, a hard trachytic stone not otherwise present in any idol or sculpture in the place.

The most sacred spot in the Sun-temple had been reserved for this gate and, although the monolith was not actually discovered there, the site had been prepared for its erection. In fact, the gate was found lying overturned a short distance away. It was in 1908 that the Congress of Americanists re-erected the gate on the spot where it had been found — in other words, in the place where the Tiahuanacu people had once chiselled it out of solid stone.

In view of its sacred character the priests of Tiahuanacu presumably had the huge block of stone for their Gate of the Sun brought from far away, from some place which played an important role in their mythology. Yet if Tiahuanacu stood at its present altitude of 12,000 feet in those days, we are still left to wonder how the immense monolith could possibly have been trundled hundreds of miles up into the soaring heights of the Andes, when, despite all our modern technical aids, the task would present us with almost insuperable difficulties today.

We shall never know.

IN RAREFIED AIR 12,000 FEET UP

The Incas

WE do not know the reason for Tiahuanacu's downfall. This civilization, with its most impressive buildings concentrated around Lake Titicaca, enjoyed a second great prime between A.D. 800 and 900 and then dwindled away to nothing. Tiahuanacu's many uncompleted buildings may be an indication that its end was a sudden and unexpected one. The pre-Tiahuanacu civilizations of Peru and Bolivia, Chavin, Nasca, Mochica and the rest, had long ago passed their prime and relapsed into the dust of ages.

The short lifetime of all these civilizations is in sharp contrast to the splendour of their artistic and architectural achievements. The artists and craftsmen of Peru and Bolivia lived as wretchedly as though they expected to die on the morrow, yet they built for eternity. Between A.D. 900 and about 1200 lies a dark 'medieval' period of roughly three hundred years' duration, which produced, and about which we know, very little. Then came the Inca period.

The artistic history of Old Peru impresses one as having retrogressed from its earliest beginnings. Chavin, Nasca and Mochica represent a brilliant and magnificent start, Tiahuanacu an intermediate stage, and the Inca period — at least in the artistic sphere — a feeble end. Where architecture was concerned, on the other hand, Tiahuanacu only represents a modest level of attainment when compared with the remarkable achievements of the Inca period, with its vast drainage installations, fair-sized towns and almost unique road system.

Who were the Incas, and what was Inca civilization?

The Incas and their civilization suddenly appeared out of nowhere about A.D. 1000. By the time Pizarro had landed at Tumbez in 1532, by the time Atahualpa, the last Inca king, had been taken prisoner and Cuzco had been captured, the Incas were finished. Inca civilization only lasted about three hundred years, but, almost 'mythical' as it may seem to us today, it does not lie very far in the past. Its beginning more or less coincided with Dante, and its end with Calvin.

The word *Inca* was in reality the king's title. The Inca rulers were of Quichua stock and spoke the Quichua language. About A.D. 1000, they lived in the neighbourhood of Cuzco, the late 'cradle' of the Incas. From there they proceeded, in the course of five centuries, to carve out a mighty empire which ultimately extended for well over two thousand miles from northern Ecuador, through the whole of Peru and Bolivia, down to central Chile.

Before the time of these conquests, the whole Andes area had been split into countless political units. Almost every valley and range of hills possessed its own language. In order to do away with this confusion, the Inca rulers made their own Quichua tongue the official language of the whole empire. When the Spaniards landed, they soon ascertained that Quichua was the only language which could get them anywhere, much as English is today. They therefore took no trouble to learn the numerous local languages and dialects, and dealt with the natives exclusively in Quichua. Since then, dozens of ancient Indian languages have vanished into oblivion.

This, then, was the overall picture: the Incas were a small upper class, the rulers, governors and military leaders of an immense region inhabited by native Indians. They were foreign overlords, aristocrats, men with paler skins than their Indian subjects, men with greater knowledge and wisdom, men with their own language, a language with which the subject peoples of their empire were not always conversant. The people of the Andes had no form of writing, and all we know of Inca history is what later authors of the sixteenth century can tell us. These Spaniards learned something of the Incas' ancient traditions by word of mouth, and obtained further information from narrative poems and 'statistics', which were preserved in the form of knotted strings. Apart from these records, the Incas also had professional 'history memorizers', learned men who carried their 'libraries' in their heads.

The Incas handed down legends about their gods and heroes, the origin of mankind and the adventures of their ancestors, by word of mouth. They were also familiar with their table of kings, which began with Manco Capac and ended with the luckless Atahualpa. This dynasty, which comprised thirteen kings, was founded about A.D. 1200, but its members are all somewhat shadowy figures until the year 1438, which saw the coronation of a certain Pachacutec. So we are, in fact, only conversant with a hundred years of Inca history. Like all others of its kind, it is a very human story, a story of wars, conquests, the enslavement of prisoners, subjugation, tribute, tyranny, and disputes over the right of succession. But it is also a story of brilliant colonization and efficient government.

The genius of the Incas displayed itself less in the arts than in political organization. In a sense, they were the Romans of the South American continent. They built a magnificent network of roads running through the rugged highlands and coastal deserts of their empire. Alexander von Humboldt described these roads as the most remarkable and useful installations ever to have been effected by human hand. And indeed, looked at as a whole, the Incas' was a more impressive road network than that which any other ancient people — including the Romans — ever produced. For a period of four hundred years — that is to say, until Napoleon renovated the Roman roads of Europe — the royal highways of the Incas constituted the only good road system in the world. While the cultural communications of Europe were bogged down for centuries in mud and sand, Inca couriers were trotting comfortably along over the ridges of the Andes carrying dispatches between Tiahuanacu and Cuzco, almost 1250 miles apart. A postal service such as this only took a week to cover this distance, even though the Incas lacked one of the most important devices known to man: the wheel. That is why they built the longest foot-paths in the world. They were not really paths, of course, but dead straight roads built on solid foundations, roads designed for mass communication along which passed llama caravans, columns of troops, messengers and royalty borne along in sedan-chairs on the sturdy shoulders of porters, swaying over plaited suspension-bridges and through tunnels from one chain of hills to the next.

The Incas laid down a coast road between twenty-three and twenty-six feet wide which ran for over 750 miles through deserts which hardly ever saw any real rain — once every seven to twenty-five years, in fact. This road was bordered by a waist-high wall, a little South American version of the Great Wall of China. In constructing this desert road, as in building their mountain roads, the Inca engineers followed a simple plan. They never let themselves be deterred by any natural obstacle, but took it in their stride and built as the crow flies. If a marsh lay in their path, they built interminable stone causeways across it, causeways so solid that people still use them today. They spanned lakes with pontoons and precipices with daringly constructed bridges. One such bridge survived until July 20th, 1714, when it parted, hurling a band of travellers down into the waters of the Apurimac. On coming to cliffs, the Incas either tunnelled beneath them or cut flights of steps leading conveniently over their ridges.

Results like these were achieved at heights of 12,000 feet, where the extremely rarefied air makes breathing difficult, the sun beats down mercilessly, and the snow-capped peaks are almost blinding in their brightness. The Incas' suspension-bridges were supported by fibre cables nearly six inches thick. Half way between heaven and earth, their plaited structure paved with matting, these miracles of elasticity made excellent walking.

At intervals of between four and eleven miles along the whole road system (nearly 2000 miles long) stood rest-houses, where meals could be obtained. There were also post-stations for the royal express messengers, who were trained to run at record speeds in the rarefied atmosphere. The messengers operated in relays, each of which could put 150 miles behind it in a single day.

Where there's a will, there's a way. But where there's a way, it may inspire a will to exploit it. It was the very convenience of the Incas' magnificent system of roads which tempted the Spaniards to complete their conquest of the country. Thus the Incas' greatest achievement was destined to determine the speed of their own destruction. Spanish ox-carts, horses' hoofs and lack of maintenance eventually led to the roads' dilapidation.

The Incas were not only brilliant road constructors, but also made their country the finest horticultural centre in the contemporary world. They grew over forty different kinds of plants and cereals, and installed remarkable systems of irrigation. Their principal source of fresh meat was the guinea-pig. This creature was kept on the spot in the kitchen, and reared on scraps and greenstuff. It was clean, and its meat was tender and even fat. The Incas always abominated dog's meat, but they regarded duck as a great delicacy.

The Incas built their houses out of stone, usually in groups of six, with a central courtyard and a surrounding wall. Their armies used tents. Only high officials who had been appointed by the king sat on chairs, while the king himself sat on a throne.

Ruins of massive stone palaces and Sun-temples are to be found throughout the Inca empire. Inca cities were seldom fortified, but usually possessed a place of refuge on some hill near by. The city of Cuzco consisted of a religious centre where noblemen, priests and government officials lived with their servants, and a ring of small villages around it.

The male Inca's wardrobe comprised an armless cape, a second, larger cape for cold weather, a cloth apron and leather sandals with woollen laces. Women wore a long gown tied about the hips with a sash, and a cape like that of the men. They also had skirts reaching to their calves, and their hair was held in place by a head-band. All Inca aristocrats wore huge cylindrical 'ear-plugs', frequently made of gold and about two inches in diameter. Boys' ears were pierced when they were only fourteen years old. Women never wore ear-ornaments. The Incas used to paint their faces for war, mourning and religious ceremonies.

The Incas worked in many metals, including copper, gold, silver, tin and lead. All gold-mines belonged to the State, and inspectors were posted at their entrances to guard against theft.

The number of wives a man owned was an indication of his wealth and authority. The king often rewarded men who had served him well by giving them several wives.

The king of the Incas was an absolute ruler by divine right. He could trace his ancestry back to the sun, and was worshipped as a deity throughout his lifetime. He demanded slavish obedience from his subjects, and his position was carefully secured against the dangers of revolution. There was scarcely any private property. The nation was organized on collectivist lines, all agricultural land being owned by various clans whose chieftains shared it out among individual citizens. The latter farmed their 'allotments' for a year, at the end of which time the land was distributed afresh. The whole system was a kind of communism supervised by an autocratic god-king. One government department was responsible for the public highways, another for game and hunting, and another for the forests. The design and construction of towns, temples and bridges was in the hands of a corps of engineers, while public 'statisticians' kept a register of crops, births and able-bodied labourers. A certain number of children were trained by the State to become soldiers, another group was earmarked for the priesthood, and yet another for the civil service. The Incas' communistic regime was very highly organized.

In addition to his chief wife, every king possessed a large harem. From the time of Topa Inca onwards, the chief wife was invariably the king's own sister. The secondary wives won special privileges according to the number of children they bore. These children were responsible for the upkeep of the royal palace and the ruler's personal cult. (There were about five hundred persons of direct royal descent alive at the time of the conquest.) The propagation and maintenance of the 'royal ideology' was in the hands of a team of learned men, who were in a sense directors of State propaganda, and from whose ranks the highest officials in the administration were as far as possible drawn. Where succession to the throne was concerned, the king generally selected the most able of his chief wife's sons and trained him for his future task. The royal throne took the form of a low chair only eight inches high, carved out of red wood and covered with fine rugs. The king's titles ran: 'Only Inca', 'Son of the Sun', 'Friend of the Poor'. His chief wife was known as 'Queen' or 'Mother'. Each new king built a palace at Cuzco during his reign, since his predecessor's automatically became a temple of remembrance. Anyone who wished to see the king had to take off his sandals and put a burden on his back before entering the royal presence. The king normally sat behind a folding screen, and it was a great honour if he showed a visitor his face. When the king died his body was embalmed, and it was considered only natural that the wives and servants whom the king had esteemed most highly during his lifetime should voluntarily follow him into the grave. His devoted entourage were first made drunk and then strangled. The dead ruler enjoyed the same attendance in his burial-palace as he did during his lifetime. Young women were always stationed on either side of his mummy armed with fans to drive away the flies. The Spaniard Polo de Ondegardo discovered the bodies of all the former Inca kings in 1559, during the course of his campaign against the Inca religion.

The empire was continuously combed for talented men to fill the many thousands of State appointments in the royal dictatorship. Anyone with the slightest signs of leadership or administrative ability suddenly found himself transplanted into a strange village where he was obliged to govern according to the principles dictated by the sovereign.

All taxes were demanded and paid either in work or in kind. There was no money. Taxpayers had to cultivate land whose yield went to the Inca government and the Inca priesthood. In addition, a certain portion of their life was devoted to compulsory military service, public works, or personal attendance on the king and the nobility. The fortress of Sacsahuaman, which was probably the most impressive of all the Incas' buildings, required a labour corps of 30,000 men to construct it. In the mines, the usual term of compulsory labour was only a month.

One of the king's greatest worries was how to find enough work to keep his labour corps continually occupied. Huayna Capac, for instance, had a hill moved from one site to another merely because he was temporarily devoid of any ideas for a better project. The Inca kings knew that a nation with too much leisure may start to criticize its government. Revolutions occurred even when they kept their subjects well occupied, so they dreaded to think what would happen if they allowed them any long spells of idleness.

Women were quite as strictly controlled under the Inca regime as men. All girls were 'classified' at the age of ten by royal officials who visited each village in turn. Girls who were particularly well-favoured were brought up by the government, while the rest were obliged to stay in their home towns and marry tax-payers. Marriages were conducted on a communal basis under the auspices of the State. All the young men and girls of marriageable age were drawn up in two rows, and an official allotted one girl to each young man. The girls who had been selected for government service entered State boarding-schools where they learned spinning, weaving, cooking and other domestic arts. Then they were released, some for service in temples and for religious duties connected with Sun-worship, which entailed their perpetual chastity as 'Virgins of the Sun', and others as wives for deserving noblemen and warriors. Still others became the royal concubines who prepared the king's meals and made his clothes.

At the time of their selection at ten years of age, some girls were straight away earmarked for sacrifice on sundry ceremonial occasions. As always in such cases, the State religion taught that they were 'especially privileged' and offered them the prospect of a life of joy and contentment — if not there and then, at least in the world to come.

AT MIDNIGHT...I SHALL COME

That was how people lived on the west coast of South America under their Inca rulers. It was all eerily reminiscent of something much nearer our own day.

GREAT though the power of the Inca kings was, wide though the bounds of their mighty empire were set — from the highland plateaux of the Andes down to the Pacific — and absolute though their authority seemed, they still dreaded revolutions. After all, there has never yet been a tyrant or dictator in the history of the world who could sleep peacefully at night.

The Inca kings did not see the conquest of new territory as any very great achievement. Not only was there universal military conscription, but the conviction of each individual that he was merely the volitionless property of the king was so deep-seated that the latter felt he could lead his armies to the ends of the earth, if need be. Conquering countries was easy: the difficulty lay in holding them down.

The kings accordingly adopted a policy which has only recently come back into fashion. The seething unrest which prevailed in every newly conquered country was calmed, cooled and finally rendered innocuous by mass deportations. No sooner had a new province been occupied than it was depopulated. Thousands upon thousands of Indians, burdened with their most treasured possessions and accompanied by their wives and children, trudged along the magnificent straight roads of this empire which lasted half a millennium (A.D. 1000–1532). And as these homeless D.P.s of the Inca period wandered along in their endless columns, they met the future occupants of their own homes going in the opposite direction, the colonists, the people with what Goebbels called the 'spontaneous pioneering spirit'. They, too, were sad to be leaving their homes, but they were reliable, orthodox veterans of the Inca will, and trusty devotees of the 'New Order'.

These settlers were called *mitimaes*. The new occupants of the strange villages and fields never got on very well with the few original inhabitants who were allowed to stay behind. The latter owed their rights to inheritance, while the former had received theirs by royal edict. The Inca State expected its loyal colonists to set the defeated peoples and the 'converts' among them a good example. The new arrivals spread the Quichua language and established Inca garrisons. As a mark of royal gratitude, they were permitted to appropriate as many local girls as they wished. But the Inca kings went even further in their efforts to preserve their Hitlerian trinity — one people, one State and one Inca god. Each of the provinces high up in the region of

283

Lake Titicaca and on the highland plateau of Bolivia was allotted some fields in the warm lowlands, which meant that even up in the Andes its citizens could still enjoy the sub-tropical fruits of their native valleys.

By the time the Spaniards conquered Peru, the colonists in many provinces outnumbered the original inhabitants. The Inca king recruited a large proportion of the colonists he dispatched in every direction from his royal capital, Cuzco. By using his own people, he provided himself with a source of inside information on what was going on among the deportees in all the provinces in his empire, and could study their customs and character without moving from his armchair, so to speak.

The Inca Empire was the New World's first true melting-pot of humanity, a vast, whirling vortex of many different nationalities. If the Spaniards — the 'white gods' — had not arrived upon the scene when they did, the Inca people would have become fused into a homogeneous nation with Quichua as its universal language. In the Inca Empire, the apportioning of work and leisure rested with the State alone, which saw to it that no one starved, no one froze to death, and no one had too good a time, either. There was no such thing as unemployment, even among those who might have enjoyed a spell of it. Even women had to go on working between the ages of fifty and eighty, and when men became so old that their teeth fell out, they were still considered fit for the task of feeding and breeding guinea-pigs. These ancients were known as 'old sleepers' or *puñucrucus*, probably because they went about their duties in a permanent doze.

The Indian author Felipe Huaman Poma de Ayala reports that the Incas allowed absolutely no one to be idle, not even the infirm, blind, deaf, deaf-mutes, cripples or feeble-minded. It was the State's constant concern to increase its man-power, and not even men with the disabilities listed above were allowed to remain celibate. However, since a healthy young woman was unlikely to want to marry an aged cripple, the State decreed that a lame man should marry a lame woman, a blind man a blind woman, an aged stutterer or a deaf-mute a wife with the same defects.

Trade was a State monopoly in the Inca Empire. Taxpayers used to run small village markets where they bartered their surplus goods and such articles from the State workshops as the government had allotted them. Money did not exist, but, since the government only demanded taxes in the form of manual labour and did not levy them on 'turn-over', a hard-working family could amass a considerable quantity of goods and chattels. Precious metals and objects of artistic or ornamental value were the exclusive property of the king and the aristocracy.

Anyone who imagines that the Inca citizen could travel around freely on his country's magnificent roads is much mistaken. These roads were reserved for government traffic only. Taxpayers were not permitted to use them, partly to avoid traffic congestion, but, even more important, because in doing so they would be interrupting their labours.

Law-enforcement in the Inca Empire was strict but just. Every misdemeanour was regarded as a crime against the State or the king. Punishments included public reprimand, removal from office, banishment to the coca plantations, torture and death. One method of torture – a sort of divine ordeal – was the *hiwaya*. This punishment involved the dropping of a very heavy stone on to the condemned man's back, a procedure which usually resulted in his death. Capital punishment took the form of hanging up by the feet, stoning, hurling from a cliff, or blows on the head with a club. Cruel as these methods may seem, it must be remembered that sentence of death could only be passed by government officials of the highest rank or by the king himself. There was no right of appeal. In Cuzco, the capital, there was a subterranean cave inhabited by jaguars, pumas, bears, foxes, poisonous snakes, and scorpions, into which traitors to the State were thrown. Despite the manifest dangers of such a sojourn, these men still had a slender chance of survival, and if they managed to stay alive for two days they were released, and even honoured, as being under the protection of the gods.

The Inca penal code distinguished between aristocrats and commoners. The dignity of the aristocracy had at all costs to be upheld. A convicted nobleman might only lose his office, for instance, whereas a commoner would be subjected to torture. In cases of adultery, however, positions were reversed. A man or woman of the people was merely whipped, but if the adulterous wife belonged to the nobility both guilty parties were executed. The incidence of crime seems to have been generally low in the Inca empire, partly because penalties were so severe, and partly because the State provided for all material needs.

The Inca army had no cavalry or siege-engines. Soldiers were equipped with thick woollen shirts and a kind of bandaging which took the place of armour. They carried shields, slings for firing stones, clubs and spears, and marched into battle helmeted, shouting abuse at their foes, beating drums, and blowing clay trumpets and bone flutes. The king had his personal bodyguard, known as the 'Big-ears', who were recruited from the aristocracy. The Spaniards christened the whole of the nobility *orejekes*, after their heavy 'ear-plugs'. We are involuntarily reminded by them of the stone figures on Easter Island with their long, mysterious faces and large ears.

Prisoners of war were normally brought back to Cuzco, where a few of them were sacrificed to the gods as a thank-offering. The king attended the ceremony in the Sun-temple walking on a carpet of prisoners' necks.

285

Particularly dangerous enemies were cast into the cave of snakes. Dead prisoners were stuffed with straw and ashes and used as trophies, while the skin from their stomachs was used as drum-parchment — hence the phrase so frequently encountered in the Incas' verbal traditions: 'He defeated him and made him into a drum.' Noblemen who had distinguished themselves in battle were granted the right to carry an umbrella or sit on a chair.

If there is much that seems harsh or inhuman about the Incas, we should remember that most people in the past five thousand years have possessed about the same measure of good and evil. They all had their worries, they all wept, laughed and loved. Garcilaso de la Vega recorded a little poem which he heard from Indians of the Inca period: 'This is where you shall sleep. At midnight . . . I shall come.' Sarmiento de Gamboa translated a small and dramatic song which ran: 'I was born like a lily in the garden. Like a lily I was reared. I blossomed, my season came, I withered, and I died.' The little love-letter and the observations on the impermanence of life both go to prove that the Incas were far from devoid of soul or feeling. They believed in a supreme god, Viracocha, the creator and maker of all supernatural beings. He was portrayed as a man, and his statues were worshipped in the Inca temples. One such statue stood in Cuzco, made of solid gold. Viracocha had command of all divine power, although he delegated the government of his creation to numerous supernatural viceroys. Tradition has it that when Viracocha saw what he had made, he travelled throughout the land and taught the people many good things. After performing a number of miracles he went to Manta in Ecuador, and eventually found his Gennesaret in the Pacific Ocean, wandering away over it dry-shod.

The Creator's most important 'angels' were the sun, moon, thunder, stars, earth and sea, but the Incas also worshipped various places and objects. The Spaniards found *huacas* or shrines everywhere they went.

The State made sacrifices to Viracocha the Creator, the holy ceremonies being administered by priests. Only the most important gods received human sacrifices, and then only at times of crisis like plagues, famine, unsuccessful wars, or when the king was ill or going into battle in person. Coronation celebrations included the sacrifice of two hundred children. They were plied with plenty of refreshments before the ceremony to ensure that they did not arrive at 'Viracocha's' in an unhappy or hungry condition. In the case of older children, intoxication preceded sacrifice.

The idea of sacrificial atonement and propitiation of the gods was very widespread in the Inca empire. A man who was extremely ill and for whom the soothsayers forecast certain death sometimes sacrificed his son, begging God to be content with one life and to spare the life of the sacrificer. If even that was of no avail, the man had to die anyway. After death one either lived on with the sun in the higher world, which had plenty of food and drink to offer, or went as a sinner to a hell in the centre of the earth, where it was cold, and stones took the place of bread. It was only the aristocracy who had no choice in the matter. They went to heaven willy-nilly, however rascally they had been on earth. The dead were buried either in rock graves or in stone graves with their entrances blocked by a boulder.

So there the Incas sat with their knees drawn up, waiting for their souls to go to heaven, or their tombs to be ransacked by Spanish conquistadors. The aristocrats attained both ends, of course, for they were assured of heaven, even though it was the same heaven which sent the Spaniards to plunder their graves.

ATAHUALPA TUMBLED INTO THE DUST

'It was the will of Heaven.' Pizarro to Inca Atahualpa after the massacre at Cajamarca on November 16th, 1532.

AN icy wind races over Flanders, forces its way into the narrow streets of Ghent, and moans high in the lofty tower of Saint-Bavo Cathedral. It is February 24th in the year 1500. By the time the sun's first rays fall upon the roofs of the city, the world will have witnessed the birth of a child destined to rule over Germany, Austria, Italy, Burgundy, Spain, the Netherlands and parts of America and North Africa.

Though you are still lying in your cradle, Charles, you will one day be 'Holy Roman Emperor', the mightiest ruler the world has ever seen. Yet before you die even your world will have collapsed, and you will spend the evening of your days in humility, a monk kneeling in a monastery. The Venetian painter Titian has dropped one of his brushes; you pick it up. 'It is only fitting that Titian should be waited on by an emperor,' you say. Your beloved clocks tick on, tick on ceaselessly; you peer into their mechanism. 'What is the time?' you ask. 'God is the time,' the clocks reply. Night after night you peer into the cold clockwork of their tiny hearts. And then, Charles V, contrite little man and mighty emperor, you die.

It was a great moment in a great year, the year 1500, a pinnacle in the history of Western civilization one and a half thousand years after the birth of Christ. It was the golden age of the Renaissance, the rebirth of classical antiquity. Michelangelo built St Peter's, Albrecht Dürer carved his great Passion, Copernicus realized that the world was only a planet among other planets, Raphael joyously painted his beautiful Madonnas. Luther, Calvin and Zwingli reformed the Church. Leonardo da Vinci's genius seemed to embrace in its elemental greatness all the artistic and creative impulses of his age. Paracelsus was the doctor of these times, Hans Sachs their shoemaker and poet. Jakob Fugger financed papal elections, wars and the largest merchant fleet in the contemporary world. But the greatest explorers and conquerors of the day were three sons of Spain and a Genoese, men who added to the wealth of the Western world — with its glorious paintings, sculptures and cathedrals — a whole new continent and the largest of all the oceans.

It is instructive to picture the world as it was at the turn of the century. The year 1500 saw Columbus a man of forty-five with snow-white hair. He had been through interminable periods of suffering and hardship, and now he was lying in chains. The discoverer of America was lying in chains

Melanesian ancestor-figures from New Ireland in the Bismarck Archipelago. Ancestor-worship has existed there from time immemorial. [Völkerkunde-Museum, Munich. *Photograph:* Herbert List

A Melanesian from New Caledonia

The face of a Central American Indian (A.D. 200–300); a sculpture from the district round Vera Cruz, it exhibits a striking resemblance to the Guatemalan Indians of today. [*Photograph:* Schapowalow

Face of a modern Central American Indian, a porter from the Guatemalan highlands, where Mayan civilization began

Mexican stone mask from the 2nd century A.D. [*Photograph:* Susanne Schapowalow

A face of classical Mayan style. It dates from the 9th century A.D. and comes from a priest's grave recently discovered inside a pyramid at Palenque

Burial-accessory found on the northern coast of Peru,
a product of the *Mochica civilization* (*c.* A.D. 500–800)

Figurine from the Yucatan Peninsula, probably of a pre-Mayan period. Nine inches high and carved in greenstone. It was probably made sometime during the first five centuries A.D.

Clay model of a head found on the coast of Vera Cruz. It dates from the Toltec period (*c.* A.D. 900) and is assumed to represent Xipe Totec, the God of Spring. The ears are adorned with pale blue knots

A clay figure from Oaxaca Museum reminiscent of ancient Egyptian sculptures. It was the work of the Zapotecs, who lived on the southern coast of Mexico at about the same time as the Maya

Scene on a door-post from Yaxchilan, Chiapas, Mexico, in the British Museum, London. The penitent on the right is pulling a rope of thorns through his tongue, and the blood runs down into a sacrificial basin. The standing priest wields a stylized maize plant

his photograph shows us what is really the ost gigantic calendar in the world. Engineers the Nasca civilization used this dry and fertile desert as a gigantic drawing-board, arking out a series of dead straight lines any miles long in the arid soil. Nasca tronomers then sighted along them and served their relationship to particular stars they rose above the horizon, using the results to fix dates

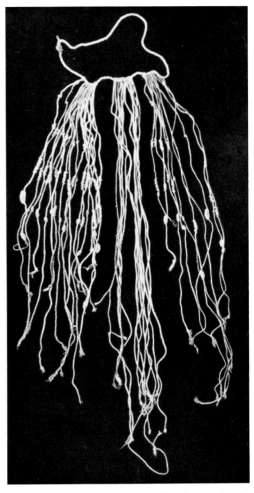

he Incas' slaves and oppressed tributary oples betrayed all their other secrets to the vaders, yet Machu Picchu, overgrown with opical vegetation, eluded discovery. It mains a mystery why the Spanish con- uistadors never heard about this town. It as not until 1911 that Hiram Bingham discovered these ruins

Inca knot-writing. Principal strings had sub- ordinate strings attached to them. Different coloured strings signified different categories of articles. Countless combinations could be achieved by varying the colours and types of knot. This was the Incas' sole form of writing and numerical system

mask of high-carat gold, from the Chimu vilization of the 14th and 15th centuries, hich was found on the northern coast of eru. Masks like these were attached to ummies as a kind of artificial face. They ere more commonly made of wood or cotton cloth than of gold or copper

Atahualpa, the last Inca, who spent many years as Pizarro's prisoner, and was finally executed

Francisco Pizarro, conqueror of Peru, born in 1471 at Trujillo, Spain, and murdered at Lima on June 26th 1541

A small clay head of the Teotihuacán civilization, now in the British Museum, London. We know almost nothing about the inhabitants of this temple-city, which reached its prime in the 5th and 6th centuries A.D.

The pyramid at Cholula, Mexico. Its cubic capacity (38,820,000 cubic yards) is larger than that of the Pyramid of Cheops

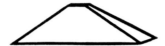

The Sun-pyramid at Teotihuacán, the ruined city's largest building (drawn to scale)

The Moon-pyramid at Teotihuacán, probably the city's most important building

The Pyramid of Cheops, Egypt. Its capacity is about 35,402,790 cubic yards

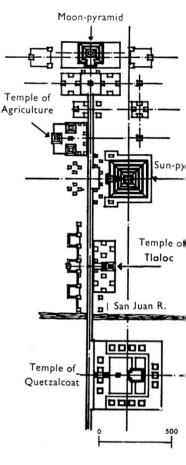

Moon-pyramid

Temple of Agriculture

Sun-py

Temple of Tlaloc

San Juan R.

Temple of Quetzalcoat

0   500

Plan of Teotihuacan

This overgrown hill is really the pyramid of Cholula, in cubic capacity the largest building in the world. It is now surmounted by the church of Los Remedios

at Cadiz, hearing again and again in his dreams the voice of Rodrigo de Triana crying: 'Land, land!' Cortez, destined to conquer Mexico, was fifteen at this time, Balboa twenty-five. It was Balboa who was later to discover the Pacific, and Pizarro, as yet poor and unknown, who was to seize Peru, the gold-mine of the world, and see the legendary Inca king brought before him in chains. All four men belonged to the same period — and what a rich, courageous and splendid period it seems in comparison with our own poor, pale age of drab masses, where there are no more unexplored continents, no more uncharted seas, and no more heroic figures like those who once used to charm the angels down from heaven to earth.

Pizarro was born at Trujillo, a town in the Spanish province of Estremadura. His mother Francisca wept, for he was an illegitimate child, and she was too poor to support him. Not knowing what to do, she laid him down outside the door of a church. No one took him in, however, and he should by rights have died. But in an age of so many marvels, when the Madonna's portraits looked down on suffering humanity and occasionally worked miracles, the child survived — nourished, so the Spaniards used to relate, by Nature. No one taught him to read or write, and he became a swine-herd.

The harbour of Seville was a hive of activity. Tall-masted caravels used to weigh anchor there, bound for far-off lands across vast and little known oceans. The place was a rendezvous for thirsty sea-captains and a wild rabble of Spanish adventurers, fortune hunters and treasure seekers. The poor, hungry herdsman wandered through the busy streets, his mouth agape at the seafaring men's tales of the New World. His fertile imagination grasped the boundless possibilities of this New World, but year after year went by and still no captain would take him there.

Pizarro was thirty-nine before he reached America. He entered the service of a bold caballero called Morales, the founder of a New World settlement. When next we see him, he is at Balboa's side in Darien, south of the isthmus of Panama. It was an arduous trek over the mountains. With Balboa, Pizarro was one of the first Europeans to set eyes on the Pacific Ocean. Feverishly he set about collecting gold and pearls from the islands off the coast of Panama. It was loot, loot all the time — not for his own benefit, however, but for Morales, his knightly master.

Pizarro early recognized that the New World spelt hardship, danger and privation, and that his plans and dreams could only be fulfilled by dint of incredible exertion and foresight. And age was creeping up on him. He was already fifty years old. Soon it would be too late. He was the owner of an unhealthy strip of land, but he had no gold. He had become renowned as a daring knight, yet he was still dogged by his past, the beggar-woman at the church door, the stigma of his illegitimacy. He was stranded on the shores of an alien world like a rotting hulk which is slowly becoming clogged with sand. In despair, he offered a little golden shoe to the Madonna, and wept. Cortez had just conquered the whole of Mexico. Had Pizarro not seen for himself how Balboa waded down the beach into the surf and claimed the vast Pacific for the King of Castile? Had not Magalhães imperiously given the ocean its name, 'el Mar Pacífico'? Was not Andagoya always talking about his journey south, about a fabulous Inca Empire and the gold which lay beyond the slopes of the Cordilleras? And all this while he, Pizarro, was sitting wretchedly on the isthmus of Panama, getting himself devoured by mosquitoes! All he needed was money, ships, a royal charter and some stout hearts, and there might still be a chance, down in the south, of making his name a thing to be whispered with awe in the streets of Seville.

In the end, Pizarro found the men he needed. Diego de Almagro was a foundling like himself, a soldier who had carved out a career without the assistance of noble birth. The third member of the party was Hernando de Luque, a curious blend of schoolmaster and priest who was the administrator of public funds in the small community of Darien, east Panama. Luque supplied the money, Almagro manned the ships, and Pizarro, burning with ambition, took command of the expedition. By a quirk of history, one of his ships had been built by Balboa, who died five years before. The caravel was still lying unrigged in Panama harbour. We know what Balboa, the discoverer of the Pacific Ocean, had in mind when he built it. His intentions were identical with Pizarro's: the conquest of the Inca Empire.

Pizarro weighed anchor in the middle of November 1524 and, sailing southwards, eventually steered his small ship into the mouth of the Biru. It was from this river, or so Zarate reports in his *Conquista del Peru*, that the Spaniards derived the name 'Peru'. Pizarro and his companions made repeated marches into the unknown Inca Empire. Sailing on and on down the coast, they landed at several points and pushed forward into the Peruvian interior armed only with swords, for they were not yet equipped with muskets. They returned to Panama, only to sail southwards again, solemnly pledging their lives to their bold undertaking and swearing to kill one another if they were ever disloyal. Before their departure Father Luque administered Holy Communion to his companions, dividing the consecrated bread into three pieces so that each received a third of it. Standing before an altar in Panama, the three men shared an unknown empire amongst themselves, an empire of which they were almost completely ignorant.

The moment Pizarro saw his first Indian in the tropical forests of Peru, his belief that people lived in them and that gold must exist there was confirmed. Whenever he and his party entered a village the Indians fled, leaving their gold behind in their houses. The conquistadors' appetite grew with eating, while the Peruvians, as though motivated by some curious urge towards self-destruction, received their dangerous white visitors in a submissive and friendly fashion, showing them remarkable courtesy and hospitality. In one place, which they named Santa Cruz, the Spaniards were met by an Indian princess who came on board their ship of her own free will. Pizarro gave her a few worthless little presents, and she begged him and his companions to return the visit, which they did. On going ashore, they found that the princess had erected arches of sweeping branches intertwined with scented flowers and sweet-smelling shrubs. For the first time in his life, Pizarro enjoyed Peruvian cooking and tasted the unfamiliar fruits of the country with their strange and exotic colours. He heard strange music and watched graceful young girls in simple costumes performing dances which no European had ever seen before. He showed his gratitude by presenting the princess with a Castilian flag, and bidding her fly it as a token of submission to the ruler of his country — which she did.

In the summer of 1528 Pizarro, now a man of fifty-seven, went back to Seville. On arrival, he was thrown into prison on a charge of debt lodged by a scholar called Enciso. Pizarro had been away from his native land for twenty years. He left it as a poor and unknown adventurer destined to undergo incredible sufferings and hardships. Now he had returned, only to be clapped into gaol.

Pizarro's name came to the ears of the Emperor, who summoned him to court and inspected the astonishing things which the strange man had brought back with him. He was shown the first llama ever to be brought back to Europe, and examined various articles in gold and silver, whose metallic lustre greatly augmented his interest. Pizarro comported himself in a grave and dignified manner as a true son of Estremadura should, and spoke like a man who had really seen something of the world.

Unfortunately for Pizarro, the court of the world empire received another visit, also from a man of the New World. It was Hernando Cortez, the conqueror of Mexico. With a whole new empire to lay at his imperial master's feet, he rather put Pizarro's achievements in the shade. Cortez was by this time at the end of his career, fifty-six-year-old Pizarro at the beginning. Both men overthrew powerful Indian ruling houses in their time, but they were as yet ill-matched rivals. For all that, Pizarro enjoyed some measure of success. He was granted the rank and title of governor and commander-in-chief in the New World, with a salary for life of 725,000 *maravedis*. It was his duty as a sort of viceroy to maintain a civil service and an army, and he was also empowered to erect fortifications. Meanwhile, dispatches arrived in the New World from far-off Spain appointing Pizarro's associate Almagro as commander of a fortress, with the rank of *hidalgo* and a salary of 300,000 *maravedis*. Reverend Father Luque got the bishopric of Tumbez and the title 'Protector of the Peruvian Indians'. One of Pizarro's navigators was made 'Grand Pilot of the Southern Sea', and one of his cannoneers became commander-in-chief of the artillery. The rest of his men became hidalgos and caballeros. Emperor Charles was not stingy with the Spanish conquerors of a land which did not belong to him where titles, offices and governorships were concerned. Money, however, was another matter. It is said that Pizarro had considerable difficulty in raising enough funds to put to sea again, and that he was helped out of his predicament by Cortez, who was enormously wealthy.

So Pizarro went back to the land of the Incas once more, this time equipped with the musket, a miraculous new weapon of which South America was as yet ignorant in A.D. 1532.

At the head of his small band of adventurers, Pizarro thrust far inland towards the Incas' main encampment. Ordering his men to treat the natives well, he led his stout-hearted little troop on a daring and successful march into the heart of the country. Inca Atahualpa sent them an envoy, who bade them welcome in the name of his master and invited them to visit him in his mountain encampment. Pizarro requested the man to inform his master that he, Pizarro, had been sent by a mighty prince who lived across the sea. Furthermore, he wished to pay his respects to the Inca and would shortly be presenting himself in person. The natives offered no resistance, and immediately took to their heels whenever Pizarro appeared. However, Pizarro's brother Hernando caught a Peruvian, stretched him on the rack, and extracted from his prisoner the fact that the Inca's invitation had been nothing but a ruse to get the foreigners into his clutches.

Pizarro's column wound its way up steep roads into the Andes and along the crest of the Cordilleras. More messengers arrived from Inca Atahualpa bearing their master's greetings and the information that he was stationed near the town of Cajamarca, famous for its warm springs. The Spaniards marched on, gazing in surprise at the carefully tended fields of a countryside inhabited by a civilized, cleanly dressed population which included many graceful girls. At last, ranged in lines along the slopes of a mountain, the Spaniards made out a large number of white tents, quite unlike anything they had seen in Indian country before.

Pizarro marched into Cajamarca on November 15th, 1532. Between the town and the royal encampment lay a meadow. Only this meadow now separated Pizarro from the legendary Inca.

It was an immensely interesting moment in the history of mankind. Picture these two men, the white conqueror and the Indian king, as they

292

assured each other of their mutual friendship, each hesitating before entering the other's trap. Picture the scene inside the town as Pizarro prepared his soldiers for battle, and the Spaniards sang: 'Arise, O God, and plead thine own cause.' After a period of anxious waiting, Atahualpa informed the Spanish commander that he would visit him accompanied by his armed warriors. When he was about half a mile from the town, however, he came to a halt.

He pitched camp.

He hesitated.

Could he trust Pizarro?

Shortly before sundown he set his column in motion again. Borne aloft on the shoulders of his vassals in a sedan-chair, Atahualpa entered the town on a throne made of solid gold, his throat adorned by a necklace of huge emeralds. When the king finally swayed into the main square, there was not a Spaniard to be seen. Everything was very still. 'Where are the strangers?' asked the king. At that moment, Father Vicente de Valverde, a Dominican monk, appeared. Stepping up to the Inca with a Bible in one hand and a crucifix in the other, he announced that he was there on the orders of his commander, to convert the king to the true faith. The monk gave a detailed account of the Creation, the Fall, the Redemption by Jesus Christ, the Crucifixion, the Ascension and the Trinity. Furthermore, he called upon Atahualpa to pay tribute to Emperor Charles V.

The Inca's reply was translated by Felipillo the interpreter. It was short and to the point: 'The Christians believe in three gods and one god. That makes four. I will pay tribute to no man. I am greater than any other prince in the world. The Pope must be a madman if he gives away countries that do not belong to him. I shall not change my faith. You say yourselves that your god was killed by the very people he had created. My god is alive. He lives in heaven. He looks down on his children below. What gives you the right,' Atahualpa asked the monk, 'to put forward all these claims?'

The monk pointed silently to the Bible in his hand. Atahualpa snatched it, leafed through it for a moment, and then threw it into the dust. 'Tell your companions that I call them to account. I demand satisfaction for all the injustices they have committed in my country.'

The monk picked the Bible up and went off to tell Pizarro what had happened. 'I give you absolution,' he cried to the assembled Spaniards. 'Strike now!' At a signal from Pizarro, the heavy Spanish cannon at the top of the fortress opened fire. 'Sant' Iago!' shouted the Spaniards. 'To the attack!' And they poured out of their places of concealment into the square, hurling themselves into the midst of the Indian ranks. A bloody carnage ensued.

Atahualpa stared at the massacre in horror. Most of the Indians were cut down, and blood flowed like water. The Inca watched the scene uncomprehendingly. Strange weapons flashed before his eyes like lightning, and their thunder rolled about him. His sedan-chair swayed to and fro on the shoulders of his loyal retainers like a ship about to founder. A few of the noblemen who were supporting it fell. The rocking throne tilted, and Atahualpa was tipped out. He tumbled into the dust, and his badge of royalty, the *borla*, was immediately torn from his forehead.

The greatest ruler in South America, the most mighty Inca, the god-king, was Pizarro's prisoner. Not one Spanish life had been lost.

'It is the fortune of war,' the Inca said. Pizarro told the king to be of good cheer, and lodged him in a large building where he had him closely guarded but allowed him to retain some of his Indian servants.

'Heaven willed it so,' Pizarro told Atahualpa, 'because you insulted the Holy Book. Take courage and trust me. We Spaniards are a magnanimous people. We have come to this land to spread the religion of Jesus Christ. No wonder we are victorious.'

Atahualpa sat there in grave and kingly composure. No one saw that he was inwardly a broken man. His eyes stared out of his massive head, blood-shot and unnaturally bright.

All the fight went out of the Peruvians when once their king had been captured. Men, women, a multitude of female servants, and the wives of the Inca all lay encamped round the prison which housed their king, as though under a spell. They gazed in wonder at the 'white gods'. The Inca's power had been smashed, and with it his people's belief in miracles. Victory had dropped into the Spaniards' laps like a ripe fruit. It was as though some uncanny power had mysteriously chained the Inca and his people and driven them inexorably to their own self-destruction.

What had been happening in the Inca Empire before Pizarro's landing, and how did all this come about?

PIZARRO'S DEATH

Men do not know the world they live in, nor do they know what else besides themselves God has created upon the earth they tread. Atahualpa did not know then, any more than we know today.

MANKIND has never been able to grasp more than it can directly perceive. Anything outside our field of vision, outside the space which we have been granted to live in, lies beyond the range of thought.

Let us try to imagine what it would be like if in these days of apparently insoluble conflict between East and West the inhabitants of another planet landed on earth tomorrow, and, equipped with weapons a thousand times more powerful than our own, arrogantly constituted themselves our sole judges and our destiny. It seems improbable, doesn't it? Yet something very like that happened in Peru during the years 1532-33.

The throne had been occupied by a powerful ruler called Inca Huayna Capac. In addition to his main wife, who was also his sister, he owned a large number of subordinate wives. One of these was a princess of Quito, an extraordinarily beautiful woman and a foreigner at court, being the choicest prize of one of the Inca's military conquests. She was now the king's foster-daughter, his slave and his wife. The relationship which linked the Inca king to this princess was a somewhat uncomfortable one. He, the Inca, had annexed her parents' country, and they had died of grief. The Inca had now come to love the princess with the possessive passion of a victor, coupled with a sympathy which sprang from a wish to atone for injustice done. And he loved Atahualpa, too, the son who had been born of their union.

When the king felt that his end was drawing near, it occurred to him that he must name his successor. It was no easy task. On the one hand there was his beloved son Atahualpa, and on the other Huascar, the son of his chief wife, who should by rights accede to the throne. Lying there on his death-bed, the king came to a dangerous decision. Both his sons were to succeed him as joint rulers, Atahualpa reigning at Quito in the north, his mother's native land, and Huascar in the southern portion of the empire. Having made his decision, Inca Capac died, a powerful and benevolent ruler greatly mourned by his subjects. They cut the dead king's heart out and buried it at Quito, the place where it had always been, but his body itself they buried in the south, at Cuzco. The Sun-king was followed into death and the 'gleaming abode of the sun' by thousands of his concubines.

Atahualpa should have been well satisfied with his inheritance, for Huascar

295

was the legitimate heir. But Atahualpa wanted glory and the whole empire to himself – perhaps motivated even at this late stage by a wish to avenge his maternal grandparents. And so the two brothers joined battle. In the spring of 1532, Atahualpa's army rolled southwards and eventually took Cuzco, the southern capital. Huascar was captured and imprisoned in the fortress of Xauxa.

Even then Atahualpa was not satisfied. He invited the whole of the Inca aristocracy to visit him and, when the noble lords were duly assembled, had them massacred. In order to banish the possibility of any future disputes about his right to the throne, he had nearly all the women of the blood royal executed – sisters, aunts, nieces and cousins alike. At last Atahualpa could rule as sole and undisputed master of the strongest empire South America had ever known. No power in the world, as the Indians of those days knew it, could have hoped to shake Atahualpa's authority.

But men do not know the world they live in, nor do they know what else besides themselves God has created upon the earth they tread. Atahualpa did not know then, any more than we know today.

A few months after Atahualpa's coup d'état, the Spaniards landed under Pizarro. The strangers from another planet had arrived. We have already learned how they conquered the Inca Empire, and how Atahualpa was finally discovered sitting before Pizarro listening to his conqueror as, Bible in hand, he told him of the new god. Atahualpa was Pizarro's prisoner, just as Huascar was Atahualpa's prisoner, still languishing at Xauxa in the keeping of the defeated king's soldiers.

Atahualpa racked his brains night and day for some means of regaining his liberty. He knew that the Spaniards loved two things above all else: their own god, and other people's gold, so he told Pizarro that if he would release him he would fill the room in which he was imprisoned with gold as high as he could reach. In demonstration of this, he stood on his toes and stretched his hand towards the ceiling. The room was over sixteen feet wide and twenty-three feet long, and the tall king's finger-tips reached a point on the wall more than nine feet above the floor. Pizarro agreed to this proposal, and had a notary draw up in writing what must be the most peculiar contract in world history. The Inca sent messengers to all the towns in his empire and, before long, endless caravans were winding their way towards Cajamarca laden with the most magnificent articles of gold as ransom.

Meanwhile, Huascar had learned of Pizarro's arrival and the capture of his half-brother. He sent Pizarro a secret message offering a much higher ransom for his own release. On learning this, Atahualpa spent many sleepless nights and, when he did sleep, it was only to be tormented by dreams. He saw his brother standing menacingly before him, saw the blood of the Inca

296

royal house rise from the dust and take shape, screaming for vengeance, saw his gaoler Pizarro smiling and pointing to the nine-foot mark on the wall. The gold had not yet reached the specified height. Plagued by these dreams, Atahualpa sent a messenger to the fortress of Xauxa with orders to remove the higher ransom-bid once and for all — in other words, to kill his brother. A defeated king never lives long in the clutches of his conqueror. Huascar was murdered. 'The white men will avenge me,' he gasped as he was dying. Here and there in the country, small bands of men gathered to oppose the Spaniards. Pizarro accused the captive Inca of treachery, and his advisers searched for some pretext to get rid of Atahualpa. At the same time, there were a number of Indians in the royal prisoner's entourage who had been supporters of Huascar and wanted to avenge his murder. The most dangerous man of all, however, was Pizarro's interpreter Felipillo. He was having an affair with one of Atahualpa's concubines.

When Atahualpa learned of this, he found it a harder disgrace to bear than his captivity. From that moment on, Felipillo translated everything Atahualpa said so unfavourably that every cross-examination brought him nearer to a death sentence. A Spanish court of inquisition was set up, before which Atahualpa was obliged to defend himself against twelve charges: usurpation, the murder of his brother Huascar, extravagance, idolatry, adultery, affairs with prostitutes, rebellion against the Spaniards and five more of the same calibre. The verdict was 'guilty', and the sentence, burning at the stake in the main square of Cajamarca. At first Atahualpa begged Pizarro for mercy with tears in his eyes. Then he recovered his composure. He was tied to the stake, piles of faggots around him ready for kindling.

Father Valverde approached the doomed man with an upraised cross. The man of God promised Atahualpa that if he embraced the cross and let himself be baptized, his painful sentence would be commuted to one of garrotting, or judicial strangulation. Atahualpa was baptized — and strangled. A Mass was read for the dead king's soul. From the small church which the Spaniards had built came the sound of weeping and wailing. Thousands of Indian girls, the dead man's wives and such of his sisters as still survived, crowded round his corpse. The Spaniards drove them out of the church. Back in their huts, they took their lives and accompanied their beloved Inca into the 'gleaming abode of the sun'.

The regime which had become such second nature to every Peruvian Indian collapsed like a house of cards. For centuries the Inca had dominated everything that went on in the State. Even the most secret thoughts of the individual ran along the lines prescribed by the Inca regime. 'The foreign god must be stronger!' That was the whisper which ran from the little townships along the Pacific coast to the cities up in the Andes. The Peruvians began to burn their villages. They ransacked their temples and palaces. They realized the value of gold and, for the first time in their country's history, began to hoard it. Feeling that the downfall of the old regime threatened to bring disorder and revolution in its train, Pizarro hastily summoned the Indian noblemen together and presented them with a new Inca in the person of Toparca, one of Atahualpa's brothers. When Toparca had been duly crowned, Pizarro installed him in a sedan-chair and started off with his army on the arduous journey to Cuzco, the legendary Inca capital. The smoke of burning villages accompanied the Spaniards throughout their march, and here and there the spirit of resistance flared up. Just to make matters worse, the new Inca died, and the Spaniards quickly had to look around for a scapegoat, which they found in the person of Challcuchima, a Peruvian prince. Challcuchima was burned alive. The murder of Atahualpa and Challcuchima was only the start of a series of such executions. A Spanish court of inquisition was always held, and an attempt always made to convert the condemned men before their death. Father Valverde was always in attendance, complete with promises of Paradise and baptismal water. The requiem was always read, and the executed men's bodies given a Christian burial.

When Father Valverde tried to convert Challcuchima by describing the fate of unbelievers in the next world and the splendour of life in Paradise, the chieftain only answered coolly: 'I cannot understand the white man's religion.' He endured all his torments with true Indian stoicism and died calling upon the name of Pachacamac, his own god.

The subsequent history of the conquest of Peru is more dramatic than any fictional drama could ever have been. It could have provided a genius like Shakespeare with enough material for dozens of plays and kept him busy for the whole of his life. Try to picture the course of events in the land between the shores of the Pacific and the High Andes. Pizarro received an unexpected visitor in the shape of Manco, who was the murdered Huascar's brother and, as such, the legitimate heir to the throne. Pizarro imperiously crowned him, and the conquistadors instituted and directed a great national festival to celebrate the occasion. The Indians joined in the coronation festivities, little guessing that they marked the end of their glorious history. And even the ancient Inca rulers of long ago joined in the celebrations, too. Their mummies sat in eerie state round the main square, decked out in all their jewels and finery, each mummy surrounded by a large retinue of attendants. They sat there stiffly, staring out of empty eye-sockets at the throng of revellers who danced, drank and made merry the whole night long.

Wherever the Spaniards went they built Christian churches and monasteries. The temples of the old Peruvian gods were demolished and their images destroyed. Dominican monks preached, prayed and baptized. A Roman Catholic nunnery was erected on the site of the Sun-virgins' temple at Cuzco, and Father Valverde was appointed bishop of the city. This devil in priest's clothing is one of the most terrifying figures in the deluded age of Don Quixote.

'I need a harbour,' thought Pizarro, 'a large harbour here by the Pacific, where it can form a link between Spain and the New World.' So he went down to the sea and founded a capital of his own. In honour of Epiphany on January 6th, 1535, he called his foundation 'City of the Kings' — Ciudád de los Reyes. It stood on the site of a small Indian township called Rimac. City-names always become modified in any language, and only fifty years after its foundation the Spaniards had abandoned the name Ciudád de los Reyes and Rimac had become 'Lima'. Pizarro's original ground-plan is still discernible today as a triangle based on the river, with perfectly straight streets intersecting at right angles, and the remains of stone pipes which once formed part of the sewage-system.

The history of Peru plunged ever deeper into a welter of senselessly spilt blood. The Cain of this conquest was Almagro, the man who had been in on the Peruvian venture from its very beginning. He was by now a prominent man, a Marshal of Emperor Charles V, ever ambitious, ever envious of Pizarro's fame, and ever greedy for power and property. Reflecting that the Emperor awarded most power to those who in his eyes had won the most glory and could guarantee him the most gold for his coffers, Almagro secretly introduced one of his trusted servants into Pizarro's brother's retinue before the latter went back to Spain. This man was to call the Emperor's attention to his, Almagro's, services. On reaching court, Hernando Pizarro described his brother Francisco's prowess, the great hardships he had undergone, the battles he had fought. Emperor Charles confirmed Pizarro's governorship and generally fulfilled all that Hernando and Francisco had hoped for. Meanwhile, however, Almagro's precautions had not been in vain. His governorship was to begin in the south of Peru, where the limits of Pizarro's authority ended. Hernando set sail again for Peru with one of the finest fleets which ever weighed anchor from the shores of Spain. Almagro's man was with him and, when he reached Cuzco and told his master of the Emperor's reward, Almagro was overjoyed. His new appointment made him feel independent, and he persuaded himself that Cuzco was now his own personal property. Pizarro and Almagro enjoyed one last spell of reconciliation before they finally resorted to open hostilities. Almagro secured Cuzco with an armed force and threw Pizarro's brothers, Gonzalo and Hernando, into prison.

To escape from Spanish custody was not easy. It entailed steady nerves and a clear head. Hernando Pizarro sat in his dungeon and passed the time in card-play. His opponent was a certain Alvarado, one of Almagro's men. The prisoner and his visitor played for high stakes, and Hernando won 80,000 gold castellanos. Alvarado wanted to pay him immediately, but Hernando modestly refused to take the money. So much generosity in a prisoner charmed Alvarado and he put in a good word for him with his master.

Almagro, too, had decided to build himself a harbour on the Pacific, and he left Cuzco, taking his prisoner Hernando with him. In the meanwhile, Francisco Pizarro had been ruminating day and night how to get his brother Hernando out of Almagro's clutches. After two parleys between Pizarro and Almagro, Hernando was finally freed.

The Pizarros were not the sort of men whom one could offend with impunity. They never forgot an injury. Hernando had hardly been released before his brother Francisco sent him off with an army against Almagro. The battle took place on the salt-flats of Las Salinas, near Cuzco. Almagro was a very sick man by this time, and followed the battle from a deck-chair while his general, Orgonez, conducted it. Half delirious, he was obliged to watch his forces routed by a victorious Hernando. The boot was now on the other foot, and Almagro was Hernando's prisoner. Once in gaol, Almagro showed every symptom of being about to die. He was very weak, and suffering either from gout or syphilis. It could not be, thought the Pizarros: Almagro had to get well, so that he could be well and truly executed. Hernando therefore sent his prisoner friendly and encouraging letters and had him served with the choicest food from his own table. Almagro was soon on his legs again. But he had scarcely left his bed when a monk entered his cell and read out his sentence of death: he was to be publicly beheaded in the city's main square. Almagro winced. 'Surely no one could be so unjust,' he said. 'I cannot believe it.' Calling Hernando to his cell, he pleaded with him to spare his grey hairs and not to rob him of the little time which remained to him. 'I am astonished,' Hernando said coldly, 'that you, as a brave knight, should behave in such an unworthy fashion. God in his mercy made you a Christian. Make your peace with Heaven.' Almagro tried to say a great deal more, but Hernando cut short the uncomfortable interview with the words: 'The sentence is irrevocable. Reconcile yourself to it.'

Hernando was not a cruel man, however. He charitably commuted Almagro's sentence from public execution in the square to garrotting. Almagro was to be throttled. At twilight that evening, priests and executioners slipped quietly into the prison. Almagro was given Communion, then the garrotte. The gloomy dungeon passages were quiet once more.

The sentence had been carried out, but the Pizarros were still uneasy. Almagro's authority had been guaranteed by Charles V. Perhaps they should first have consulted the Emperor and sought his decision. So Hernando set off for Spain once more. The glittering court was residing at Valladolid. Once again Hernando made a ceremonious entrance into the city, and once again Almagro's secret representatives went with him, almost as though their master had dispatched them from the grave. Almagro's friends described to Charles V the injustice which their master had suffered. Hernando gave his account of the feud, backing it up with visible arguments in the shape of gold. Even so, the scales tipped in Almagro's favour. Hernando was committed to the fortress of Medina del Campo. This tough eldest brother of Pizarro was confined in the fortress for twenty years, until 1560. His life passed before his eyes again and again during that time. He saw deaths and executions, and survived them all. He even lived on for some years after his release, reaching an age of over a hundred.

To restore order in Peru, Charles V sent over to the Inca Empire Vaca de Castro, a member of the imperial court. Meanwhile, Francisco Pizarro had been governing the country with a heavy and despotic hand. The new Inca, Manco, had long ago lost all faith and confidence in the Spaniards and was secretly stirring up rebellion everywhere. Pizarro failed to capture him, but, to bring him to his knees, he caught one of his wives. She was young and beautiful and the Inca loved her very dearly. Pizarro had her stripped to the skin, tied to a tree, flogged, and then shot to death with arrows. No word of complaint, not a single sob escaped the Indian girl's lips throughout the whole of these proceedings. She endured her torments in silent composure.

Pizarro now had many enemies. They included not only the Indians, but a large number of Almagro's former adherents, who had come to be called 'the people of Chile'. They were universally oppressed in Peru, being excluded from holding office or serving in the armed forces. They were the outlawed knights of the conquered land. They starved, and they brooded on revenge. Eventually they decided to assassinate Pizarro. Sunday, July 25th, 1541, was agreed on as the day of reckoning, the '20th of July' for Lima and for that period of history, as it were. The conspirators assembled at the house of Almagro's son. Pizarro was to receive the death-blow as he emerged from Mass. The plan was betrayed to Pizarro. He laughed. He let his old, harsh, confident laughter ring out until his whole palace echoed with it. For all that, he stayed away from Mass. Intoxicated by their lust for revenge, the conspirators rushed to the palace and, racing up the steps, surprised Pizarro at table. Greatly outnumbered, Pizarro grabbed his sword and dispensed some lethal blows among his adversaries before he was finally hit in the throat and fell to the ground. 'Jesus!' he gasped, not wanting to die before he had kissed the cross. But there was no cross to be seen, and all he could hear was the cry: 'Death to the tyrant!' He drove his finger into his wound, drew a cross on the floor in his own blood, and kissed it. Then one of his enemies dealt him a last terrible blow, and he died.

It was almost as though the ancient gods of the Incas were still alive and holding vengeful court in heaven, for, from then on, the Spaniards themselves drowned the glorious deeds of their knights in a sea of murder, blood and executions. The best way of assessing the extent of the subsequent executions is to ask who survived. In fact, no one escaped the executioner's sword.

It was the man who had been sent out from Valladolid, Vaca de Castro, who settled the score with young Almagro and the murderers of Francisco Pizarro. Just twenty-four years old, Almagro's son was executed on the spot where his father had died before him, devoutly inclining his head to receive the executioner's stroke. The next figure of note to die was a certain Francisco Carbajal, whose hoary head and eighty-four years rather unnerved his executioner. As always, a father confessor was in attendance. The old man was conveyed to the place of execution in a pannier slung between two mules. It was *Pater Noster . . . Ave Maria . . .* and then the scaffold.

Gonzalo Pizarro, who regarded himself as his brother Francisco's rightful heir, gambled away his chances at the battle of Xaquixaguana, after Charles V had sent a priest to arrest him as a rebel. Impeached and convicted of lese-majesty and high treason, he was brought to the place of execution on a mule. The day before his death, he asked whether he could rely on spending another night alive. 'Your Honour can sleep easy,' they told him. Next day he knelt before the cross and kissed it. 'Do your job well, brother Juan,' he said. 'You have my word upon it,' said the executioner, and down came his sword.

You may be interested to know what happened to Pizarro's assiduous military chaplain Vicente de Valverde, the man who had pronounced the benediction over so many condemned prisoners. Pursued by Almagro's supporters, he fled to the island of Pina, where he was captured by the Indians. 'We will show you what you have been wanting to see all your life,' they told him. Then they poured molten gold into his eyes and murdered him.

And Pizarro's interpreter Felipillo, who stole Atahualpa's favourite wife and then translated what the captured Inca said so unfavourably that he was inevitably sentenced to death? Almagro had long ago had him quartered for treachery, an art in which Felipillo was a master.

Anyone who travels to Lima, the magnificent Peruvian capital on the Pacific, and stands in the cathedral before Pizarro's marble sarcophagus will feel how strongly the history of the place has been influenced by three factors: a lust for gold; a stubborn and unbending code of chivalry; and the will to spread Christ's teachings by the sword.

Only seven years ago, some learned archaeologists made an interesting find at Cuzco, Peru's erstwhile capital. They discovered the skeletons of Gonzalo Pizarro, Almagro the elder, and Almagro the son. Almost nothing remained of the three heroes. Not far away, in the heart of the city, the Sun-temple is still standing. During the earthquake in 1950 the church which had been erected on top of the temple's foundation wall collapsed. A few of the Inca walls remained standing. Like the church above them, they are now being restored. The three heroes are to be left in peace.

CENTRAL AMERICA

ℵ

THEIR GODS WERE ALWAYS HUNGRY
The Maya

The Maya were the 'Greeks' of Central America, just as the Aztecs can be compared with the Romans. At the time of Cortez' conquest of Mexico there were still scholars who could read Mayan script. Today, no one can decipher it.

ANYONE who crosses the neck of land which links North and South America comes first to Panama. Then, passing through Costa Rica, Nicaragua, Honduras and Guatemala, he finally reaches Mexico. Mexico is the northern half of what is the most interesting bridge in the world, the bridge of land between the two Americas. Deserts and mountains account for two-thirds of Mexico, and the few clouds that drift across the blue Mexican sky only bestow a scanty amount of rain – enough, in fact, for a mere tenth of the thirsty land.

When Cortez, the conqueror of Mexico, went back to see Charles V, the Spanish king asked him: 'What is this Mexico of yours like?' Without speaking, Cortez gave his king the best description anyone could give. He took a piece of paper, crumpled it up, and threw it on to the king's desk.

Mexico is at once poor and rich, happy and unhappy. It is the greatest silver-producing country in the world, but the Mexicans know only too well that what Fate gives with one hand, she takes away with the other. It has always been so in this country. The Mexicans are a race with thousands of years of practice in the art of patience. Toughness, endurance and resignation to the inevitability of Fate – the American Indians of both continents may owe these invaluable qualities to the earliest discoverers of America who migrated there over the Bering Straits. The German expert Humboldt summed up Mexico in an expression which has lately become rather hackneyed: 'A land of contrasts.' Ignorance, superstition and cruelty have dominated Mexico for thousands of years, and her highlands have always been at the mercy of a destiny which never afforded them any security. Nothing is certain in Mexico, absolutely nothing. 'Who knows?' the Mexicans say, 'Quién sabe?' No one knows when he will be born, and no one knows when he will die. Anyone who tries to fathom the civilizations or the soul of this country will meet a darker veil of obscurity the further he probes. Even the American expert Prescott, who studied the history of ancient Mexico as thoroughly as he did that of the Incas in Peru, had to admit that as a scientist he found it extremely hard to deal with a field which was so woven about with romantic fiction. Anyone seeking to establish cultural or historical facts about Mexico will find himself confronted at every turn by the aura of myth, legend and poetic fiction which surrounds all her ruins, picture-writings and archaeological sites. When a Mexican lady was asked whether her country got as much rain in summer as in winter, she answered: 'There are no firm rules, señor.' And, in fact, Mexico provides no firm rules for history, culture, or the origins of her peoples, no firm rules for her past whatsoever.

There were writings here, to be sure, but we cannot decipher them. When Cortez landed, the people of Mexico had already reached man's estate, and about a thousand years of history and culture lay behind them.

. . . About a thousand years of history and culture. What does that mean? We first see the clear outlines of an advanced civilization in Mexico from about A.D. 300 onwards, the Mayan civilization. But to have reached such a level the Mayan race must first have passed through an evolutionary period lasting several hundreds, if not thousands, of years. And of this evolutionary period we know virtually nothing.

The Mayan civilization first emerged from the obscurity of the past and began to take distinct shape about A.D. 300, reaching its classical period about A.D. 600. Then something remarkable happened: at the end of the seventh century, still before A.D. 800, this amazing civilization simply dissolved. The masterbuilders stopped building, the sculptors stopped modelling, the painters laid down their brushes, and all the large towns were abandoned. There was a complete cessation of activity in every field.

The reason remains a mystery to this day. Perhaps the Maya were overwhelmed by enemies, perhaps they destroyed themselves in civil wars, perhaps most of the population died off in epidemics, perhaps famine broke out, perhaps such a severe climatic change occurred that the Maya were forced to abandon their country. Perhaps, perhaps. . . .

At all events, Mayan civilization did not wither gradually away as in Spengler's *Untergang des Abendlandes*, but collapsed within the span of fifty years. The large towns lay there forlorn and desolate, just as their inhabitants had abandoned them.

Their inhabitants? Here we come to another question which cannot be answered unequivocally. All we know is that the citizenry and the intelligentsia were poles apart. They wandered forth never to return again, leaving a vast accumulation of capital behind, massive temples, palaces, dwelling-houses, all the things which had been laboriously built up and created over the centuries. But someone always stays behind in such cases. In this

particular instance it may have been the slaves, or the poor, or perhaps just the sick. These remaining inhabitants probably supported themselves by agriculture and hunting in the local forests. Certainly, all planning and creative activity ceased.

The seat of advanced Mayan civilization lay in the region bounded by the once large towns of Uaxactún (in Guatemala), Palenque (in Chiapas) and Copán (in Honduras). After the old empire had been abandoned, part of the nation roamed into the Guatemalan highlands, where they founded several small States. The majority of the Maya, however, made for the northern part of the Yucatan Peninsula and established a new Mayan Empire there. This new Mayan Empire was a form of rebirth or renaissance patterned on the ancient glory of the past. However, it was only a pale reflection of it, and the splendid prime of the old culture was never again achieved.

How do we know anything at all about Mayan history?

Well, first of all there are the Mayan manuscripts, texts which were written by Mayan priests long before the conquest of Mexico. The Spaniards unfortunately regarded them as 'works of the Devil', and the Spanish bishop Landa organized a great bonfire of them in the plaza at Merida. That is why only three manuscripts have survived. One of them is, or was, in Dresden. It is by far the most interesting, since it dates from the best period of the new Mayan Empire. The second, of later date, is in Paris, and the third in Madrid. However, none of these three texts contains anything more than entries dealing with the calendar or religious rites. All the texts containing religious, medical and mathematical treatises went up in smoke when the Spaniards decided to exorcize the Devil. The hieroglyphs in the three surviving texts present us with more problems than information. If more of these manuscripts had survived, we should probably have found the key to their solution.

Apart from this, there are some notes made shortly after the Spanish conquest. However, they suffer from the disadvantage that Mayan civilization was already on the wane when they were compiled.

Then there are also a few historical dates which were noted down by the Maya in hieroglyphs before the conquest and translated into Spanish.

Finally, we still have the stone pillars which the Maya erected in their towns every five, ten and twenty years, and on which they carved a record of the most important events. Unfortunately the Maya had quite a different chronological system from ours, so it is not easy to relate individual events to our own measurement of time.

Among the first Spanish ecclesiastics in Yucatan were one or two astute men who learned how to read the Mayan script, and some of them even knew how to write it. In the course of time, however, this art became lost, and today even the foremost Americanists are groping in the dark. On the other hand, the Mayan numerical system has been solved. It contains only four symbols: a dot for a unit, a horizontal dash for the figure 5, and two other symbols for 20 and 0. With great ingenuity the Maya used these simple aids to express figures up to several millions, a fact which has only recently been established. To do this, they did not range the numbers horizontally, but vertically. The bottom figure was taken at its simple face-value, while the second, fourth and succeeding rows represented twenty times the value of the row immediately beneath. The third row was only eighteen times the value of the second. In their possession of this numerical system the Maya were the superiors of every other race in America, and even of the Greeks and Romans.

The Maya were also far advanced in the writing of words, as the elegant characters in their manuscripts go to prove. Even if we cannot decipher these manuscripts, they do at least help us to know what objects, buildings and sculptures belong to the Mayan cultural orbit, for the Maya adorned not only their buildings and sculptures with inscriptions, but even their pottery.

The Maya had squat skulls and retreating brows, a physical characteristic which they greatly prized and even attempted to produce by artificial means. Their skin was a pale cinnamon colour. They were small in stature, but sturdy and well-built. Their hair was black. A squint was regarded as a mark of great beauty. Girls and women adorned their faces with red, white and black paint. From his birth to the hour of his death, the Maya was dominated by religious cults and a large and powerful priesthood.

The Maya worshipped everything which seemed powerful and mysterious in Nature. Over the centre of every town towered step-pyramids with temples enthroned on their squat summits.

If one were to arrange the gods of all the pagan races in order of their performance, the Mayan gods would come in very nearly last, only beating the Aztec gods by a short head. The Mayan gods were always so hungry and did so little to earn their keep that it was no wonder their worshippers finally came to grief, though not before they had offered up an enormous number of human sacrifices. For a long time, scholars believed that no human sacrifices were made under the old Mayan regime. This fallacy rested upon the assumption that a highly cultured race would shrink from such barbarity. But even a highly developed civilization needs food and drink — especially drink — and, since the Maya believed that by offering their Sun-, Earth- and Rain-gods blood they could put them into a good humour, they made human sacrifices. Victims were stretched out on a sacrificial block high up on the pyramid's altar, and their hearts torn out. The lifeless bodies were then thrown over the edge so that they tumbled all the way down the pyramid's steps to the ground, where the waiting public cut them up. Each individual took a piece home to boil and eat.

There is a certain spot at Piedras Negras where this procedure is illustrated in stone. Victims included captured warriors, children and young girls. Whenever harvest prospects looked bad or there was a prolonged drought, the Maya hastily sacrificed a few virgins. Virgins were likewise considered ideal as a placatory offering for wells and springs, and the Maya threw them in with little regard to the insanitary consequences of such an action. It should never be forgotten that these races only had the most rudimentary notions of medicine and hygiene, even if they did know how to extract quinine from tree-bark and were familiar with certain medicinal herbs. A thorn in the foot could lead to fatal blood-poisoning, there was no remedy against epidemic diseases, and Mayan babies were put straight on to an adult diet after a short period of breast-feeding. It seems a miracle that these races survived for as many centuries as they did, and that their descendants are still living today. The Maya knew nothing about dairy-farming or draught-animals and they were probably even ignorant of the wheel, although there is some evidence to the contrary. All loads had to be carried on men's backs. At the same time, the Maya were good arithmeticians and had an astonishingly accurate calendar. They had an official State year of 360 days and an astronomical year of 365 days. The moon's passage round the earth served as the basis of the Mayan lunar calendar, in which 405 lunar revolutions corresponded to 11,960 days. Modern astronomical computations put it at 11,959.888 days — or only 0.112 of a day less than the Mayan estimate. Mayan astronomers also worked out a Venusian calendar based on a remarkably accurate knowledge of the movement of the planet Venus. There are only tiny discrepancies between their figures with regard to Venus and our modern computations, a fact which becomes all the more impressive when we remember that the Maya made their observations with the naked eye. We know the Mayan hieroglyphs for sky, earth, sun, moon, Venus, Mars and Jupiter. We know the symbols for the twenty days of their month and the eighteen months of their year. We know the hieroglyphs for certain gods and ceremonies, and for the four cardinal points of the compass. It is interesting to note that some of these hieroglyphs owe their elucidation to astronomy, since Mayan calculations and modern science agree in this particular field.

The Maya were brilliant craftsmen, wore clothes and shoes, manufactured cotton fabrics and even velvet, and were great artists in general. Their architectural achievements, their temples and their town-planning were most remarkable. Temples and houses, mostly built upon pyramids, public squares, whole networks of streets, palaces with numerous rooms, corridors and open courtyards, pillars up to forty feet in height with statues carved into them — all these things are identifiable in the ruins which still stand today. The Maya themselves lived in huts of reed-work and mud built on level ground. The silent ruins of the metropolitan cities of Uaxactún, Tikal, Palenque, Copán (the Athens of the old Mayan Empire) and Piedras Negras, still seem to reverberate with the life which once pulsed through them in all its animation, laughter, suffering and blood-letting.

One of the riddles which has not yet been solved is the so-called 'stele B' at Copán. Above the head of the god portrayed upon it are the distinct outlines of elephants' heads complete with trunks. They are Indian elephants, with mahouts perched on their necks. Americanists have been racking their brains as to how the Maya got hold of them, since elephants have long been extinct in America. The indigenous American elephant died out thousands of years before the first dawning of Mayan civilization.

Where did it come from, the Mayans' urge to design things in the particular way they did, and the inspiration which engendered ornamental and pictorial styles reminiscent of Egypt, India and even of Buddhism? Was it a piece of cultural flotsam which drifted thousands of miles across the Indian Ocean and the Pacific?

We do not know, and we shall never know.

THEY BUILT PYRAMIDS

The Teotihuacáns and Toltecs

It was built in honour of the god Quetzalcoatl. 'Are you weary? It is only granted us to venture into the world for a short time, just so that we become hot. . . .' Translated from the Aztec by Sahagun.

BROTHER BERNHARDINO DE SAHAGUN was a pious monk. He had the nose of a Spanish aristocrat, very dark and weary-looking eyes, and the energy of a man undeterred by any obstacle. He came to Mexico as a missionary in 1529, arriving only eight years after the capture of Mexico City, a time when the history of the Aztecs, Toltecs and Mayans was still vividly remembered.

Any attempt to convert the native inhabitants to the Christian faith entailed a knowledge of their innermost being, their thoughts, their legends, their religion, their gods. Realizing this, Brother Sahagun spent years listening to all that the Aztec scholars could tell him about such things. To write it all down would have taken one man a hundred years, so Sahagun ordered his young pupils to take down the Aztec accounts phonetically in Latin characters. They worked night and day, and it was their parchment transcripts which formed the basis of the famous historical work hastily translated into Spanish by Brother Sahagun himself. Eduard Seler translated several chapters of the work into German, and Professor Leonhard Schultze-Jena has done a translation and commentary on the greater part of it.

Anyone who turns the pages of this 'first-hand source' will feel very close to the vanished empires of the Mayans, Toltecs, Aztecs and many other races. He will find descriptions of the gods, their attire and their idiosyncrasies. He will find lists of annual festivals. He will meet Quetzalcoatl, king and god, the mysterious prince and prophet of the Toltecs. He will read about the abodes of the dead, the education of boys, about sorcerers, conjurers, soothsayers and, finally, about the conquest of Mexico City by the Spaniards.

Four advanced civilizations join hands in Mexico: Teotihuacán, Mayan, Toltec and Aztec.

The builders of the city of Teotihuacán are an unknown race. We do not even know the original name of this metropolis of a once great civilization. Teotihuacán is probably a late-Aztec translation of the city's original name, but we have no idea what language it was translated from. Even the language of its inhabitants remains a closed book.

Teotihuacán civilization coincided with the so-called 'Late Archaic' period, and its authors lived about A.D. 500. The Teotihuacáns have left us the ruins of their city, and very remarkable they are, both in design and constructional planning. They lie some twenty-two miles to the north-east of Mexico City, and a visit to Teotihuacán is a 'must' for every foreign visitor to Mexico. Everyone has to 'do the pyramids' at least once.

Teotihuacán was laid out along both sides of a broad avenue. This dead straight road formed the city's axis, and certainly possessed some religious significance. Known as 'The Way of the Dead', it was a sort of terrestrial copy of the Milky Way. At its northern end the road met the 'Moon-pyramid', while to the east of it lay the much larger 'Sun-pyramid'. Also on the east, but at the southern end, stood the temple of the god Quetzalcoatl, the so-called *ciudadela*, or fortress. Ciudadela may be a misnomer, since there were probably no fortifications at the time of its building. This massive quadrangular complex is really a pyramid-city composed of the bases of two large pyramid-temples and fifteen smaller temples. The whole sacred place was erected in honour of the Wind-god, who controlled the rain-clouds and, consequently, fertility. Magnificent stone sculptures were found here, including heads of snakes and other grotesque portraits ascribed to the Rain-god Tlaloc. All these sculptures were at one time painted in glowing colours. The massive friezes, galleries, flights of steps and platforms also found here are products of an art which may not have achieved great intricacy of detail, but nevertheless creates an elemental and dramatic impression. Quetzalcoatl himself is to be found here, carved in stone. He is always represented as a plumed serpent, and the eyes which stare out of his head were once carved from obsidian.

The Sun-pyramid has a ground-plan roughly similar in proportions to that of the largest Egyptian pyramids, covering about the same area as the Pyramid of Cheops. On the other hand, it is only half as large in height and cubic capacity. The Teotihuacáns' Sun-pyramid is also surpassed by numerous Mayan pyramids, both in construction and building-materials. Nevertheless, where the transportation of large masses of stone and earth and the achieving of special effects was concerned, the Sun-pyramid shows us that there were some unrivalled architects among the people of Teotihuacán. The most impressive thing about it was its bulk and its apparent height. It gave an amazingly good simulation of infinite height and mass. The pyramid consisted of five steps or terraces linked by a series of very steep stairways which added to the monumental impression of the structure. If a religious procession mounted these stairs, it seemed to disappear into the sky. At a height which was outside the range of vision of anyone standing at the foot of the pyramid stood the Sun-god's shrine. This was where the communication between priests and gods took place. When a procession arrived at each of the five terraces, it had to traverse the whole pyramid before it could mount the next flight of steps.

Archaeologists have driven shafts into the heart of the Sun-pyramid, but they discovered no vaults or tunnels such as are common in the Egyptian pyramids. The whole construction was solidly packed with mud and earth throughout. It was not erected one section at a time and then enlarged, like so many other American pyramids, but built in one operation according to a preconceived plan. The greatness of the Teotihuacáns' project proves that they were impelled to undertake it by religious convictions of great strength. The same rule is valid throughout the cultural history of the whole world: the most monumental and impressive pieces of building were never merely the result of forced labour, since religious fanaticism has always been stronger than coercion. This principle applies equally to the great era of pyramid building in Egypt under the Third Dynasty.

The outer surfaces of the pyramid were faced with stone, but even the rubble of old mud bricks and earth in the interior proved a valuable source of information to archaeologists, for it contained clay vessels, clay figurines and stone implements, all of which must once have belonged to the ancient Teotihuacáns, and indicate that the pyramid was built at a very early stage in Teotihuacán civilization. Exactly when this was, we shall never know. The only certainty is that this artificial mountain was erected to a god, and not as the tomb of some king.

Less excavation has been carried out on the Moon-pyramid than the Sun-pyramid, although the location of the former at the end of the 'Way of the Dead' points to its greater importance, even if its cubic capacity is only a quarter as large.

Even today not all the buildings in Teotihuacán have been excavated. Several of the ruins possess subterranean chambers containing extremely fine frescoes. The walls of one group of buildings, called the 'Temple of Agriculture' are decorated with sculptures of various fruits and flowers which used to be sacrificed to the gods but only exist today in replica. Excavation has revealed the remains of walls which probably belonged to dwellings once inhabited by priests. Such huts as may have stood on the outskirts of the religious metropolis would have fallen into ruin long ago during the course of the past 1400 years.

It is impossible to determine the exact beginning and end of Teotihuacán civilization. It may be that the Sun-pyramid was built in the 2nd century A.D., and that Teotihuacán was destroyed in the year A.D. 856. We do know that the city met its end in a terrible conflagration.

It may be asked why the date has been set at 856.

The year A.D. 856 is traditionally regarded in Central America as the foundation-date of a city which was only excavated in 1940, and whose discovery marks one of the greatest archaeological successes of our age. This was the city of Tollan, which succeeded Teotihuacán as a cultural metropolis. The ruins of Tollan stand in the vicinity of what is today Tula in the Mexican province of Hidalgo, some sixty miles north of Mexico City. Tollan was founded by people who stormed out of the northern deserts, 'barbarians' who spoke the Nahua language and were ethnologically related to the later Aztec Chichemeces. The Toltecs got their name from Tollan, their capital, and their sole connection with the old city of Teotihuacán was that they conquered it. Excavations at Tollan soon showed that the legendary capital of the Toltecs had really been discovered at last, the metropolitan city whose erstwhile existence was still remembered all over Central America. It is only a short time since the ruins of Tollan was fully unearthed. They disclosed pyramids, palaces, gigantic stone colossuses, portrayals of human beings in stone reliefs and murals, and friezes depicting jaguars and eagles devouring hearts. An extremely efficient sewage-system was dug up here, too, but perhaps the most interesting finds were two arenas where ball-games used to be played. Hans Dietrich Disselhoff, who wrote a fascinating history of the early American civilizations, alludes to the rubber ball as having originated among the early South American Indians. Hard, heavy and not un-dangerous, the india-rubber ball could not be touched with the hand or foot, but had to be played with the hip. The game undoubtedly had a religious significance, and the first balls were certainly meant to represent stars. Thus the ball-game was really a divine sport, since only gods could throw the stars about.

The principal importance of Tollan lay in the fact that it was the residence of the Toltecs' priest-king, Quetzalcoatl. This individual has been responsible for a great deal of bewilderment in the world, both among historians and archaeologists, and among men who were in other respects orthodox Christians. In Teotihuacán civilization Quetzalcoatl appears as a god, while to the Mayans and the Toltecs he was a priest-king. In Yucatan he went by the name of Kukulkan, and during the Aztec period Quetzalcoatl became a title.

Many imaginative authors have tried hard to see Quetzalcoatl as Mexico's Christ in a new shape, as it were. In fact one particular author, the Irish archaeologist Lord Kingsborough (1795-1837), devoted his whole life to this theory. He collected all the information about the ancient advanced civilizations of Mexico available to him, and then compiled a monumental work in nine volumes entitled *The Antiquities of Mexico*. Kingsborough's aim was to prove that the ancient peoples of Mexico were of Jewish origin, being the descendants of the ten lost tribes of Israel. He collected literary works of both the Old and the New Worlds, together with Mayan and Aztec accounts dating from before Columbus. He got hold of the volumes which the Spanish Fathers had so diligently compiled at the time of the conquest. He spent such an enormous amount of money on the work of collection, research and publication that he eventually went bankrupt, and his printer had him thrown into the debtors' prison at Dublin. Even in gaol, he still yearned and dreamed of demonstrating to the world that Christ had appeared among the Toltecs. But the prison was damp and swarming with insects, and Kingsborough finally caught typhus and died.

Nevertheless, many people supported Kingsborough in his attempt to prove that the ancient Mexicans were familiar with the Book of Genesis. Mexico had its own tradition about a Flood. The last surviving Aztecs together with the ancient sculptures of their forefathers were held to exhibit Semitic traits. Like the Jews, the Itza Maya worshipped one supreme god whom they never anthropomorphized in stone, and like the Jews, they directed their prayers towards the east. Again, the Toltecs revered the snake, just as the heathen of the Old Testament used to. And, finally, a virgin called Chimalman from the Toltecs' capital, Tollan, gave birth to a son. It was Quetzalcoatl, who became the Toltecs' king, priest, astronomer, bearer of civilization, prophet and god.

Even without any embroidery of the facts, the parallels between the Christ of the West and the Toltecs' Quetzalcoatl are striking enough. Quetzalcoatl is reported to have been a white man, not dark-skinned like the Toltecs. Tradition has it that he was sent to mankind by God, became a human being, learned all the arts, and taught wisdom and everything that was good. He brought the Toltecs a golden age, and even Nature shared in his good works. He is said to have introduced the Toltecs to the Mayan calendar, which he brought back with him from a visit to that race.

According to Toltec tradition, Quetzalcoatl eventually incurred the wrath of his divine superior. This meant the end of the Toltecs and their destruction. Quetzalcoatl was forced to flee to the 'eastern ocean' (i.e. the Atlantic coast), interrupting his flight to spend twenty years in the city of Cholula, where 'the greatest pyramid in America was erected in his honour'.

Today this pyramid is no more than a hill covered with undergrowth. Nevertheless, it still remains the largest building in the world from the point of view of cubic capacity. Cholula was still a religious centre in Aztec times when the Spaniards arrived. There is no doubt that it was the Teotihuacán people who built the pyramid, even though it is more recent than the Sun- and Moon-pyramids of that oldest city in Central America. A solid mass of earth, bricks, stone and cement, it is too vast to allow of thorough investigation, but shafts which have been driven into the pyramid indicate that it is composed of several buildings superimposed one on top of the other. As for Quetzalcoatl, when the 'Son of God' arrived at the Atlantic, he built himself a boat out of snake-skin and sailed away over the ocean in the rough direction of Europe to the legendary country called Tlapallan. Nobody knows where this land was supposed to lie.

Quetzalcoatl's moral teachings, which he never wrote down, seem to have been of a high standard. He was opposed to any form of human sacrifice, and taught that only fruit and flowers should be sacrificed. He preached peace, and was even familiar with the saving power of brotherly love.

The disappearance of Quetzalcoatl never quenched the hope that he would return, not just some time, but at a predetermined season.

He never did come back, but in the precise year when his second coming had been predicted someone else arrived. It was Cortez.

Even if we discard the fanciful supposition that the prophecies of the Old Testament were in some mysterious manner translated to South America long before Columbus, and after him Cortez, ever reached the new continent; even if we discard the fable that the people of the Old Testament were themselves cast up on the shores of Mexico; the achievement of the Toltec race only appears the more amazing. There in the Valley of Mexico, a race of men unwittingly and unconsciously found their way to a supreme religious morality and the belief in a *single* supreme and invisible god.

I OVERTHREW LARGE AND POWERFUL NATIONS

Hernando Cortez

'Perhaps it had been resolved that he should receive his reward in a better world. I firmly believe so. For he was a goodly knight, and most sincere in his prayers to the Virgin, Peter the Apostle, and the other holy ones.' Bernal Díaz del Castillo in his *Historia Verdadera de la Conquista de la Nueva España*, 1568.

THE long, sweeping arc formed by Florida, Cuba, the Antilles and the coasts of Venezuela and Panama was at least vaguely known in the year 1518. Only one country awaited discovery: Mexico and its large peninsula, Yucatan, the nearest land to the western tip of Cuba. It is still an undiscovered, undisturbed world, even today.

Here I must mention Gerónimo de Aguilar, a man whose experiences put even those of Robinson Crusoe in the shade. In the year 1511 or 1512 a sailing-ship put out to sea from Darien, bound for Hispaniola. The vessel foundered in a storm, and a few members of her crew managed to reach the coast of Yucatan. Believing that they had found safety, they gave thanks to God, only to be seized by natives and borne off to their pyramids. The prisoners stood there on the summit for a moment, looking down on a vast city and a strange new world. Then they were thrown down on to the sacrificial slab and priests tore the hearts from their bodies.

As for Aguilar, he managed to escape into the interior, where he fell into the hands of a powerful Indian prince. Having at first treated him with the utmost severity, the chieftain gradually became touched by his prisoner's humility and powers of endurance, and in the end offered him a woman of his own race as a wife. Being a priest, Aguilar remained true to his vow and declined. This made the chieftain suspicious, so he submitted the unfortunate priest to a series of temptations, all of which, like St Antony, Aguilar steadfastly resisted. When the prince finally realized that Aguilar really was continent he regarded him as a saint, and assigned him the office for which he seemed logically most suited: keeper of his harem. Aguilar became an important man in Mexico, but he lived, as it were, behind the iron curtain of an uncharted world.

The conquest of Mexico was to be the prerogative of another. It was Hernando Cortez whom the Governor of Cuba entrusted with an expedition into the country, the first rumours of whose gold and treasure were just beginning to filter through into the outside world. Cortez was a young man of thirty-four, and fired with a true spirit of adventure. The Governor had scarcely commissioned Cortez to start preparations for the expedition when

318

he became jealous and tried to cancel his orders. By that time, however, Cortez and his men were already on board their hastily assembled and ill-provided ships. Cortez was half way out of the harbour when the astonished Governor arrived at the water's edge. 'A truly courteous way to take your leave, I must say!' stuttered the Governor. 'Your pardon,' shouted back Cortez, 'but time presses, and there are some things which have to be done without too much reflection. Has your Excellency any further orders?'

Cortez and his fleet set sail for Yucatan in February 1519. Arriving at the island of Cozumel, he immediately had the natives' idols destroyed and erected an altar in one of the Indian temples, complete with effigies of the Virgin and Child. The first Mass ever to be held in 'New Spain' was conducted in an Indian temple. It was here that Cortez met a most peculiar man, a poor creature who touched the ground and then lifted his hand to his head in the Indian mode of greeting. He was very wretchedly clad and Cortez wrapped him in his own cloak. Both men thought a miracle had happened. The stranger was a white man, and spoke Spanish. It was Aguilar, the 'Crusoe' we have already met. After so many years in Mexico he had lost all hope of regaining contact with Europe.

At Tabasco, Cortez and his small party were obliged to do battle with a greatly superior force of Indians. This was the first time the natives had ever seen horses or come into contact with cavalry. Taking rider and steed for a single creature, they imagined that they were dealing with monsters and fled. Next day, however, they approached again, this time bringing gifts. Among these gifts were twenty women, and among the twenty women an extremely beautiful Aztec princess called Malinche, whom the Spaniards renamed Marina.

Marina stood before Cortez with downcast head. It soon became clear that she and Aguilar could understand one another, and the latter translated what she said into Castilian. Cortez soon learned that Marina could speak several native Mexican dialects, and that she could be extremely valuable to him as an interpreter. As for Marina, she knew from the very first moment that she was in love with Cortez and, since there is no finer teacher than love, she quickly learned Castilian. Marina at first acted as Cortez' secretary, but it was not long before she became his mistress. She was uncommonly beautiful, she was young, she was clever, and she remained unswervingly loyal to the Spaniards from the very first. During Cortez' campaigns she often rescued the Spaniards from the most difficult situations, and at the same time frequently managed to preserve her own people from disaster. Although she had a son by Cortez, Don Martín, Cortez never married her, being already married to a Spanish woman.

Cortez sailed down the coast with his fleet, and the Spaniards saw the snow-capped peak of Orizaba for the first time. On Good Friday, April 21st, 1519, they landed at the spot where Mexico's modern seaport Vera Cruz now stands.

The Spaniards had long ago heard of the powerful Aztec king, Montezuma, and Montezuma, who was expecting the return of the white god Quetzalcoatl in that year, had already been informed by his scouts that Quetzalcoatl's ambassadors had landed. The king's learned soothsayers declared that there were two possibilities: if the king met the strangers with hostility, he would perish, and if he welcomed them with open arms, he would lose his throne. The king decided to welcome the strangers, so he sent them gifts. As soon as Cortez set eyes on them, he knew that this was the land of which the rulers of Spain had been dreaming for so long, the land which must be won, whatever the cost. Solid gold lay heaped before him, huge basins of it as big as wagon-wheels, gold dishes representing the sun, silver dishes representing the moon, turquoises, feather cloaks, gold and silver animals and a helmet filled with gold. The gifts acted like a loadstone, drawing Cortez and his men ever deeper into the country's interior.

Meanwhile, Cortez sent King Montezuma some presents in return. They included a decorated arm-chair, beads, two shirts, a red cap with a medallion on it – and the assurance that he, Cortez, would not leave Mexico without first paying Montezuma a courtesy visit.

Cortez soon learned that the great Montezuma had many enemies, the tribes, in fact, against whom the Aztecs were continually waging war to obtain the prisoners they sacrificed to the gods on the lofty summits of their pyramids. One of the tribes which immediately threw in their lot with Cortez was that of the Totonacos. The Spaniards found their capital, Cempoala, a true feast for the eye with its splendid streets, magnificent buildings and luxuriant gardens, not to mention its friendly inhabitants who showered their guests with roses and garlands. But Cortez realized that from now on he would be advancing, with only a small body of men, into a country fraught with a thousand dangers. There would be an ever-present threat of war and mutiny, and death itself would be his constant companion. So he came to a decision almost without parallel in world history. There in a country as yet completely strange to him, and separated from his native land by a whole ocean, he made up his mind to convince his men of the impossibility of retreat, to show them that they must fight and win – or die. He accordingly had every one of his ships destroyed except one small vessel which was to carry dispatches. The trek into the mountains began. Men groaned as they dragged their cannons up the steep defiles, and packhorses panted under the weight of their loads. The Spaniards' route took them through a trackless desert which later gave way to fields of maize.

They met some resistance in the country of the Tlaxcalans, but the latter ultimately became their allies.

The day came when the Spaniards reached Cholula, the sacred city of the Toltecs. The pyramid of Quetzalcoatl was an incredible sight in those days, as was the broad avenue with its busy stream of traffic. At night, Marina slipped out of the temple courtyard where the Spaniards were encamped. She learned that Cholula was in league with Montezuma, and that the Spaniards were to be ambushed as they left the city. Cortez replied with a wholesale massacre. The temple on the great pyramid was overthrown and a massive stone crucifix immediately set up in its place. Soon afterwards Montezuma sent envoys to Cortez inviting the Spaniards to visit him in his capital, Tenochtitlan, or what is today Mexico City.

It must have been a breathtaking moment when the Spaniards looked down from the mountain heights into the Valley of Mexico for the first time, with its sparkling lakes and steaming forests, bright houses and numerous townships. Far in the distance towered the pyramids of Teotihuacán, while nearer at hand stood Tenochtitlan, the Venice of ancient Mexico. Montezuma welcomed the Spaniards in person, and Cortez at last saw before him the ruler of an empire which had surpassed his wildest dreams. As for Montezuma, he saw Cortez as an emissary of his god, the Quetzalcoatl whose return the oracle had so long ago foretold, and quartered the Spaniards in one of his palaces. When the great king climbed into his sedanchair once more the crowds prostrated themselves on the ground and lay motionless.

'I shall never forget this spectacle', wrote Bernal Díaz, the Spanish chronicler who had come to Tenochtitlan with Cortez. Crowds of people surged through the streets. Countless faces peered from every gateway and window. The inhabitants stood shoulder to shoulder on the roof-tops and gazed at the Spaniards in wonder. The city boasted a huge market-place, long rows of buildings and streets which were cleaned daily by thousands of sweepers. Since the lake on which Tenochtitlan lay was brackish, drinking-water was conveyed into the city through earthenware pipes from a reservoir in the mountains. This clean water supplied the fountains which played everywhere in Tenochtitlan.

Montezuma owned numerous spacious palaces, as well as an armoury stocked with weapons and military accoutrements. Young Aztec noblemen fought duels, and warlike spectacles were enacted. There were granaries, huge warehouses and an aviary containing brightly feathered birds from all over the empire. Parrots of a thousand varieties, their plumage ranging over every colour in the rainbow, filled the air with their incessant chatter. Every known bird was represented in the aviary, from golden pheasants down to tiny humming-birds. The place kept three hundred attendants busy, for the birds' feeding-stuffs often had to be brought from far afield. In the moulting-season the valuable feathers were collected for the feathered robes whose manufacture the Aztecs had brought to such a fine art. Special houses were set apart for birds of prey, such as the vultures and various species of eagle which were captured in the chilly wastes of the Andes. There was also a zoological garden containing wild beasts and snakes. Some of these reptiles were housed in long cages lined with down and feathers, while others lived in tubs full of mud and water. The keepers knew their charges well, and the zoo was pervaded by an atmosphere of well-being and cleanliness. Montezuma also kept a sort of curio-collection, a human menagerie full of monstrosities, dwarfs and other unfortunate creatures. All the buildings housing the various collections were enclosed by vast gardens filled with flowers, shrubs, trees and medicinal plants. (The Aztecs had raised pharmaceutics and botany to the status of a science.) Sparkling fountains shed their refreshing dew on the luxuriant gardens. Water-fowl and fish of every description inhabited the king's ten large fish-ponds, some of which contained marine amphibians and were filled with sea-water.

Montezuma's palaces were equipped with every conceivable amenity. The ladies of his harem had their own quarters, where they were provided with everything they needed for their comfort. They were experts at weaving and knitting, and produced the most elaborate garments of feathers. These ladies lived under the supervision of old women whose particular responsibility was to see that their charges took plenty of baths. Montezuma himself changed his clothes four times a day, and garments which he had worn once were immediately given away to his servants. Noblemen were always on duty in the palace antechambers, ready to serve him.

Henry VIII would have envied Montezuma. He used to dine sumptuously, sitting in solitary state with hundreds of dishes piled on the mats in front of him. When he had indicated the dishes of his choice, they were heated for him. Venison from distant forests, fish from sea and river — the Aztec chefs had an inexhaustible repertoire of dishes. Serving-men of noble birth used to carry in the food, which was served by girls especially selected for their grace and beauty. The king sat on a cushion with an umbrella above his head, while venerable old counsellors stood at a respectful distance, ready to answer his questions. Golden table-requisites were laid on a cotton table-cloth, and the dining-room was illuminated by torches supplied with a special resin which gave off a sweet perfume as it burned. The royal menu included sweet dishes, pastry, waffles (prepared on the spot by two young girls) and chocolate flavoured with vanilla, so frothy that it melted in the mouth. After his meal, the king was handed finger-bowls and then pipes, from which he inhaled the smoke of a soothing herb called tobacco, blowing it out again through his nose. During this pleasant after-dinner smoke the king amused himself by watching jugglers whose technique surpassed anything the contemporary world could have produced. The king also had a court jester, an individual who frequently combined clowning with sound advice. The dancers employed by the palace occupied one whole quarter of the city, and the expense of maintaining the court swallowed up vast sums. Nevertheless, a strict account of income and expenditure was kept, and the king's household functioned in an exemplary manner.

Meanwhile, a game of cat and mouse was going on. Montezuma showed Cortez over a pyramid. They stood by the jasper slab on which human sacrifices were made. The air reeked of stale blood. As Cortez and Montezuma stood there, the king turned to Marina. 'Climbing our great temple has made you both tired,' he said. It was a rather uncomfortable moment. 'Spaniards never grow weary,' Cortez replied hastily.

On top of the sacred towers Cortez saw the Aztec gods with human hearts lying in golden basins on the altars before them, still warm and only recently plucked from the prisoners' bodies. 'An atmosphere like that in a Castilian slaughter-house reigned there,' wrote Díaz. The priests' robes were stiff with blood. . . .

Cortez wanted to sweep all this idolatry aside without more ado and replace it with the cross of Christianity, but Montezuma was greatly enraged at the idea. 'These are the gods which have led us Aztecs to victory,' he protested. Perhaps he remembered that the old god Quetzalcoatl had been opposed to human sacrifice, and that it was the new god Huitzilopochtli who had first demanded these streams of blood.

The Spaniards inspected Montezuma's private treasury. 'It looked to me', wrote Díaz, 'as though all the riches in the world had found their way into one place.' Montezuma visited the Spaniards in their palace. The Spaniards visited Montezuma. Finally, Cortez decided on a plan to take Montezuma prisoner. Choosing five courageous knights as his companions, he went to call on the king. Montezuma received the party amicably and even offered Cortez one of his daughters in marriage. Cortez replied that his religion forbade polygamy and that he already had one wife in Cuba. We are left to wonder how Marina must have felt when translating this last sentence!

Cortez found it hard to abandon friendly conversation for more serious matters, but he eventually requested Montezuma to leave his own palace and move in with the Spaniards. Montezuma was absolutely dumbfounded by this demand and made no reply, whereupon one of Cortez' knights cried out: 'Why are we wasting words on this savage? Let us seize him, and if he resists, kill him!' Montezuma asked Marina what the furious Spaniard had said, and Marina translated it in the mildest and most friendly way she could manage. In the end, Montezuma consented to leave his palace. He was never to see it again.

The Aztecs started to murmur at this, and, when they finally appeared outside the Spaniards' quarters brandishing their weapons, Montezuma, the Pétain of his day, went out on to the balcony to pacify them. They looked at their king as though he were some wild beast which had been tamed and was standing submissively in its enemies' cage.

'Vile Aztec!' they shouted, 'Woman, coward! The white men have turned you into a woman, fit only for spinning and weaving.' Spears flew quivering through the air and a volley of stones and arrows pattered down on the king. The Spaniards hurriedly covered him with their shields, but it was too late. Montezuma had been mortally wounded.

Father Olmedo knelt at the dying man's side. 'Embrace the cross,' the priest said, 'the symbol of man's redemption.' Montezuma pushed it away. 'I have only a few more moments to live. I will not spend them in disloyalty to the beliefs of my forefathers.'

Montezuma died on June 30th, 1520, in the arms of the noblemen whom the Spaniards had allowed to stay with their king.

The rest of the story was uprising and rebellion, massacre and blood, the siege of the starving Aztecs, the filling in of the city's canals and the dismantling of nearly all her buildings, temples included, to make room for Cortez' cavalry charges, room for slaughter and death. The Aztecs' temples toppled to the ground, and churches and monasteries arose on their ruins, built out of their ancient stones. Using Tenochtitlan as a base, the Spaniards spread their influence in every direction. In another twenty years Spanish towns were established on the Yucatan Peninsula.

That was how the Aztec Empire met its end, more dramatically than any product of the imagination could ever have done.

Even in old age, Cortez continued to earn his living at sea by conquest and exploration. Accusations, impeachments, secret investigations – his enemies plotted against him with every means at their disposal. It was always the same story. He was for ever fitting out squadrons for new voyages of discovery, but his enterprises were no longer attended by their former success. On one occasion, he and his companions nearly starved to death. On another, he was beset by storms and his ship cast up on to rocks. Only his indomitable will-power brought the old man ashore alive. Cortez sent yet another squadron off to sea under the command of Ulloa. But Ulloa never came back, and the 300,000 gold castellanos which Cortez had invested in the expedition did not bring him a ducat in return.

Cortez went to the Castilian court to fight for his rights. But he was old now, as everyone could see, and a grey-haired old man like him could not be expected to render his king any further useful service. He had met with nothing but bad luck in recent years and, besides, his limelight had now been stolen by a man whom he had himself once outshone, Pizarro, who had achieved such brilliant successes in Peru.

Cortez sent letters and petitions to the Emperor. He had hoped, he said, that the hardships of his youth would have assured him of an untroubled old age. He had spent forty years of his life on continuous active service, sleeping little and eating badly. He had brought many large and powerful nations under the Emperor's dominion. Now he was old, infirm and encumbered with debts.

No response came from court. Week after week went by, and month after month. The weary conquistador spent another three years penning humble letters, arguing, making petty proposals and waiting, always waiting . . . 'It is much harder to defend oneself against officers of the Crown than to wrest huge countries from powerful foes,' said Cortez in the twilight of his days.

So much embitterment and mental unrest brought on stomach trouble. Cortez was living in Seville with his fifteen-year-old son when he was attacked by dysentery. The last item in his will stated that it had long been questionable whether anyone could own Indian slaves with a clear conscience. Cortez enjoined his son to spare no effort in clarifying this problem, 'for it is a matter which touches every man's conscience no less than my own'.

Growing weaker day by day, Cortez went back to the village of Castilleja de Cuesta, where his young son nursed him with childish solicitude. Cortez confessed, received extreme unction, and died on December 2nd, 1547, in his sixty-third year.

CRETE

X

A LABYRINTH 5000 YEARS OLD

Did King Minos really exist? Was there really a labyrinth at Knossos? And where did people literally 'take the bull by the horns'? Minoan civilization was only unearthed fifty years ago by Sir Arthur Evans.

ROUGHLY equidistant from the coasts of Europe, Asia and Africa lies the island with the oldest advanced civilization in Europe: Crete, 'a land set in a wine-dark sea', as Homer described it.

Crete is in fact the first and oldest link in the splendid chain of European civilizations. By the time Greece had reached her prime, Crete was almost submerged in a sea of legend and fable. When battles were raging round Troy (1194-1184 B.C.), Crete could already look back on 2000 years of advanced civilization. When Christ was born, the laughter of the elegant ladies-in-waiting and courtesans in the palace at Knossos had been silent for 1400 years. The gorgeous clothes, the rustling skirts and petticoats which could have competed with the most modern Paris creations, the bodices, lace and puffed sleeves had all returned to dust long ago. Crete was as good as a myth. For almost 2000 years, everything which was told about Crete was regarded as a piece of fanciful invention — until fifty years ago, when it became clear that it was all absolutely true.

In 1878, a Cretan merchant with the resounding name of Kalokairinos dug up several objects of great antiquity on a hill south of Candia. Eight years later, in 1886, a stranger visited the district. A very gaunt, rather worried-looking man, he examined the district restlessly through weary eyes. He had an uncannily sharp nose for ruins which had lain forgotten under the ground for many thousands of years. He was a German, and his name was Heinrich Schliemann. He had already rediscovered Mycenae and Troy, and now he stood there in Crete and asserted that the legendary palaces of Knossos were lying beneath his feet and must be excavated.

Schliemann was a painstaking reader of the Greek classics. Before he started digging, he always knew where he had to dig and what he was looking for. He opened negotiations with the proprietors of the land, wanting to start excavations without delay. The proprietors tried to demand too high a price, however, so Schliemann abandoned the project, and with it the chance of following up his success at Troy by personally excavating yet another age-old seat of civilization. He died shortly afterwards. In 1893, the British archaeologist Dr Arthur Evans bought a few moonstones from a Greek woman in Athens. His wife wore the stones as a lucky charm, but Evans was more interested in the undecipherable hieroglyphs which were scratched on them.

A good archaeologist must also be something of a detective. By a process of comparison, Evans succeeded in establishing that the hieroglyphic trail led in the direction of Crete. He went to the island and travelled about collecting such objects as had accidentally come to light there from time to time. Finally he purchased the land beneath which Knossos lay buried and employed 150 labourers to excavate it.

They dug for nine weeks. At the end of that time Evans had brought to light the richest of all the treasures of modern archaeology, the palace of Minos.

'We were entering a completely undiscovered world,' Evans wrote. 'Each step forward was a step into the dark. There were no buildings which could serve as a pattern, and systematic digging was therefore impossible. The palace put into the shade all that was known about European antiquity or had been supposed to exist here.'

Evans found thousands of bricks and clay tablets bearing the same hieroglyphics as those on the amulet which had brought him from Athens. The magnificent civilization of a race uncommonly gifted both in the intellectual and artistic sphere unfolded before his eyes, exposed to the Mediterranean sun once more.

We already know that cities 'grow', and that past civilizations lie in layers on top of one another, the top layer being the most recent, and the lowest layers the oldest. Evans established that while the Minoan Bronze Age civilizations went back to the year 3000 B.C., there were late Stone Age civilizations lying beneath them which embraced the fantastic span of 10,000 years. The palace at Knossos and Minoan civilization must therefore have taken shape in a prehistoric era which makes us, with the scope of our thought limited by historical boundaries, slightly dizzy when we contemplate it. Advanced Minoan civilization did not just suddenly appear two or three thousand years before the birth of Christ. After all, wherever we go in the world, we can nearly always be sure that we are treading upon a vast accumulation of debris left behind by man's exertions and his struggle for advancement. Like many others, therefore, Minoan civilization must have spent many thousands of years in slow and independent evolution.

It was only in 1936 that Evans, by that time Sir Arthur Evans and the proud possessor of many honours and academic awards, finally completed his monumental six-volume work *The Palace of Minos at Knossos*. It is a marvellous work, the work of a lifetime's endeavour, and it has a mysterious

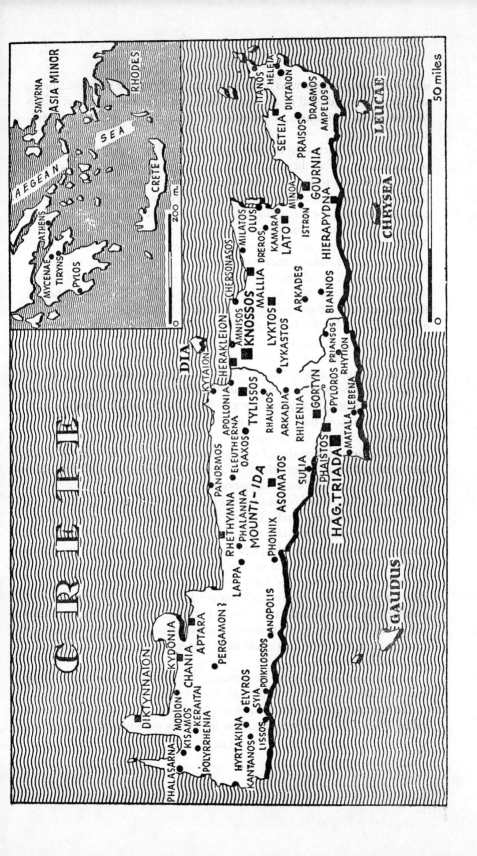

way of drawing anyone who reads it ever farther down the path to a strange and fabulous world until he eventually finds himself at the very heart of this Mediterranean civilization, wandering in the legendary realm of the sea-kings of Knossos.

Evans presupposes a great deal, however, and his readers must know a certain amount before they can find their way about in his thick volumes. It is perhaps natural to inquire why any archaeologist should have hit upon Crete and nowhere else in his search for the palace at Knossos and, in particular, for the palace where a king called Minos was reputed to have reigned.

The truth is that we should never write off every ancient legend as mere fiction. We should have the courage to take the information given in ancient narratives and accounts at its face-value and follow it up. Our oldest legendary sources of information about Crete are Homer's *Iliad* and *Odyssey*. Homer lived about 800 B.C. He mentions King Minos, the palace at Knossos, and many things relating to the Cretan king. Herodotus, the 'father of history', who lived between about 484 and 425 B.C., also gives an account of Minos, his fleets and a Cretan expedition against Sicily. Thucydides, an Athenian aristocrat and an extremely objective student of history who was born in 455 B.C., tells us about Minos' sea-power. Aristoteles, a Greek doctor's son who was born in a small Macedonian town in 384 B.C., wrote that Crete's geographical location was so convenient that it had enabled King Minos to dominate the whole Aegean area, i.e. the islands in the Aegean Sea and the countries bordering it.

Greek sagas and legends tell us a great deal more. Apparently Knossos was inhabited by a raging 'Minotaur', a monster half man, half bull. Was this a mere figment of the imagination?

The word 'Minotaur' is a compound of King Minos' name and the Greek word *tauros*, meaning bull. During the excavations at Knossos, many different portrayals of the bull were found, and it became apparent that the animal possessed an especial significance there. The palace of King Minos displayed bull-fighting scenes in which young girls and men seized the bull by its horns and vaulted over the savage beast in mid-career. One mural shows a girl impaled upon a bull's horns while in the act of jumping. It is possible that captured children were also trained in this sport. If King Minos did at one time subjugate Athens and receive tribute from her, it is easy to imagine how the Athenians could have combined the king and the bull in one terrible creature.

King Minos, so the legend goes on, confined the Minotaur in a building called a 'labyrinth'. Was this fiction? By no means.

The Cretans' most sacred being was a Mother-goddess whom the Greeks called 'Rhea'. The goddess was almost invariably portrayed in the company of a male deity who may have been her son. Both god and goddess had a symbol, a kind of fetish or lucky charm into which they could vanish at will. This was the two-bladed axe. The Carian expression for this double-axe was *labrys*, and the symbol of the labrys or double-axe was found everywhere in the excavated palace at Knossos, so it is no wonder that the palace itself came to be called *labyrinthos*. Our expression 'labyrinth' therefore originated at Knossos and is a good 5000 years old – if not considerably older.

We do not know whether our palace really was the original labyrinth, or whether the Minoans could remember another labyrinth which had disappeared long before. Coins found at Knossos and in the palace of Minos bore the regular outlines of a building, sometimes round, sometimes square, which contained a single long passage twisting and turning at right angles. It must have meant a long walk before one reached the heart of the building, and once inside one could never have got out. This was without doubt the ground-plan of the celebrated labyrinth.

Far away in Italy on August 24th, A.D. 79, Vesuvius erupted, completely engulfing the famous city of Pompeii. Preserved under ash and masses of lava lay another clue to our mystery. On one of the walls a little Roman child had scratched the drawing of a maze. Underneath, written in his own hand, were the words: 'Labyrinth Here dwells the Minotaur.' So this Roman child, too, was familiar with the Cretan labyrinth and the story of the Minotaur. We know something else: the curriculum of Roman schools still included this 'fairy-story' under the heading of history.

King Minos' architect, the man who built the palace at Knossos and invented the labyrinth, is reputed to have been Daedalus. He was undoubtedly an authentic person, and seems to have been a kind of Leonardo, always surprising his royal master with new inventions and feats of ingenuity. He was also a talented sculptor and produced statues so lifelike that, according to the Greeks, his works would have stepped down from their pedestals if they had not been secured to them by chains. Daedalus was also the world's first aviator. It is said that when King Minos imprisoned him and his son Icarus in the impenetrable labyrinth, he contrived some wings for them both, with the aid of which they soared over the walls of the labyrinth and flew away far above the sea, climbing towards the sun. Icarus died on the flight, but Daedalus landed in Sicily, where he introduced the inhabitants to Cretan culture and executed some noble statues, among them a marble relief of Minos' daughter Ariadne dancing. These works are said to have been in existence as late as A.D. 200, and the Greeks never doubted that Daedalus was an historical personality

I believe, too, that the 'legend' of Theseus and Ariadne really occurred.

Once every nine years, it ran, King Minos required the city of Athens to provide seven girls and seven young men for sacrifice to the Minotaur. Theseus, the son of King Aegeus, volunteered to go to Crete as one of these victims with the intention of slaying the monster. King Minos' daughter Ariadne had no sooner set eyes on the young Athenian prince than she fell in love with him. She gave him a sword and showed him how to unwind a reel of thread behind him as he advanced into the labyrinth, so that he could later use it to find his way out. Theseus killed the Minotaur, followed Ariadne's thread out of the labyrinth, and escaped with the king's daughter to Naxos. He married her as he had promised, but then sailed away with his companions while she was asleep.

Stories like that of Theseus and Ariadne are hardly ever pure invention, and ideas as complex as the labyrinth are very seldom the products of poetic fiction. It is still not clear exactly when the labyrinth existed, and whether the people of Knossos were still familiar with it or only remembered it dimly. If the latter supposition were correct, it would explain their uncertainty as to whether it was square or round.

It was because King Minos reigned in the palace at Knossos and was master of a large maritime empire, because Minos in all probability existed, and because his name was possibly a king's title — as Pharaoh was for the Egyptians — that Evans designated the civilization of ancient Crete the 'Minoan' civilization. He established in the course of his excavations that the late Stone Age lasted there until about 3400 B.C., when the Bronze Age began, and he divided Minoan civilization into three periods: early Minoan (3400-2100), middle Minoan (2100-1580) and late Minoan (1580-1250). This classification was extremely difficult to make, since the people of the Minoan civilization left no form of chronological guides or dates behind them. The Egyptians, on the other hand, have supplied us with very accurate dates, and so the commercial and cultural relations which existed between Egypt and ancient Crete make it possible to place the occurrence of certain historical events with reasonable accuracy in Crete, too.

In or about 2100 B.C. the princes of Knossos, Phaistos and Mallia erected massive palaces containing innumerable rooms, workshops, store-chambers, courtyards, staircases and balustrades. Altars and temples were constructed also, together with complex systems of water-supply. The walls of the various palaces were adorned with bright frescoes, and a linear script began to evolve from the hieroglyphics of past millennia.

In 1700 B.C. a great catastrophe seems to have occurred, and the palace at Knossos was destroyed. Was it an earthquake, or had the inhabitants of Phaistos attacked the city? The latter question is allowable because curiously enough the palace at Phaistos did not collapse until a later date. The earth is yielding up one secret after another. Some time afterwards more cities tumbled down, including Mochlos, Gournia, Palaikastro and many others. Then, about 1600 B.C., life started afresh. New buildings arose out of the ruins, grander and more beautiful palaces were built at Knossos, Phaistos, Tylissos, Hagia Triada and Gournia. The same kind of opulence began to prevail which Greece was not to know until a thousand years later. Plays were performed in the palace courtyards, gladiators fought with wild beasts, fashions in dress grew more and more sumptuous, craftsmanship and literature flourished, and the wealthy discovered ever new outlets for their extravagance. Between 1600 and 1400 B.C. Crete and the Minoan civilization enjoyed a golden age, and the whole of the Aegean Sea basked in the rays of the Cretan sun. And then, about 1400 B.C., everything suddenly disintegrated. An appalling catastrophe annihilated all the products of human ingenuity, thought and endeavour which it had taken hundreds, nay, thousands of years to create.

What had happened?

⊢	⊢	ta
Λ	↑	ti
‡	‡	pa
𝖦	𝖲	po
+	+	lo
𝖼	𝖹	ra
¥		ni
⟲		re
𝖠	Ⲙ	ma
𝖬	Ⲙ	mi

Oldest syllabic characters of Europe
Left: Cretan. *Middle:* Cypriot. *Right:* Equivalent deciphered
by Ernst Sittig.

UNITS – I = *1,* ||| = *5*
         ||

TENS |⁻ • OR ⁻ } = *10,* •••, ---, ☰, = *50*
              OR _ }   ••   ☰

HUNDREDS – O = *100,* OOO = *500*
                          OO

THOUSANDS – ◇ = *1000,* ◇◇◇ = *4000*
                            ◇

EXAMPLE : ◇◇ OO ☰☰☰||| = *2496*
              OO |||

Cretan numerals. One can see that any sum may be expressed
by this system. Our own system derives from the Arabs.

THE MYSTERIOUS DOWNFALL

Before his departure Heracles was magnificently honoured by the natives, and wishing to show his gratitude to the Cretans he cleansed the island of the wild beasts which infested it . . . This deed he accomplished for the glory of the island, which, the myths relate, was both the birthplace and the early home of Zeus.

Diodorus Siculus iv, 17

IN 1400 B.C. Minoan civilization disintegrated as though it had been smashed by some superhuman fist. The catastrophe which demolished the cities of Crete was an all-embracing one. Knossos, Phaistos, Hagia Triada, Gournia, Mochlos, Mallia and Zakros, all these places of varying size exhibit traces of simultaneous demolition and fire, while other towns, like Palaikastro, Pseira and Tylissos, collapsed without being burnt.

We know no people of this period, about 3350 years ago, who have left us a first-hand account of the disaster. There are no contemporary descriptions of the collapse of advanced Minoan civilization, and no indications as to its exact date. We are solely dependent upon the researches of archaeologists in this respect, and it is an astonishing fact that, although archaeology can only supply us with the approximate year in which the catastrophe occurred, it has been able to name the precise month.

The year 1400 B.C. was arrived at after an extremely careful examination of individual layers of subterranean debris, and was confirmed by the last portrayals of Cretans (*Kefti*) found in Egypt, which date from the time of Pharaoh Amenophis III (1401-1375). This estimate may be a few years out, but if the great disaster did not actually take place in 1400 B.C., it certainly occurred shortly thereafter. We come now to the traces of burning, which is to say, the smoke stains still clearly visible on the walls of the excavated ruins. They actually enable us to 'see' the wind which swept the clouds of smoke through the palace while it was on fire. The smoke has left such clearly defined traces on the blocks of masonry that we can deduce that the fire and billowing smoke which raced along the tottering walls were driven from south-west to north-east by a south-easterly gale. The Moslems of today call this south-east wind *gharbis*. It blows in the spring months, bringing with it vast clouds of sand from the distant Sahara, and reaching its full force in March. Only a gharbis of that strength could have left traces of smoke like those which were found on the walls of Knossos. That is how we know the month when the city was destroyed. It was March. Only in March could so many cities have gone up in smoke at the same time, for only a very strong wind could have assisted the fires so effectively.

But how did the fires occur? Sir Arthur Evans, the archaeologist who excavated Knossos and the first man to bring the dead city back to life, as it were, is convinced that Knossos, like the other cities on Crete, owed its collapse to a great earthquake, and that the terrible conflagration was a consequence of that earthquake. Certainly everything points to a swift and sinister end, and to the fact that the inhabitants were taken completely by surprise. The most sacred spot in Knossos, the throne-room, showed signs that an extraordinary drama was enacted there at the very last moment. Alabaster oil-jars such as were only employed at the most sacred ceremonies were evidently standing in readiness at the very moment of disaster. We do not know exactly what was going on, but it is apparent that the catastrophe coincided with a sacred ritual of some kind. The condition of the city's workshops likewise indicates that her craftsmen and artists were suddenly overtaken by disaster in the middle of their work. If an enemy had been approaching the island, surprise would not have been so complete – at least in Evans's astute judgment, and his arguments carry great conviction.

Another very conscientious archaeologist, J. D. S. Pendlebury, who knows Knossos extremely well and conducted the excavations at Tell el Amarna, has put forward a different theory. He holds that in ancient times earthquakes were not inevitably followed by fire, and that fire as the result of an earthquake only came in with gas and electricity – a clear example of this being the great earthquake at Tokyo in 1923. Furthermore, an earthquake would have destroyed the grand staircase at Knossos, yet it was demonstrable that this structure had survived for a long time after the date of the alleged disaster.

While studying these different points of view, I was struck by an idea which no investigator – so far as I know – has yet ventured to put forward. Since the Cretans were an able and ingenious race and technically very advanced, it might fairly be supposed that they used petroleum, probably for purposes of illumination, and possibly even in their smithies and kitchens. If there was an earthquake and their oil-conduits burst, the theory that fire resulted then becomes quite tenable.

Be that as it may, Pendlebury believes that all the evidence points to intentional destruction by some human agency.

Let us assume that in 1400 B.C. it was not Crete which ruled the mainland, but the mainland – or what is today Greece – which ruled the island of Crete. It is then quite conceivable that the cities of the island, conscious of their own ancient civilization, one day came to the conclusion that they had had enough of foreign domination and decided to shake it off by means of a concerted revolt against everything foreign. We know that the Cretans rebuilt their cities after the disaster and lived on relatively undisturbed, and we also know that two hundred years after the event they were importing far fewer products of foreign culture than they had done formerly. All

Tenochtitlan (*now Mexico City*) *as it was in* 1519, when Cortez entered it.
The large pyramid on the left was where Cortez and Marina stood with
Montezuma. *Centre:* an altar for human sacrifice

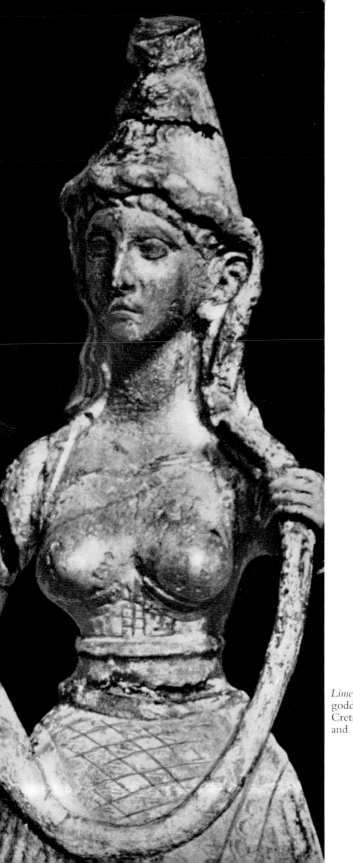

Limestone figure of a Minoan snak
goddess dating from 1500 B.C. T
Cretans had a household snake-cu
and there was a snake-room in t
palace at Knossos

In the Minoan civilization women's clothing displayed great opulence and refinement of taste. The waist was kept very slim, and elaborate corsets were worn, but the breasts were always exposed. This was the Goddess of Sport

The head of a snake-goddess, adorned with a lioness, an animal greatly revered by the Cretans

Tight bodices were the height of fashion. Note the wealth of beautiful embroidery

A gown with six flounces, surmounted by a short hip-piece and a sort of apron. The beautiful long black hair is carefully dressed

A Knossos 'creation', 2000 B.C. Skirt adorned with crocuses, bodice vertically striped, waist narrow

these facts are substantiated by excavation, so the 'revolution theory' seems well-founded.

If, on the other hand, Crete still controlled the whole of the Aegean area in 1400 B.C., and if her 'dominions' decided to break their mother-country's supremacy, then an actual landing and invasion becomes conceivable. In that case, the hostile armada which destroyed the cities of Crete must have been brilliantly organized. The motive for this planned devastation would seem to have been a political one, quite divorced from any intention to settle down and colonize, for as soon as destruction was complete the enemy abandoned the island, leaving the Cretans to rebuild their cities and lead a shadowy existence for another two hundred years. This second theory, the 'invasion theory', is the one which Pendlebury favours, and it marches well with the 'legend' of Theseus.

If Crete really did demand that a number of young Athenian men and girls be sent at certain regular intervals to Knossos as human sacrifices, and if there really was such a person as the Theseus who decided to kill the man-eating Minotaur in the labyrinth at Knossos, it may well be that the 'myth' of Theseus' revengeful visit to Crete was a factual occurrence which has been transmuted into legend. Pendlebury describes the scene as he imagines it. It was a spring day in late April or early May when the hour of retribution struck. A fierce wind drove the flames almost horizontally through the palace at Knossos. The throne-room was a scene of frightful confusion. The celebrated King Minos may himself have hurried there at the last moment, thinking to save his people by performing some sacred ritual, when Theseus rushed in and killed him. Perhaps Theseus saw the king as the Minotaur, a man with a bull's head, or perhaps it was legend which later turned the dead king into a monster. In any case, Crete had fallen. After vegetating for another two centuries as a satellite of the Greek world, she was then swamped by the greater vigour of Hellenic culture and assimilated into a new world whose life was only just beginning.

The Cretans were a Mediterranean race. They were a seafaring people and maintained commercial relations with Egypt, the Near East and all the members of the Aegean and Mediterranean communities as far as Italy and Spain. Their navy was so powerful that they never felt the need to fortify Knossos. It was an unfortified city just as London or New York is today.

The Cretans never wore beards. That in itself is enough to discourage any talk of a 'Cretan-Mycenaean' civilization, for the Mycenaean Greeks were very fond of beards. The Cretans, on the other hand, were so attached to their razors that they took them into their graves.

The ladies of the Minoan civilization used to wear massive sugar-plum hats, white leather shoes with ornamentation (if they were well-to-do), and very lovely narrow-waisted gowns which covered their bodies completely, except for the breasts. Waists had to be extremely slim, and the ladies who lived in Crete 4000 years ago laced themselves up tightly in elegant bodices. Their skirts were stiffened with metal ribs to keep them spread out, just like crinolines. The colours of various articles of dress were very carefully selected, and young Cretan women's heads were coiffed and their pretty faces painted and powdered with a finesse which could hardly be rivalled today, 5000 years later. Youths and men also drew in their waists with a metal belt, but they only wore a loin-cloth, and were very scantily clad by Greek standards.

Cretan women wore valuable jewellery, a form of personal adornment which their menfolk did not despise either. The men of ancient Crete almost undoubtedly held their women in great esteem, and even the ladies of Egypt could seldom have been pampered with such taste and sophistication. It is no mere coincidence that the supreme member of the Cretan pantheon was a Mother-goddess.

One cannot fail to be amazed by the towns which have been dug up in Crete, with their well-kept streets, their facilities for water-supply, baths and drainage, their shops, their smithies, potteries, carpenters' and shoe-makers' workshops, their oil refineries and textile factories. Knossos could boast houses of up to five storeys, partitioned by folding doors and artificially lit by oil-lamps supplied with fuel in a most ingenious manner. The Cretans used to play an interesting game on the lines of chess. In general, we can recognize the symptoms of a joyous and lively quest for charm and delicacy of effect in every field of art. It was particularly in small things that the Cretans showed their greatness, for they delighted in the pretty little minutiae of everyday life much as the people who live beneath the skies of Paris do today.

Sir Arthur Evans had succeeded in giving us back a highly developed European civilization which was three and a half thousand years old and yet gave an amazing impression of modernity. But it was not Evans's intention to bring Europe's *prehistory* back to life. He had a much bolder end in view. He wanted to enlarge the span of European *history* by a thousand years. History always begins with writing and, on that basis, the history of Greece began in 776 B.C. If Evans wanted to push the frontiers of European history back into the past, therefore, he was going to have to find some much older examples of a European script than had existed hitherto. In fact, it was a wish to discover European documentary evidence that prompted him to visit Crete in the first place.

Actually, he found two sorts of script, which he named 'Linear A' and 'Linear B'. Linear A was in use on the island of Crete as early as 1600 B.C.

That fact alone enlarged the written history of Europe by a span of 800 years.

Linear A was discovered at fourteen places on the island. Thirteen of these sites produced a total of 51 different inscriptions between them, while the fourteenth, Hagia Triada, yielded 168. Of the group of 51 inscriptions, all of which are quite brief, 14 were found on terracotta tablets, 8 on terracotta vases, 6 on sacrificial tables and another 6 on seals. Of the 156 inscriptions found at Hagia Triada in a prince's summer villa situated near the centre of the south coast, 154 were inscribed on clay tablets. They are trivial little memoranda about the running of the villa, written in crude and sketchy characters which give a far from copy-book impression. In fact, it can be said that not one single decent piece of handwriting in Linear A exists.

Why were so few examples found? Well, if Linear A was only discovered at fourteen sites and on seventeen kinds of article, it is fair to assume that we only possess a ten- or hundred-thousandth part of all that was ever written in that script. Moreover, we do not know whether any kind of paper or ink had been invented and whether all that have survived are the less perishable specimens. The Cretans probably wrote upon palm-leaves, as Pliny the Elder informs us in his Natural History. Yet if so much more writing was done than our finds indicate, it is still hard to understand why the characters in the inscriptions impress one as having been executed by very inexperienced hands, if not by complete novices in the art of writing. It is probably nearer the truth to assume that throughout Crete the art of writing was only practised by a select few.

Besides, it is apparent that in spite of the very high degree of culture and the equally advanced state of artistic development in Crete during this period — i.e. between 1600 and 1400 B.C. — writing was regarded as something infra dig and only fit for bureaucrats. The fact that the script was only employed for unimportant housekeeping records suggests that it was considered relatively worthless. All this would explain why not many examples of Linear A exist. It was not 'exported', either. Linear A has hardly ever been found elsewhere in the Aegean area. Two inscriptions at Melos and one at Thera are the only ones to have been unearthed outside Crete. It appears scarcely likely, therefore, that the reason why so few specimens of Linear A have been found on Crete itself is that not enough excavation has been done there.

An even greater mystery surrounds the script known as Linear B. Whereas Linear A was employed all over the island from 1800 B.C. onwards, Linear B first appeared in 1450 B.C., but *only in one place*: the palace at Knossos. All the Linear B inscriptions found in Crete come from the palace at Knossos, and all of them date from the period immediately preceding 1400. They therefore represent the government records of one generation at the most.

While the whole of the rest of Crete went on using Linear A, the palace scribes at Knossos used Linear B for making calculations and inventories and for recording transactions of all sorts. All the examples we have found are practical book-keeping entries, calculations or accounts relating to financial administration. Evans found 2000 small oval clay tablets in the palace, mostly lancet-shaped and all bearing Linear B inscriptions of this type. They were stored in sealed wooden chests.

In 1939 the American archaeologist Carl W. Blegen and his Greek associate Kourouniotis came upon a remarkable find. They dug up a set of archives very like those at Knossos — comprising 600 clay tablets — in the mainland Peloponnesian district of western Messenia. This sensational discovery was made eleven miles north of the city of Pylos. The ruined palace at Pylos itself yielded items very similar to those at Knossos, including business statements, bills and labels, all drawn up in Linear B and dating from the fourteenth century b.c. Blegen dug up another 400 tablets in 1952 and over 50 more in 1954, making an approximate total of 1050 tablets found in this region.

Finally, in 1952, the English archaeologist Alan Wace discovered some more examples of Linear B in the 'House of the Wine-merchant' at Mycenae. They were the tradesmen's accounts. Wace thinks that we can expect to find tablets like these in every house and palace of this period — 1300-1200 b.c. (L.H. III). In Bennett's opinion, the tablets found in the house of the wine-merchant were written by six different people.

All these tablets, that is to say, the 2000 Knossos tablets, the 1050 Pylos tablets, and the 42 Mycenae tablets, display very marked similarities. All three groups are in Linear B. Before 1400, the date when Linear B first turns up on the mainland, the Greeks had no sort of script at all. In 1300 or perhaps even in 1400, people on the mainland began to write. Then, in 1100 b.c., writing died out again in Greece. In Crete, the general disaster of 1400 destroyed both Linear A and Linear B. It is the only case in the history of Europe where the art of writing has completely disappeared after several centuries of use. It was not until 800 b.c. that the Greeks again adopted a script, this time from the Phoenician inhabitants of Thera on the island of Santorin.

For decades the Cretans' notes remained unreadable. No one had managed to decipher their script. In 1928 Eduard Meyer, the German authority on ancient history, wrote: 'Whether the discovery of a successful combination will one day make it possible for us to decipher this script remains uncertain, and what makes it even more problematical is that we know absolutely nothing about the basic language or even the names. . . .'

The English philologist Michael Ventris said in 1940: 'The Minoan inscriptions of Knossos and elsewhere remain . . . the only wide-spread script in the ancient world which can neither be read nor understood.'

The American woman philologist Kober said in 1948: 'We are dealing with three unknown quantities: language, script and meaning . . . An unknown language written in an unknown script cannot be deciphered, either with or without a bi-lingual text.'

In company with other scholars of many nationalities, the German philologist Ernst Sittig struggled to decipher the Cretan script. His studies of the classical, Semitic, Slavonic, Etruscan, Cyprian and other rare idioms, including those of Asia Minor, made him well fitted for his task. During the First World War Sittig was engaged in breaking down code-systems.

As Evans, Myres and Sindwall had done before him, Sittig presupposed a similarity between the script of ancient Crete and another script belonging to Cyprus. This ancient syllabic script was used until 1000 years later, almost exclusively to express a Greek dialect, but also for a pre-Greek language for which it must originally have been designed. Employing a statistical analysis of the individual characters, Sittig next compared the construction of this pre-Greek language with ancient Cretan, established that they exhibited a similar structure, and thus managed to obtain reliable phonetic values for a number of Cretan syllabic symbols. By doing so, Dr Ernst Sittig of Tübingen University had laid the foundations of a technique for deciphering the Minoan script of ancient Crete and ancient Cyprus.

In 1951 the Pylos inscriptions were published in America by Bennett, and in 1952 the Knossos inscriptions appeared, taken from Evans's papers after his death by John Myres, who was a friend of his. Then, in 1953, a truly sensational development came from London. J. Chadwick and Michael Ventris demonstrated that the main language found on the tablets at Knossos, Pylos and Mycenae was not only Indo-European, but actually Greek. Ventris and Chadwick deciphered 65 out of an approximate total of 80 symbols, and their interpretations have recently been corrected and amplified by Hans L. Stoltenberg of Giessen.

Without wishing to minimize the services rendered by Ventris and Chadwick, it must be said that the assumption that Greek was the language which lay behind the Linear B symbols was never very remote from the minds of past researchers. For example, if one put together three of the Minoan symbols whose value Sittig had already discovered, *ti, ri* or *re*, as the case might be, and *po*, making the compound *tiripo = tripos =* the Greek for 'tripod', it became fairly clear that one was dealing with a Greek dialect of some kind, especially since on one of the Pylos inscriptions a tripod had been painted in behind the three symbols in question. The assumption which Wace and Blegen had already made on historical grounds, namely that a Greek language was spoken in Mycenae and Pylos and perhaps Tiryns too — i.e. in the fortified towns of the Mycenaean period — had now been proved beyond all reasonable doubt.

But how did Linear B script come over from Knossos to Pylos and Mycenae?

What had happened in 1400 B.C.?

Well, some people in Knossos had adopted Linear A script and developed from it a script which could express Greek words. The result of this adaptation was Linear B. It was the first time a script had been adjusted to suit Greek. Since the Cretans were not originally Greek, the question arises, who inhabited Knossos at that time, and who was interested in inventing a script suitable for Greek?

It seems likely that in 1400 at the latest, rulers from the Greek mainland were resident at Knossos, that a mainland dynasty had conquered Knossos and no other city on the island, and that it was these rulers who introduced the new invention to Pylos and Mycenae.

Of course, it could equally be argued that the new script, Linear B, was imported into Knossos from the mainland. What militates against this theory, however, is the fact that Linear B is related to the earlier Cretan Linear A script (in fact, nearly half the symbols in Linear A also appear in Linear B), and that Linear B must thus have evolved from Linear A. The further fact that most of the clay tablets in Linear B were found at Knossos — 2000 as opposed to the 1050 found at Pylos — also speaks for its Knossos origin. So Linear B was adapted for Greek out of Linear A, a script designed for Cretan, a foreign language quite unlike Greek.

But what sort of 'Greek' was spoken at this time?

We should expect the inhabitants of Pylos and Mycenae to have spoken an Old Achaean dialect something like the language of the later Achaeans. In fact, the language on these little clay tablets is early Achaean of the early Arcadian variety.

The Minoans had adopted the decimal system, deriving it either from the Egyptians or from their own ten fingers. They had no single symbol for 5, but then even our own Arabic 5 really consists of five separate symbols. The Minoans had no nought sign, either. For 1, they used a simple vertical stroke | , for 2, two strokes || , for 3, three strokes ||| , for 4, two strokes on top and two below ¦¦ , 8 was represented by four vertical strokes with another four beneath ¦¦¦¦, 9 by three groups of three strokes one beneath the other ¦¦¦ . If they wanted to change 9 to 8, they did not just strike out one of the nine strokes, but erased all nine and replaced them by four strokes on top of another four. 10 was a horizontal stroke ⌐ , 20 was expressed by two horizontal strokes = , and so on up to 10,000, ⏀, the Greek myriad.

Numerous miscalculations were discovered on the clay tablets. A lot of tablets exhibit crosses which look like our own multiplication sign ×. However, these were only a sort of 'tick' made by those who checked the figures. They were found on 39 Linear B documents.

Their inconvenient arithmetical system did not allow the Minoans to pursue higher mathematics, but it was quite adequate for lists of tributary payments, accounts and registers of craftsmen and labourers.

Ventris announced, after spending years on this script: 'The more one studies Linear B, the more amazed one becomes at the stereotyped nature of the tablets, which goes far beyond the similarity of characters and language.' Ventris assumes the existence of a permanent writing tradition with a common origin and environment. As long as Linear B went on being used in Knossos, Pylos and Mycenae, people retained the awkward characters unmodified in the slightest detail, with much more conservatism than the Phoenicians later showed. The Minoan civilization can hardly be called a literary civilization. Artistic as the Minoans were, all that they left behind in the way of writing were book-keeping entries.

Be that as it may, the deciphering of Linear B will gradually open our eyes to pre-Homeric Greece, a Greece almost a thousand years older than we have known hitherto. It will exert an immensely strong influence on our ideas about Greece's earliest times, and there will come a day when her history will no longer begin in 776 B.C., but in 1400 B.C. at the very latest.

Reproduction of the characters on a tablet inscribed in 'Linear B'. Carl W. Blegen and K. Kourouniotis found hundreds of such tablets at Pylos in West Messenia in 1939

GREECE

✗

THE CITY OF PRIAM

Troy

So then I said: 'Father, if walls like those were there at one time, they cannot have been completely destroyed, but are probably hidden beneath the dust and rubble of centuries.'
Heinrich Schliemann, at the age of eight.

IN the north-west corner of Asia Minor, two and a half miles from the shores of the Dardanelles, stands a hill which the Turks call 'Hissarlik'. This hill makes an ideal site for a fortress, citadel, or town, since it stands some way from the sea, where it is not directly exposed to naval attack, yet commands the approaches to the Dardanelles. In fact, the ruins of no less than ten towns and villages lie buried in the hill of Hissarlik. It was originally believed that the hill only contained nine periods of building, but archaeologists later realized that the seventh layer comprised two distinct kinds of rubble, and they accordingly divided it into two categories, VIIa and VIIb.

The lowest layer was composed of ruined buildings on which the sun last shone a good 5000 years ago. The second layer, or Troy II, was burned down by some enemy hand about 4200 years ago. The third, fourth and fifth layers, Troys III-V, covered the period 2200-1750 B.C., while Troy VI was a vanished civilization which flourished between 1750 and 1300 B.C. Research undertaken by the American archaeologist Blegen indicates that the gigantic walls of the latter period, which are still in a relatively good state of preservation today, were demolished by an earthquake. This assumption is based on the fact that a large number of unconnected walls all exhibit cracks running in the same direction. Dörpfeld took Troy VI for the Troy of Homer, but he was mistaken.

Troy VIIa was destroyed by enemies about '1200 B.C., which would agree nicely with the ancient tradition giving the date of Troy's destruction as 1185 B.C. Blegen presumes that Homer's city lies in that layer, and it would in fact seem that that is where the greatest heroic epic in human history is buried. Professor Brandenstein of Graz also considers City VIIa to be Homeric Troy. He did not allow himself to be misled, like Dörpfeld, by the much more impressive walls in the sixth layer. The remaining three layers, Troys VIIb-IX, embrace the period 1200 B.C.-A.D. 400. The hill has been repeatedly raked around, and the various layers have eaten into one another. Anyone visiting the mound today will find it difficult to imagine how archaeologists could ever have succeeded in separating the ten periods from one another, or have recognized that the seventh layer contained two completely distinct cities, and so shed light on the almost inconceivable life-span of a place which existed from the dawn of prehistory until Roman times.

The archaeologist Wilhelm Dörpfeld wrote: 'There is, to my knowledge, no other place in the world where so many distinctly perceivable layers of buildings and masses of debris have been preserved as on the hill of Hissarlik ... That the remains of ancient buildings should reach a height of fifty feet, and that this rubble should allow of a clear differentiation between nine or more chronologically distinct layers, is something which occurs only at Hissarlik ... Here are ruins dating from a far distant time when we in Europe were still ignorant of any kind of building ... To wander over this ruined site is as if to find yourself in a great museum ...' But Dörpfeld's remarks are already out of date. We have since unearthed the ruins of many more ancient settlements in the East, places which were inhabited without interruption for far longer than Hissarlik.

The tenth or uppermost layer of rubble belongs to Roman times, to the period when Christ was alive. Cultured Romans considered it good form to have paid a visit to 'Troia'. Roman tourists were shown Paris's lyre and a stone which depicted the Trojan heroes playing on a gaming-board. Troy was an object of the greatest interest to the tourists of ancient Rome, especially after the publication of Virgil's *Aeneid*, which told how, after the fall of Troy, Aeneas and his son Ascanius wandered off to Italy, where Ascanius founded the city of Alba Longa in Latium – later to become Rome.

When Constantine the Great transferred his residence from Rome to Constantinople in A.D. 350, his first thought had been to erect his new capital at Troy. However, the Byzantines for unknown reasons allowed Troy to fall into decay, and the Turks, to whom the land has belonged since 1306, have never settled there. The village which now stands near the ruins only came into being in recent times. Troy represents an interesting exception among the age-old city foundations of mankind, for a site whose convenient location has encouraged many generations of people to build cities on it is usually still occupied by an important metropolis today – as in the case of Alexandria, for example (founded in 332 B.C.), or Paris (once the Lucotecia of 3000 years ago), or Jerusalem (founded about 2000 B.C.), or Lo Yang in China (5000 years old). But Troy was already a legend by the time Greece reached her prime. Absolutely nothing remained of her pristine glory – or rather, nothing of *ancient* Troy was visible to the human eye.

But if nothing visible remained of Troy, and if mankind did not know

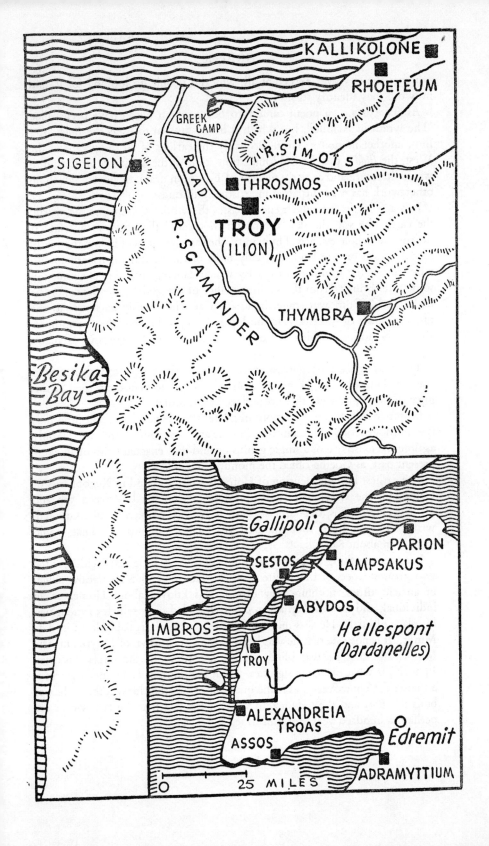

whether the city ever existed at all, why did people go looking for it, and how did they identify its site?

About 850 B.C., a poem came into being which might have been called 'The wrath of Achilles', but which is better known to us as the *Iliad*, after Ilios, another name for Troy. Probably the earliest of all the poems of the West, the *Iliad* is the classical foundation-stone of the West's contribution to world literature and an early nucleus of European dramatic poetry which no other work has ever surpassed in artistic significance.

It is a work of art which encompasses the whole contents of the world, the earth, the sea, the sky, the round moon and the unwearying sun. It mirrors the whole essence of humanity, the cares and joys of living, the yearly round of toil on the land, the daily tasks of the herdsman, fisherman and woodcutter, the moments of ecstasy which dancing or the poet's song can sometimes bring. From the sublime reality of the gods to the depths of the underworld, from war, rage, infatuation and inexorable harshness to the finest impulses of sympathy, friendship and conjugal love – there is nothing, absolutely nothing which lies outside the scope of this colossus of man's poetic art.

The *Iliad* is always regarded as the work of the poet Homer. But who was this Homer? Did he exist? And was only one man concerned in this gigantic work, or were there countless contributors?

In spite of all the interpolations of a later date which it contains, the *Iliad* is so homogeneous and so uniform in style and composition that we can only assume the existence of a single genius behind this 'enacted truth of an ever-present past' as Goethe called the monumental epic.

The earliest known mention of Homer's name is found in Xenophanes of Colophon, the Greek poet and philosopher who lived between 570 and 480 B.C. Herodotus, the 'father of history' whom we have so often quoted, writes: 'Homer lived four hundred years before my time.' That would have been about 850 B.C.

It is an astonishing thing, but we know extremely little about either of the two greatest poets of the Western world, Homer and Shakespeare. Even in ancient times, nothing very certain was known about Homer as an individual, and no less than seven cities wrangled over which of them was his place of birth. He was undoubtedly a Greek and probably lived in Asia Minor. It is possible that he was born in the Greek town of Smyrna in Asia Minor, and that he was blind, which, according to the Greek historian Ephorus, is what his name signifies. Even the number of Homer's works is a matter for controversy, as is the question of whether he was the author of both the *Iliad* and the *Odyssey*, in view of the fact that the two works are perhaps a hundred years apart in time.

The *Iliad* describes the battle of Troy. The poet does not deal with the whole ten years which elapsed between the arrival of the Greeks and the fall of Troy, but only with fifty-one days, during which period we live through the whole of the war up to and including the destruction of the city. The division of the *Iliad* into twenty-four books is not attributable to Homer, but to the Alexandrine scholars of a later age who split it up according to the number of letters in the Greek alphabet. This arrangement bears little relation to the text, and the blind genius would have shaken his head sadly at it. It is likely that the 'old *Iliad*' was somewhat shorter than its present 'Alexandrine setting', and that it was expanded at Athens even as early as Pisistratus' day, or 550 B.C. A mass of varied material has undoubtedly been interpolated into the work, including, for instance, legends which originated in the southern part of Asia Minor.

Just as Shakespeare culled the plots of most of his plays from collections of old stories or historical works, so Homer built his amazing poems out of ancient folklore and traditions. The warlike events described in Homer's *Iliad* must have taken place in 1184 B.C., for that is the year in which the scholars of antiquity set Troy's destruction.

Homer's genius fell prey to the pardonable temptation of painting his compatriots in a more favourable light than their enemies. When the casualties of the two warring races are counted, for instance, the Greeks only lose fifty dead as compared with the Trojans' two hundred. Even the Trojans' victories are never entirely honourable. The valiant Greeks are often fated to be ambushed by concealed bowmen. Achilles himself was shot down by an arrow (although it is true that the *Iliad* contains no reference to this), whereas Hector, the Trojans' greatest hero, appears to have been worsted in fair fight.

Europe saw Troy as a piece of poetic fiction on Homer's part, and the ruins of the city slept on undisturbed beneath the hill of Hissarlik. Never-theless, since the long Trojan war could not have been a mere invention of Homer's, since such a detailed story must have had an historical basis, and since both the Greeks and the Romans assumed that 'Homeric' Troy must lie in the vicinity of the hill which became known much later as Hissarlik, the ancient city had to be somewhere near there.

In the last four hundred years, many scholars have attempted to find out where the ancient city must have stood. Particularly favoured as a possible site was the village of Bunarbashi, only two and a half miles south of the hill of Hissarlik. Helmuth von Moltke was a prominent supporter of this theory. 'We simply let our military instincts lead us to the spot which, then just as today, would most have lent itself to the construction of an unscalable fortress.' Moltke was wrong, however.

The Bunarbashi theory conflicted with the traditional view of the local peasants, which was that Troy lay beneath Hissarlik. Frank Calvert, an Englishman acting as United States Consul in the Dardanelles, eventually bought part of the hill of Hissarlik with a view to excavating it, his principal aim being to prove that Bunarbashi could *not* be Troy. The project involved considerable expense, however, and when the British Museum declined to associate itself with the trial diggings Calvert abandoned his idea. Then one day he was visited by a millionaire, a remarkable man who told him quite simply that he wanted to dig up Troy and find King Priam's treasure. Calvert was delighted to be relieved of his worries. The odd stranger's name was Heinrich Schliemann.

Schliemann was one of the most interesting personalities of the last century. A German who later became an American and a poor man who worked his way up to millionairedom, he was at once tradesman and scholar, visionary and realist, genius and pedant, a restless globe-trotter and one of the most tenacious archaeologists who ever excavated the site of his youthful dreams: Troy.

His daughter, significantly named Andromache, who lives in America, recently described an incident which occurred in her childhood. She remembers how her father once asked her what she was reading. '*Ivanhoe,* by Sir Walter Scott,' she replied. 'Read me a sentence,' said her father. Little Andromache had only read a few words when her father interrupted her and began to recite page after page of the book from memory. He had learned the great thick book by heart at the age of nineteen, and even at the age of sixty he could still remember it word for word.

Heinrich Schliemann's life-story sounds like a fairy-tale. He was a poor parson's son from Neu-Buckow, Mecklenburg-Schwerin. As a boy, he fell in love with a little girl of fourteen called Minna Meincke. She returned his affections, a happy circumstance which kindled his ambition hugely. Heinrich was a shop-assistant in a small general store in Fürstenberg, where he sold herrings, butter, potatoes, brandy, milk, salt, coffee, sugar, oil and, last but not least, tallow candles. It was also his job to sweep out the shop, and he later recalled sadly that his occupation only brought him into contact with the humblest strata of society. One day, while lifting a tub which was too heavy for him, Schliemann suffered an injury to his chest. He roamed off to Hamburg, where he signed on as cabin-boy on the small brig *Dorothea.* The ship sailed from Hamburg on November 28th, 1841. During the night of December 11th-12th, it foundered. Schliemann was rescued, and later secured a post with a commercial house in Amsterdam. He learned how to write correctly from a calligraphist in Brussels. 'There is no greater incentive to study,' he said in after life, 'than poverty, and the sure conviction that strenuous work can free one from it.' He evolved an interesting method of learning languages, which entailed much reading aloud, no translating, writing essays on enthralling subjects in the foreign language in question and, above all, committing a great deal to memory. Nightly repetition was of the greatest value, said the persevering Schliemann, and he added: 'I recommend this method to everyone.'

He first learnt Dutch, then English, and then French, Spanish, Portuguese, Italian, Swedish and Polish. It all seemed to take far too long, thought Schliemann impatiently, even though he learned these languages in a matter of months. Russian he mastered by committing to memory an old Russian translation, *The Adventures of Telemachus*. 'It occurred to me that I would make better progress if I had someone to whom I could recite *The Adventures of Telemachus* aloud, so I paid a poor Jew four francs a week to visit me for two hours every evening and listen to me declaiming in Russian – a language of which he understood not a syllable.'

Schliemann was eventually doing so well as a commercial agent in Petersburg that he decided to propose to Minna. However, he learned that his childhood sweetheart had contracted a marriage only a few days before. 'I felt completely incapable of any form of activity and became quite ill,' wrote the disappointed suitor. On July 4th, 1850, during his stay in California, the country became part of the United States, and all the people staying there, including Schliemann, became American citizens. In 1852 he opened an agency in Moscow to handle wholesale purchases of indigo. He did huge deals in indigo, dye-woods, saltpetre, sulphur and lead. He learned Greek and read all the Greek classics (in particular the *Iliad* and the *Odyssey*) over and over again in their original tongue. To his dying day, Schliemann knew both the *Iliad* and the *Odyssey* by heart with such accuracy that he could recite them forwards or backwards line for line.

By this time Schliemann had become a very wealthy man. He retired completely from active business and began for the first time in his life to take a good look at the world. Starting in Sweden, he travelled to Denmark, Germany, Italy, Egypt and Nubia, where he speedily learned Arabic. He roamed through Syria and visited Smyrna, the Cyclades, Athens and the islands of Ithaca. Back in Russia once more, he estimated the value of the goods he imported in six months at no less than ten million marks. They were gold marks in those days, too, worth twenty times their modern value. When his Russian wife refused to desert the land of the Tsars, he divorced her, advertised the fact that he was looking for a Greek wife, and, at the age of forty-seven, picked himself a nineteen-year-old Greek girl from one of the photographs he received. He christened their son Agamemnon.

In 1864 he travelled to Tunis and visited the ruins of Carthage. Then, revisiting Egypt on the way, he journeyed to India. His subsequent itinerary included Ceylon, Madras, Calcutta, Benares, Agra, Lucknow, Delhi, the Himalayas, Java, Saigon and China. Schliemann climbed the Great Wall, travelled on to Japan, and then sailed off across the Pacific to San Francisco, California. During the passage, which lasted fifty days, he wrote his first book, *China and Japan*. After that, he settled down in Paris and devoted himself to the study of archaeology.

Then came the day when the millionaire went to see Frank Calvert, the man who owned half the hill of Hissarlik. On October 11th, 1871, Schliemann began the first of his four extensive excavations of the mound. They covered eleven months out of the next two years, and by the end of that time Troy had been discovered.

In the course of his researches, the brilliant scholar fell prey to an error. He worked his way through all the layers of Troy until he came to the lowest. Then, while rummaging about in the past, he came upon some fortifications, the ruins of a very ancient city which had been burnt down, and immense treasures of gold and jewellery. Schliemann dubbed this find 'the treasure of Priam'. (The collection was almost completely destroyed in Berlin during the last war.) Schliemann believed that he had discovered Homeric Troy, but his city belonged to a much earlier period. In fact, of course, he *had* found Troy. His only error lay in mistaking which layer he was dealing with. Astonishing as it may seem, Schliemann had dug down *past* Homer's Troy (VIIa), for the gold and silver and the ruined palace which he found belonged to Troy II, destroyed about 2200 B.C. However, he had gained his main objective. He had found out where the legendary city had been sleeping its millennial sleep. It was only shortly before his death that Schliemann realized his error, but by that time it was too late for him to start digging again.

Before he took leave of his fascinating life, Schliemann carried out excavations at Mycenae, Ithaca and Orchomenos. He unearthed a portion of Tiryns and intended to excavate the palace of Minos in Crete. But one lifetime was not long enough, and Schliemann had to leave it to others to complete the projects which he had started or planned.

Schliemann's closest associate was Wilhelm Dörpfeld, the brilliant archaeologist who only died in 1940, at the age of eighty-six. It was Dörpfeld who excavated Old Olympia and Pergamum, and he carried on Schliemann's work at Hissarlik with such perseverance that Troy came to life under his hands stone by stone. This gifted man was the author of a theory of method in excavation which is used by archaeologists all over the world today. He was an architect, and could form such an accurate mental picture of whatever the earth did not immediately disclose that subsequent excavations always proved him right. Dörpfeld wanted to be linked with Greece even in death, and he lies buried in his own plot of ground of Leukas, the place which he identified with Ithaca.

Schliemann was buried in Athens, which was equally appropriate, for it was he who proved what had for centuries only been dimly suspected: that Troy and the heroic epic called the *Iliad* were not merely the products of Homer's wild imagination. They really existed in terms of stone and gold, flesh and blood.

GRAVES TELL SECRETS: PREHISTORY

Agamemnon really existed, and so did Heracles, the strongest man in world history. Mycenae was not just legend, nor Tiryns mere imagination. The whole prehistory of Greece,
with its legendary figures and Homeric cities, is being dug up stone by stone. It was all true.

ISTORY is the written past. It is tied to paper, metal and stone. It
takes us back only as far as writings and inscriptions exist to tell us
of human activity on earth.

Yet the greater part of humanity's past lies in times when there was no
writing, only verbal tradition. It is these interminable ages without written
records or firm dates which we call prehistory. They are the periods of
time which precede our written sources of historical information. Only the
ground can tell us what happened during those times, and the true historians
of prehistory are field archaeologists.

Techniques of investigation have now reached the stage where a single
fragment of pottery, the particular way in which a stone has been flaked,
the bones of a little bird, or even the radio-carbon method (C_{14}) evolved by
Professor Libby of Chicago, can often give us a pretty accurate idea of dates.
Investigators of the ground are the 'criminologists' of the good and — far
more frequently — the evil deeds which men committed in distant times.
Even the tiniest clue can be enough for them to identify religious beliefs,
often of the strangest kind, or superstitions, or various aspects of human
activity — in short, the deeds and misdeeds, large and small, which make up
the period generally termed prehistory.

The history of Greece as it is known to us from written evidence only
covers a span of about 600 years. It begins with the first Olympiad in 776 B.C.
and ends in 133 B.C., the date when Greece and Asia Minor became Roman
provinces.

Before this lies a very much more extensive period, embracing a span of
approximately 3000 years, which is lost in a darkness only illuminated by
legends, myths and heroic sagas which were passed on by word of mouth
and not written down until much later.

Taking as a basis the materials used for man's most important tools and
weapons, science has divided prehistory into the following main categories:
the Stone (or Palaeolithic) Age, the Ceramic (or Neolithic) Age, the Bronze
Age, and the Iron Age. At first men shaped their weapons and implements
out of stone, then they invented pottery and learned how to bake clay vessels
and, finally, they discovered the application of metals and their alloys. Stone
came before bronze and bronze before iron. It was the same the whole
world over.

354

Greece does not appear to have been inhabited during the Palaeolithic Age. Achilles' native land, fertile Thessaly, played a decisive role in bringing settlers into the area, for during the Neolithic Age people arrived there from Asia Minor and made it their permanent abode. The earliest civilization in Greece is known, from its chief site of discovery in Thessaly, as 'Sesklo civilization'. It lasted from 3000 until 2800 B.C. and expanded over the whole Greek area.

The next immigrant invasion came from the abode of Danubian civilization in the Seven Hills region of Hungary, arriving in two waves. People have attempted on insufficient grounds to designate these immigrants as proto-Indo-Europeans. In reality, they only got as far as Thessaly. Their civilization is called the 'Dimini civilization' from the main site of its discovery. The second wave reached the northern Peloponnese. The remainder of Greece was at that time dominated by the first stages of an early Helladic civilization which roughly lasted from 2500 to 2400 B.C., and coincided with the transition to the age of metal.

The two stages which follow are only evolutionary stages, and are known as Early Helladic II and III (2400-1900 B.C.). They represent the link with the Bronze Age. In 1900 B.C. a new race appeared from the north and devastated many settlements. There is reasonable justification for assuming that they were Indo-Europeans, but there is still no proof that they were already 'Greeks' proper. Their arrival coincided with the beginning of the pre-Mycenaean Bronze Age (also termed Middle Helladic). The cultural transition to the Late Helladic period or Mycenaean Bronze Age followed about 1600 B.C. The appearance of the so-called war-chariot, however, a light two-wheeled racing and fighting vehicle introduced into the Near East by the Indians at about the same time, is probably an indication that a new race had arrived: the Mycenaean Greeks to whom the heroes of Homer belonged.

Mycenaean civilization, which was strongly influenced by Crete, was completely annihilated about 1200 B.C. by the so-called Aegean Migration. This racial cataclysm was undoubtedly connected with the greatest of all the prehistoric migrations, that of the Urn-field People — so termed by students of prehistory because they cremated their dead and buried their remains in large urns. These urns were then sunk into the ground in regular cemeteries, forming the large urn-fields which are their authors' legacy to us today. The great migration had its exit in Central Germany, and eventually led to an upheaval in almost every seat of civilization in the contemporary world. One race after another was set in motion, a phenomenon which brought about, for instance, the total destruction of the Hittites as a great power in the Near East. Even Egypt became threatened by the convulsion, and it is possible that the Indian migration from the area between the

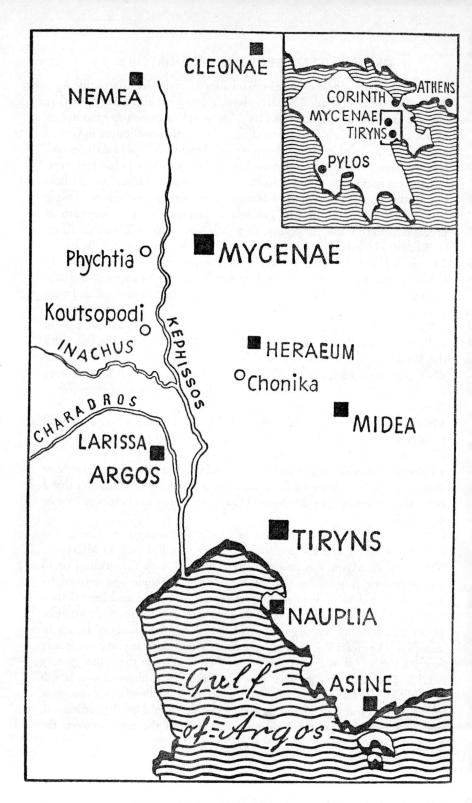

The large fortified towns of the Mycenaean period

Caucasus and the Urals north of the Caspian Sea should also be linked with it. The whole of Greece was burned down by these invaders in 1200 B.C. Some hundred years later, the Dorian Greeks roamed into the country in company with Illyrian tribes.

Two cities were pre-eminent during the Bronze Age of prehistoric Greece: Mycenae and Tiryns. Both stood in the district of Argolis in the Peloponnese. Modern archaeologists might never have looked for either of them if Homer had not mentioned them in his *Iliad*. According to Homer, Mycenae was the stronghold of Agamemnon, the prince who besieged Troy.

It had long been disputed whether Agamemnon was an historical character or only a legendary figure. Perhaps the worst sign of our times is a propensity to banish everything we cannot measure or count to the realm of myth, imagination or poetic fiction. Of course, it is a trait which makes for scientific accuracy, but in giving it free rein we miss something of immense value. We miss realities which cannot be measured, we have no more respect for myths and no more affinity with the real roots of life. Yet at one time, in an age when the dangerous art of writing and the even more dangerous art of printing were still unknown, words carried weight.

All the Greek myths originated in the Mycenaean period, a prehistoric era when men were forging bronze, a time between 1000 and 2000 years before the birth of Christ. The work of archaeologists during the past hundred years has translated one legendary city and one mythological hero after another from shadowy existence into reality. We know today that Agamemnon, the man who besieged Troy, really existed. Alan J. B. Wace dates him at about 1200 B.C. Homer gives us the names of Agamemnon's father, Atreus, and his brother, Menelaus. These men, too, must have been authentic figures.

Legend also tells us about Heracles, whose descendants the Heraclides were the heroes of the Dorian migration, the last major influx into Greece. He settled down at Tiryns in the service of the lord of Mycenae, his wicked uncle Eurystheus. Heracles was the strongest man in the whole of world history. At some period more than 3000 years ago, such a man must have existed, for a titanic figure like his could never have been pure invention. Even in Roman times, schoolchildren were still told about the days of Heracles, or Hercules, as they called him. It appears that Eurystheus of Mycenae was uneasy about having such a strong retainer as Heracles virtually on his doorstep, for the popular hero only lived nine miles away in neighbouring Tiryns. Eurystheus accordingly set his nephew twelve tasks, each one harder than the last, designed to put an end to him. Heracles' labours eventually took him to the Straits of Gibraltar, the gateway to the Atlantic which the ancients called 'The Pillars of Hercules'.

It seemed that a city which was linked with names such as Eurystheus and Heracles, Atreus and Agamemnon, must exist somewhere or other, but the place where the city was supposed to have stood was now occupied by an insignificant-looking hill. Undiscouraged, two Englishmen and a Turkish governor began to dig there. They were Lord Elgin, Lord Sligo and Veli Pasha. These gentlemen were less concerned with digging up evidence of prehistory, however, than with finding sculptures, antiques and treasures which they could take away and turn into cash.

Unlike them, Heinrich Schliemann was prompted by motives of respect for mythology and a belief in the truth of prehistoric traditions. He was convinced that he could produce proof of the authenticity of Homer's descriptions. In 1874, with the excavation of Troy already behind him, he started trial diggings on the hill at Mycenae with the intention of finding Agamemnon's grave and the treasures of Atreus. It was a bold venture, much as if someone set out to dig up the treasure of the Nibelungs today. When Schliemann began serious excavation in 1876, he opened up a whole new world for archaeology. He found five royal graves dating from the 16th century B.C., graves damaged only by the ravages of time but not by any human agency. They had neither been broken open nor plundered. Schliemann's excavations were costing him 100,000 gold marks a year by this time, but he knew only too well how great and enduring a reputation he was winning. As he himself wrote: 'I could not abandon the excavations at Mycenae before I had thoroughly explored all the royal graves. It is well known what a wonderful measure of success attended my excavations, and how immense and remarkable were the treasures with which I enriched the Greek nation. Far in the distant future, travellers from all quarters of the world will still be flocking into the Greek capital to visit the Mycenaean Museum and marvel at and study the fruits of my disinterested labours.' Between 1877 and 1878, the Greek archaeologist Stamatakes continued the work and found a sixth grave, which he christened 'The grave of Agamemnon or the treasure of Atreus'. At the turn of the century a second Greek called Tsountas followed in Heinrich Schliemann's footsteps, and a fairly accurate picture of Mycenaean civilization began to take shape. Keramopoullos and the German archaeologist Rodenwaldt also set their spades to the task, the British School at Athens worked on the hill from 1920 onwards, and, finally, the site was dug and explored by that gifted British archaeologist Alan J. B. Wace, the man who clearly recognized that Mycenaean culture between 1400 and 1200 B.C. was an early expression of the spirit of Greece, and who found the forty-two tablets in Linear B script.

Archaeology thus shed light first on prehistory and then on people who had actually left written records.

GRAVES TELL SECRETS: PREHISTORY

The citadel at Mycenae was already occupied by men in 3000 B.C. — 5000 years ago. The first 'Greek' tribes appeared on the scene about 2000 B.C. Their arrival marked the beginning of the city's golden age. Mycenae gradually established links with Crete and adopted the island's customs, habits, art, technical experience and script — in short, everything which we know as civilization. Nevertheless, it was only after Crete's power had been broken and the mainland States were free to develop independently that Mycenae attained her greatest heights. In 1350 B.C. the city was enlarged, and the legendary Cyclopean walls with their Lion Gate were built. Later Greek generations did not think it possible that ordinary mortals could have piled such massive blocks of stone on top of one another, and so they ascribed the work to giants, one-eyed Titans whom they called *Cyclops*, or 'round-eyes'. The citadel of Tiryns was also surrounded by Cyclopean walls like these. Tiryns and Mycenae probably represent the very earliest large fortified towns in Europe.

A whole chain of fortresses extended across the district of Argolis, from Tiryns via Nauplia, Asine, Midaea, Argos and Prosymna to Mycenae, the largest and strongest of them all. The majority of these sites exhibit traces of the violent spate of destruction which engulfed everything in 1100 B.C. The fortresses were first pillaged and then burned down. We do not know how long Mycenae remained unoccupied, but people were living there again somewhere between 1100 and 750 B.C. In 468 B.C. Mycenae was attacked by her jealous neighbour Argos and eventually razed to the ground. When the Greek geographer Pausanias visited the site in the 2nd century A.D., he found it in ruins. And, remarkably enough, the site was never rebuilt but lay buried under rubble, where it turned into an insignificant-looking hill like Tiryns or Troy.

It is astonishing how many details of daily life become evident from graves. The six Mycenaean shaft-graves of the 16th century B.C. tell the story of a whole civilization. The human skeletons lay stretched out on their backs, most of them with their heads pointing towards the east, that is to say, looking westwards. The faces were covered by golden masks. They are, as Hermann Bengtson has pointed out, the first essays at portraiture in Europe. The skulls had crumbled away, but the masks survived, and so we are virtually able to look into the faces of the Mycenaean princes as they were during their lifetime. They belong either to a Nordic or Mediterranean race, and the varying beard-styles are clearly distinguishable. Similar golden masks, dating from the 6th century B.C., were found at Trebenishtshe in the Balkans.

The shaft-graves of Mycenae contained numerous fragments of gold-leaf scattered about above and below the skeletons. These little pieces of gold-leaf had obviously been sewn on to the cloths which had once swathed the corpses. Weapons and implements lying beside the dead men included metal receptacles, clay utensils, breast-plates, swords, daggers, knives and chisels. The graves were obviously family vaults. Grave IV contained the bodies of five adults and two children. The three corpses in Grave III were loaded with golden ornaments. Large golden crowns were found on two of the skulls. Thirty-five arrow-heads lay in a heap, and the corpses of two babies were completely encased in gold. It was evident that the children had been laid to rest with loving care.

The women of the Mycenaean civilization used to set great store by cosmetics, as their silver tweezers and little cosmetic jars and spoons go to prove. A semi-circular ivory comb, ear-rings, necklaces, finger-rings and thirty-seven golden buttons in an alabaster bowl all indicate that a feeling for jewellery and dainty little fashion accessories existed here 3500 years ago. However, it seems that the ladies of Mycenae seldom, if ever, looked at themselves in the mirror. One metal mirror was all that was found, and archaeologists are even in doubt as to whether the object really was a mirror at all.

The men wore short aprons or a kind of short trousers. Nakedness was considered unseemly, and the women of the upper class wore long chemises and tight, short-sleeved jackets which sometimes left the breasts bare. We know nothing about footwear in the early and middle Bronze Age, even though fragments of linen have managed to remain preserved over this amazingly long lapse of time. Among other things which the graves yielded up were pieces of wood (mainly tiny fragments of cypress), razors, a gaming-board, gaiter-fastenings, helmet-crests in gold, and a thousand articles of daily use.

We know that the Mycenaeans were familiar with eagles, swallows, butterflies, the nautilus and the octopus. Sea-monsters seem to have played a prominent role in their thoughts. The walls of their stone burial-places bore the earliest representations of a two-wheeled war-chariot ever to be found in Hellas. Oxen, sheep, pigs, goats and donkeys were the principal domestic animals, but chickens, ducks and geese were also kept, and portrayals of horses are frequently found. It appears that, then just as now, man's most loyal companion was the dog. The rulers of those days used to take their favourite dog with them into their graves, as canine skeletons indicate.

The graves have disclosed a life of amazing diversity and richness. The heroes of antiquity are throwing off their shroud of dust, debris and ruins and a prehistoric world four thousand years old which had long ago entered the realm of legend is coming to life once more.

THE WORLD'S FIRST DEMOCRACY

We Athenians fought the Persian at Marathon single-handed. When he returned, and we were not strong enough to defend ourselves against him on land, we boarded our ships one and all, and in company with the other Greeks, fought the sea-battle at Salamis.' *Thucydides,* I, 73.

GREECE is a rocky peninsula, almost treeless and mainly barren. It stands there, insignificant, small and rather forlorn in its corner of the Mediterranean. Yet Greek history, the history of this peninsula, forms the basis of Western civilization, regardless of whether it is confined to a span of 600 years, as the convention used to be, or whether, as the latest excavations strongly suggest, it is assigned a span of about 1300 years.

The real history of Greece was always assumed to have begun in 776 B.C., with the first Olympiad. It ended in 133 B.C., when the Greek world passed under Roman domination. In these 600 years the Greeks made more concentrated history than any other race in the Western world. In the beginning was Greece: twenty centuries have lived off the fruits of her experience.

It was here that a little band of men dethroned the blind and incalculable deities of the East which had ruled the world for so many thousands of years. The Greeks fought their way through the tangled misconceptions of oriental mythology to the conviction that the Universe has a pattern, and that by the exercise of reason man can comprehend it. The Greeks recognized the concept of virtue. The Greeks were the first men to make scientific truth the object of thought. It is the Greeks whom we have to thank for our notions of freedom within the State and equality before the law; 2000 years have done nothing to pale the glory of this inexhaustible and amazing heritage. It is this bed-rock of remarkable historical vivacity, this 'classical civilization' existing at the very beginning of all European thought, this spiritual marvel which was Greece, which must still form the indispensable basis of any understanding of the present, whether today, tomorrow, or countless years hence when you and I have long since turned to dust and ashes.

The Greeks passed on their store of knowledge to the Romans, and the Romans united the spiritual order of Greece with Christianity. It is this unity which supports the edifice of Western civilization — which *is* Western civilization, in fact, for without it we should plunge back two thousand years in time.

In the 2nd millennium B.C., wave upon wave of migrants invaded Greece. They were Indo-European mountain tribes who pushed farther and farther

GREECE

southwards until they eventually reached and occupied the Peloponnese. The Achaeans were followed by the Aeolians and the Ionians, and finally by the Dorians, who settled in the Peloponnese, as well as on Crete, Rhodes and many other islands. The 'Dorian Migration' burst in on the ancient civilizations of the Minoans and Mycenaeans and swamped the Achaeans who had arrived some centuries earlier.

The numerous Greek races never established a common capital, but they nevertheless regarded themselves as a single people and called everyone else *barbaroi*, or foreigners. Despite all their differences, the Greek races were united by a common language, common religious beliefs, the oracle at Delphi, a kind of league of nations (the Amphictyonic League), and their great national festivals: the Olympic, Isthmian, Nemean and Pythian, the most famous of which were the Olympic games. All the tribes which spoke Greek and were linked by Delphi, the League and the Games, called themselves by the common name *Hellenes*, and their country *Hellas*. The name 'Greeks' comes from Italy, where the first people to build a Greek city on Italian soil were probably the Graei. The Latin development of this name was *Graeci*, which was how our own word 'Greeks' originated.

The majority of historical works merely tell us about the amazing evolution of the Greek peoples. If we want to get behind the secret of the immense cultural achievements of Greece, however, we must try to identify the characteristics of her two largest component races, the Dorians and Ionians. The Dorians were mountain people. The Ionians came from the sea-coasts. The Dorians – as Sparta demonstrated – were a practical, hardy, conservative, helpful and good-natured people. The Ionians were probably more temperamental and imaginative. They were seafarers, merchants, 'cosmopolitans', and formed the intellectual side of the blend. They travelled widely, they saw a great deal of the world and talked about their experiences, they were fond of finery and they invented the drama. It was these two large and utterly different races which determined the ultimate destiny and success of Greece. They made as fortunate a combination as Anglo-Saxon and Celt have done in the United Kingdom – the English and Scots of today.

As time went on, the Greeks founded colonies on the coasts of Asia Minor, in southern Italy and Sicily, and on the northern shores of Africa. They even went as far as Gibraltar, significantly named the 'Pillars of Hercules'. The Italian settlements of Tarentum, Sybaris, Croton, Cumae and Neapolis were all Greek foundations, as were Syracuse in Sicily and Cyrene on the North African coast. Massilia (modern Marseilles) was also a Greek commercial centre.

The Greeks' 'motherland' was not Hellas or Greece, but the *polis* or city-State. Greece was split up into hundreds of such political microcosms. The city-States passed through four phases of evolution. They began by being monarchies, but the kings gradually disappeared, until in the 8th and 7th centuries B.C. they had ceased to exist. Monarchy was replaced by oligarchy, or 'government by the few'. Oligarchy in its turn gave way to tyranny. One social group or another was always discontented, and a tyrant rose to power on the strength of his 'programme'. When he had broken every one of his promises, he was overthrown (normally assassinated), and it was then the people's turn: a 'democracy' or 'government by the people' came into being. Greek history has shown that *tyrannis* or rule by a tyrant was the surest precursor of democracy, and that a tyrant always came between oligarchy and democracy.

When the tyrant Pisistratus died a natural death at Athens in 527 B.C., at a ripe old age, he handed over the reins of government to his two sons, whose names were Hippias and Hipparchus. Hippias, the elder, devoted himself to State affairs, and Hipparchus to poetry and amorous escapades.

There lived in Athens at this time a beautiful young man called Harmodius, who was in love with a middle-class citizen by the name of Aristogeiton. The course of these two Athenians' passionate friendship ran smooth until one day when royal Hipparchus took a fancy to Harmodius' exceptional charms. Harmodius sent him about his business, however, and told everything to his friend Aristogeiton, who immediately flew into a jealous rage.

When Hipparchus' overtures had been rejected a second time, he decided to wound his idol's feelings. It happened that the object of his passion had a young and virginal sister who had been chosen to 'carry the basket' in the religious procession during the great Panathenaea of 514 B.C. Hipparchus saw to it that this honourable privilege was taken away from the young girl on the grounds that 'she was far too wicked for it'. This insult brought Harmodius and his friend Aristogeiton to such a pitch of fury that they decided only to wait until the day of the Panathenaea before revenging themselves on Hipparchus and overthrowing the tyranny. It was an ideal occasion, since no one could attend the festival armed without arousing suspicion. When the time came, they fell upon Hipparchus in blind fury and stabbed him to death.

Aristogeiton managed to escape temporarily, although Harmodius was killed on the spot. But if two tyrants are in power, and they are brothers to boot, there is little point in only killing one of them. An attempt on the life of Hippias, the elder brother, miscarried in the general confusion. Hippias now became cautious and uneasy. He had numerous Athenians executed and tortured Aristogeiton to death. It is related that a girl called Leaena was also in love with the handsome Harmodius. The beautiful girl was subjected to torture, but she would not reveal the names of the other conspirators. Instead, she bit off her tongue and spat it in the faces of her captors.

The tyrant Hippias controlled the administration for another three years until 510 B.C., when he was forced to abdicate. Closely escorted, he managed to reach the court of the Persian king Darius, and twenty years later when he was a very old man, he had an opportunity of seeing the striking-power of democracy in action. From the Persian ranks, he watched his Athenian compatriots winning their victory at Marathon. Harmodius' and Aristogeiton's action became the symbol of Athenian liberty. Cleisthenes took Athens and gave her the first democratic government in world history. That was in the year 507 B.C. From then on, dangerous individuals — i.e. men who exhibited any tendency towards becoming demagogues or tyrants — could be exiled. Any citizen whom a majority of at least 6000 votes declared to be dangerous was obliged to leave the country for ten years. People cast their votes by scratching their names on pieces of clay. This was 'ostracism', a system 2500 years old which might well come into fashion again sometime!

Meanwhile, Sparta had grown into the most powerful military State in Greece. Still clinging to a primitive monarchical form of government prescribed in the strict legal code laid down by Lycurgus, she watched her democratic rival Athens with mounting jealousy.

It was at about this time that the Greeks began to develop the talents which were to make them unique in the history of the world: science and philosophy.

Thales, the first Greek philosopher, was a citizen of Miletus. He won universal admiration in Greece by predicting a solar eclipse for May 28th, 585 B.C., which duly occurred. Thales believed that each tiny component of the world was alive, and that plants, metals and animals were inhabited by an immortal soul just as human beings were. When he was once asked what he considered difficult, Thales answered: 'To know myself.' And when he was asked what he considered easy, he replied: 'To give advice.'

Pythagoras, who was born on the island of Samos, was a Greek philosopher, but he lived from 529 B.C. onwards at Croton in Italy. He is reported to have been the most ardent scientific investigator of all his contemporaries. This man became the focus of a sort of religious brotherhood at Croton devoted as much to philosophy as to a new moral order. It is worthy of note that, half a thousand years before the birth of Christ, Pythagoras' most important precept was the immortality of the soul. His amazing intellect was not directed towards mathematics and geometry alone. He also laid down rules for music, engaged in the study of harmony, and was an astronomer of repute.

Heraclitus was a recluse and a meditator. This philosopher from Ephesus lived between 540 and 475 B.C. He was possibly the founder of metaphysics, or the doctrine of the ultimate unity and coherence of all life. To him, heat and cold, good and evil, day and night, all formed a unity and were merely complementary halves of one and the same thing. Fire was the basic substance and rhythm the reason of the Universe. Heraclitus' lonely life, his contempt for humanity, the profundity of his philosophy and his dark and oracular pronouncements won him the name of 'the dark philosopher', while Democritus of Abdera in Thrace was christened by the Greeks 'the laughing philosopher'. Democritus' genius gave birth to seventy-two works whose subjects included atomic science and cosmology, the origins of the Universe, the soul, feeling, ethics and theology. He believed that the upper air was inhabited by beings composed of the finest atoms, beings who were much less susceptible to decay than human beings, but nevertheless mortal. Democritus lived about 450 B.C.

The poet Anacreon was born in 563 B.C. at Teos, an Ionian city on the coast of Asia Minor. He was a bon viveur who went through life in a state of permanent good humour, much as Lao-tse did in China. He was fond of wine, girls, boys, good food and singing. Although — or perhaps because — he indulged in every conceivable excess, he was reputed by the Greeks to have reached the age of eighty-five. He often got drunk, and his poems reflect their author's tipsy joviality. We only possess a few fragments of his five lyrical works. His headstone bore the legend: 'O Vine, wax full and ripe over Anacreon's grave.'

The Greeks' greatest poetess was Sappho, who was born in about 635 B.C. on Lesbos, the island of wine and flowers. She is said to have composed nine books of poems, epigrams and elegiac verse, but until recently her compositions were only known to us from quotations in ancient authors. It is only in the last fifty years that papyrus rolls have been found in Egypt which bear authentic texts of Sappho's works. Fragments of these rolls are now in Oxford, Berlin, London, Florence, Halle and Graz.

Sappho was one of the great lovers of history. But she lived for the love of others, and was perhaps the first and last woman in Europe to keep aloof from men, devote herself entirely to the service of Aphrodite, the dispenser of love, and at the same time to immortalize that love in verse. She was at once priestess and poetess. On Lesbos, young girls were enrolled in societies in preparation for marriage. The members of these sacred societies were called *thiasoi*. They worshipped Aphrodite, prepared future brides for marriage, saw to their instruction, and fostered all the fine arts, including music, singing and choral dances. These societies were institutes of conduct and deportment, 'charm schools', in fact. There were several such girls' societies at Mytilene, the capital of Lesbos, and Sappho directed the most important of them. She won a world-wide reputation and attracted girls from all quarters because, in spite of all the mistaken vilifications of later centuries, she was the greatest and most dedicated educator of girls in history. And in her devotion to the refinement and education of young girls, she was really the first to bear the cross and experience the ecstasy which is the lot of all women teachers. She saw the eternal failings of humanity and knew how to forgive them. She worried and grieved, yearned and prayed. She was patient, gentle in her reprimands, and ever ready to console. She saw her girls come, only to go again for ever. She alone remained solitary and unfulfilled, yet she was always moved and fascinated by the lives of others. She drained her cup of bitterness to the dregs of deadly resignation.

The famous Greek geographer Strabo (63 B.C.–A.D. 19) said of Sappho: 'There is, to our knowledge, no other poetess in the long ages of history to equal her.' Plato called her 'the tenth Muse'. On her death at Mytilene she was accorded the honour of a hero's burial. The life's work of this great woman is fragmentary and shattered by time. The verses of 'pure, gently laughing Sappho', as the contemporary Greek poet Alcaeus called her, will never be known to us in their entirety. She must remain silent. Yet our own era, which trusts nobody and is disinclined to believe in anything, has once more taken Sappho's shy love and perfect piety, her secret life of dreams and visions, her whole fragile frame which yearned for eternal love and goodness, and burned it on a great funeral pyre of abuse and misrepresentation. In A.D. 1073, Sappho's poems were publicly committed to the flames by the Church at Rome and Constantinople. It was not until 1897 that Grenfell and Hunt discovered some burial-shrouds made of papier mâché at Oxyrhynchus in Egypt. This material was composed of ancient rolls of papyrus, and on them were the texts of some of Sappho's poems.

With the spirit and statecraft of Greece well on the way to achieving immortality, ominous storm-clouds began to gather in the east. Persia, the great Asian power of the day, had noticed the awakening of the free peoples of Greece, for Athens had been sending aid to the oppressed Greeks in Asia Minor. The wars between Persia and Greece formed a dramatic climax in the conflict between the two great contemporary world-powers and their ways of life.

Neither sympathy nor understanding existed between the peoples of Greece and Persia. The Greeks' successful repulse of the Persian invasions under Datis and Artaphernes in 490 B.C. were simply victories of the better moral cause, or so it appeared to the Greeks. They felt that the subjects of a dictator must ultimately prove inferior to the citizens of free States. The Persians fought under compulsion, the Greeks out of conviction.

THE WORLD'S FIRST DEMOCRACY

The battles of Marathon, Thermopylae, Salamis, Plataea and Mycale were contests between the Persian giant and the Greek midget. In the end the midget won. Why? Because his morale was higher than the giant's.

Germany's great classical scholar Ulrich von Wilamowitz-Möllendorff wrote: 'The days of Marathon and Salamis decided whole epochs. They determined for the moment and for perpetuity that there was to be an individual European culture and a political and social system at once superior to and unlike any which the East—its Aryans and its Semites included—had ever possessed.'

I went to see the brilliant old man shortly before his death. He was very weak, and one of his shoulders hung down slightly. 'You know,' he said, 'they draw a very sharp distinction these days between those who work with their hands and those who work with their brains. But do you know why my shoulder is so crooked?' He gestured towards his filing-cabinet. 'I've made this movement 8,000,000 times. It's a fact, I've worked it out.'

THAT IS WHAT EARTHLY IMMORTALITY
MEANS

'... that one of the great ages of civilization be designated by the name of Pericles. Men of high standing can never be replaced.' *Leopold von Ranke, 1795-1886*

HE was the greatest Greek statesman, one of the first flesh and blood personalities to appear on the stage of European history, and the founder of Athens' importance in world history. Gifted to a degree where his wisdom became foolhardy and bordered on high treason, Themistocles was indifferent to the means he employed. He had an unusually flexible mind. No one before him had ever rendered Athens such great services, and no one before him had ever been so determined to extract due payment for them. He was considered self-seeking, avaricious, incalculable and unapproachable. Even as a young man he was so eager for fame that after the battle of Marathon he went around lost in melancholy thought during the day and was unable to sleep at night. When friends asked him what was wrong, he replied that he could not stop brooding about the reputation Miltiades had won by his victory.

Themistocles was probably born in 514 B.C., but almost nothing is known about his early years. Later, however, he elbowed his way ruthlessly into power. He had certain ideas, and he was determined to carry them out. All Greece could see the danger which threatened, the vast resources at Persia's disposal, and the way the mighty Persian armies and fleets were rolling on relentlessly out of the east. Only Themistocles knew what had to be done. Only he devised any effective counter-measures. He talked the Athenians into building two hundred ships, fortifying their harbour, and erecting higher walls. He decreed that Athens should exert all her energies in becoming a naval power. And so the Piraeus became a naval station, Athens a naval power, and Themistocles the first statesman of Greece.

Athenian merchant-ships sailed off all over the known world, to Asia in the east and as far as the Pillars of Hercules in the west. The city's coffers began to fill with gold. Even women and children worked on the new walls, for every minute was precious. Huge quays and massive granaries arose, together with ship-yards and the first dry-docks in the world.

The Spartans watched the growing strength of Athens with mixed emotions, for Athens and Sparta were rivals. However, Themistoclean diplomacy proved more than a match for Spartan envy. It was Themistocles who won the sea-battle at Salamis. When the immense Persian fleet appeared off the coast like some inevitable storm, Themistocles ordered every citizen to collect his possessions and take to the ships. Everyone who

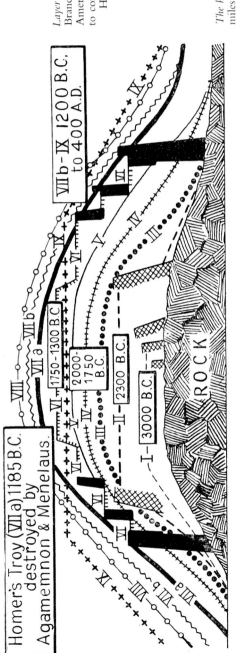

Layer VIIa is believed by Professor Brandenstein of Graz and the American archaeologist Carl Blegen to contain the city of Troy which Homer described in his Iliad

The hill of Hissarlik, two and a half miles from the shores of the Dardanelles in Turkey. Under it was found the debris of ten separate Trojan settlements

Homer's Troy (VIIa)1185 B.C. destroyed by Agamemnon & Menelaus.

VIIb-IX 1200 B.C. to 400 A.D.

1750-1300 B.C.

2000-1750 B.C.

II-2300 B.C.

I-3000 B.C.

ROCK

Ivory carving found at Mycenae, in the Peloponnese. It probably dates from the late Bronze age, or about 3,500 years ago. This period produced some remarkably fine workmanship in **ivory**

Statue of the goddess Persephone from the period 540–530 B.C., on the Acropolis, the sacred citadel of Athens

This statue was erected in the Temple of Zeus at Olympia in 460 B.C., ten years after the birth of Socrates. It shows a Lapithae girl, one of the legendary people of Thessaly. At the wedding of their king, Peirithoos, the guests included some centaurs (creatures half horse, half man), who got drunk and tried to rape the ladies. The disembodied hand of a Centaur is still in the girl's hair

Left: a two-drachma piece in silver with Nike's head. *Centre:* A Syracusan ten-drachma piece from the year 405 B.C. (a bull cost about five drachmas). *Right:* an Achaean two-drachma piece bearing the head of the goddess Artemis

An Attic mixing-bowl from the middle of the 6th century B.C., now in the Museo Archeologico, Florence. It represents a Babylonian hunting scene, a chariot battle for Patroclus' body, a cortege of gods going to the wedding of Thetis, Achilles pursuing Troilus, and pygmies fighting

Head of Athena from the eastern pediment of the Temple of Aphaea on the island of Aegina. In 490 B.C., Aphaea (Britomartis) was the island's tutelary goddess. [Antikensammlungen, Munich

Large copper water-jug from Grave IV in the citadel of Mycenae. The jug had been repaired

This golden beaker also came from Grave IV at Mycenae, which contained five bodies

A Greek painting dating from 440 B.C., in the lifetime of Themistocles

could bear arms had to report for service with the fleet. The Delphic oracle had prophesied that all was lost. In desperation, the Athenians consulted it for the last time. It replied that Athens should take refuge behind wooden walls. Themistocles, never at a loss, had an immediate interpretation ready: the wooden walls were ships. The whole of Athens must go on board. Thousands of Athenians abandoned their homes, leaving the Persians free to land and burn the Acropolis with its temples and sacred trees.

Leopold von Ranke, the great German historian, believes that in adopting this course of action Themistocles made one of the greatest military decisions of all time. He compares the evacuation of Athens with the burning of Moscow, which forced Napoleon to turn back.

The Persian king, Xerxes, had a throne set up on the cliffs overlooking the Bay of Salamis, from which vantage-point he hoped to watch the heroic deeds of his victorious seamen. He wanted to see with his own eyes the final blow being struck against Hellas, the sinking of the Greek fleet, and the victory of his own Phoenician ships. But the immense Persian fleet could not deploy properly in the narrow gulf. It fell into disorder and confusion, and the day was lost.

Although the Greeks began by showering Themistocles with honours after his victory at Salamis, they later started to have their doubts about him. It was the Spartans, Athens' greatest rivals, who finally managed to discredit the statesman. They discovered that their ruler Pausanias had been conducting a clandestine correspondence with the Persians, and alleged that Themistocles was also involved in a conspiracy with the Persian king. The information was passed on to the Athenians, and a warrant was issued for Themistocles' arrest. That was how the Spartans revenged themselves on the great Athenian wall-builder. As for their own ruler Pausanias, they incarcerated him in the temple of Athena Chalcioicos and left him there to starve to death.

Themistocles fled to Asia Minor and informed Artaxerxes, the son of Xerxes, that he was being persecuted by the Greeks 'on account of his friendship for the Persians'. The oriental king admired Themistocles' sharp-wittedness (he had learned Persian in the meanwhile), consented to receive him, and made him prince of numerous cities in Asia Minor. Themistocles promised the Persian king that he would help him to conquer the whole of Greece, both in an advisory and a practical capacity. He was obviously never able to refrain from plotting new intrigues. However, before he could realize his final plans for revenging himself on his native country, he died at Magnesia in 459 B.C.

Themistocles was sixty-five years old when he died, and an object of admiration and hatred throughout the Mediterranean world. The inhabitants of Magnesia deified him and erected a magnificent memorial in his honour. The Greeks forbade his body to be buried in his native soil, but friends secretly brought his remains home to Attica, and his grave at the Piraeus was later decorated and honoured.

The Athenian historian Thucydides, writing approximately forty years after Themistocles' death, considered that he merited far more praise than any of his contemporaries. He could reach swift decisions when faced by sudden disaster, he possessed the gift of accurately forecasting events, and his judgment, even in spheres where he had no direct experience, was extremely sound. Thucydides also opines that Themistocles poisoned himself because he found that he could not keep his promise to the Persian king to overthrow Greece. Thucydides was a Greek, and it is understandable that he was not over-eager to mourn Themistocles as a 'Persophile', despite the great admiration which he accorded him as the victor of Salamis. It is more probable, however, that the founder of the Greek navy died a natural death in luxurious surroundings.

Teachers can exert a very great influence on the development of their pupils, but the mental constitution of the pupil is often quite as important in this respect as his instructor's. The Greek philosopher Anaxagoras, who was born about 500 B.C., had a pupil who bore out the truth of this statement to a signal degree. Anaxagoras offered him some extremely good advice which could well prove of great value in our own day.

We all know that fear is the ball and chain which each of us drags along with him throughout life. Anaxagoras taught his pupil that the things which fill us with apprehension for the future are all really quite natural events and developments. We should therefore fear them as little as we do Nature, and never allow anything to disrupt our peace of mind. The pupil in question was Pericles. He took this precept to heart at an early age, and that was why he grew into a man who was free from superstition, free from fear, and fairly free from doubt. It is not surprising that someone who followed the great philosopher's teachings so faithfully soon reached the top of the political ladder. Pericles was a democrat, and he regarded *demos*, the people, as an entity for whose assent and understanding a continual battle should be waged. It was no easy task to guide and influence the people of Athens. Thucydides says that Pericles was never followed by the masses, but they by him. Power was vested in the people, but Pericles guided the assembly in such a way that the power of the people became the basis of his own authority. It was a brilliant example of co-operation between nation and individual which has scarcely ever been equalled in the whole course of world history.

Pericles knew no other road than that which led from his house to the assembly, where he spoke better than any man had done before him. It was his constant prayer that no unseemly word should ever escape his lips. He never indulged in temperamental outbursts or exhibited any signs of agitation. He must have been the Churchill of his day, a brilliant parliamentarian who ignored abuse and insults and steadfastly resisted any temptation to digress. It was he who presided over the ten *strategoi* or generals who were the highest officials in the administration. He was responsible for the maintenance of public order within the city-State, he had to conduct public festivals, which was very important, and — which was even more important — he controlled the public purse.

Like Themistocles before him, Pericles realized that sea-power was worth more to Athens than land-power, and that a permanently mobilized fleet was indispensable to her security.

Under Pericles, the plastic arts reached a zenith which they never attained in Greece either before or subsequently. The Acropolis or citadel of Athens which the Persians had destroyed was rebuilt during his time.

A miraculous building arose on the Acropolis between 447 and 437 B.C., under the direction of Callicrates and Ictinus. It was the Parthenon, the great new marble temple for 'Athena Parthenos', the tutelary goddess of Athens. This temple is probably the finest piece of architecture which the European art of building has ever produced. The horizontal lines of its stepped substructure were intentionally given a slight upward curve in the centre, to counteract an optical illusion which would otherwise have made them seem slightly sunken. Again, the Parthenon's pillars were not perpendicular, but leaned towards the centre, since perpendicular pillars would have looked as though they were slanting outwards. In 438 B.C. a colossal statue of the goddess Athena, nearly forty feet high, was installed in the temple's main hall. It was a work in wood, gold and ivory by the sculptor Pheidias; 873 years later, after the banning of all heathen cults by Emperor Theodosius II, the statue was brought to Constantinople. That was in A.D. 435. Since then, it has disappeared without trace. The sculptural ornamentation of the Parthenon was executed by sculptors from every studio in Athens working under the direction of Pheidias. The Greeks used to hold important national festivals at Olympia, Delphi, Nemea and on the Isthmus, and Athens had her own festival, the Panathenaea, which took place every four years. This Attic national festival became an event of world renown, and it was the ceremonial procession of the Panathenaea which formed the theme of the Parthenon's frieze. It was originally 525 feet long, but only a portion of the narrow western side survives in situ. The greater part of the frieze, together with most of the remaining sculptures, was dismantled and brought to London in 1816 by Lord Elgin. It is now in the British Museum.

371

The Erechtheum on the Acropolis was named after King Erechtheus. At one time there were several shrines on the site of this ancient royal palace: Athena's sacred olive-tree, the place where Poseidon split the rocks, the tomb of King Cecrops, and altars to Athena, Poseidon, and Erechtheus himself. It was Pericles' idea to bring all these holy places within the confines of a single building, the Erechtheum, but his plan was only carried out after his death, between 421 and 406 B.C.

Pericles was also responsible for initiating the Propylaea, the large gateway which formed the entrance and western façade of the Acropolis. He entrusted its building to his architect Mnesicles, and it has served as a model for all forms of gate-construction until very recent times.

North-west of the Acropolis on the market hill arose the Theseum, a shrine dedicated to Hephaestus which was mistakenly regarded in earlier times as being the temple of Thesus – hence its name. It is the best preserved temple in Greece. To the south-east, at the foot of the citadel, the Odeum was erected. This concert hall was considered the loveliest building designed for musical performances which the Greek cult of Dionysus possessed. The Odeum was excavated, but only its foundations had survived.

The Athenians, like all the members of the Attic League, made great financial sacrifices in order to pay for the building of these shrines. Building costs which have been preserved for us chiselled in stone tell us that the Parthenon alone cost 469 talents, or about £180,000 – little enough to pay for such a truly eternal work.

Our expressions 'gymnasium', 'lyceum' and 'academy' all originated in Greece. Under Pericles, institutions like these, which were dedicated to the mental and physical training of youth, grew up stone by stone on the barren soil of Athens. They blazed an educational trail for the whole of Western civilization. The mental energy with which Pericles set about turning Athens into a cultural centre cannot fail to excite our astonishment and admiration today. While other places in Greece still remained large villages or towns, Athens became a veritable metropolis, tiny though it was in comparison with our large modern cities. To remember this is only to feel an even greater respect for the numerous men of genius and talent who transformed Athens into a cultural wonder of the world during the Periclean age. In the forefront of all these engineers and artists stood Pheidias, who created so many glorious statues out of bronze, gold and ivory. He also supervised the progress of building on the Acropolis, and most of the sculptural decoration in the Parthenon was his work or that of his pupils. Pericles wanted his buildings to outshine the palaces at Persepolis – another facet in the rivalry between Greece and Persia.

The history books which we read at school only show us the many-sided

372

genius of Pericles, painting him as a man of great self-control, gravity and discretion. In doing so, they neglect the human angle. Pericles' first marriage does not seem to have been too happy. It had probably never occurred to him that he might one day fall in love with a non-Athenian woman, for he was himself the sponsor of a law prohibiting marriages between Athenians and non-Athenians. On divorcing his first wife, however, he chose as his second a woman of Miletus called Aspasia. He was now a victim of his own law, for as a non-Athenian she could never become his wife. It was only natural that the Athenians should gossip unceasingly about his relationship with her. She was a foreigner, after all, and it may also be true that before her friendship with Pericles, Aspasia had pursued a rather disreputable career as madame to a large establishment of hetaerae. These hetaerae were girls without any family life, but often of great intellectual attainments.

Aspasia was a beautiful and cultured woman. She opened a school of rhetoric and philosophy, drew young girls, women and men into her circle, and became such a focus of attention that even the philosopher Socrates declared he had learned the art of speaking from her. Aspasia gathered around her all the major scientists, artists and scholars of her day, not to mention the sophists, 'these impudent innovators who disputed the ancient beliefs'. (Eduard Meyer.)

The historian Herodotus, the philosopher Anaxagoras of Clazomenae, the most progressive town-planner in the contemporary world, Hippodamus of Miletus, and its greatest sculptor Pheidias, all belonged to Pericles' and Aspasia's circle, as did the dramatist Euripides, that earliest and finest portrayer of the soul of woman. He had met Aspasia in his youth and must have learnt a great deal from the emancipated Ionian woman about the psychology of woman and her social repression in Attica. He was therefore able, in contrast with his predecessors Aeschylus and Sophocles, to deal for the first time with the real nature of women's problems and to venture an authentic treatment of relationships between the sexes and the theme of marital love. 'Women are the best things about which one speaks least' (Thucydides), and 'Women had no share in Attic society' (Bengtson). However, Aspasia the Ionian woman had set a new fashion in Athens. The poet Cratinus called her a 'sweetheart', while Aeschines tells us of a cattle-dealer, a wicked and despicable person, whose association with Aspasia transformed him into one of the most highly esteemed men in Athens. So world-wide did Aspasia's reputation become that Cyrus the Younger, the pretender to the Persian throne, renamed his favourite girl-friend Milto after her.

The last two years of Pericles' life lay in the shadow of the titanic struggle which has been called 'the Thirty Years War of the ancient world'. This was the war between Athens and Sparta, which lasted from 431 until 404 B.C., and in which Sparta held the upper hand. The true victor, however, was a third party: the Persian Empire.

In Thucydides, the great struggle found an historian who for the first time treated history as a science 'not pleasant or amusing, it is true', as he himself wrote, but instead 'reliable, profitable, and of enduring utility'. Hegel went so far as to assert that Thucydides' work is the profit which humanity gained out of the Peloponnesian War. The war brought with it such extensive upheavals and such frightful atrocities, disease and misery, that from then on Greece withdrew from the stage of world history and watched from the wings while Persia, Macedonia and, finally, Italy, stepped forward into the bright footlights to play their part in the pre-Christian evolution of mankind. The war was made more tragic by the fact that neither Sparta nor Athens wanted it. Sparta's population was decreasing at the time, and she feared fresh uprisings among her helots, or serfs. Her sources of economic and financial aid were none too abundant, and her Peloponnesian League was less reliable than Athens' maritime Attic League. It is obvious that she did not go to war of her own volition.

On the Athenian side, Pericles was equally reluctant to fight. No, the instigators of the war were clearly Corinth and her associates, who could not tolerate Athens' thriving world trade. Corinth brought in Sparta with her, and Pericles could not avoid a conflict without great humiliation to Athens. Such were the immediate causes. The underlying reasons, however, were to be found in the impingement on each other of Athens' and Sparta's expanding spheres of influence, and in the contrasting political systems of the two States.

Pericles' object during the second year of this suicidal conflict had become limited to the defence of the city of Athens. Since Sparta was the land-power and Athens commanded the sea, Pericles decided to sacrifice the open country to the enemy. He ordered the country-dwellers to abandon their farms and take to the triangular area enclosed by the two long walls linking Athens with the Piraeus and Phaleron. As long as the Athenian fleet remained undefeated, this immense twin stronghold could never be successfully blockaded, since its only exposed side, the sea side, could not only be protected by naval forces, but also served as an ideal supply-line. A great migration began. Laden with their goods and chattels, thousands of people poured into Athens to take refuge behind the walls. Many of them even dismantled their houses and dragged them into the safety of the triangular defence-zone.

Then a fate overtook Athens which no one could have foreseen. A plague-like epidemic suddenly broke out. The inhabitants of the Piraeus were the first to be attacked by it. The exact nature of the disease is still in dispute today. At all events, it began with 'high fever, redness and smarting of the eyes, a raw throat, and a foul and fœtid-smelling breath'. The next symptoms were 'hoarseness, a racking cough, secretions of bile, great pain and convulsions' followed by 'abscesses on the abdomen, diarrhoea, exhaustion' and death. Many sufferers lost their limbs, others their eyes, and still others their memories. All these symptoms are listed by Thucydides. The sick were in the grip of such high fever that they threw themselves headlong into cold water. Groups of desperate and tormented men threw themselves into the water-tanks, racked by unquenchable thirst. The epidemic spread at lightning speed. There were too many sick people to nurse, too many dead to bury. People were afraid of coming near those who had been attacked, and many households were completely wiped out. It was hot, that dreadful summer in the year 430 B.C. The huts were cramped, small and stifling. Corpses lay everywhere, and people in the last throes of disease tottered along the streeets and thronged the fountains. In their fear, men turned into animals, made raids on other people's funeral pyres and laid their own dead upon them, or threw them on to the first pyre whose flames caught their eye.

Almost everyone succumbed to the temptation to have one last fling at life. No one was any longer ashamed to publicize his most secret lusts, indulge in a frenzy of sensuality, and hastily squander his money. No one feared the gods any longer, for they were sparing no one, and no one respected the laws either, since it seemed unlikely that anyone would live long enough to be punished for breaking them. Yet the courts went on sitting in spite of the general panic, and the daily round of accusation and counter-accusation continued, even in the face of imminent death. Dense clouds of smoke from funeral pyres hung over the centre of the city day and night, and the plague spread to the Athenian fleet.

Curiously enough, Sparta and the Peloponnese remained unaffected by the epidemic, although the Peloponnesians refused to take any more prisoners and killed everyone who fell into their hands for fear of catching it. Equally curious is the fact that during this time an epidemic was also raging in an unknown place in Italy – clearly the same sickness which had attacked Athens. This insignificant township was destined later to become master of all Greece. Its name was Rome.

What with a second Peloponnesian invasion, the fresh devastation it caused, the general hardships of war, and the particular hardships brought by disease, the Athenians had now lapsed into a mood of apathetic despair. They began to see Pericles as the sole author of their frightful predicament. Had he not advised them to go to war? Had he not described the risks as slight? Had he not underestimated the Spartans' war-potential? They murmured and grumbled and shook their fists at him.

For all the danger, Pericles kept his head. He still had some reserves of strength left. He was still guided by his genius. Above all, he still had Aspasia. He kissed and embraced her every day as he left his house for the assembly, as Plutarch tells us in Book 24 of his biography of Pericles. But the Athenians would not leave her alone. Comic dramatists poked fun at her. Dirty jokes were whispered about her. In fact, she was even brought to trial for alleged impiety and procuration, charges against which Pericles defended her in person with amazing eloquence. Aspasia was acquitted, but from then on Pericles seemed to have lost something of his old inviolability, infallibility and powers of persuasion. The Athenians were really a most difficult and critical people. They wore down nearly all their greatest men by their eternal intrigues, slanders and accusations.

Since Pheidias was a friend of Pericles and had many envious rivals, the next attempt to undermine Pericles' reputation took the form of a law-suit against the sculptor. He was accused of having falsified certain costs in respect of his statue of Athena. He was convicted, and died in prison. The Athenians' next victim was the philosopher Anaxagoras of Clazomenae, who had ascribed the creation of the Universe not to chance, but to a single, pure, disinterested mind. He was charged with having propagated godless doctrines. Pericles defended Anaxagoras, but his friend was convicted and had to pay a fine of 5 talents, or nearly £2000.

By now the people of Athens were in such an embittered, unstable and desperate frame of mind that they were willing to lend an ear to any kind of slander, and finally even the incorruptible Pericles was convicted of embezzlement. He was relieved of his office in the autumn of 430 B.C., after the terrible summer of plague. He ceased to be a *strategos* of Athens. However, only one year passed before he was reinstated. In their hour of need, the Athenians realized that he was their ablest man. 'The people being what they are,' says Thucydides, 'they made him *strategos* once more and entrusted him with the administration of all affairs.' But Pericles' strength was gone. The plague had robbed him of his two sons. Now it attacked him. The Black Death carried him off in the midst of his labours, in the year 429 B.C.

'That is what earthly immortality means,' Ranke wrote, 'that one of the great ages of civilization be designated by his name. Men of high standing can never be replaced.'

ALCIBIADES, ATHENS' MOST DANGEROUS FRIEND

THEMISTOCLES was the greatest Greek statesman, the saviour of Athens, the victor of Salamis, and the man who banished the Asiatic peril, Persia. Pericles was Athens' greatest master-builder, an aristocrat by birth and nature, the most brilliant Greek parliamentarian, and the man who gave the golden age of Greece its name, 'the Periclean age'. Alcibiades was Athens' idol, Athens' Mephistopheles, Athens' seducer and Athens' destroyer. All three men were impeached and betrayed by Athens. Pericles alone remained true to himself and true to Athens. Themistocles and Alcibiades died on Persian soil, enemies of their native land.

Alcibiades was nineteen years old when the Peloponnesian War broke out. By the time he was murdered, Athens had been decisively defeated by Sparta. There is a queer logic in the fact that Alcibiades' death coincided with Athens' defeat.

Alcibiades was an uncommonly handsome person. Handsome as a child, handsome as a youth and handsome as a man, he never lost his power to fascinate and endear himself to others. He combined a magnificent physique with an extraordinary number of faculties, both physical and mental. He had a lisp, yet the Athenians found everything about him charming – even his lisp, and the whole city made a fetish of lisping like him.

He was passionate and impetuous, hot-blooded and ambitious. On one occasion in his childhood, when he was fighting a bigger boy, his opponent pushed him away, saying: 'Shame on you, Alcibiades! You bite like a woman.' Young Alcibiades' eyes flashed. 'Like a woman?' he said, 'Like a lion, you mean!' On another occasion, when Alcibiades and his companions were playing dice in a narrow alley in Athens, an approaching cart threatened to run the children over. 'Wait!' called Alcibiades to the driver, but the man paid no attention. While the other children ran off in dismay, young Alcibiades calmly lay down in front of the cart, his face to the cobble-stones. The waggoner reined in hard, dumbfounded by his audacity, just as the whole of Athens and the contemporary world were to be in later years.

As a young man, Alcibiades weaned the Athenians from playing the flute. 'The flute stops up the mouth and voice. It distorts the face,' said Athens' young idol. To a man, the Athenians stopped playing the flute. From then on, only the lyre was played.

In his heart of hearts, Alcibiades despised the Athenians. Everyone loved him, but he loved only two people: himself and Socrates, the greatest Greek philosopher. Everyone flattered the youth, everyone sought his company and his friendship, everyone tried to pamper him. For his part, however, he kept his rich and aristocratic admirers at arm's length, took his meals with Socrates every day, practised wrestling with him, and shared his tent with him on military campaigns. With everyone else he remained disdainful and reserved.

Alcibiades once received an invitation to dine with an extremely wealthy man called Anytus. He declined it, got drunk with some friends of his at home, and then decided to go to Anytus' house after all. When he entered the banqueting-hall and saw the tables loaded with gold and silver drinking-vessels, he ordered his slaves to take half of them away. Anytus' guests were outraged, but Anytus himself declared equably that Alcibiades had behaved in a kind and sociable manner. He had only taken half, when he could have taken everything!

Alcibiades' mad escapades knew no bounds. The only time he wept was when Socrates reproved him. If he tried to escape from Socrates, the old philosopher chased after him and caught him. Then he was ashamed and afraid. Socrates saved his pupil's life on two occasions, once on the campaign against Potidaea, and once at the battle of Delion.

For a while the young man lived at Pericles' house. 'When I was your age,' Pericles told him, 'I was wiser.' 'What a pity,' Alcibiades replied coolly, 'that I never knew you at your best!'

Once, when Alcibiades asked a schoolmaster if he could borrow a copy of Homer, and discovered that the man did not own one, he gave him a box on the ears.

In return for another box on the ears, Alcibiades received a wife. He punched Hipponicus, a rich and highly respected Athenian, to win a bet he he had made with some friends. The next morning he knocked on the affronted man's door and announced that he was ready to be thrashed for what he had done. The rich man was so touched by this that he offered Alcibiades his daughter Hipparete's hand in marriage. The worthy girl had nothing to laugh about. She was virtuous and loved her husband dearly, but he for his part carried on such a lively association with the hetaerae of Athens that she eventually sought refuge in her brother's house. When Hipparete appeared before the magistrate to sue for divorce, Alcibiades also turned up and, seizing her, carried her forcibly home across the market-place. From then onwards she stayed with him, contenting herself with such crumbs of affection as he deigned to bestow on her. She died of a broken heart soon afterwards.

Alcibiades owned a very large and handsome dog. He cut off its tail, whereupon everyone became angry and was sorry for the animal. 'Good!'

said Alcibiades. 'They'd find still worse things to say about me otherwise.'

Alcibiades was a brilliant speaker, but since he insisted on selecting only the best words or expressions possible and they did not always occur to him immediately, it often meant that he had to stop short and spend a moment in silent thought. He did so with a complete lack of embarrassment, thinking for a while in silence, and then continuing as eloquently as before. He was fond of horses and owned a large number of chariots. He sent seven teams of horses to the Olympic Games, a thing which no rich man or king had ever done before. He not only won, but gained second and third places as well.

Even at the very start of his career, Alcibiades had some powerful rivals. Principal among them was Nicias, a much older man who was regarded as the finest general Athens had. It was he, so the Greeks thought, who had successfully terminated the war against Sparta, and the armistice was termed a 'Nician peace'. This appellation was a source of constant annoyance to Alcibiades, and in his jealousy he decided to break the peace treaty. He succeeded in doing so with brilliant success, of course, for the public assembly could always be relied on to applaud him, and every speech he made ended in his winning unanimous approval.

There was a man living in Athens at this time whose fame rested on the fact that he hated everyone and avoided friends and hangers-on. His name was Timon, the same Timon to whom no less a person than Shakespeare gave the title-role in one of his great plays. When Alcibiades was walking home after his successful speech accompanied by an admiring crowd, Timon the misanthrope accosted him. 'It is good, my son,' he said venomously, 'that you are becoming so important, because you will become great through the misfortunes of all these men here.' Some laughed and others were annoyed, but Timon was right.

The island of Sicily had been the object of all Athens' dreams and aspirations even in the time of Pericles. Every city on the island was under the control of Syracuse. Well knowing how alluring and attractive a proposition Sicily was to the Athenians, Alcibiades advised them to send a great fleet to conquer the island. He painted a glowing picture of great prospects and brilliant successes. Sicily was to be only the start. From there they could go on to conquer Carthage, Africa, Italy and the treasures of the whole western Mediterranean. Nicias cautioned the assembly and pointed out the difficulties involved, but it did not rob the young men of their enthusiasm for Alcibiades, nor prevent them, when they were sitting together at their wrestling-schools, from wistfully drawing the outlines of Sicily in the sand. Socrates, too, advised against the undertaking, and as for the astronomer Meton (he was also an astrologer), Alcibiades' crazy plans drove him to such a pitch of fury that he seized a burning torch and set fire to his own house. The Athenians probably regarded Alcibiades as too headstrong and Nicias as too cautious to conduct the campaign single-handed, because they entrusted its leadership to them both, and added a third general to their number, a certain Lamachus, whose advanced age had detracted nothing from his bold and fiery spirits. That done, the conquest could proceed.

All was ready for departure, when something happened which was really responsible for Athens' subsequent defeat.

The worthy citizens believed in their gods. In front of their houses and before the doors of their temples stood sacred statues called *Hermae*. They were merely stone pillars surmounted by a head, and were not exactly objects of beauty, but the Athenians venerated them greatly. On the night of the 'Adonia', a festival dedicated to Aphrodite and Adonis, the sacred stone images were mutilated by an unknown hand.

Since the Athenians were always inclined in such cases to suspect or accuse the most important men in their city, and since Alcibiades naturally had enemies in Athens, the blame was laid on him and his cronies. Alcibiades asked to be allowed to defend himself, but his enemies knew that, if he once got an opportunity to speak, he would win his case. They therefore declared that it would be pointless to bring the leader of a projected expedition before a court. Let Alcibiades sail away for the time being, they said. There would be time enough to defend himself after the war was over.

Alcibiades did not like the idea of setting out under such a cloud of suspicion, but he received orders to embark, and so 140 galleys weighed anchor. He reached Italy, captured Rhegium and, crossing to Sicily, forced Catania to surrender.

At this juncture, the Athenians recalled Alcibiades to face a judicial inquiry. His enemies at Athens had no positive charges to bring against him, admittedly, but absence was always dangerous in such circumstances, and slanderous rumours about him were growing rife. A ship arrived to fetch him. The morale of the Greek soldiers in Sicily dropped abruptly, for they were well aware how tedious the campaign would become with Nicias in sole command. Once on board ship, Alcibiades found out that the Athenians had already condemned him to death *in absentia*. He decided to show them that he was still very much alive, and so, when he reached Thurii, he slipped ashore and went into hiding. Then he travelled across the Peloponnese and sought asylum in Sparta, promising to help the Spartans against Athens. He advised them to send a general to Sicily to crush Athenian power there. In the meanwhile, he began to incite a direct war against Athens herself. It was not long before he became an object of great respect and admiration among the Spartans.

Alcibiades was a fine actor. His brilliant intuition told him exactly how to adapt himself to each new situation as it presented itself. Life in Sparta was simple, plain and frugal — 'spartan', in fact. The pampered Alcibiades had his hair shaved down to the scalp, bathed in cold water, ate barley-bread, and even acquired a taste for the Spartans' famous 'black blood-soup'. People could scarcely believe their eyes. They were astounded to see the man who had once maintained the best chef and perfumier in Athens, suddenly living a more spartan life than the Spartans themselves. Alcibiades enjoyed playing the part. There was no mask he could not assume. Only one thing remained beyond his powers: he could not control his sensuality. His roving eye lighted upon Timaea, the wife of Agis, the Spartan king. This Spartan 'hero', had, it must be explained, been thrown out of his wife's bedroom by an earthquake, and the experience so unnerved him that he did not touch her again for ten months. Alcibiades took advantage of Timaea's enforced period of solitude to seduce her and, when she gave birth to a son, there was no doubt about its fatherhood. Moreover, Timaea herself was so much in love that she whispered to all her women friends that the child's name should really be Alcibiades.

Meanwhile the Athenians in Sicily had suffered a terrible defeat. What was more, Alcibiades had managed to alienate the whole of Ionia from Athens. King Agis was doubly enraged, both by the great reputation Alcibiades was winning and by his wife's adultery. Alcibiades' position in Sparta was no longer secure. He betook himself to the Persian satrap Tissaphernes, a ferocious barbarian who was greatly feared and cherished an unrivalled hatred of the Greeks. His new guest's dexterity and cunning appealed to him. Alcibiades now exerted all his eloquence and great powers of persuasion in an attempt to incite the satrap against Sparta. Simultaneously he began to conspire with the council of the Four Hundred, the body which ruled Athens.

The whole of Athens' naval power was at this time concentrated at Samos, where her fleet was engaged in crushing defections among her allies and defending Greek possessions. Alcibiades joined the Athenian fleet and eventually became commander of a naval squadron on the Hellespont. He defeated the Spartan navy once at Abydos and twice at Cyzicus, and conquered Chalcedon and Byzantium for Greece. By this time he was yearning for his native land and, with all these victories behind him, he decided to show his face in Athens once more.

It was a triumphal home-coming. All his ships were decorated with captured enemy shields. Yet Alcibiades' heart thumped apprehensively and he did not dare leave his galley until his cousin and a large number of friends had arrived to welcome him. He was accompanied through the city by loud and joyful cheers. The Athenians decked him with garlands and held their children up to see the great hero in his hour of triumph. An assembly of the people was convened. With tears in his eyes, Alcibiades described the injustice he had suffered. The people presented him with golden crowns and elected him supreme commander of their land- and sea-forces.

But if ever a man was undone because of his own fame, it was Alcibiades. People regarded him as infallible. It was thought at Athens that anything Alcibiades set his hand to was bound to succeed. It only needed one failure now to destroy his halo once and for all.

The Spartans ordered out their fleet under the command of Lysander. Seeking an opportunity to levy funds for the payment of his seamen, Alcibiades temporarily handed over command of the Greek fleet to a helmsman called Antiochus, with strict injunctions not to engage the Spartans during his absence. Antiochus disregarded this warning, however, and was defeated, losing his life in the process. Thanks to the Greeks' usual fickle-mindedness, Alcibiades immediately fell into disgrace again. People started to collect material for an indictment. Alcibiades took to his heels once more. Lysander surprised the Greek fleet at Aegospotami (405 B.C.), besieged Athens, starved the city out, and captured it. He burned all the Athenians' ships and had the long walls dismantled. The destiny of Greece had run its course. Athens fell and Greece collapsed with her. She dragged all Hellas down into the abyss.

As for Alcibiades, he had once more fallen between two stools. He could expect nothing more from the Athenians, and now he had the Spartans to fear as well. Then he remembered Themistocles. Had not Themistocles found asylum with the King of Persia in the evening of his days? Alcibiades decided to make his way to the court of Artaxerxes. He travelled across Phrygia to see the Persian satrap Pharnabazus, hoping to get a recommendation to the Persian king.

But Alcibiades was not the sort of man the world leaves in peace. As long as he was alive, the Spartans could never feel that the conquest of Greece was complete. They were afraid of him. They had defeated Athens, yet they were still afraid of his genius. He loomed over them like a menacing shadow. They feared him just as the English still feared Napoleon, even when he was a prisoner on St Helena. Lysander accordingly requested Pharnabazus to have Alcibiades done away with.

Alcibiades probably had a presentiment of his approaching death. Living alone with his mistress, Timandra, he was troubled by a recurrent dream in which he saw himself beheaded and his body burnt by Magaeus, the brother of Pharnabazus.

The men who were detailed to kill Alcibiades did not dare to tackle the

Odysseus of their age in hand-to-hand combat. Instead, they surrounded his house and then set it ablaze. Alcibiades hastily bundled clothing and rugs together and threw them on to the flames. When the fire threatened to as-phyxiate him, he wrapped his cloak about his left hand and, taking his sword in his right, plunged out through the inferno. The barbarians gave ground. They shrank back before the lone figure of the most dangerous man in Greece. None of them dared to stop him or oppose him, but when he had reached a safe distance they shot arrows and threw spears after him. Alci-biades fell with blood streaming from a dozen wounds. He died in 404 B.C., when he was only thirty-six years old. Timandra wrapped his body in her own garments.

In that moment, the power of Greece was broken once and for all. In that moment, the curtain fell on her glorious history. In that moment, the first world-power in Eкrope left the stage.

SOCRATES, THE SAINTLY TEACHER

FOUR hundred and seventy years before the birth of Christ a man was born who embodied insight, reason, intellect and morality to a degree unequalled in any man before him. He brought mankind closer by several hundred years both to true humanity and to God. This man was Heaven's gift to the world. Heaven is very sparing with such gifts, however. It only bestows them once every thousand or two thousand years.

Socrates' father was called Sophroniscus. He was a sculptor and a good citizen. His mother's name was Phainarete. She was a midwife by profession, and probably a good-hearted person by nature. Both parents died a natural, final and irrevocable death.

Their son, on the other hand, came into conflict with the laws, was sentenced to death — and became immortal.

Our sources of information about the life and activities of Socrates are the Greek historian Xenophon and the Greek philosopher Plato. Since they were both about forty-five years younger than Socrates, their accounts, authentic and apocryphal, were based upon personal contact with him over the last ten or twelve years of his life.

Xenophon was a keen sportsman, a land-owner and an officer. Being an aristocrat, he did not feel at home in democratic Athens, so he went off to Persia and took part in a campaign against the younger Cyrus. He later fought for the Spartans and was on that account exiled from Athens. When he died in 354 B.C., he left behind an extensive library of books of his own authorship. They included a history of Greece; a work on the Spartan State; the *Cyropaedia*, a novel with a pedagogic-cum-political bias; the famous *Anabasis*, which described the march to Thrace made by ten thousand Greek mercenaries; a text-book on the duties of a cavalry officer; a work on domestic science and the duties of a housewife; the *Banquet*; and four volumes of memoirs, the *Apomnemoneumata*. In the latter, Xenophon defends Socrates against the charges levelled at him. The books are no literary masterpieces. They do not do justice to the philosopher, for they give us a small-scale picture of Socrates, whereas Plato heightens his stature and enhances it. The truth is, of course, that Xenophon was a man of only moderate talent, while Plato was one of the greatest thinkers in world history.

Almost all Plato's works are written in the form of dialogues and, except in one of them, Socrates is always the chief protagonist. It is hard to distinguish in Plato between imagination and actual experience, but his portrayal of the philosopher is so realistic and convincing that he would have been a greater genius than Socrates if he had invented it all. Like his great teacher, Plato was always searching for a firm basis for thought. All his prose works have survived. They form a gigantic edifice of human knowledge, as well as the finest memorial Socrates could ever have been accorded.

Socrates himself never wrote. He knew a little about geometry and astronomy, and may also have had a bent for sculpture. He was very far from despising the sciences, but he refused to undertake any research himself so that he could devote himself entirely to the ethics of mankind and the betterment of the individual. He tried to steer clear of politics, and successfully managed to avoid holding office under the State. He asserted that a public appointment would force him to compromise his convictions—and compromises were not for Socrates. He spent only one year, 406-405 B.C., as a member of the council of the Four Hundred at Athens. The man who wishes to fight for righteousness, he said, must lead a private, not a public life. 'For it is certain, Athenians, that if I had taken part in public affairs I should long ago have been done away with, and thus been of no more use either to you or to myself.'

The poets of Athens poked fun at Socrates' poverty in their comedies. He obviously cared nothing for personal property. It is probable that he only married Xanthippe, who bore him three sons, quite late in life. As so often happens, these offsprings of a genius were mere insignificant shadows of their titanic father, who had expended enough mental energy for several generations. The story that Socrates was henpecked and that Xanthippe was a shrew may not be authentic, although Xenophon tells us that she had a somewhat fiery disposition. On the other hand, it must be reflected that married life with Socrates as a husband could not have been all beer and skittles! Although Socrates was a good soldier (he took part in three campaigns), his outward appearance seems to have been rather grotesque. Small and rotund, with prominent eyes, a snub nose, wide nostrils and a large mouth, he was scarcely a beauty. Inwardly, however, 'this shrewdest and most intelligent man of the whole era', as Plato described him, seethed and sparkled, shone and glowed with a mysterious fire. His self-control and powers of endurance were unrivalled. He had practised self-denial so assiduously that he was well content with the very barest necessities of life. At the same time, he was no ascetic. He was familiar with the so-called pleasures of life even if he did not run after them, and he could be so gay and witty when he was at a banquet or with friends that he was always the centre of attention. He was firmly convinced that he was as imperfect as the next man, but he considered it his god-given mission in life to serve his fellow-men by showing them the way to reason, and therefore to goodness. He was also well aware that his best method of winning people over was not to wag his forefinger at them, but to gain their friendship and confidence. Moreover, he could sympathize with and feel for the weak, the ingenuous, and the mentally less well endowed.

Socrates spent nearly all his life in the open air, in the streets and the market-place or at the gymnasium. He had no taste for country life, and left his native Athens as seldom as Kant his Königsberg. Socrates said of himself: 'I know that I do not know.' When he was speaking with people who fancied they were wise, and had deduced by means of clear and logically conducted conversations that they could offer no convincing proof of their wisdom, he became more than ever certain that he was wiser than everybody else, since only he was conscious of his ignorance. Knowledge — that was to Socrates the supreme thing, and he was so utterly bound up in his mission to explain its meaning to all men that anything else seemed of little importance. Poverty, spells of starvation, unkind laughter — he endured them all with the same splendid equanimity. He was even willing to suffer death rather than betray his convictions. He never wore a shirt or shoes, and his one coat served him all the year round. He was completely independent of the thousand-and-one things which his circle of acquaintances found so important. His contemporary Antiphon asserted that even a slave would run away in disgust if he were forced to live like Socrates.

Socrates was a loyal and devoted son of his native Athens, a true patriot, and a man of uncommonly high personal courage. Regardless of popular trends, etiquette, and public opinion, and uninfluenced by prevailing habits of thought and action and the signs of the times, Socrates resolutely took up his lone stand and taught that the only source of all concepts and all ethical ideas was the human mind. Quite independent of the Old Testament prophets and their age-old perceptions, and totally ignorant of the god-seekers of Mesopotamia and Canaan, he recognized that there were some things which only God could understand, and that there existed a single divine intelligence which operated in all things. One of the creations of this supreme intelligence, and related to the gods, was the human mind. And there was something else, something mysterious which could only be sur-mised but not known, an invisible link between the human and the divine, a measure of which he could detect in himself: his 'I'. And there was some-thing still further, which gave him warning whenever he went astray: his soul. Socrates firmly believed that the soul was immortal. Living 400 years before Christ, he led Greek thought a remarkably long way towards the New Testament, and it is no mere chance that our Western civilization has its roots both in Greece and in the Christian religion, for it was Socrates who unwittingly linked them together.

Before Socrates, philosophy had been exclusively devoted to the investigation of natural phenomena. Ever since his time, philosophers have had to concern themselves with 'virtue', with man's actions and conduct. Socrates was something of a saint in this respect, for he strove not only to acquire knowledge but also to employ it for purposes of education. He taught that the only end of all study was the improvement of man, and he was the first to pluck philosophy out of the clouds and implant it in towns, houses and people. He became the founder of philosophical 'ethics', which comes from the Greek word *ethos*, meaning disposition, morality and character.

During the lifetime of Socrates there flourished at Athens a school of philosophers who were the authors of an important intellectual movement called sophism. The Greek word *sophistes* means 'man of wisdom', and the sophists were itinerant teachers who went about giving instruction in return for high fees. Their kind of education was thus available to the wealthier classes only. They taught philosophy, literature, art, grammar, mathematics, astronomy and, above all, political science. In this way they encouraged specialization in individual sciences, and turned their pupils into men well qualified both for private and public careers. In their opinion there was no such thing as absolute truth or absolute morality. The sophists' teachings destroyed the ties which linked the individual to religion and society, and their insistence on specialization finally created a situation almost as dangerous as that which exists today. Egoism gained the upper hand, and people followed the precept: 'the means justifies the end'. The sophists taught their pupils to be able to argue for or against any proposition. Naturally enough, such an ability could also be used to further the wrong cause, and in the end the sophists threatened to become the quite unintentional authors of a universal breakdown in morality. Socrates recognized this danger and spiritedly went into action against the sophists.

It should not be forgotten that during Socrates' lifetime Greece was still worshipping her ancient demons, idols, gods and spirits. What was more, her gods were endowed with extremely human and extremely immoral characteristics. Fables and legends told of the wildest love-affairs and amorous intrigues in Heaven, and Greece was a hot-bed of thriving Mystery-cults and Eros-cults. The Athenians' fury at the mutilation of their Hermae and the fact that Alcibiades' enemies chose that crime because its very heinousness made it an ideal means of getting rid of him, proves how deeply entrenched in her primitive polytheism Athens still was. Socrates was far in advance of his time. He publicly declared that the whole of Greek mythology was poetic fiction. Buttonholing every man he met, he demonstrated to him with inexorable logic that the only source of knowledge was a wholesome human intelligence, and that the only thing superior to human knowledge was God. Socrates became the terror of the city, only admired and revered by a small number of adherents. He was misunderstood. He was laughed at. Aristophanes, the greatest comic dramatist of his age, misrepresented the barefooted philosopher in his comedy *The Clouds*. Designed to show how Socrates was leading Athenian youth along the road to godlessness and dishonesty, the play tells how a furious father makes up his mind to burn the philosopher.

The Athenians could have tolerated all Socrates' irritating eccentricities if only he had not come out against the basic tenet of democracy. If moral knowledge meant good sense, as King Solomon taught in the Old Testament, then only the most sensible man should rule, and never the people. Perhaps it was just Socrates' bad luck to have lived at a time when there was no administrator of superlative intelligence to be found. Alcibiades certainly did not correspond to this ideal.

In the year 404 B.C. Sparta forced Athens to capitulate, and the walls of Athens were razed to the ground. Sparta had triumphed.

Who was to blame? Who had occasioned it all?

Alcibiades.

And who was Alcibiades?

A pupil of Socrates.

But who recalled Alcibiades from exile?

Critias. And Critias, one of the Thirty and the man who played Quisling to the Spartans in 404 B.C., was also a pupil of Socrates.

In 403 B.C. a universal amnesty was declared, which meant that Socrates could no longer be indicted for anything which had occurred prior to that date. His indictment in 399 B.C. was therefore couched in very general terms: 'corrupting the young, scorning the old gods and worshipping new'.

The prosecutor Meletus was an insignificant and rather obscure person, but behind the prosecution stood the influential figure of Anytus and the defeated, miserable people of Athens, apathetic prisoners of their ancient beliefs. Behind it, too, stood the whole of the contemporary world.

BUT I WILL OBEY GOD

'You will put me to death heedlessly and then go on sleeping out your lives, unless God in his mercy sends you another.' Socrates, in 399 B.C. – Plato's *Apology*.

JUST as great lovers only win purity and immortality in the memory of mankind when they have sealed their love with death, so it appears that before people will believe them, the world's great moral teachers must also sign their supreme desire with death – death by torture, at the stake, in the arena, or on the cross. Socrates had to drink a cup of hemlock, the umbelliferous plant containing coniine, an alkaloid poison. Again, just as Greece was the pattern on which our Western civilization has been modelled, so the human frailty displayed in the market-place and streets of Athens has likewise served as a pattern for succeeding ages of man. Four hundred and thirty years after Socrates' execution, the self-same cry rang through the narrow streets of Jerusalem: 'Crucify him!' And another 1500 years later it was heard in Rouen: 'To the stake with the witch!'

Like Joan of Arc, Socrates was executed for heresy. He was a heathen in our sense of the word, of course, and the term 'heresy' had not yet been invented, but he was accused of not recognizing the gods which Athens worshipped and serving others of his own. What the prosecutors called 'other gods' were in fact the inner voice which Socrates obeyed, which spoke to him in dreams, and which he took for a divine message. He called this heavenly sign his *daimonion*. The indictment also referred to his having corrupted the young. If it were really 'corrupting' to make virtue the supreme end of philosophy instead of mere natural science, then the prosecutors were right. But then prosecutors are always right – as long as the object of their accusations is still alive. Later on, the picture changes – in favour of truth.

Death was the punishment demanded. The result of the trial was a verdict of guilty (by 281 votes to 220), and a sentence of death (by 300 votes to 201). In Plato's famous *Apology* we have the full text of Socrates' defence. He conducted it in such a manner that he virtually compelled his judges to find him guilty and at the same time demonstrated that they were in the wrong. It is quite untrue to say that Socrates made no serious attempt to defend himself because he was indifferent to whether he lived or died. It is true that he was seventy years old and that he had 'completely lived himself out', as Ranke puts it, but that does not mean that he tamely surrendered. He forced his judges to condemn him despite his innocence in order to engrave his teachings on the hearts of men for all time to come, and, by doing so, he ranged himself among the great saints of this world. Socrates' speech, as

390

Plato has handed it on to us, is one of the grandest and most moving vindications any lonely genius whose sole struggle was for a better world could ever have had.

'And this is what will overthrow me, if I am overthrown: not Meletus, nor Anytus either, but the prejudice and envy of the multitude. They have been the destruction of many good men before me, and I think that they will be so again . . .' It is almost as though Socrates had a presentiment of Christ's coming. 'It is just this frankness of mine which makes me enemies, but that is only a proof that my words are true . . . He among you is the wisest who, like Socrates, knows that his wisdom is really worth nothing . . . I have never had any leisure, but live in extreme poverty by reason of my service to God . . . I have gone about doing one thing and one thing only — exhorting all of you, young and old, not to care for your bodies or for money, but for your souls . . . Athenians, I hold you in the highest regard and love, but I will obey God rather than you, and, while I still have life and strength, never cease to seek wisdom and admonish you . . . Best of men, you are a citizen of Athens, a city famous for its wisdom and power. Are you not ashamed of caring so much for money-making and fame and reputation? Will you not think or care about truth and understanding and the welfare of your souls? . . . Acquit me or acquit me not. I shall not change my ways, not if I have to die a hundred times . . . Meletus and Anytus can do me no harm. They have no power to, for I am sure it is not permitted that a good man be injured by a bad . . . So it comes about, men of Athens, that I am not arguing in my own defence at all, as you might expect me to, but on your behalf, that you may not lose God's gift by condemning me . . . But you are probably irritated, as sleepers are when suddenly awakened. Following Anytus' advice, you will put me to death heedlessly and then go on sleeping out your lives, unless God in his mercy sends you another . . . I have often seen men of reputation behaving in the strangest way at their trial, as if they thought it a terrible fate to be killed, and as though they expected to live for ever if you did not put them to death . . . For all that men can tell, death may be the greatest good that can happen to them. . . .'

That was how Socrates spoke before the verdict, and this is what he said after he had been sentenced: 'Perhaps it was right for these things to be so: and I think that they are well so . . . If death is a journey to another place, and the common belief be true, what good could be greater than this, my judges? . . . If a man were to go to the abode of death, leaving all these self-styled judges to find the true judges there, would that journey be ill to take? . . . I, at least, am willing to die a hundred deaths if that be true. . . It would be particularly interesting for me there, comparing my experiences with the men of old who have died by an unjust decree . . . they are happier than we of this world, for they are immortal . . . No evil can come to a good man, either in life, or after death . . . Punish my sons when they come of age, my friends. Trouble them as I have troubled you, if you think they care more for money than for virtue . . . But now it is time for us to go, I to death, and you to life: and which goes to the better condition is hidden from all save God.'

During the days following his sentence, Socrates lived as he had lived all the years that preceded it. He conducted the same discourses as he had always done. In fact, he was very contented with his term of confinement because the gaol and its fetters were actually conducive to philosophical thought. 'You see,' he said, 'when I am in the market-place I am distracted by all kinds of people.'

'But tell us, in what manner shall we bury you?' Crito asked him. 'As you please,' answered Socrates, 'only you must catch me first, and not let me escape you.' Socrates watched his friend and laughed gently as he said this. 'My friends,' he said, 'I cannot convince Crito here that I am the Socrates who has been conversing with you. He thinks I am the Socrates he will presently see a corpse. All the arguments which I have used to demonstrate that I shall not remain with you after I have drunk the poison, but that I shall depart to the happy abode of the blessed, have been thrown away on him.'

After he had bathed and they had brought his children and the women of his family to see him, he spoke to them in Crito's presence, and gave them his last commands. Then he bade them depart. It was close to sunset when the gaoler came to him and said: 'Oh Socrates, I know that I shall not have to worry about you as I have to do with other men. They are angry with me and curse me when I summon them to drink the poison. In my eyes, you are the noblest, gentlest and most admirable of all those who have ever been here. Farewell, and try to bear what must be as lightly as you can.' The warder turned away weeping, and went out. Socrates looked after him. 'How courteous the man is. He has visited me constantly all the time I have been here, and now he weeps for me.' Crito said: 'The sun is still shining on the hills. It has not yet gone down. I know that other men do not take the poisoned cup until quite late. They dine and drink heartily, and some even have girls brought to them. So do not be over-hasty, there is time enough.' But Socrates replied: 'The men you mention were quite right to do as they did, for by doing so they thought to gain something. But I do not think to gain anything by drinking a little later. I should only seem ridiculous in my own eyes if I clung to life.' Crito motioned to his slave, who went out and soon came back with the man who was to administer the poison to Socrates. He brought it in already prepared in the cup. When Socrates saw him, he said: 'Well, my good friend, I expect you understand how one does these things?' 'You have only to drink this,' the man replied. 'When you have drunk it, walk around until your legs become heavy, and then lie down. It will act of itself.' So saying, he handed the cup to Socrates, who took it confidently, without the slightest tremor or change of colour or expression. 'I suppose that I may, and must, pray to the gods that my journey hence be prosperous. That is my prayer: let it be so.' As he said this, he put the goblet to his lips and calmly and cheerfully drained it.

Here Plato makes Phaedo take up the story. 'Until that moment, most of us had been able to control our grief fairly well. But when we saw him drinking, no more. As for myself, the tears flowed not just by drops but with all their might, so that I had to cover my face in order to weep my fill . . .' Apollodorus burst right out weeping and made everyone else break down — everyone, that is, save Socrates himself. 'What are you doing, you remarkable people?' he exclaimed. 'That was why I sent the women away: because I have always heard that a man should die in silence.'

When they heard that, they were ashamed and controlled their weeping. As for him, he walked around, and when he noticed that his legs were becoming heavy he laid himself down on his back, just as he had been advised. The man who had given him the poison touched him from time to time, and examined his feet and legs. Then he pressed his foot hard, and asked whether he had any feeling in it. Socrates said: 'No,' whereupon he touched his knee, and so higher and higher, showing us that he was cold and rigid. When his lower body was almost completely cold, Socrates covered his face. And these were his last words: 'Oh, Crito, I owe a cock to Asclepius. Do not forget to pay it.' 'It shall be done,' answered Crito. 'Have you anything further to ask?'

Socrates made no reply. Shortly afterwards he stirred. Then his eyes dimmed.

LITTLE HORSES OF VENUS

'. . . those music-loving, money-grubbing bird-catchers the smart little horses of Venus, as they stand on parade in their ranks clad in diaphanous gossamer, like nymphs by the sacred waters of Eridanus. . . .' From the *Deipnosophists* or *Dinner-table philosophers* by Athenaeus (d. A.D. 192).

EVEN those who have read the greatly over-publicized works of the sexual statistician Dr Alfred Kinsey will be at a loss to tell you what a 'handle-kiss' is. Figures abound in Kinsey's pages: only charm is lacking. And charm was what the Greeks had in plenty.

There used to be a comedy popular in ancient Greece entitled *Anteia*, by a playwright called Eunicus. Only one verse of this play has survived, but it is like a ray of light from 2400 years away in time, illuminating the joyous zest for life of a race which really knew how to laugh and love. The line I refer to, runs: 'Take me by the ears and give me a "handle-kiss"!'

A lucky chance has preserved for us a dainty little shoe which once, 2500 years ago, belonged to a Greek street-walker. Written in nails on the sole of this shoe is: 'Follow me'. This pert invitation used to be imprinted in the soft dirt of the streets as the girl strolled along. The Greeks were an ingenious race, there is no denying – and they were no prudes, either. 'Yearning Love was there, and Desire, sweet Dalliance and ingratiating Entreaty, which infatuates even the wise.' So Homer wrote of Aphrodite, and his words might well have been applied to the Greeks as a whole.

Homer lived about 800 B.C., and the times he describes lie 1200 years before the birth of the Man of Nazareth. It appears from his descriptions that the women of those early days occupied a much more respected position both at home and in public than the women of the so-called historical period of Greece (800-167 B.C.).

Who had deposed them? How had the Greek woman of historical times come to be accorded no more than the conventional 'oriental' treatment? What had caused the whole of womankind to find contempt in the eyes of men? Why was it that women were obliged to live in their own allotted part of the house, the *gynaeconitis*, under conditions of semi-slavery?

These questions have never yet been answered, but there is no mistaking the fact that within the span of a few dim centuries the women of Greece had fallen from the status of 'subject' to that of 'object'. The best way of ascertaining what sort of standing women enjoyed in any particular epoch of human history is to find out how they were acquired in marriage. In Homer, a girl still had to be bought from her parents. As time went by, however,

394

brides became cheaper, until finally the positions were reversed, and a father either provided his daughter with a dowry, or was obliged to keep her.

The men of Greece set great store by their freedom and, as man's personal liberty increased, so woman lost hers. At the same time, an aberration came into fashion which was still quite unknown in Homer's day, namely pederasty, or love of boys.

The male Athenian spent his life in the open air, in the *agora* or market-place, in the gymnasium, at his place of business, or at public assemblies. Athenian women spent most of their lives shut up at home. Girls and young women were not permitted to see any men, or be seen by any. Hence they never got a chance to fall in love, and very few love-matches were made. The only time amorous glances were ever exchanged was at public festivals, religious ceremonies, burials, or during temple-sacrifices. That was why Greek girls got as excited over the prospect of a funeral as a cloistered girl of today does over a ball. It was not in question *whom* a girl should marry. The only thing that mattered was that she should be very young when she did — between sixteen and twenty, in fact. As for the man, he was not considered ready for marriage until he had reached the age of thirty or thirty-five. As a rule, men were twice as old as their brides.

The Greek philosopher Aristoxenus, who lived in the 4th century B.C., held that boys should be kept so effectively occupied and fatigued by constant exercise in every kind of sport that they would never feel any hankering after amorous delights, nor even have any inkling of them until their twentieth year. And even when they reached that age, they should only indulge in the ecstasies of love at rare intervals.

The Greeks regarded the fair sex as inferior, intellectually ill-endowed, incapable of participation in public life, and fit only for sensuality and procreation. Nature, it was thought, had allotted women a station in life far beneath that of men, and the life and activities of women were scarcely noticed except by their immediate circle inside the home. A woman was expected to obey her husband, bring up her children, supervise the slaves' housework, spin, weave, embroider, and keep herself looking as attractive as possible. The Athenian woman had no civil rights, and was treated throughout the whole of her life as though she were a minor. Nothing a man did on the advice or at the request of a woman carried any legal validity.

The education of girls was left to their mothers and their female attendants, which meant that cultured women were a rarity. While the 'woman-chamber' or gynaeconitis was not exactly a prison or a sealed harem, it was still a confined space assigned to women as quarters for the duration of their lives. Girls were kept under lock and key until their marriage, and a young wife could never leave the house without her husband's permission. A husband was allowed to lock his wife in, and her society was thus chiefly limited to her slave-women. In Sparta it was the other way round. Girls were intentionally left fairly free to associate with men, while married women had to live in seclusion. The symbol of Athenian womanhood's segregated existence was the tortoise, which the sculptor Pheidias portrayed under the feet of his Urania. Many Greek men kept their wives constantly under lock and key and, if even that precaution were not enough for them, they carefully sealed the door of the gynaeconitis.

All this seclusion led, particularly among young girls, to great inexperience and timidity, and frequently to ingenuousness and exaggerated reserve. Yet it also lent the Athenian teenager a certain touching charm, a spirit of uncomplaining resignation. Perhaps the only modern women who still bear a resemblance to the girls of classical Greece are the Japanese. The shy timidity of the Attic maiden was in sharp contrast to the forward behaviour of her Spartan and barbarian sisters. It will be remembered that the Greeks divided everyone into 'Hellenes' and 'barbarians'. Anyone who did not speak Greek was automatically a barbarian, regardless of whether he was a savage Thracian tribesman, a highly civilized Egyptian, or a sophisticated Persian. To a Greek, all the languages of the non-Greek world sounded like *bar-bar*, and 'Barbara' was originally a name given to foreign slave-girls.

A married woman of Athens blushed and drew back from her window if ever a man's glance fell upon her. The Athenians were certainly no 'gentlemen' where women were concerned, being only too convinced of their superior worth and dignity. Yet the respect for marriage and propriety was so universal that it was not often that men actually did cast glances in the direction of upper windows. Unmarried men had been penalized by Lycurgus, the strict Athenian legislator. They were forced to run naked around the market-place in winter while the crowd sang a satirical song about them. Procreation was necessary to the continued existence of the State and as such, was a duty. This was yet another factor conducive to stable marital relationships.

It was therefore a girl's lot to be given in lifelong marriage to a man she did not know, to bear his children, and to form part of the 'body of his estate' when he died. The evening before their marriage, brides — generally 15, 16, or 17 years old — used to bring their dolls and a lock of their hair to the temple and sacrifice them to Artemis.

The Greeks regarded the physical aspect of love as a sort of disease, a more or less violent form of madness. Love, they thought, involved a disturbance of the wholesome equilibrium between body and soul, and erotic desire was a temporary clouding of the intelligence.

Of course, this did not stop the Greek male from openly admitting to this clouding of the intelligence or from giving it free rein. There was no embarrassment in such matters, and numerous Greek texts describe associations with hetaerae, hired women who were not wives at home but mistresses in public. The expression *hetaera* means comrade or companion. That was the nicer term for them, but there were also 'bridge-girls', or girls who hung round the bridges, 'strollers' who roamed the streets, 'she-wolves', 'street-sweepers' and 'dice', who passed from hand to hand. Some hetaerae were highly educated women of wide accomplishments who were conversant with literature, philosophy and music. No stigma attached to an association with them, and it was in their company that the men of Greece found the mental stimulus which they lacked at home.

Probably the most intelligent hetaera of all was Aspasia of Miletus, who became Pericles' mistress. Glycera (literally 'sweet one') was the poet Menander's lover. The hetaera Gnathaena ('little cheek') wandered happily about the streets with her young grand-daughter, on whom she set a price twice as high as that which she charged for her own services. The whole of Greece 'languished', to use Properz's expression, before the door of Lais, another famous hetaera. There were two courtesans of that name. The elder Lais gave her love to the poor Cynic Diogenes gratis, although she was somewhat recompensed when the wealthy philosopher Aristippus of Cyrene came and visited her for two months on the island of Aegina and paid ready cash for what Diogenes had been receiving free of charge. When people remonstrated with Aristippus about his affair with Lais, reminding him that he was a philosopher and should not indulge in such diversions, he retorted: '*I* own Lais, not she me!' Phryne, whose real name was Mnesarete, was the most beautiful, celebrated, and at the same time, dangerous of all the Athenian hetaerae. Even the great sculptor Praxiteles succumbed to her beauty, and he used her as a model for his Aphrodite. Her goings-on were the subject of a thousand scandalous stories and formed a daily topic of Athenian conversation. Indicted for sacrilege, she was defended by the orator Hypereides. When he saw that his oratory was getting him nowhere, he tore his beautiful client's robe from her body and revealed 'the priestess of Aphrodite' to her judges, who dared not convict her. That shows how great an influence feminine beauty wielded in Athens in those days. Phryne affected the *chiton* — a body-hugging chemise — and never used the public baths, although on one occasion, when all the people of Greece were assembled for the Festival of Poseidon, she took off her clothes in full view of the public, unbound her hair, and stepped naked into the sea. It was this which inspired Apelles to create his 'foam-born' Aphrodite stepping from the waves.

Naturally enough, the hetaerae were not a faithful bunch of women, and the frequency with which they changed their lovers caused great unrest in male circles. We are told, for instance, about the hetaera Nico who promises to visit her lover at nightfall. When she does not turn up, her lover complains: 'The perjured creature! The last night-watch is nearly spent. Turn out the lights. She will not be coming now.' Again, when the hetaera Pythias invites the poet who is her current lover to visit her, the unfortunate man finds the doors locked. He calls upon the Goddess of Night to witness the wrong he has suffered, and prays that the faithless Pythias will one day meet with like treatment at the hands of a lover. The hetaera Philomene writes to Crito: 'Why do you trouble to write long letters? I need fifty gold pieces, not epistles. If you love me, give! But if you love your money, then do not trouble me further. With that, farewell!'

The hetaerae curled their hair, manicured their nails, and wore handsome purple robes. A certain Lucillus gibes at one of them: 'A lot of people are saying that you have dyed your hair, Nicylla. But it was already black when you bought it at market!'

Aristophanes has left us an inventory of feminine toilet requisites, the stock-in-trade of the Athenian 'geisha-girl', as it were. It included scarves, ribbons, mirrors and scissors, veils and hair-nets, belts and pyjamas, dressing-gowns, chemises and dresses with trains, wax cosmetics, soda, white lead, pumice-stone and rouge, foot- and ankle-bangles, beauty-patches, ear-pendants, jewelled chains, precious stones and a thousand other things. There were regular handbooks for hetaerae. We find one madame instructing her charges as follows: 'Above all, you must never be faithful. You must learn the art of lying and dissembling. And as for shame — you do not know the meaning of the word. If your lover becomes violent and plucks out your hair, re-conciliation must then be purchased with gifts. Let your doorkeeper be well schooled. He must shut the poor out and only open to the rich. Even slaves are not to be disdained, providing their pockets are well lined. That is the main thing. What good is a poet who only adorns you with verses but not with gifts?'

Yet even a poet sometimes had his uses. The fair Archeanassa, a hetaera from Colophon, achieved immortality through the medium of an epigram by Plato, who was in love with her. A hetaera's activities usually fell far short of immortality, of course, but Pythionice was another who gained posthumous fame. After her death, the governor Harpalus erected two memorials in honour of the girl who had squandered his money so extravagantly during her lifetime, one at Athens and one at Babylon. He dedicated a shrine, a temple-precinct, a temple and an altar to her, and, overcome with grief, inscribed the words 'Pythionice Aphrodite' on the marble.

Important as the role of the hetaerae may have been, the Greeks also loved their wives, and they have provided us with many fine examples of true conjugal fidelity. No matter how many thousands of years go by, this grave-stone erected by one Marathonis to his wife Nicopolis will never lose its moving appeal: 'Under this stone Marathonis laid his Nicopolis to rest and spilled tears upon the marble coffin. They were useless. For what remains for a man whose wife has departed, leaving him alone in the world?'

'Divine power reposes in slaves' hearts, too.' *Aeschylus*

OTHER races saw only themselves, stared at their own kings' citadels, prayed in their own temples, danced about their own gods, made sacrifice to their own particular Moloch. The Greeks, by contrast, tried to understand not only their own world but that of other nations as well. If it had not been for them, we should only have gleaned the scantiest information about early times.

The Greeks had a wonderful instinct for the things which matter in life. In their view, the supreme thing was to be free. Everything the Greeks did or endured, they did and endured in freedom. This was yet another respect in which they differed from all their contemporaries. They regarded personal liberty as the first and foremost earthly blessing.

They also tried to be just. If they did not always succeed, perhaps it was because the question 'What is justice?' was as nearly unanswerable then as it is nowadays. The race which had more than any other recognized the value of personal liberty robbed millions of foreigners of their freedom, moulded them into mere tools without a will of their own, and transformed them into articles of merchandise or useful domestic animals. The Greeks were incapable of imagining a world without slaves.

Opinions vary as to the number of slaves owned during the classical age of Greece. Our best information concerns Attica, where the volume of grain consumed and distributed provides us with a firm basis for calculation. We know, for example, that the annual imports of grain into Attica in 335 B.C. totalled 800,000 medimnae (900,000 bushels). We know that Attica's domestic grain production in 330 B.C. was 370,000 medimnae. If we deduct the allowance for seed-corn (70,000 medimnae), we then find that the total annual grain consumption of the Attic population was 1,100,000 medimnae. We also know that a census taken by Demetrius of Phaleron in Attica in 310 B.C. gave totals of 21,000 adult males with full citizenship, 10,000 metoikoi or foreign immigrants, and 400,000 slaves. The figure 400,000 appears to be a textual corruption, however, for if we put an adult male's yearly consumption of grain at $7\frac{1}{2}$ medimnae and that of women and children at 6 medimnae, the following sum results: total population = 1,100,000 (annual consumption) ÷ (average individual consumption) = approximately 180,000 persons. If we subtract 21,000 full citizens, 10,000 metoikoi, and 60,000 women and children from 180,000 we are left with a figure of 90,000. So there were from 90,000 to 100,000 slaves living in Attica between 350 and

Boeotian terracotta statuette of a cape-dancer dating from the middle of the 3rd century B.C. [Antikensammlun Munich. *Photograph:* Hirmer

The so-called *Athena Lemnia* in the Museo Civico, Bologna; commissioned by Athenian settlers in Lemnos, the bronze original was considered to be Pheidias' finest work. This is a copy. [*Photograph:* Alinari

A very early copy of the bronze statue of Socrates erected by remorseful Athenians in 380 B.C., nineteen years after his execution

Detail of the 'sorrowing companion' from the grave of Mnesarete (Phryne), shown below. This Attic tomb dates from about 380 B.C. [Antikensammlungen, Munich

The Parthenon on the Acropolis at Athens was dedicated to the virgin goddess Athena. Ictinus built it for Pericles using plans drawn up by Pheidias. The building was completed in the year 438 B.C.

Top of a tomb portraying a stout Etruscan, found at Chiusi, on the route from Rome to Florence. Date: possibly 3rd century B.C. [In Florence Museum. *Photograph:* Carlo G. Mundt

An Etruscan married couple adorning the clay sarcophagus in a grave in the ancient Etruscan town of Caere. [*Photograph:* Carlo G. Mundt

Bronze head of an African, 350 B.C. These were the sort of men who worked as government-owned slaves in the wooden galleys of the Carthaginians

A Roman trireme in the time of the Punic Wars. The heavy ship was propelled by slaves rowing sixty a side, and the deck was manned by legionaries armed with spears and shields. During the course of the Punic Wars, these ancient 'ships of the line' were superseded by quinqueremes, five-deckers capable of greater speeds

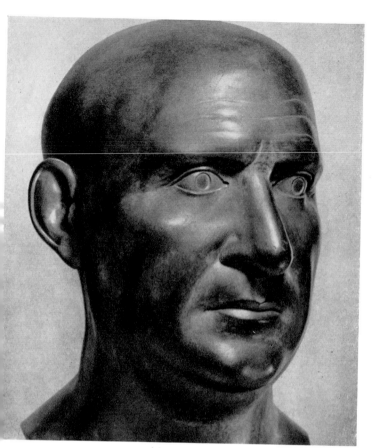

Publius Cornelius Scipio (237–183 B.C.), who defeated Hannibal, was the first really outstanding figure in Roman history

1 and 2. *Golden stater.* 1 stater = 2 drachmas, Obverse: the nymph Arethusa with dolphins

3 and 4. *Silver tetradrachm,* or four-drachma piece, Sicily

5 and 6. *Golden double-stater* minted in Africa, showing the head of Demeter. Punic script on the reverse

330 B.C., together with an equal or slightly smaller number of free men, women, foreigners and children. I have set out this sum in considerable detail because it is sometimes interesting to make an accurate examination of problems like these.

Born and bred in humility for generation after generation, the slaves formed a social stratum of their own. Without slaves, the Greeks thought, neither the individual nor the State could continue to exist. The question whether slavery was just or unjust never arose. Where did the Greeks get their slaves from?

People could be born into slavery. This was not the most productive source of slaves, however, because there were far fewer female slaves than male, and it was cheaper to buy a slave than bring one up from birth. Children could be sold into slavery by free parents, a practice which was universally permitted except in Attica. Foundling children became slaves, free men could sell themselves into slavery, and, until the time of Solon (638-588 B.C.), a debtor whose resources were exhausted automatically became his creditor's slave. But the most important source of slaves was provided by prisoners of war. So it came about that there were not only Asiatic and Thracian, but also Greek slaves, men who had been captured during the numerous fratricidal wars of Greece. In conclusion, kidnappers and pirates were always on the look-out for marketable human prey, and life on the coasts of the Mediterranean was not without its dangers. The slave-trade was a flourishing industry. The principal exporting countries were Syria, Pontus, Lydia, Galatia and, in particular, Thrace, but Egypt, Ethiopia and Italy were also sources of two-legged merchandise. Asiatics made the most popular slaves because they were considered adaptable and were experts at manufacturing luxury articles, but Greek slaves were the most expensive of all. The slave-trade kept the courts of Eastern potentates supplied with courtesans, female musicians and dancers. Athens was an important slave-market, and the State benefited from a high rate of purchase-tax. Other noteworthy slave-markets existed on the islands of Cyprus and Rhodes, at Ephesus, and above all, on the island of Chios.

Slaves who had been put up for sale were either exhibited naked or had to take their clothes off for the benefit of the purchaser. A trader was not allowed to conceal the physical defects of his human wares. Prices varied according to age, capabilities and character. A male or female slave cost between 1 and 10 minas. To give you an idea of what an Athenian had to pay for a slave, here is a small sum. There were a hundred drachmas in one mina. A drachma's purchasing-power at the time of Pericles roughly corresponded to that of £1 14s. today, which would make a Periclean mina worth about £170. On that basis, a slave would have cost between £170 and £1700. There were far fewer poor people in those days than there are now, and any well-to-do family maintained seven slaves at the very least. Indeed, only to possess seven slaves was regarded as a token of poverty. It was considered unseemly if the lady of the house was only accompanied by four female slaves when she went out, and not to have any slave attendants with you when you went for a walk was thought a sign of the greatest poverty. When the wife of a certain Phocion went around with only one slave-woman, the 'scandal' of it became a topic of conversation in the theatre. Men, too, were often attended by three or more slaves, especially when travelling.

Plato treats it as quite normal that a man should own fifty slaves or more. Nicias had a thousand of his slaves out on hire to the mines of Attica. As a matter of fact, most Greek slaves were manual workers whom their owners hired out to factories, farms, or building-contractors. They were regarded as a form of interest-yielding capital.

Slaves who worked as manual labourers were more independent than household slaves. In general, the lot of the Greek slave was happier than that of the Roman, and it is probable that there was a better relationship between slave and master in Athens than later prevailed in Italy. Plutarch speaks of the 'mute obedience' of the Roman slave and the 'familiar garrulity' of the Greek. Everything naturally depended on the disposition of the master. Aristotle recommended that slaves should be treated neither with excessive harshness nor excessive familiarity. The Athenians were of the opinion that masters or mistresses should never engage in banter with their slaves, since that would result in a weakening of their authority. Plato said that a man should affect the utmost formality in his relationship with his own slaves. Slaves should always be allowed to cherish the hope of eventual emancipation, it was advised, and in fact most of them did cherish such a hope, even though very few were ever freed.

A master could beat, chain or punish his slave. The only thing he was not allowed to do was kill him. Alternatively, he could hand him over to a magistrate for punishment. In cases of extreme personal hardship, a slave could request that he be resold, but he could not appeal to the courts. If his master treated him very cruelly, his only recourse was to flee to a temple and take sanctuary at the altars of the gods, waiting there until his owner was compelled to sell him. Household slaves were often beaten, regardless of their sex, but the slaves who had the worst time of it were usually those who worked in the factories of the day, where the overseers and foremen were slaves like themselves.

Slaves who worked on the land or in the mines often wore fetters on their feet, not as a form of punishment, but simply to prevent them from escaping.

There were also inter-State agreements in force under which escaped slaves were recaptured and extradited. Those who had escaped once were branded to prevent any further bids for freedom. Educated slaves like those whom the Romans later employed in scientific work did not exist in the Greek household. Teachers were always free men, never slaves. However, reliable slaves and those who were not fit for heavy work were entrusted with the care of children, and intimate and rather touching relationships often grew up between such slaves and their charges. Luxury-slaves, like musicians, dancers or actors, only came into fashion in later times, when Roman influence was already making itself felt in Greece. Negroes and eunuchs were very popular with the wealthy. Being vain, people liked to make a parade of their slaves, and eunuchs were in particular demand. They were regarded as especially trustworthy, and often administered their master's finances. On the other hand, we find no evidence that they were ever entrusted with the custody of women.

Some women kept slaves as lovers. The Greek poet Herondas, who lived in the 3rd century B.C., has left us some pictures of everyday life written in iambics (so-called 'Mime-iambics'). He describes the case of a jealous woman who accused her slave-lover of infidelity. She had him bound and ordered him to be given 2000 lashes.

Although there were far fewer female slaves than male, much of the work in every prosperous household was performed by slave-women. Besides being responsible for domestic order and cleanliness, they cooked and spun, served as nurses and attendants, and waited on the lady of the house. One especially privileged slave acted as lady's-maid proper.

Particularly sad was the lot of the girls who had to operate the hand-mills for grinding grain whose characteristic hum filled the air in every Greek village. These poor girls often worked until they dropped because their overseers had forgotten all about them. The hand-mill was the constant nightmare of every slave-woman in Greece.

It was not uncommon to find free men living with slave-women, but the children of such unions were only free in very rare cases. Slaves were regarded as mere tools of the free, and the virtues of a male or female slave (the Greeks were quite positive about this) ranked far below those of the free — about as far as animals are below human beings. This attitude was in part due to the fact that people went in perpetual fear of the slave population. In Attica, for instance, there were twice as many slaves as free men, while the district of Corinth alone contained 150,000 slaves (if one included those that were brought to market there), and there were about the same number on Aegina. Whenever war broke out there was always the threat of a slave uprising 'behind the front line'. After the Athenian army's defeat in Sicily and the occupation of Deceleia in 413 B.C. by the Spartans under King Agis, 20,000 slaves deserted the Greeks in Attica at one fell swoop.

There was constant friction between various city-States because one of them had given asylum to escaped slaves from another. In war-time, attempts were always made to incite the enemy's slaves to desert, and generally speaking it was only during periods of complete peace and quiet that the Greek city-States could feel happy about their slaves and exploit their man-power to the full.

Slaves who showed bravery in battle were frequently rewarded with emancipation, but their main concern was usually less to display valour than to stab their Greek masters in the back. One is continually meeting instances in Greek literature of slaves who murdered their masters. Xenophon tells us that the citizens voluntarily set up a mutual protection society to combat the slave menace, and that a property-owner could only feel really safe if he was the first to rise in the morning and the last to go to bed at night.

The dialogue between Xanthias and Aeacus in the celebrated *Frogs* by the comic dramatist Aristophanes gives us some indication of how slaves thought and felt. 'They stick their finger into every pie, listen to what their master says, and then twist it round the wrong way. They grumble outside after they have been beaten, and their greatest delight is in cursing their master behind his back.'

ITALY

THE MYSTERIOUS ETRUSCANS

ABOUT 3000 years ago, men of an alien race landed on the western shores of Italy. Gradually overrunning the present provinces of Toscana and Umbria, they founded cities, evolved their own culture, interpreted the meaning of the stars, built gigantic walls, and produced unique sculptures and paintings which still survive today. They were the very first race to create an advanced civilization on Italian soil.

The Etruscans were a strange people, a people whose language is only now being rediscovered and most of whose enthralling secrets accompanied them to the grave. They maintained their existence for seven hundred years, and then vanished from history once more. The more people excavated, the more they explored, the more they strove to understand the forgotten language of the Etruscans, the harder the task of comprehending their true nature seemed to become. Why did the Etruscans never record their history? What impelled them to come to Italy? Where did they come from?

In the year 1200 B.C., something occurred in the countries of the eastern Mediterranean which violently convulsed the whole of the known world. It was a fearful catastrophe under whose impact governments collapsed, nations were scattered, and cities tumbled into dust and ashes. Whole populations migrated on a scale hitherto unknown, inundating Greece, Asia Minor, Syria and countless islands. An incessant stream of invaders surged from north to south. Assyrian inscriptions, the Old Testament and Egyptian sources shed but scanty light on the obscurity surrounding this vast racial upheaval, which has been christened 'the Aegean Migration' because the area of the Aegean Sea was particularly affected by it.

The various migrations were not conducted on military lines. The migrating races roamed along with all their goods and chattels, travelling in carts or on board ship and bringing the whole of their portable or transportable property with them. It is presumed that the home of these marching hordes was in Europe and that they were of Indo-Germanic stock. The Aegean Migration was responsible for bringing the Dorians into Greece, for destroying the ancient Mycenaean civilization, and for starting the metronome which has regulated Europe's pulse-rate until the present day. It was by the agency of this human cataclysm, too, that a race was set in motion whom the Greeks called the *Tyrsanoi* and from whom the 'Etruscans' of Italy were descended.

Our earliest and in fact only information about the origins of the Etruscans comes from the Greek historian Herodotus, who lived about 500 B.C. Herodotus tells us that in the time of King Atys a great famine broke out in the land of the Lydians. (Lydia lay on the Aegean Sea, near the centre of the western coast of Turkey.) The famine lasted for eighteen years. Wishing to put an end to it, the King of the Lydians commanded half his subjects to emigrate, appointing his son Tyrsanus as their leader. These homeless people procured ships at Smyrna, loaded them with all kinds of useful household equipment, and sailed off over the high seas to look for a new home. 'After sojourning with many nations in turn, they came to the Umbrikoi, where they founded cities and have dwelt ever since. They no longer called themselves Lydians, however, but Tyrsanians, after the name of the king's son who had led them thither.'

The Umbrikoi resided in the present Italian province of Umbria, so we are apparently dealing with a journey from Asia Minor to Italy. Almost all the historians of antiquity derived their views on the origins of the Tyrsanians from the foregoing passage in Herodotus. The Tyrsanians are, in fact, the race whom we call by the later Roman name of 'Etruscans'.

But who were these Tyrsanoi, Tyrsenoi or Tyrrhenoi — as the Greeks used variously to write the name? The Greeks themselves did not always connect the designation with Tyrsanus, the king's son, but sometimes with *tyrsis*, a word meaning fortified town or citadel. However, since the Etruscans never built any fortified towns in Italy it may be fair to assume that there once existed an ancient city called 'Tyrsa', an Etruscan metropolis, a sort of proto-city whose location is unknown to us. If it ever proved possible to find the vanished city of Tyrsa, and if some archaeologist were to dig in the right spot, we should probably then know the Etruscans' exact place of origin. In Tyrsa we are confronted by the very interesting case of a city still awaiting discovery and exploration, a 'Sleeping Beauty' of a city which this unromantic age of ours ought one day to see roused from her slumbers.

The German Etruscan scholar Schachermeyer has even given us a hint where to dig. He tells us to look for the city in the general vicinity of Jamanlar dagh, the area of archaeological discovery in the ancient province of Mysia, on the Aegean coast of modern Turkey opposite the island of Lesbos.

Would it be worth while digging there? Perhaps there never was a city called Tyrsa. Perhaps the Etruscans had been in Italy from time immemorial. Perhaps they were autochthonous. (The Greek word *autos* means 'self' or 'own', and *chthon* means 'earth', so an autochthonous race is one that originated in and has always been indigenous to its present habitat.)

The Extension of Etruria

However, scholars have recently become increasingly convinced that the Tyrsanians or Etruscans were not originally resident in Italy, but were foreign immigrants from Asia Minor. They are, in fact, reverting to the old theory about a long sea-voyage which Herodotus once espoused. Etruscan culture, art, religion and mythology all point in the direction of Asia Minor. The Etruscans were either orientals or semi-orientals. Their art bears a resemblance to that of Mesopotamia, Syria, Crete, Cyprus and Egypt. Their gods and mythological personages appear to be the heroes and gods of the Asiatic sagas. The style in which the Etruscans' mural paintings depict demonic figures comes from the Cretan-Mycenaean world, and their divination and astrology from Babylon. Their chronology was Chaldean in conception, while the 'inspection of livers' which was the focal point of all their religious rites is only to be found among the Babylonians and Hittites, and nowhere else. The Etruscans' towns were laid out in terraces after the Babylonian manner, and their method of burial, which consisted in conserving the ashes of the dead in cloths and open bowls, has its roots in Asia Minor. Furthermore, phenomena such as the Etruscans' 'twin-graves' had never occurred in Italy before their arrival, yet we are familiar with this method of grave-construction among the Mycenaeans. And finally, the Etruscan language also appears to come from Asia. But here we are confronted by some mysteries which have not yet been solved.

There is already in existence today a fairly extensive literature dealing with the problems raised by the Etruscan language and script, and the tomes written by the numerous scholars who have attacked them so energetically and ingeniously in their time would fill a large library.

We can identify those letters of the Etruscan alphabet which are derived from early Greek, it is true, but until recently the full meaning of the inscriptions has remained obscure.

We are today in possession of some 9000 Etruscan inscriptions, most of them being just names, brief title-deeds, or epitaphs. Carved in stone, scratched on clay, or engraved in metal, they have managed to survive the passage of thousands of years. The only text of any length in our possession is the so-called 'Zagreb mummy-bandage'. This is a roll of linen bearing the 1500 words of a sacrificial calendar. The linen had subsequently been used in the embalming of an Egyptian princess, and now reposes in Zagreb Museum.

Berlin Museum owns a clay tablet from Santa Maria di Capua with about 300 words on it, also containing sacrificial instructions. A large stone from Perugia carries a family agreement about the use of a burial-vault. The bronze liver from Piacenza, with its numerous names of gods, is of particular importance since it gives us a picture of the methods used by the Etruscans in divination from the liver of animals. Our recent success in elucidating these inscriptions was based upon an interpretation of the Etruscan numerical terms as used in recording death-statistics.

The scholars who used to include Etruscan among the Indo-European languages were mistaken. On the contrary, we are here dealing with a language very similar in construction to the Uralian (Finno-Ugrian) language. It is well known that Etruscan exercised a measure of influence upon the Italian language, and even Rome, the name of Italy's capital, is Etruscan in derivation.

The Roman emperor Claudius, who was born in the year 10 B.C., was himself the author of an Etruscan history in twenty volumes. This work has unfortunately disappeared, but even if we did have it its value would be doubtful, since the golden age of Etruria lay more than 500 years before Claudius' time. Moreover, the Emperor could scarcely have drawn upon Etruscan sources, since the Etruscans had no historians and never recorded their history.

The Etruscans were the first people in Italy to establish towns. Their favourite sites were hills on whose slopes they could lay out their towns in terraces. Cortona, Chiusi (Clusium), Cosa and Perugia are examples of such hill-side sites. Whenever the Etruscans built a town above a river, they installed their necropolis or cemetery on the opposite bank, so that the abode of the dead was always in view of the living. Examples of this arrangement were Vulci, Cerveteri (Caere) and Tarquinia. Massive walls enclosed each town and, just as in Babylonia, the temple was always situated at its centre. So that the living could commune with their dead, shafts were sunk deep into the ground to enable them to be near those who had passed away.

Italy was still thickly wooded in Etruscan times, and almost everything the Etruscans built was made of wood: their houses, their temples, their gates, their bridges and their sacred precincts.

The Romans described Etruscan men as a race of fat, drunken, dissolute gluttons. They were not a particularly congenial bunch, it seems. We should never forget, however, that the Romans had spent hundreds of years fighting the Etruscans, and had never been exactly fond of their tough enemies. Veii, the most important city in southern Etruria, was besieged by the Romans for ten long years and did not fall into their hands until 396 B.C. Although bitter fighting continued for another three hundred years, this city's capture really marked the beginning of the Etruscans' end. At the battles of Fidenae (426 B.C.) and Sutrium (356 B.C.), the Etruscans were led into action by priests who charged the Romans with an amazing disregard for danger, brandishing live snakes and flaming torches. The Romans fought bitterly against the city of Tarquinia for eight years. The Etruscans sacrificed 307 Roman prisoners of war to their gods, and the Romans retorted in 353 B.C. by stoning and decapitating 358 members of the Etruscan aristocracy in the Forum. It was not until 265 B.C. that the Romans finally managed to capture the Etruscan town of Volsini. The Etruscans received Roman citizenship in the year 89 B.C., but even after that time a few isolated Etruscan cities were still offering resistance. It took Sulla three years of savage fighting before he finally captured Populonia and Volaterrae in 79 B.C. The Etruscan people certainly put up an heroic defence, and it seems improbable that such men could really have been as flabby and self-indulgent as the Romans painted them.

Etruscan women had the same rights as their menfolk and took part in festivals, games and assemblies. Many sculptures and paintings testify to the death-transcending affection and harmony which existed between Etruscan married couples. It has even been suggested that Etruscan society was matriarchal — in other words, one in which the mother of a family took precedence over everyone else. There was once an Etruscan queen of Rome called Talaquil, who seems to have been one of the really great feminine personalities of the ancient world. She had the gift of clairvoyance and is reputed to have possessed magical powers which enabled her to direct the amorous impulses of the young women of Rome as she pleased. Etruscan women were universally famed for their beauty. Anyone with an eye for physiognomy who travels through modern Italy can even now recognize traits in the features of many Italian women which are reminiscent of the Etruscan beauties of long ago.

The whole life of Etruria was governed by thoughts of the life to come. The Etruscans did not just live carelessly from day to day, but kept the prospect of death constantly before their eyes. Just as in Babylon and Egypt, the citizenry were guided and led by a powerful priesthood. Every street, temple, gate and public square was consecrated to one or other of the three most important gods, Tina, Uni and Minerva. Funerals were marked by great festivals held in honour of the dead, by competitive sports, dancing, flute-playing and pantomimes. Much of our knowledge of the Etruscans' civilization is attributable to their habit of living for eternity, and building, modelling and painting for their dead.

The cemeteries and Cerveteri and Tarquinia disclosed complete residences for the dead which had been hewn out of the ground. Precious objects, glorious vases, golden ornaments and magnificent paintings have been unearthed in the cemeteries of Etruria and, whereas Roman slaves were buried in communal graves, the remains of Etruscan slaves were often found in funeral urns grouped round their master's sarcophagus.

Whatever wisdom and culture Rome may have derived from the East she owed mainly to the Etruscans. It was from them that the Romans learned the art of building cities. They adopted the realism of Etruscan sculpture, and the artistic life of Rome was dominated by Etruscan fashions, style of dress, music and drama. The Etruscans were responsible for the introduction into Italy of soothsaying, astrology, natural science and a well formulated theory about lightning. Indeed, the influence of the Etruscans survived long after their cities had been destroyed by the Romans. The Roman emperors Galba, Vespasian, Hadrian, Alexander Severus and Diocletian were all supporters of the Etruscan method of 'entrail-inspection', the method whereby the future was divined from the intestines of animals. Dante, whose facial characteristics were supposed to have resembled the Etruscan type, drew upon murals in Etruscan burial-vaults for his visions of hell.

Etruscan sovereignty in Italy only lasted for 700 years. Yet the culture of this mysterious race of seers and diviners lives on. More and more of their graves are being opened. The highly intelligent faces sculpted on their sarcophagi regard us smilingly with eyes which seem to look into eternity. There is much wisdom written in these faces, much nobility and a hint of irony. Their mute lips whisper to us: 'Your life too will last but a day. To whom does eternity belong?'

THE LAND OF CALVES

At the foot of the Palatine, one of the seven hills of Rome, lay a marsh where the 'first Romans' used to bury their dead. This burial-ground was the site on which the Forum later arose. A few years ago, the urns of men who had been dead for 3000 years were dug up there. Eternal Rome.

THE history of Rome, and with it the history of a world empire, begins with a bridge.

About six miles from the Tyrrhenian Sea, the Tiber — the river the Italians call the 'Tevere' — meets a small but stubborn obstruction. It is an island which has been there since time immemorial and marks the erstwhile site of a wooden bridge which once enabled people to cross the Tiber in comfort. It was a very old bridge, older even than the Bronze Age which was succeeded by the Iron Age in about 1000 B.C. Not a single nail had been driven into the bridge and nothing but wood had been used in its construction, for wood was still invested with the sanctity which the great forests of Europe once possessed in the misty obscurity of prehistoric times. It still held the magical properties of the sacred trees which had been worshipped by the white inhabitants of primeval Europe.

It was there, at the left end of the bridge and in the heart of the fertile plain of Latium, that the eternal city of Rome arose. It was there, too, that the Roman dancers used to gather each spring. They pranced and leapt in wild war-dances, their weapons clanged, the woodwork groaned, and a weird singing rang out across the river to the other bank. Priests guarded the sanctity of this bridge and supervised its cults, and one of these priests was the 'bridge-maker' himself, the *pontifex*. That was so a thousand and perhaps even two thousand years before Christ's birth, yet today, four thousand years later, the man who guards the bridge to heaven which all true believers must tread is likewise called pontifex. And this man, the Pope, resides in the same Rome where the first bridge was once thrown across the Tiber. No wonder Rome is called an eternal city!

To look down from the streets of modern Rome, with its maze of houses, palaces and churches, on to the ancient Forum Romanum, that ruined confusion of marble columns, Roman arches and stonework, is to be forcibly and almost frighteningly reminded of the city's eternal past. As one stands there, it seems as though the clock were racing backwards in time at an irresistible pace over hundreds and thousands of years towards the moment when the first stone was laid, and one is struck by a thought which has probably occurred to countless millions of men in countless ages: two or three thousand years ago people like ourselves trod these same stones, people with cares and joys, good and evil thoughts very like our own. One has to look down a little to see the Forum, for it lies rather below modern street-level. Cities not only grow downwards into the depths of their burial-vaults and catacombs, but on the surface as well, rising above the debris left behind by generation after generation of their inhabitants.

Yet another thought occurs to one. How small ancient Rome really was, despite the magnificence of her buildings, and how cramped and confined everything was.

Among the seven hills of Rome (they are now partially flattened) were two called the Palatine and the Capitoline. Between them lay a valley, and in the valley brooded a dismal marsh and three small lakes. To the north-east of the Capitoline stood the Quirinal hill. The Quirinal was inhabited by a tribe called the 'Sabini', and the Palatine by the 'Latini'. These people were not yet townsmen, and Rome was still far from being a city. Her inhabitants lived in mud huts with steep thatched roofs, and left the smoke of their fires to drift out through the door. Living-quarters were surrounded by stables, and cows wandered in the streets. They were a race of sturdy peasants, these unwitting ancestors of the future masters of the world.

In the valley below the Palatine hill, on the present site of the Forum, there once used to be a burial-ground. The Romans of Cicero's time were aware that their Forum surmounted an age-old cemetery, and called it the 'Doliola'. It was forbidden to spit or speak aloud there, for far below lay the sinister relics of prehistoric times, the funeral urns of the first inhabitants of Rome.

This ancient tradition encouraged the Italian archaeologist Giacomo Boni (d. 1925) to dig there. On the northern side of the valley at the foot of the temple of Antoninus and Faustina, he unearthed a burial-ground dating from the early Iron Age, from the 9th to 6th centuries B.C. It is the earliest token of human presence in the Forum.

The Latins on the Palatine and the Sabines on the Quirinal were not well-disposed towards each other. Wars were waged between the two hills just as they were later waged between towns, later still between principalities, later still between countries, and as they will probably some day be waged between continents or planets. However, there came a day when they made peace. And when peace had been made, they drained the marsh below the two hills. The villages expanded and the centre of the marsh became a communal forum or market-place.

On the rocks which projected from the lower slopes of the Capitoline hill the early Romans erected altars for their gods Saturn and Vulcan, and on the Palatine hill they built a shrine to the goddess Vesta and a house for her priestesses, the Vestal Virgins.

ITALY

The early inhabitants of Rome had a curious collection of gods. There was Pales, the tutelary god of cattle, Deverra, the goddess of sweeping, and Janus, the twin-headed god who guarded the front door, which was itself sacred. Then there was Faunus, a woodland god. The sacred festival of Faunus was celebrated by 'wolf-men' who pranced about naked on the Palatine hill and lashed women with thongs to stimulate fertility.

Wolf-men . . . That is a story on its own.

Italy was still, it must be remembered, a land of unbroken forests. Wolves used to wander into the town of Rome, howl eerily at night on the slopes of the seven hills, and occasionally steal a child or two. The twin brothers Romulus and Remus, to whom legend attributes the founding of Rome in 753 B.C., were suckled in their infancy by a she-wolf, and there used to be a shrine on the Palatine called the 'Lupercal' which was sacred to that animal.

The Romans of those days were a wild race of men who dressed themselves in clothes and caps of skins. They were probably acquainted with altars and holy shrines, but had not yet started to build temples or set up idols. Just as cattle were used as a form of money among the Greeks of Homer in 1000 B.C., so they were in Rome, too, and *pecunia*, the Roman word for money, derived its name from *pecus*, meaning ox. At a time when Greek civilization was already in its prime, the Latins were forging primitive weapons in bronze, sacrificing bulls on the Mons Albanus, and (something they probably did as well then as they do nowadays) making cheese. The tribe which spoke the language we now call Latin was probably more industrious than its neighbours. The dialects spoken by this group of tribes were so closely related that they are now all classified as 'Italic', and the people who spoke them 'Italici', or Italians.

As we have already seen, the Italici were principally cattle-breeders, and ancient tradition has it that this occupation originally gave the land of Italy its name. *Italos* was the Greek for 'bull-calf': thus 'Italia' was 'the land of calves'.

The boundary between the Latins and the Etruscans was marked by the river Tiber. The Etruscans were constantly launching attacks on the village of Rome, which meant that the Romans learned the arts of defence, and war in general, at a very early stage in their history. It was from the Etruscans that they adopted the 'phalanx', an infantry battle-formation designed for heavily armed troops wearing helmets and armour and carrying spears and shields. The Etruscans, in their turn, had taken over this battle-formation from the Greeks.

Even as late as 700 B.C. the Romans could not read or write. This was yet another art which they learned from the Etruscans, for they modelled their own letters on the Etruscans' Greek alphabet. In contrast to the Etruscans, however, they wrote from left to right. It is this Roman modification of the Greek alphabet which we ourselves have inherited.

In 600 B.C. the Latins fell completely under the sway of their dangerous neighbours, and the Etruscan Tarquins became the first kings of Rome. In 509 B.C., however, these kings were overthrown, and Rome became a republic.

The Romans had succeeded in throwing off Etruscan domination, but southern Italy and the island of Sicily were occupied by Greek colonists. This portion of the peninsula was known as Magna Graecia or 'Great Greece'. Tarentum, Heraclea, Rhegium and Locri were all Greek cities during this period.

But how could these cities maintain their strength, when the ancient glory of their Greek motherland was giving way to fatigue and collapse, and when the King of Macedonia, Alexander the Great, had been carried to his grave? Greece and the East in general were still the home of great numbers of artists, scholars and poets. The Greek theatre could still boast magnificent acting. But the actors were now better than the plays they performed; and when the executive side of an art is stronger than the creative, its end is always near. Greece and the countries of the eastern Mediterranean had never held more splendid banquets, displayed a higher standard of cuisine or enjoyed a more pampered standard of living. Trade flourished. Yet, militarily, the East was weak. Rome gained the upper hand in the Greek part of southern Italy because Greece had left the stage of world history.

It was at this juncture, when little Rome, the future ruler of the world, was at the very beginning of her irruption into history, that she was opposed by Pyrrhus, the last of the great Greek generals.

Pyrrhus was the king of Epirus and a relation of Olympias, the mother of Alexander the Great. Throughout his life (318-272 B.C.), Pyrrhus referred to himself as a descendant of Achilles, the hero who fought at Troy. Pyrrhus was also a hero, but he was obsessed by the tragic impulses of one who was born too late, of a man who at heart still embodied the Greece of long ago, but belonged to an age when Greece luxuriated on rugs and cushions and regarded any man with ambitions for world conquest as an unnatural son.

Pyrrhus came to the throne when he was still a boy. His only education was life itself, which made him shrewd and adaptable. He was brought to the court of Ptolemy as a hostage by Demetrius. Ptolemy was another man who occupied a throne which had once ruled the world, being the founder of the Ptolemaic empire of Egypt. It was at his court that Pyrrhus married Antigone, Ptolemy's step-daughter.

The stronghold of Hellenism in Italy and the pride of all the Greek colonial foundations was the splendid city of Tarentum. In 281 B.C. Tarentum was attacked by Rome, a youthful Rome which was just beginning to flex its mighty limbs. Tarentum appealed to her mother-country for aid, whereupon Pyrrhus was dispatched to Italy, and marched to the attack with 25,000 men, including cavalry and an elephant corps. He engaged the Romans at Heraclea, and in the ensuing battle defeated the Roman consul Valerius Laevinus. The encounter cost him so many casualties, however, that his triumph went down in history for all time as a 'Pyrrhic victory'.

Pyrrhus very nearly reached the outskirts of Rome. He defeated the Roman legions yet again, but the Romans obstinately refused to sue for peace. In the end, gallant Pyrrhus gained so many victories that he became completely exhausted. He crossed to Sicily with the intention of driving the Carthaginians out of the island, but the Romans allied themselves with the Carthaginians and the Sicilian cities rebelled against the Greek general's tyrannical methods. He stayed in Sicily for three years before trying his luck in Italy once more, only to be defeated at Beneventum in 275 B.C. Five years later, in 270 B.C., the whole of southern Italy was under Roman control.

Before Pyrrhus left Italy to make his way disconsolately homewards, he uttered a very interesting prophecy. He foretold the dreadful wars which were later to break out between Rome and Carthage. Looking eleven years ahead, he saw a war which was destined to drag on for more than a century. He saw the faces of drowning, dying men, and his prophetic words were these: 'What a battle-field I am bequeathing to Rome and Carthage!' It has always been so in world history: at first, two powers unite against a common enemy. But when once that enemy has been disposed of, a conflict arises between the victors – first a cold war, then a hot war and then . . . who knows? There is a depressing similarity between the cases of Rome and Carthage and America and Russia!

The Romans had captured so much booty in their wars against Pyrrhus that they used the material to build the most famous aqueduct in the history of the world. It was over thirty-four miles long, and brought fresh water to Rome from the mountains. Large portions of this aqueduct can still be seen today. It was so well built, so firmly supported by the Roman arches which carried it on its lofty journey through the countryside, that sections of it have survived for more than 2200 years.

For centuries the Romans drank water which had travelled to them along their canal in the sky, and even today people stand lost in wonder before this bridge with its innumerable arches, before this miracle wrought by an aspiring nation, before this symbol of a strength which clothed itself in beauty and passed it on to later European millennia as civilization.

CARTHAGE

§

ELEPHANTS AND GALLEYS

The millionaires of Carthage sat there on the terraced roofs of their skyscrapers, an enlightened, shrewd and rather pampered race of men. They were still the masters of the world. Meanwhile, an endless column was making its laborious way across the Alps. Hannibal, the Carthaginian cavalry general, was marching to war with his elephants.

'FROM now on there will be no more progress,' people said. 'We have reached the zenith of erudition, knowledge and ingenuity.' That was in the year 300 B.C.

Berossus, the Babylonian priest, historian, astrologer and astronomer, was constructing a gigantic sun-dial. In the 'Bright Hall' at Athens the Stoics were discoursing on the meaning of life, and on virtue, the only source of happiness. The Greek astronomer Aristarchus had recognized that the sun is the centre of our planetary system, but he had an even greater announcement to make: that the earth does not simply rotate upon its own axis, but whirls in a circle round the sun's orb as well. Manetho, the Egyptian priest and student of history, was striving to communicate the former greatness of Egyptian history to the West. In Rome, there was jubilation among the crowds whose hubbub filled the Forum, for from now on no State appointment was barred to plebeians. A mysterious race invaded Rome's northern territories, plundered them, and finally settled there. They were the Celts. Meanwhile, the fields of central Europe witnessed the appearance of a strange new invention, an iron plough with round things attached to it — the first wheels the northern part of the Western world had ever seen.

Three hundred years before Christ!

The Carthaginians lolled on the terraced roofs of their six-storeyed skyscrapers, quaffing wine from the island of Samos and feeling that they were masters of the world. They found it impossible to believe that anyone could be richer, more powerful or more magnificent than they. Yes, the zenith of progress had really been reached.

Italy and the island of Sicily divide the Mediterranean into an eastern and a western half. At the point where North Africa juts closest to Sicily lies the Gulf of Tunis, and by the shores of this North African bay, twelve and a half miles from the modern city of Tunis, the landscape has from time immemorial been broken by a projecting hill. Today this high ground is surmounted by the French convent of the 'White Fathers', the cathedral of St Louis, and

O   417

an archaeological museum housing the treasures of ancient Carthage which were dug up by Père Delattre.

Our word 'purse' has an interesting etymological ancestry. The Greek word *bursa* used to mean 'leather' or 'leathern money-pouch'. Later on, the term was applied to the actual site of commercial transactions (cf. the French *Bourse*), and so it is easy to see how the heart of Carthage, the largest commercial city in the Mediterranean, came to be called 'Byrsa'. Byrsa was the name of the hill which carried the citadel and the oldest quarter of this most amazing metropolis in the ancient world. It was there that the earliest Punic graves were found. For the Carthaginians were Punians, the same people whom we know as 'Phoenicians' or 'Poeni', from the adjective *Punicus*. They were the same Semites who called their original home 'Chanaan', after the Canaan of the Bible, and whose oldest capital cities were Tyre and Sidon. Carthage was founded by Phoenician colonists from the city of Tyre in 800 B.C., and its name literally means 'new city'.

Anyone visiting Tunis should once make the twelve-and-a-half-mile trip by sea to the hill of Byrsa. It is only a little under two hundred feet high, but the view from its summit is most rewarding. What immediately strikes one is the decisive command Carthage must have had over the sea and the undulating hinterland which stretches westward to Tunis and the Lake of Tunis, now a salt-water lagoon.

The Greek author Polybius, who wrote a forty-volume history of the world in about 150 B.C., described Carthage as the wealthiest city in the world. Carthage was the Phoenicians' most important commercial centre, and possessed capacious harbours which were proof against any storm. Walls over sixty feet high have been dug up on the hill of Byrsa. The city dominated the whole of the North African coast from Egypt to Gibraltar, as well as southern Spain, the islands of Sardinia and Corsica, and the western half of Sicily. From Sicily to Gibraltar, in fact, the Mediterranean was a 'Carthaginian sea'. Through the warehouses of the merchants of Carthage passed the gold and pearls of the East, purple from Tyre, ivory, lion and leopard-skins from the African interior, incense from Arabia, linen from Egypt, clay vessels and aromatic wines from Greece, copper from Cyprus, silver from Spain, tin from England, iron from Elba. Her ships sailed far out into the Atlantic, putting in at the Canary Islands and probably the Azores too. Was it any wonder that Carthage became a world power?

The citizens who walked the streets of Carthage in 300 B.C. were an enlightened, shrewd and, one might almost say, rather pampered folk. Their city could look back on half a thousand years of thriving evolution. Foreign visitors stared in awe at the splendid marble temples with their gold and silver pillars and gilded statues of Greek workmanship, at the largest harbour installations in the contemporary world, the wharves and docks, the warehouses, workshops and factories. (The magnificent cathedral at Pisa was constructed of blocks of marble brought to Italy from the ruins of Carthage.) The Carthaginians formed joint stock companies, developed the most up-to-date financial economy in the ancient world, and invented the first money to have only a conventional but not an intrinsic value. They owned well-stocked arsenals, knew how to build machinery, and manufactured weapons which possibly represented the earliest 'modern' artillery in the world. The casemates at Carthage contained stabling for 300 elephants. The sturdiest negro slaves and the loveliest slave-girls in Africa were sold in the city's market. Carthaginian planters owned the fertile land of Libya and used chain-gangs to work it, some citizens owning as many as 20,000 slaves.

There were villas and palaces at Carthage, together with tall blocks of apartment and office buildings. The city had a rectangular street system just like Manhattan's, each block measuring 36 yards by 136 yards. The astonishing symmetry of the street network was disclosed by archaeological excavation. There were berths for 220 warships in the naval station at Carthage. In the middle of the harbour stood an island from which the Punic admiral could survey his fleet in comfort.

If there were ever such a thing as a plutocracy, a State where government was exercised by the rich, Carthage was a prime example of it. The wealthiest families made the laws and directed policy. The two presidents who were elected annually well knew that gold and silver were the decisive factors in war. It was gold and silver which enabled the Carthaginians to build ships and recruit the foreign mercenaries who were willing to sacrifice their lives for their wealthy masters, gold and silver which allowed them to win sea-battles without having to expose themselves to the risk which such unpleasant work involved. A few of the aristocratic families supplied the admirals, it was true, but by and large the millionaires of Carthage preferred to stay at home, drinking Greek wine from the island of Samos on their magnificent terraces and roof-gardens. They preferred to sit there, fanned by slave-girls, and admire the purple robes of their elegant womenfolk, ladies who never let their dressmakers touch any material which was not a dream by contemporary Mediterranean standards.

There was no doubt about it, Carthage was the richest city in the world. Her inhabitants had implicit faith in the power of gold, and it was only when very considerable danger threatened the masters of the world in their lofty houses that they became ready to sacrifice anything beyond gold to combat it. In such cases, the Carthaginians cremated their children alive to placate Baal Moloch and appease the hunger of the goddess Tanit. On the whole, however, the Carthaginians knew of better ways to win wars than the sickly sweet smell of burnt sacrifices which filled so many aristocratic families with dread. They relied on the courage of hired barbarians, on large elephant corps, on their splendid navy and on gold — especially gold.

How did this commercial metropolis become so wealthy? It was quite simple. Foreign ships and, in particular, Roman ships, were permitted to carry on trade with Carthage direct, but not with her colonies. This shrewd measure ensured that all merchandise passed through the city's books — and on the assets side, too. Any ships which disregarded the embargo on colonial trade were captured by the Carthaginians and their crews thrown overboard. One Carthaginian admiral said with pride: 'The Romans cannot even wash their hands in the Mediterranean without our sanction.'

Three wars were fought between Carthage and Rome. These were the celebrated Punic Wars, World Wars 1, 2 and 3 of that particular era. They covered a span of 119 years. The sanguinary performance began in 264 B.C. By 146 B.C. it was all over. Carthage was destroyed and became a Roman province in Africa.

Were the Carthaginians a cowardly race? Did this city of merchants produce no heroes at all?

It needed stout hearts to sail across the uncharted and even the charted seas of the world in those days, and the Phoenicians demonstrated time and again that they did not lack for such men. These Semites — Mommsen describes them as 'Aramaeans' — 'defended their national integrity against all the lures of Greek civilization as well as against all the forceful methods of oriental and occidental despots with a stubbornness unequalled by any Indo-Germanic race, both with the weapons of the spirit and with their blood'.

What the Carthaginians lacked was political organization. We read in the Bible: 'They dwelt careless, after the manner of the Zidonians, quiet and secure' (Judges). The men who had witnessed the First Punic War and those who had fought in the Second were all long since in heaven or hell when Rome was finally victorious.

How did the wars start in the first place?

The city of Messina in Sicily supplied the immediate cause. The Roman tribune Caius Claudius landed there and took the Carthaginian general Hanno prisoner, and the Carthaginians, after lengthy deliberation, declared war.

The Roman Senate were naturally well aware that any interference in Sicily could mean war with Carthage. However, the war-party in Rome gained the upper hand, and so began a bloody chapter in world history which terminated in Roman supremacy in the Mediterranean.

The Carthaginians were at that time superior to every other nation in the world where ship-building was concerned. Carthage built quinqueremes, ships with five banks of oars manned by government-owned slaves. These galley-slaves were excellently drilled, and the ships' captains were skilful and daring men.

The Romans were still not much more than a race of peasants in those days. An up-to-date warship seemed as weird and wonderful a device to them as a Flying Saucer does to us, and they were quite ignorant of how to build one. However, there came a day when a 'Flying Saucer' fell into their hands. A Carthaginian ship was driven up on the Italian coast. With this wreck to serve them as a pattern, the Romans began to cut down their forests for the first time, and before long they had constructed 120 galleys, each manned by 300 oarsmen and 120 soldiers.

At that time, naval engagements were won by ramming enemy ships. This manœuvre demanded considerable experience, and naval experience was just what the Romans lacked. But necessity is the mother of invention, and in this case the Romans hit upon what may have been the most important invention in their history. On the forward part of their galleys they installed 'flying bridges', triple ramps which could be let down over the prow or on either side. If an enemy ship rammed a Roman galley, the Romans dropped the appropriate bridge down on to the enemy deck, where it stayed, firmly held there by an iron spike which embedded itself in the woodwork. The Carthaginian captains, who were only schooled in the ramming technique, had about three hundred oarsmen and a mere ten soldiers on board. Once the Romans had driven their hooks into the enemy deck, some 120 legionaries charged across the gangway and set to work with their swords. Thus the Romans turned the sea-battle of Mylae (260 B.C.) into a sort of land-battle. The date is important because it marks the Romans' first great naval victory — if so it can be termed.

For all that, the Roman admirals lost one fleet after another as time went by, until no less than 700 Roman ships and 200,000 men lay scattered on the Mediterranean sea-bed. Rome summoned up her last reserves of strength, built a new fleet, defeated the Punians, and Carthage surrendered. The First Punic War came to an end in 241 B.C., having lasted twenty-four years. Carthage had to pay no less than 2300 gold talents in reparations, and her possessions in western Sicily were annexed by Rome. It looked as though Carthage was finished. Her naval power had been shattered. Mutiny broke out, and flames painted the sky above Carthage a sinister red. Finally, order began to be restored. The Carthaginians once more took to drinking wine on their terraces in the cool of the evening. . . .

The man who quelled the post-war mutiny was a general called Hamilcar. When he had completed his work at home, he set sail for southern Spain and defiantly began to fortify and extend Carthaginian possessions there. The Spanish silver-mines supplied the necessary funds.

In 237 B.C. we see Hamilcar with a nine-year-old son at his side. The boy swore on his father's hand 'never to be a friend of the Romans'. It was the oath of his lifetime, an oath which Hannibal never broke.

Hamilcar died, and young Hannibal rose in the world as no Carthaginian had ever done before him. At the age of twenty he was a cavalry general, at twenty-five he was commander-in-chief of the Carthaginian army in

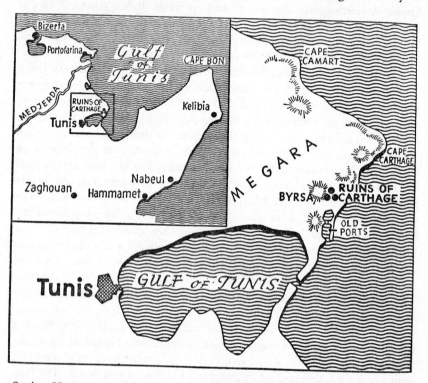

Spain. He conquered large tracts of territory there and eventually besieged Saguntum, a city south of the Ebro. Saguntum had concluded a defensive pact with Rome, and Roman envoys warned him that the place was a 'Roman sphere of interest'. Hannibal was undeterred, however, and after eight months Saguntum fell into his hands. A Roman delegation appeared in Carthage and demanded satisfaction. Bunching his robe together, the Roman spokesman declared that it contained either peace or war, and that it was for Carthage to choose which. The shrewd Carthaginians answered that they left the decision to the Romans. The Roman envoy was no diplomat: he chose war. The Carthaginians nodded assent, and the Second Punic War had begun.

Rome shipped troops to Spain and simultaneously prepared to attack Carthage herself. Hannibal, the Carthaginian, devised an even bolder plan. At the head of his battle-tried veterans, he marched through Spain, across the Pyrenees, through southern France, and finally across the Alps and into Italy, taking an elephant corps with him. Thousands of his soldiers, only accustomed to the warm climates of Spain and Africa, died of cold and hunger in the high Alpine passes. Even so, Hannibal eventually reached the Po Valley with half his army intact.

This enterprise is one of the most interesting military achievements in world history. In these days we should term it a masterpiece of logistics. Hannibal's crossing of the Alps has been so hotly debated by geographers, historians, military experts and ethnologists, that we will take the trouble to accompany the great cavalry general, organizer and strategist on his journey across the snow-covered heights of the St Bernard Pass.

THE TRAGEDY OF HANNIBAL

The Carthaginians defended their city of skyscrapers street by street and block by block, until everything was submerged in blood and debris. Carthage blazed and her walls tottered and fell. She was never to rise again.

THE Roman historian Titus Livius, a contemporary of Christ, left behind him a monumental work in 142 volumes. Livy was born in 59 B.C. and died in the seventeenth year of our era. Thirty-five of his books have survived, together with the tombstone which reposes in the Museo Civico at Padua, the city of his birth and death. Livy had this stone engraved during his lifetime with the words: 'Titus Livius, son of Caius, for him and his.'

A Roman to his very marrow, Livy extolled the traditional Roman virtues, idealized Rome's past, and wrote what the ancient world regarded as the 'crowning glory of Roman historical writing'. As a patriotic Roman, Livy must have had good reasons for his admiration of Hannibal, the most dangerous adversary in his country's history. Most other Roman and Greek historians hounded Hannibal through their pages with a mixture of hatred and envy.

It is astonishing that Hannibal still occupies such a resplendent place in the recollections of men, when we consider what poor memories they generally have and how eager they are to misrepresent the facts.

Let us listen to what Livy, a Roman, says about the Carthaginian general: 'Hannibal met dangers with the most painstaking precautions, but conducted himself in moments of dire emergency with the greatest possible equanimity. He never allowed any difficulties to fatigue his body or curb his spirits. He ate and drank only as much as was absolutely necessary, never for pleasure. His times of rising and retiring were independent of day and night. He rested when he had time, and needed neither a soft bed nor quiet for sleep. He was often to be seen lying on the ground between guard-posts, wrapped only in a short military cape. His dress was scarcely different from that of his men, although his weapons and his charger were objects of universal admiration. He was always by far the best cavalryman and by far the best foot-soldier in the whole of his great army. He rode into action ahead of everyone, and was the last to leave the battle-field. The older soldiers always had the feeling that a youthful Hamilcar — Hannibal's father — had been given back to them, with the same radiant look, the same fire in the eyes, the same splendid bearing and physique.'

It was Hannibal who as a cavalry general had supplied the occasion of the Second Punic War by his capture of Saguntum in Spain, and it was he, burning with the same hatred of Rome which Roman historians later lavished upon him, who wanted to win that war for Carthage.

The Romans' plan was to transport their main army from Sicily to Africa by sea and attack Carthage, while sending a second army to Spain to keep the enemy occupied there. Under no circumstances did they want to fight on Italian soil. And Hannibal? Hannibal decided to do just what the Romans were striving at all costs to avoid. He resolved to carry the war to the very gates of Rome.

It was a daring and dangerous project, for ever since Rome's victory in the First Punic War her navy had been far superior to that of Carthage. Hannibal was thus faced by the problem of how to carry the war to Italy without shipping his soldiers across the Mediterranean. He solved it by devising a plan — it was in the year 218 B.C., never forget — which must be numbered among the most audacious pieces of military strategy in world history. If he could only succeed in marching an army all the way across Spain and southern France, over the Alps and down into the valley of the Po, he would then give the Romans so much to do that they would have to abandon all idea of attacking Carthage. Then the merchants of Carthage could go quietly about their business again, earn mountains of money, and drink wine on their lovely terraces.

Hannibal did not plunge blindly into his vast undertaking. He pondered it carefully, planning it down to the last detail. Indeed, he prepared his Italian expedition with much more care than Alexander the Great ever devoted to his Asian campaigns. There was one other thing in his favour. The north of Italy was occupied by the Gauls whose presence there was a source of constant irritation to the Romans. If he could only reach the southern side of the Alps he would be able to count on Gallic support.

If we reflect on the care with which Hannibal planned his enterprise, we cannot fail to be astonished at the blind fury with which certain 'great generals' of our own day have plunged into their military escapades.

Hannibal assembled a powerful army in Spain. He did not rely on mercenaries but collected Carthaginian soldiers of long service and equipped them with the most up-to-date weapons available. He sent scouts across the Alps to explore various routes and passes, for the area was scarcely known at all in those days. He dispatched envoys to the Gauls of northern Italy to interest them in his plans long before he himself arrived. He concluded pacts of friendship with numerous Gallic tribes, established embassies among them, and sent them financial aid. He was never for one instant in doubt about the immense risks he was running, but he was also aware of the advantage of surprise.

The Romans were subtle in small things but careless in big. They had given Carthage twenty years in which to recuperate, twenty years in which they could have attacked Africa. The respite was sufficiently long for the Punians' spirit of aggression to revive. Rome failed to recognize the dangers inherent in the Punic conquest of Spain. Engaging in a senseless feud with Macedonia, she neglected to put down the Celts and secure the Alpine passes. Her only resolve was to fight the next Punic war on African soil, and she went on nursing that idea until the Carthaginians decided to select their own battle-ground. The Romans were as careless in their historical infancy as they were over-cautious when they reached man's estate.

In May 218 B.C., Hannibal was thirty-one years old. He was at the best possible age for the hardest undertaking of his life, and it was a noble army which he led out of Cartagena, or New Carthage. The hard core of this army was composed of Carthaginian veterans, Libyans and Spaniards. Two-thirds of it were Carthaginian Africans, battle-hardened, disciplined men who were loyally devoted to their cavalry general. It is fully in keeping with our picture of this tough general, with his strength of character and self-discipline, that he sent his beautiful Spanish wife Imilcea and his little son back to Carthage before his departure. Sixteen years were to pass before he embraced them again. At the end of May, Hannibal crossed the Ebro and marched on over the Pyrenees. Hostile tribes contested every foot of his way through northern Spain. Crossing the Rhône, he passed through the valley of the upper Isère and reached the High Alps at a point near the Little St Bernard. Throughout this march, and especially in the mountains of Tarentaise, he was under incessant attack by hostile Celtic tribes.

Historians and geographers have fiercely debated which pass Hannibal used when he crossed the Alps. No less distinguished a student of ancient history than Professor Gaetano de Sanctis of Rome University has given it as his opinion that Hannibal used the Alpine pass of Mont Genèvre. This must be an error, however, and the *Encyclopaedia Britannica* should amend its article on the subject. Our most reliable source is the Greek historian Polybius, born in 201 B.C., who actually saw Carthage burning in 146 B.C., and died in 120 B.C. as the result of a fatal riding-accident. His treatment of the Second Punic War contains very precise details of the distances which Hannibal covered on his march. Livy, too, describes Hannibal's march across the Alps, but he lived 200 years after the event, and his account is much too good to be true. Polybius, on the other hand, was a soldier, and he was writing only a generation after Hannibal's campaign. Lieutenant-Colonel Theodore Ayrault Dodge, an American, took the trouble to follow out both Polybius' and Livy's accounts. He clambered around over the Alpine passes with their texts in his hand until he finally settled on the Little St Bernard. Dodge then wrote a first-class book on Hannibal. He was even able to refute Napoleon, who displayed a significant interest in Hannibal's route and came to the conclusion that he chose the pass over Mont Cenis. It may serve to illustrate how many great minds have applied themselves to this detail of history if we cite yet another name, that of Theodore Mommsen, the great German historian. He always had an infallible instinct for solving such problems, and rightly sends Hannibal over the Little St Bernard.

At the foot of the St Bernard rises the celebrated 'White Rock', *La Roche Blanche*, a chalk cliff which commands the approaches to the pass. It was there that Hannibal bivouacked with his infantry and spent a whole night covering the laborious ascent of his cavalry, pack-mules and elephants. There were a series of sanguinary engagements during the night, but the top of the pass was reached on the following day. There, by the shores of a small lake at the source of the Doria, Hannibal allowed his army to rest.

How large was this army? It consisted of 50,000 infantry, 9000 cavalry, and a corps of 37 elephants. These elephants present us with another interesting historical problem. The Carthaginians had adopted the elephant as a weapon of war from the Greek kings, perhaps from Pyrrhus or even Alexander. They used African, not Indian elephants, although the drivers were Indian. It may be that the habitat of the wild elephant extended farther north in those days than it does now (they are still to be found in Central Africa), or again, it may be that the Carthaginians had them brought from Central Africa along the caravan-routes leading through the Sahara.

One thing is certain: Hannibal brought these elephants with him more to impress the Celts and Gauls than with the intention of using them seriously in battle. One could never be too sure how the beasts would behave in action. They struck terror into races who had never encountered them before, but if they turned savage they were often more of a menace to the Carthaginians than to their foes. That was why elephant-drivers in the Second Punic War always kept a heavy mallet and some long iron pegs handy, so that they could drive one home behind their beast's ear and kill it the moment it threatened to get out of control.

When Hannibal reached the top of the St Bernard he found the pass already deep in snow — huge masses of it, probably deposited there by avalanches. In Mommsen's estimate, Hannibal crossed the pass at the beginning of September. Dodge puts it at the beginning of November. At all events, the climate up there was undoubtedly much more severe 2000 years ago than it is today. Men died like flies in the intense cold, many soldiers stumbled into the yawning chasms which bordered their route, and the elephants starved.

Hannibal had crossed the Alps, but he had lost more than half his army en route. The Carthaginian general could only muster 20,000 infantry, 6000 cavalry, and 15 to 20 elephants. Furthermore, he was now inside the borders of a country which could in theory mobilize 280,000 men and recruit about twice that number from among its allies. However, the Romans only had 40,000 men under arms, and the first Roman army had no sooner taken up its stand in the Po Valley than the Carthaginians overwhelmed it.

The Gauls joined forces with Hannibal according to plan, which doubled the army at his disposal. He annihilated a second Roman army at Lake Trasimene. This meant that Rome had now lost 40,000 men on each of two separate occasions. In their hour of direst necessity the Romans hastily levied some more troops and put them under the command of the Dictator Fabius. This cautious aristocrat has gone down in history as the *Cunctator*, or 'Delayer', because although he followed Hannibal's army everywhere it went he never ventured to engage it in pitched battle.

Rome then gave the supreme command to two Consuls, who were to annihilate Hannibal once and for all. Battle was joined in a narrow plain near Cannae in 216 B.C. The Romans greatly outnumbered the Carthaginians, but Hannibal was the greater tactician and had the better cavalry. Taking the Roman army in the flank, a manœuvre which turned the heavily armed and ponderous Roman soldiery into an impotent mass, he butchered it. Fifty thousand Roman and allied soldiers fell that day, and 10,000 were captured.

When the news reached Rome, the Senate forbade the women who had lost their fathers, husbands and sons to weep. The city made ready for a siege. But Hannibal never appeared. His cavalry could win battles, it was true, but they could not charge walls, and he had not been able to bring any catapults or battering-rams with him on his long-range expedition.

Some of Rome's allies deserted her, as was usual in such cases. The large cities of Syracuse and Capua and a few smaller places left Rome in the lurch. The Roman Senate remained unperturbed, however. While Hannibal was marching through Italy leaving a trail of destruction in his wake, the Romans were mustering more and more legions with every year that passed. The fields of Italy had been devastated, and grain had to be imported at war-time prices. The Romans eventually besieged Capua and Syracuse to make an example of them and stiffen their other allies' resistance. Capua was starved out, and Syracuse was looted and her glorious marble statues borne away to Rome.

In her hour of need, Rome found a young and brilliant general in Publius Cornelius Scipio, the man who captured Cartagena in Spain.

Hannibal was now in southern Italy, waiting for Rome to capitulate or his younger brother Hasdrubal to arrive from Spain with reinforcements. Hasdrubal crossed the Alps in Hannibal's footsteps, but he was defeated by the Roman legions at the Metaurus and killed. The Romans were so embittered by their years of defeat that they catapulted Hasdrubal's head into Hannibal's camp.

Hannibal waited. He was undefeated, but without reinforcements he was becoming weaker every year. In Spain, young Scipio annihilated one batch of reinforcements after the other, and he was finally able to return to Rome in triumph. He was given an army and a fleet and sailed off to attack Carthage. The tables were turned. Scipio the Roman stood before the gates of Carthage. Carthage was forced to capitulate, to sue for peace, and to recall Hannibal from Italy. Hannibal's story is a tragic one. In all of fifteen long years in Italy he had not lost a single battle. On one occasion he had got to within three miles of Rome. Nothing but weeds grew in the fields of Italy. Hundreds of towns lay in ruins. The bones of Carthaginian soldiers and Carthaginian pack-animals bleached in the Alpine passes. Hundreds of thousands of Romans and Roman allies had been killed. All this Hannibal had achieved. He was the greatest military genius in the ancient world, perhaps second only to Alexander the Great. And it had all been in vain.

Hannibal returned to Carthage and immediately persuaded the leading men of his country that the struggle must continue. He engaged Scipio at Zama, and suffered the first defeat of his career. Carthage was forced to pay the fabulous sum of 10,000 talents. She was further obliged to relinquish all her warships and all her elephants except ten. Furthermore, she had to make a solemn declaration that she would never go to war again without Roman sanction. All the Carthaginian possessions in Spain went to Rome.

Hannibal was given an important government post at Carthage, but the Romans insisted that he be banished. He made his way to the East. Always true to his oath of eternal hatred, he incited foreign nations against Rome. The Romans pursued their indomitable enemy, however, and, in order not to fall into Roman hands, Hannibal eventually took poison.

Fifty years later, the story of Carthage was at an end. The Carthaginians were rich once more and had regained their courage. They attacked Massinissa, the King of Numidia, who was a friend of Rome. In Rome at that time was an old peasant, a member of a wealthy plebeian family. He was not a handsome man. In fact he probably looked something like the Hunchback of Notre Dame. His name was Cato and he discharged his duties as censor with the utmost severity, hounding everyone whose conduct offended against his standards of respectability. He conducted interminable tirades against any Roman whose tastes lay in the direction of Greek culture, philosophy or luxury. He wanted to see nothing but peasants and tough soldiers in Rome. Women existed to work and obey, he thought, and slaves should be sold as soon as they became old and weak. He travelled to Carthage, ascertained what a wonderful economic recovery Rome's former enemy had made, and brought back some Carthaginian agricultural products. From then on he constantly advocated war against the Romans' dangerous rivals, concluding every speech he made with the words: 'For the rest, I vote that Carthage must be destroyed.'

In the end, the Romans followed his advice. When Carthage rose against Massinissa they sent their legions to Africa, and the Third Punic War began. The Carthaginians offered the Romans three hundred of their most prominent citizens as hostages, but the Romans insisted that Carthage be demolished. The Carthaginians could build a new city, they said, but it must be at least ten miles inland. The only effect this request had upon the Carthaginians was to start them forging every rusty nail they had into a weapon. Once more they summoned up their courage and offered resistance. The Romans besieged the city for two years. In the third year they stormed it.

The Carthaginians defended their 'New York of antiquity' house by house and block by block. This miraculous city, inhabited by nearly 500,000 people, did not surrender until everything had been engulfed in blood and debris. Only 50,000 Carthaginians survived to be sold into slavery. Everything went up in flames. Houses, temples and splendid terraces tottered and fell. Jetties crumbled and lighthouses collapsed in ruins. Carthage was never to rise again. . . .

So ended the last Punic War. The year was 146 B.C. If Carthage had not been destroyed, if she had remained a world power, it would have been the Carthaginians who handed the ancient civilizations of the Mediterranean on to us, and the Carthaginians who bequeathed to Europe the heritage of the ancient world. As it was, world supremacy passed to the Romans, and Rome became middleman between the heritage of the Mediterranean and modern Europe.

INDEX

INDEX

ABDERA, 365
Abraham, 121 ff, 134, 168
Absalom, 125
Abu-Chalchalan, Map p. 31
Abydos, Battle of, 382
Acapana, 272
Achaeans, 342, 362
Achaemenes, 101
Achaemenides, 101-8, 113 ff
Achilles, 348, 349, 355, 415
Acropolis, 369, 371, 372
Adab, Map p. 31
Adonis, 381
Aegean migration, 84, 355 ff, 405 ff
Aegeus, King, 332
Aegina, 397, 403
Aegospotami, Battle of, 383
Aelana, Map p. 123
Aeneas, 346
Aeneid, The, 346
Aeolians, 362
Aeschylus, 373
Afghanistan, 105, 155
Agamemnon, 357, 358
Agis, King, 382, 404
Aguilar, Geronimo de, 318, 319
Ahasuerus, King, 106
Ahiram, King, 96
Ahmosi, King, 62
Ahriman-Angramanyu, 112-13
Ahu statues, 258
Ahura-Mazda, 102, 106, 109, 112-14, 116
Ainoids, 208 ff, 260
Ainu, 207-12
Akhen-Aten, 64-8, 88-9, 147
Akhet-Aten, 65
Akkad, 37, 42, 102
Akkadian period, 37, 42 ff, 87
Akki, 37
Alba Longa, 346
Alcaeus, 366
Alcibiades, 378-84, 388-9
Alexander the Great, 45, 47, 71, 95, 97, 102, 107-8, 114, 118, 155, 181, 415, 425, 427
Alexandria, 69, 346

Alexandrinus manuscript, 140
Almagro, Diego de, 290, 292, 299-303
Alphabets: Egyptian, 77; Etruscan, 414-15; Indian, 148; Phoenician, 97
Al'Ubaid, 29
Al'Uqair, 33
Amarna, 66, 67, 81, 83, 93, 122, 336
Amarna period, 65 ff
Amarna tablets, 83, 93, 122, 134
Amaterasu (goddess), 214
Amenemhet I, 61
Amenhotep II, 63
Amenhotep III, 63-4, 66
Amenhotep IV, 64, 66
Amenophis III, 122, 335
Amenophis IV, 61, 122
American Indians, 247, 258, 265-8, 269-76, 277-82, 283-7, 288-94, 295-303, 305-11, 312-17, 318-25
Ammon, 118
Ammon, Oasis of, Map p. 111
Amos, 129, 130, 131
Amphictyonic League, 362, 372, 374
Amu, 62
Amun, 61, 63, 64, 65, 67, 68
An Lu-shan, 191
Anacreon, 365
Anahita (god), 112
Anatolia, 37, 81 ff
Anaxagoras, 370, 373, 376
Anazarba, Map p. 31
Angkor Thom, 167
Angkor Vat, 166-8
Anglo-Saxons, 127, 362
Animism, 209-12, 261
Anitta, King, 84-5
Ankara (Angora), 81, 203
Antoninus Pius, 413
Antonius, Marcus 57
Anu (god), 32-3
Anyang, 171
Anzan, 101
Aphrodite, 365, 381, 394
Apollodorus, 393
Apostles, Christian, 137, 138, 139, 140

433

INDEX

Aqueducts, Roman, 416
Arabia, Arabs, 24, 37, 118, 126, 128-9, 176, 188
Arachosia, Map p. 111
Aradus, 97
Aramaeans, 420
Aramaic, 19, 105, 123, 134, 139
Aranyakas (Vedic), 149
Arban, Map p. 31
Arbela (Erbil), Map p. 31
Archeanassa, 398
'Archive A', 83
Areia, Map p. 111
Argolis, 357
Argos, 104, 359
Ariadne, 331-2
Ariki Ngaara, 256-7
Ariosto, 165
Aristarchus, 16, 417
Aristippus, 397
Aristophanes, 389, 398, 404
Aristotle, 19, 402
Aristoxenus, 395
Armenia, 109
Arpad, Map p. 31
Arsinoe, 79
Artaphernes, 366
Artaxerxes I, 107, 369, 383
Artaxerxes II, 107, 114, 115
Artemis, 396
Artystone, 115
Aryans, 99, 110, 142, 148, 367
Asakusa, 224, 234
Ascanius, 346
Asia Minor, 18, 81 ff, 114, 116, 117, 341, 345 ff, 354, 355, 362, 366-7, 369, 406 ff
Asiatics, 62
Asine, 359
Askalon, 125
Aski Mosul, Map p. 30
Aso-také crater, 213
Asoka, King, 155
Asosi, King, 79
Aspasia, 373, 376, 397
Assur, 33, 40
Assurbanipal, King, 28, 44, 133
Assyria, Assyrians, 42-3, 64, 69, 88, 109, 117
Astarte, 96
Astrology: Etruscan, 411; Sumerian, 33
Astronomy: Chinese, 195; Colla, 275; Egyp-
tian, 18-19, 70; Greek, 18-19, 20, 364, 386, 417; Mayan, 310; Phoenician, 94; Polynesian, 250
Astyages, King, 100-1
Atahualpa, 277, 292-4, 295-7, 302
Atchana, Map p. 31
Aten, 64-5, 67
Atharva-Veda, 149
Athena: Chalcioicos, 369; Parthenos, see Parthenon
Athens, 19, 330, 332, 349, 353, 364, 366, 368 ff, 378 ff, 385 ff, 390 ff, 401 ff
'Atlantis', 242, 247, 267
Atossa, Queen, 104, 115
Atreus, 357, 358
Attica, 370, 400, 401 ff
Attila, 199
Atys, 406
Auckland (N.Z.), 252
Australia, 218, 241-5, 260
Avesta, see Zend-Avesta
Ay, King, 67
Aymará tribe, see Collas
Azores, 418
Aztecs, 121, 265, 312-17, 318-24

BAAL, 124, 130
Baana, 126
Babylon, 33, 41 ff, 96, 102, 105, 127, 408, 410
Babylonia, 38-9, 62, 64, 96, 117, 132, 409
Babylonia-Assyria, 40-6
Bactra, 109, 155, 185
Bactria, 102, 110
Badari, 50
Baghdad, 27-8
Balboa, 289, 290
Balis, Map p. 31
Baluchistan, 109, 142
Banks Islands, 261
Barca, Map p. 111
Baru (priests), 32
Bashan, Map p. 123
Basho, 220
Bathsheba, 125
Bayezid, 203
Bear-cult, 210-12
Beersheba, Map p. 123
Behistun, 28, 105
Beirut, 93
Bejat, Map p. 31

INDEX

Beneventum, Battle of, 416
Bengtson, Hermann, 359, 373
Bennett, Wendell C., 272-3, 340, 341
Bering Straits, 265, 267-8, 305
Berossus, 27, 114, 417
Bethlehem, 131, 137, 167
Bible, The, 33, 41, 43, 93, 95, 106, 110, 121-7, 128-32, 133-6, 293, 420
Bimbisara, King, 151
Birth-control (Japan), 218
Biru, River, 290
Bittel, Kurt, 82-4, 87
Bokhara, 201
Bolivia, 269 ff, 277
'Book of the Dead, The', 121
Borsippa, 33
Borubudur, 167
Bortai (wife of Jenghiz Khan), 202, 203
Bosphorus, 105
Bossert, H. T., 87
Bougainville (Solomon Islands), 260-1
Brahmanas (Vedic), 149
Brahmanism, 159-60
Brahmi script, 148, 154
Bricks, Babylonian, 41, 44
Bricks, Harappa, 141
British Museum, 29, 77, 350, 371
Brunton, John and William, 141
Buddha, 141, 151-3, 154-8, 160-2, 174, 188, 197
Buddhism, 141, 145, 153, 154-8, 163, 166, 216, 311
Burial practices: American-Indian, 270-1; among Magi, 112; among Parsees, 112; Chinese, 184; Egyptian, 48-51, 54-6, 60-2, 71-2; Etruscan, 408, 410; Inca, 281, 287; Mycenaean, 359-60; Persian, 112; Phoenician, 96; pre-Egyptian, 48, 50, 51; Sumerian, 33-6
Buriats, 199
Burma, 166
Byblos, 93, 95, 96
Byrsa, 418
Byzantium, Byzantines, 60, 346, 382

C₁₄ (radio-carbon method), 354
Cabral, 247
Cadiz, 94, 289
Cairo, 52
Cajamarca, 288, 292-4

Calah, Map p. 31
Calasasaya, 272, 274, 275
Calendars: Mayan, 310, 316; N. American-Indian, 316; pre-Inca, 275
Callicrates, 371
Calvert, Frank, 350, 352
Calvin, Jean, 288
Cambodia, 165-8
Cambyses, 69, 100-1, 103-4, 115, 116
Camões, Luíz de Vaz de, 165-6
Canaan, 122 ff, 387, 418
Canaanites, 62, 93, 122 ff, 418
Canals: Babylonian, 43; Chinese, 183; Egyptian, 61, 68; Mongolian, 205
Canary Islands, 418
Candia, 327
Cannae, Battle of, 428
Cannibalism, 250, 262
Canton, 183
Cape of Good Hope, 94
Capitoline Hill, 413-14
Cappadocia, 109, 118
Capua, 428
Carchemish, 86
Caria, 102, 117
Caricature sculptures, 30-1, 73
Caroline Islands, 259
Cartagena, 426
Carthage, Carthaginians, 94, 95-6, 182, 351, 416, 417-23, 424-30
Catalaunian Fields, Battle of the, 60
Catania, 381
Cato, 429-30
Caucasus, 109
Celts, 362, 417, 426, 427
Ceramics: American-Indian, 268, 272, 275, 309; Chinese, 170-1, 195-6; Egyptian, 48-50; Indian, 146; Sumerian, 29, 30, 32, 35
Cerveteri, 409, 410
Ceuta, 165
Ceylon, 154
Chalcedon, 382
Chaldeans, 135, 408
Challcuchima, Prince, 298
Ch'ang An, 185, 188, 190
Chang Ch'ien, 185
Chantre, E., 81
Charles V (Holy Roman Emperor), 288, 291-292, 293, 299, 300-1, 302, 305
Chavin civilization, 16, 266, 270, 277

INDEX

Chefren, *see* Khafre
Cheops, 53, 57-60
Ch'i, 175
Chichemeces, 315
Ch'ien Lung, Emperor, 195
Chimalman, 316
Ch'in dynasty, 175, 182
Ch'in Shih-huang-ti, Emperor, 182-4
China, Chinese, 19-20, 37, 121, 127, 154, 155, 157, 167, 169-73, 174-9, 180-7, 188-92, 193-197, 200, 202, 203, 216
Ching, Emperor, 185
Ching-te-Chen, porcelain factory, 413
Chios, 401
Chiusi, 409
Chorasmia, Map p. 111
Cholula, 316-17, 321
Chou Hsin, Emperor, 172-3
Chou K'ou Tien, 169, 170
Christ, Jesus, 19, 29, 110, 115, 120, 124, 132, 137-40, 151-2, 157, 168
Christianity, 114, 121, 127, 137 ff, 163, 361, 387
Churri, 62
Chwang-tsze, 178
Cicero, 413
Cieza de León, 274
Cilicia, 87, 117
Circesium, Map p. 31
Claudel, Paul, 133, 166
Claudius, Caius, 420
Claudius, Emperor, 409
Cleisthenes, 364
Cleopatra, 57, 69
Clothing: Ainu, 209; Aztec, 322; Chinese, 170; Cretan, 327 ff, 337-8, 360; Egyptian, 70, 73-75; Inca, 280-1; Indian, 145; Mayan, 310; Median, 100; Mohenjo-Daro, 145; Mongolian, 204; Mycenaean, 360; Persian, 99; Polynesian, 251
Cochise civilization, 266, 267
Codex: Alexandrinus, 140; rescriptus, 140; Sinaiticus, 140; Vaticanus, 140
Collas, 275-6
Colossi in Central America, 315
Colossi on Easter Island, 257, 267
Colossi of Memnon, 64
Colossus of Rhodes, 182
Columbus, 167, 268, 288-9, 317
Confucianism, 121, 176 ff, 186

Confucius, 174-9, 182, 188, 189
Constantine the Great, 346
Cook, Capt. James, 218, 242-3, 250, 253
Copán, 307, 310
Copernicus, 16, 288
Corinth, 374, 403
Cornwall, 94
Corroboree, 245
Corsica, 94
Cortez, Hernando, 127, 289, 290, 291, 292, 305, 306, 317, 318-25
Cortez, Martin, 319, 325
Cortona, 409
Cosa, 409
Cosmetic utensils: Egyptian, 48, 75; Greek, 398; Mycenaean, 360; Sumerian, 35
Courty, Georges, 274-5
Cozumel, 319
Cratinus, 373
Crete, Cretans, 65, 327-33, 334-43
Critias, 389
Crito, 392, 398
Croesus, 103-4
Croton, 362, 364
Ctesiphon, Map p. 31
Cumae, 362
Cuneiform script, 27-8, 40, 46, 86 ff, 110, 142
Cuzco, 277, 280, 281, 284, 285-6, 298, 299, 303
Cyaxares, King, 100
Cyprus, 94, 401
Cyrene, 362
Cyrescata, 102
Cyrus I, 45, 101
Cyrus II, 101-3, 108, 115, 127, 373, 385
Cyrus, River, Map p. 111
Cyzicus, Battle of, 382

Daedalus, 331
Daigo, Emperor, 216
Damascus, 138
Dante, 165, 411
Danube, 105
Darien, 290, 318
Darius I, 104-7, 109, 113-14, 115, 116, 117, 118, 364
Darius II, 107, 132
Darius III, 107-8, 118
Daschur, Map p. 49
Datis, 366
David, King, 95, 125-6

INDEX

Decimal system (Egypt), 77
Decimal system (Minoan), 342 ff
Deioces, King, 100
Delion, Battle of, 379
Delphi, 362, 369, 371
Democedes of Croton, 104
Democritus, 14, 365
Demons (daevas), 113
Deverra (god), 414
Díaz del Castillo, Bernal, 318, 321, 323
Diban, 124
Dilwara temple sculptures, 162
Dimini culture, 355
Diocletian, Emperor, 411
Diodorus Siculus, 17, 79, 335
Diogenes, 397
Dionysus cult, 372
Dnieper, River, 201-2
Dniester, River, 105
Doria, Dorians, 357, 362, 405, 427
Dostoievski, 177
Doumer, Paul, 166
Dur Sarrukin, Map p. 31
Dürer, Albrecht, 288
Dzungaria, 199

EA (god), 33
East India Railway, 141
Easter Island, 167, 247, 248, 253-8
'Ebers Papyrus', 77
Ecbatana, 100, 103, 105
Edel, E., 89
Egypt, Egyptians, 43, 47-51, 52-6, 57-70, 71-80, 103, 118, 122 ff, 146, 168, 332, 335, 337, 355, 401, 410
Elba, 418
Elgin, Lord, 358, 371
Elijah, 127, 128-9, 130
Elisha, 130
England, 94, 418
Enlil (god), 33, 37
Enoch, 127
Ensi, 36-7
Ephesus, 139, 181, 365, 401
Ephorus, 348
Erech, see Uruk
Erechtheum, 372
Erhardt, Sophie, 83
Eridu, 28, 30, 33
Eskimos, 170

Esther, Queen, 106, 115, 119
Ethiopia, Ethiopians, 69, 118, 401
Etruscans, 37, 405-11
Eunicus, 394
Eunuchs, 115, 183, 184, 191, 403
Euphrates, 30-1, 40, 63
Euripides, 19, 373
Eurydice, 214
Eurystheus, 357, 358
Excavations: Asia Minor, 82 ff, 345 ff; Australia, 242; Carthage, 419; Central America, 314-15; China, 169-71; Crete, 328 ff, 335 ff; Egypt, 52-6, 335, 366; Greece, 155, 358, 372; India, 141-7; Iraq, 30 ff; Italy, 413; Java, 241-2; Mesopotamia, 27 ff, 142; Palestine, 126; Persia, 105-6; South America, 269-70; Syria, 96; Troy, 345 ff
Exogamy, 261-2
Eyraud, Eugène, 253-4
Ezekiel, 130, 132, 174

FABIUS CUNCTATOR, 428
Falcon (symbol), 51
Faunus (god), 413
Fayum, 50
Fidenae, Battle of, 409
Fiji, 259, 260, 261
Fleet, Athenian, 368 ff, 374, 380 ff
Flint tools, 47-8, 50, 58, 170, 208, 261
Flood, The, 28, 124, 316
Folsom, civilization, 266, 267
Forrest river caves (Australia), 245
Forum (Rome), 412-13
France, French, 96, 417-18, 425
Fugger, Jakob, 288
Fuji (goddess), 207, 212
Fuji-no-yama, 193, 207, 213, 239
Fujiwara family, 216

GALATIA, 401
Galba, Emperor, 411
Galilee, 139
Gandhara, 155-7
Ganges, River, Map p. 123
Gathas (Avesta), 113
Gauls, 425, 427, 428
Gautama, see Buddha
Genesis, Book of, 121, 316
George III (England), 243

INDEX

Germans, 37
Gerrhaeans, 118
Gerzeh period, 50
Gibraltar, 357, 362, 368
Gilgamesh Epic, 28, 124
Gilgamesh, King, 28
Giluhepa, Princess, 66
Gizeh, 57, 181
Glenelg river caves (Australia), 245
Glycera, 397
Gobi Desert, 199
Goethe, 134, 348
Goliath, 125
Gondwana, 17, 241, 242
González y Haedo, Felipe, 253
Gournia, 333, 335
Graei, 362
'Great Medical Papyrus', 77
Great Wall of China, 180-7, 194, 201, 203, 279
Greece, Greeks, 60, 62, 97, 106, 110, 156-7, 168, 174, 327, 333, 336, 337, 345-53, 354-60, 361-7, 368-76, 378-84, 385-9, 390-3, 394-9, 400-4, 415-16
Guatemala, 308
Gudea, King, 37, 42
Güterbock, 87, 89
Guti tribe, 37

HADRIAN, EMPEROR, 139, 411
Haggai, 132
Hagia-Triada, 333, 335, 339
Haikai (poems), 220
Halaf, 30
Halys, River, 81, 84
Hamilcar, 421-2, 424
Hamonurabi, 38, 42-3
Han Dynasty, 191
Hanging Gardens of Babylon, 44-5, 181
Hannibal, 95-6, 182, 417, 422-3, 424-9
Hanno, 420
Haragla, Map p. 31
Harappa, see Mohenjo-Daro
Harpagus, 101
Harris Papyrus, 68, 79
Hartog, Dirck, 242
Harunobu, 234-6, 239
Hasdrubal, 428-9
Hassuna, 30
Hatiay, 71
Hatran, 122

Hatshepsut, Queen, 62-3, 123
Hattusa, 81-5, 88 ff
Hattusilis, King, 89-90
Hawaiki saga, 248
Hawaii, 247, 251
Head-hunting, 262
Heba, Map p. 123
Hebrews, 138
Hector, 349
Hegel, 374
Heliogabalus, 172
Heliopolis, 64
Helladic period, 355 ff
Heraclea, Battle of, 415-16
Heracleopolis, Map p. 123
Heracles (Hercules), 96, 335, 357, 358
Heraclitus, 365
Herod, King, 137
Herodotus, 27, 41, 44, 46, 57-8, 72, 78, 93, 99, 100, 104, 112, 115, 116, 118, 119, 330, 348, 373, 406, 408
Herondas, 403
Hetepheres, Queen, 54
Hideyoshi, 217-18
Hieraconpolis, 51
Hieroglyphics: Chinese, 171; Cretan, 328, 332; Egyptian, 74; Hittite, 86-7; Jewish, 127; Mayan, 308-10; Old Persian, 27, 101; Polynesian, 257-8; Sumerian, 27-8, 38, 142
Hinduism, 153, 159, 161, 163
Hipparchus, 19, 363
Hipparete, 379
Hippias, 363-4
Hippodamus of Miletus, 373
Hiram of Tyre, 95
Hiroshige, 221, 237, 239
Hissarlik, 345 ff
Hittites, 64, 67, 81-97, 355
Hokkaido, 207, 208, 209, 212, 213
Hokusai, 224, 229-32, 233-4, 237
Holland, 241, 288
Homer, 93, 94, 132, 345, 348-9, 353, 357, 394
Honan, 171, 175
Honolulu, 251-2
Horemheb, King, 67
Horses: among Medes, 118; in Mexico, 319; at Mycenae, 360; under the Shang, 172
Horus (god), 51
Horus Ahai, King, 51
Horus Kaa, King, 51

INDEX

Horus Wadjet, King, 51
Horus Zer, King, 51
Hosea, 130, 131
Hotu Matua, Prince, 256, 258
Hrozny, Bedrich, 82
Hsien Yang, 183, 185
Hsüan Tsung, Emperor, 188-91
Huaman Poma de Ayala, Felipe, 284
Huascar, Prince, 295-6
Huayna Capac, 282, 295
Hugo, Victor, 134
Hui-te-Rangiora, 250
Huitzilopochtli (god), 323
Human sacrifice: Aztec, 320, 323; Canaanite,
    121-2; Carthaginian, 419; Inca, 281, 285-6;
    Mayan, 309-10; Phoenician, 96; Polynesian,
    250; Sumerian, 34-5; Toltec, 317
Humber river caves (Australia), 245
Huns, 62, 155, 185
Hunting, 76, 172
Hydaspes, River, Map p. 111
Hyksos race, 62
Hyrcania, Map p. 111

ICA VALLEY, 270
Icarus, 331
Ictinus, 371
Iliad, The, 148, 330, 348-9, 351, 353, 357
Illyrians, 357
Imhotep, 51, 52
Imilcea, 426
Inanna (goddess), 32
Incas, 265, 270, 274, 275, 277-82, 283-7, 288-
    294, 295-8, 306
Incense, 118, 418
India, 109, 116, 141-7, 148-53, 154-8, 159-63, 176
Indo-China, 154, 166, 167, 183, 248
Indonesia, Indonesians, 167, 248, 250
Indra (god), 149
Indus, River, 105, 109, 142, 147
Insignia of State (Japan), 215
Ionia, Ionians, 102, 362
Iran, 42, 99, 112, 200
Iraq, 27, 30-1, 40
Isaac, 122, 134
Isaiah, 130, 131, 174
Ise (shrine), 215
Isin, Maps pp. 31, 111
Ishmael, 122
Ishtar, 33, 42, 90, 96

Islam, 168, 200
Israel (Kingdom), 62, 125-7, 316
Israel (Republic), 93
Issus, Battle of, 107
Istakhr, Map p. 111
Italy, 62, 337, 362, 374, 401, 412-16, 417, 423,
    424-9 and see Etruscans, Rome
Ithaca, 352, 353
Iyomande (Ainu), 211
Izanagi (god), 214
Izanami (goddess), 214

JACOB, 121, 134
Jainism, 159-63
Janszoon, W., 242
Janus (god), 413
Japan, Japanese, 153, 154, 155, 157, 170, 208,
    209, 213-19, 220-3, 224-8, 229-32, 233-9
Jarmo, 30
Jaussen, Tepano, 254
Java, 157, 169, 241
Jaxartes, 102
Jebeil, 96
Jemdet-Nasr period, 50
Jenghiz Khan, 186, 194, 199-205
Jeremiah, 130, 131-2, 174
Jericho, Map p. 123
Jeroboam, 126
Jerusalem, 125, 126-7, 346
Jesus, see Christ
Jewellery: American-Indian, 280; Chinese,
    184, 186, 196; Cretan, 338, 360; Egyptian,
    50, 55-6, 70, 75-6; Greek, 398; Inca, 280;
    Indian, 147; Mohenjo-Daro, 145-6; Mon-
    golian, 196; Mycenaean, 360; Persian, 119-
    120; Polynesian, 258; Sumerian, 35-6;
    Trojan, 352
Jews, 102-3, 121-7, 128-32, 133-6, 316
Jimmu, Emperor, 207, 214-15
Joan of Arc, 390
Job, Book of, 23, 133-6, 163
John, St, 138, 139-40
Jonathan, 125
Josephus, 62
Judaea, 126, 176
Judah, 121 ff
Julius Caesar, 57, 69
Jupiter Olympus (Pheidias), 181
Jurja, Map p. 31
Justin (Martyr), 138

INDEX

Ka, 59-60
Kabuki (theatre), 238
Kadesh, Map p. 123
Kaimakoi, Prince, 257
Kalaat-Mahul, Map p. 31
Kalmucks, 199
Kamakura, 157-8, 217
Kamosi, King, 62
Kampfer, Engelbert, 28
K'ang-Hsi, Emperor, 195
Kanishka, King, 156
Kansu, 171
Karachi, 141
Karnak, 63, 68
Kassites, 42, 62
Keme, 69
Kerulen, River, 200
Kesakambalin, Ajita, 151
Ketubim, 124, 133
Khafaje, 33
Khafre, 57, 58, 61, 76
Khmer, 167-8
Khufu, 57, 59, 181
Khuta Kuan, 167
Kiangsi, 191
Kirghiz Steppes, 199
Kish, 37
Kisurra, Map p. 31
Knossos, 327 ff, 335 ff
Knudtzon, J. A., 81
Koran, 129, 204
Korea, Koreans, 157, 200, 217-18
Kreffer, Friedrich, 107
Kublai Khan, 167, 186, 194, 202
Kufa, Map p. 31
Kupe, 248
Kush, 68
Kutalla, Map p. 31
Kyoto, 216, 239
Kyushu, 207, 213

LABYRINTH, CRETAN, 327, 330-2
Laevinus, Valerius, 416
Lagash, 28, 36-7
Lahore, 141
La'ipu, 37
Lais, 397
Lamachus, 381
Lao-tse, 177-9, 188, 197, 365
La Perouse, 253

La Paz, 274
Laroche, E., 87
Larsa, 33
Last Judgment (Zarathustra), 110, 113
Latini tribe, 413
Latium, 346, 412
Laws: Babylonian, 42-3; Hittite, 91; Inca, 280-2, 284-5; of Jenghiz Khan, 200; Melanesian, 261; Persian, 116-19; Sumerian, 36, 38
Leah, 121
Lebanon, 88, 93
Lemuria, 242 *and see* Gondwana
Leonardo da Vinci, 229, 288
Lesbos, 365-6
Li Ling, Prince, 191
Li T'ai-po, 19, 186, 188-92
Libraries: Assyrian, 40, 133; Chinese, 186, 188; Egyptian, 77; Greek, 385; Inca, 278; Khmer, 168; Persian, 110
Libya, Libyans, 69, 419, 426
Lien Koku O, King, 217-18
Lima, 298, 301, 302
Linear 'A' and 'B', *see* Scripts, Cretan
Linear measure, prehistoric, 146
Lisht, 61
Literature: Aztec, 316; Canaanite, 93; Chinese, 185-6; Egyptian, 61-2, 64-5, 68, 76-8, 79; Greek, 19, 364-6; Hebrew, 124 ff, 133-6; Inca, 278, 286; Indian, 148 ff; Japanese, 220, 229, 232; Mayan, 308, 316; Median, 100; Persian, 110; Phoenician, 93, 97; Polynesian, 253 ff; Roman, 424
Livy, 424, 426
Locri, 415
Lope de Vega, Carpio, 229
Loyalty Islands, 261
Lo Yang, 191, 346
Lugalzaggisi, King, 37
Luke, St, 138, 139
Luque, Hernando de, 290, 292
Luther, 288
Luvian language, 86-7
Luxor, 64, 68
Lycia, 102
Lycurgus, 396
Lydia, Lydians, 102, 103, 117, 401, 406
Lysander, 383

MACEDONIA, 374, 426
Magalhães, 290

INDEX

Magellan, 247
Magi, 15, 110-11, 114
Magnesia, 369-70
Mahabharata, 121, 149, 168
Mahavira Vardhamana, 160-1
Maka, Map p. 111
Malaya, 259
Malinche, *see* Marina
Mallia, 335
Malta, 94
Mamelukes, 203
Manchu dynasty, 186-7, 194
Manchuria, 186
Mancolapac, King, 278
Manco Inca, 298, 301
Mandane, Princess, 100-1
Manet, 237-8
Manetho, 62, 417
Manistusu, King, 37
Mao Tse-tung, 197
Maoris, 248
Marathon, Battle of, 104, 106, 364, 367, 368
Marathus, 93
Marduk, 33, 41, 42, 46, 102, 134
Margada, Map p. 31
Margiana, 102
Mari, 30 ff, 42
Marina, Princess, 319, 321, 323-4
Mark, St, 138, 139
Marriage: Babylonian, 46; Egyptian, 78-9; Greek, 394-6; Hittite, 88, 91; Inca, 280-1, Melanesian, 261-2; Persian, 119; Polynesian, 251
Marseilles (Massilia), 94, 362
Mass re-settlement (Inca), 283-4
Massagetae, 103
Massinissa, King, 429, 430
Mastaba, 51
Mathematics: Egyptian, 77-8; Greek, 364; Mayan, 268, 310
Matthew, St, 138, 139
Mauka, 207
Mausolus, King, 181
Maya (mother of Buddha), 151
Mayan race, 265, 266, 268, 305-11, 312
Media, Medes, 44-5, 88, 99 ff, 114, 119
Medicine: Aztec, 322; Chinese, 171; Egyptian, 70, 78, 104; Greek, 104; Khmer, 167; Mayan, 310; Persian, 119

Medina, Map p. 123
Megiddo, 126
Mekong, River, 165-6
Melanesia, Melanesians, 167, 250, 259-63
Melitene, Map p. 111
Melos, 94, 339
Melqarth (god), 96
Memnon, 64
Memphis, 52, 61
Menander, 397
Menelaus, 357
Menes, King, 47, 51
Menkaure, King, 57
Merimde-beni-Salaam, 50
Merv al-Shahidshan, 201
Mesa, King (Stele of), 124
Mes-Kalam-Dug, Prince, 34
Mesopotamia, 27-39, 50, 62, 176, 387
Messina, 420
Metaurus, The, Battle of, 429
Meton, 380-1
Mexico, 127, 266, 305 ff, 312 ff, 318 ff
Micah, 131
Michelangelo, 288
Micronesia, Micronesians, 250
Midaea, 359
Miletus, 364
'Millingen Papyrus', 61
Miltiades, 368
Mina (Greek), 401
Mina (Sumerian), 38
Minaeans, 118
Minamoto family, 216
Minerva, 410
Ming dynasty, 186, 194
Minoans, 362
Minos, King, 327 ff, 337
Minotaur, 330, 337
Miru tribe, 257
Missions: Buddhist, 167-8; Christian, 251, 253-254, 298 ff, 312; Persian, 186
Mitanni, 18, 62, 64, 66, 88
Mithra, 112, 114
Mnesicles, 372
Moab, 124
Mochlos, 333, 335
Mohammed (prophet), 115, 129, 168, 188
Mohammed II, Sultan, 60
Mohenjo-Daro, 141-7, 148, 170
Moloch, 96, 130, 419

INDEX

Monet, Claude, 228
Money: Greek, 401; Persian, 117-18; Sumerian, 38
Mongolia, 20, 154, 180, 199
Mongols, 62, 167, 170, 171, 180, 182, 186, 194, 201, 207, 267
Montezuma, 320-4
Moortgat, Anton, 86, 87
Moscow, 200, 203, 369
Moses, 37, 42, 122-4, 127, 168
Mu (Pacific 'Atlantis'), 247, 267
Multan, 141
Mummies: Egyptian, 71-2; Inca, 287, 298
Mursuli II, 81, 89-90
Muskets, 292
Mycale, Battle of, 107, 367
Mycenae, Mycenaeans, 327, 342, 343, 352, 355, 357-60, 362, 405, 408
Mylae, Battle of, 421
Mylitta (goddess), 96
Mysia, 117, 406
Mystery religions: Asia Minor, 114; Greece, 388
Mytilene, 366

NABONIDUS, KING, 43, 102
Nabu (god), 128
Naga (snake), 168
Nahua group, 315
Naksh-i-Radjap, Map p. 111
Naksh-i-Rustam, 106
Nanking, 186, 191
Napoleon I, 57, 58, 105, 200, 369, 383, 427
Nara, 216
Naramsin, King, 37
Nauplia, 359
Nasca civilization, 270-1, 277
Navigation: Cretan, 337; Greek, 368; Phoenician, 93 ff; Polynesian, 247 ff
Naxos, 332
Nazareth, Map p. 123
Neanderthal, 265
Neapolis, 362
Nebkaure, 61
Nebiim, 124, 128
Nebo (god), 33
Nebuchadnezzar, 42, 43, 95, 127, 128
Nefertiti, Queen, 66-7, 89, 147
Negade civilization, 50-1
Negeb, Map p. 123

Nelson, 165
Neolithic age, 48-9, 208, 354, 355
Nepal, 154, 155-8
Nero, 172
Nestorians, 186
New Britain, 260
New Caledonia, 260, 261, 262
New Guinea, 260, 261
New Hebrides, 261
New Testament, 137-40, 387
New Zealand, 247
Ngaure tribe, 257
Nicias, 380-1, 402
Nile, River, 47 ff, 62, 68, 69-70, 103, 124
Nimrod, 124
Nimrud, Map p. 31
Ningirsu (god), 36-7
Ninigi-no-Mikoto (god), 214-15
Nineveh, 28, 100, 133
Ninlil (goddess), 33
Nippur, 29, 33, 37, 38
No (plays), 238
Noah, 28, 149
Nobunaga, 217
Numerical systems: American-Indian, 309; Arabic, 268; Cretan, 334, 340 ff; Egyptian, 77-8; Roman, 268
Numerology, 124

OBELISKS, EGYPTIAN, 63
Oceania, 259 ff
Ochus, King, 107
Odeum, 372
Odyssey, The, 94, 148, 165, 330, 348, 351
Ogotai, Khan, 202
Old Testament, 106, 119, 121 ff, 124-7, 128-32, 133-6, 174, 316, 317, 387, 405
Oligarchical government, 363
Olympia, 19, 352, 371
Olympiads, 361-2, 380
Olympias, Queen, 415
Onon, River, 200
'Orbiney Papyrus', 77
Orchomenos, 352
Orizaba, Mt, 320
Osorkon, King, 54
Otten, Heinrich, 84, 85
Ottshigin, 202
Oxus, River, Map p. 111
Oxyrhynchus, 140, 366

INDEX

PACHACAMAC (GOD), 298

Pachacutec, King, 278

Painting: Chinese, 186; Egyptian, 70; Etruscan, 405, 408, 410; Indian, 157; Japanese, 214-15, 220-1, 224-8, 229-32, 237-9; Nasca, 272, 277

Palaeolithic age, 47-8, 169, 170, 354

Palaic language, 86

Palaikastro, 333, 335

Palatine Hill, 413, 414

Palenque, 307, 310

Pales (god), 414

Palestine, 42, 63, 121-7, 128-32, 133-6, 137-40, 174

Palm Islands, 245

Palmyra, Map pp. 31, 111

Pamir, 205

Panama, 289, 305

Panathenaea, 363, 371

Paper, Japanese, 237

Papini, Giovanni, 137

Papuans, 260-1

Papyrus, 61, 65, 68, 69, 76-80, 95, 96, 139-40, 366

Paracelsus, 288

Paradise (in Bible), 29, 124, 298

Paricanians, Map p. 111

Paris, 346

Parsagarda (Pasargadae), 101, 113

Parsees, 112

Parthenon, 371-2

Parthia, Map p. 111

Pathala, Map p. 111

Paul, St, 137-8

Pausanias, 369

Pausanias (geographer), 359

Peking, 62, 169-70, 186, 193-7, 201

Peloponnese, 355, 357, 362

Peloponnesian War, 373 ff, 378

Pelusium, Map p. 123

Pergamum, 42, 140, 352

Pericles, 368, 370-6, 378, 379

Perry, Matthew C., 219

Persepolis, 105, 106-8, 110, 114, 119, 372

Persia, Persians, 69, 95, 99-108, 109-20, 124, 174, 203, 366-7, 368 ff

Persian Gulf, 37, 40

Persis, 101, 105, 117

Peru, Peruvians, 253, 256, 265-6, 269 ff, 277-300 (passim)

Perugia, 409

Peter, St, 138

'Petersburg Papyrus', 77

Petra, Map pp. 111, 123

Petrarch, 165

Petroleum, 45, 336

PG/800 (Grave), 34

PG/1054 (Grave), 34-6

Phaedo, 393

Phainarete, 385

Phaistos, 332-3, 335

Pharnabazus, 383

Pharos, 181-2

Pheidias, 371, 372, 373, 376, 396

Philippines, 259

Philistia, Map p. 123

Philistines, 125

Phoenicia, Phoenicians, 77, 93-7, 343, 418 ff

Phrygia, 109, 383

Phryne, 397

Picture writing, 28, 77, 172, 258, 275

Piedras Negras, 309, 310

Pijusti, King, 85

Piracy, Phoenician, 94

Piraeus, 368, 370, 374

Pisa, 419

Pisistratus, 349, 363

Pithana, King, 84

Pithecanthropus erectus, 241, 265

Pithom, Map p. 123

Pizarro, Francisco, 277, 289-94, 295-303, 325

Pizarro, Gonzalo, 299, 302, 303

Pizarro, Hernando, 292, 299-301

Plataea, Battle of, 107, 367

Plato, 19, 366, 385 ff, 390 ff

Pliny, 110, 339

Plutarch, 376, 402

Polis, 362-3

Political organization: Carthaginian, 419; Chinese, 183-4; Egyptian, 69; Greek, 362 ff, 370-1; Inca, 278-82, 284 ff; Japanese, 218; Persian, 116 ff

Polo, Marco, 186

Polyandry, 210

Polybius, 418, 426

Polygamy, 210

Polynesia, Polynesians, 23-4, 167, 207, 223, 247-52, 253-8

Pompeii, 33

Pompey, 97

Pontus, 401

INDEX

Populonia, 410
Porcelain, Chinese, 195-6
Portugal, Portuguese, 165-6, 217
Poseidon, 372, 397
Postal services: Inca, 279-80; Persian, 116-17
Potidaea, 379
Praxiteles, 397
Prexaspes, Prince, 103
Priam, King, 345 ff
'Prisse Papyrus', 79
Prophets, 110, 128-32, 387
Propylaea, 372
Prosymna, 359
Proverbs, 133
Psalms, 126, 133
Pseira, 335
Psusennes, King, 54
Ptah-Hotep, 79
Ptolemy (mathematician), 19
Ptolemy I, 415
Punic Wars, 182, 420-30
Punians, 418 ff
Punin, 269
Punjab, 141
Pura, Map p. 111
Purana Kashyapa, 151
P'u Yi, 187
Pygmoids, 259-60
Pylos, 340, 341, 342, 343
Pyramids: American-Indian, 309, 313-15, 316-317; Egyptian, 50, 52-6, 57-62
Pyrrhus, King, 415-16, 427
Pythagoras, 19, 364
Pythias, 398
Pythionice, 398

QUEENSLAND (AUSTRALIA), 245
Quetzalcoatl (god), 20, 312, 313, 315-17, 320, 321, 323
Quichuas, 277-8
Quirinal, Hill, 413
Quito, 295

RA, 64-5
'Radio-carbon method', see C$_{14}$
Raga, Map p. 111
Rama, King, 149
Ramaseum, 68
Ramayane, 149, 168
Rameses II, 67, 76

Rameses III, 68-9
Ramses, Map p. 123
Raphael, 288
Ras Shamra, Map p. 31
Rebecca, 122
Rehoboam, 126-7
Rhea (goddess), 330-1
Rhegium, 415
Rhodes, Island, 94, 401
Rhodesia, 265
Rig-Veda, 149
Rimus, King, 37
Rio de Janeiro, 193
Road-construction: Chinese, 183; Inca, 278-80; Persian, 116
Roggeveen, Jakob, 253
Rome, Romans, 37, 62, 69, 96, 157, 168, 185, 346, 361, 375, 409-11, 412-16, 417, 420-4, 425-30
Romulus and Remus, 413
Rousseau, Jean Jacques, 178
Roxane (wife of Cambyses), 103
Roxane (wife of Alexander the Great), 108

SABINI TRIBE, 413
Sachs, Hans, 288
Sacsahuaman, 282
Sagartia, Map p. 111
Saguntum, 422, 424
Sahagun, Bernhardino de, 312
Sahure, King, 58
St Bernard Pass, 423, 426, 427
Sais, Map p. 123
Sakhalin, 207, 208
Sakkara, 51
Salamis, 99, 107, 367, 368-9
Samaria, 126
Samarkand, 102, 201, 204
Samarra, 30
Sama-Veda, 149
Samoa, 248
Samos, 364, 382
Samuel (prophet), 121, 125, 129
Sandia civilization, 266, 267
Sanskrit, 109, 128, 159, 168
Santa Cruz, Islands, 261
Santa Cruz (Peru), 291
Sappho, 365-6
Sapporo, 207

444

INDEX

Sardis, 100, 102, 103

Sargon I, 37

Sargon II, 126

Satraps, 109, 116-18

Saturn (god), 413

Saul, King, 124-5

Scales, prehistoric, 146

Schopenhauer, Artur, 150

Scipio, Publius Cornelius, 428-9

Scripts: Akkadian, 87, 89-90; Andean, 278;
Aztec, 312, 313; Babylonian, 46, 105;
Brahmi, 148, 154; Chinese, 171-2; Cretan,
332, 334, 338-43, 358; Egyptian, 76-7;
Elamitic, 105; Etruscan, 341, 408-9; Greek,
139-40, 340, 365, 366; Hebrew, 124, 341;
Hittite, 86 ff; Japanese, 216; Mayan, 308-9;
Persian, 105, 106; Polynesian, 248, 253-8;
Roman, 414-15; Semitic, 124, 148 ff;
Sumerian, 36, 38

Sculpture: American-Indian, 272, 314; Assyrian, 42; Cambodian, 166-7; Chinese,
157, 186; Egyptian, 58, 61-2, 65-6, 69;
Etruscan, 405, 410; Greek, 372; Indian, 157,
162; Japanese, 157; Sumerian, 30 ff

Scythians, 19, 103, 105, 155

Sebastian, King of Portugal, 165-6

Sekhem-khet, 52-6

Selebije, Map p. 31

Seler, Eduard, 312

Seleucia, Map p. 31

Semenchkare, King, 67

Semiramis, Queen, 44-5

Semites, 37, 93, 367

Senmut, 63

Sennacherib, King, 44

Septimus Severus, Emperor, 57

Sesklo culture, 359

Sesostris, King, 61, 77

Seville, 290, 291, 325

Severus, Emperor, 58, 411

Shakespeare, 78, 132, 229, 348, 349

Shamanism, 210

Shamash (god), 33, 42, 46

Shammuramat, see Semiramis

Shamsi-Adad, King, 44

Shang (yin) dynasty, 19, 171-3

Shanghai, 222

Shansi, 175, 202

Shantung, 174, 175, 189-90

Sharaku, 238-9

Shekel (Sumerian), 38

Shensi, 175, 188

Shinto, 215, 222

Shiraz, 105

Shogun, 217-18

Shub-ad, Queen, 34-6

Shuddhodana (father of Buddha), 151

Shunsho, 230

Shuruppak, Map p. 111

Siam, Siamese, 157

Siberia, 183

Sicily, 331, 362, 380, 381, 404, 415-16, 417,
420-1, 425

Sidon, 93, 95, 97, 126, 418

Silk: Chinese, 186; Japanese, 221

Sin (moon-god), 33

Sinai, 122 ff

Sinaiticus Manuscript, 140

Sinanthropus Pekinensis, 169-73, 265

Sinope, Map p. 111

Sinuhe, 77

Sippar, 33, 133

Siva (god), 145, 168

Skisei-koro-Ekashi (god), 207

Slaves: Babylonian, 45; Carthaginian, 419;
Egyptian, 68, 73, 74-5; Etruscan, 410;
Greek, 400-4; of Jenghiz Khan, 201;
Khmer, 168; Persian, 119; Phoenician, 94;
Roman, 402, 403

Sligo, Lord, 358

Smerdis, Prince, 103, 104

Smith, Dr S. A., 242

Smyrna, 406

Socrates, 18, 23, 102, 151, 174, 373, 378-9, 380,
385-9, 390-3

Soctria, 109

Sogdiana, 102, 185

Solomon Islands, 260, 261

Solomon, King, 79, 95, 125, 178, 389

Solon, 103, 401

Sommer, Prof. Ferdinand, 85, 87

Sophists, 388

Sophocles, 373

Sophroniscus, 385

Spain, Spaniards, 94, 258, 270, 277, 284, 286,
288-94, 295-303, 312-17, 318-24, 337, 421,
422, 423, 425-6

Sparta, Spartans, 362, 364, 368, 369, 373 ff,
378, 380, 381 ff, 404

Sphinx, The, 58, 63

INDEX

Step-mastaba of Zoser, 51, 52-5, 57
Stoltenberg, Hans L., 341
Strabo, 366
Stupas, 145, 154
Sulla, 410
Sumer, Sumerians, 23, 27-39, 42, 102, 142, 146
Sun Yat-sen, 197
Sung dynasty, 186
Suppiluliuma, King, 81, 88-90
Suryavarman II, 168
Susa, 42, 101, 106, 119
Susa-no-o (god), 214
Susiana, Map p. 111
Sutras (Vedic), 149
Sutrium, Battle of, 409
Sybaris, 362
Syracuse, 362, 380, 428
Syria, Syrians, 42, 63, 68, 93, 203

Taduchepa, Princess, 66
Tahiti, 251
Taia, Queen, 64-5
Taira family, 216
T'ai Tsung, Emperor, 186, 188
Talaquil, Queen, 410
Talgai, 242
Tamerlane, 199, 203-5
Tang Dynasty, 185, 188-9, 216
Tanis, Map p. 123
Tanit (goddess), 419
Tao-te-king, 178
Taranto, see Tarentum
Tarato, 207
Tarentum, 362, 415-16
Tarquinia, 409-10
Tarquins, 415
Tarsus, 137
Tartars, 185, 189, 194, 199-205
Tartessus, 17, 94
Tása, 48-9
Tasso, 165
Tattooing: Ainu, 210; Polynesian, 257
Teispes, 101
Tell el Obed, see Al Ubaid
Telloh, see Lagash
Tenochtitlan, 321, 324
Teos, 365
Teotihuacáns, 312-15
Tepe Gawra, 29
Thales, 364

Thebes, 62, 63-7, 71
Themail, Map p. 31
Themistocles, 368-71, 378, 383
Theodosius II, 371
Thera, 339, 340
Thermopylae, Battle of, 367
Theseum, 372
Theseus, 331-2, 337
Thessaly, 355
Thrace, 105, 401
Thucydides, 370, 374, 375, 376
Tiahuanacu, 269-76, 277 ff
Tiber, River, 412
Tibet, 153, 157
Tigris, River, 27, 28, 30, 40, 43
Tiglath-Pilezer, King, 44
Tikal, 310
Timaea, Queen, 382
Timandra, 383, 384
Timon, 380
Tina (god), 410
Tiryns, 342, 357
Tischendorf, 140
Tissaphernes, 382
Titian, 288
Titicaca, Lake, 272, 274, 275, 277, 284
Tlaloc (rain-god), 313
Tlaxcalans, 321
Tokugawa-Iyeyasu, 217, 218
Tokyo, 193, 213, 218, 222, 336
Tollan, 315
Tolstoy, 122, 132
Toltecs, 312, 315-17
Tonga Islands, 247, 248
Topa Inca, 281
Toparca, Inca, 298
Torah, 123
Toromiro tablets, 253 ff
Totemism, 262
Totonaco tribe, 320
Tower of Babel, 38, 41, 275
Town-planning, Earliest, 44, 144, 313
Toys: Egyptian, 73; Prehistoric, 146, 346
Trade: Phoenician, 420
Trajan, Emperor, 117
Trasimene, Lake, Battle of, 428
Trebenishtshe, 359
Tripolis, 97
Troy, 327, 345-53, 358
Trujillo, 272, 289

INDEX

Tsingtao, 193
Tu Fu, 190
Tuamotu Islands, 259
Tula, River, 200
Tule (son of Jenghiz Khan), 202
Tumbez, 277
Tunguses, 20, 37, 186, 210
Tunis, 351, 417-18
Tupahotu tribe, 257
Turkestan, 103, 199, 203
Turkey, Turks, 81 ff, 346, 406
Tushratta, King, 66
Tutankh-Amun, 54, 67, 89, 199
Tuthmosis III, 63, 76
Tylissos, 333, 335
Tyranny as form of government, 363-4
Tyre, 93, 95, 97, 126, 418
Tyrsanus, 406
Tze-Kung, 175

UAXACTÚN, 266, 307, 311
Ugarit, 87, 93
Uigirs, 201
Ukiyo-e school of painting, 234, 236, 237
Ukiyo Matabei, 234
Umbria, 405, 406
Uni (god), 410
Upanishads (Vedic), 149, 150, 159
Ur, 28, 33 ff, 121
Uratru, Map p. 111
Urn-field people, 355-6
Ur-Nammu, King, 38
Ur-Nanshe (singer), 32
Uruk, 28, 32, 33, 37
Urukagina, King, 36-7
Ur-Zababa, King, 37
Utamaro, 226-8, 230, 237, 239

VACA DE CASTRO, 301, 302
'Valley of Kings', 63
Valmiki, 149
Valverde, Vincento de, 293, 297, 298, 299, 302
Vasco da Gama, 94, 247
Vedas, 110, 148-53, 159, 160, 168
Veddas, 260
Veii, 409
Veli Pasha, 358
Venice, 193
Ventana Cave, 266
Vera Cruz, 320

Vespasian, Emperor, 411
Vespucci, Amerigo, 247
Vesta (goddess), 413
Victoria, Queen, 141
Viracocha (god), 286
Virgil, 346
Vishnu (god), 168
Vladivostok, 187
Volaterrae, 410
Volga, River, Map p. 111
Volsini, 410
Voltaire, 178
Von Kotzebue, Otto, 253
Von Moltke, Helmuth, 349
Vulcan (god), 413
Vulci, 409
Vulgate, The, 133

WALDSCHMIDT, 160
Wan Li Ch'ang Ch'eng, see Great Wall
Wedge script, see Cuneiform script
Wen, Emperor, 185
Wends, 37
Wheel, Invention of the, 417
Wigs, Egyptian, 75
Woman, status of among: Ainu, 210; Australian aborigines, 244; Babylonians, 46; Cretans, 338; Egyptians, 79-80; Etruscans, 410; Greeks, 373, 394-9; Incas, 282; Japanese, 221, 223, 396; Melanesians, 261-2; Persians, 119; Polynesians, 251
Wonders of the Ancient World, 43, 181-2
Woodcuts, Japanese, 23, 233 ff
Wu-Hu, Empress, 186, 188
Wu Shan, 191
Wu Ti, Emperor, 185

XAQUIXAGUANA, BATTLE OF, 302
Xanthippe, 174, 386
Xenophanes, 348
Xenophon, 102, 385, 386, 404
Xerxes I, 95, 99, 106-7, 115, 119, 369
Xerxes II, 107

YAHWEH, 41, 103, 114, 122-7, 128-32
Yajur-Veda, 149
Yamato, 207
Yang Kuei-fei, 186, 188, 190-1
Yangtze, River, 188, 189, 191
Yasakuni shrine, 215

447

INDEX

Yedo, 234, 235, 238, 239
Yen Hwui, 174-5
Yorimoto, 216-17
Yoshiwara, 224-8
Yozei, Emperor, 215-16
Yucatan, 307 ff, 318 ff
Yulun Eke (mother of Jenghiz Khan), 200
Yung Cheng, Emperor, 195
Yung Lo, Emperor, 194

'ZAGREB MUMMY-BANDAGE', 408

Zagros Mts, 105, 116
Zakros, 335
Zama, Battle of, 429
Zarathustra, 109, 110-15, 118, 174
Zechariah, 129, 132
Zen priests, 153
Zend-Avesta, 109 ff
Zikkurats, 32, 38
Zoser, 51, 52-5, 57
Zoser-Atoti, see Sekhem-khet
Zwingli, 288